Entrepreneurship: Launching and Managing New Ventures

Entrepreneurship: Launching and Managing New Ventures

Edited by Scott Gibson

www.clanryeinternational.com

Clanrye International,
750 Third Avenue, 9th Floor,
New York, NY 10017, USA

Copyright © 2019 Clanrye International

This book contains information obtained from authentic and highly regarded sources. Copyright for all individual chapters remain with the respective authors as indicated. All chapters are published with permission under the Creative Commons Attribution License or equivalent. A wide variety of references are listed. Permission and sources are indicated; for detailed attributions, please refer to the permissions page and list of contributors. Reasonable efforts have been made to publish reliable data and information, but the authors, editors and publisher cannot assume any responsibility for the validity of all materials or the consequences of their use.

Trademark Notice: Registered trademark of products or corporate names are used only for explanation and identification without intent to infringe.

ISBN: 978-1-63240-787-0

Cataloging-in-Publication Data

Entrepreneurship : launching and managing new ventures / edited by Scott Gibson.
 p. cm.
Includes bibliographical references and index.
ISBN 978-1-63240-787-0
1. Entrepreneurship. 2. Industrial management. 3. New business enterprises.
I. Gibson, Scott.
HB615 .E58 2019
658.421--dc23

For information on all Clanrye International publications
visit our website at www.clanryeinternational.com

Contents

Preface IX

Chapter 1 **An Analytical Analysis of Entrepreneurial Skills in Some Selected Small Scale Businesses in the Southern Region of Nigeria** 1
Anifowose Oladotun Larry

Chapter 2 **Innovation and SME Development: Indonesian Experience in Uzbekistan Context** 5
Golibjon Y

Chapter 3 **E-Government Success Factors: Views of Saudi Professionals** 9
Fahad Bin Muhaya, Saad Haj Bakry and Suhail M AlAlmaee

Chapter 4 **Green Energy in Turkey** 15
Yeter Demir U and Ufuk E

Chapter 5 **Impact of Factors of Family Business on the Performance: A PLS-SEM Study** 18
Bharti Motwani

Chapter 6 **Challenges of Technological Entrepreneurship in Africa: The Case of Tunisia** 29
Walid Ghodbane

Chapter 7 **Joynal and Mizan (J.M.) Model for Cluster Development** 35
Md. Joynal Abdin and Md. Mizanur Rahman

Chapter 8 **Human Resource Orchestration for the Implementation of Entrepreneurial Opportunities** 42
Rinne T

Chapter 9 **Leadership Management among Construction Professionals in the Context of Nepal** 49
Khet Raj Dahal and Manoj KC

Chapter 10 **Enterprenurship Development Under Government Support in India through Business Incubation** 58
Siva Kumar A

Chapter 11 **Assessing and Developing Entrepreneurs' Self-Leadership and Super-Leadership** 65
Sibylle Georgianna

Chapter 12 **Learning Curve Spillovers and Transactions Cost in the Microfinance Industry of the Philippines** 70
Jovi Dacanay C

Chapter 13	**Entrepreneurial Passion as Mediator of the Entrepreneurial Self Efficacy and Entrepreneurial Performance, Relationship: An Empirical Study in Small Medium Businesses**..90 Muhammad Awais Siddiqui	
Chapter 14	**Compare the Characteristics of Male and Female Entrepreneurs as Explorative Study**..97 Abdulwahab Bin Shmailan	
Chapter 15	**Impact of MBA on Entrepreneurial Success: Do Entrepreneurs Acquire Capacity through the Program or Does MBA Only Signal Gifted Talent and Experience?**..104 Matsuda N and Matsuo Y	
Chapter 16	**Effects of Leadership Behavior on the Organizational Commitment and Job Satisfaction: A Public Sector Research**..111 Mehmet Sahin G and Büşra K	
Chapter 17	**Medical Value as a New Strategy to Increase Corporate Viability: Market Chances and Limitations in the Diagnostic Industry**..116 Schäfer H Hendrik, Filser Ludwig, Rohr Ulrich P, Laubender Ruediger P, Dieterle Thomas, Maitland Roger and Zaugg Christian E	
Chapter 18	**The Effect of Supervisor Support on Employee Voice Behavior based on the Self-Determination Theory: The Moderating Effect of Impression Management Motive**...124 Jui-Chih Ho	
Chapter 19	**Role of Relational Capital and Firm Performance: Analysis of a Cluster of Bell-metal Enterprises in a Rural Region in West Bengal, India**..........................132 Soumyendra Kishore Datta and Tanushree De	
Chapter 20	**Technology Innovation and Global Competition-evidence from Global 500 Strong Construction Enterprise**..138 Lai Xiao-Dong	
Chapter 21	**The Effects of Non-interest Banking on Entrepreneurship in Nigeria**....................147 Larry Anifowose	
Chapter 22	**Personal Variables and Perception of Customers on Service Quality of Commercial in Madurai**...150 Selvaraj N	
Chapter 23	**Transnational Entrepreneurship and Ghanaians Abroad: What are the Motives?**..156 Elvis Asiedu and Patrick Dede Nyarkoh	
Chapter 24	**The Influence of Decision Making in Organizational Leadership and Management Activities**..166 Nichodemus Obioma Ejimabo	
Chapter 25	**The Consequences of Entrepreneurial Outlook on Business Initiatives: The Case of Restaurant Operators**..179 Yeboah AM and Alhaji A	

Chapter 26	**Stimulating Innovation within Social Sector Organizations: The Application of Design Thinking**..186 Berzin SC and Catsouphes MP	
Chapter 27	**Performance of Entrepreneurs' Involvement of Industrial Estates in Southern Districts of Tamilnadu - A Study**..193 Selvaraj N	
Chapter 28	**Psychological Need Satisfaction as a Pre-determinant of Entrepreneurial Intentionality**..200 Francoise U, Donghong D and Janviere N	
Chapter 29	**Study on the Bank Finances to Small Scale Industries in Theni District in Tamil Nadu**..206 Selvaraj N and Balajikumar P	
Chapter 30	**Prospects and Challenges for Small-Scale Mining Entrepreneurs in South Africa**..215 Zandisile Mkubukeli and Robertson Tengeh	

Permissions

List of Contributors

Index

Preface

Entrepreneurship refers to the launch, administration and management of a new business venture. It is achieved by a combination of capital, human and material resources, undertaking risks and by developing an understanding of market demand and supply. It is also associated with designing of business and management strategies, recognition of opportunities, leadership and team building. This book is a compilation of chapters that include several significant topics relevant to entrepreneurship and the launch and management of new ventures. It also includes the research areas that are being explored in entrepreneurship and consists of contributions made by experts across the world. With its thorough approach and detailed analyses, this book is an ideal reference text for enterprising businessmen, students and experts.

This book unites the global concepts and researches in an organized manner for a comprehensive understanding of the subject. It is a ripe text for all researchers, students, scientists or anyone else who is interested in acquiring a better knowledge of this dynamic field.

I extend my sincere thanks to the contributors for such eloquent research chapters. Finally, I thank my family for being a source of support and help.

Editor

An Analytical Analysis of Entrepreneurial Skills in Some Selected Small Scale Businesses in the Southern Region of Nigeria

Anifowose Oladotun Larry*

Department of Entrepreneurship Management of Technology, Federal University of Technology, Akure, Ondo State, Nigeria

Abstract

The objective of this paper is to investigate entrepreneurship skill development through the apprenticeship scheme in some selected small scale business in the Southern region of Nigeria. The paper describes entrepreneurship skills development and also analysis the apprenticeship scheme in Southern region of Nigeria. In order to achieve the objectives, a well-structured sampling technique was employed. A total of number of 112 questionnaires were administrated to the selected small scale business owners in the southern region states which were all properly completed and analyzed using simple percentage.

The results obtained revealed that there is low level of education among the majority of the selected small scale businesses in the Southern region of Nigeria. And majority acquired their skills through the apprenticeship. The sources of apprenticeship recruitment are mainly friends and associates. The paper therefore recommends that attention there is need for regular seminars, conferences and workshops for the owners of the small scale business among the Igbo community in order for the region to experience rapid and sustainable economic transformation desired.

Keywords: Entrepreneurial skill development; Small scale business; Southern region

Introduction

Entrepreneurial skills development is a significant contributing factor of the economic growth and transformation of any society mostly in especially in a developing economies like Nigeria where the level of unemployment has reached its peak. Most graduates do not secure employment many years after they have concluded the training in their various institutions of higher learning.

The attitude of the graduates is to secure a ready-made white collar job immediately after the completion of their studies but often time these jobs are not available. The apprenticeship scheme, a systematic method of acquiring skills in a trade, has therefore been part of the culture of most African countries including Nigeria. Entrepreneurship development is therefore a means to create job opportunities for the swarming unemployed young school leavers. This paper is particularly interested in investigating the entrepreneurial development in the following selected small scale business–clothing related business, Electronics, food related business, phone related and Agriculture related business in the southern region of Nigeria [1].

It is an tries to examine the how the skills in these business were acquired, how the capital was raised, to what extent the current entrepreneurs had trained others, the line of business most Igbo-tribe are interested in this 21st century and the sources through which the apprentices are enlisted. Previous studies on entrepreneurial skills and development are mostly concentrated on large-scales business. This research work is divided into five chapters. The first chapter introduction of the topic, chapter two will focus on the theoretical framework of entrepreneurial development and the apprentice ship scheme in Nigeria. The third Chapter would be based on the methodology to be used for the data analysis. Chapter four would focus on the interpretation and analysis of the data collected using simple Southern region here denotes South East states and South –South states of Nigeria for this study percentage while the final chapter, which is chapter five, shall comprise the summary of findings, conclusion, and recommendations.

Theoretical Framework

Entrepreneurship development

Entrepreneurship development is practice, where a group of individual or group of people accepting the risk of starting and running of business. It is a means of through which jobs are created and huge benefits are derived by the public [2]. Acknowledged four reasons why people take entrepreneurial task namely, opportunities, profit, independence and challenge. Rutashobya also recognized the qualities required of a successful entrepreneur. Such a person should be self–disciplined, self-assertive, action-oriented, highly energetic and tolerant Kurtako [3]. Quoting Olomi also describing the entrepreneur from two different perspectives. Firstly, the entrepreneur is seen as the factor of production that attracts and coordinates the other factors of production. The entrepreneur is therefore the individual who has the ultimate responsibility for the overall direction of a business and bears the risks and rewards of the business.

In addition Kurtako [4], identified two major schools of entrepreneurial though, namely, the macro view and micro view. The macro view identifies a number of environmental variables that may determine the success and failure of modern entrepreneurial ventures. Most of the factors are always beyond the control of the entrepreneurs. The Macro view is also subdivided into three schools of thought, and the financial/capital school of thought identifies the following environmental factors as elements of entrepreneurial development institutions, values, socio-political and legal structures

---

*Corresponding author: Anifowose Oladotun Larry, Department of Entrepreneurship Management of Technology, Federal University of Technology, Akure, Ondo State, Nigeria, E-mail: anifowosedotun@yahoo.com

etc. The financial / capital school of thought emphasizes the financial management of entrepreneurship activities while the third the displacement school of thought, focuses on someone who feels "out of place" or is displaced from the group. A person with this kind of experience will seek for ways out of frustration by venturing into an entrepreneurship pursuit with the aim of high success to prove the critics wrong. Three major types of displacement were identified. They include political displacement, cultural and economic displacement. Other theories of entrepreneurship that thrive in the literature as summarized by Ogundele [5], include the economic theory, socio-cultural theory, political theory and historical theory. Others include the experimental theory, innovation theory, network theory, structural theory and multi-factor approach. According to Nichels et al. [2], small businesses create 75% of the new jobs in America account for more than 40% of the Gross Domestic Product (GDP) and more than 80% of Americans find their first job in small scale businesses. Nigeria's experience is not suggestively diverse especially where small scale traders, hawkers, subsistence agricultural farmers, poultry farmers, fish farmers, commercial telephone operators and various other small businesses dominate over 50% of the national economic activities.

Methodology

This chapter describes the data used in this study, the data source, and the estimation methodology.

Description of area of study

This study is performed in the framework of some selected small scale businesses which includes the followings- **clothing-related businesses, electronics business, Food related businesses** (e.g. selling of raw food stuffs plus cooked food items), **Phone related business** (Selling of recharge cards, repairing and sales of phones) and **Agriculture related business** (i.e. fish pond business, piggery business, poultry business etc.) in the Southern region of Nigeria. The states covered in this study include Rivers State, Abia State, Imo State, Anambra State, Edo State and Akwa- Ibom State. Ebonyi State was excluded due to perceived low small scale businesses thus leading to low volume of trade. The volumes of trade in these selected small scale businesses are enormous in these selected states.

Employment generation and entrepreneurial development is high as most business owners in the sector at one time or the other have at least some apprentices. These apprentices do not only acquire skills in the business but are also economically empowered to provide for themselves and other people who want to learn the trade. The unique feature of skill is that interested applicants for the apprenticeship skill know before the commencement of the training. However, this cannot be said of the higher institutions in Nigeria as the curriculum does not actually prepare graduates for self-employment but for job seekers.

Sampling procedure and analytical tool

A suitable sampling technique was employed as the questionnaires distributed to those that were available at their business locations.

The questionnaires were distributed in Rivers State, Abia State, Imo State, Anambra State, Edo State and Akwa- Ibom State. One hundred and twelve (112) questionnaires were distributed to clothing-related businesses dealers, electronics business dealers, Food related businesses dealers, Phone related business dealers and Agriculture related business dealers.

A total of 112 questionnaires, representing 100% were acutely completed and collected from the respondents. The questions were structured is such a way that respondents were required to supply information in such as qualifications, numbers of years in business, numbers of years used in acquiring the skills for the business, number of apprentices already training and average required amount of capital required to establish the apprentice. The responses were analyzed using Simple Percentage.

Data Presentation and Discussion of Findings

The qualification of the majority owners /dealers in the selected small scale businesses in the Southern region of Nigeria fall within senior school certificate and OND/NCE/A.L certificate holders. For instance, 57% have senior school certificate (WASC/SSCE), while 22% are OND/NCE/A.L certificate holders (Table 1). The educational qualification of the majority of the respondents therefore falls within senior school certificate and OND/NCE/AL certificate holders. This is likely have a slight negative on the ability to keep adequate records and it is possibly going to limit the growth of the selected small businesses. This is similar to results obtained by Madichie [3], for most Nnewi indigenes of South East Nigeria in which majority often enroll into one of form of apprenticeship immediately after their primary school education. He also stressed that lack of adequate formal education is a major barrier from transforming small scale businesses in large scale businesses (Table 2).

The number of years that the respondents have been in the business is as shown in Table 2. A total number of 60 respondents representing 53% have been in the business between 1 and 5 years, while 18% have been there for between 6 and 10 years. Majority have therefore been in business for upward of between 5 and 15 years. The implication is that the respondents must be enjoying a level of profitability that is why they have recorded a long stay in the selected small- scale business (Table 3).

The process of acquiring skills for the selected small scale business in the Southern region of Nigeria is shown in Table 3 below. Vast majority of the respondents (52%) acquired their skills through the apprenticeship, 26% acquired their apprenticeship through family business while only 22% said through formal education (i.e. government entrepreneurial centers and NGO centers). The choice to trade. The choice of trade in which an individual is to be trained is often dictated by the trade that is peculiar to the family [6], and environment.

Qualification	Frequency	Percentage
Primary School	8	7
WASC/SSCE	64	57
OND/NCE/ A.L	24	22
B.Sc./ B.A./HND	6	14
M.Sc./M.Phil.	-	-
Ph.D.	-	-
Total	112	100%

Table 1: Qualification of the Respondents.

Years of Experience	Frequency	Percentage
1-5	60	53
6- 10	20	18
11-15	16	14
16-25	12	11
Above 25	04	4
Total	112	100

Table 2: Number of years in the Business.

Method of skill acquisition	Frequency	Percentage
Formal school	25	22
Apprenticeship	58	52
Inherited family business	29	26
Total	112	100

Table 3: Method of Skill Acquisition.

The number of years used for the training (Table 4) ranged between 1 and 3 years for 62 respondents, representing 55%. Forty–five of the respondents, representing 40% claimed that they have spent between 4 and 6 years. The training, according to the respondents, does not follow a defined and structured syllabus. As good as the apprenticeship scheme is in enhancing the development of entrepreneurs and skills acquisition, the educational level of the boss is low and the rudiments of teaching are essentially lacking [7] (Table 5).

The major sources of apprentice recruitment into the apprenticeship scheme are the community through friends and Business associates. These accounted for 80% of the sources of recruitment for apprenticeship. This is because master-craftsman often accommodates their apprentices as more than 98% of them either partially or fully provided accommodation for their apprentices. In Igbo land, the master (boss) always train and set-up the apprentices. According to Madichie [3], it was confirmed that the extended family system which the Igbo society often bestows responsibility on the successful entrepreneur to train younger members of the family and community. In addition, it is mandatory to recruit members of the family and community, especially those ones who are found to be the reliable, hardworking and trustworthy compels the master-entre to co-opt his extended family members into his business chain.

Table 6 shows that about 53% of boss entrepreneurs in the selected business gave between ₦50, 000 and ₦100, 000 as a take-off grant to graduating apprentices while 36% gave between ₦101, 000 and ₦300, 000 as take-off grant. The implication of this is an increased number of entrepreneurs. It was also revealed through observation that the Igbo tribe business is usually concentrated in a location since their boss will ensure a good location for the business of his/her apprentice. Also, family members provide the major source of direct and indirect financing to make sure that the young entrepreneur matures into success after the period of apprenticeship [8].

Summary of findings

The followings observation were made

- Low levels of education exist among the entrepreneurs as majority of them have school certificate as their highest qualification.
- The majority of the entrepreneurs have been in business for between 5 and 15 years.
- A greater percentage of respondents (over 50%) acquired their skills through the apprentices' scheme.
- The duration of training ranges between 3 and 6 years.
- Friends and associates are the major source of recruiting in the apprenticeship scheme among the Igbos.
- The take-off grant the apprentice ranges between ₦ 100,000 and ₦ 300,000.
- The line of business of often considered among the selected small scale business is Food related business, followed by Clothing and Electronic business while the least considered line of small scale businesses are Phone and Agriculture businesses.

Conclusions and Recommendations

The contribution of these selected small scale businesses entrepreneurs as employer of labour and as agent for skill acquisition cannot be overemphasized. The contribution of this sub-sector to Nigeria Southern region economic transformation cannot be ascertained as most of the businesses transactions are have no database. However, one thing is certain their contribution is substantial.

Since the contribution of the sub-sector is enormous in the area already mentioned, it is appropriate for the following recommendations to be made.

- Since apprentice schemes have become a popular means of skill acquisition in many small scale businesses, it has become necessary for government and other stake holders to find a way of developing a curriculum appropriate for each selected small scale businesses and appropriate ways of evaluating the apprentices.
- Secondly, the take-off grant given to apprentices after completion of their mandatory period of training ranges between ₦100,000 and ₦300,000. In summary, an average sum of ₦200,000 (two hundred thousand naira) would have been given out as a take-off grant to set up personal businesses by the graduating apprentices. The apprenticeship scheme among the Igbo should therefore be encourage for South East and South-South to experience a total and sustainable economic transformation as a nation.
- Thirdly, regular workshops, seminars and conferences on latest Science and technology for entrepreneurs in various small scale businesses must be encouraged by the government in order to form a synergy between agriculture sector and industrial sector in which is currently dominated by the small scale businesses.
- Finally, no nation can experience any meaningful industrialization without the availability of stable and affordable power supply for these small scale businesses. Based on the above

Years of Training	Frequency	Percentage
1-3	62	55
4-6	45	40
7-10	5	5
Total	112	100

Table 4: Number of years used in Training.

Sources	Frequency	Percentage
Advertisement	8	7
Friends	44	39
Relations	28	25
Business Associate	32	29
Total	112	100

Table 5: Sources of Apprentice Recruitment.

Capital (₦)	Frequency	Percentage
50,000-100,000	60	53
101,000-300,000	40	36
301,000-500,000	8	7
501,000-1,000,000	4	4
Above 1,000,000	0	0
Total	112	100

Table 6: Capital Used to Set up Apprentice.

these recommendations but not limited is required for Nigeria experience a total and sustainable economic transformation.

Refernces

1. Enukwu EU, Mgbor M (2005) The National Directorate of Employment's Open Apprenticeship Scheme in Nigeria: New Wine in Old Wine Skin? Education+ Training 47: 325-336.

2. Nichels WG, Mchug JM, Mchugh SM (2002) Understanding Business. (6thedn), Boston: McGraw-Hill Companies Inc:164-199.

3. AnayoNkamnebe D, Nnamdi Madichie O (2003) "Entrepreneurial training and Development in Africa: Reflections on Critical Issues from Nigeria". 51 Iweka Road (Onitsha, Nigeria): could this single African address redefine business cluster development?

4. Kurtako DF, Nodgetts (2007) Entrepreneurship: Theory Process Practice. United States: Thomson South-Western 37-41.

5. Ogundele OJK (2007) Introduction to Entrepreneurship Development, Corporate Governance and Small Scale Business Management. Lagos: Molofin Nominees 71-102.

6. Obidi SS (1995) Skill Acquisition through Indigenous Apprenticeship: A Case study of the Yoruba Blacksmith in Nigeria".Comparative Education 368-394.

7. Uwameiye R, Ede Iyamu OS (2002) Methodology used in Nigeria Apprenticeship System. Education and Development 59.

8. Nwanoruo CC (2004) "Towards the Improvement of Informal Apprenticeship Scheme for Self-Reliance in Nigeria" Journal of Technology and Education in Nigeria 9: 65-70.

Innovation and SME Development: Indonesian Experience in Uzbekistan Context

Golibjon Y*
Tashkent State Institute of Oriental Studies, Uzbekistan

> **Abstract**
> Under the current increased interdependence and market globalization product and service markets have been in constant change. These changes in their turn contributing to the rise of the level of competition putting enormous pressures on enterprises of all sizes to respond quickly to the changes and developments in market affairs. One of the crucial factors of survival in this highly competitive world economy is to find the way to increase the productivity and efficiency while reducing the costs. Thus, the key for success has become enterprise's capacity to innovate and come up with innovative solutions to the production processes. It is nowhere as obvious as in the case of small and medium sized enterprises (SMEs) whose share and contribution to the overall economy have been increasing, especially, in the developing or transition economies.

Keywords: Innovation; Innovation and small and medium-sized enterprises; Research and development; Innovation development; Small and medium-sized enterprises development; Indonesian experience; Interdependence; Association of Southeast Asian nations

Introduction

Under the current increased interdependence and market globalization product and service markets has been in constant change. These changes in their turn contributing to the rise of the level of competition putting enormous pressures on enterprises of all sizes to respond quickly to the changes and developments in market affairs. One of the crucial factors of survival in this highly competitive world economy is to find the way to increase the productivity and efficiency while reducing the costs. Thus, the key for success has become enterprise's capacity to innovate and come up with innovative solutions to the production processes. It is nowhere as obvious as in the case of small and medium sized enterprises (SMEs) whose share and contribution to the overall economy have been increasing, especially, in the developing or transition economies.

Since gaining its independence in early 90s, government of Uzbekistan has paid serious attention to encouraging innovative activities of enterprises through direct and indirect state assistances and legal support. It is especially case with small and medium sized enterprises as their stake in the national economy is increasing sharply. However, although the concept of innovation is widely discussed and mostly used by the politicians, as a theoretical notion little attention has been given by the academic community. Very little, if any, scholarly work has been done on innovation in the context of SME and its likely contribution to national economy. Therefore, the current paper intends to propose new insights for further research by highlighting recent trends in innovation literature and some ASEAN countries' policy in the development of innovation in the context of SME.

Literature Review

There are wide range of definitions have been proposed on 'innovation', however, general logic of the term is quite straightforward. Innovation is a process which involves creating or re-engineering products or services to meet new market demand, introducing new processes to improve productivity, developing or applying new marketing techniques to expand sales opportunities, and incorporating new forms of management systems and techniques to improve operational efficiency (Bologna SME Conference, 2000). Or, putting it simple, innovation is a commercial exploitation of new ideas as products, processes and organizational techniques [1]. Innovation takes many forms, from investing in research and development (R&D), to gaining knowledge and experience from others' investments. The main goal of the innovation is to ensure higher productivity through investing in knowledge capital, because markets that rely on input resources and price signals alone cannot be effective in ensuring higher productivity.

Innovation, be it in small or bigger scale, has a direct impact on overall national economic performance. Innovation is considered to be vital in addressing market failures, ensuring higher productivity, and contributing to overall economic growth. Thus, governments have been doing their best to establish a favorable climate for product and service innovation in order to create a more progressive economy and greater employment opportunities. However, it is not to say that any state policy aimed at promoting innovation will bring desired outcomes. State innovation policy is deemed effective when the benefits exceed the costs of deployed resources, and social returns are greater than their alternative uses. Therefore, in evaluating the efficiency and effectiveness of innovation policy one should compare the level of spending and ultimate social returns. More often than not, according to some studies, social returns to innovation are high and exceed private returns by a wide margin [2,3].

The role of innovation in economic progress is undeniable and there is body of literature that proves it. The initial scholarly interest in the role of innovation in economic dynamism arose from the work of Schumpeter [4]. The topic further developed by Solow with a new emphasis on explaining the origins of innovation. In contrast to neo-

---

*Corresponding author: Golibjon Y, PhD researcher, Tashkent State Institute of Oriental Studies, Uzbekistan
E-mail: golibhackerjon@yahoo.com

classical economists who believe that capital accumulation is the main driver of economic progress, innovation theorists contend that evolving institutions, entrepreneurs and technological change lay at the center of the growth. As Schumpeter's remarkably put it, creative destruction is crucial to economic progress.

However, it took some time until Schumpeter's ideas on the role of innovation in economic growth has gained greater acceptance amongst scholarship. The literature on innovation is now vast. Leading scholars of innovation economics include Paul Romer, Elhanan Helpman, W. Brian Arthur, Robert Axtell, Richard R. Nelson, Richard Lipsey, Michael Porter, Christopher Freeman, Igor Yegorov and etc. Common belief is that innovation is an important answer to the fundamental issue of economics - puzzle of total factor productivity growth.

For the innovation theorists' economic growth could no longer be sustained through the traditional ways of increasing inputs used in the production process. Instead, creativity and new ideas are needed for generating growth and ensuring economic prosperity. Proponents of innovation claim that the notion of capital accumulation is no longer relevant to the current knowledge-based world economy. The only way to prosper is innovative capacity facilitated by knowledge and technological externalities [5].

For a group of scholars, the impact of innovation tends to explain labor productivity [6]; Roper et al. [7]. Some of them use value added per labor as an independent variable [8], while others give a bigger credit to the turnover per worker [9]. Both approaches provide evidence that innovation contributed to the increased welfare. Contribution is of twofold: it may lower the costs or expands the demand, or both. If enterprise faces a perfectly inelastic demand then the price cuts resulted from the successful introduction of innovation would impact productivity increase and, hence, the increase in welfare. Consequently, a price reduction expands sales and turnover, and productivity increase understates the value of the innovation [10].

Needless to stress, until recently development of innovation and formation of knowledge-capital have been attributed exclusively to the large manufacturing firms and studied through this prism [11-14]. This stems from the fact that introduction and diffusion of innovation used to be costly, and small and medium sized businesses could barely afford it. Likewise, lack of sufficient human recourses is also one of the reasons that SMEs usually record weak performances in terms of research and innovation.

Lessons from Indonesia

However, more recently due to the technological advancement and development of information-communication technologies, coverage of the innovation has been expanded to small and medium sized businesses, and hence their matter for the national economy is rising steadily [9]. Innovation, Schumpeter [15] put it, has become a competitive stake for SMEs in terms of their place in the productive system of economies. Today investment in new technologies and know-how is strongly associated with innovation by smaller businesses and this has been contributing to the overall national economic progress. It is especially true with some ASEAN economies where small and medium sized enterprises account for more than 90% of all enterprises and whose share and contribution to the overall economy is utterly enormous.

Speaking particularly of Indonesian case, SMEs account for up to 97% of employment and contribute to 58% of country's overall GDP. Thus, particular attention of the Indonesian government has been paid to boosting competitiveness and productivity of SMEs through promoting innovation. And country's Science, Technology and Innovation (STI) policy aim at transforming the entire national economy into knowledge-based economy (KBE) as it is recognized to be an important determinant of the national wealth and prosperous future. Recent economic downturns have made innovation far more important to target challenges, enhance country's competitiveness and ensure greater employability [16]. According to the data, so called Gross Expenditure Research and Development (GERD) was accounted for about 8.09 Trillion IDR in 2014, which is roughly 49% greater than it was in 2009 and much higher that previous years [17]. Moreover, according to innovation sub-index of the Global Competitiveness Report, Indonesia ranked 30th amongst the 144 countries in 2014 which is also a remarkable achievement as compared to other developing economies.

Enterprises of sizes, be it state-owned or private, are highly encouraged or urged to closely collaborate with the national and independent research institutes and country's leading universities. Indonesian government is also improving the intellectual property system, creating supportive schemes that encouraging and boost patent applications. The state ministry which responsible for research and technology (RISTEK) is trying to increase the capability and capacity of leading research institutes through supporting them improve their research infrastructures and build networks with their counterparts in abroad, and hence, enhance their contribution to the national innovation system. Indonesian STI policy is multidimensional and many agencies are involved in this process. Furthermore, in 2010 Indonesian government established an independent National Innovation Committee in order to ensure efficient and effective coordination of the collaboration between respective agencies. Along with this, in 2012, it was established Indonesia Endowment Fund for Education which was aimed at effectively managing the budget provided for research and related infrastructure development.

It is important to stress that a wide-scale governmental measures to promote innovation in SMEs have made an impact on the Indonesian national economy and the data clearly proves it. For instances, according to the estimates of McKinsey Global Institute [18], Indonesia has become 16th largest economy in the world and it is expected to become 7th by 2030. Moreover, based on World Bank Data [19], years right after the global financial crisis, Indonesia has been able to sustain relatively high GDP growth rate, averaging 5.8% between 2010 and 2014 (6.2% in 2010, 6.2% in 2011, 6.0% in 2012, 5.6% in 2013 and 5.0% in 2014). Indonesia's admission to the G20 club is another recognition of its position in the world economy.

The relationships between Uzbekistan and Indonesia was officially established on June 23, 1992. Both countries have recognized the importance of each other's potential. The government of Uzbekistan recognized the strategic importance of Indonesia, Southeast Asia's largest economy, the world's 10th largest economy in terms of purchasing power parity (PPP) and the world's biggest Moslem population. Meanwhile, the government of Indonesia is aware of Uzbekistan strategic importance as the gate to Central Asia, and a growing economy also a potential market. In terms of diplomatic relations, Indonesia has an embassy in Tashkent, while Uzbekistan has an embassy in Jakarta. Both countries have Moslem-majority population and both are members of Organization of Islamic Cooperation. The bilateral trade between Indonesia and Uzbekistan is about US$ 13.6 million in 2014. The export volume from Indonesia to Uzbekistan reached US$ 8.7 million in 2014, while import from Uzbekistan to Indonesia reached

US$ 4.7 million. Based on Indonesian Ministry of Trade data [20], the main export commodities from Indonesia to Uzbekistan in 2014 were refrigerators, freezers and other refrigerating or freezing equipment (total export US$ 5 million); margarine (USD 1.6 million); nonwovens, whether or not impregnated, coated, covered or laminated (US$ 0.3 million); tea, whether or not flavored (US$ 0.3 million); and soap, organic surface-active products for use as soap, in bars, cakes (US$ 0.1 millions). While the main import commodities from Uzbekistan to Indonesia in 2014 were spark-ignition reciprocating or rotary internal combustion piston engines (total import value US$ 3.5 million); pulps of fibers derived from recovered (waste and scrap) paper or paperboard or of other fibrous cellulosic material (US$ 1.1 million); and cotton, not carded or combed (US$ 0.09 million).

During the years after gaining independence from communist system, Uzbekistan has also undergone serious transformations towards building of a democratic state based on market economy. Legal and institutional foundations of the market economy have been established with the aim of enhancing competitiveness of national economy and ensuring greater progress in terms of national wealth. Due to the state economic policy and programs, Uzbekistan's economy has been developing on average of 7 % throughout past decades, which is higher than global average. However, the main issue at stake is to determine the core driver and/or source of factors that have contributed to this stable growth. Needless to stress, not all the credit could be given to the innovation policy. Natural resources and industrial policy of the government have a bigger share in the economy progress during the early decades of national development.

However, in recent years, greater emphasis has been put towards creating the conditions and prerequisites for fostering the development of innovation pillar of national economy. In 2006, in accordance with the decree of the President of Uzbekistan it was established the Committee on Coordination of the Development of Science and Technology under the Cabinet of Ministers of Uzbekistan. The main task of the committee is to coordinate the activities on the development of science and technology in national as well as local levels, to ensure effective coordination between state agencies involved in research and development, to monitor the effective implementation of research programs and projects, to ensure the use of the results of researches and innovations, to develop mutually beneficial international scientific and technical cooperation, and etc.

Another remarkable step to foster the development of innovation is the President Decree "On measures to stimulate innovative projects and technologies in production" from July 15, 2008, which sheds light upon the creation of mechanisms to facilitate the promotion of applied research and innovation, and provision of closer collaboration between science sector and enterprises, especially SMEs. Today, more than 200 organizations are involved in research and development activities to support enterprises. These organizations deal exclusively with conducting fundamental and applied researches, experimental-design development and implementation of their results in the production.

However, vast majority of the organizations involved in research and development mainly collaborate and have an agreement of cooperation with bigger businesses and industries. Innovative development in SME sector has gained lesser acceptance not due to the lack of attention from the government or miscalculation of the impact of such innovation, but rather due to the cost associated with such research and development which small businesses not always able to afford. Another issue is that there is insufficient studies and research in local level on the role of innovation in SME development and scientifically proven recommendation on how to foster innovative development of small and medium sized enterprises. Additionally, the system of state stimulations and preferences for innovation in the context of SMEs does not meet the desired level yet.

For the stated reasons, it is recommendable that the state innovation policy should provide serious attention to the following measures:

− On the issue of access to financing for research and development, government should provide support for venture capital and other types of risk financing through tax incentives;

− Government should establish a clear mechanism to work directly/exclusively with SMEs through offering special financial arrangements for research activities, particularly in the early stages of development of SMEs;

− Access to new technologies and know-how should focused on cooperative information-sharing at the local, regional, national and international levels;

− National patent system should be effective, user-friendly and with lower cost. Special patent regime for SMEs could be very efficient;

− High priority should be given to the education and training in order for providing a competitive foundation for the economy in general;

− Scientific research and studies should be promoted and, if necessary, financed in order to involve researchers in the applied research to come up with scientifically proven recommendation on how to foster innovative development in SME sector;

− Finally, regulatory and administrative burdens should be seriously reduced.

References

1. OECD (2003) Tax Incentives for Research and Development. Trends and Issues, Paris.
2. Griffith R, Redding S, Van Reenen J (2001) Measuring the Cost-Effectiveness of an R&D Tax Credit for the UK. Fiscal Studies 22: 375-399.
3. Wieser R (2005) Research and development productivity and spillovers: empirical evidence at the firm level. Journal of Economic Surveys 19: 587-621.
4. Schumpeter JA (1950) Capitalism, socialism and democracy. Harper & Row, New York.
5. Antonelli C (2003) The Economics of Innovation, New Technologies, and Structural Change. Routledge, London.
6. Belderbos R, Carree M, Lokshin B (2004) Cooperative R&D and Firm Performance. Research Policy 33: 1477-1492.
7. Roper S, Du J, Love JH (2008) Modelling the Innovation Value Chain. Research Policy 37: 961-977.
8. Crepon B, Duguet E, Mairesse J (1998) Research, Innovation, and Productivity: An Econometric Analysis at the Firm Level. Economics of Innovation and New Technology 7: 115-158.
9. Hall B, Lotti F, Mairesse J (2009) Innovation and Productivity in SMEs: Empirical Evidence for Italy. Small Business Economics 33: 13-33
10. Foreman-Peck J (2010) Effectiveness and Efficiency of SME Innovation Policy. Cardiff Economics 41: 55-70.
11. Jones C, Williams J (1998) Measuring the social return to R&D. Quarterly Journal of Economics 113: 1119-1136.
12. Lee S, Park G, Yoon B, Park J (2009) Open innovation in SMEs-an intermediated network model. Research Policy 39: 290-300.
13. Spithoven A, Clarysse B, Knockaert M (2010) Building absorptive capacity to organise inbound open innovation in traditional industries. Technovation 30: 130-141.

14. Parida V, Westerberg M, Frishammar J (2012) Inbound open innovation activities in high-tech SMEs: the impact on innovation performance. Journal of Small Business Management 50: 283-309.
15. Schumpeter JA (1983) The theory of economic development. Transaction Publishers, New Brunswick.
16. Kuncoro A (2012) Globalization and Innovation in Indonesia: Evidence from Micro-Data on Medium and Large Manufacturing Establishments.
17. OECD (2014) Indonesia, in OECD Science, Technology and Industry Outlook 2014, OECD Publishing.
18. McKinsey Global Institutem (2012) The Archipelago Economy: Unleashing Indonesia's Potential.
19. Word Bank (2014) GDP Growth (annual %) by country.
20. Indonesian Ministry of Trade (2015) 'Indonesian product got preference tariff 50 percent cheaper in Uzbekistan's market'.

E-Government Success Factors: Views of Saudi Professionals

Fahad Bin Muhaya, Saad Haj Bakry and Suhail M AlAlmaee
King Saud University, Riyadh, Saudi Arabia

> **Abstract**
>
> E-Government success is associated with various factors. This paper is concerned with exploring such factors and investigating, through a survey, how e-government professionals view them, as this would help finding ways for the future promotion of e-government success. The work identifies "35" success factors associated with seven levels including: "the international level, the national level, the sector level, the organization level, the requirements level, the services level, and the user level". The survey asks e-government professionals to assess each factor from the viewpoints of importance and current state or impact. This assessment has six grades starting from "no" importance or impact and moving up to: "low, below average, average, above average, and high". "88" Saudi e-government professionals participated in the survey. The results obtained show that the importance of most success factors considered has been above average or close to "high", except for few which were slightly less. The results also emphasized the gap between importance and current state or impact for each factor. This gap ranged from "40%" to over "80%". The work provides useful knowledge for the future development of e-government. It is an example of a knowledge sharing exercise that should become a normal practice for the purpose of achieving development based on collective wisdom. This practice can be expanded to include users for whom the services are provided.

Keywords: e-Government: importance; Impact; Knowledge sharing; Future development

Introduction

This section introduces the work presented in this paper in three steps. It starts by emphasizing the importance of e-government. This is followed by viewing the support e-government development is receiving at various levels. The problem considered by the paper and its benefits are then presented.

Importance of e-government

It is widely accepted that using information and communication technology (ICT) to provide various government and business services provides: faster, cheaper, better, different, and more secure (FCBDS) services [1]. This provides advanced efficiency and enhanced effectiveness not only to those concerned, but also to society as a whole [2]. In this respect, government services have special importance, as every government is the sole organization in its own country, where it provides services to all businesses and individuals that no other organization can do.

Figure 1 provides an illustrative view of the various dimensions of e-government services [3]. It shows that these services can be made available 24 hours for citizens (G-C) and for businesses (G-B); and that they support interaction among government departments (G-G), in addition to directly or indirectly enhancing interaction among citizens and businesses (C-B).

E-government should enable anyone visiting a city website to communicate and interact with city employees via the Internet with graphical user interfaces (GUI), instant-messaging (IM), audio/video presentations, and in any way more sophisticated than a simple email letter to the address provided at the site" and "the use of technology to enhance the access to and delivery of government services to benefit citizens, business partners and employees". The focus should be on:

• The use of information and communication technologies, and particularly the Internet, as a tool to achieve better government.

• The use of information and communication technologies in all facets of the operations of a government organization.

• The continuous optimization of service delivery, constituency participation and governance by transforming internal and external relationships through technology, the Internet and new media.

Whilst e-government has traditionally been understood as being centered on the operations of government, e-governance is understood to extend the scope by including citizen engagement and participation in governance. As such, following in line with the OECD definition of

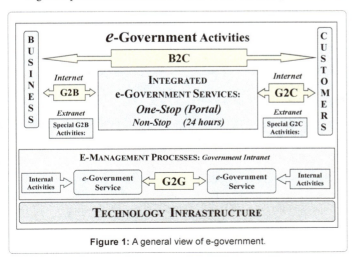

Figure 1: A general view of e-government.

*Corresponding author: Saad Haj Bakry, King Saud University, Riyadh, Saudi Arabia, E-mail: shb@ksu.edu.sa

e-government, e-governance can be defined as the use of ICTs as a tool to achieve better governance.

Development of e-government

Development of e-government has been receiving support at different level; and here are some examples:

➢ At the international level, support has come through the following:

o The Millennium Development Goals (MDG) issued by world leaders after their United Nations (UN) meeting in the year 2000, at the turn to the third millennium [4].

o The World Summit on Information Society held in Geneva in 2003 and subsequently in Tunis in 2005 [5].

o The United Nations Department of Economic and Social Affairs (UNDESA), which publishes an annual worldwide survey of e-government development [6].

➢ At the national level, various governments have produced plans and initiated e-government development programs, like the various national plans [7,8] and "YESSER" e-government program [9] in Saudi Arabia.

➢ At the sector level, various sectors have been developing their own e-services such as the government health sector of Saudi Arabia [10].

➢ At the researchers' level, a group at King Saud University has produced a framework for the development of e-government [3], and this has been highly sighted and used [11]. In addition, YESSER researchers have published a planning initiative for e-government services at a specialized international conference in Ireland [12]. It should be noted that the development of e-government is not a start-stop process, but it is a cyclic continuous process that requires continues response to accumulated experience, advancement of technology, changing demands, and other dynamic issues.

This Paper

This paper is concerned with the assessment of e-government success factors using the experience of those who have been involved in e-government development and management in Saudi Arabia since 2005 when "YESSER" program was initiated. For this purpose, the paper presents a multi-level framework that incorporates basic e-government success factors. It provides a survey questionnaire that enables the e-government professionals to assess the importance and current state or impact of these factors. The outcome of the work would be useful in supporting the future development of e-government toward enhanced success.

Success Factors: A Multi-Level Framework

The levels of the framework of the basic e-government success factors considered here are illustrated in Figure 2. This section presents these factors according to each level; and it also shows how the assessment of these factors has been enabled through a survey questionnaire.

The international level

This level is concerned with factors related to international influence; they involve the following:

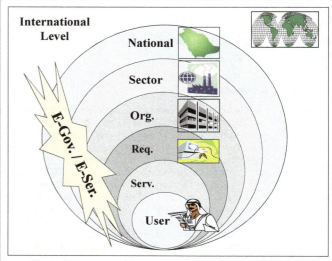

Figure 2: The levels of the framework incorporating the basic e-government success factors considered.

❏ The MDG direction toward supporting the utilization of ICT for development [4].

❏ The WSIS direction toward enhancing ICT services and expanding their use [5].

❏ The UNDESA annual assessment and ranking of the e-government state in different countries [6].

❏ The existent of international cooperation or an international center for sharing knowledge, skills, and experience at the world level, with respect to e-government implementation.

❏ The presence of international technical and management standards for the various issues of e-government implementation.

The national level

This level is related to factors concerned with national influence; and they include the following.

❏ The direction of the Saudi national science and technology policy toward ICT development and use [7].

❏ The direction of the Saudi national ICT policy toward enhanced and expanded ICT services [8].

❏ The direction of "YESSER" program toward supported e-government development all over Saudi Arabia.

❏ The existent of national cooperation or a national center for sharing knowledge, skills, and experience, with respect to Saudi e-government implementation.

❏ The presence of Saudi national technical and management standards for the various issues of e-government implementation.

The sector level

In e-government, various sectors have their own special issues, in addition to the general issues. This level is related to factors concerned with sector specific issues; and these include the following.

❏ Sector directions toward e-government and e-services development.

❑ Directions of professional societies associated with the sector.

❑ The actual sector plans and projects.

❑ The existent of sector-level cooperation or special sector center for sharing knowledge, skills, and experience for enhanced implementation.

❑ The presence of sector technical and management standards.

The organization level

This level is concerned with factors associated with individual organizations issues; and these include the following.

❑ Organization directions.

❑ Top management attitude.

❑ Actual plans and projects.

❑ The existent of clearly identified implementation responsibilities.

❑ The presence of organization's technical and management standards.

The requirements level

This level is concerned with factors associated with e-government requirements issues; and these include the level of readiness of the following issues.

❑ Financial resources.

❑ Human resources.

❑ ICT infrastructure.

❑ E-government technical requirements.

❑ Information security.

The services level

This level is concerned with factors associated with delivering e-government services; and these include the level of availability of the following.

❑ Download of needed information.

❑ Exchange of information.

❑ Delivery of simple direct services.

❑ Delivery of sophisticated services that involve multi-party interaction.

❑ Delivery of smart services, such as those of grid computing [13].

The user level

This level is concerned with factors associated with the e-government user; and these include the following.

❑ User awareness and skills in using the e-government services.

❑ User drive toward using the services.

❑ The existent of cooperation or user groups to promote making use of the services.

❑ The existent of help, feedback and cooperation channels between users on the one hand and those at the levels above on the other.

❑ User behavior in making use of the services.

Assessment issues

The above proposed "35 e-government success factors" have been incorporated in a questionnaire, according to their levels, for the purpose of enabling Saudi e-government professionals to give their views of each one of them. Two issues are considered for each factor: its importance; and its current state or impact. Each issue is assessed according to the six grades given in Table 1.

Assessment of Success Factors: A Survey

The questionnaire of the framework has been presented and distributed in a "YESSER" meeting attended by Saudi professionals responsible for e-government services in Saudi Arabia. The questionnaire was answered by "88 professionals"; and the results obtained are presented in the following.

The international factors

Figure 3 presents the collective outcome of grading for each international success factor considering: its importance, and its current state or impact. The results obtained illustrate the following:

❑ The grades concerned with the importance of the international factors range from average to above average, and do not go beyond above average except for international standards.

❑ The grades of the impact or current state of these factors range from below average to average, which is clearly much lower than the grade for the importance.

❑ The relative differences in grades between importance and impact or current state range from "50%" for MDG to around "70%" for cooperation.

The national factors

Figure 4 presents the collective outcome of grading for each national success factor including: its importance, and its current state or impact. The results obtained indicate the following:

0	1	2	3	4	5
Non-existent	Low	Below Average	Average	Above Average	High

Table 1: The grades of assessing the success factors used for both: factor importance and its current state or impact.

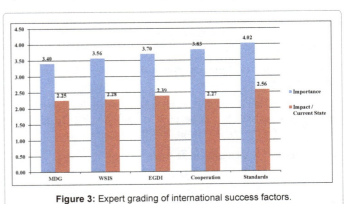

Figure 3: Expert grading of international success factors.

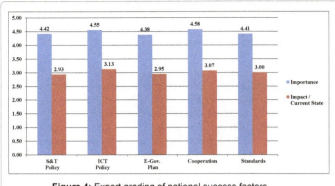

Figure 4: Expert grading of national success factors.

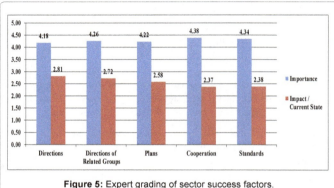

Figure 5: Expert grading of sector success factors.

❏ The grades concerned with the importance of the national factors are well advanced with all exceeding the grade of above average toward the high grade.

❏ The grades of the impact or current state of these factors are around average.

❏ The relative differences in grades between the importance of the national factors and their impact or current state range from around "45%" for the national ICT policy to over "50%" for the national science and technology.

Assessment of sector factors

Figure 5 shows the collective outcome of grading for each sector level factor including: its importance, and its current state or impact. The results obtained illustrate the following:

❏ Like the national factors, the grades concerned with the importance of the sector factors are well advanced with all exceeding the grade of above average.

❏ The grades of the impact or current state of these factors do not reach the grade of average.

❏ The relative differences in grades between the importance of the sector factors and their impact or current state range from around "50%" for sector directions to over "80%" for cooperation.

Assessment of organization factors

Figure 6 shows the collective outcome of grading for each organization level factor including: its importance, and its current state or impact. The results obtained illustrate the following:

❏ Like the above two levels, the grades concerned with the importance of the organization factors are well advanced with all exceeding the grade of above average.

❏ The grades of the impact or current state of these factors range from below average to around average.

❏ The relative differences in grades between the importance of the national factors and their impact or current state range from around "45%" for the organization directions, management and plan to over "70%" for responsibility.

Assessment of requirements factors

Figure 7 shows the collective outcome of grading for each requirements level factor including: its importance, and its current state or impact. The results obtained illustrate the following:

❏ Like the above three levels, the grades concerned with the importance of the requirements factors are well advanced with all well exceeding the grade of above average.

❏ The grades of the impact or current state of these factors range from below average to around average.

❏ The relative differences in grades between the importance of the national factors and their impact or current state range from around "50%" for the financial resources to over "70%" for human resources.

Assessment of services factors

Figure 8 shows the collective outcome of grading for each services

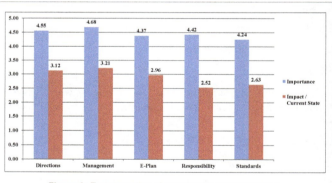

Figure 6: Expert grading of organization success factors.

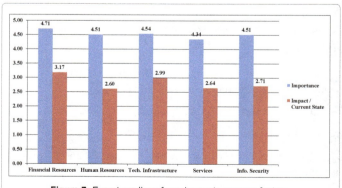

Figure 7: Expert grading of requirements success factors.

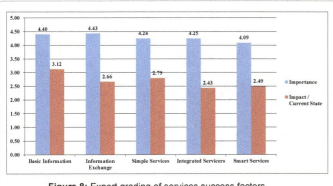

Figure 8: Expert grading of services success factors.

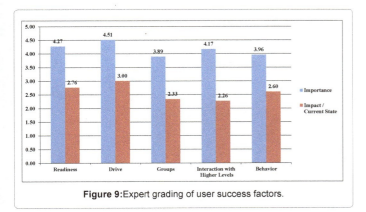

Figure 9: Expert grading of user success factors.

level factor including: its importance, and its current state or impact. The results obtained illustrate the following:

❑ Like the above four levels, the grades concerned with the importance of the services factors are well advanced with all exceeding the grade of above average.

❑ The grades of the impact or current state of these factors range from below average to around average.

❑ The relative differences in grades between the importance of the services factors and their impact or current state range from around "40%" for basic information delivery to over "70%" for integrated services.

Assessment of user factors

Figure 9 shows the collective outcome of grading for each user level success factor including: its importance, and its current state or impact. The results obtained illustrate the following:

❑ Three out of five grades concerned with the importance of the services factors are exceeding the grade of above average, while the rest are slightly less.

❑ The grades of the impact or current state of these factors range from below average to around average.

❑ The relative differences in grades between the importance of the services factors and their impact or current state range from around "50%" for user drive to over "80%" for user interaction with higher levels.

Conclusions and Future Work

The work presented in this paper is one example of a knowledge sharing exercise concerned with e-government success factors among Saudi professionals in charge of e-government services. Such exercises would support e-government success through views and feedbacks that promote future development with collective wisdom. While the work explores "35 potential success factors", other factors may be explored in other knowledge sharing exercises in the future. In addition, future knowledge sharing exercises may be extended to include not only e-government professionals, but also e-government users. This would provide a richer knowledge base and enhanced collective wisdom for the future development of e-government services.

Within the scope of the work presented in this paper, the collective views on the importance of "29" factors exceeded the grade of above average toward the high grade; while "6" factors did not reach above average, but exceeded average on the scale considered. "4" out of these "6" factors are associated with the international level, while the other "2" are related to the user level.

The gap between the importance and the impact or current state for all "35" factors was quite wide. It reached no less than "40%" and went up to over "80" percent. This leads to the conclusion that future e-government plans should consider the promotion of the current state and impact of all "35" factors considered. Ways for doing so, would involve various development issues that need to be studied including: human, technical, and management issues, which are of dynamic nature.

In summary, future integrated action is recommended for Saudi Arabia and other countries on the following main issues:

❑ The development of a program of knowledge sharing exercises for the continuous assessment and improvement of e-government. Such exercises should not only involve e-government professionals but also users.

❑ The initiation of research work concerned with finding better human, technical and management ways for enhancing the impact of the important success factors on e-government development.

❑ Building a dynamic knowledge base that considers the continuous changes of e-government technology, management practices, innovative applications, demands and other dynamic issues.

❑ These integrated work dimensions would provide useful tools for the future development of e-government for the benefit of building an efficient and effective knowledge-based society.

Acknowledgement

The authors acknowledge the support of QIYAS Project of Saudi E-Government Program (YESSER)-and-King Abdullah Institute for Research and Consulting Studies of King Saud University. They wish also to thank the Saudi e-government professionals who shared their views on e-government success factors.

References

1. Aldeen JR, Bakry SH, Nouh A (2000) Performance-based evaluations of the tangible benefits of information networks with applications. International Journal of Network Management 10: 91-101.

2. Bakry SH, Muhaya F (2011) Assessing the benefits of e-government. Second Kuwait Conference on e-Services and E-Systems, Kuwait.

3. Bakry SH (2004) Development of e-government: a STOPE view. International Journal of Network Management 14: 339-350.

4. ITU (2003) World Telecommunication Development Report: Access Indicators

for the Information Society. International Telecommunication Union, Switzerland.

5. WSIS (2003) Declaration of Principles: Building the Information Society: a global challenge in the new Millennium. World Summit on the Information Society (WSIS), Geneva 2003-Tunis 2005.

6. United Nations Department of Economic and Social Affairs (UNDESA) (2014) UN E-Government Survey.

7. STNP (2013) Science and Technology National Policy, King Abdulaziz City for Science and Technology.

8. NCITP (2013) National Communication and Information Technology Plan, Saudi Ministry of Communication and Information Technology.

9. YESSER (2003) E-Government Program, Saudi Ministry of Communication and Information Technology.

10. NEHS (2013) National E-Health Strategy, Saudi Ministry of Health.

11. Esteve J, Joseph RC (2008) comprehensive framework for the assessment of e-Government projects, Government Information Quarterly 25: 118-132.

12. Al-Almaee SM, Khayyat WR (2010) Strategic planning and supporting initiatives department: Saudi e-government program. 10th European Conference on e-Government, National Centre for Taxation Studies, University of Limerick, Ireland.

13. Arafah MA, Al-Harbi H, Bakry SH (2007) Grid computing: a STOPE view. International Journal of Network Management 17: 295-305.

Green Energy in Turkey

Yeter Demir U* and Ufuk E

Giresun University Management, Ordu, Turkey

Abstract

As in the world, Turkey has also improved the renewable energy backed by the government as well as supporting institutions and organizations which build a project and do research on renewable energy.

Turkey is a pretty rich country due to both stream wealth and geographical position. Turkey being known countries as hydroelectric energy potential in the world, owing to the streams has an important position in terms of solar, wind and geothermal power, too.

This study aims to emphasize the importance of green energy in Turkey and create awareness the impacts of renewable energy on provinces having green energy potential, especially in an economic sense with green energy studies.

Keywords: Energy resources; Renewable energy; Green energy; Wind power; Solar power

Introduction

Energy is among the essentials of our lives. The nature is damaged by humankind in voluntarily so that the energy we use in our daily life is produced.

During green energy production and consumption, which is less harmful to the nature doesn't damage the environment. As in the world also in Turkey the tendency to green energy increased and consequently the private sector and public institutions are supported.

The aim of this study is to raise awareness revealing the renewable energy potential in Turkey.

Green energy

From past to present, notion of energy and sustainable energy resources are one of the important issues in the world. Rapidly the depletion of energy resources and insensibly the consumption of non-renewable sources such as petrol, coal and atomic energy and all of this sources' effects on environment and atmosphere lead people to use renewable energy sources [1].

Renewable energy is usually defined as energy resources that can be mostly supplied above ground without needing any production process and do not come from fossil resources and are lower harm to environmental in contrast with conventional energy resources and can renew continuous kinesis and exist on earth at the ready [2].

In other words, renewable energy is a type of energy obtained from flow of energy that exists on natural periods. In contrast with conventional energy sources, renewable resources provide a lot of environmental profits [3].

When it is examined Turkey's energy profile, the concept of renewable energy sources has a highly important position. However, the use of renewable energy sources has quite low levels and these types of energy are not adequately interested. Particularly, the use of solar and wind power contribute substantially to Turkey's energy budget. The importance of plan, policies and strategy in order to benefit properly and healthfully from renewable energy resources gradually increases [4]. We can range the types of renewable energy producing energy in Turkey as solar energy, wind power, hydro-electric power and geothermal energy.

Solar energy

Solar power is electromagnetic energy that comes constitutively from the sun. Sun is a plasmic energy resource that consists of 92% hydrogen and 8% helium and a trace of other some atom and elements. Plasma is one of the states of matter that electrons separate from nuclear because of ultra-high temperature (Figure 1) [5].

According to studies made by General Directorate, renewable energy is low levels in Black-Sea and Marmara regions in Turkey. Sunshine durations in Black Sea region vary approximately maximum between 8 and 10 hours in June. Even if Solar Power that is 1.168 KWh/m 2-years in Marmara region is under country average, it is a high rate in contrast with Europe. While sunshine durations in eastern Marmara region are average 10 hours, it can rise till 11 hours in Istanbul province. And also, the durations determine as 12 hours in Çanakkale and around.

According to a report studied by Ege University Institute of Energy, with regard to solar energy potential, Izmir is one of the most

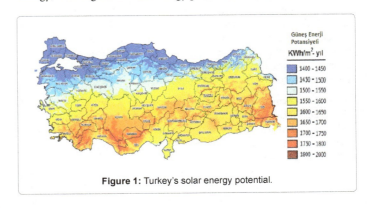

Figure 1: Turkey's solar energy potential.

---

*Corresponding author: Yeter Demir U, Giresun University Management, Ordu, Turkey, E-mail: dryeterdemir@gmail.com

advantageous after the provinces in Mediterranean and southeastern Anatolia region [6]. While sunshine durations are till 12 hours in the region, utilization of durations from solar power rise [7].

Mediterranean that is one of the most advantageous regions of solar energy is determined as 13 hours. The region is at the southern, therefore, Mediterranean being one of the regions that solar radiation is the most intense is a crucial region for solar power. It is observed that is benefited from solar energy in the region, particularly in heating and greenhouse cultivation activities.

It is observed that both Mediterranean and southeastern Anatolia regions improve close rates. In contrast to the other regions, Mediterranean and southeastern Anatolia regions have markedly the advantage thus they separate easily. Consequently, it is anticipated that development policies about power generation produced from solar energy in Mediterranean region play an active role. According to the ministry of energy and natural resources' studies, it is understood that average monthly sunshine duration is more than Turkey's average sunshine durations for each one month. When it is examined across the provinces, it is understood that only Hatay's sunshine duration in month of July and August is less than Turkey's average. However, it is seen that Kahramanmaraş and Osmaniye have more sunshine durations for one each month according to Turkey's average [8].

According to a report made by Serhat Development Agency (SERKA), Agri and Igdir come into prominence in terms of solar power potential in the region. And also, it is stated that Both Agri with its solar radiation values and Igdir with its long sunshine duration are pretty convenient for solar power investments. According to reviews, Igdir's the average annual of Sunshine duration is 9.149. It is high than 7.49 which is Turkey's average annual sunshine duration. Moreover, it is determined that Igdir's sunshine duration in the summer month increases above 12 hours and Agri has annual average 1700 kWh solar radiation values. Within this scope, the report says that it should be encouraged investments feasibility for power generation via photovoltaic panels and to be done feasibilities based upon greenhouse cultivations via solar power in these provinces and to popularize water heater system via solar energy throughout the region [9].

Wind energy

Wind power consists of replacing air mass that has different heats. 1-2% of Energy, which comes from sun to the world, converts into wind power. Taken into consideration Turkey's geographical features, it can be seen that Turkey is a rich country in terms of wind energy potential. In result of measurements made by meteorology, it is determined that southeastern Anatolia and the Marmara regions' wind power density is rather rich in contrast with other regions [10].

It is confirmed that Marmara region has maximum value with 3.29 m/sec and 51 W/m² with regard to average annual wind speed and power density in 10 meter-high. On the other hand, Eastern Anatolia region has the lowest level with 2.12 m/sec speed and 13.19 W/m² power densities. 11 certified wind farms that are above 50 W/m² with not exceeding 20 W/m² 14 items and 15 items between 30-40 W/m² have been activated in Turkey in 2014. Examined Wind power committee's power table, it is in evidence 41% of power to intensify in Aegean region while wind power committee in Aegean region says that 40% of power intensifies within İzmir provincial borders. This rate that corresponds to formed power 312, 4 MW, points out electric power production annual 826.500.000 kWh. Moreover, wind electricity, acquired from Aegean region, is 2.000.000.000 kwh/year, and it is sufficient to supply İzmir's domestic-based electricity energy demand [6].

In consideration of velocity distribution of wind power that the cities have in Southeastern Anatolian region, it is observed that Hatay is the most advantageous one in terms of wind power in that region. As a result of studies, it is confirmed Hatay's formed wind energy power as 216 MW. Furthermore, it is determined that Gokcedag RES which has formed power 135 MW in Osmaniye, is third big wind energy switchboard of Turkey after Balıkesir RES that has formed power 143 MW and Soma RES that has formed power 141 MW [11].

Canakkale's wind energy potential comes into prominence due to location in Marmara region. It is confirmed the total to be established power capacity in Canakkale [12].

Hydro-electric power

Hydro-Electric switchboards (HPP) convert running water force into electricity. Water flow velocity or water flow arranges energy amount in running water. Running water which flows in a big river has vast amount of energy. Or, when water flows from a high point, it is acquired high amount of energy. In both ways, water, taken into the ducts or pipes, flows towards turbines, and it supplies to turn turbines that have column like a propeller for power generation. Turbines bases upon generators and they convert mechanical energy into power generation [8].

According to information taken from Energy Market Regulatory Authority, it can be seen in process of operation of HPP's energy power in Table 1. While Black-sea region is in the first place as region that produces more than energy 50 MW, Marmara region takes place last row. When we look at Sequences of HPP that produce low energy than 10 MW, Black-sea region ranks first. While Black-sea comes first in the number of HPP in the form of total operating, Mediterranean region comes second.

Statistical information in Table 2, that is acquired from Energy Market Regulatory Board shows that Black-sea region comes first in continuing HPP, while Marmara region comes second. When continuing HPP completes, 1656 HPP will have already begun energy generation.

There is among Turkey's 2023 targets to use overall potential for Hydroelectricity in energy generation. According to a report made by Turkish Electricity Transmission Corporation (TEIAS in Turkish), examined energy map in compliance with Turkey's formed hydraulic power, Although Hatay in Southeastern Anatolia region has under 100 MW formed hydraulic energy power, it can be shown that Kahramanmaras ve Osmaniye have between 100 MW and 1000 MW formed hydraulic energy power. Accompanied by actualizing

	≤10 MW	10-50 MW	≥50MW	Toplam
Marmara Region	21	8	2	31
Aegean Region	13	9	4	26
Mediterranean Region	41	30	17	88
Central Anatolia Region	25	21	9	55
Black Sea Region	57	64	28	149
Eastern Anatolia Region	42	27	8	77
Southeastern Anatolia Region	8	9	7	24
Total	207	168	75	450

Table 1: Distribution by licensed businesses in the region and hydroelectric power plants installed capacity.

	≤10 MW	10-50 MW	≥50MW	Toplam
Marmara Region	168	83	86	337
Aegean Region	75	100	61	236
Mediterranean Region	88	67	48	203
Central Anatolia Region	94	60	33	187
Black Sea Region	186	157	53	396
Eastern Anatolia Region	99	68	34	201
Southeastern Anatolia Region	40	32	24	96
Total	750	567	339	1656

Table 2: Ongoing construction of the hydroelectric distribution by region and council of power.

Figure 2: Turkey geothermal resource distribution and application map.

Hydraulic energy potential projects, it is anticipated that Hatay via HPP that produced the amount of electricity rises from 10 MW to 46 MW and Kahramanmaraş rises from 842 MW to 1.402 MW and Osmaniye rises from 774 MW to 844 MW [13].

Geothermal energy

It is understood that Turkey being seventh of the world in terms of geothermal energy potential can supply whole electricity demand till 5% and radiant density demand in heating till 30% [11].

Examined Figure 2, it is showed that geothermal energy resources have parallels with tectonic faults. Hence, it should be indicated that Aegean region is a crucial point in terms of geothermal energy. Particularly, Izmir has richest geothermal field of Turkey and Aegean region. Notably Balcova, the towns of Seferihisar, Cesme, Dikili, Bergama, Aliaga and Bayindir are important geothermal fields [6].

Discussions

Acar et al. [14], were determined the green energy to reduce environmental pollution, and as energy that the line technology and requirements will develop rapidly.

Ozkaya [15], when intending to say that the main features of the renewable energy are to reduce carbon dioxide emission and helpful to protect the environment, because it is domestic resource, it must reduce foreign dependency and make a contribution to increasing employment and also get support from public opinion widely.

Kumbur et al. [16], were determined as great importance energy resources the green energy resources due to the continuous and sustainable, and also were defined that environmental effects of green energy resource is more slightly than non-renewable energy resources.

Conclusion

It is tried to determine the regions' current situation and important sub-regionals that constitutes renewable energy resources in the studies made by Development agencies and other institutions. In continuation of the these studies, it should be formed healthy and reliable data sets belonging to renewable energy resources and supplied the data sets continuity and updating. For instance; the measurements of renewable energy sources should be locally and uninterruptedly done and recorded. It should be realistically reviewed the regions' gross, technique and economical potential according to emerging technologies [17].

• After it is created required awareness by way of being encouraged renewable energy investments, it will be supplied to get locals' electrical demand through a cheaper process and it will be a perfect example in Turkey those who will establish renewable energy coops. Moreover, it is considered that renewable energy switchboards' building and operating period plays an important role in employment and economy.

Refernces

1. Kulekci OC (2009) Place of Geothermal Energy in The Content of Renewable Energy Sources and it's Importance for Turkey. Ankara University Journal of Environmental Science 1: 83-91.
2. Adiyaman C (2012) Turkiye'nin Yenilenebilir Enerji Politikalari Nigde University, Institute of Social Sciences, Department of Public Administration, Nigde.
3. Ata R, Fatih O (2014) Manisa'nin Yenilenebilir Enerji Potansiyelinin Analizi-potential Analysis of Renewable Energy Sources in Manisa. Celal Bayar University Journal of Science 1: 1-10.
4. Ozturel RZ, Ecevit A (2001)"Turkey's Strategic Planning Monitoring Policies Needed for Renewable Energy Sources and Their Social and Political Consequences". Renewable Energy Resources Symposium: 28-32, Istanbul.
5. Tuba YA, Gor HP (2013) Investment Project With Analytic Hierarchy Process Method. Journal of Suleyman Demirel University Faculty of Economics and Administrative Sciences18: 89-110.
6. Anonim I (2012) Izmir ili Yenilenebilir Enerji Sektor Analizi. Ege University Solar Energy Institute, Izmir.
7. Anonim I (2015) Maden Tetkik Ve Arama Genel Mudurlugu.
8. Anonim I (2015c) YEGM carried out by the Engineering Services Hydroelectric power plant projects.
9. Muhammad AY (2015) TRA2 Bolgesi Yesil Enerji Kaynaklari Sektor Raporu. SERKA, Yesil Enerji Potansiyelini Arastirdi.
10. Ata R, Rashid (2010) "Development of Geothermal and Wind Energy from Renewable Energy Sources and Environmental Assessment". CB Soma Vocational School of Technical Sciences Journal 2: 47-54.
11. Dogak A (2014) Yenilenebilir Enerji Raporu.
12. Anonim I (2015) Canakkale Anakkale ili Ruzgar Kaynak B Zgar Kaynak Bilgileri.
13. Ayranc E (2011)"TR42 East Marmara Region Renewable Energy Report". BRAND Development Agency, Kocaeli.
14. Acar E, Dogan A (2008) "Evaluation of Potential Environmental Effects", VII National Clean Energy Symposium, December 17-19: 675-682, Istanbul.
15. Ozkaya SY (2015) Yenilenebilir Enerji Kaynaklari.
16. Kumbur H, Ozer Z, Ozsoy HD, Hunter ED (2015) Turkiye'de Geleneksel ve Yenilenebilir Enerji Kaynaklarının Potansiyeli ve Cevresel Etkilerinin Karsilastirilmasi.
17. Anonim I (2015d) Gunes Enerjisi Potansitel Atlasi (GEPA).

Impact of Factors of Family Business on the Performance: A PLS-SEM Study

Bharti Motwani*

Institute of Management and Research, Information Technology, Vijay Nagar Indore, Madhya Pradesh-452010, India

Abstract

Family Business is seen as significant source for economic growth and development in today's world. Family businesses have the potential to outperform any other form of business organization through their inherent synergies between capital and management. Performance is an essential indicator of the organisational success and competitive advantage of firms. If firms are able to identify the factors that determine improved performance, they could take advantage of their specific features. The purpose of this research is to give insight in the determinants of family business that contribute in meeting/exceeding performance objectives of the firm. Structural Equation Modelling is used for the analysis.

Keywords: Transparent; Communication; Family business

Introduction

Family Business is seen as significant source for economic growth and development in today's world. Family businesses have the potential to outperform any other form of business organization through their inherent synergies between capital and management. Family businesses are essentially people businesses and are the backbone of the world economy. They generate wealth, offer jobs, and exist for longer periods of time. A family business is a commercial organization in which management is a prime concern by multiple generations of a family. It is any type of business operation in which a group of relatives have controlling interest in the organization.

In a family business, the business is passed from one generation to the next, with younger generation given training to enter the business and taking different duties from their parents over time. Family Business enhances the prospects for firm survival [1], by helping to create and sustain conditions of trust, identity, and norms of reciprocity and obligation [2,3]. Typically, family members will hold key roles in terms of being decision makers, improving their skills and talents by hiring employees that are capable of managing other tasks. Family firms may also be viewed by family members as a source of socio-emotional wealth.

Family Business is guided by the desire to build a healthy business that they want to pass on to their children. Scholars of family business argue that the firm succession is a vital part of the family business and succession can lead to an important infusion of entrepreneurial energy based on the potential of new owners and managers to rejuvenate their firms [4]. However, the nature and degree of involvement will depend on the responsibilities that family members has within the organization.

Family businesses (FBs) represent the majority of firms around the world, and the research focusing on the implications of family involvement in business ventures is growing exponentially [5-7], But, according to Carlos [8], the field of family firms has been of interest to management researchers and writers as a topic of scholarly inquiry since the 1980s; however, the discipline has been largely ignored until the last decade. Also, according to Bhalla [9], research into family businesses is considered to be in an evolutionary phase and is not as voluminous as in other management areas [10].

Due to the importance of their presence into the economy many researchers [11-25], still consider FBs as an increasing topic into the business management research. Family firm research has been growing over the last decade but is still an emerging field of study [26-28] it has experienced similar growth in recent years. Besides, families who have built sustainable businesses over generations are facing a problem in determining the contributing factors for meeting performance objectives. Hence, more effort is necessary to address the complexity of family companies and to understand the reasons of their excellent/poor performance.

Researches had also been made in some parts of the world [29] investigated the moderating effect of family CEOs on the family ownership-firm performance relationship in Asia, in which family CEOs were found to positively moderate the relationship in some countries (e.g., Indonesia and Taiwan), and negatively moderate the relationship in Hong Kong. Maury [30], investigated the relationship between family ownership and firm performance of eleven Western European countries and revealed that family ownership positively affects firm profitability in terms of return on assets, particularly in economies having stringent regulations [31], demonstrated that family firms listed in eleven Continental Europe countries have superior performance in terms of return on assets. Ben-Amar and Andre [32], show similar findings in the context of Canada. But, this area of research is lacking in other parts of the world including India.

On the other hand, performance is an essential indicator of the organisational success and competitive advantage of firms. If firms are able to identify the factors that determine improved performance, they could take advantage of their specific features. Family business may want to know the key drivers of success to direct their efforts to the accomplishment of those measures. Based on the above rationale, this study extracts new evidence from a blooming emerging area -family

---

__Corresponding author:__ Bharti Motwani, Institute of Management and Research, Information Technology, Vijay Nagar Indore, Madhya Pradesh 452010, India
E-mail: bharti_motwani@pimrindore.ac.in

business. Hence, the purpose of this research is to give insight in the effects of the influence of a family on the aforementioned components, and how these are related to success of a firm and to have a better picture of the ambiguous and imperfect literature on family businesses. The outcome of our research will be formed by answering the following research question: "Which determinants of family business contribute in meeting/exceeding performance objectives of a firm?"

Literature Review

Le Breton-Miller and Miller [33] argue that family governance and leadership creates unique conditions which can make them more effective than non-family firms. Family-led enterprises might then be better able to create products or to enter markets that outside investor-controlled or managerially led firms cannot, and to better adapt to changing environments [34]. Some scholars [35], threw light on the difference between corporate governance structures used in family-funded and non-family-funded firms. They further discuss that firms without the burden of agency costs may be able to take advantage of different, and perhaps more lucrative, opportunities than firms dealing with outside investors. Other studies explore the family effect on firm performance and compare firm value between family companies and widely held corporations [36-39].

Research papers focused on family business performance reveal mixed results. According to some authors, family firms outperform non-family peers, while other papers show the opposite. The family enterprise must be a remarkably efficient and robust organizational form: it is the world's most common form of economic organization and, as noted by Shleifer [24], family-controlled corporations dominate the global economic landscape. Miller and Le Breton-Miller [40] included studies that show superior performance of family firms along various performance dimensions. Bennedsen et al. [5], found that non-family CEOs provide valuable services to the organizations they head, thereby supporting the case that family managed firms have lower performance than non-family firms.

Yet, despite the many positive aspects of family businesses, there are some negative effects. Family conflicts, lacking ability in next generation and profit sharing etc. are few criticisms about family businesses. Family businesses more frequently use written employee policies rather than written succession plans or hiring plans for family members [41]. In general, there is a lack of strategic planning and professionalization in family businesses that has contributed to their high failure rate. Professionalization is related to the succession-planning process and involves transitioning from an informal management style to a more formal management style for economic growth.

Although, family involvement is an essential attribute of a family business [42,43] but, more family members mean more complexity, since they bring a diversity of interests, skills and needs. The situation becomes difficult, when a strong and successful leader disappears and an ill-prepared next generation comes into role. Besides, managing authority and responsibilities of family members is also a matter of concern. Very few families in business translate their fear into a pro-active approach by providing training to the younger generations and evaluating them, with the clear objective of ensuring that future generations wisely exercise their rights and responsibilities.

Conflict is related to interpersonal family dynamics. It can cause a high cost in family enterprises because family members are 'locked' in a firm, thereby making conflicts more persistent and interests more difficult to align [44]. Family business research often utilizes this broad systems view because many issues affect family members both in and out of the business [45-49]. Other dimensions of family business include succession[50-52], corporate governance [3,53] strategic management [54], etc. For exiting from the family business, owners can decide to (i) sell their firms to an external party [55], (ii) hand over the business to family members and/or relatives [56], or (iii)) to close down their business [57].

Barth, Gulbrandsen [58], suggested that future researchers concentrate on who runs the firm as opposed to who owns it; many supports have been reported for the impact of family ownership on the firms' performance. One possible explanation for why the results were inconsistent may be related to the lack of understanding of the moderating effect of a family CEO and founder CEO. Sharma noted that the rigors of academic research did not accommodate the solutions needed by consultants in solving the problems which occur in family businesses and emphasized on more work needed to understand the determinants of family firm performance.

Garcia-Castro et al. [59], have investigated different studies towards FB and FP, conducting three different relationships between FB and FP (positive, negative and neutral). But they concluded that the contradicting results emerged from empirical research, was plagued by the way the relationship between FB en FP was measured. But that family involvement has influence on the business is for sure. It only depends on the conditions how the family business is build. With a solid build structure of ownership and proper management, a family business is able to create unique competences to create superior financial firm performance.

With regard to the relationship between family involvement in management and performance, the results are mixed. Some of the research has confirmed that FBs offer superior performance [60,61]. However, it seems that the relationship between performance and ownership is not linear. In particular [33,62], suggest that family ownership positively affects firm performance, exhibiting an inverted U-shape relationship. On the other hand, some scholars have found hardly any differences between FBs and NFBs [7,39], have even confirmed that NFBs performed better than family owned firms. Whereas [61,62], suggest that family management has a positive effect on profitability, other authors such as Barth [58,63-66] found that firms with family members who serve as managers underperform firms that are managed by outside managers.

Collins [67], reported about gaps in family business research. Among these gaps is the link between family involvement and its effect on the performance, which is still under debate [68]. Despite the fact that SEM is an increasingly popular approach in business research and related social sciences, family firm researchers have used the method sparingly [69]. Several family business researchers have called for more sophisticated and rigorous statistical analysis techniques, such as SEM [70-73] revealed that only 13 empirical studies investigating family businesses published between 1989 and 2013 used SEM methodologies, seven of which (from a total of 183 empirical articles) were published in Family Business Review.

Research Methodology

The study

The study is exploratory in nature and intends to discuss the factors affecting success of family business. The objective of the study was to analyze the relationship of meeting/exceeding performance objectives of family business with selected constructs such as Distinguished

Documentation, Enhanced Transparency, Conducive Environment, Professional Attitude, Communication Integration, Innovative Training, Financial Management, Immense Trust, Entrepreneurship Development and Evaluation Standards. Non probability judgemental sampling method was used for the collection of data.

Tool for data collection

Self-structured questionnaire was used for the collection of data. For measuring the variables related to success of family business, the list of 36 items were formed. These items in the tool were employed on 5-point Likert scale, ranging from strongly disagree to strongly agree. Because, the study incorporated tools that were new to family business research, further retesting of these tools was deemed necessary to assess their robustness to a different population of firms, and to derive confidence in subsequent analysis, a pilot survey was executed before conducting the main survey. The purpose of the pilot survey was to examine whether or not the proposed model was well developed and suitable to analyze family business success. In the pilot study, Item-total-correlation was calculated on data collected for 36 items to find out which items significantly contribute towards measuring the factors contributing to the success of family business. In the first iteration four variables were found insignificant at 0.05 level of significance were dropped and the remaining items were retained to explore the factors. The data were finally, subjected to Principal Component Method of Factor Analysis. The results of the pilot study using Principal Component of Factor Analysis explored 10 factors Appendix 1.

Empirical data for testing the proposed constructs on success of family business were examined using a mail to the owners of family business. Initially, the questionnaire was mailed to 500 owners of only large scale enterprises, but with a response rate of 46.4%, only 232 owners participated in the survey. This survey was used for confirmatory analysis and hypotheses testing of the model shown in Figure 1. In both cases, the survey questionnaire was mailed to the family members in family firm, along with a letter outlining the purpose of the research and soliciting their participation in the survey. No specific incentive was provided to participants for completing the survey, beyond promising them a copy of the aggregated results. The statistics of firms is displayed in the following Table 1.

Tools for data analysis

After ensuring the content of the items selected, the reliability of the tool was determined by Cronbach's alpha method and the reliability coefficient alpha (α) was 0.95 showing high reliability of tool. The analysis of pilot data was carried out using Exploratory Factor Analysis from the Statistical Package of Social Science (SPSS 16.0).

Partial Least Squares-Graph was used to test the hypothesized relationships among the study variables. The choice was motivated by several considerations. Partial Least Squares is a non-parametric estimation procedure Wold 1982. Its conceptual core is an iterative combination of principal components analysis relating measures to constructs, and path analysis capturing the structural model of constructs. The structural model represents the direct and indirect causal relationships among constructs. It is more appropriate for analyzing moderating effects because traditional techniques cannot

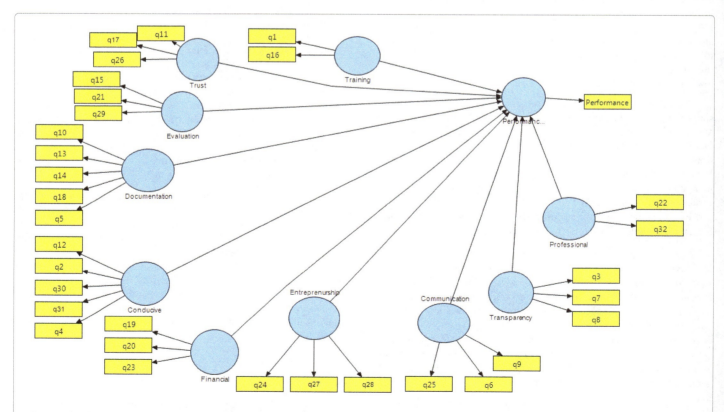

Figure 1: Initial Model Displaying Relationship Between Distinguished Documentation, Enhanced Transparency, Conducive Environment, Professional Attitude, Communication Integration, Innovative Training, Financial Management, Immense Trust, Entrepreneurship Development and Evaluation Standards with Performance of Family Business.

No. of Family Members	<10	76
	Between 10 and 50	130
	> 50	26
Year of Establishment	< 1975	42
	Between 1975 and 2000	173
FA	> 2000	17

Table 1: statistics of firms.

account for measurement error in exogenous constructs [74], allows for modeling latent constructs under conditions of non-normality, and is appropriate for small to medium sample sizes [75-77].

Construct development and framing of hypotheses

Communication Integration construct was framed of the following 3 items: There are regular scheduled meetings within the family members for the discussion related to business; we are able to sort out the persistent, uncomfortable issue with proper professional methodology and Communication among family members is critical to maintain family harmony and has been ideal. Family businesses are places where parties, while working together, can experience disagreement about task priorities and about how to accomplish them and can experience interpersonal incompatibilities on values and attitudes. It has been shown that the family adds complexity to business conflicts and conflict resolution, as family members can be concerned not only about business performance but also about their involvement in and satisfaction with the business [78]. Therefore the following hypothesis is proposed:

H_{01}: Communication Integration has an association with performance objectives of the family business.

Conducive Environment construct is made up of 5 items including Potential leaders are given projects to lead despite of being a non-family member; We do hire some new talent to do the job effectively in absence of ineffective family member; Policies for management of corporate profits between employee and non-employee shareholders are clearly defined; Regular senior management meetings to discuss strategic business plan involving family and non-family members are held and Data integration and information circulation is given a due importance in our business.

Several researchers [61,79], examined the family involvement in the management of family firms. Owing to the family's legacy being one and the same with the firm's welfare, family owners are often disinclined to relinquish their power to external managers. According to Al Masah [80], most Arab family businesses have their management in the hands of family members. This can be achieved through the goal alignment between owners and managers [81], manager's identification with the firm [82] and family managers' trustworthiness, as postulated by the stewardship theory Dalton et al. [83], Similarly, Lee [84] revealed that family firms underperform non-family firms with the exception of situations where family members were CEOs. According to Block this is because of management's identification with the firm. When the CEOs have greater identification and possess more incentive not to employ actions that may tarnish the firm's reputation, their identification encourages them to expend effort and work together for the protection of the welfare and reputation of both the family and firm. Thus, we can propose that;

H_{02}: Conducive Environment has an association with performance objectives of the family business.

Distinguished Documentation construct is framed of 5 constituents. There is a need to define document clearly all the policies because family owners may block non-family members from gaining key managerial positions in the company [72]. Moreover, family owners opt to keep the decision making process in their hands Ward [85] to prevent the occurrence of any conflict between them and external managers that would consequently impact the performance of the firm in a negative way [42].

According to Jiang et al. [29], a family member has more chance of being a CEO as opposed to non-family members in family firms owing to their alleviation of agency cost and provision of support to family control. They also state that ownership influence the role of the CEO, because a family business may choose who they want as an CEO. The way the CEO behaves, active or passive, has influence in the firm performance. For example, the CEO can influence the performance by having a longer investment intention, so the business has a long term vision, what is good for the continuity of the firm. Therefore, it is reasonable to assume that there is a relation between distinguished documentation integration and performance objectives of the family business which leads to the following hypothesis:

H_{03}: Distinguished Documentation Integration has an association with performance objectives of the family business.

Entreprenurship Development is another construct which is composed of three items namely: We are aware of the critical success factors and our weakness; Only those family members who are active in the business are eligible for ownership and We look for new opportunities like a watch-dog and take advantage of opportunities as and when they arise.

Anderson and Reeb [62], expressed that family ownership has some unique competitive advantages, that causes the positive relationship. According to Filatotchev et al. there is a negative relationship between a family member being a CEO and the firm's performance, because family managers select other mechanisms on how to run the business, compared to nonfamily firms. It is also stated that the family is tempted to do what is profitable for the family, but not to the minority shareholders in the business. But the family does not negatively influence the firm's performance [29,40,62,66] suggested family firms whose dominant family shareholder (founder) is the CEO outperform their non-family (non-founder) counterparts. Similarly, Ward et al. [85] revealed that family firms underperform non-family firms with the exception of situations where family members were CEOs. Therefore, we can predict that there is a relation between Entreprenurship Development and performance objectives which leads to the following hypothesis:

H_{04}: Entreprenurship Development has an association with performance objectives of the family business.

Evaluation Standards is comprised of 3 items namely Financial standards to evaluate financial performance are used; Proper evaluation of potential of strengths and weaknesses of younger generation for being a successor is done and All stakeholders are evaluated and receive positive and negative results. This seems to be true since enrolling poorly educated family members in the management team may also lead to resentment on the part of senior nonfamily managers because they would not see tenure, merit, and talent as requisite skills and hence is the importance of evaluation. Thus, we can propose that evaluation standards help in meeting the performance objectives of the firm. Hence the hypotheses:

H_{05}: Evaluation Standards has an association with performance objectives of the family business.

Financial Management is comprised of 3 items. This seems to be an important construct because [1], also found that Family businesses bring financial stability. Those financial resources (survivability capital) can be used during a crisis, when economic times are hard and can be used to sustain the business during economic hardship or after unsuccessful strategic moves [34]. In addition, family CEOs help to align family shareholders' incentives with managers' incentives, which eventually results in positive firm performance [62]. Also, family managers have the possibility of substituting monetary for nonmonetary returns [86], they often follow nonmonetary goals, such as independence, employment for family members [87,88], prestige has presented evidence that family business entrepreneurs tend to value emotional factors and consequently substitute them for the above-mentioned nonmonetary outcomes.

On the other hand, [72,89,90], did not observe significant differences on financial performance measures between family and non-family managed firms. Others were not able to confirm a relationship between ownership concentration [79,91] and firm profitability, on the other hand Vaninsky et al. [92], found that nonfamily managers running a firm generate a higher net income compared to family managed firms, since family managed firms are not run by professional managers (most of the time). Professional managers promote firm performance, especially, it secures a higher net income. In addition, as recently argued by Zellweger [93], the extended time horizon that characterizes family firms reduces the marginal risk of an investment and therefore the corresponding risk-equivalent cost of equity capital [94]. Consequently, family-owned firms can seize investment opportunities their nonfamily competitors do not consider as sufficiently attractive or consider too risky; "such a situation offers family-owned firms the possibility of developing their activities unhindered by aggressive competitors and of conquering markets that competitors cannot enter" [93], expressed that the greater profitability in family firms, relative to non-family and found that firm performance is increasing when the family ownership is about one-third of the firm's outstanding shares. Hence, we propose that;

H_{06}: Financial Management has an association with performance objectives of the family business.

Professional Attitude comprised of 2 items namely we do not give importance to preserving harmony in family at the cost of loss in business and different measures for increasing profitability in our family business are employed. According to Dyer [95] professional management competencies can be a major constraint in the success of family business. Successful management requires the development of plans, effective control systems for performance evaluation. This raises the need for competencies in strategic and financial planning sometimes missing in family-managed firms [96-98], found that responses to disruptions explained more of the variance than did family resources and expressed that hiring temporary help during hectic periods increase business revenue. Hence, it is reasonable to assume that;

H_{07}: Professional Attitude has an association with performance objectives of the family business.

Innovative Training construct comprises of 2 items namely Proper training to the family member is provided on a regular basis to younger generation and Employee performance reviews and customer feedback are conducted regularly. This seems to be true since either providing a training to family members or hiring nonfamily managers with previously developed capabilities can be a method of overcoming some problems and running the company more successfully. Therefore, the hypothesis formulated is:

H_{08}: Innovative Training has an association with performance objectives of the family business.

Enhanced Transparency is comprised of three items namely Company's' missions and vision are clearly documented which is known to all family members; Guidelines and mechanisms exist for liquidating ownership position in the family business during their lifetime. Rules and regulations for compensating family members employed in the business have been established. Sirmon et al. [98] found that family influenced firms maintain higher levels of research and development investments and internationalisation, and thus, they enjoy higher performance. Therefore, it is reasonable to assume that there is a relation between enhanced transparency and performance objectives of the family business which leads to the following hypothesis:

H_{09}: Enhanced Transparency has an association with performance objectives of the family business.

Immense Trust is also a strong construct of family business because trust in family business finally leads to better firm performance [84], also showed that high levels of trust and commitment can lead to higher profitability and greater efficiency. According to Dollinger, Family managers' trustworthiness is usually known by customers and suppliers, who may establish and cultivate long-lasting relationships because of the goodwill generated by the family commitment. Based on this argument, it is formulated that:

H_{10}: Immense Trust has an association with performance objectives of the family business.

Results and Discussion

The model was designed to study the effect of different factors including Distinguished Documentation, Enhanced Transparency, Conducive Environment, Professional Attitude, Communication Integration, Innovative Training, Financial Management, Immense Trust, Entrepreneurship Development and Evaluation Standards on meeting/ exceeding performance objectives of the family business (Figure 1). To assess the psychometric properties of measurement model, individual item loadings, internal consistency, convergent validity, and discriminant validity were examined of the reflective factors.

The loadings of the measurement items on their respective factors were examined (Figure 2). Finally, the model included the items whose loading were above the threshold value of 0.65 on their respective factor and were statistically significant at the 0.001 level, which provides support for convergent validity (Figure 3). Three items were deleted which include Wills and associated trusts documents are been regularly updated, Financial standards to evaluate financial performance are used and Communication among family members is critical to maintain family harmony and has been ideal.

The study assessed convergent validity by examining composite reliability and average variance extracted from the measures. Although many studies have used 0.5 as the threshold reliability of the measures, 0.6 is a recommended value for a reliable construct [75-77] For the reflective measures, rather than using Cronbach's alpha, which represents a lower bound estimate of internal consistency due to its assumption of equal weightings of items, a better estimate can be

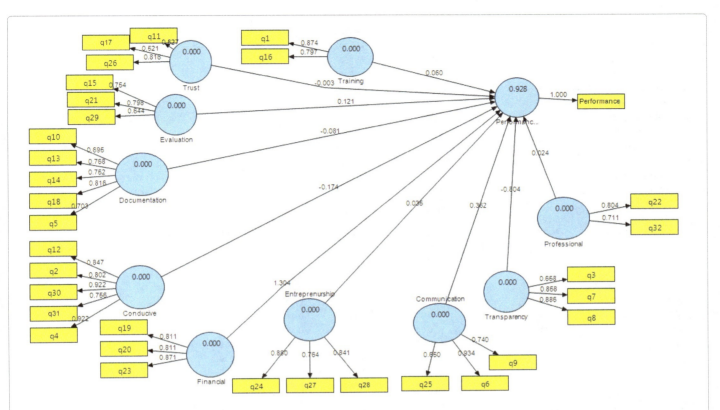

Figure 2: Initial Values on the Model Displaying Distinguished Documentation, Enhanced Transparency, Conducive Environment, Professional Attitude, Communication Integration, Innovative Training, Financial Management, Immense Trust, Entrepreneurship Development and Evaluation Standards with Performance of Family Business.

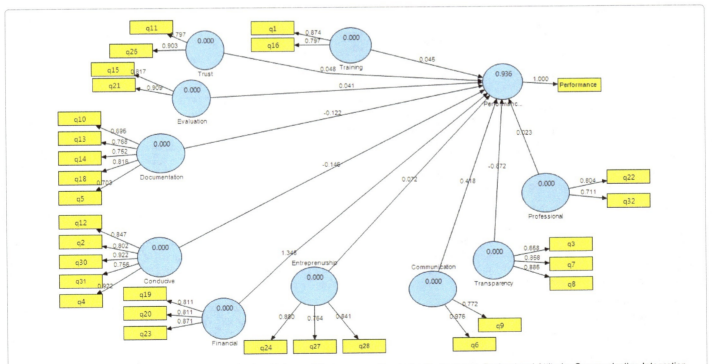

Figure 3: Model Displaying Distinguished Documentation, Enhanced Transparency, Conducive Environment, Professional Attitude, Communication Integration, Innovative Training, Financial Management, Immense Trust, Entrepreneurship Development and Evaluation Standards with Performance objectives after Removal of Some Items.

	AVE	Composite Reliability	R Square	Cronbachs Alpha	Communality
Communication Integration	0.77452	0.871426		0.762463	0.774528
Conducive Environment	0.72674	0.929671		0.910508	0.726741
Distinguished Documentation	0.55958	0.863583		0.804025	0.559583
Entrepreneurship Development	0.68861	0.868632		0.801841	0.688617
Evaluation Standards	0.74731	0.855035		0.669568	0.747318
Financial Management	0.69107	0.870181		0.825901	0.691073
Performance Objectives	1	1	0.9356	1	1
Professional Attitude	0.57615	0.730349		0.666704	0.576151
Innovative Training	0.69949	0.822878		0.674417	0.699498
Enhanced Transparency	0.65169	0.846731		0.748142	0.651692
Immense Trust	0.72537	0.840305		0.630542	0.725373

Table 2: Verification of Convergent Validity.

	Comm.	cond	doc	Entp	eval	fin	prof	trg	trans	Trust
q1	0.8	0.78	0.64	0.221	0.56	0.45	0.372	0.874	0.7	0.76
q16	0.5	0.6	0.7	0.598	0.61	0.4	0.121	0.797	0.55	0.06
q6	1	0.64	0.67	0.436	0.52	0.61	0.312	0.707	0.75	0.57
q9	0.8	0.72	0.73	0.092	0.6	0.41	0.197	0.67	0.67	0.64
q11	0.7	0.58	0.53	0.027	0.53	0.28	0.256	0.625	0.56	0.8
q26	0.5	0.33	0.15	0.011	0.11	0.18	0.382	0.339	0.33	0.9
q12	0.5	0.85	0.63	0.363	0.63	0.49	0.415	0.655	0.62	0.37
q2	0.8	0.8	0.64	0.305	0.57	0.5	0.238	0.757	0.69	0.64
q30	0.6	0.92	0.69	0.183	0.74	0.48	0.239	0.731	0.68	0.36
q31	0.4	0.76	0.59	0.146	0.68	0.31	0.295	0.613	0.49	0.24
q4	0.6	0.92	0.69	0.183	0.74	0.48	0.239	0.731	0.68	0.36
q10	0.7	0.71	0.79	0.155	0.59	0.45	0.244	0.648	0.64	0.6
q13	0.4	0.46	0.77	0.689	0.54	0.39	0.146	0.646	0.5	0.02
q14	0.5	0.45	0.75	0.65	0.49	0.52	0.185	0.572	0.55	0.01
q18	0.5	0.6	0.82	0.348	0.62	0.48	0.141	0.493	0.54	0.22
q5	0.7	0.67	0.7	0.32	0.57	0.41	0.212	0.662	0.61	0.58
q15	0.4	0.5	0.58	0.319	0.82	0.45	0.175	0.581	0.55	0.23
q21	0.6	0.8	0.7	0.253	0.91	0.59	0.254	0.618	0.67	0.33
q8	0.6	0.64	0.61	0.318	0.64	0.78	0.312	0.566	0.79	0.29
q7	0.7	0.66	0.68	0.419	0.54	0.61	0.312	0.716	0.76	0.56
q3	0.4	0.6	0.54	0.093	0.63	0.45	0.208	0.578	0.66	0.37
q22	0.2	0.25	0.04	0.249	0.17	0.35	0.804	0.239	0.26	0.32
q32	0.3	0.27	0.36	0.397	0.23	0.37	0.711	0.232	0.28	0.26
q19	0.6	0.71	0.68	0.333	0.7	0.71	0.309	0.625	0.69	0.29
q20	0.6	0.71	0.68	0.333	0.7	0.81	0.309	0.625	0.79	0.29
q23	0.4	0.26	0.37	0.482	0.35	0.87	0.473	0.262	0.46	0.16
q24	0.4	0.33	0.5	0.88	0.26	0.52	0.512	0.346	0.35	0.1
q27	0.3	0.24	0.45	0.764	0.32	0.3	0.162	0.491	0.31	-0.1
q28	0.3	0.13	0.52	0.841	0.24	0.31	0.2	0.383	0.29	-0.1

Table 3: Cross Loadings Table.

gained by using the composite reliability measure Chin and Gopal As shown in Table 2, the internal consistency of all reflective constructs clearly exceeded 0.60, suggesting strong reliability. For the average variance extracted by a measure, a score of 0.5 indicates acceptability. From the table it is clear that AVE by all reflective measures is greater than 0.5, which is above the acceptability value.

Finally, in the study, Discriminant validity is also confirmed, when items related to a particular factor have the highest load on that factor. When we look at the cross loadings (Table 3), we find that these conditions holds good.

The PLS modeling approach involved two steps - validating the measurement model and then fitting the structural model. The former is accomplished primarily by reliability and validity tests of the measurement model, followed by a test of the explanatory power of the overall model by assessing its explained variance, and the testing of the individual hypotheses (structural model). The model shows that the explanatory power of the model is 93.6% (Figure 3). For testing the individual hypotheses, a bootstrap re-sampling procedure was conducted and coefficients were estimated (Figure 4).

It is evident from the Table 4 and Figure 4 that all the hypothesis except H_{01}, H_{02}, H_{06} and H_{09} stands rejected at 5% level of significance because the calculated value of t is more than tabulated value (1.95). Thus, Enhanced Transparency, Conducive Environment, Communication Integration and Financial Management are associated with meeting/exceeding Performance objectives of family business, while Distinguished Documentation, Professional Attitude,

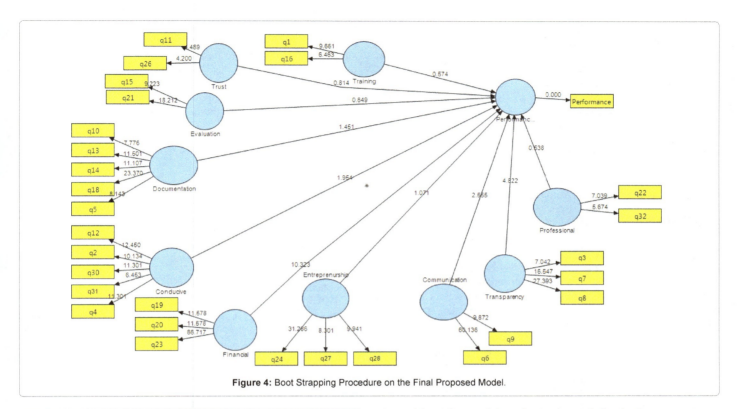

Figure 4: Boot Strapping Procedure on the Final Proposed Model.

	Standard Deviation (STDEV)	Standard Error (STERR)	T Statistics (|O/STERR|)
Communication Integration-> Performance Objectives	0.17156	0.17156	2.438118
Conducive Environment-> Performance Objectives	0.067424	0.067424	2.163242
Distinguished Documentation -> Performance Objectives	0.080488	0.080488	1.51872
Entrepreneurship Development -> Performance Objectives	0.055135	0.055135	1.299446
Evaluation Standards -> Performance Objectives	0.061518	0.061518	0.664713
Financial Management-> Performance Objectives	0.119598	0.119598	11.270112
Professional Attitude -> Performance Objectives	0.040026	0.040026	0.584798
Innovative Training -> Performance Objectives	0.08359	0.08359	0.535159
Enhanced Transparency -> Performance Objectives	0.187612	0.187612	4.649003
Immense Trust -> Performance Objectives	0.056305	0.056305	0.861114

Table 4: Correlation between Distinguished Documentation, Enhanced Transparency, Conducive Environment, Professional Attitude, Communication Integration, Innovative Training, Financial Management, Immense Trust, Entrepreneurship Development, Evaluation Standards and Performance objectives of the firm.

Innovative Training, Immense Trust, Entrepreneurship Development and Evaluation Standards are not associated with meeting/exceeding Performance objectives of family business.

The study reveals that Financial Management is vital to the success of family business. The assumed overlapping of family and business could produce particular attitudes in relation to financing strategies. In this regard Sa´nchez-Andujar [99], suggested that typical agency costs derived from the possibility of using free cash flow by the managers can be drastically reduced in family businesses due to the control exerted by the family members involved in the company.

The study revealed that conducive environment, enhanced transparency and communication integration are also important factors for determining the success of the family business. This seems to be true since management teams that are fully dominated by family members outperform mixed family nonfamily management teams due to the effective culture within the team. McConaughy et al. [100] ,present evidence that family ownership control is associated with higher firm performance. But when these authors split family control of a firm into different sub-factors, such as ownership concentration and monitoring, they find that the positive effect of family control on firm performance is not clearly due to managerial ownership. Bloom and Reenen [101] also find that that poor management practices are more prevalent when family-owned firms pass management control down to the eldest sons. Few families effectively manage this difficult transition. The key to success is accepting the diversity rather than suppressing it and putting in place a practical, transparent and effective governance structure.

In accordance with our study Zellweger [102], finds that in contrast to family influence in ownership and on the supervisory board, family influence on the management board is beneficial to the return on equity of a firm, Perez-Gonzalez [65] also finds that firms where incoming CEOs are related to the departing CEO, undergo large declines relative to firms that promote unrelated CEOs. Similarly, Villalonga and Amit [66], presented that family ownership only develops value in situations where the founder is the CEO of the firm and this value dissipates once the descendants take the founder's place as the CEO.

The study showed that Distinguished Documentation, Professional Attitude, Innovative Training, Immense Trust, Entrepreneurship

Development and Evaluation Standards are not associated with meeting/exceeding Performance objectives of family business. This might be true because this research was primarily done on large scale enterprises in which these parameters might have lost their meaning with passage of time. However, these paramters seems to be important and of prime concern , if the company size is small and is in growing stage. These paramters might have weightage earlier at the time of start of the venture. Also, because large scale family business are more stable and experienced and since owners of these business are more qualified and knowledgable, they might give more focus on the other crucial parameters like financial management, conducive environment, enhanced transparency and communication integration for meeting and exceeding performance objectives.

Suggestions and Conclusion

In today's era, family business needs to be carefully managed. With changing mindsets of the people, their lifestyle, rules and regulations in accordance to product specification, government laws, there seems to be a tough competition around the globe. Since, the success of a family business is driven by different organizational factors and set of policies, this project was deliberated to study to understand the impact of different factors on the success of the family business. It is very important to consider the financial management in a company hence the management should pay more attention to it. Each family member has its own strength and weaknesses, which can help to business to grow. The problem arises when the people are not aware about the transactions that are happening in the company, future planning which finally grow into conflicts among family members. This study could also help to the owners, in understanding and improving the factor on which they are lacking behind.

Finally, successful families understand that they need to add value to the business, for meeting/exceeding performance objectives. This added value on the part of family members comes in different shapes and forms, including actively leading the business, supporting the business strategies, maintain transparency in the business, making the environment affable, understanding the business and industry deeply, and, last but not least, conflict resolving between the family members.

Limitations

This research paper surveyed only the large scale family business enterprises. However, to have a better understanding of family business, small and medium scale family business should also be surveyed. A comparative study of family business of different company sizes will also show a better picture. This research paper could not focus on a variety of important questions that, re fundamental to the field and merit investigation.

Such questions relate to ownership transitions, difference in the managerial issues of small and big family business, influence of family business on the achievement of nonfinancial goals, the roles and responsibilities of family members, issues related to succession, family composition and management, evolution of firm governance across generations, the influence of family on firm financial structure, and a host of matters concerning family disputes and the successors. Moreover, more effort is needed to identify and analyze the distinctive resources and competences that make it possible for family firms to outperform non-family companies.

Also, different studies can be conducted at different geographical areas. On the basis of the present empirical analysis, the researchers can have a base for a further study to be conducted. Although, the traditional family business model of growing organically within a geographic region is rapidly becoming outdated as customers, suppliers and even employees spread across the globe. This also limits the scope of the research as it may yield different results if done at a different time and place. Like every study involving human feedback, there is always a big room for bias. Respondents could have provided with false information due to the thought that it might reflect their personality.

Refernces

1. Sirmon DG, Hitt MA (2003) Managing resources: Linking unique resources, management, and wealth creation in family firms. Entrepreneurship: Theory and Practice 27: 339-358.
2. Pearson AW, Carr JC, Shaw JC (2008) Toward a theory of familiness: A social capital perspective. Entrepreneurship Theory and Practice 32: 949-69.
3. Miller D, Le Breton-Miller I (2007) Kicking the habit: Broadening our horizons by studying family businesses. Journal of Management Inquiry 16: 27-30.
4. Habbershon TG, Williams M, MacMillan IC (2003) A unified system perspective of family firm performance. Journal of Business Venturing 18: 451-465.
5. Bennedsen M, Nielsen KM, Perez-Gonzalez F Wolfenzon D (2006) Inside the family firm: The role of families in succession decisions and performance. Working Paper, Columbia University 647-691.
6. Sirmon DG, Arrègle JL, Hitt MA, Webb JW (2008) The role of family influence in firms' strategic responses to threat of imitation. Entrepreneurship Theory and Practice 32: 979-998.
7. Chrisman JJ, Chua JH, Litz RA (2004) Comparing the agency costs of family and non-family firms: Conceptual issues and exploratory evidence. Entrepreneurship Theory and Practice 28: 335-354.
8. Carlos A, Benavides-Velasco, Cristina Quintana- García, Vanesa F, Guzmán-Parra (2011) Trends in Family Business. Small Business Economics: 40: 41-57.
9. Bhalla A, Henderson S, Watkins D (2006) A multi paradigmatic perspective of strategy: A case study of an ethnic family firm. International Small Business Journal 24: 515-537.
10. Bird B, Welsch H, Astrachan JH, Pistrui D (2002) Family business research: The evolution of an academic field. Family Business Review 15: 337-350.
11. O'Boyle Jr EH, Pollack JM , Rutherford MW (2012) Exploring the relation between family involvement and firms' financial performance: A meta-analysis of main and moderator effects. Journal of Business Venturing 1-18.
12. Shepherd DA (2009) Grief Recovery From the Loss of a Family Business: A multi -and meso- Level Theory. Journal of Business Venturing 81-97.
13. MassMutual FG (2003) New Nationwide Survey Points to Bright Spot in American Economy-family Owned Business.
14. Smyrnios K (2006) The MGI Family and Private Business Survey. Melbourne: RMIT.
15. Alpay G (2008) Performance implications of institutionalization process in family-owned businesses: Evidence from an emerging economy. Journal of World Business 235-448.
16. Cubico S, Togni M, Bellotto M (2010) Generational transition guidance: support for the future of family firms. Procedia Social and Behavioral Sciences 1307-1311.
17. Floren R , Uhlaner L, Berent-Braun M (2010) Family Business in the Netherlands Characteristics and Success Factors . Centre for Entrepreneurship Nyenrode Business University.
18. Basco R, Perez-Rodriguez MJ (2011) Ideal types of family business management: Horizontal fit between family and business decisions and the relationship with family business performance. Journal of Family Business Strategy 2: 151-165.
19. Hearn B (2011) The performance and the effects of family control in North African IPOs. International Review of Financial Analysis 140-151.
20. Leung S, Horwitz B (2010) Corporate governance and firm value during a financial crisis. Review of Quantitative Finance and Accounting 459-481.
21. Chen CJ, Yu CMJ (2011) Managerial ownership, diversification, and firm performance: Evidence from an emerging market. International Business

Review 1-17.

22. Arosa B, Iturralde T, Maseda A (2010) Ownership structure and FP in non-listed firms: Evidence from Spain. Journal of Family Business Strategy 1: 88-96.

23. Ducassy I, Prevot F (2010) The effects of family dynamics on diversification strategy: Empirical evidence from French companies. Journal of Family Business Strategy 224-235.

24. La Porta R, Lopez-de-Salines FL and Shleifer A (1999) Corporate ownership around the world. Journal of Finance 54: 471-517.

25. Sharma P, Chrisman JJ, Gersick KE (2012) 25 Years of family business review: Reflections on the past and perspectives for the future 1-6.

26. Chrisman JJ, Chua JH, Keller manns FW, Matherne CF, Debicki BJ (2008) Management journals as venues for publication of family business research. Entrepreneurship Theory and Practice 32: 927-934.

27. Katz JA (2000) Databases for the study of entrepreneurship. Advances in Entrepreneurship, Firm Emergence and Growth.

28. Sharma P, Hoy F, Astrachan JH, Koiranen M (2007) The practice driven evolution of family business education. Journal of Business Research 60: 1012-1021.

29. Jiang Y, Peng M (2011) Are family ownership and control in large firms good, bad, or irrelevant? Asia Pacific Journal of Management 28: 15-39.

30. Maury B (2006) Family ownership and firm performance: Empirical evidence from Western European corporations. Journal of Corporate Finance 12: 321-341.

31. Barontini R, Caprio L (2006) The effect of family control on firm value and performance: Evidence from continental Europe. European Financial Management12 : 689-723.

32. Ben-Amar W, Andre P (2006) Separation of ownership from control and acquiring firm performance: The case of family ownership in Canada. Journal of Business Finance and Accounting 33: 517-543.

33. Le Breton-Miller I, Miller D, Lester RHS (2011) Stewardship or agency: A social embeddedness reconciliation of conduct and performance in public family businesses. Organization Science 22: 704-721.

34. Dyer WG (2006) Examining the family effect on firm performance. Family Business Review 19: 253-273.

35. Randoy T, Nielsen J (2002) Company Performance, corporate governance, and CEO compensation in Norway and Sweden. Journal of Management and Governance 6: 57-81.

36. Kellermanns FW, Eddleston KA, Sarathy, Murphy F (2012) Innovativeness in family firms: A family influence perspective. Small Business Economics 38: 85-105.

37. Chu W (2009) The influence of family ownership on SME performance: Evidence from public firms in Taiwan. Small Business Economics 33: 353-373.

38. Saito T (2008) Family firms and firm performance: Evidence from Japan. Journal of the Japanese and International Economies 22: 620-646.

39. Sraer D, Thesmar D (2006) Performance and behavior of family firms: Evidence from the French stock market. Journal of the European Economic Association 5: 709-751.

40. Miller D, Le Breton-Miller I (2005) Managing for the long run: Lessons in competitive advantage from great family businesses.

41. Harris RID, Reid RS, and McAdam R (2004) Consultation and communication in family business in Great Britain. International Journal of Human Resource Management 15: 1424-1444.

42. Chrisman JJ, Chua JH, Sharma P (2003) Current trends and future directions in family business management studies: Toward a theory of the family firm.

43. Minichilli A, Corbetta G, MacMillan I (2010) Top management teams in family-controlled companies: familiness, faultlines, and their impact on financial performance. Journal of Management Studies 47: 205-222.

44. Schulze WS, Lubatkin MH, Dino RN (2003) Exploring the agency consequences of ownership dispersion among inside directors at family firms. Academy of Management Journal 46: 179-194.

45. Cole PM (1997) Women in family business. Family Business Review 10: 353-371.

46. Dumas C (1989) Understanding the father–daughter and father–son dyads in family-owned businesses. Family Business Review 2: 31-46.

47. Heck RKZ, Trent ES (1999) The prevalence of family business from a household sample. Family Business Review 12: 209-224.

48. Heck RKZ , Walker R (1993) Family-owned home businesses, their employees, and unpaid helpers. Family Business Review 6: 397-416.

49. Rosenblatt PC (1985) The family in business: Understanding and Dealing with the Challenges Entrepreneurial Families Face.

50. Handler W (1994) Succession in family business: A review of the research. Family Business Review 7: 133-157

51. Lansberg I, Astrachan J (1994) Influence of family relationships on succession planning and training: The importance of mediating factors. Family Business Review 7: 39-59.

52. Sharma P, Chrisman JJ, Chua JH (2003) Predictors of satisfaction with the succession process in family firms. Journal of Business Venturing 18: 667-687.

53. Dino RN, Lubatkin M H, Schulze WS, Ling Y (2005) The effects of parental altruism on the governance of family-managed firms. Journal of Organizational Behavior 26: 313-330.

54. Chrisman JJ, Chua JH, Sharma P (2005) Trends and directions in the development of a strategic management theory of the family firm. Entrepreneurship Theory and Practice 29: 555-575.

55. Wennberg K, Nordqvist M, Bau M, Hellerstedt K (2010) Succession in private firms as an entrepreneurial process – A review and suggestions of new research avenues.

56. Sharma P, Chrisman J, Chua J (2003b) Succession planning as planned behavior: Some empirical results. Family Business Review 16: 1-15.

57. Shepherd D, Zacharakis A (2000) Structuring family business succession: An analysis of the future leader's decision making. Entrepreneurship: Theory and Practice 24: 25-39.

58. Barth E, Gulbrandsen T, Schone P (2005) Family ownership and productivity: The role of owner-management. Journal of Corporate Finance11: 107-127.

59. Garcia-Castro R Aguilera R (2014) Family involvement in business and financial performance: A set-theoretic cross-national inquiry. Journal of Family Business Strategy 5: 85-96.

60. Martinez JI, Stohr BS, Quiroga BF (2007) Family ownership and firm performance: Evidence from public companies in Chile. Family Business Review 20: 83-94.

61. Maury B, Pajuste A (2005) Multiple large shareholders and firm value. Journal of Banking and Finance, 29:1813-1834.

62. Anderson RC, Reeb DM (2003) Founding-family ownership and firm performance: evidence from the S and P 500. Journal of Finance 58: 1301-1328.

63. Filatotchev I, Zhang X, Piesse J (2011) Multiple agency perspective, family control, and private information abuse in an emerging economy. Asia Pacific Journal of Management 28: 69-93.

64. Morck R, Strangeland D, Yeung B (1998) Inherited wealth, corporate control, and economic growth, in The Canadian Disease.

65. Perez-Gonzalez F (2006) Inherited control and firm performance. American Economic Review 96: 1559-1588.

66. Villalonga B, Amit R (2006) How do family ownership, management and control affect firm value? Journal of Financial Economics 80: 385-417.

67. Collins L, O'Regan N (2011) Editorial: The evolving field of family business. Journal of Family Business Management 1:5.

68. Filatotchev I, Lien YC, Piesse J (2005) Corporate Governance and Performance in Publicly Listed, Family-Controlled Firms: Evidence from Taiwan. Asia Pacific Journal of Management 22: 257-283.

69. Wilson SR, Whitmoyer JG, Pieper TM, Astrachan JH, Hair JF, et al. (2014) Method trends and method needs: Examining methods needed for accelerating the field. Journal of Family Business Strategy 4-14.

70. Debicki BJ, Matherne CF, Kellermanns FW,Chrisman, JJ (2009) Family Business Research in the New Millennium An Overview of the Who, the Where, the What, and the Why. Family Business Review 151-166.

71. Dyer WG, Dyer WJ (2009) Putting the family into family business research. Family Business Review 22: 216-219.

72. Westhead P, Howorth C (2006) Ownership and management issues associated with FB performance and company objectives. Family Business Review 19: 301-316.

73. Claudia B, Patel V, Wanzenried G (2014) A comparative study of CB-SEM and PLS-SEM for theory development in family firm research. Journal of Family Business Strategy 5: 116-128.

74. Fornell C, Bookstein FL (1982) Two Structural Equation Models: LISREL and PLS Applied to Consumer Exit-Voice Theory. Journal of Marketing Research 19: 440-452.

75. Chin WW (1998) Issues and Opinion on Structural Equation Modelling. MIS Quarterly 22: 7-16.

76. Chin WW (1998) The Partial Least Squares Approach to Structural Equation Modelling. Modern Methods for Business Research 295-336.

77. Chin WW, Newsted PR (1999) Structural Equation Modelling Analysis with Small Samples Using Partial Least Squares. Statistical Strategies for Small Sample Research 307-341.

78. Sorenson RL (1999) Conflict management strategies used in successful family businesses. Family Business Review 12: 133-146.

79. Sciascia S, Mazzola P (2008) Family Involvement in Ownership and Management: Exploring Nonlinear Effects on Performance. Family Business Review 21: 331-345.

80. Al Masah (2011) MENA Family Businesses: The Real Power Brokers? Al Masah Capital Management Limited. Dubai, UAE.

81. Davis JH, Schoorman FD, Donaldson L (1997) Toward a stewardship theory of management. Academy of Management. The Academy of Management Review 22: 20-47.

82. Block J (2010) Family Management, Family Ownership, and Downsizing: Evidence From Sand P 500 Firms. Family Business Review 23: 109-130.

83. Dalton DR, Daily CM, Ellstrand A E, Johnson JL (1998) Meta-analytic reviews of board composition, leadership structure, and financial performance. Strategic Management Journal 19: 269-290.

84. Lee J (2006) Family firm performance: Further evidence. Family Business Review 19: 103-114.

85. Ward JL (1987) Keeping The Family Business Healthy. San Francisco: Jossey-Bass.

86. Adams FA, Manners GE, Astrachan JH, Mazzola P (2004) The importance of integrated goal setting: The application of cost-of-capital concepts to private firms. Family Business Review 17: 287-302.

87. Sharma P, Chrisman JJ, Chua JH (1997) Strategic management of the family business: Past research and future challenges. Family Business Review 10: 1-35.

88. Zellweger T (2006) Risk, return and value in the family firm.

89. Daily CM, Dollinger MJ (1992) An Examination of Ownership Structure in Family and Professionally Managed Firms. Family Business Review 5: 117-136.

90. Blanco-Mazagatos V, de Quevedo-Puente E, Castrillo LA (2007) The trade-off between financial resources and agency costs in the family business: An exploratory study. Family Business Review 20: 199-213.

91. Castillo J, Wakefield MW (2006) An exploration of firm performance factors in family business: do family value only the "bottom line?" Journal of Small Business Strategy 17: 37-51.

92. Lauterbach B, Vaninsky A (1999) Ownership structure and firm performance: Evidence from Israel. Journal of Management and Governance 3: 189-201.

93. Zellweger T (2007) Time horizon, costs of equity capital, and generic investment strategies of firms. Family Business Review 20: 1-15.

94. McNulty JJ, Yeh T D Schulze WS, Lubatkin MS (2002) What's your real cost of capital? Harvard Business Review 80: 114-121.

95. Dyer JG (1989) Integrating professional management into a family-owned business. Family Business Review 2: 221-235.

96. Smyrnios KX, Walker RH (2003) Australian family and private business survey.

97. Olson PD, Zuiker VS, Danes SM, Stafford K, Heck RKZ, et al. (2003) The impact of the family and the business on family business sustainability. Journal of Business Venturing 639-666.

98. Sirmon DG, Arrègle JL, Hitt MA, Webb JW (2008) The role of family influence in firms' strategic responses to threat of imitation. Entrepreneurship Theory and Practice 32: 979-998.

99. Ló´pez-Gracia J, Sa´nchez-Andujar S (2007) Financial structure of the family business: Evidence from a group of small Spanish firms. Family Business Review 20: 269-287.

100. McConaughy D, Matthews C, Fialko A (2001) Founding Family Controlled Firms: Performance, Risk, and Value. Journal of Small Business Management 39: 31-49.

101. Bloom N, Van Reenen J (2006) Measuring and explaining management practices across firms and countries.

102. Zellweger T (2007) Familieneinfluss und Performance privat gehaltener Unternehmen.

Challenges of Technological Entrepreneurship in Africa: The Case of Tunisia

Walid Ghodbane*

Department of Management Science, University of Tunis, Tunisia

Abstract

Technology parks are a strategic tool to spill over knowledge and skills. The rise of technology parks around the world and especially in developing countries, has addressed concerns on the technopreneurial activity and its impact on developing locations and regions, especially in developing countries in Africa, where private and public sector are joining efforts to create a sustainable ecosystem for technology entrepreneurs. Hence, numbers of challenges are facing Africa, particularly the cross-cultural factors and the ICT infrastructure. This research was conducted on Technology Park El Ghazala in Tunisia. We will try to assess the impact of cross-cultural variables such as age, communication and social networks influence on prospective technology entrepreneurs.

Keywords: Entrepreneurship; Technopreneurial; Technology Park El Ghazala; Tunisia

JEL Classification: I22, I25

Introduction

The recent change in economic and managerial thinking has led to questions relating to the context of entrepreneurship in light of the radical change in the global economy, as well as the development of science and technology. This scenario has opened up new opportunities and stressed on the restatement of the prosperity principles on the basis of the new vision of the global economy.

Porter's studies [1-3] show that a well-known strategy for global competition is recognizing that science and technology are central aspects of excellence and the source of competitive advantage. The transition from macro to micro level, induced by technological progress, has resulted in a revised competitive strategy at the global level [4]. Competition is now based on the concept of global city regions [5]. Performance associated with science and technology parks has become global because of the high added value provided by the ICT industry.

Due to the globalization of technology and economy in general, ICT job shifts are occurring worldwide [3]. It is, therefore, important to examine the impact of ICT job shifts all over the world and particularly in developed countries. However, the empirical evidence on this topic is scant [6]. Also, the shift from a macroeconomic to microeconomic perspective has led to the assessment of this phenomenon from a human resources-based view [4].

Multinational companies ("MNCs") have historically favored countries where economies of scale can be achieved. However, their preference criteria have grown to include the presence of organizational and managerial skills and techniques, in addition to the financial gains brought by lower labor costs [7-9]. This has allowed them to establish direct links with the talents with which synergies can develop innovation [10].

Literature Review

The 'ICT job shifts' phenomenon can be described as the transfer of ICT jobs from developed countries to developing countries. This can be attributed to the globalization of (ICT) jobs where environments conducive to innovation, such as the technological and the scientific parks, become relevant within a business context. The globalization of (ICT) jobs can be defined as a phenomenon of off-shoring or outsourcing jobs to procure human skills and talents [11,12]. The globalization of ICT jobs includes job creation and a resulting economic and social prosperity. This approach is based on the creation of enterprises favored by the social connections of talent and exceptional individuals [5,9,13,14]. Indeed, the globalization of the ICT industry is not based solely on technological innovation, but also on its location [15]. According to many researchers, location is very important in developing the ICT industry [5,16,17]. Combining the late elements, the location, the talent and skills' availability, and a special capability to commercialize innovation allows some regions with their technology parks to be successful.

Various authors and researchers on technological entrepreneurship [18-20] have proposed studies on technological innovation as an evolutionary approach that aims to solve the problem of technological innovation from a cultural perspective and social development [21,22]. It can be seen that social connection is a key factor in the development of entrepreneurial activity in technology parks, allowing other countries to gain a competitive advantage in the globalization of trade in technology information and communication. In the Tunisian context, there has, in recent years, been a development of entrepreneurial activity in technology; however, in light of the fact that such entrepreneurial activity is in its early stages, along with the influence that societal and cultural factors play, it will be interesting to see how and to what extent these changing environments of innovation will affect technology parks.

Globalization had an influence on the spread of science and technology, so developing countries are struggling to compete by building capabilities toward gaining the competitive advantage. The ICT job shifts can allow developing countries to gain an advantage

---

*Corresponding author: Walid Ghodbane, Assistant professor, Department of management science, University of Tunis, Tunisia
E-mail: 06.waleed@gmail.com

by allowing a more specialized workforce that is informed about the technological advancements of the developed countries.

Talents are not easy to find or maintain, and this is where social and cultural factors come into play [7]. For example, Multinational Firms (ICT) seeks to transfer knowledge in technology through the human capital of the host country. Audia and Rider [23] reviewed various theories in psychology regarding organizations and entrepreneurship to examine the notion that entrepreneurs are the products of existing organizations.

Tunisia

Tunisia has around 700 ICT companies, one-third of which specializes in IT services and engineering. Most of these are small companies, employing fewer than 20 skilled workers. Reselling is the main activity for 45% of channel partners; 42% are focused on services, and IT manufacturers represent only 1%[1]. Tunisia has the most developed telecommunications infrastructure in Africa, and has boosted its IT and telecom sector through some incentives offered to foreign investors, including a 50% tax break for IT investors, and subsidies and incentives for both hardware and software investments. The public sector also plays an important role[2]. The most important Technology Park is El GhazalaTechnolopole-located in the capital region-followed by Sousse and Sfax. Major investments are planned in telecommunications, with a focus on mobile and internet offerings and data transmission networks. The proposed services include software development, system integration, website design, and network engineering and support. Technology Park El Ghazala in Tunisia is considered a key tool for Tunisia to establish a competitive strategy with the ICT industry. The aim is to provide Tunisia with a place of excellence enabling it to harness the growing opportunities for investment and entrepreneurship in developing new technologies. There are currently more than 90 firms and 12 multinational firm subsidiaries located at the park[3].

The weaknesses of El Ghazala Technology Park is that it does not currently implement valid assessments of human competencies and talent. Despite internationally standardized ICT infrastructure, El Ghazala Technology Park has two major problems (1) the institutional background and bureaucracy, and (2) the lack of strategic vision and leadership.

At El Ghazala, there is a scarcity of advanced university research labs and they did not develop relationships with industry and the broader economy in general. This might be explained by the nature of the technology parks such that, in El Ghazala, technology parks are MNC oriented, rather than technology-entrepreneurship oriented. Thus the problem is structural specifically, it is created or compounded by the lack of involvement of state agencies and the government. On the one hand, an ecosystem designed for MNC exists which aims to develop their technological activities; on the other hand, there is the need to develop technology entrepreneurship from the ICT jobs created by MNC. Cross-cultural variables such as strength of weak ties and social networks might be able to have a deeper role but only with the support of state-owned agencies and universities.

Methodology

The present research is partially concerned with the emergence of technology artifacts in a technology park in Tunisia. Specifically, the novelty of the phenomena associated with artifacts of technology and emerging issues relating to the strategic use of ICT led to the birth of the sub-discipline of information systems. Although the study of entrepreneurship in technology is concerned largely with economic and psychological factors, it is, nevertheless, a field that is suitable for analysis from the perspective of information systems.

The case study is the most appropriate research method in the context of this research, firstly because it is exploratory in nature; secondly, because it is a comparative study of two technology parks and; thirdly, because the research aims to examine a novel (rather than old) phenomenon (namely, ICT job shift globalization).

Yin [24] stressed the importance of distinguishing the case study from other types of qualitative methods, such as ethnography, participant observation, and grounded theory. In particular, he explains that, unlike ethnography, in a case study the researcher does not necessarily go into the field or conduct direct observations of the phenomenon studied and detailed. In general, Yin says that we should not locate the case study in terms of data collection techniques; rather the case study should be regarded as a "comprehensive research strategy "with a" logic design research, data collection techniques and specific approaches in relation to data analysis." However, the case study does possess limitations, the most notable of which relate to representativeness and generalization[4].

The objective of this research is to examine the role of cross-cultural factors in the development of entrepreneurial activity in technology parks. The development of these factors is dependent on the phenomenon of ICT job shifts. This results in the emergence studies, from either single or multiple designs, stems on theory rather than on populations of another phenomenon-namely, the globalization of technology entrepreneurship through technology parks [25,26].

As part of the present research, an assumption of research focuses on test statistics and their interrelationships:

H1: The technology park is a concentration of companies combined, and pursuing goals such as the development of entrepreneurial activity in technology.

H2: Technology Park has a developed infrastructure, including tools for developing

H3: The role of the government is to ensure the sustainability of entrepreneurial activity in technology planning and development Technology Park.

H4: Universities are the core of innovation and creative entrepreneurship. They allow the linking of talents and skills with industry and donors.

H5: The mechanisms of financing are donors who are willing to risk their funds in investment in technological innovations, particularly in startups.

H6: Managerial and technical skills can be acquired from people who have academic training and experience in the field of technology or management.

The foundation of the conceptual model is ICT job shifts, with five elements that are related to ICT clusters: ICT infrastructure, state

---

[1] http://www.tunisieindustrie.nat.tn
[2] The public sector investments in ICT infrastructure.
[3] http://www.elGhazala.tn

[4] The main problem with generalization from studied to unstudied cases is that it is potentially subject to high and unknown levels of error. This problem obviously increases with heterogeneity in the population. (I.e. two different contexts are being compared in Tunisia and in France). According to Yin (1994), generalization of results from case

agencies, universities, and talents and human competencies. Cross-cultural elements are proposed as moderators of the relationship between technology park elements and dependent variables[5] (1) the entrepreneurial process split into opportunity development and managing the start-up); these cross-cultural variables include: (1) race, (2) ethnicity, (3) gender, and (4) strength of weak and strong ties. Communication and social networks are final moderator elements. The aim is to establish a link between cross cultural variables and the ICT job shifts phenomenon[6]. It is anticipated that the findings from the study will help to explain how ICT jobs are shifted from one ICT cluster to another and how they contribute to sustaining competitive advantage in technology entrepreneurship.

Data

In order to collect data, semi-structured interviews were administered to the personnel at technology- based companies and research development centers (managers and staff, students, and administration staff). A quantitative questionnaire survey was then designed and administered. Thus, the present study involved a triangulation of methods. Qualitative (interview) data were analyzed using the manual analysis approach [27], and quantitative (questionnaire) data were analyzed using XLStat[7]. Data was collected via an online questionnaire survey and by the researcher's participation in seminars organized by the El Ghazala technology park. Between 2008 and 2011, qualitative data was collected by means of small focus groups (5 to 15 people in each group). Focus groups were provided with the same semi-structured questions in order to facilitate the discussion.

Sampling procedure

The sampling procedure was very simple. First, we reduced data from the qualitative data already collected and this enabled the results to be triangulated. Then, individuals' choices are based on personal profiling[8]. This sampling methodology led us to the sampling procedure. We organized our questionnaire to fit with information needed from our sample as it fits our qualitative research outcomes.

The sample comprised 81 individuals from the El Ghazala Technology Park. This table describes our sampling procedure (Table 1):

Results

By comparing triangulated results we were able to confirm, in relation to El Ghazala Technology Park, that University/ research laboratories have played only a minor role in establishing bridges with industry, and that there were infrastructure problems (lack of offices and ICT building capabilities). The cross-cultural variables could lead graduate students to find a venture for their ideas. However, it could also impede any initiative or marginalize human talents by fostering the attitude that if anybody takes the initiative it will be against cultural norms and standards. Therefore, Hypothesis 1 is confirmed while hypotheses 2, 3, 4, 5 and 6 are not supported with regard to El Ghazala Technology Park. Indeed, the qualitative results demonstrated that cross-cultural influences on ICT infrastructure, universities and financial mechanisms are very significant.

However, government incentives and efforts are not taking into consideration the endogenous side of technology parks, but it is still significant for entrepreneurial initiative with respect to financial mechanisms as well as the ICT infrastructure. Those initiatives are not coming from the ICT job creation or shifts but, rather, are planned actions from institutions. Thus, it seems that the strategy behind technology park development does not take cross-cultural factors into account. Results (both qualitative and quantitative) provide support for this contention. In El Ghazala, age, gender and ethnicity are the most influential factors in relation to entrepreneurial activity stimulated by ICT job shifts. These findings might best be explained by the fact that MNCs (formed by foreigners, rather than Tunisians or Tunisian Diaspora) are the principal component in El Ghazala.

El Ghazala Technology Park has two telecommunications schools: Supcom[9] and the ISETcom[10] for the technicians in the telecommunication industry. The principal mission for both Supcom and ISETcom is to produce technical graduates and prepare students to embark on a career in the IT sector (Tables 2 and 3).

There are two state agencies in El Ghazala Technology Park among the administration: (1) CERT and (2) ANCE. They depend on their department of origin: the national telecom operator for the first agency and the ministry of telecommunication and defense for the second (Tables 4-8).

Conclusion

Entrepreneurship is created by innovation and business initiative woven with risk taking strategies. One of the novel ways of doing business is Technology entrepreneurship. Technology entrepreneurship is based on some important steps to establish business ventures, such as: following the patterns and efficacy of existing Technology Parks, identifying the prospective regions, human capital equipped with ICT skills, social interactions with corporations, operational financial resources, productivity, adoption of policies and best management practices.

Technology entrepreneurship in Africa and especially Tunisia faces huge challenges to operate successfully. The major hurdles are ICT policies, regional infrastructure to promote business, identifying skilled human labor, and technology and product promotion.

---

[5]A consideration is the relationships moderated by cross-cultural variables.
[6]Cross-cultural variables play a "mediating" role; A mediator variable is a variable that explains (comes in the middle of) the relationship between two variables
[7]http://www.xlstat.com
[8]Personal profiling of selected candidates for our interviews and questionnaire based on (1) Leadership capabilities, (2) importance and influence in entrepreneurs 'community and (3) Availability.

9 http://www.supcom.mincom.tn
10 http://www.isetcom.mincom.tn

Sample	Description	Extraction and Representativeness	The use of PCA methodology
El Ghazala (EG)	The sample is composed of 81 respondents: -15 CEO, MNCrepresentatives. -55 prospective technology entrepreneurs. -12 Administrative and organisational staff [1].	At El Ghazala Technology Park, the sample was extracted and then selected in the basis of technology 10 entrepreneurship process[2].	Moderator variables (cross-cultural factors) are confirmed to have a high impact on ICT job shifts[3].

[1]Employees of the technology park el ghazala including the two agencies for telecom and electronic certification.
[2]Selection of relevant profiles for our questionnaire was based on the assessment made by qualitative methodology. Respondents who are close to Graduate, seeking "opportunities" was given a special attention.
[3]See appendix 4 (i.e., el ghazala statistics) Contribution of the variables (%) and Squared cosines of the observations.

Table 1: Sampling procedure description and use of PCA methodology.

Universities	Moderator variables					ICT job shifts
	Code	SWT	ETH. RACE. Gender	Communication Social Networks	Research Propositions[1]	Impacts
SUPCOM	SCOM	Strong	No ethnic or racial problems	Fair researcher communities	P1, P2, P6 OK P3, P4, P5 Non confirmed	Strong
ISETCOM	ICOM	weak	Female challenges	Poor job prospects	P1, P2, P3, P4 confirmed P5, P6 non confirmed	Moderate

Note: SWT=Strength of Weak Ties

[1]P1: spin-off and start-ups arise from an ecosystem of skills of highly qualified academic and professional human resources.
P2: the technology park objective is to develop entrepreneurship through the ICT job shifts phenomenon.
P3: managerial skills and techniques influence the interaction between businesses in the technology park.
P4: the development perspective of the ICT job shifts depends on technology entrepreneurs.
P5: Cross-cultural factors influence the establishment of a technological trajectory between technology parks, including those of France and Tunisia.
P6: the development of entrepreneurial activity depends on the underbody of cross-cultural technology entrepreneurs. The location of technology parks, including El ghazala in Tunis-Tunisia- and Sophia Antipolis in Nice-France- contribute to the emergence of the technology entrepreneurship process.

Table 2: Role and impact of cross-cultural variables on universities.

University	Themes	Interpretations
SUPCOM	Educational role of university.	The management role of university is dominant in the educational purpose of university. This role is very important for engineers and MNC present in thetechnology park el Ghazala. University has an educational role and "institutional" one by delivering their student an engineer diploma after finishing their studies. Cross-cultural variables are very significant in this university. As education is open and free for all, the access and the success are based on "diploma" itself. The entrepreneurial role of academia and scientific research is minimal.
	Entrepreneurial role of University. The knowledge diffusion.	The entrepreneurship process is very complex to establish within university. However, it seems that knowledge diffusion plays an important role in the technology transfer for established companies and MNC. This transfer is very weak as the relationship between university and industry is not well defined and clear.
	Aspiring role of university teaching programs to apply the knowledge gained and identify opportunities	This sub-variable is related to the appropriateness of technology education and its outcomes. We categorized this sub-variable from different sources and we found that knowledge diffusion at educational level does not play a role in the entrepreneurial process. Furthermore, MNC has established standards and norms by which they catch the sticky knowledge in the educational background of engineers. Thus, the role of the university as an entrepreneurial "hub" does not work.
ISETCOM	Employment prospects	Students link their education with their first employment. This sub-variable demonstrates that employment and success in finding a job after graduating is very important for students. As employment prospects for ISETCOM students are limited to MNC and some established companies outside the technology park, unemployment problems arise. The student does not see entrepreneurial opportunity because there are no associations or organizations that support entrepreneurship inside the technology park.

Table 3: Results relating to the role cross-cultural variables in technology entrepreneurship development in the university.

State Agencies	Moderator Variables					ICT Job Shifts
	Codes	SWT	Ethnicity; Race; Gender	Communication Social Networks	Research Propositions	Impacts
ANCE	ANCE	Strong	No ethnic or racial problems	strong influence of internet (bandwidth)	P1, P2, P3, P5 OK P4, P6 Non confirmed	Very significant
CERT	CERT	Weak	Female challenges	No effective role	P1, P2, P3, P4 confirmed P5, P6 non confirmed	Non-Significant

Table 4: Mixed impacts of cross-cultural variables and state agencies on technology entrepreneurship.

State agencies	Themes	Interpretations
Role of state's agencies in fostering technology entrepreneurship in el Ghazala technology park: ANCE and CERTcom	Factor of development of entrepreneurial opportunity	While the institutions of El Ghazala are very weak and with no incidence on technology entrepreneurship, the telecom valley organization is very influential in this respect. Hence, the development of the entrepreneurial opportunity is blocked by institutional barriers in Tunisian techno park.
	Problems faced by new firms in the park.	There are some problems faced by entrepreneurs. At El Ghazala we found that cross-cultural variables are very influential. However, they are not managed sufficiently to attract and retain new entrepreneurs.

Table 5: The role of state agencies in technology entrepreneurship development with ICT job shifts

During data collection, the research team had the opportunity to meet with several individuals in the ICT domain. These people are directly or indirectly involved in the entrepreneurial ecosystem of El Ghazala.

Technical and Managerial Competencies	Moderator Variables					ICT Job Shifts
	Codes	SWT	Ethnicity; Race; Gender	Communication Social Networks	Research Propositions	
Technical competencies	TOCO M	Strong	No ethnic or racial problems	Strong	P1, P2, P3, P5 OK P4, P6 Non confirmed	Strong
Managerial competencies	MCOM	Strong	Female challenges	Fair	P1, P2, P3, P4 confirmed P5, P6 non confirmed	Strong

Table 6: The impacts of cross-cultural variables in technical and managerial skills: The role of Universities in creating ICT job shifts.

Sub-Sample	Themes	Interpretations
Students	Culture and skills	The ICT talents are very important to foster technology entrepreneurship. The cross-cultural variables impact the students' path. The consequence of culture and lack of efficient institutions drive El Ghazala university students to search for employment rather than searching for an entrepreneurial opportunity.
	Special ecosystem	The special ecosystems that drive innovation and entrepreneurship are impacted by cross-cultural variables. We argue that El Ghazala requires institutional support and social mechanisms that help create and prepare students to be entrepreneurs and take initiative.
Managers (both technical and managerial competencies)	Experience and extra professional activities	Experience influences the engineers and ICT managers. At El Ghazala we met with ICT technical and managerial staff of all levels. It seems that the cross-cultural variables such as strength of strong ties and communication are related to the academic background.

Table 7: Influence of cross-cultural variables on ICT job shifts and ICT skills and talents in El Ghazala.

Cross tab analysis was used to summarize the statistical findings. The main statistical instrument was principal component analysis or PCA which was conducted in order to conceptualize important variables for use in testing the hypotheses.

Variables	El Ghazala-Tunisia	
ICT infra-structure	Hypothesis	Cross-cultural variables' impacts
	H2- Non confirmed[1]	The role of university is very significant with the cross-cultural variables. The ICT infrastructure is negatively influenced by the ICT job shifts. Race, SWT, communication and social networks are influencing the ICT infrastructure positively; ethnicity, age and gender are influencing this variable negatively. This can be interpreted as a threat to entrepreneurship development in the technology park El Ghazala, because of the quality of ICT infrastructure that does not encourage technology entrepreneurship. Younger students and researchers need an up-to-date ICT infrastructure. ICT job shifts are influenced by cross-cultural variables and by ICT infrastructure. At El Ghazala this influence is negative. It means that ICT infrastructure impedes technology entrepreneurship initiatives.
State agencies	H3-Supported[2]	Age, gender and communication play a positive role with 'State agencies'. However, race, SWT and social networks have a negative impact on it. This is due to the nature and the role assigned to the state agencies. Indeed, the PCA, previous results, has supported it.
Human talents and competencies	H1, H6	Age, gender and social networks positively influence technology entrepreneurship with the help of the ICT job shifts. (The PCA results demonstrate that those variables are very influential in regard to technical and human competencies).
	H1 supported. H6 is not supported[3]	The results of the linear regression analysis demonstrated that race, age, gender and social networks are helping to implement efforts to build human talents capabilities. However, SWT and communication are negatively influencing the role of the technology park in dealing with the strategic use of human capital. There is no special ecosystem that could help build this strategic capability.
Universities	H4 Not supported[4]	Race, gender and age have a positive impact through universities at El Ghazala Technology Park. Communication, social networks and ethnicity play a negative role in establishing entrepreneurial linkages between university and MNC. This is due to the role of research facilities based in both isetcom and supcom. Communication is very weak and social capital is not appreciated. Universities are marginalized because of the lack of vision. Research labs are influenced by race, gender and age. This constitutes an opportunity to get hold of universities at El Ghazala technology park.
Summary	H1 supported H2,3,4,5,6 Not supported	We tested the impact of seven cross-cultural variables upon the dependant variables in our conceptual model. The use of PCA as a statistical exploratory tool helped us to confirm that independent variables (cross-cultural) have a strong impact upon the dependant variables (elements of the technology park). At El Ghazala technology park we pointed out three main issues (1) university/ research labs play a very minor role in helping establish bridges with industry, (2) financial mechanisms are limited (this is a real challenge for technology entrepreneurs), and (3) infrastructure problems (lack of offices and ICT building capabilities). The cross-cultural variables could help graduate students to find a venture for their ideas. However, it could also slow down any initiative or marginalize human talents by conveying the message that if anybody take the initiative it will be against cultural references and standards.

[1]See appendix 2.
[2]See appendix 5.
[3]See appendix 4.
[4]See appendix 3.

Table 8: Results of the cross tab analysis.

The study demonstrates a strong relationship between cross-cultural variables and technology entrepreneurship development. However, in Tunisia the ICT infrastructure problems might be impeding progress in the further development of the technology park at El Ghazala.

In the light of present study and in order to overcome the major barriers found in this sector, we recommend that El Ghazala Technology Park should develop its existing financial mechanisms; enhance competitive edge over technology parks by employing cross cultural variables; project the contribution of States agencies; adopt effective communication channels; formulate Technology entrepreneurship incentives; explore technology outsourcing possibilities by coordinating with corporate and leadership should play a visionary role to uplift the global ICT market.

Future research should include studies of Technology Parks should focus on their institutional or managerial weaknesses undermining their potential growth. The Governments should support for basic science in Universities. In fact, regions with ICT capable of human capital should be explored without any racial and gender bias. Research on public-private partnerships and their impact on technology entrepreneurship should be established for emerging applied technologies. Other research considerations are the leadership contribution to the ICT strategy based on Technology Park development, with the purpose of advancing science and technology and sustenance of global economy.

References

1. Porter M (1990) The Competitive Advantage of Nations. The Free Press, New York pp: 255-364.
2. Porter M (1998) Clusters and Competition, in On Competition. Harvard Business School Press, Cambridge 7: 197-271.

3. Porter M (1998) Clusters and new economics of competition. In On Competition, Harvard Business School Press, Cambridge pp: 77-90.

4. Porter ME, Et Stern S (1999) Understanding the Drivers Of National Innovative Capacity. MIT Sloan School p: 10.

5. Scott AJ (2001) Global City-regions: Trends, Theory, and Policy. Oxford University Press pp: 137-169.

6. Bernhard M (2007) Potential ICT-enabled Offshoring of Service Jobs in Belgium. Federal Planning Bureau, Kunstlaan/Avenue des Arts 47-49, 1000 Brussels pp: 1-16.

7. Andersen PH, Christensen PR (2005) From localized to corporate excellence: How do MNCs extract, combine and disseminate sticky knowledge from regional innovation systems? DRUID Working Paper pp: 05-16.

8. KohFrancis CC, Winston TH K, Feichin TT (2005) An analytical framework for science parks and technology districts with an application to Singapore." Journal of Business Venturing 20: 217-239.

9. Steve L (2007) Silicon Valley Shaped by Technology and Traffic, New York Times p: 5.

10. Chesbrough H, Vanhaverbeke W, West J (2006) The inter-organizational context of open innovation. Open innovation researching a new paradigm pp: 1-22.

11. Saxenian AL (2000) Silicon Valley's New Immigrant Entrepreneurs, The Center for Comparative Immigration Studies. University of California, San Diego, Working Paper pp: 1-30.

12. Martin R, Aldrich HE, Carter N (2003) The structure of organizational founding teams: Homophile, strong ties, and isolation among US entrepreneurs. American Sociology Review 68: 195-222.

13. Granovetter M (1985) Economic action and social structure: the problem of embeddedness. American Journal of Sociology 91: 481-510.

14. Granovetter M (2005) The Impact of Social Structure on Economic Outcomes. Journal of Economic Perspectives 19: 33-50.

15. Florida R (2002) The economic geography of talent. Anals of the association of the American geographers 92: 743-755.

16. Moretti E (2012) The New Geography of Jobs. Houghton Mifflin Harcourt Edn p: 304.

17. Van Der Linde C (2003) The Demography of clusters: Findings from the cluster Meta-Study. Innovation, Clusters and interregional competition, Berlin, Heidelberg, Springer-Verlag, New York pp: 130-149.

18. Zahra SA, Gerard G (2002) International entrepreneurship: The current status of the field and future research agenda. Entrepreneurship Theory and Practice 41: 50.

19. Richtermeyer G (2003) Emerging themes in entrepreneurship research, Business Research and Information Development Group (BRIDG). Outreach and extension, University of Missouri, Lincoln University p: 29.

20. Zahra S, Bogner W (2000) Technology Strategy and Software New Venture Performance: The Moderating Effect of the Competitive Environment. Journal of Business Venturing 15: 135-173.

21. Florida R (2002) The rise of the creative class. Basic Books, NY, USA.

22. Parnell JA (2006) Global Entrepreneurial Strategy. In: Carraher (ed.) International Entrepreneurship.

23. Audia PG, Rider CI (2005) Entrepreneurs as organizational products: Revisited. Robert Baum, Michael Frese, and Robert Baron (eds.) University of California, Berkeley pp: 1-33.

24. Yin RK (2003) Case Study Research. (3rdedn) Sage Publications, London, England.

25. Schramm C, Ballmer S, Bernd D, Blanchard J, Buckley G (2008) Innovation measurement: tracking the state of innovation in the American economy: A report to the US secretary of commerce. Kauffman Symposium on Entrepreneurship and Innovation Data pp: 1-19.

26. Athreye S (2010) Economic Adversity and Entrepreneurship-led Growth, Lessons from the Indian Software Sector. World Institute for Development Economics Research (UNU-WIDER) pp: 1-20.

27. Miles MB, Huberman AM (1994) Qualitative Data Analysis. (2ndedn) Newbury Park, CA, Sage pp: 10-12.

Joynal and Mizan (J.M.) Model for Cluster Development

Md. Joynal Abdin[1] and Md. Mizanur Rahman[2]*

[1]*Deputy Manager at SME Foundation in Dhaka, Bangladesh*
[2]*Assistant Manager at SME Foundation in Dhaka, Bangladesh*

Abstract

Cluster is a geographical location (5 km radius) having 50 or more manufacturing or service providing units of interrelated and interdependent firms along with their backward and forward linkage industries. Manufacturing or service providing firms are co-located and experience unique strengths, weaknesses, opportunities and threats in a cluster. Clusters could be naturally grown due to the availability of raw materials, skilled labor, historically inherent professional uniqueness etc. reasons. On the other hand government or concerned agencies may establish a pre-planned co-located cluster of a particular sub-sector in a specific place. Where firms are co-located and linked with each other through the value chain of a particular product. Clusters, either naturally grown or man-made, require development interventions in different phases to perform better than its existing situation. Cluster development interventions could be different based on specific needs of a cluster. Implementation modalities of cluster development interventions could be different due to the explicit features of a cluster. There are several models for cluster development offered by different international bodies, expert groups, practitioners to guide clusters into a particular benchmark of development. The J.M. Model for cluster development was offered by both the authors to guide cluster managers toward success in a challenging environment. This model was initially offered by the authors through their publication titled 'Cluster Development Models: Challenges and Opportunities" published by the International Journal of Economics, Finance and Management Sciences. It comprises of five phases and twenty one steps for comprehensive development of a selected cluster. The J.M. Model for Cluster Development is described elaborately here in this article for better understanding of the cluster managers, practitioners, academicians and other relevant stakeholders.

Keywords: J.M. Model for cluster development; Cluster development model; Cluster development process; Steps and phases of cluster development; Different steps of cluster development

JEL Code: C38; O14

Introduction

Many least developed countries (LDCs) including Bangladesh wants to foster economic development through entrepreneurship development. Because it is one of the most powerful means for employment generation, new employment creation, increasing GDP growth, export earnings and finally poverty alleviation. Governments are trying to promote enterprise development, industrialization for the same reason. But they have limited resources to deploy after taking care of basic needs like foods, clothing, housing, education and healthcare facilities to the mass people. As a result, scarcity of budget allocation or inability to mobilize entrepreneurship development is a common phenomenon in almost every LDC's.

It is difficult to provide all industrial logistics including lands, electricity, gas, water, infrastructure to 100 enterprises located scattered all over an Upzilla. But government could easily ensure these industrial logistics into a particular location for the same number of enterprises. At the same time it is difficult for the revenue collectors to collect tax and VAT from 100 small enterprises located at different parts of a town than collecting the same from a particular location. Business cost is much lesser in a co-located industrial cluster than that of the scattered located industrial environment. Therefore cluster based enterprise development concept is becoming popular around the world [1].

Problem statement and research questions

Cluster based industrial development is a comparatively economic, swift, comprehensive and result-worthy method for entrepreneurship development, employment generation, increasing GDP growth and export earnings. But, what is a cluster? How a co-located industrial cluster could be established? Or, how a naturally grown cluster could be further developed? What are the steps of cluster Development? How many processes involved in cluster development? etc. All of the above mentioned questions will be focused and answered here in this article.

Objective

Objective of this paper is to describe the J.M. Model for Cluster Development elaborately to make it easy to understand for the cluster managers and practitioners. Helping the stakeholders to initiate and implement cluster development activities successfully in any economies of the world especially least development economies.

Methodology

This paper is the result of a number of SME Cluster development initiatives in Bangladesh. Experiences of "SME Cluster Mapping" study in 2013 and "Needs Assessment for Cluster Development" at 30 SME clusters located at 30 districts of Bangladesh. Secondary materials were collected and analyzed to identify a suitable cluster development model. As we have experienced difficulties to adopt any of the models completely here in Bangladesh then we have decided to offer a new model based (J.M. Model for Cluster Development) on the needs assessment results and a series of focus group discussions (FGD) and key informant interviews (KII) with the stakeholders.

*****Corresponding author:** Md. Mizanur Rahman, Assistant Manager at SME Foundation in Dhaka, Bangladesh, E-mail: rubelbclt@gmail.com

Scope of work

The authors are two key members of SMEF cluster development team. Having experiences to identify and map SME Clusters. Conducted Needs Assessment for SME Cluster Development at different SME clusters of Bangladesh. The authors were engaged with conducting Censuses and Surveys at various SME clusters. Both the authors have analyzed most of the available models for Cluster Development and offered this J.M. Model for Cluster Development to foster cluster based SME/enterprise development in any LDC like Bangladesh.

Limitation of this study

Main limitation of this model could be the uniqueness of it. It is still in the primary stage of implementation. After completing every steps in some clusters we may have to think of revision for this model. But it will take ten to fifteen years to complete the whole process in a cluster and identify the improvement opportunities of this model. But this model has flexibility to adopt any new component or changes as and when required. With all potential limitations in mind till now, we believe that, this model can guide cluster managers/development agencies/authorities toward successful development of a cluster based on predetermined benchmarks.

Literature review

Michael Porter who is recognized as the founder of industrial cluster concept defined cluster as a "Geographically proximate group of interconnected companies, suppliers, service providers and associated institutions in a particular field, linked by externalities of various types" [2]. Clusters contain a mix of industries related by knowledge, skills, inputs, demand, and other linkages. United Nations Industrial Development Organization [3] defines industrial cluster as: "Geographic and economic concentration of manufacturing activities which produce and sell a domain of interrelated and complementary products and having common problems and opportunities" [4]. Cluster could be defined based on different parameters like activities, origin, size wise, technology wise, linkage wise, market wise, state of development and based on entrepreneurs etc. For example manufacturing cluster or service providing cluster, naturally grown cluster or man-made cluster, growing cluster or declining cluster, export oriented cluster or domestic market based cluster etc. parameters could be used to define nature of a cluster.

Cluster development practitioners introduce several models for cluster development. Notable models for Cluster Development includes, the UNIDO [5] Cluster Development Approach-1 and 2 offered by the United Nations Industrial Development Organization [6]. Five Phase Twelve Steps Model for Cluster Development offered by the Cluster Navigator – New Zealand [7]. Cluster Development approach in Republic of Croatia offered by Maxwell Stamp Plc. [8]. Cluster Development Model offered by the International Trade Department, World Bank [9]. Cluster Map of an Agri-business cluster offered by the World Bank. Cluster management strategy by the European Cluster Observatory [10]. Cluster Based City Economic Development Concept offered by the ADB [11]. Besides these there are contributions of Cluster Plus – India, TCI Network – USA in cluster development models. None of the above mentioned model is fully implementable in a least developed country like Bangladesh. Having limitations in financial, technical knowledge, technological, managerial capacity to dedicate for cluster development etc. With all these limitations in mind the authors would like to propose a pro-poor, flexible and equally effective in any least developed country and developed economies as well model (J.M. Model for Cluster Development) for cluster development. This model is offering a pro-poor, comprehensive and flexible guideline for developing clusters around the world irrespectively in a developed or developing or least developed economy.

Joynal and Mizan (J.M.) model for cluster development

This is a model to guide cluster development authorities/practitioners/cluster managers to develop a newly identified cluster or develop a cluster in a particular location. It includes 5 phases and 21 steps from identification to making the cluster self-guided. J.M. Model for Cluster Development is as follows [1] (Table 1).

	Phase-I Identification and Maping	Phase-II Cluster Analysis	Phase – III Intervention Designing and Piloting	Phase-IV Implementation and Monitoring	Phase-V Networking and Evaluation
Phases					
Steps	1. Defining cluster as per national stage of industrialization, 2. Identify cluster's location in countries administrative map 3. Educating Stakeholders with the cluster development process 4. Developing a database with cluster information	5. Collecting data regarding cluster's existing features, development barriers, potentials etc. through FGD and KII. 6. Preparing Cluster's Resource Map. 7. Prioritizing cluster's development barriers. 8. Listing problems as per short, mid and long term basis.	9. Designing development interventions to solve/overcome the barriers. 10. Identifying concern agencies to take the lead. 11. Piloting a cluster with identified interventions. 12. Monitoring outcome. 13. Revising/updating the list of interventions as and when required.	14. Implementing determined interventions at a cluster. 15. Monitoring output 16. Fixing benchmark 17. Initiative for further value addition 18. Preparing leadership groups for future course of action.	19. Networking with local and international stakeholder organizations. 20. Evaluating progress and taking corrective measures. 21. Handing over the leadership into the leadership group.
Outputs	Latest database of Clusters across the country	Updated information about the problems and prospects of each cluster.	Cluster Development Action Plan	A growing/developed cluster	A sustainable and well established cluster with value chain linkage
	Source: Abdin MJ, Rahman MM Cluster Development Models: Challenges and Opportunities, International Journal of Economics. Finance and Management Sciences 3: 358-366. [1]				

Table 1: Joynal and Mizan (J.M.) Model for Cluster Development.

Phase-I: Identification and Mapping

The first phase of this model starts with the identification and mapping of clusters across the country's territory. This can be initiated first by constructing and adopting an acceptable and applicable definition of cluster in the context of that country's socioeconomic condition. After that the administrative map of the country will be used to identify the naturally grown clusters across the country by using suitable communication method. Government authorities has vital role in assisting the cluster mapping process as there are many mechanisms where govt. can work with private firms for locating and gathering information. The identified clusters are to be screened out as per the adopted definition. Cluster members have to put their inputs in the development process. Thus a final database of clusters countrywide with all elementary information will be constructed at the end of this phase. Phase-I involve the following four (04) steps:

Defining cluster as per national stage of industrialization (Step-1)

Clusters can be defined based in various terms like as occupancy of geographic area, number of entrepreneurs within the cluster, volume of gross production and revenue generated annually, type of business in the cluster, nature of supply chain network, cultural, religious or social groupings etc. Although the clusters are to be defined as per the macro economic conditions related to industrialization of the concerned country such as the scale of industrialization, expansion of industrial proximities, scale of investment in manufacturing of the country and so on. In such way, considering the factors and based on the industrial economy an acceptable definition of cluster has to be adopted.

Identify cluster's location in countries administrative map (Step-2)

After all ways acceptable definition of cluster in hand the identification step has to be followed. This can be done with the help of the Country's administrative map. Division of all geographic location should have contained clusters of various industrial activities. Newspaper, Local Govt. offices, Journalists, Businessman, Local Development agencies etc. can be the source of information on the presence and location of clusters on that divisional area. According to those information, the clusters are to be visited physically for verification and finally listed with some elementary information like Name and address, Products/ Service description, no of entrepreneurs, communication directions, trade body, supply chain, raw materials, types of machines used, general market data and other information as far as possible. This data can be used as baseline data in future for progress tracking and used to build up KPIs for interventions. The more quantifiable date could be collected the better.

Educating Stakeholders with the cluster development process (Step-3)

The stakeholder of a cluster may include entrepreneurs, suppliers, marketing personnel, labors and maintenance workers, local govt. officials, teachers, trade body representatives, journalists and other professionals etc. They have key role in the development process of the cluster. Hence, the stakeholders are to be engaged into the development strategy for selected cluster. To do so, first there should be communications and informal discussions between stakeholders and cluster development authority on planning, strategy set up, availability of cooperation, mutual benefits etc.

Developing a database with cluster information (Step-4)

In this step, all the elementary information on clusters being in hand, a concrete database has to be built. A common format has to be used to describe each identified cluster. There should be clear indexing system to easily seek for a cluster information according to category like as location in administrative map, product/ service type, size of cluster, cluster by founding period, exporting or non-exporting, rising or declining cluster and many more as categorical as it can be. With all the collected background data for each of the clusters, there would be a basic prioritizing of importance based on cluster size in terms of number of entrepreneurs, area, investment volume, production volume, employment ratio etc. This database has to have an upgradation period of say 05 years.

Output of Phase-I: Latest database of Clusters across the country divided into categories to find out information easily and conveniently. The database has all information verified and which will be regarded as the base data for all future activities.

Phase-II: Cluster Analysis

The cluster analysis phase comes up with in depth study on selected clusters. However, selecting the right cluster to start the initiative with is a very critical issue. But clusters can be selected based on leveraged existing activities and business environment strengths [12]. Priority would be given to the clusters which came first by screening in step-04. This study may be combined with census, interviews, surveys and other statistical tools. There would be a sketch up on the clusters' resource map which reveals the pertinent economic features for a selected cluster. In the end of these studies, the barriers and opportunities of development are listed, sorted, prioritized and categorized according to short, mid and long term goals.

Collecting data regarding cluster's existing features, development barriers, potentials etc. through FGD and KII (Step-5)

At the very beginning of the cluster analysis phase, the step 5 focuses on extensive rapport build up with the stakeholders of the selected cluster. There would be focus group discussions (FGD) with cluster members which include entrepreneurs, trade body representatives, supplier and buyers, intellectuals and professionals who are related to appraisal of that cluster. Also, there should be key informant interviews which targets persons who are learned and acknowledged about the cluster's SWOT for long and better than anyone. This step will bring about the differential features, general business environment, supply chain, role players, barriers of development, hidden opportunities, and urged development needs of the concerned cluster.

Preparing cluster's resource map (Step-6)

Resource map is a graphical information bank that represents data about each active player operating the Clusters' either from inside or outside of a cluster. It is to be built with the information gathered in step 5 in such a way that, it can be easily understandable. The map includes raw materials suppliers, machineries and tools suppliers, technology and maintenance support suppliers etc. located at the left. Also the marketing agents, packaging, transporting service providers, finance providers, public relations etc. are shown at the right part of the map. At the top, the local and regional govt. institutions that support the activities of the cluster are placed. At the bottom, education, training, technological and business research providers of the cluster are plotted. The middle part of the cluster map focuses on the manufacturers and processors, lead role players and sub-contractors etc. who are directly involved through the conversion process. Actually this map gives us complete overview on the operational framework, overview on active network players and external service providers of that cluster [13]. A typical example of agricultural processing cluster resource map can be shown as follows (Figure 1).

Prioritizing cluster's development barriers (Step-7)

A naturally grown or initiative based planned cluster may have many barriers for a smooth development. As a matter of fact, all development initiatives need proper time to complete and all barriers of development can't be addressed simultaneously. Hence the barriers identified, has to be properly prioritized based on some factors. These factors include the measurement of impact of resolving a problem in terms of economic and social benefit that it may bring for the cluster. Also the barriers easier to understand and solve are to be given top most priorities. It is possible that some barriers can be flagged not solvable for the current period and considered for future development projects.

Listing problems as per short, mid and long term basis (Step-8)

Prioritized problems carry definite goals with them. But all are no to be addressed in same time range. Some should come first in considerations, some are dependent to another. Hence, the goals are divided into shot, mid and long terms. Generally, the short term goals are achievable within 3-12 months. Midterm goals need 12 to 36 months whereas long term goals can take 36 to 60 months to address. Most importantly, all the goals are to be specific, measurable, attainable, and relevant and time bound (SMART).

Output of Phase-II: The output expected from this phase is updated information about the problems and prospects, the complete resource map for each cluster and enough background knowledge for intervention design based on the prioritized cluster problems and needs.

PHASE – III: Intervention Designing and Piloting

In this phase of cluster development, with all analyzed data and known factors of improvement, the cluster development agent will design various interventions targeting the resolution of identified issues and new development projects. Although the interventions are to be taken under implementation only with necessary involvement of implementation authority. Prior to go for full phase implementation, there need to be necessary piloting for verifying the applicability and effectiveness of interventions. Implementation activities will be monitored for measuring progress and making necessary adjustments. Every intervention will be time bound and each cycle of similar interventions will come up with revised framework for more effective outcome.

Designing development interventions to solve/overcome the barriers (Step-9)

With the clusters being properly analyzed and the problems and prospects are being sort out, there need to be measures for addressing those problems. The measures include interventions related to infrastructural and institutional development, financial support, technological upgradation, human resource development by skill sessions and on the job training, tracer study of growth and so on that may apply. Interventions' applicability and effectiveness for solving real world problems can be problematic to justify, but proper brainstorming can help overcome. All the designed interventions are focused on time bound short, medium and long term goals with the problem statements properly defined. Each intervention has to target in achieving justified value of pre-defined KPIs at the end of the implementation term.

Identifying concern agencies to take the lead (Step-10)

As the interventions designed are of various discipline in nature, each of these need to be handed over to proper agency/ implementation authority for taking the lead. Intervention leadership is of top most importance as this will define the rate of success at the end of the day. The knowledge pool and expertise of the intervention authority have to be at required level to come up with lower risk of failure. Leading authority can be a cluster development agent, or a department of concerned discipline, Govt. or Local organizations, NGOs or Financial

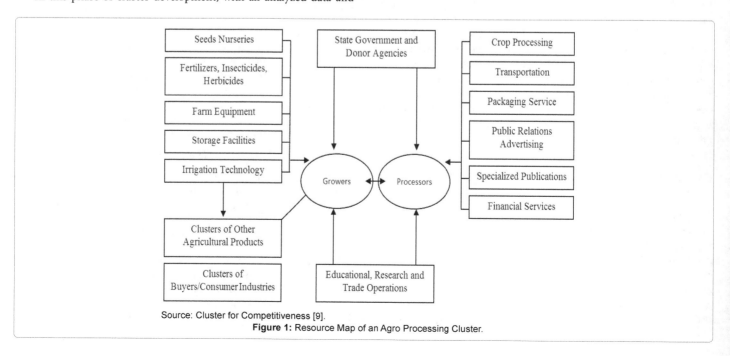

Source: Cluster for Competitiveness [9].
Figure 1: Resource Map of an Agro Processing Cluster.

institutions, Training academy or a department of Government for concerned development works.

Piloting a cluster with identified interventions (Step-11)

Piloting is very important for making sure the effectiveness and applicability of a designed intervention for a definite cluster. Some interventions may seem appropriate and the output may found to be very much necessary for the cluster, but can come up with failures right at its piloting state. Some may success in piloting for an individual cluster but may bring failure for another one. Considering all these facts, prior to implementing in full phase, all the interventions should begin with a proper time bound piloting and if success follows, to the full phase implementation. Although piloting will help decide in making necessary corrections and adjustments in the design of the intervention.

Monitoring outcome (Step-12)

Monitoring here actually means keeping the track of pilot projects for necessary interventions. It can be done by assessing the increase or decrease in KPIs, physical observations, interviewing the cluster members and graphical performance monitoring [3]. Monitoring results will help us make to re-design, adjust, correct or improve the intervention designs.

Revising/updating the list of interventions as and when required (Step-13)

This step simply helps to decide the revision or update needs for the intervention designs based on the piloting outcome. In this way, perfection can be achieved and an effective number of interventions can be found applicable for the cluster development. Interventions from all disciplines will combine into a complete action plan practically applicable with achievable effective results.

Output of Phase-III: This phase intends to produce the final and refined version of cluster development Action Plan. This plan will be the base line of the development of initiatives for every cluster. There would be enough flexibility for making necessary alteration of any type for the sake of increased effectiveness and applicability of this action plan. This will enable the continual improvement of the action plan in flow with development economics. After this plan, real implementation stage will begin.

Phase-IV: Implementation and Monitoring

This phase will turn a cluster into a fast growing cluster having remarkable momentum of development. With a proper cluster development action plan, the implemented interventions will continually improve each cluster's performance specifically economic, social, and environmental, productivity and quality, human resource development, market expansion and so on. All the outputs from those interventions will be regularly monitored and measured for further improvement and modification. The performance of clusters will also be benchmarked with some successfully established clusters located locally or internationally. Also the phase will have significant focus on further value addition through the entire value stream of the cluster and build up a leadership group capable enough to take over the responsibilities to carry out the development process of the respective cluster keeping the vision intact.

Implementing determined interventions at a cluster (Step-14)

Actual momentum of cluster development will get at its peak with the implementation of determined interventions from cluster development action plan. These interventions are targeting either to resolve cluster's existing and future problems or to make improvement of exiting situation or to achieve a desired level of KPIs. Interventions are of different disciplines as of mentioned earlier and has time bound objectives to achieve. Implementation role players i.e. agents were already settled and gone through with the piloting intervention-wise. So this step starts the actual implementation of designed interventions according to the final cluster development action plan at full pace and involves all the stakeholders in this process role-wise.

Monitoring output (Step-15)

As the implementation goes on, a monitoring team will be formed to continuously monitor the progress of implementation. Monitoring should always be aligned to the comparison of achievement of objectives and according to this, criteria for progress tracking has to be developed. The team can perform their activities at end of small milestones of each intervention or periodically as the development progresses. There will be necessary tools and equipment for collecting data while monitoring upon the brainstorming and discussion of applicability. It is expected that the monitoring data conforms the effective implementation of the interventions to impervious growth of clusters' macro-economic and social condition.

Fixing benchmark (Step-16)

Benchmarking is a process of comparison of performances between or among two or more subject matters under similar circumstances and conditions. Cluster growth performance with respect to individual interventions as per the implementation by KPI data has to be compared with local or internally situated clusters for that similar interventions to get a mark of baseline performance standard. There would be many criteria to compare and each criteria will give best upper or lower values for any KPI based performance scale. The best performance score will be the benchmark for a development initiative for further continuation. It will establish a standard performance scale for clusters across the country or even the globe for a definite intervention what will be performance goal to achieve at the end of the intervention. There are several benchmarking tools used in many cluster initiatives in Europe base. Such tool can be helpful for going for the local cluster benchmarking.

Initiative for further value addition (Step-17)

All clusters has a natural set up of value streams since form the establishment. But as the value stream is not efficient enough, there will be more and more opportunities for further value addition. This will increase profits, increase employment and make the value stream more stable. Integrating backward and forward linkages into the cluster's value chain is a better way. Other may find non-value added activities and wastes and remove those gradually to increase value addition process efficiency of that cluster. Also, introducing innovation initiatives by starting innovation centers such as RandD and intermediate services such as designing, prototyping and intellectual property reservations etc. can foster the value addition process a way further [14]. Other than adding more fruits to the basket, its rally hard to become competitive in global market economy.

Preparing leadership groups for future course of action (Step-18)

Cluster development is a continuous process and the leadership of cluster members can only make the process stable. Also, the whole process is initiated and nurtured by cluster development agent with the necessary participation of cluster members. With the course of time, the clusters' entrepreneurs and leaders will become skilled enough to handle this continuous development process. This motto is built within the cluster development strategy right from the beginning which can only become operational by correct engagement of potential leadership groups into planning, designing, implementation, monitoring, evaluation, restructuring and many other processes of cluster development.

Output of Phase-IV: At the end of phase IV, it is expected that the cluster will be at stronger growth potential and renowned as a fast growing / developed cluster across the country and world as well. Also, both supply chain network and market will be at their most stable state. Interventions with induction of modern technology and skill education will make the cluster a model of successful cluster with appropriate development strategy to follow.

Phase-V: Networking and Evaluation

In this final phase of development clusters will be enough matured to enter evolution with distinctive economic features at a higher scale. Supply chain network will expand over the national boundaries and stakeholders from both local and international communities will continuously increase in number and integrate into the development frame. The cluster development agency and implementation authority will evaluate the stage of development until they find that opportunity and scope for handing over the leadership to internally established leadership group.

Networking with local and international stakeholder organizations (Step-19)

Clusters as they grow with immense economic growth potential with well-established supply and market linkages, more and more local and international stakeholders need to be conglomerated within the network for gain share. Many development partners, financial organizations, NGOs, Academic and Research Partners, Local and International Corporate groups, Business cartels and MNCs etc. are some example of such stakeholders that creates global value chain linkages [15].

Evaluating progress and taking corrective measures (Step-20)

In this step, the cluster development agent will perform a cross platform i.e. social, economic, environmental etc. evaluation of the entire development progress right from the beginning till phase V. According to the evaluation there might need some corrective measures for some key principle of cluster development strategy. Also the evaluation will give a pathway to be ensured about handing over the lead of cluster development to the locally developed leadership group.

Handing over the leadership into the leadership group (Step-21)

The final phase of cluster development has enormous indications in favor of the cluster to be at its most enriching features of development. As this is been known all over the world as a role model of cluster based economy, the development will go on with progress with its in-built momentum of growth potential. More and more other clusters from around the world will be integrated into the system and as the days go by, it will be more and more matured. Hence the lead of development procedure has now the time to be handed over to locally developed cluster leadership group for continuation of its growth.

Output of Phase-V: There will be strong level of vertical cooperation along the value chain where the enterprises will perform complementary tasks of the same production process [5]. And the rise of inter-personal trust and vocabulary sharing because of repeated interactions facilitates will enhance the flow of knowledge among the enterprises and it will emphasis the scope for specialization in the use of all inputs. It will result complete agglomeration among the cluster members as well as forward and backward supply chain networks. The phase V cluster will provide a complete lesson learnt and hands on experiences on cluster development for the development agency that will be followed for the development of other clusters across the country.

Justification

There is a long list of models for cluster development. But none of these are comprehensive with detailed description of activities, inputs, outputs etc. The Joynal and Mizan (J.M.) Model for Cluster Development is designed to guide a layman cluster manager from beginning to the end without any confusion. There is enough space for evaluation and adoption of new measures as and when required.

Conclusion

Joynal and Mizan Model for Cluster Development is a new model proposed by both the authors of this article. Authors are confident that this model can guide cluster managers from beginning to the end without any confusion. It has enough flexibility to address any new issue and take corrective measures as and when required. The model is equally applicable at developed or least developed economies. It describes specific object oriented output in each of the phases to measure effectiveness of the initiative.

Refrences

1. Abdin MJ, Rahman MM (2015) Cluster Development Models: Challenges and Opportunities. International Journal of Economics, Finance and Management Sciences 3: 358-366.
2. Porter ME (2003) The Economic Performance of Regions. Regional Studies 37: 549-578.
3. UNIDO (2013) The UNIDO Approach to Cluster Development, Key Principles and Project Experiences for Inclusive Growth.
4. Small and Medium Enterprise Foundation (2013) SME Clusters in Bangladesh.
5. Clara M (2008) Going Beneath the surface: UNIDO industrial cluster programme and a new research agenda for the study of industrial districts. UNIDO.
6. Murali BP, Banerjee S (2011) Fostering Responsible Behavior in MSMEs in Clusters: Role of Cluster Development Agent III, Foundation for MSME Clusters.
7. Williams I (2005) Cluster Development: The How, TCI Annual Conference. Hong Kong.
8. Ministry of Economy, Labor and Entrepreneurship (MELE) (2013) Central Finance and Contracting Agency (CFCA), Government of the Republic of Croatia Guidelines for Cluster Development A Handbook for Practitioners.
9. World Bank (2009) Cluster for Competitiveness- A Practical Guide & Policy Implications for Developing Cluster Initiatives.
10. Gamp TL, Köcker GM, Nerger M (2014) Cluster Collaboration and Business Support Tools to Facilitate Entrepreneurship. Cross-sectoral Collaboration and Growth, European Cluster Observatory.
11. Choe K, Roberts B (2011) Competitive Cities in 21st Century: Cluster based local economic development. Urban Development Series, ADB.
12. Solvell O, Lindqvist G, Ketels C (2003) The Cluster Initiative Greenbook (1st edn).
13. Federal Ministry of Economics and Technology (2009) Cluster Management Excellence 1, Under the Kompetenznetze Deutschland Initiative, Germany.

14. Yonghui Y, Haixiong Q, Qiang C (2010) A Case Study of Innovations at the Xiqiao Textile Industry Cluster, Chinese Sociology and Anthropology 42:3.

15. Contreras OF, Carrillo J, Alonso J (2012) Local Entrepreneurship within Global Value Chains: A Case Study in the Mexican Automotive Industry. World Development 40: 1013-1023.

Human Resource Orchestration for the Implementation of Entrepreneurial Opportunities

Rinne T*

Department of Management Studies, Aalto University School of Business, P.O. BOX 21230, 00076 AALTO, Finland

Abstract

Entrepreneurial service firms continuously seek new opportunities, trying to integrate identified opportunities as part of their service portfolio. Successful implementation of new opportunities requires effective management of human resources and development of competences required in these firms. The concept of resource orchestration offers a theoretical framework for strategic human resource management in entrepreneurial firms. However, there is limited research on how the firms orchestrate their human resources in the process of implementation of entrepreneurial opportunities. This paper is a case study of five small technology service firms. The paper examines how the case firms have managed and developed their human resources while implementing new business opportunities and how they have adopted the concept of resource orchestration. Results of this study show that the importance of different sub-processes of resource orchestration varies among small service firms and that often several sub-processes must be managed simultaneously. Successful implementation of new business opportunities requires good managerial abilities and is connected to the sub-processes of resource orchestration. Based on the findings of the study, this paper proposes a revised model for human resource orchestration for the process of entrepreneurial opportunity implementation.

Keywords: Management; Human resources; Resource orchestration; Strategic entrepreneurship; Service business

Introduction

Human resource management is an important part of *strategic entrepreneurship* (SE). Intangible resources, and specifically human resources, are the most important factor in creating competitive advantage for a firm [1]. Continuous opportunity seeking and exploitation processes are the core of SE, and all management activities related to entrepreneurial opportunities are critical for small firms. Human resource management in SE has been strongly based on Resource-Based View (RBV) [2, 3, 4]. In recent years, the concept of *resource orchestration* has contributed to SE by introducing an alternative approach to resource management [5]. Resource orchestration introduces the process of structuring, bundling, and leveraging resources in a firm [5, 6, 7].

However, literature in the area of resource orchestration has had a strong theoretical approach, and only few empirical studies have been published in this field. Specifically, empirical research of resource orchestration in the context of implementing entrepreneurial opportunities is missing in this field. Additionally, earlier research [7, 8] argues that feedback loops exist among structuring, bundling and leveraging, and these phases do not necessarily follow each other in sequence. Also it is emphasized that the leaders need to synchronize their resource orchestration actions properly and that it is possible to implement different phases in different order. However, empirical research is missing on how the leaders synchronize their resource management actions in practice and how different phases and sub-processes of resource orchestration are implemented for opportunity implementation.

This paper aims to develop a deeper understanding of the resource orchestration concept by examining how human resources are managed during the process of opportunity implementation. We examine the challenges faced by small technology services firms over the life-cycle of opportunity implementation in those firms and link them with the resource orchestration process. In this paper, we also study what is the value of different phases in the resource orchestration process for small service firms and which phases and sub-processes these firms have implemented as well as how they have done it. In addition, we study how small service firms synchronize the different phases of resource orchestration process in their human resource management activities.

This paper is a case study of five small service firms and their activities in human resource management in the implementation of new entrepreneurial opportunities. Because this paper draws its theoretical background from SE, the focus of the research is specifically on the process of human resource management activities through the theoretical lens of the resource orchestration concept.

This paper provides several theoretical and managerial contributions. This study shows that, for opportunity implementation, some selected sub-processes of resource orchestration are more important than others and some sub-processes practically do not exist in the context of case firms. Sirmon et al. [8] suggest that the order of sub-processes is at least partly sequential. This study shows that sequential order for sub-processes is very limited and that most of the sub-processes must be managed simultaneously. It was also found that entrepreneurial leadership is an important part of the resource orchestration process and actions of entrepreneurial leaders are critical for successful opportunity implementation. Based on the findings of the study, this paper proposes a revised model for human resource orchestration in new opportunity implementation.

This paper is structured in the following way. The beginning of the paper discusses the theoretical background for this study. First, we review

---

**Corresponding author: Rinne T, Department of Management Studies, Aalto University School of Business, P.O. BOX 21230, 00076 AALTO, Finland
E-mail: timo.p.rinne@aalto.fi*

the process of entrepreneurial opportunity implementation and then focus on human resource management from the perspective of SE, specifically on the concept of resource orchestration and its sub-processes. Theoretical background is followed by an introduction to research methodology, and major part of this paper reviews the results from the empirical part of the study. The paper is concluded with analysis of theoretical and managerial implications, and also limitations of the study.

Theoretical Background

In this paper, we analyze human resource processes and activities in case firms during implementation of new entrepreneurial opportunities. Several concepts and theories are developed for entrepreneurial opportunities, specifically for identification, recognition, discovery, and creation of opportunities [9, 10, 11]. If business potential of an opportunity is evaluated high enough, the next step in the process is implementation, i.e., exploitation of an opportunity. According to Buenstorf [12], the entrepreneur's subjective perception of an opportunity has an influence on the decision about how to pursue an opportunity. Also, the characteristics of organizations affect the management of opportunity exploitation and the evolution of the organization during this process [12].

Strategic planning and management is an important part of the process of opportunity implementation, for which a firm can choose different strategies. Strategic choices can be based for example on transaction costs, real options, market positioning, product diversification and usage of resources [13, 14], or superior competitive advantages, available market opportunities, and creation of business opportunities [8]. The need for integration of strategic management and entrepreneurship has been pointed out by several researchers [15]. One of the most recognized development in this field is *strategic entrepreneurship* (SE). SE is a process of simultaneous identification and exploitation of opportunities, which results in a firm's superior performance [2]. SE has theoretical roots in economics, international business, organization theory, sociology, and strategic management [15]. Strong integration between SE and a firm's strategy is evident, and SE is considered as a process of entrepreneurial activity with a strategic perspective [15]. Resource management is an important part of SE; 'Resources are managed strategically when their deployment facilitates the simultaneous and integrated use of opportunity- and advantage-seeking behaviors.' [2]. This definition summarizes the spirit of human resource management in SE; in parallel with the use of human resources in strategic projects and operations, resources are continuously used also for searching and implementing new business opportunities.

In the early days of SE, resource management was based on the theory of *resource-based view*, RBV [2, 4, 16]. In an RBV-based strategy, a firm creates competitive advantage by using and developing its unique resources, which are difficult to copy by competitors [17]. Resources can be tangible like financial capital, land, or machines, or intangible like human resources or social connections [2, 18]. Intangible resources can create a unique resource position and competitive advantage more effectively than tangible resources, because intangible resources are often rare, tacit, and socially complex, and for this reason more difficult to copy [15, 18].

Teece and Shuen [19] have criticized RBV for not taking fully into account the influence of rapidly changing business environment. The concept of dynamic capabilities was introduced by them to complement resource management theories from the perspective of environment. Dynamic capabilities are managerial and organizational routines for reconfiguring and developing existing competences of a firm [20]. Development of dynamic capabilities has a strong link to a firm's strategy, because decisions about which resources the firm should further develop have an impact for the firm's future position [19,21]. The process of competence development and resource reconfiguration is intertwined with the firm's strategy process [22].

One of the latest developments in resource management is *resource orchestration* [6,7,8], which is a process driven by the actions of managers. It integrates two concepts: *resource management* and *asset orchestration*. Resource management is *'the comprehensive process of structuring the firm's resource portfolio, bundling the resources to build capabilities, and leveraging those capabilities with the purpose of creating and maintaining value for customers and owners.'* [8]. Asset orchestration is derived from the concept of dynamic capabilities, and it has two components: search/selection and configuration/deployment [6]. Integration between resource management and asset orchestration is known as resource orchestration [6,8].

According to Sirmon et al [6,8], the resource management framework includes three components; *structuring, bundling, and leveraging* resources. Each of these process components is further divided into three sub-processes. Structuring includes the sub-processes of *acquisition, accumulation*, and *divestment*. Firstly, resources in strategic markets must be identified, and the firm must make an investment to get some of those resources. Human resources can be acquired for example from competitors, customers, universities, or from open labor markets. After the acquisition, a resource portfolio for the firm is formed, and the acquired resources become a part of the strategic assets of the firm. *Accumulation* of resources requires actions for internal development. New employees can be trained to their duties through formal education or by making them to work together with other employees. *Divestment* of resources means continuous evaluation of the existing resources and figuring out how these resources could support the firm's strategy. Leaders need to evaluate whether unproductive resources could be reconfigured to support a new strategy and new objectives of the firm, or if the existing resources would need to be replaced by new resources to create a better match with the firm's future strategy. From human resource perspective, divestment includes training and relocation of personnel, or, for example in case of cost-cutting in an uncertain economic environment, also laying off a part of the unproductive human resources. Divestment must be planned very carefully so that it does not negatively affect the firm's competitive advantage[6,8].

Bundling resources has three sub-processes: *stabilization, enrichment, and pioneering*. During bundling, acquired resources are used to form new capabilities for the firm [8]. *Stabilization* aims to preserve the acquired resources and the competitive advantage of the firm. Continuous training is important in order to maintain the acquired competences. The purpose of *enrichment* is to extend the existing capabilities with new capabilities which are in line with the firm's existing strategy and operations. In the enrichment process, new resources with new competences are mixed with the existing capabilities of a firm. For example, a service firm can extend its value chain by making available services so far supplied by other firms. Another example of enrichment is to learn new competences and integrate these competences with existing capabilities. *Pioneering* means integration of completely new capabilities with existing capabilities. For identifying potential synergies of the firm's new capabilities, pioneering requires specific creativity and deep knowledge of the business field. According to Sirmon et al [8], when environmental uncertainty is high, the sub-processes of enrichment and pioneering are more likely to create competitive advantage and optimum value for customers than stabilization is [6,8].

The purpose of the *leveraging* process is to match internal resources with challenges from external business environment. The focus of the leveraging process is to use the firm's resources and capabilities for exploiting market opportunities and, in this way, create value to the customers. Leveraging includes the sub-processes of *mobilization, coordination, and deployment* of resources. These sub-processes have sequential links with each other. Firstly, resources must be *mobilized* before they can be coordinated and deployed. During mobilization, a firm tries to identify the resources needed for exploiting identified business opportunities. According to Sirmon et al. [8], during mobilization, the firm may plan its leveraging strategy, which requires particular capability configurations. A chosen strategy can be based on superior competitive advantages (*resource advantage strategy*), available market opportunities (*market opportunity strategy*), or creation of business opportunities (*entrepreneurial strategy*). Each strategic option involves different capability configurations, which are formed as a result of mobilization and coordination. The purpose of *coordination* is to integrate capabilities together to form required capability configurations. Effective coordination of capabilities requires creation of strong internal social capital in the firm. Social capital facilitates sharing of tacit knowledge and experience. Also, effective cross-divisional communication within the firm is needed to build social capital and to enable effective coordination of capabilities. *Deployment* is the final step in the leveraging process. Deployment means using the capabilities which were first mobilized and then integrated to the firm with the help of coordination. Deployment is the final step of implementation of the chosen leveraging strategy [6,8].

Synchronization of resource management activities is particularly important in the leveraging phase [7]. Previously acquired and bundled resources need to be synchronized in order to create a performance advantage [23]. Need for synchronization is based on dependency between the phases and sub-processes. If a certain opportunity requires specific resources which first must be acquired, bundled and then leveraged, the processes will be dependent on each other, and a high level of synchronization is needed for using these resources efficiently [23]. High level of synchronization also results in a competitive advantage, because synchronization between the processes makes resource bundles more complex and more difficult to imitate by rivals [8,23]. However, not all resources need to be synchronized. If the processes are independent from each other, synchronization does not provide added value in the efficiency of resource deployment [23].

Methodology

The purpose of this study is to understand how the leaders of small service firms manage their human resources in the process of new business opportunity implementation. Empirical data was collected from five case studies and then analyzed. A multiple-case study method was chosen, because the use of multiple cases helps to improve constructive validity of the study and can result in a deeper understanding of the research problem [24,25, 26]. Also, when using multiple-case studies and multiple realities, different standpoints are considered, which helps to avoid accepting too simple models or answers [27].

Because the purpose in this study is to understand the activities of people and social phenomena in organizations which they represent, an interpretive research approach was used. Interpretive approach offers a holistic view to social problems by close participation in the actors' realities and by interpretation of their experiences and perceptions [28]. The researcher also had an opportunity to observe activities in the case firms by attending meetings and in other situations during the process.

Observing is considered a useful research method: in interpretive research approach, the researcher may interact closely with the actors, which provides opportunities for deep insights into the research problems [25].

The case firms were selected from a field of business where the researcher had a good access to empirical data. A fairly specific business field was chosen: payment card services. Payment card services are normally provided through a technical infrastructure including IT servers and payment card personalization machines. In addition, the service process normally includes visual design of payment cards and planning of logistic processes for payment card distribution. Services include both standardized and configurable components.

Three criteria were used to select the case firms. Firstly, the number of employees in the firm should be small, fewer than 30 employees. Size of the firm is an important criterion, because in small firms resources are usually limited and all resources are in continuous use. Secondly, the firms must have endured in the market for more than two years. Strategic thinking is normally involved in a firm's operations once it has succeeded to stay alive the first years of its operations [29]. Thirdly, the firm must have implemented at least one new business opportunity which has created strategically important business operations in the firm. By using this set of criteria, it was possible to study strategic resource management in small service firms for the process of new business opportunity implementation.

Two primary sources of empirical data were used in this study. The first primary data source was face-to-face interviews of the managers in the case firms. Two persons from each case firm were interviewed, some of them more than once. In all case firms, the managing director and also either sales or operational director were interviewed. In most cases, the interviewees were also minority shareholders of their firms. Interviews were semi-structured and followed the themes identified from theoretical frameworks of strategic entrepreneurship and human resource management. The second primary source of data were observation memos from the researcher during participation in different meetings and other daily situations in the process of new opportunity implementation in the case firms. The secondary data sources included meeting memos and other confidential documents which were directly received from the firms. These documents complemented the findings from the primary data sources and supported the researcher's interpretation of the human resource processes in the case firms.

The interviews took place during 2012-13. All interviews were recorded and transcribed. Some details were checked with the interviewees after transcription in order to clear out possible misunderstandings. Data analysis was performed in parallel with data collection as an interactive process. Interactive process of collection and analysis of the data allows researchers to make adjustments to data collection methods if it is thought that the method requires changes to make the data more reliable, or its collection more efficient or more flexible [24].

Following the case-study approach by Eisenhardt [24], data-analysis was performed in two phases. At first, the researcher got detailed knowledge of the case firms with a within-case analysis approach. All possible data was gathered from each case firm and the process of opportunity implementation was minutely studied. The second step was cross-case analysis, which was tightly coupled with the process of within-case analysis. In the cross-case analysis, the tactic was to classify data by their source (interviews, observation data, and secondary data like company documents) and in this way to identify similarities between the cases and their patterns. The purpose of this approach was to get to know well each case and its unique patterns and then to analyze the data through multiple diverse lenses. This approach makes a better fit between data and theory more likely, and also the likelihood of capturing novel findings from the data will increase [24].

Findings

Human resource management in small service firms is a complex process which requires managers to pay special attention to single individuals: their competences, capabilities, and individual needs. It is particularly challenging for a manager to develop human resources for implementing new entrepreneurial opportunities, while simultaneously using human resources for ongoing activities in business operations and customer projects.

The results of this study are summarized in Figure 1. By following the sub-processes of resource orchestration, resources can be managed successfully during opportunity implementation. Resource structuring, bundling, and leveraging each have their own particular role in the total process of human resource management. However, the results of this study show that different sub-processes are of different importance for the case firms, and some sub-processes are practically missing from the total process. In the structuring phase, only the sub-process of acquisition can be identified. Similarly, the bundling phase includes only the sub-process of enrichment. In the leveraging phase, the sub-processes of mobilization and coordination are intertwined and deployment is the most important sub-process. Three elements of managerial ability influence successful resource deployment: responsibility combined with trust, simultaneous management of sub-processes, and motivation of employees. Managerial ability influences all phases of resource orchestration, most importantly the leveraging phase. Details of the findings are discussed in the following chapters.

Resources structuring

Structuring includes the sub-processes of *acquisition, accumulation* and *divestment*. Among these three sub-processes, resource acquisition is the most important and critical activity for a firm [7]. For a small service firm, almost all employees are key people, playing important roles in a firm. These kinds of firms usually have limited budgets for resource acquisition. Due to small number of employees, each single person in the organization is a strategic resource, and each single person has a big influence to organizational activities in a firm.

All case firms used a similar approach in the selection process of new employees and prioritized personal characteristics and work experience ahead of formal education. Good communication skills, creativity, innovativeness, and personal self-responsibility were considered as key characteristics of a person. On the other hand, as payment card business is based on complex technologies, good understanding of these technologies was considered an important indicator of the related competence of that person. During acquisition, all case firms emphasized the importance of interviews in selection process. The case firms interviewed candidates several times before final selection. Referee statements were verified in all case firms, and all firms preferred to recruit persons known personally to them from the past whenever these kinds of people were available. People were hired from the open market and sometimes also from competitors. The managing director of Firm A commented on the importance of positive attitude:

"I think it is good to have technical background in this business. For marketing and commercial people, it is so hard to understand this business. It would be good to have people with a background in IT, electronics, and related areas. It is also important that the people have a strong will to learn new things themselves. It is very challenging to teach something in this business, so it is important that the people are willing to study themselves, too."

Accumulation of new human resources was not considered an important sub-process for the case firms. The main reason was lack of time for a long internal competence development process. At the start-up stage, the most important thing for a firm was to hire people who could successfully perform their tasks without needing an education or training process. New employees were expected to be productive almost

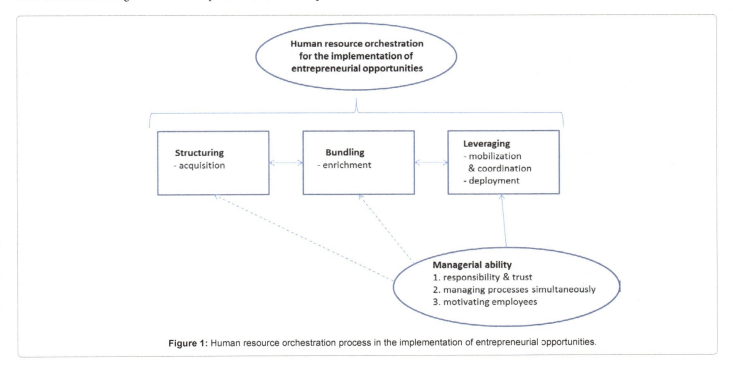

Figure 1: Human resource orchestration process in the implementation of entrepreneurial opportunities.

immediately when they started to work for the firm. CTO of Firm B:

"When we want to hire an experienced person, we have to find a specific person who knows almost everything already. If you have enough time, you can educate and train a person for two years, maybe. But, if you need new resources right now, you have to hire someone who already can do the job."

Managing director of Firm C adds:

"Our activity is very, very specific. It is not normal for a generic IT manager to have the knowledge about our activity. If this is the case, then this person needs to have almost all knowledge already from the beginning and then to spend only a minimal time to learn the specific details."

However, all case firms recognized the importance and challenges of transferring tacit knowledge, and new employees started to work closely together with more experienced colleagues after joining the firm. All leaders in the case firms supported Hansen's [30] argument that transferring tacit knowledge is more efficient when experienced and inexperienced employees work together.

Divestment was not considered a critical phenomenon in the case firms either. Competences which were needed at the firm in the beginning were still needed and valid for the operations of current business activities. Therefore, employees did not change their tasks in these firms that frequently, and very few people had left their firm since they had joined it. The firms were continuously seeking for new opportunities, and they had also implemented some of them. The original business idea and operations were still important for the case firms, and the firm could deploy original resources for these activities.

Based on the findings from the case firms, the structuring process consists only from one sub-process, that of acquisition of resources. Acquired resources are expected to be productive immediately after acquisition, without a dedicated period for competence development after acquisition.

Resources bundling

Resource bundling is closely connected to a firm's strategy process and opportunity implementation process. In strategically entrepreneurial firms, continuous seeking of opportunities is an important part of overall strategy. During resource bundling process, new and existing resources are developed in preparation for future challenges. Human resources need to have good education and knowledge of the business field, but they also need to learn new competences that are important for the implementation of new business opportunities.

Resource bundling includes the sub-processes of *stabilization, enrichment and pioneering*. As in the resource structuring process, there was only one sub-process which was considered important by the case firms. While enrichment was considered very critical, it was not possible to identify the sub-processes of stabilization and pioneering.

The case firms found enrichment to be a very critical sub-process for them. Leaders of the case firms actively collected information on new competences which were identified during the firms' strategy process. The case firms considered different types of training for developing new competences. They used academic education in universities, professional courses offered by training firms, knowledge transfer between partner firms, and self-learning. Academic education was considered to be an important source for basic knowledge of underlying technologies and for capabilities to understand new technologies. However, the case firms considered that internal training was the best option for competence development.

All case firms preferred either self-learning or knowledge transfer with partner firms. All case firms had close relationships with their partner firms in the same business field. Relationships between the firms had been established during joint sales activities and development projects. While offering services to big customers, the case firms felt that they are too small alone, and they decided to prepare joint offers with partners in order to be more competitive against big firms. The case firms had agreed to use an open dialogue and co-operation model with their partner firms in order to transfer knowledge from one firm to another. Both firms involved in the scheme named the contact persons who would be responsible for the process of knowledge transfer between the firms. If a firm decided to implement a new opportunity, it was possible for the other firm to involve their employees in the project in order to learn this new technology from the partner. Co-operation between the partners also included co-financed training sessions mainly for technical employees. CTO of Firm C says:

"External training is a bit tricky, because this kind of business is not taught anywhere. In this situation, we need to get help from our partners. As a result, we learn new technologies and we can store new information that we can replay later to new people. For example, some training sessions are recorded on video tapes. This is in order to guarantee that we can refresh some things later and to show the same to new persons."

As discussed, the sub-process of stabilization was missing from the case firms' resource orchestration process. The reason for the missing sub-process of stabilization was lack of time. All resources needed to be productive all the time, and there was no time for stabilization activities in the firms. Transfer and further development of existing competences was mostly based on co-operation between senior and junior colleagues, who worked together as pairs for long periods.

Also the sub-process of pioneering was missing in the case firms during opportunity implementation process. The main reason for neglecting pioneering was lack of time and resources. Small organizations in the case firms were continuously occupied by day-to-day operations and evaluation of new business opportunities, and they did not have R&D type of teams or activities. It was not possible to allocate time for searching opportunities from different business fields which had little bearing with the case firm's strategy. For this reason, the leaders of the case firms did not actively develop employees and their competences for pioneering type of activities.

Resources leveraging

Once human resources and their competences are ready for new business opportunities, resources need to be leveraged, that is, *mobilized, coordinated,* and *deployed*. If the structuring and bundling processes are planned and implemented properly, it is fairly easy for a firm to exploit new opportunities from resource management perspective. However, it was found that many times the leveraging stage was achieved without proper completion of previous acquisition or bundling processes. This meant that a firm often faced new opportunities without having the necessary quantity of people or required competences. In this case, structuring and bundling processes would be very short and as effective as possible, and structuring and bundling would include only one sub-process in each of the main phases. In addition, especially the bundling process is often implemented partly in parallel with the leveraging process.

In the case firms, the sub-processes of mobilization and coordination were intertwined with deployment. In small firms, it is normal that the same persons and teams contribute to the majority of the projects. In addition, from resource management perspective, the case firms did not experience any differences if the opportunity was based on different strategies: i.e., on superior competitive advantages, available market opportunities or business opportunities. Therefore, mobilization and coordination activities were needed mainly to verify the availability of the resources which already were being employed in other projects despite of a later strategic choice that had focused on a specific opportunity. In case of resource shortage, the managers needed to prioritize the projects and other activities where the same resources were needed. As a result, in some cases, selected tasks and projects were delayed due to prioritization, but most often it was possible to exceed the normal productivity rate of resources and handle all the tasks and projects in the agreed time schedule. Managing director of Firm D says:

"Some people in the company are able to stretch themselves, to work temporarily with 120-130% load for some time. This is the case if prioritization is not possible and there is more work to do than we have time. If I can get new resources, I use them to release others for the new project and put new people to existing tasks. In this way, I have more experienced people in the new projects, and new people are growing up with normal routine work, so they are capable of doing some other new things in the future. Then everybody is learning something new and everybody have positive pressures."

Deployment was identified as the most important sub-process during leveraging. Due to limited resources in small organizations, the leaders had a critical role in efficient deployment of resources. Holcomb et al. [23] argue that managerial ability is positively associated with resource productivity. Holcomb's main argument is that superior managers are able to add resource productivity specifically in situations where the quality of resources is low. When the quality of resources increases, positive influence of managerial ability for resources' productivity decreases. In other words, good managers are needed more when resources are not good; if resources are high in quality, managers are not needed that much.

Managerial abilities

The case firms recognized the importance of managerial ability in resource management. They identified managerial ability as a very important factor for resource orchestration in general and specifically for the leveraging phase. Three factors of managerial ability were found important for a successful leveraging process; 1) responsibility combined with trust, 2) management of overlapping processes, and 3) motivation of employees. These factors are explained more in detail in the following paragraphs.

All the leaders in the case firms strongly supported a leadership style where the responsibility of new opportunity implementation is given solely to one single person. The leaders argue that, if they put a single person in charge of implementation of a new business opportunity, it is easier for them to manage the development of that business case. Giving full responsibility for the implementation process requires a high level of trust from the manager towards the chosen employee. Traditional management models have favored different control mechanisms in order to monitor employees' performance [31]. These controls are often quantitative in nature, like detailed reporting or tracking of working hours. When the managers trust their employees, they do not need to monitor employees' performance by special controls made for that purpose. Spreitzer and Mishra [32] argue in their study that managers' trust towards their employees increases both individual and organizational performance. CTO in Firm D supports this approach:

"This is a good way. I think it is good to have freedom to do the things in my own way, but it is also very important to have the support available all the time, especially in the areas which are a bit outside of my core competence. I think responsibility for one person is better than to share the responsibility among a team."

No case firms had slack resources which could have been assigned for implementation of new opportunities. Also, the firms were suffering from the lack of required knowledge for opportunity implementation. Finally, all case firms needed, at the same time, to acquire more resources *(acquisition)*, to develop new knowledge *(bundling)*, and to implement new opportunities into profitable businesses *(leveraging)*. Simultaneous management of the acquisition, bundling, and leveraging processes became a critical factor for the success of each project.

Despite of the resources having been fully allocated, all case firms were able to assign people for new opportunity implementation, even though these people needed to contribute considerably more time and efforts than their working agreements required them to do. This kind of working attitude requires high motivation. Entrepreneurial leaders have a key role in motivating employees in their duties [4,7,33]. Firstly, the leader must be able to communicate her vision to the other members of the organization to ensure that the activities of the employees are consistent with each other and with the firm's overall mission [34]. Managing director of Firm E says:

"It requires strong motivation to work overtime for a long time, and from the manager's point of view, you need to make the target intellectually attractive, interesting and motivating for the people. Then people can get enthusiastic about the new opportunity, and they want to do their best."

Secondly, by showing and sharing his/her passion for new business opportunities, the leader can motivate employees to share the same goals and objectives, and with the same level of passion, as the leaders themselves [7]. Passion itself is a significant source of energy for entrepreneurs. In a context of entrepreneurship, passion is understood as *love of work* and *love for the venture itself* [35]. Communication between the leader and the employees has a key role in this process. By clearly communicating the vision about a new opportunity and about the importance of each person's role in the implementation process, passionate thinking and entrepreneurial behavior can be leveraged in an organization. Passionate feelings arise among people engaged in activities which relate to meaningful and salient self-identity [35]. Passion has a direct relationship to entrepreneurial behavior, including goal commitment, persistence, and creativity, and, through these factors, passion can increase entrepreneurial effectiveness [7,35].

Conclusions

This paper identifies several areas which can be used either to further support or further develop theoretical frameworks. Firstly, this paper supports the core elements of the resource orchestration concept by Sirmon et al [6,8]. It was found that the case firms manage their human resources in opportunity implementation by following the main phases of resource orchestration. However, it was found that all the sub-processes of research orchestration are not in place or their usage is very limited. In the structuring phase, only the acquisition sub-process could be identified, while the sub-processes of accumulation and divestment were not adopted at all by the case firms. Similarly, in the bundling phase, only the enrichment sub-process could be identified, while the sub-processes of stabilization and pioneering were not a part of human resource management processes in the case firms. In the leveraging phase, the deployment sub-process was considered to be the most important. The sub-processes of mobilization and coordination could not be identified separately in the case firms, but these were intertwined with each other with strong connection to deployment. The sub-processes of mobilization and coordination were more concerned with prioritization of tasks than with coordination of resources. All case firms recognized the importance of managerial abilities in resource synchronization. Responsibility combined with trust, simultaneous management of different phases and sub-processes of resource orchestration, and increasing employee motivation were found to be the most important characteristics of an entrepreneurial leader. These three elements helped the case firms to significantly increase productivity of human resources for the challenging projects in opportunity implementation.

Limitations of this study are mostly related to case study methodology and to the case firms themselves. The business field of the case firms, payment card services, is very narrow and specialized, there being only some hundreds of active firms globally in this business field. In addition, the business field is regulated and controlled by global payment card organizations, and therefore the access to the field is limited. Additionally, the selection of case firms was based on the researcher's personal access to those firms, and it was not possible to select the firms randomly.

As this study shows, there is need for further empirical research in the field of resource orchestration and strategic entrepreneurship in the future. Further empirical studies are needed to understand how the concept of resource orchestration is implemented in entrepreneurial opportunity implementation. Based on the results of this paper, it is likely that the contents of resource orchestration will differ between small and big firms, and also in different business fields. That said, empirical studies in other business fields are needed to develop the theoretical concept of resource orchestration further.

References

1. Hitt M, Bierman L, Uhlenbruck K, Shimizu K (2006) The Importance of resources in the Internationalization of Professional service firms: The good, the bad and the ugly. Academy of Management Journal 49: 1137-1157.
2. Ireland D, Hitt M, Sirmon D (2003) A model of strategic Entrepreneurship: The construct and its dimensions. Journal of Management 29: 963-989.
3. Kraus S, Kauranen I (2009) Conceptualizing a configuration approach based model of strategic entrepreneurship. International Journal of Strategic Management 9: 1-20.
4. Foss N, Klein P, Kor Y, Mahoney J (2008) Entrepreneurship, subjectivism and the resource-based view: toward a new synthesis. Strategic Entrepreneurship Journal 2: 73-94.
5. Barney J, Ketchen D, Wright M (2011) The Future of resource-based theory: revitalization or decline? Journal of Management 37: 1299-1315.
6. Sirmon D, Hitt M, Ireland R, Gilbert B (2011) Resource orchestration to create competitive advantage: breadth, depth, and life cycle effects. Journal of Management 37: 1390-1412.
7. Hitt M, Ireland R, Sirmon D, Trahms C (2011) Strategic entrepreneurship: creating value for individuals, organizations, and society. Academy of Management Perspectives 25: 57-75.
8. Sirmon D, Hitt M, Ireland R (2007) Managing firm resources in dynamic environments to create value: looking inside the black box. Academy of Management Review 32: 273-292.
9. Ardichvili A, Cardozo R, Ray P (2003) A theory of entrepreneurial opportunity identification and development. Journal of Business Venturing 18: 105-123.
10. Sarasvathy S, Dew N, Velamuri R, Venkataraman S (2003) Three views of entrepreneurial opportunity. Handbook of Entrepreneur Research; An Interdisciplinary Survey and Introduction. Kluwer Academic Publishers.
11. Baron R (2006) Opportunity recognition as pattern recognition: How entrepreneurs "connect the dots" to identify new business opportunities. Academy of Management Perspective 20: 104-119.
12. Buenstorf G (2007) Creation and pursuit of entrepreneurial opportunities: An evolutionary economics perspective. Small Business Economics 28: 323-337.
13. Morris M, Schindehutte M, Allen J (2005) The entrepreneur's business model: toward a unified perspective. Journal of Business Research 58: 726-735.
14. Plummer L, Haynie J, Godesiabois J (2007) An essay on the origins of entrepreneurial opportunity. Small Business Economics 28: 363-379.
15. Hitt M, Ireland D, Camp M, Sexton D (2001) Entrepreneurial strategies for wealth creation. Strategic Management Journal 22: 479-491.
16. Kraus S, Kauranen I (2009) Strategic management and entrepreneurship: friends or foes? Int. Journal of Business Science and Applied Management 4: 37-50.
17. Wernerfelt B (1984) A resource-based view of the firm. Strategic Management Journal 5: 171-180.
18. Barney J (1991) Firm resources and sustained competitive advantage. Journal of Management 17: 99-120.
19. Teece D, Shuen A (1997) Dynamic capabilities and strategic management. Strategic Management Journal 18: 509-533.
20. Eisenhardt K, Martin J (2000) Dynamic capabilities, what are they? Strategic Management Journal 21: 1105-1121.
21. Teece D (2007) Explicating dynamic capabilities: the nature and microfoundations of sustainable enterprise performance. Strategic Management Journal 28: 1319-1350.
22. Borch O, Huse M, Senneseth K (1999) Resource configuration, competitive strategies, and corporate entrepreneurship: an empirical examination of small firms. Entrepreneurship Theory and Practice 24: 49-70.
23. Holcomb T, Holmes R, Connelly B (2009) Making the most of what you have: Managerial ability as a source of resource value creation. Strategic Management Journal 30: 457-485.
24. Eisenhardt K (1989) Building theories from case study research. Academy of Management Review 14: 532-550.
25. Diaz A (2009) Interpretive research aiming at theory building: adopting and adapting the case study design. The Qualitative Report 14: 42-60.
26. Piekkari R, Welch C, Paavilainen E (2009) The case study as disciplinary convention: evidence from international business journals. Organizational Research Methods 12: 567-589.
27. Perren L, Ram M (2004) Case-study method in small business and entrepreneurial research – mapping boundaries and perspectives. International Small Business Journal 22: 83-101.
28. Leich C, Hill F, Harrison R (2010) The philosophy and practice of interpretivist research in entrepreneurship: quality, validation and trust. Organizational Research Methods 13: 67-84.
29. Kuratko D, Audretsch D (2009) Strategic entrepreneurship: exploring different perspectives of an emerging concept. Entrepreneurship Theory and Practice 33: 1-17.
30. Hansen M (1999) The search-transfer problem: the role of weak ties in sharing knowledge across organization sub-units. Administrative Science Quarterly 44: 82-111.
31. Raelin J (2011) The end of managerial control? Group and Organization Management 36: 135-160.
32. Spreitzer G, Mishra A (1999) Giving up control without losing control: trust and its substitutes' effects on managers' involving employees in decision making. Group and Organization Management 24: 155-187.
33. Monsen P, Boss R (2009) The impact of strategic entrepreneurship inside the organization: examining job stress and employee retention. Entrepreneurship Theory and Practice 33: 71-104.
34. Witt U (1998) Imagination and leadership – the neglected dimension of an evolutionary theory of the firm. Journal of Economic Behavior and Organization 35: 161-177.
35. Cardon M, Wincent J, Singh J, Drnovsek M (2008) The nature experience of entrepreneurial passion. Academy of Management Review 34: 511-532.

Leadership Management among Construction Professionals in the Context of Nepal

Khet Raj Dahal[1]* and Manoj KC[2]
[1]*Centre for Post-Graduate Studies, Nepal Engineering College, Kathmandu, Nepal*
[2]*Civil Engineer, Kathmandu Valley Development Authority, Nepal*

Abstract

This study, "Leadership in Construction Management among Construction Professionals in the Context of Nepal", was conducted during the period from March to November in 2015. For this purpose, field survey was conducted through semi-structured questionnaire. Sample survey among professional practitioners was conducted in Kathmandu valley. The findings of the study reveal that construction professionals realize the effective leadership in different levels and dimensions in Nepalese construction industries. In addition, the study has shown the relevancy of authentic leadership in order to overcome challenges like corruption and unsophisticated organizational context. At the same time, the study highlights the various requirements to update the priority of leadership traits towards skills, such as, communication, motivation rather than limiting only to hard core skills. Similarly, leadership behavior was found out to be oriented towards higher level people of management. Furthermore, the study has also demonstrated that construction professionals are not adequately strong in key dimensions of authentic leadership. Hence, leadership development should be given equal emphasis on technical and managerial aspects in construction industries along with the professionals in the circumstance of Nepal.

Keywords: Construction industries; Clients; Contractors; Leadership management; Professionals

Introduction

Construction is a human attempt to build facilities for the people's welfare. The term 'Construction Leadership' is defined as the leadership relevant to the management of construction process, projects and products. Leadership is important in all fields of human endeavor. Features of the construction process and construction projects render leadership even more essential [1,2]. Leadership occupies a broader meaning than the than the leaders [3]. Leadership needs in every sector of human society along with construction industries.

The construction industry has a greater need for leadership than, arguably, any other field of endeavor. Many reasons support this contention and are evident in the nature of the construction projects, industry and constructed products [4]. Developing countries have an even greater need for leadership in construction for abundant reasons such as poor project performance deficiencies, problematic operating environments, direct relation of constructed products with long term socio economic development and finally the stakeholders are unaware of the many aspects of construction [1,2]. Nepalese Construction Industry has its own challenges of its own in many levels and dimensions of construction and development such as poor design and quality of projects [5], inappropriate construction policy, lack of professional development justifying the need for research on construction leadership in Nepalese Construction industry.

Despite this recognition that leadership is important at all levels of the construction industry, emphasis is placed on the technical aspects, as well as management and leadership receives inadequate attention [6,7].

"Leadership is a process of motivating people to work together collaboratively to accomplish great things" [8]. "Leadership is something larger than the leaders-that leadership encompasses all there is that defines who a leader may be" [3].

Finding one specific definition of leadership is very complex task as studies on this topic are varied and there is no single generally accepted definition [9].

Despite these differences in definitions, there is consensus in common leadership notions such as influence, motivation, common goals.

Leadership and management are two terms that are often confused. Not all leaders are managers and not all managers are leaders [10]. While highlighting the importance of both [11], argues that "managers promote stability while leaders press for change and any industry that embraces both sides of the contradiction can survive in turbulent times." This research shall use the terminology construction leadership as the leadership relevant to management of construction process, projects and products.

Early theories of leadership developed before 1980s focused on supervisory nature of leadership. They were namely i) trait theories ii) behavioral theories, iii) Contingency theories [12].

There are three well known studies on leadership behavior. They are i) Ohio state studies, ii) Michigan studies, iii) Blake and Mouton's Leadership Grid studies. First two studies were done around 1940s and 1950s which consider two dimensions by which leadership behavior can be characterized : i) Orientation towards people and ii) Orientation towards task. Using these two dimensions Blake and Mouton developed a graphical portrayal called leadership grid showing various ranges of leadership styles.

This managerial grid is widely used by practitioners and management trainers because of its simplicity and intuitive appeal,

---

*Corresponding author: Khet Raj Dahal, Visiting Professor, Centre for Post-Graduate Studies, Nepal Engineering College, Kathmandu, Nepal
E-mail: dahal.khetraj@gmail.com

although there is little empirical evidence to suggest which of the style is best in all situations [10].

In construction Industry there is no one best style of leadership and construction managers have to wear different hats in dealing with the stakeholders both within the industry and outside the industry. The main objective of this study was to explore the understanding of the concept of "construction leadership" among practitioners in the context of Nepal.

Materials and Methods

The Study Area was entities such as Government organizations, contractors /developers organizations, Engineering and Architectural Firms, Professional bodies, Educational Institutions involved in construction Industry of Nepal. Kathmandu valley and its vicinity was selected as the area of study since most of the interest of this study were stationed here in the valley and thought to be sufficient for the scope of this Study.

The study followed perception based sample survey method. The answers to seven specific research questions were found out by careful observation of the phenomenon of construction leadership among selected samples through the responses to Four (4) sets of carefully designed leadership questionnaire in addition to separate set for obtaining demographic information of the construction professionals. The survey included research variables such as (i) need for leadership (ii) dimensions of problems in construction,(iii) causes of poor construction, iv) appropriate solutions to overcome poor performance (v) leadership skills/traits (vi) leadership behavior orientation/styles, and (vii) key dimensions of authentic leadership development. Also relationship of these variables was established with various situational factors such as level of industry, age and experience, job type and position, organization type etc. obtained through the demographic information of respondents. This Study simply explored the various construction leadership trends prevalent among Nepalese Construction Industry practitioners and assumed sample survey method would be appropriate to find the answers to these research questions.

Mixed method of research approach was taken to meet the objectives of this research. Basically Descriptive statistics such as Measures of centre and location like Mean, Frequency analysis, Percentages, Relative Average Index, Standard Deviation were used to measure the research variables while measures such as ANOVAs Table and Paired T-test were used to demonstrate the relationship between some of these variables and situational factors like level of industry, organization type, Age and experience etc.

The study population were the practitioners involved in three typical participants of Nepalese construction industry i.e. (i) client, government departments and organizations (ii) contractor, which this study included general contractors, developers and subcontractors, which are working in various construction projects, and (iii) consultant, which included engineering and architectural consultant firms, experts working as freelancers giving consultancy services to the client.

Again, the population was selected in order to assimilate professionals involved in all three levels of the industry which this study categorized into (i) policy/institution level professionals involved in policy making and promoting professionalism taking executive positions in various professional societies, Joint secretaries of ministries, retired high government officials and faculties of engineering institutions (ii) organization level professionals involved in leading their organizations with innovation and competency such as managing directors and top executives of private firms, senior divisional engineers and architects of government organizations, fresh engineer/entrepreneurs and lastly (iii) project level professionals involved directly in construction projects in various positions ranging from project manager, site manager, project engineer, procurement manager

This study preferred convenient quota sampling technique as the best fit technique for selecting sample population. Quota was given to each three typical participants; client, consultant and contractor and care were also taken in order to involve all levels of professionals. Samples were interviewed as per the convenience and availability of the respondent's (i.e. willingness to participate in the survey).

Results and Discussion

Need of leadership in construction industries

The respondents were asked about the importance of leadership in Nepalese construction industries. The answer was different. There were three options of this question: agree, disagree and don't know. The result is presented in Figure 1. Ninety one percent of the total respondents (91%) agreed to the statement i.e. effective leadership is one of the primary answers to the problems in Nepalese construction Industry. This statistic indicated that maximum number of respondents realized the need of leadership in construction in Nepal. These responses from all three levels of the industry as categorized by this study were analyzed to find out if need for leadership is felt at all levels of Nepalese construction industry (Figure 1). Similarly, the realization of leadership in different three levels: organization level, policy level and project level. The respondents answered differently. The result is presented in Figure 2. More than 85% answered it was necessary in organization level, more

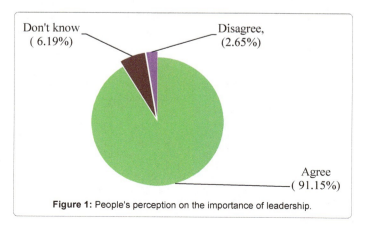

Figure 1: People's perception on the importance of leadership.

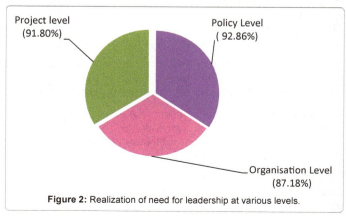

Figure 2: Realization of need for leadership at various levels.

than 92% answered that it was necessary in policy level, and more than 91% felt that it was necessary in organization level. The result is presented in Figure 2.

Reasons justifying the need for leadership

In this regards, respondents were asked to choose among the best reason/s justifying the need for leadership in Nepalese construction industry. There were five options to choose from. Some respondents selected more than one options as their answers to this question. The distributions of responses among the five options are illustrated in Figure 3.

The results indicated that Nepalese construction industries have many unique problems, which suggest that Nepal has even greater need for leadership in many levels and dimensions as in the case of many developing countries [1,2,13]. More than 55% (55.75%) of respondents pointed out all the four reasons listed in the questionnaire as equally justifiable for the need of leadership in Nepalese construction industry. Similarly, 24.78% of respondents pointed out the project performance deficiencies were the main issue to be addressed through effective leadership. Remaining 7.96% of respondents saw the problems in Project management itself, which need to be addressed while equal percentages of respondent pointed out the need to educate many aspects of construction to end users, clients themselves through effective leadership. While meager (5.31%) of the respondents considered long term implications of the completed projects or products are critical to socio-economic development of Nepal. Hence, poor performances have adverse implications to the nation as a whole.

Major causes of poor construction performance

In this regard, maximum number of respondents accepted that construction performance is poor in many levels and dimensions of industry and considered effective leadership as one of the primary answers to these problems. The specific major causes of poor construction performance were investigated through the answers given by the respondents. The results from the respondents are represented in Figure 4.

Many respondents selected more than one reason for poor construction performance. Among them corruption and inappropriate construction policy stand out at the top with 30.97% for each. Next 25.66% of the respondents felt ethical leadership is decreasing among the professionals. Lack of political will from the leaders occupying formal leadership position stands as next at 22.12%, while poor operating environment comes at 18.58% and lastly weak bureaucratic structure comes at 15.04% (Figure 4). Negative trends like corruption, decrease in ethical leadership, and lack of political will on the one side reflect negative psychology among practitioners, while inappropriate construction policy, weak bureaucratic structure and poor operating environment reflect under developed organizational context in Nepalese construction industry. These results indicate the relevancy of authentic leadership in Nepalese construction industry because authentic leadership is a process that draws from both the positive psychological capacities and a highly developed organizational context, which results in both greater self-awareness and self-regulated positive behaviors on the part of leaders fostering positive self-development [14].

Solutions to overcome poor construction performance

The last question of this part of questionnaire was about recommended solutions to overcome poor construction performance. There were 5 (five) options to choose from. The respondents answered differently and the result is presented in Figure 5.

The respondents were also asked to recommend solutions other than that specifically mentioned in the questionnaire under "others" option. The answers ranged from (i) effective monitoring and evaluation (ii) proper incentives and effective reward system (iii) awareness of quality consciousness (iv) technically as well as managerially competent project manager (v) accountable to one's duty by each citizen (vi) high level of ethics (vii) good governance in each area (viii) trained construction workers, and (ix) strong leadership in all phases of project.

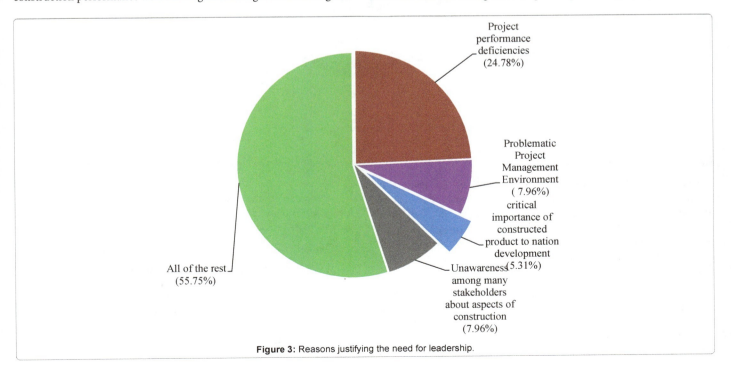

Figure 3: Reasons justifying the need for leadership.

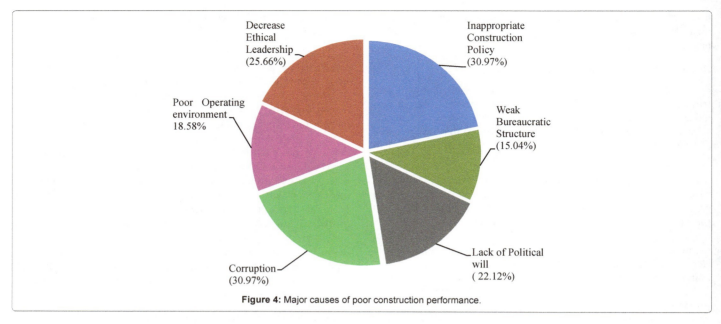

Figure 4: Major causes of poor construction performance.

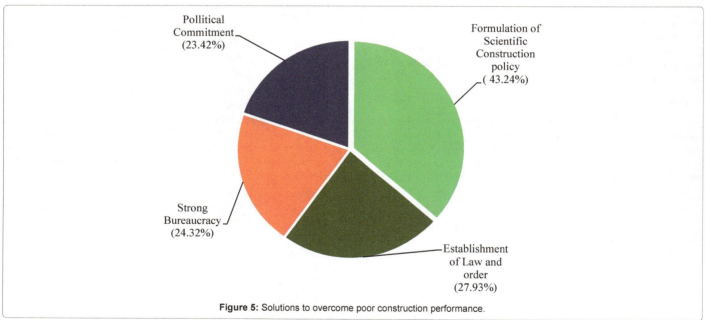

Figure 5: Solutions to overcome poor construction performance.

Leadership qualities

Now, since the respondents realized the need for leadership in construction with reasons prevalent in many dimensions and levels, the study next examined the individual leadership qualities prevalent among Nepalese construction professionals with multi dimension approach (i) leadership traits (ii) leadership behavior and contingency approach, and (iii) authentic leadership development.

One of the objectives of the research was to find out the relative importance of leadership traits as its value to construction professionals in order to get positive construction business results. Twenty number of leadership skills were listed and respondents were asked to rank them according to its value to them. Relative Important Index (RII) statistic was used to rank the leadership Traits. The result of RII is presented in Figure 6.

According to the results of this study Top 7 Most Important leadership traits as preferred by Nepalese Construction professionals are shown in Table 1.

Similarly, Top 5 least important traits are presented in Table 2.

According to Chartered Institute of Building priority of skills said to be required in Construction Industry because of its unique nature are different from those required in other businesses [15]. However, Top 7 leadership traits valued by construction professionals according to this study are similar to the survey results carried out in other businesses such as in the survey results of 200 CEOs preferable leadership traits is presented in Table 3.

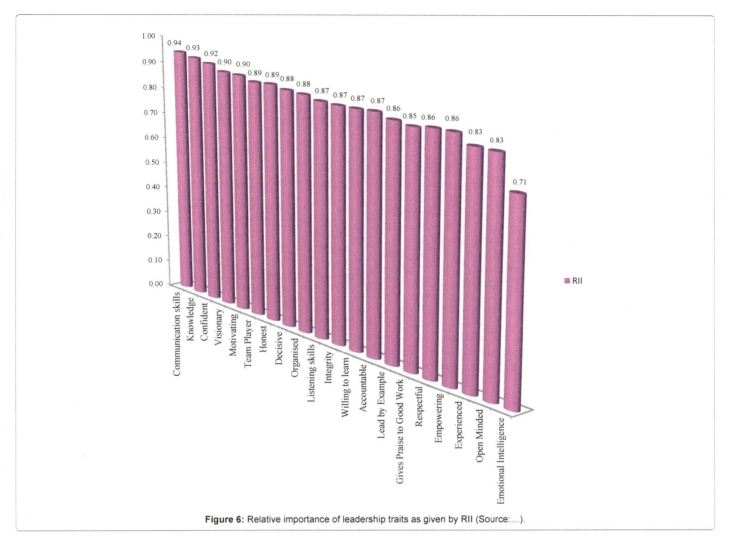

Figure 6: Relative importance of leadership traits as given by RII (Source:....).

Table 1: Top 7 most important construction leadership traits.

Leadership Traits	RII	Rank
Communication skills	0.94	1st
Knowledge	0.93	2nd
Confident	0.92	3rd
Visionary	0.90	4th
Motivating	0.90	4th
Team Player	0.89	6th
Honest	0.89	6th

Source: CIB, 2009.

Table 2: Top 5 Least important construction leadership traits.

Leadership Traits	RII	Rank
Emotional Intelligence	0.71	20th
Experienced	0.83	18th
Open Minded	0.83	18th
Gives Praise to Good Work	0.85	17th
Empowering	0.86	16th

Source: CIB, 2009

The fact that the communication stood up at the top most position ahead of knowledge, majority of leadership traits that came within top seven are rather soft skills, and the scores given by RII to all the listed 20 skills are in proximity to each other indicates softer skills such as communication skills, honesty, motivation, which are equally important than hard core skills such as experience and knowledge. The results highlight the importance of softer skills even in the construction sector which is said to give emphasis upon technical skills as well as the management of money, Machine and materials called three M's. This once again proves that leading man with effective leadership skills comes in front in every construction management. Another interesting finding is that communication skills came at the top in the similar studies done by Bhangale and Devalkar and Xiong [16]. Some argue that the traits of leaders in the construction industry are unique Chartered Institute of Building [15]. The department of construction management, University of Washington D. C. shows that construction leaders are similar, have similar skill sets, and face similar leadership obstacles as other business leaders.

Leadership behavior and style

Part IV of the survey dealt with the ranges of leadership behavior preferred by the respondents while doing their job. Thus, determining (i) their style of leadership, and (ii) orientation of their leadership behavior i.e. towards people or towards task.

The answers given by the construction professionals to the leadership behavior were the preferred/habitual style of leadership. One would find himself/herself close to while discounting the effects of situational variables [17]. The results obtained for the preferred styles of leadership can be summarized as in Figure 7.

Majority of the respondents (72.81%) said they practice team management in their leadership style which indicates maximum no. of practitioners' leadership behavior are oriented towards both high task and high people meaning they unequivocally value task at hand while establishing smooth relationship with people. This high task and high person style of leadership is compatible with the theory of Blake and Mouton Leadership Grid, which suggests team management is the best approach in getting results from committed people who have common stake in the organization purpose. Also quite number of respondents (19.30%) favored middle of the road management in their leadership style which suggests they acquire to maintain balance between task and relationship in order to obtain adequate organizational performance. And 4.39% respondents said they practice country club management which means they give priority to people rather than task and believe satisfying relationship promotes friendly atmosphere and work tempo. Meager (2.63%) of respondents suggested their behavior are oriented towards high task. Few people represented by authority obedience i.e. they focus on job design where there is minimum people interference. During survey only one respondent suggested his behavior is oriented towards low task and low people i.e. he preferred exerting minimum effort and delegate their jobs to others, which falls into the category of impoverished management.

In this study, maximum number of respondents (92%) preferred either high task and high people (Team management with 72.81%) or medium task and medium people (Middle of The Road management with 19.30%). Perfect Team Management has score of (9.9) according to leadership grid developed by Blake and Mouton while in this study the respondents falling into team management grid scored not that perfect of meager 6.5 meaning they are not much high either in task or in people i.e. they preferred medium task and medium people just enough for organizational performance or that is to say they do not put that extra little effort or are not motivated/empowered to go beyond self and look for the shared vision as investigated by contemporary theories of leadership.

Leadership Orientation

However, in construction, evidence, from leadership researches, suggest that different styles of leadership are needed in different situations [18]. The manager may therefore find that one can lead successfully in some settings but not in others. There are several key variables that may have an influence in determining the suitable leadership style in construction projects such as nature of the project, size of the project, time perspective, organization structure etc. But the present study examined the effect of two variables. They are (i) Type of organization, and (ii) Nature of project on the leadership styles of the professional practitioners.

Type of organization

Three typical participants of Nepalese construction industry namely client organization, consultant organization, and contractor organization were surveyed in order to see if the organization structure/type affects the style of leadership of professionals involve in these organizations. The average leadership orientation score (people score and task score) for each type of the organization is presented in Figure 8.

It is found from the results, contractors scored highest in both people and task score (6.60 and 6.67). Clients scored lower score than the contractors in both task and people (6.45, 6.38). In the consultant organizations, score for task is relatively lower than score for people, which means leadership orientation is slightly oriented towards people rather than task.

Nature of work

Respondents were asked to specify the nature of work they were

Quality	CEOs Rating (as most important), %
Communication Skills	52
Ability to Motivate People	47
Honesty	34
Ability To Listen	25
Team Building Expertise	24
Analytical skills	19
Aggressive in Business	10
Source: Vancouver, 2000	

Table 3: What CEOs identify as key leadership traits.

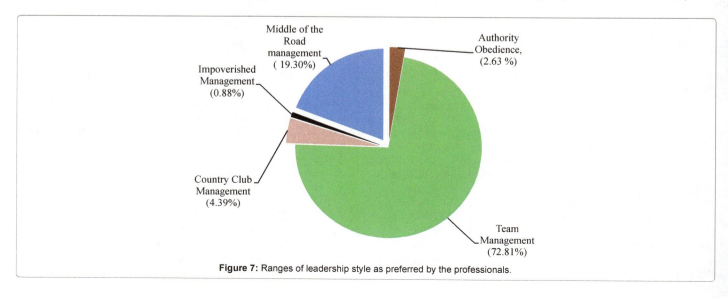

Figure 7: Ranges of leadership style as preferred by the professionals.

involved in. They had three options to choose from (i) Design (ii) Design and construction, and (iii) Construction supervision. The data were analyzed to see if there is significant difference between the leadership behaviors exhibited by these three groups of practitioners. The results obtained were as shown in Figure 9.

Results showed practitioners involved predominantly in construction were more oriented towards people rather than task while practitioners involved predominantly in Design as well as Design and Construction scored almost equal both in people as well as Task.

These results indicated that the professionals preferred not significantly varied style of leadership irrespective of the nature of work they are involved in or the type of organization they work for. This result contradicts with studies undertaken on the effect of situational variables existing in construction [19]; which emphasizes on switching approaches to leadership as the situation demands?

Strength positions in key dimensions of authentic leadership development

Another part of field survey titled "Authentic leadership self-assessment questionnaire" dealt with the strength position in key dimensions of authentic leadership development namely (i) self-awareness (ii) internalized moral perspective (iii) balanced processing, and (iv) relational transparency among the respondents. The results obtained are presented in Figure 10.

Overall Average Authentic leadership score obtained from among the responses of 114 respondents in each of the four dimensions was less than 16 which indicated that the respondents were weaker in each aspect of authentic leadership. Two key dimensions i) Self Awareness of (Average score 15.54) and ii) Internalized moral perspective (Average score 15.12) can be considered as Average strength but not stronger which requires the range of 16-20 while the other two dimensions Balanced processing and Relational Transparency score below 15 with 14.97 and 14.69 respectively which fall into the lower range of 15 and below indicating weaker Authentic leadership.

The research assumed Successful Practitioners are strong in Authentic Leadership. Successful respondents were selected from the sample population. The criterion of selection of successful practitioners was the formal leadership position they occupied in their respective job. Average authentic leadership score of successful practitioners are presented in Figure 11.

The results showed that successful practitioners of Nepalese construction Industry score high in two dimensions i) Self Awareness and ii) Balanced Processing. They also scored near to 16 in Internalized

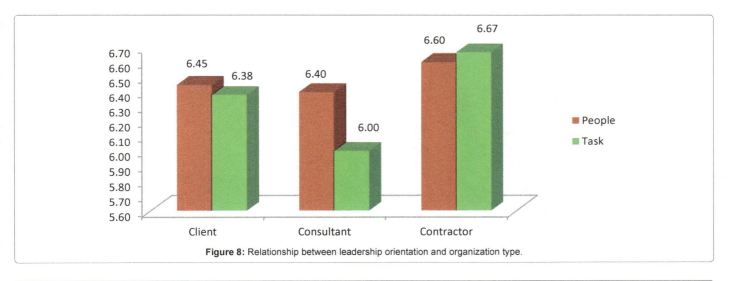

Figure 8: Relationship between leadership orientation and organization type.

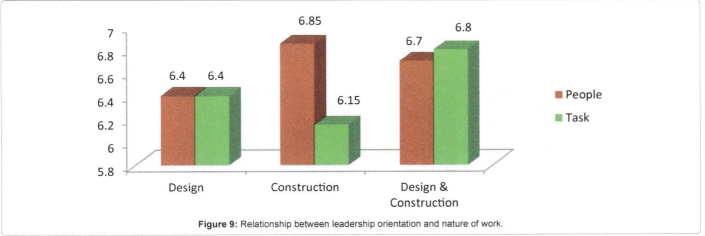

Figure 9: Relationship between leadership orientation and nature of work.

Moral perspective. And as in the cases of all the respondents surveyed, score in Relational Transparency is the lowest of all. Also, the authentic leadership scores were compared among the respondents of varying age and experience. The results are shown in Figures 12 and 13.

The results showed that there is no significant difference between the Authentic Leadership strength of various Age Groups. However, results shown in Figure 12 indicate that Authentic Leadership strength is much lower (less than 15) in the fresh group of engineer (less than 5 yrs. of experience). The results indicated experience does matter in development of Authentic Leadership and the fresh Engineers lacked leadership qualities which owes partly to the impractical engineering education system that gives too much emphasis on technical aspects and totally ignores softer part of engineering such as leadership in undergraduate engineering curriculum.

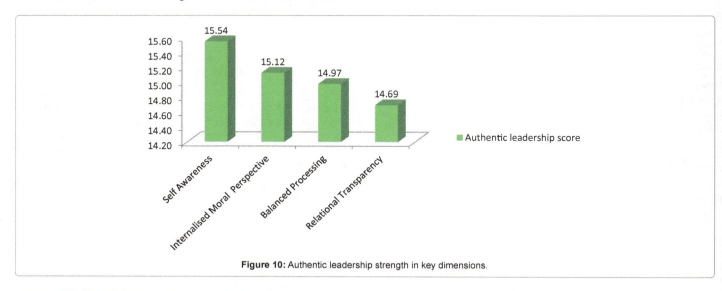

Figure 10: Authentic leadership strength in key dimensions.

Figure 11: Authentic leadership strength of successful practitioners.

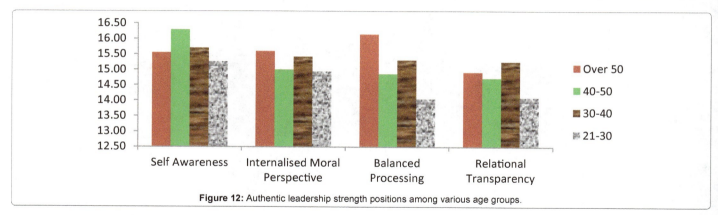

Figure 12: Authentic leadership strength positions among various age groups.

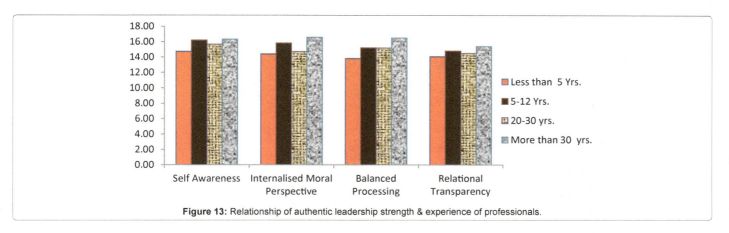

Figure 13: Relationship of authentic leadership strength & experience of professionals.

Conclusions

Despite there is recognition of leadership at all levels of the construction industry, emphasis is placed on the technical aspects. Thus, management receives inadequate attention. This is very common case in many Nepalese construction industries. The study has found out the realization of need for leadership in many levels and dimensions of Nepalese construction industries. Furthermore, it has also concluded that there are problems in many levels and dimensions of Nepalese construction industries along with effective leadership. Moreover, authentic leadership, softer leadership traits, such as, communication and honesty, and team management. There are contradictory views regarding similarity of valued leadership traits/skills in construction as compared to other businesses because of the unique nature of construction industry. However, this study found out that Nepalese construction practitioners prioritize similar sets of leadership traits. Nepal has the pressing need for infrastructure development of the nation. Thus, there is a need for new breed of professional leaders. Hence, leadership development should be given equal emphasis on technical and managerial aspects in construction industries along with the professionals in the context of Nepal.

Acknowledgements

We would like to acknowledge Dr. Khem Raj Sharma, Mr. Anjay Mishra, and Robert Dangol, for their contribution during preparation of this paper.

References

1. Ofori G, Toor SUR (2012) Leadership and Construction Industry Development in Developing Countries. Journal of Construction in Developing Countries 1: 1-21.
2. Ofori G, Toor SUR (2012) Leadership Development for Construction SMES Rheden. The Netherlands, Engineering Project Organisations Conference.
3. Fairholm MR (2004) Different perspectives on the practice of leadership. Public administration review 64: 577-590.
4. HilleBrandt P (2000) Economic Theory and the Construction Industry (3rdedn), Basingstoke, Macmillan, London.
5. Panthi K, Farooqui RU, Ahmed MS (2010) An investigation of the leadership styles of Construction Managers in south Florida. Florida International University, Miami, Florida.
6. Skipper C, Bell L (2006) Assessment with 360 degree evaluations of leadership behavior in Construction Project Managers. Journal of Management in Engineering 22: 75-80.
7. Skipper C, Bell L (2006) Influences impacting leadership development. Journal of management in Engineering 22: 68-74.
8. Vroom VH, Jago AH (2007) The role of situation in leadership. American Psychologist 62: 17-24.
9. Bass B, Avolio B (1997) The Full Range of Leadership development. Bass/Avolio and Associates, New York.
10. Gomez-Mejia L, Balkin D (2012) Management: People/Performance/Change. Pearson Education Inc, New Jersey.
11. Kotter J (1990) What Leaders really do? Harvard Business Review pp: 103-111.
12. Anon (2012) Constructiong futures.
13. Toor S, Ofori G (2008) Taking leadership research into future: A review of empirical studies and new directions for research. Engineering, Construction and Architectural Management 15: 352-371.
14. Luthans F, Avollio B (2003) Authentic Leadership: A positive Developmental approach. In: Cameron, eds. Positive Organisational scholarship: Foundations of a New Discipline. San Fransisco: CA: Berrett -Kohler, pp: 241-58.
15. Spatz DM (1999) Leadership in the construction industry. Practice Periodical on Structural Design and Construction 4: 64-68.
16. Xiong R (2008) Leadership in Project Management. Georgia.
17. Rowlinson S, Ho K (1993) Leadership style of Construction Managers in Hong Kong. Construction Management and Economics 11: 455-465.
18. Bresnen M (1986) The leader orientation of Construction site Managers. Construction Engineering and Management 112: 370-386.
19. Hammuda IM, Dulaimi MF (1997) The Effects of the situational variables on the leadership styles in Construction Projects. Association of Researchers in Construction Management, Cambridge.

Enterprenurship Development Under Government Support in India through Business Incubation

Siva Kumar A*

Bharathidasan University, Environmental Engineering, Palkakalai Nagar, Pallavakam, Chennai, India

Abstract

The specific requirement of the project, the structure of the instrument and its accuracy levels in measuring data, from business incubation community. The source of data needed to come from the four different important incubation players such as Business Incubator Managers, Incubatee Entrepreneurs, Academicians who are engaged in Business Incubation Activities and Policy Makers.

Keywords: Incubation manager; Entrepreneurship development; Government

Introduction

Importance of this study

This study is the first of its kind in India and therefore it is hoped that this study will provide some useful insights, policy implications and recommendation for new entrepreneurs who are attempting to introduce change and development to attract our nation's growth. This study is also expected to extend our understanding about the extent of successful entrepreneurship development and change polices in improving performance.

Research Methodology

The research methods involved in this study should be based on three phases.

In Phase I, crucial concepts to be generated using a variety of means such as literature review, focus group interviews and content analysis of relevant documents. In Phase two, the themes of the research are elaborated through open ended, non-standardized interviews. Finally, in Phase three, data are gathered using appropriate measuring instruments.

Phase II of the research was essentially qualitative in its design. Interviews to be conducted for the purpose of understanding the view of the Incubator Managers, Incubate Entrepreneurs, Academicians and Policy Makers.

Phase III of the research consisted of a quantitative survey, a questionnaire to be distributed to various Incubator Managers, Incubate Entrepreneurs, Academicians and Policy Makers. Survey research is particularly well suited for studying attitudes, opinions and orientations. A high response rate increases the probability that the respondents will accurately represent sample, thereby reducing the chance of bias Moore.

Five Generation of Innovation

1. Technology Push
2. Market Pull
3. Coupling of R&D and Marketing
4. Integrated Business Process
5. System Integration and Networking

Results, Discussion and Conclusion

Defining entrepreneur

A person who organizes and operates a business or businesses, taking on greater than normal financial risks in order to do so.

Someone who basically:

1. Becomes aware of a need (product or service)

2. Creates a business to fulfil that need

Due to the nature of entrepreneurs, they cannot be summarized in one definitive way but they all have common traits. These are some of the most common:

• **Flexible**-able to work whenever needed

• **Self motivated**-can motivated themselves to take action

• **Good Common sense**-Can make judgments sensibly and accurately

• **Good timing**-requires patience and know when to jump in and get things done!

There are also multiple types of entrepreneur and these can be broken down to the acronym

'SMILE'

S System, someone who is happy to buy a proven system and use it (eg. franchisee)

M Money, someone who measures their success by the number in the bank

I Innovator, the creative among you who enjoy developing new ideas

---

***Corresponding author:** Siva Kumar A, Bharathidasan University, Environmental Engineering, Palkakalai Nagar, Pallavakam, Chennai-600 041, India
E-mail: ashivaa@hotmail.com

L Lifestyle, for those who want their hobby as their job and to earn money from it

E Empire builders, those who want power and influence and to see their brand.

Ups and downs of being an entrepreneur

Can make a lot of money: The richest people in the world are entrepreneurs of one business type or another.

Risk: The financial risk in starting up a company does not guarantee a fixed flow of income for yourself or your loved ones at first.

Independence: Many people don't like to be answerable a boss and prefer being in control of their working lives. They are leaders as opposed to followers.

Time: Running a business may be heavily demanding on your time.

Control: Being in charge of how time is spent and other areas of work management lead to greater autonomy and control over life.

Isolation: Many people starting their own business may feel lonely of not properly supported. It is a different work culture and requires a great deal of self-motivation. To reduce the risk factor to the budding entrepreneurs Government of India launched DST in 1997 which objectives give below.

Literature Survey

Department of Science and Technology (DST)

Department of Science and Technology (DST) was established in May 1971, with the objective of promoting new areas of Science and Technology and to play the role of a nodal department for organizing, coordinating and promoting S and T activities in the country.

The Department has major responsibilities for specific projects and programmes as listed below:

1. Formulation of policies relating to Science and Technology.

2. Matters relating to the Scientific Advisory Committee of the Cabinet (SACC).

3. Promotion of new areas of Science and Technology with special emphasis on emerging areas.

a) Research and Development through its research institutions or laboratories for development of indigenous technologies concerning bio-fuel production, processing, standardization and applications, in co-ordination with the concerned Ministry or Department.

b) Research and Development activities to promote utilization of by-products to development value added chemicals.

4. Futurology.

5. Coordination and integration of areas of Science and Technology having cross-sectoral linkages in which a number of institutions and departments have interest and capabilities.

6. Undertaking or financially sponsoring scientific and technological surveys, research design and development, where necessary.

7. Support and Grants-in-aid to Scientific Research Institutions, Scientific Associations and Bodies.

8. All matters concerning:

(a) Science and Engineering Research Council;

(b) Technology Development Board and related Acts such as the Research and Development Cess Act, 1986 (32 of 1986) and the Technology Development Board Act, 1995 (44 of 1995);

(c) National Council for Science and Technology Communication;

(d) National Science and Technology Entrepreneurship Development Board;

(e) International Science and Technology Cooperation including appointment of scientific attaches abroad (These functions shall be exercised in close cooperation with the Ministry of External Affairs);

(f) Autonomous Science and Technology Institutions relating to the subject under the Department of Science and Technology including Institute of Astro-physics and Institute of Geo-magnetism;

(g) Professional Science Academies promoted and funded by Department of Science and Technology;

(h) The Survey of India, and National Atlas and Thematic Mapping Organization;

(i) National Spatial Data Infrastructure and promotion of G.I.S;

(j) The National Innovation Foundation, Ahmedabad.

9. Matters commonly affecting Scientific and technological departments/organizations/institutions e.g. financial, personnel, purchase and import policies and practices.

10. Management Information Systems for Science and Technology and coordination thereof.

11. Matters regarding Inter-Agency/Inter-Departmental coordination for evolving science and technology missions.

12. Matters concerning domestic technology particularly the promotion of ventures involving the commercialization of such technology other than those under the Department of Scientific and Industrial Research.

13. All other measures needed for the promotion of science and technology and their application to the development and security of the nation.

14. Matters relating to institutional Science and Technology capacity building including setting up of new institutions and institutional infrastructure.

15. Promotion of Science and Technology at the State, District, and Village levels for grass- roots development through State Science and Technology Councils and other mechanisms.

16. Application of Science and Technology for weaker sections, women and other disadvantaged sections of Society.

India is one of the top-ranking countries in the field of basic research. Indian Science has come to be regarded as one of the most powerful instruments of growth and development, especially in the emerging scenario and competitive economy. In the wake of the recent developments and the new demands that are being placed on the S and T system, it is necessary for us to embark on some major science projects which have relevance to national needs and which will also be relevant for tomorrow's technology. The Department of Science and Technology plays a pivotal role in promotion of science and technology in the country. The department has wide ranging activities ranging from promoting high end basic research and development of cutting edge technologies on one hand to service the technological requirements of the common man through development of appropriate skills and technologies on the other.

Hon'ble Minister for Ministry of Science and Technology and Ministry of Earth Sciences.

The best solution to solve a problem of unemployment, in country like India, is to have as many Job Creators as possible, so we need Entrepreneurs. Various Government and Non Government agencies are doing lot of work to promote Entrepreneurship. Particularly Government of India is doing great work to promote Techno Entrepreneurship by providing support through various agencies under the umbrella of Department of Science and Technology (DST). Even it has established National Science and Technology Entrepreneurship Development Board under DST.

I will try to give information and study, mainly exploratory, related to these support activities to convert Techno-innovation to Techno Entrepreneurship by keeping main focus on Technology Business Incubation approach in India. Here I am trying to give conceptual model to establish relationship between Techno Innovation and Techno Entrepreneurship. And this will be substantiated by various Techno Innovation and Techno Entrepreneurship illustrations of real life.

Here, the major focus is given to Technology Business Incubation approach to support and create Techno Entrepreneurship from Techno-innovation. This paper will show a research gap, in the context of India, in the area of Techno -entrepreneurship through Technology Business Incubation. This can be further useful for research in broader sense in future in this context [1].

Entrepreneurship

Definition Entrepreneurship is neither science nor an art. It is the practice. It has acknowledged base. Peter Drucker Entrepreneurship is the practice of starting new organizations or revitalizing mature organizations, particularly new businesses generally in response to identified opportunities. Entrepreneurship is a creative human act involving the mobilization of resources from one level of productive use to a higher level of use. "It is the process by which the individual pursue opportunities without regard to resources currently controlled."Entrepreneurship involves a willingness to take responsibility and ability to put mind to a task and see it through from inception to completion. Another ingredient of entrepreneurship is sensing opportunities, while others see chaos, contradiction, and confusion. Essence of Entrepreneurship is going against time with maturity and serving as a change agent.

Scope of entrepreneurship development in India

In India there is a dearth of quality people in industry, which demands high level of entrepreneurship development programme throughout the country for the growth of Indian economy. The scope of entrepreneurship development in country like India is tremendous.

Especially since there is widespread concern that the acceleration in GDP growth in the post reforms period has not been accompanied by a commensurate expansion in employment. Results of the 57th round of the National Sample Survey Organization NSSO) show that unemployment figures in 2003-04 were as high as 8.9 million. Incidentally, one million more Indian joined the rank of the unemployed between 2005-06 and 2007-08.

The rising unemployment rate (9.2% 2008 est.) in India has resulted on growing frustration among the youth. In addition there is always problem of underemployment. As a result, increasing the entrepreneurial activities in the country is the only solace. Incidentally, both the reports prepared by Planning Commission to generate employment opportunities for 10 crore people over the next ten years have strongly recommended self-employment as a way-out for teaming unemployed youth. We have all the requisite technical and knowledge base to take up the entrepreneurial challenge. The success of Indian entrepreneurs in Silicon Valley is evident as proof. The only thing that is lacking is confidence and mental preparation. We are more of a reactive kind of a people. We need to get out of this and become more proactive. What is more important than the skill and knowledge base is the courage to take the plunge. Our problem is we do not stretch ourselves. However, it is appreciative that the current generations of youth do not have hang-ups about the previous legacy and are willing to experiment.

These are the people who will bring about entrepreneurship in India. At present, there are various organization sat the country level and state level offering support to entrepreneurs in various ways. The Govt. of India and various State Government has been implementing various schemes and programmes aimed at nurturing entrepreneurship over last four decades. For example, MCED in Maharashtra provides systematic training, dissemination of the information and data regarding all aspects of entrepreneurship and conducting research in entrepreneurship. Then there are various Govt. sponsored scheme for the budding entrepreneurs. Recognizing the importance of the entrepreneur development in economic growth and employment generation, Maharashtra Economic Development Council (MEDC) has identified entrepreneurial development as the one of the focus area for Council activities two years ago. Various Chambers of Commerce and apex institutions have started organizing seminars and workshops to promote entrepreneurship. Incidentally, various management colleges have incorporated entrepreneurship as part of their curriculum. This is indeed a good development. This shows the commitment of the Govt. and the various organizations towards developing entrepreneurial qualities in the individuals

History of Entrepreneurship in India

The history of entrepreneurship is important worldwide, even in India. In the precolonial times the Indian trade and business was at its peak. Indians were experts in smelting of metals such as brass and tin. Kanishka Empire in the 1st century started nurturing Indian entrepreneurs and traders.

Following that period, in around 1600 A.D., India established its trade relationship with Roman Empire. Gold was pouring from all sides. Then came the Portuguese and the English. They captured the Indian sea waters and slowly entered the Indian business. They forced the entrepreneurs to become traders and they themselves the role of entrepreneurs. This was the main reason for the downfall of Indian business in the colonial times which had its impact in the post-colonial times too. The colonial era make the Indian ideas and principles rigid.

A region of historic trade routes and vast empires, the Indian subcontinent was identified with its commercial and cultural wealth for much of its long history. Gradually annexed by the British East India Company from the early eighteenth century and colonized by the United Kingdom from the mid-nineteenth century, India became an independent nation in 1947 after a struggle for independence that was marked by widespread nonviolent resistance. It has the world's twelfth largest economy at market exchange rates and the fourth largest in purchasing power. Economic reforms since 1991 have transformed it into one of the fastest growing economies however, it still suffers from high levels of poverty, illiteracy, and malnutrition. For an entire generation from the 1950s until the 1980s, India followed socialist-inspired policies. The economy was shackled by extensive regulation, protectionism, and public ownership, leading to pervasive corruption and slow growth. Since 1991, the nation has moved towards a market-based system. Entrepreneurship is the result of three dimensions working together: conductive framework conditions, well-designed government programmes and supportive cultural attitudes. Across these three perspectives of entrepreneurship, two major conclusions are apparent. Firstly, the economic, psychological and sociological academic fields accept that entrepreneurship is a process. Secondly, despite the separate fields of analysis, entrepreneurship is clearly more than just an economic function.

There were three distinct classes in village India: (i) the agriculturists, (ii) the village artisans and menials, and (iii) the village officials. The agriculturists could be further divided into the land-owning and the tenants. Labor and capital needed was either supplied by the producers themselves out of their savings or by the village landlord or by the village moneylender. These credit agencies supplied finance at exorbitant rates

Graphics analysis: It is a most crucial part the incubators must associate himself with various organizations like ISBA–Indian Science Park and Business Incubators Association, APIN–Asia Pacific Incubation Network, AAIN–Asian Association of Incubation Network etc (Figures 1-6).

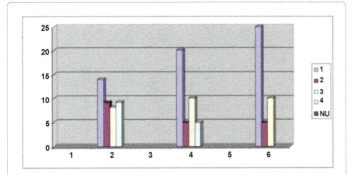

Figure 1: Your feedback on the perceived value of physical resources on facility related services.Incubation centre provide you with: if you are not utilizing any facility please write not used (nu).

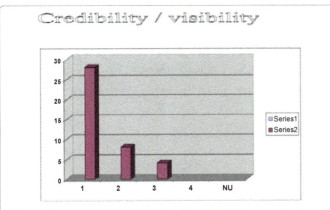

Figure 2: Incubators are constantly doing road shows, seminars and advertisement to enhance their visibility.

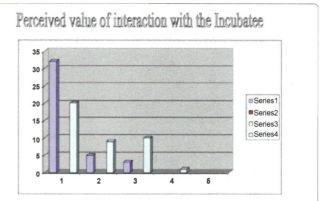

Figure 3: Incubation Managers are periodically meet their incubates through various forums to understand their needs.

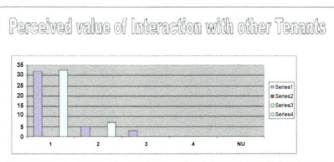

Figure 4: In the interactive meetings one incubates can meet other tenants and exchange their incubation industry experience.

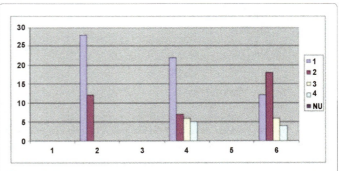

Figure 5: Perceived value of the accessibility to and networking with the resources outside incubator.

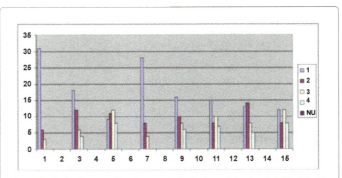

Figure 6: Evaluation must be done periodically to assist extended client facility related services.

Based the response to my questioners from Incubation Managers and Incubate I come to a conclusion that Science Parks and TBI should reach peoples more effetely to implement the scheme successfully. Also the benefited incubate should spread his experience around him. This will create a more value to the schemes. Also all colleges entrepreneurship cell should be educated to extend their services (Tables 1 and 2).

Sl. No.	Name and Address of Contact Person - TBI
1.	**Amity Business Incubator** E-3 Block ,Ist Floor, Sector 125, Amity University Campus, Noida Ph: 0120-43292242/ 243 Email: arsharma@abs.amity.edu
2.	**Society for Development of Composites** Composites Technology Park 205, Bande Mutt, Kengeri Satellite Township, Bangalore -560060 Phone:- +91 080 6599 7605, 65581005, 28482768 Fax:- +91 080 28482771 Email: drgopalan2003@yahoo.com
3.	**Technopark – Technology Business Incubator** Trivandrum 695 581 Ph: +91-471-2700222 Fax: +91-471-2700171 E-Mail: kccnair@technopark.org
4.	**Society for Innovation and Entrepreneurship** Indian Institute of Technology-Bombay Powai, Mumbai 400 076 Phone: (+91 22) 2576 7072/ 7016 Fax: +91 22) 2572 1220 Email: poyni.bhatt@iitb.ac.in
5.	**Vellore Institute of Technology (VITTBI)** Vellore - 632014 Phone :- +91 0416 2243097 Fax :- +91 0416 2243097 Email: vittbi@vit.ac.in, balac68@yahoo.com
6	**Technology Business Incubator – University of Madras** Taramani campus, Chepauk, Chennai 600113. Tel: 044-24540038/39 Email: tbi_unom@yahoo.com, tbi@unom.ac.in
7.	**Rural Technology & Business Incubator** Indian Institute of Technology Madras Chennai 600036 Tel: 044 – 2257 5441 Fax: 044-2257 0120 Email: lvaidya@tenet.res.in,office@telnet.res.in
8.	**Bannari Amman Institute of Technology – Technology Business Incubator** Sathyamangalam - 638 401. Phone:- 04295-221289 Fax: 04295-23775 Email: bitsathy@bannari.com
9.	**Periyar Technology Business Incubator** Periyar Maniammai College of Technology for Women, Periyar Nagar, Vallam-613 403, Thanjavur Tele fax-04362-264520 E-mail: info@periyartbi.org; ap_aruna@yahoo.co.in
10.	**JSSATE – Science and Technology Entrepreneurs' Park** J.S.S. Academy of Technical Education, C-20/1, Sector-62, Noida-201301, (U.P). Phone:- +91 012-2401514/16 Fax:- +91 012 – 2401516/2401451 Email: ce@jssstepnoida.org
11.	**Krishna Path Incubation Society** Krishna Institute of Engineering and Technology 13 KM Stone, Ghaziabad - Meerut Road, Ghaziabad 201206 Tel: 01232-262059 Email: tbi@kiet.edu, kumartbi@gmail.com,
12.	**Entrepreneurship Development Center** NCL Innovation Park National Chemical Laboratory Pune-411008 Phone: +91-20-2590-2185 Fax: +91-20-2590-2618 Email: v.premnath@ncl.res.in, vv.panchanadikar@ncl.res.in
13.	**SJCE – STEP** S.J. College of Engineering, Mysore - 570 006 Phone: 0821- 2548321 Fax: 0821 - 2548321 E-mail: sjce-step@rocketmail.com
14.	**Centre for Innovation Incubation and Entrepreneurship (CIIE)** Indian Institute of Management, Vastrapur Ahmedabad 380015 Phone:- +91 079 266324203 Fax:- +91 79 6324203, 26324207 Email:-kunal@iimahd.ernet.in
15.	**NITK - Science and Technology Entrepreneurs Park** National Institute of Technology – Karnataka Surathkal 575025 P.O. Srinivasanagar D.K. District. Phone:- +91 0824 2475490, 2477847 Fax:- 0824 2477590 E-mail:- directorstep@hotmail.com
16.	**Basaveshwar Engineering College** Science and Technology Entrepreneurs Park(BEC-STEP), STEP Road, Behind BTDA Campus, Bagalkot - 587102 Phone:- +91 08354 233204 Fax:- +91 08354 233204 E-mail:- mmbecstep@yahoo.com
17.	**Science and Technology Park** University of Pune, Pune - 411007 Phone:- +91 20 25699206/25693449 Fax:- +91 20 25699206 E-mail:- stppune@gmail.com, dirstp@unipune.ernet.in
18.	**Science and Technology Entrepreneurs Park - Thapar University** Patiala -147001 Punjab Phone:- +91 0175 2393011, 3314 Fax:- 0175 2393011 E-mail:- d_goyal_2000@yahoo.com; dgoyal@tiet.ac.in, ccstep@tiet.ac.in
19.	**TREC-STEP** TREC-STEP, NIT Campus Tiruchirappalli 620015 Phone:- +91 0431 2500085,2500697 Fax:- +91 0431 2500175 E-mail:- jawa_ts@yahoo.com / ed@trecstep.com
20.	**PSG-STEP** PSG College of Technology, Peelamedu Coimbatore 641004 Tamil nadu Phone:- +91 0422 4363300 Fax:- 0422 2573833 Email:- psgstep@vsnl.com
21.	**STEP - Indian Institute of Technology,** Kharagpur - 721 302. Phone: 03222-281091, 278618 Fax: 03222-278618 E-mail: dhrubes@gmail.com, mdstep@hijli.iitkgp.ernet.in, dbiswas@sric.iitkgp.ernet.in
22.	**STEP - Guru Nanak College of Engineering,** Ludhiana - 141 006 Phone: 0161 2814748/ 2814183 Fax: 0161- 2814748 E-mail: step_gnec@yahoo.com

Table 1: List of Science and Technology Entrepreneurship Parks (Steps)/ Technology Business Incubators (Tbis) Recognized By NSTEDB, DST, Government of India.

Sl. No.	Name and Address of Contact Person - TBI
1.	**Kongu Engineering College** Perundurai 638052, Erode, Tamil Nadu Phone:- +91 4294 226650, 226633 Fax No:- 226649 Email:- balamurugan@kongu.ac.in, tbi-kec@kongu.ac.in
2.	**Amrita TBI** **Amrita Vishwa Vidhyapeetham** Amritapuri Campus, Clappana P.O. Kollam, Kerala-690 525 Ph: 0476-2896318 Ex 4503 Email: kailash@amritapuri.amrita.edu

Table 2: Following Technology Business Incubators would be recognized recently.

Government to take steps to reach the right innovative entrepreneur to fine tunes their schemes. My suggestions are; Incubation Managers should conduct road shows, seminars, and events etc. in and around his region periodically. Encourage entrepreneurs who approached him is guided properly to access the government services. Government should periodically monitor and access their outreach centers to implement their schemes successfully. Government and Incubation Managers are advised to collect the feedback from their respected clients. Seed support system (sss) for start-ups in incubators Preamble: Technology Business Incubators (TBIs) and Science and Technology Entrepreneurs Parks (STEPs) are a facility to incubate technological ideas or technologies under development to enable them to reach the market place. It helps the young firms to survive and Grow by providing specialized support services during the critical period of a business venture i.e. the start-up phase. The goal is to nurture successful indigenous technologies and growth oriented entrepreneurs/enterprises. Around 55 STEPs/TBIs have been promoted at the institutions of higher learning e.g. IITs, IIMs, NITs, NID, and ICRISAT etc. by the National Science and Technology Entrepreneurship Development Board, of the DST across the country.

The requirement While the STEPs/TBIs are able to support the "Space + Services + Knowledge" requirements, wide gap exists in supporting the typical & specialized capital requirements of a technology driven startup which are not being addressed properly through existing mechanisms. The basic idea of the proposed financial assistance is to equip the STEP/TBI with the much needed early stage financial assistance to be provided to deserving ideas/technologies. This would enable some of these innovative ideas/technologies to graduate to a level where they can then be fit for seeking normal lending commercial banks /FI's route in their way to the successful commercialization process. Thus the proposed assistance is positioned to act as a bridge between development and commercialisation of technologies.

Guiding Features of the Proposed Assistance under SSS

- The Seed Support would be disbursed to incubatees (physical resident units within STEP/TBI) who are registered units and there
- Exist a proper legal agreement between the incubatee and STEP/TBI.
- The funds would cater to early stage funding for indigenous ideas and technologies requiring up-scaling and related work
- The funds would be disbursed to the deserving incubatees with proper due diligence by the STEP/TBI.
- This assistance would be used by the incubated entrepreneur only and would not be used by the incubator for facility creation.
- The fund would be managed by identified TBIs/STEPs selected by NSTEDB
- A modest seed financial support with an upper limit of Rs. 50.00 lakhs to a start-up.
- The terms of disbursement to the selected incubatees should be linked to
- Benchmarks/milestones as per the business plan/project proposal.
- The selection and disbursement of the proposed support would be based on
- ¾ Simple procedures
- ¾ Fast decisions ¾ Periodic Checks Broad Areas to be covered under the financial assistance
- The start-ups would be supported primarily on the following
- Product development
- Testing and Trials
- Test Marketing
- Mentoring
- Professional Consultancy (To attract Professors of institutions to work with small firms)
- IPR issues
- Manpower for day to day operations
- Any other area as deemed necessary and recommended by the Selection Committee of individual STEP/TBI.

Mechanism of selection, disbursement, governance and fund management of SSS

1. STEP/TBI would take measures to enhance the capacities of the TBI team to manage the seed fund and equip them about the financing process and due diligence of a start-up.

2. Normal time range of utilization of the SSS by the STEP/TBI would be three years from the date of receipt of the first installment of funds.

3. Each of the TBI/STEP implementing SSS would devise a proper mechanism and governance structure involving the right experts to evaluate the prospective incubates under physical incubation for seed fund support.

4. Each of this TBI/STEP would constitute a Management Committee and should associate good fund managers as consultants for proper implementation and management.

5. NSTEDB would disburse the financial assistance of maximum Rs. 200 lakhs in installments to the recommended TBIs/STEPs with a ceiling of Rs.50.00 lakhs for a startup, to be disbursed phase-wise based on progress milestones of the start-up.

6. The STEP/TBI CEO would be responsible for its proper disbursement and management.

7. STEP/TBI would have flexibility in disbursement of Seed Support to the potential incubatees with proper due diligence in the form of soft loan/royalty sharing /minority equity stake of the STEP/TBI depending on case to case basis.

8. The STEP/TBI would execute an agreement with the selected incubatee after sanction of the seed support and it should be signed before the release of the first installment of seed fund. Subsequent disbursement schedules should be linked to the progress milestones of the incubate venture for a period normally linked to the incubation period. The TBI/STEP should ensure that the necessary terms and conditions related to the Seed support agreement recovery schedule are clearly defined and is a part of the Seed fund agreement.

Some of the suggestive clauses on seed fund recovery already in practice by some of the

STEP/TBI is given below: a) The loan repayment period can normally vary from 2-5 years depending on the revenue model and moratorium of interest payment which can be around 6 months. In some cases STEP/TBI can also accept post dated checks as a part of the Seed fund payment recovery schedule.

b) The loan agreement provides for repayment of loan after a moratorium of one or two years after full disbursal based on the project. The interest is @6% per annum and repayment is in 5-8 half yearly installments depending on the quantum of loan. If an incubatee fails to pay the installments on time as per the schedule mentioned in the agreement, penalty of 2% on total due amount shall be charged. If an incubatee defaults in making payments repeatedly then part/full outstanding loan amount with interest shall be converted into fully paid equity. There is also a provision to right on IP in case of repeated default.

c) In case the agreement is for royalty sharing, the incubatee has to pay a royalty of 4% of Gross Revenue from sales of the product, for the period of 3-5 years from the launch of the product.

d) In exceptional cases the local selection committee would be empowered to relax certain conditions on recovery depending on case to case basis with convincing justifiable reasons, and these cases should be reported to the Department.

9. Various programmes should be organized periodically by STEP/TBIs implementing seed support to enhance the investment readiness of the incubatees.

10. Seed Fund to an incubatee is also regarded as a means to attract and raise external angel/venture capital funding. This would be an important parameter to judge the success of the seed fund being implemented by STEP/TBI. Encouragement to STEPs/TBIs who implement it successfully by way of showing growth of the seed support fund through the reflows from the loan/royalty/realization of equity stake for funding future proposals. Submission of a detailed report on the status of utilization of grants along with Utilization certificate and statement of audited expenditure for every disbursement made by Department in favor of the Seed Support [2-5].

References

1. Ringel S (2011) Trauma: Contemporary Directions in Theory, Practice, and Research
2. http://www.sagepub.com/books/Book237458
3. http://www.ediindia.org/
4. http://www.nstedb.com/
5. http://www.msmedi-chennai.gov.in/MSME/

Assessing and Developing Entrepreneurs' Self-Leadership and Super-Leadership

Sibylle Georgianna*

Vanguard University of Southern California, Office of Graduate Studies, 55 Fair Drive, Costa Mesa, CA, USA

Abstract

What processes do entrepreneurs use for leading themselves during the challenging times of building and growing a business? This article presents an assessment tool called DSLK that measures entrepreneurs' use of self- and super-leadership. The questionnaire measures the four foci of self–leadership (1) constructive thoughts; (2) natural rewards; (3) effective behaviors; and (4) Vitality and the super-leadership foci (1) coaching and communicative support and (2) facilitation of personal autonomy and responsibility. Reliability coefficients for the long and a short version of the DSLK are described. Implications for entrepreneurial assessment and training of self-leadership and super-leadership are discussed.

Keywords: Self-leadership; Super-leadership; Entrepreneurship

Introduction

Entrepreneurs' self-leadership and super-leadership

The share of people under age 30 who own private businesses has reached a 24-year-low, underscoring financial challenges and a low tolerance for risk among young Americans [1]. Roughly 3.6% of households headed by adults younger than 30 owned stakes in private companies, according to an analysis by The Wall Street Journal of recently released Federal Reserve data from 2013. That compares with 10.6% in 1989. The recent, sharp decline in business ownership among young U.S. adults, even when taking into account the aging population, is of concern.

It is difficult to pinpoint the reasons for the decline of entrepreneurial businesses among young Americans. One reason for the decline may be that young entrepreneurs face more post-recession challenges raising money. Fast-growing sectors as energy and health care likely require a significant access to credit or capital [1].

The second reason for the decline in entrepreneurial businesses may reflect a generation struggling to find a spot in the workforce. Some would-be entrepreneurs may be concerned about stiff competition in the Internet age: the broad use of the Web seems to increase the level of skills that are required to establish a business. According to the [2], the proportion of young adults who start a business each month dropped in 2013 to its lowest level in at least 17 years. People ages 20 to 34 accounted for 22.7% of new entrepreneurs in 2013, a decrease from 26.4% in 2003. Despite of a slow reversion of the U.S. startup activity from the downward trend in 2010 to 2015, the Annual Kauffman Index reports that startup activity is still below historic norms. A third reason for the decline in entrepreneurial businesses may be that younger workers may have difficulties gaining the skills and experience that can be helpful in starting a business.

However, modern economies increasingly depend on individuals with skills and experiences that induce creative developments [3]. State that "virtually all organizations – new startups, major corporations, and alliances among global partners - are striving to exploit product-market opportunities through innovative and proactive behavior". Innovation and proactivity are essential facets of successful entrepreneurial behavior [4]. Even companies in industries with little volatility need to constantly seize new business opportunities to remain viable [5].

Thus, the current study proposes a tool to assess and develop entrepreneurial leadership capacities. In particular, assessing entrepreneurs' ability to lead themselves (i.e., use self-leadership) and lead others (i.e., use super-leadership) will help identify entrepreneurs' strengths and areas of growth. Based on the assessment, trainings for entrepreneurs can be customized to provide the necessary growth in entrepreneurial self-leadership and super-leadership. This growth in skills should enhance entrepreneurs' skills to effectively deal with job related challenges.

Furthermore, that growth in skills should not only increase the likelihood of entrepreneurs' job success, but also have a positive impact on their employees' job satisfaction. In addition, existing studies show that entrepreneurs' well-developed self-leadership and super-leadership may compensate for the negative effects in the workplace (e.g., a centralized organizational structure may negatively impact the employees' work enjoyment [6,7]. Therefore, the first part of this article discusses the concepts of self-leadership and super-leadership and their relevance for entrepreneurs and entrepreneurial success. The second part of this article presents a European assessment tool that deserves cross-validation in the United States to serve U.S. entrepreneurs' assessment of self-leadership and super-leadership. The third part of the article discusses how assessment outcomes can be used to customize trainings of entrepreneurs' self-leadership and super-leadership. An increase in self-leadership and super-leadership should enhance entrepreneurs' abilities to start and run a successful business.

The concept of self-leadership was first developed and proposed by [8,9], as an extension of self-management theory [10,11]. According to current research, self-leadership includes four different types or foci of strategies to improve personal experiences and effectiveness: (1) constructive thoughts; (2) natural rewards; (3) effective behaviors; (4) physical vitality [12-15], lists the four self-leadership foci and associated self-leadership strategies (Table 1).

---

*Corresponding author: Sibylle Georgianna, Vanguard University of Southern California, Office of Graduate Studies, 55 Fair Drive, Costa Mesa, CA 92626, USA, E-mail: sibyllemzb@aol.com

The following section discusses the relevance of self-leadership foci and associated strategies for entrepreneurs.

Constructive thoughts: Examples of constructive thought self-leadership are (1) replacing negative self-talk and mental imaging by positive beliefs and expectations [11,12,16], (2) intentionally activating and directing will-power and volition and (3) using mental imagery of successful task performance [17-19], argued that using constructive thought strategies should help entrepreneurs to have a more optimistic outlook on future challenges of their business. In addition, it should be helpful for entrepreneurs to envision ways to successfully accomplish their goals and how to deal with obstacles that might obstruct the attainment of desired goals [17]. The empirical validity of these assumptions, however, has not yet been established for U.S. entrepreneurs.

Natural rewards: Through natural reward self-leadership individuals create situations in which they are motivated by self-conduct or rewarded by inherently enjoyable aspects of the task or activity [12,20]. Examples of natural reward self-leadership are

(1) To build more pleasant and enjoyable [12,20], features into a given activity so that the activity itself became more attractive and enjoyable (2) To re-attribute physiological arousal in positive terms (e.g., excitement, challenge) and utilize its proactive effects [21]. Natural rewards can be detected by an open-minded exploration of tasks and performance situations on the job [15,19], speculated that by using natural reward self-leadership entrepreneurs should create a work environment that leads to more satisfying and interesting business ideas and thereby increase the likelihood of being–economically and psychologically- successful. Recent research by Georgianna supported D'Intino speculations German entrepreneurs' made significant use of natural reward self-leadership, which, in turn, empowered them to lead their employees and experience job satisfaction. This finding has not yet been replicated with U.S. entrepreneurs.

Effective behaviors: Behavioral self-leadership targets individuals' self-awareness and planning activities accordingly [4,19]. Examples of behavioral self-leadership are (1) to systematically observe one's behavior during goal attainment [12,10,20,22]; (2) to observe role-models who show successful ways of problem solving [23], and (3) to adapt one's behaviors to situational change [16].

A recent study with German entrepreneurs found that if entrepreneurs used significant behavioral self-leadership, they empowered their employees through super-leadership behaviors and reported an increase in job satisfaction Georgianna, Will this also be found in U.S. entrepreneurs?

Physical vitality: Physical vitality self-leadership targets individuals' intentions to participate in programs that improve physical health and fitness [24]. One example of physical vitality self-leadership is to monitor one's diet by keeping records of daily food intake and associated times, settings, reasons, and feelings [15,25]. The use of physical vitality strategies was found to result in more physiological energy, psychological well-being, and potential to perform [26]. Entrepreneurs should benefit from using physical vitality self-leadership since their work is physically and mentally often more stressful than serving in a business [27]. German entrepreneurs used physical vitality self-leadership, which enabled them to empower their employees through super-leadership and report significant job satisfaction Georgianna Entrepreneurs' use of vitality self-leadership has not yet been empirically studied in U.S. entrepreneurs.

Super-leadership is described as a person's capacity to empower others [28,29], coined the term "super-leadership" to describe leadership behaviors as commonly shared within the organization and widely allocated among the entire workforce.

The German self-leadership questionnaires designed in studies by [15,16,30,31], served as a starting point for research on super-leadership in Germany. Items of the self-leadership questionnaire were screened, selected, and reformulated with reference to overt and observable super-leadership behavior. The resulting German super-leadership questionnaire consisting of 42 items was given to 175 employees from industry, services; education, sales, and administration [32]. In contrast to the four self-leadership foci (Table 1), exploratory factor analyses of super-leadership yielded two foci or factors (Table 2). One focus of super-leadership could be interpreted as "coaching and communicative support" (mostly items from scales 1 to 5), the second foci as "facilitation of personal autonomy and responsibility" (mostly items from scale 6) (Table 2) lists the two foci of super-leadership and the respective strategies.

The concept super-leadership consisting of two foci was supported by Manz and Sims conclusion that leaders need to become coaches and facilitators to help subordinates leading themselves. Support is also provided by Arnold et al. questionnaire of super-leadership that yielded a main focus called "Coaching".

Recent studies confirmed that "coaching and communicative support" was a distinct focus or dimension of super-leadership in autonomous work teams as well as in more centralized structured work settings Arnold et al. [33-35]. As documented by these studies, super-leadership was practiced within entrepreneurial teams as well as in firms led by single entrepreneurs. Entrepreneurs who show super-

Self-Leadership Focus	Self-Leadership Strategies
Constructive Thoughts	Cognitive Strategy # 1 (i.e., to use positive self-talk and mental images for replacing negative thoughts with positive beliefs and expectations)
	Constructive Thoughts Cognitive Strategy # 2 (i.e., to form implementation intentions)
	Cognitive Strategy # 3 (i.e., to mentally contrast past and future successful behaviors) Table 1: Self-Leadership Foci and Associated Self-Leadership Strategies.
Natural Rewards	Reward Strategy # 1 (i.e., to be mindful that certain circumstances can trigger negative emotions)
	Reward Strategy # 2 (i.e., re-appraise stressful events as a learning experience)
	Reward Strategy # 3 (i.e., to actively create circumstances that raise positive feelings such as joy, pride or satisfaction)
Effective Behavior	Behavioral Strategy # 1 (i.e., to systematically observe one's behavior through journaling or other forms of record keeping)
	Behavioral Strategy # 2 (i.e., to actively find and imitate positive role-models)
	Behavioral Strategy # 3 (i.e., to practice healthy behaviors in real life situations)
Physical Vitality	Vitality Strategy #1 (i.e., to use techniques that increase mental and physical relaxation)
	Vitality Strategy #2 (i.e., to exercise)
	Vitality Strategy # 3 (i.e., to monitor eating patterns)

Table 1: Self-Leadership Foci and Associated Self-Leadership Strategies.

Super-leadership Foci	Super-Leadership Strategies
Coaching and Communicative Support (CCS)	CCS Strategy # 1 (i.e., to encourage employees to pay attention to which tasks may look attractive to them) CCS Strategy # 2 (i.e., to comment positively when employees create stimulating work settings) CCS Strategy # 3 (i.e., to encourage employees to feel comfortable during task accomplishment) CCS Strategy # 4 (i.e., to support employees' reflections of their course of actions when employees tackle new tasks) CCS Strategy # 5 (i.e., to encourage employees to let him/her know which tasks they would like to focus on) CCS Strategy # 6 (i.e., to ask employees what they can learn from their mistakes) CCS Strategy # 7 (i.e., to inform employees about the consequences of their decisions) CCS Strategy # 8 (i.e., to give feedback to support the employees' pursuit of work-related goals) CCS Strategy # 9 (i.e., to emphasize how important it is to realistically judge ones' abilities) CCS Strategy # 10 (i.e., to encourage employees to derive opportunities of growth to get over their weaknesses) CCS Strategy # 11 (i.e., to talk about possible obstacles when setting own performance goals) CCS Strategy # 12 (i.e., to recommend celebrating the attainment of intermediate goals during long-term goal-attainment)
Facilitation of Personal Autonomy and Responsibility (FPAR)	FPAR Strategy # 1 (i.e., to allow employees to make their own decisions in their area of work) FPAR Strategy # 2 (i.e., to positively comment when employees take the initiative) FPAR Strategy # 3 (i.e., to provide free space to get the job done according to the employees' agenda) FPAR Strategy # 4 (i.e., to offers opportunities for the employees to learn and try out new FPAR Strategy # 5 (i.e., to welcome when employees take responsibility in their area of work) FPAR Strategy # 6 (i.e., to praises me when employees overcome obstacles during goal-striving)

Table 2: Super-Leadership Foci and Associated Super-Leadership Strategies.

leadership may be perceived by their employees as helpful coaches, facilitators of communication, personal autonomy, and positive role-models.

When leaders used coaching and communicative support and facilitated employees' personal autonomy and responsibility, employees reported greater organizational commitment and felt empowered to lead themselves toward set goals [34]. Furthermore, employees of empowering leaders were more satisfied with their job [33], felt more accomplished, and reported enhanced well-being on the job than employees in traditional work settings [36-38]. The question remains if this finding is replicable with U.S. entrepreneurs.

Current self-leadership and super-leadership measures

Fragebogen zur Diagnose Individueller Selbstführungskompetenz (FDSK) (Questionnaire to Diagnose Individual Self-leadership).

The first version of the German Self-leadership Questionnaire FDSK (The acronym standing for Questionnaire to Diagnose Individual Self-leadership in German) was partially based on Anderson and Prussia's [14].

Self-Leadership Questionnaire (SLQ) and was extended to measure Müller's concept of self-leadership. Müller's concept of self-leadership included the following four aspects or foci of self-leadership: (1) constructive thought focus; (2) natural reward focus; (3) behavioral focus; and (4) vitality focus. The foci have continuously received empirically validation [4,15,31,32,39,40]. Consequently, the FDSK is currently available in its' fourth edition. The resulting 100 items were validated using a representative sample of several hundred participants. Either participants had recently entered the workforce or were preparing to enter the workforce [40]. Self-leadership is measured in terms of a person's competency to intuitively master professional and personal challenges [33]. In our understanding, intuitive self-leadership competencies have been acquired through trial and error or another systematic variation of behavior. Intuitive competencies, however, do not equip the individual to know why they successfully (or unsuccessfully) dealt with the arising challenge. Success is increased if individuals are aware of the strategies that they used to successfully master the arising challenges.

FDSK format

The FDSK consists of five modules. The FDSK Module 1 measures individual's competencies and thereby increases individuals' awareness of their self-leadership competencies. Reliability for each focus ranges from 0.69 to 0.89 (internal consistencies), and between 0.72 and 0.78 (test-retest coefficients). A short version of the FDSK exists. That is, each focus is measured by five items. The reduced number of items yielded lower reliability scores of the short scales than found for the scales of the standard version (i.e., constructive thought λ strategies: $_{(2)}$ = 0.63; natural λ reward strategies: $_{(2)}$ = 0.79; behavioral strategies: $_{(2)}$ = 0.70; physical λ vitality strategies: $_{(2)}$ = 0.72).

The FDSK Modules 2-4 describe the participants' extent of self-leadership for each self-leadership focus (strong vs. medium vs. low). Recommendation for self-leadership development can be made accordingly. Self-leadership scores are compared to percentile ranks that exist for each self-leadership focus (separated by gender). Using percentile ranks to diagnose self-leadership allows the participant to quickly gauge the extent of self-leadership development.

The FSDK Module 5 measures super-leadership by means of the Coaching and Communicative Support (CCS) and Facilitation of Personal Autonomy and Responsibility (FPAR) scales (Table 2). The items are answered on a Likert-type rating scale ranging from "0" ("describes my own leadership behavior not at all") to "3" ("describes my own leadership behavior very well"). The internal consistency of the original scale was satisfactory (for detailed information, [40]. A short scale version of the FSDK with five items measuring super-leadership yielded α= 0.91 [33].

Implications for self-leadership and super-leadership assessment

Who wants to become an effective super-leader in organizations needs to become a competent self-leader first [11,41]. Research by [40] has shown that self-leadership is closely related to entrepreneurial trait potential and the ability to successfully start an own business. It seems plausible to assume that without a proactive mindset and personality entrepreneurial aspirations and initiatives would be hard to realize [42].

Contrary what sometimes is proposed as beneficial outcome of qualifying managers in organization [43], a mere training of coaching and communication techniques might not be of similar value for improving entrepreneurial leadership behavior. Although entrepreneurs may also benefit from competencies to coach and advice employees, benefits for entrepreneurs seem to hinge on entrepreneurs' competencies of self-leadership. Thus, diagnosing and training entrepreneurs' self-leadership competencies prior to teaching them coaching and communication techniques seems beneficial.

During the process of self-leadership and super-leadership skill acquisition, Modules 1 and 5 of the FSDK may be used to assess existing self-leadership and super-leadership, while Modules 2-4 may be used to determine areas of training and to monitor the effectiveness of training programs. The FDSK can be used to train super-leadership similarly to [43], so called coaching manager approach. The coaching manager approach describes a program of super-leadership development that teaches the use of problem-focused advice, non-directive questioning, intrinsically motivating feedback, and constructive dialogue with subordinates. In those trainings, the entrepreneurs' leadership capacities are expanded from self-leadership to super-leadership [33,34,43]. The FSDK approach to super-leadership development consists of training leaders in their use of coaching and effective communication skills as well as their ability to facilitate employees' growth of personal autonomy and responsibility. While the FSDK has been used extensively in Germany, no research exists on how U.S. entrepreneurs can benefit from this type of super-leadership development.

Implications for self-leadership and super-leadership practice

Existing studies showed that the use of self-leadership and the application of super-leadership moderated the negative effects of a highly centralized organizational structure on employees' enjoyment of work [6,34], found that supervisors' super-leadership might compensate for the negative effects of a centralized organizational structure on the work enjoyment of subordinates [7]. However, in highly decentralized organizations, the positive effects of coaching and communicative support tended to reverse. In other words, coaching and communicative support does serve employees in highly centralized organizations but may impair them in highly decentralized settings. Thus, to optimize super-leadership, one needs to combine skill training and organizational development.

Last but not least, job satisfaction is one of the major subjective indicators of successful entrepreneurship. It is related to life satisfaction, happiness, presence of positive affect or absence of negative affect, respectively, and general well-being at work [38,44]. Entrepreneurs were more satisfied with their job and general lifestyle if their aptitude potential for mastering challenges of occupational independence was developed [45]. Entrepreneurial aptitude potential not only correlated with entrepreneurs' job satisfaction but also with entrepreneurs' self-leadership [40]. If entrepreneurs were able to activate a proactive mindset and engage in self-leadership, their use of super-leadership behavior yielded personal job satisfaction [22].

Results and Conclusion

The FSDK has been proved useful and reliable to assess entrepreneurs' existing self-leadership and super-leadership in Europe. During the process of self-leadership trainings, the FSDK can be used to monitor the effectiveness of training programs. Effective self-leadership and super-leadership can positively impact organizational limitations and create job satisfaction in entrepreneurs and their employees. Validation of the FSDK in the United States is recommended so that U.S. entrepreneurs are able to benefit from the assessment and development of self-leadership and super-leadership like their European colleagues.

References

1. Simon R, Barr C (2015) Endangered Species: Young U.S. Entrepreneurs. The Wall Street Journal.
2. (2015) Ewing Marion Kauffman Foundation, Nation's Startup Activity Reverses Five-Year Downward Trend, Annual Kauffman Index Reports.
3. Dress GG, Lumpkin GT, McGee JE (1999) Linking Corporate Entrepreneurship to Strategy, Structure, and Process: Suggested Research Directions. Entrepreneurship: Theory and Practice 23: 85-102.
4. Houghton JD, Dawley D, DiLiello TC (2012) The Abbreviated Self-leadership Questionnaire (ASLQ): A more concise measure of self-leadership. The International Journal of Leadership Studies 7: 216-232.
5. Renko M, El Tarabishy A, Carsrud AL, Brannback M (2015) Understanding and measuring entrepreneurial leadership style. Journal of Small Business Management 53: 54-74.
6. Georgianna S, Müller GF, Schermelleh-Engel K, (2013) Entrepreneurs' job satisfaction and its relationship to super-leadership and self-leadership. Psychological Reports.
7. Gregory JB, Levy PE (2011) It's not me, it's you: A multilevel examination of variables that impact employee coaching relationships. Counseling Psychology Journal: Practice and Research 63: 67-88.
8. Manz CC (1983) The art of self-leadership: Strategies for personal effectiveness in your life and work. Englewood Cliffs, NJ: Prentice-Hall, Inc.
9. Manz CC (1986) Self-leadership: Toward an Expanded Theory of Self-Influence Processes in Organizations. Academy of Management Review 11: 585-600.
10. Manz CC, Sims HP (1980) Self-Management as a Substitute for Leadership: A Social Learning Theory Perspective. Academy of Management Review 3: 361-367.
11. Manz CC, Sims HR (1986) Leading self-managed groups: A conceptual analysis of a paradox. Economic and Industrial Democracy 7: 141-165.
12. Manz CC, Neck CP (2004) Mastering Self-Leadership: Empowering Yourself for Personal Excellence (3rd edn), Prentice-Hall: Upper Saddle River, NJ.
13. Neck CP, Manz CC (2012) Mastering self-leadership. (6thedn), Upper Saddle River, NJ: Prentice Hall.
14. Prussia GE, Anderson JS, Manz CC (1998) Self-leadership and performance outcomes: the mediating influence of self-efficacy. Journal of Organizational Behavior 19: 523-538.
15. Müller GF, Georgianna S, Roux G (2010) Self-leadership and physical vitality. Psychological Reports 383-392.
16. Müller GF (2006) Dimensions of self-leadership: A German replication and extension. Psychological Reports 99: 357-362.
17. Driskell JE, Copper C, Moran A (1994) Does mental practice enhance performance? Journal of Applied Psychology 79: 481-492.
18. Neck CP, Manz CC (1992) Thought self-leadership: The influence of self-talk and mental imagery on performance. Journal of Organizational Behavior 13: 681-699.
19. D'Intino RS, Goldsby MG, Houghton JD, Neck CP (2007) Self-leadership: A process for Entrepreneurial Success. Journal of Leadership and Organizational Studies 13: 105-120.
20. Manz CC, Sims HPJ (2001) The new super leadership: Leading others to lead themselves. San Francisco: Berret-Köhler.
21. Müller GF, Braun W (2009) Self-leadership. Bern, Switzerland: Huber.
22. Georgianna S (2007) Self-leadership and Goal-striving across Cultures: A Comparison of United States and Chinese Undergraduate Students. Mellen Press: New York, NY.
23. Neck CP, Manz CC (2007) Mastering Self-leadership: Empowering Yourself for Personal Excellence, (4thedn). Upper Saddle River, NJ: Pearson Prentice-Hall.
24. Neck CP, Mitchell TL, Manz CC, Thompson EC (2004) Fit to lead: the proven 8-week solution for shaping up your body, your mind, and your career. New York, St. Martin's Press.
25. Georgianna S (2005) Intercultural Features of Self-leadership. Shaker Press, Aachen, Germany.
26. Neck CP, Cooper JKH (2000) The fit executive: Exercise and diet guidelines for enhanced performance. Academy of Management Perspectives 14: 72-83.
27. Moser K, Zempel J, Galais N, Batinic B (2000) Self-employment as a burden and challenge. Entrepreneurship from the perspective of strain and challenge. In G. F. Müller (Edn.).Start-ups and entrepreneurial activity 137-152.

28. Manz CC, Sims HP (1990) Super-leadership: Leading others to lead themselves. New York: Berkeley.

29. Manz CC, Sims HPJ (2001) The New Super Leadership: Leading Others to Lead Themselves. San Francisco: Berret-Köhler.

30. Müller GF (2004) The art to lead themselves. The art of self-leadership. Personnel management 37: 30-43.

31. Müller GF (2004) Self leadership skills. Competent self - leadership. In B Wiese (Edn). Individual control of professional development 91-107.

32. Müller GF, Sauerland M, Butzmann B (2011) Leadership through self-management Concept, measurement, and correlates. Group Dynamics and Organizational Consulting 42: 377-390.

33. Müller GF (2013) Questionnaire for the diagnosis of leadership through self-management - Test Manual. Landau: Umbra.

34. Vecchio RP, Justin JE, Pearce CL (2010) Empowering leadership: An examination of mediating mechanisms within a hierarchical structure. The Leadership Quarterly 21: 530-542.

35. Seligman MEP (2008) Positive health Applied Psychology: An International Review, Special Issue on Health and Well-being 57: 3-18.

36. Turner N, Barling J, Zacharatos A (2002) Positive psychology at work. In CR Snyder and SJ Lopez (Eds.), Handbook of positive psychology 52: 715-728.

37. Bowling NA, Eschleman KJ, Wang Q (2010) A meta-analytic examination of the relationship between job satisfaction and subjective well-being. Journal of Occupational and Organizational Psychology 83: 915-934.

38. Prussia GE, Anderson JS, Manz CC (1998) Self-leadership and performance outcomes: The mediating influence of self-efficacy. Journal of Organizational Behavior 19: 523-538.

39. Müller GF (2014) Questionnaire for the diagnosis of individual self- management skills - Test Manual. German Self - Leadership Questionnaire - Test Manual, Landau: Umbra.

40. Sims Jr HP, Manz CC (1995) Company of Heros: Unleashing the Power of self-leadership. Informs 28: 191-193.

41. Neck CP, Neck H, Manz CC (1997) Thought self-leadership: Mind management for entrepreneurs. Journal of Developmental Entrepreneurship 2: 25-36.

42. Hunt JM, Weintraub JR (2002) The coaching manager: Developing Top Talent in Business. Business and Economics, SAGE Publications 1-252.

43. Wong CA, Laschinger HKS (2013) Authentic leadership, performance, and job satisfaction: The mediating role of empowerment. Journal of Advanced Nursing 69: 947-959.

44. Diener E, Suh EM, Lucas RE, Smith HL (1999) Subjective well-being: Three decades of progress. Psychological Bulletin 125: 276-302.

45. Müller GF, Gappisch C (2005) Personality types of entrepreneurs. Psychological Reports 96: 737-746.

Learning Curve Spillovers and Transactions Cost in the Microfinance Industry of the Philippines

Jovi Dacanay C*

School of Economics, University of Asia, The Pacific Pearl Drive Corner St. Josemaria Escriva Drive Ortigas Center (1605), Pasig City, Philippines

Abstract

Microfinance institutions (MFIs) in the Philippines have gained a reputation for operating as a for-profit institution reaching the poor through micro-lending. The problem or issue which the study addresses is to determine how MFIs in the Philippines are able to attain operational self-sufficiency, the established indicator for financial viability among microfinance institutions, in spite of high transactions cost. The phenomenon may be verified by the following research question: does the behavior of operational and transactions costs among group and individual microfinance lenders manifest experience or learning curve spillovers and a U-shaped supply curve? The study has two objectives. First, using appropriate measures of financial and social performance, the study shall empirically verify the phenomenon of experience or learning curve spillovers among MFIs. Second is to estimate the supply curve for loans to the unbanked poor and verify that it is U-shaped.

The results of the pooled least squares with cross-section random effects regression estimation show that both NGOs and rural banks are attaining both objectives of operational self-sufficiency and moderate to good social performance, through the spillover effects of learning, that is, fast learning for rural banks and moderate learning for NGOs. Operational and transactions costs are high but decreasing for both rural banks and NGOs. Older, more mature NGOs and rural banks are able to set transactions cost at the prescribed level of 11%-25%. Such costs ensure that the MFIs operate in order to both financial performance and outreach.

Keywords: Transactions cost; Operational self-sufficiency; Social performanc; Experience curve; Spillovers

Introduction

The Philippines maintains its standing as No. 1 in the world in microfinance regulatory environment. For four years in a row (2009-2012), the Economist Intelligence Unit's global survey has ranked the Philippines as number one in the world in terms of policy and regulatory framework for microfinance. The Philippines is also consistently ranked at the top ten for having a good microfinance business environment. The survey noted that the Philippines recorded material gains in transparency in pricing given the BSP's issuance of improved rules on transparency and disclosure. However, the microfinance industry in the Philippines suffers from the incidence of over-borrowing and the high cost of transactions.

Statement of the research problem

The study investigates the relationship between transactions cost and operational self-sufficiency in the microfinance industry of the Philippines. When micro-lenders target the entrepreneurial poor, monitoring regularity of payments of borrowers may be costly. This leads to the main problem of the paper: In spite of the presence of transactions cost, can the microfinance industry achieve operational efficiency? The study has two objectives. First, using appropriate measures of financial and social performance, the study shall empirically verify a downward sloping experience curve. Second is to estimate the supply curve for loans to the unbanked poor and verify that it is U-shaped. Both objectives shall lead the study to a verification of decreasing operations cost and transactions cost, thereby allowing MFIs to operate more efficiently.

Significance of the research question

The Philippines has a favorable regulatory environment which allows rural banks to operate in a financially viable manner in spite of allotting a certain percent of credit made accessible to the unbanked, that is, micro entrepreneurs. Reason is that the regulatory environment allows rural banks to financially include them. Why? There has been a significant increase in the number of active borrowers in the Philippines since 1994. Microfinance activities have been existing previous to the 1997 establishment the regulatory body called National Credit Council. Through microfinance, the unbanked, that is, micro entrepreneurs who do not have access to the lending activities and practices of commercial banks, had access to loans. Now, financial services to the poor are provided by NGOs, cooperative and rural banks [1,2].

Previous regulation by the Central Bank of the Philippines had directed credit, also called subsidized credit which did not work. Reason: micro entrepreneurs have to be trained and assisted in order to finance and operate a business viably. There was a need for human capital development [3].

In spite of the Philippines scoring high internationally in terms of creating a policy environment that enhances financial inclusion and effective financial access to the unbanked, it scores low on financial education and monitoring. Payments system, transparency in lending and data collection for existing NGOs can be improved so as to closely monitor and evaluate the financial and social outreach performance of these MFIs. The Philippines scored low on a supporting institutional framework which would incentivize MFIs to achieve accounting

---

*Corresponding author: Jovi Dacanay C, Economist, School of Economics, University of Asia, The Pacific Pearl Drive Corner St. Josemaria Escriva Drive Ortigas Center (1605), Pasig City, Philippines, E-mail: jovi.dacanay@uap.asia

transparency, adherence to international standards of accounting, dispute settlements for unfair and time-consuming loan processes, an integrated credit bureau and policy and practice of financial transactions through agents [1]. Even if the microfinance industry has allowed e-commerce, with the cooperation of telecommunications services such as Smart Communications and Globe Telecom, to be made available for the payment of loans, loan officers are crucial in order to monitor and ensure the regular payment of loans. All these seem to denote high transactions cost.

Such high transactions costs may hinder the further expansion of financial access to the unbanked, as there is still 2.9 million families which are unserved by microfinance institutions [4]. There is a large, about 67%, unmet demand for micro loans to the entrepreneurial poor, henceforth denoted as the unbanked.

Scope and Limitations

The study focuses on the occurrence of transactions cost as human asset specificity to explain the reason for high operating costs among MFIs. However, such types of costs also imply experience and learning. The theoretical formulation of experience, learning and transactions costs proper to the microfinance industry is non-existent to date.

Due to a lack of access to actual data per firm over the amount of loans and interest charged to each borrower, the study focused on annual data per MFI made accessible in the Microfinance Information Exchange Portal (MIX). Borrowing and payment behavior of creditors would be important in order to detect the occurrence of mission drift in an MFI. Indicators used in the regressions are based on the accepted accounting variables which are accessible through the MIX website. As a consequence, relevant variables in the study are interest rates charged to micro-borrowers, human asset specificity and social performance. The indicators used in the global industry are operating expense ratio (also known as operating cost per dollar of loan), personnel expense ratio and the social efficiency index.

The social performance indicators used in the study are number of borrowers, depth of outreach (Average loan size over GDP per capita also termed as national loan size), and the social efficiency index (Operating Expense Ratio x cost per borrower) Outreach is only one aspect of social performance for MFIs.

The phenomenon of multiple loans across various MFIs cannot be observed from the data used, as this phenomenon would involve detailed MFI data. Anecdotal information claims that some MFIs apply for a loan to other MFIs so as to repay their loans, leading to over-indebtedness. Previous to 2011, MFIs were allowed to lend only up to US$3,500. However, a BSP circular issued in 2011 has allowed rural banks to lend up to US$7,000.

Methodology

Using appropriate financial data provided by the Microfinance Information Exchange Portal, the likelihood of a U-shaped supply curve for loans to the unbanked poor, due to the high unit cost of transactions, shall be discussed. Then, an analysis of the factors explaining transactions cost, through an estimation of the appropriate/proper measure of operational self-sufficiency, an evaluation of selected social performance measures for the microfinance industry, and, indicators for cumulated output shall be done. Operational self-sufficiency is the measurement used to denote financial viability among MFIs, whereas, the social performance index and the number of women borrowers and outreach is the variables used to indicate social performance. The regression estimation procedure, using unbalanced panel data, with cross-section random effects shall be performed in order to evaluate whether or not the chosen MFIs for the study are either: (a) decreasing their transactions cost but at a constant or level of operational self-sufficiency, or, (b) improving their operational self-sufficiency and lowering their transactions cost at the same time.

Definition of Terms

The following terms are used based on the stated definitions. The conceptualization and definition of these terms are followed [5,6].

Operating expenses include the costs of implementing the loan activities personnel compensation, supplies, travel, depreciation of fixed assets, etc. Operating expenses consume the majority of the income of most micro lenders' loan portfolios, so this component is the largest determinant of the rate the borrowers end up paying.

Financial viability refers to the operational and financial sustainability of MFIs. Operational and financial sustainability refers to the achievement of cost effective strategies in order to reach the unbanked and entrepreneurial poor. Financial outcomes would indicate a lowering of portfolio at risk (90 days), constant or sustained returns to assets and cost of operations over total assets.

In a broad perspective, the social performance of MFIs is associated with their social objective, which is extending credit by targeting the poor and the excluded, the adaptation of services and products to target customers, and improvement in the equity capital of beneficiaries through the creation and strengthening of community relations. Specifically, the social performance of MFIs refers to their mission: the alleviation of poverty by extending credit to the unbanked poor, while at the same time operating cost effectively, that is, achieving operational and financial sustainability or viability.

Financial inclusion, as an objective of MFIs, refers to their capacity to extend credit to the unbanked entrepreneurial poor in a financially viable way. It is used synonymously with the social and financial performance of MFIs.

Transaction costs in credit markets therefore are indirect financial costs generated by various processes, including the cost of searching and collecting relevant information. They are indirect costs caused by frictions in the flow of credit funds, preventing credit markets from reaching efficient market equilibrium. Consequently transaction costs of lending consist of the costs of administering credit, coordination costs and the costs of the risk of default. It is further highlighted that administrative costs are those which are directly attributable to the processing, delivering and administering of loans while coordination costs are those resources a financial institution dedicates to ensuring that clients adhere to terms stipulated in loan contracts.

Literature Review

Historical development

Past government initiatives for poverty alleviation in the 60s to 80s were focused on direct credit and guarantee programs, which provided massive credit subsidies to bring down the cost of borrowing for target sectors. These programs resulted in very limited effectivity and outreach, and at a great cost to the government's budget. These programs were met with massive repayment problems, capture of funds by large-scale borrowers, neglect of deposit mobilization and huge fiscal costs for the government [7].

Learning from these experiences, the government policies of the last decade have shaped reforms to develop a market oriented financial and credit policy environment that promotes and supports private institutions to broaden and deepen their services; while government will instead focus not on the actual provision of credit but on creating the enabling policy environment. It is during this period that the National Strategy for Microfinance was created imbibing the following principles: 1) Greater role of the private microfinance institutions in the provision of financial services, 2) Existence of an enabling policy environment that facilitates the increased participation of the private sector in microfinance, 3) Adherence to market oriented financial and credit policies, 4) Non-participation of government line agencies in the implementation of credit and guarantee programs. Several laws were enacted in support of this strategy namely; Social Reform and Poverty Alleviation Act, Agriculture and Fisheries Modernization Act, Barangay Micro-Business Enterprises Act, Executive Order 138 and the General Banking Act of 2000. With the National Strategy for Microfinance and the subsequent policy issuances and laws that were passed, the microfinance market has been driven by the private sector with the government only providing the enabling policy and regulatory environment. The strategy also laid the groundwork for the establishment of a regulatory framework for microfinance as well as the uniform set of performance standards for all types of microfinance institutions [7].

Given this backdrop, there are now three types of institutions that provide microfinance services: the nongovernmental organizations (NGOs), cooperatives and rural banks. The success factor in developing a range of microfinance institutions is that the policy environment encourages the development of these different types of institutions recognizing the strength of each type in delivering microfinance services. The current players include eight microfinance oriented banks and 187 thrift and rural banks with some level of microfinance operations, approximately 300 NGOs where around 30 will have sizeable and significant microfinance portfolios, and 50 cooperatives engaged in pure microfinance activities. Together, these institutions are providing microfinance services to approximately 1.3 to 1.5 million families [7]. This number amounts to close to a third of the entrepreneurial poor [8].

Internationally, women, usually, are the clientele, low level of credit available to the poor in spite of the possibility of high returns [3,5]. The mission of the MFI is to alleviate poverty by extending credit to the unbanked poor. There are two factors which prompts an MFI to increase its average loan size over time, thereby lowering depth of outreach. First, progressive lending, which, in the microfinance jargon, pertains to the idea that existing clients can reach up to higher credit ceilings after observing a "clean" repayment record at the end of each credit cycle. Second, cross-subsidization, which entails reaching out to unbanked wealthier clients in order to finance a larger number of poor clients whose average loan size is relatively small. These two explanations are in line with the MFI social objective [5].

Policy issues

The Bangko Sentral ng Pilipinas (BSP) remains at the forefront of establishing a policy and regulatory environment conducive to financial inclusion. This stems from the recognition that financial inclusion is a worthy policy objective that could and should be pursued alongside the promotion of stability and efficiency in the financial system. It is also believed that financial inclusion is a key component of inclusive growth. The BSP is actively implementing policy and program initiatives to realize the Philippine government's vision for the financial sector: "an inclusive financial system which provides for the evolving needs of a diverse public" (Philippine Development Plan 2011-2016). The financial inclusion initiatives of the BSP are focused on the major areas of: 1) Policy, Regulation and Supervision, 2) Financial Inclusion Data, 3) Financial Education and Consumer Protection, and 4) Financial Inclusion Advocacy.

In spite of the absence of a regulatory body for NGOs, the BSP regulates NGOs through circulars and ordinances. The BSP aims at promoting transparency and good governance among MFIs through the Issuance of Rules Regarding the Relationship Between Banks and their Related Microfinance Non-Governmental Organizations (Circular 725, 16 June 2011). This issuance recognizes the possible synergy between a bank with microfinance operations and a related microfinance NGO/Foundation. While this has become a successful model for some, the issuance aims to ensure that the banks with related microfinance NGOs are able to safely and viably coexist by mitigating possible operational, governance and reputational risks. The salient features of the issuance includes a) requiring clear contractual agreements between the two entities, b) prohibiting bank personnel from holding any concurrent, full time positions that may cause them to be involved in the daily operations of related NGOs/foundations and c) issuing general principle sand standards that will govern the business relationships between banks and their related NGOs/foundations. (BSP Financial Inclusion Initiatives Year-End Report December 2011).

Traditionally, the central bank defined microfinance loans to be below P150,000 (US$3,500). In December 2011, BSP issued Circular 744 that allows banks to offer the option of "Microfinance Plus" loans of up to P300,000 (US$7,000). This is intended to lessen the occurrence of over-indebtedness among MFIs as small borrowers seem to resort to borrowing from other MFIs so as to pay the outstanding balance from a loan.

There is still, however, a need for an integrated credit bureau. Under the Republic Act 9510 (also known as the Credit Information Act (CISA)), signed into law in 2008, all regulated entities would be required to submit positive and negative information to a credit bureau under the Securities and Exchange Commission (SEC). A crucial component of the legislated is the creation of the Central Credit Information Corporation (CCIC) to receive and consolidate the credit data and to act as a central registry of credit information which will provide access to standardized information in order to overcome and replace the existing system of fragmented credit bureaus. Although the law's implementing rules and regulation were approved in May 2009, the establishment of the Central Credit Information Corporation (CICC) has not yet resulted in the operation of a functioning, active credit bureau. Under the CISA implementing rules and regulations, the proposed corporation will have a seed capital of Php 75 million. But so far, CCIC only received Php 17.5 million. The future central depositary of credit history is also still looking for an office, still forming the organization chart, and outlining plans for the rest of the year.

Meanwhile, the private sector is pursuing its own initiative. The Banker's Association of the Philippines (BAP) has its own credit bureau, which the Rural Bankers Association of the Philippines, the association of rural banks, is also using. BAP's credit information database contains approximately 3.8 million accounts and information pertaining to unpaid loans, loans under litigation, bounced checks and credit card debt. To encourage rural banks to subscribe to the database BAP-CB lowered the fee for each inquiry from Php 11 (US$ 0.25) to Php 5.6 (US$ 0.13) and removed the upfront subscription fee. As of January 2011, twenty rural banks have joined the bureau. Access to credit information can help rural banks identify whether loan applicants already have outstanding loans and avoid the problem of over-indebtedness, which can be harmful to the borrowers, the banks and the sector as a whole. BAP's credit bureau is almost exclusively for non-microfinance clients, however as a result, the system of fragmented credit bureaus remains intact. For example, cooperatives based in Mindanao have formed their own credit bureau called CCBOL. Perhaps the most promising initiative was taken by the leading MFIs. In early 2013, the seven largest microfinance providers (Taytay sa Kauswagan Inc. (TSKI), OK Bank, CARD Bank, CARD NGO, Negros Women, Ahon sa Hirap and ASA Philippines), which together serve about 70 percent of the estimated one million micro-borrowers in the country, signed a memorandum of agreement on the creation of the credit bureau called the "Microfinance Data Sharing System (MiDAS)". Initially, MiDAS is meant to focus on negative information, i.e. delinquent borrowers, with the view later on of establishing and implementing programs aimed at client rehabilitation. The business requirements of MiDAS are unique to its users, the microfinance institutions, with a special feature that allows for Barangay (town or village) level search for delinquent borrowers. It is the intention of the founders to expand the coverage of the credit bureau to other MFIs as well in the future [1].

New rules issued by the BSP and effective July 1, 2012 outlaw the use of flat interest rate calculation methods for regulated institutions. Unregulated NGO-MFIs and cooperatives are encouraged to follow suit but the BSP lacks the authority to require them to do so. This makes the calculation of an effective interest rate difficult. Through the flat balance calculation method, the interest rate is applied to the initial loan amount throughout the entire loan term. Through this method the borrower pays interest on the full loan amount even though the amount they have over the loan term is less and less as they repay the loan. Interest rates calculated using the flat balance appear much cheaper than declining balance rates, but are in fact nearly twice as expensive. For example, an annual interest rate of 15% charged on a flat balance results in almost the same amount in interest payments as an annual interest rate of 30% charged on a declining balance. This can make comparison between the prices of loans difficult, posing a serious obstacle to MFIs in terms of their ability to make informed price-setting decisions and to clients in terms of comparing the prices of the loan products available to them. Through the declining, or reducing, balance interest rate calculation method, the lender charges interest on the loan balance that the borrower has not yet repaid. This amount declines over time as the borrower repays the loan, so that interest is only charged on money that the borrower is in possession of.

Theoretical issues

When one observes the behavior of commercial lenders, there seems to be a causal link as to why there is low level of credit supplied to the poor in spite of high demand. There is a high demand for credit among the entrepreneurial poor, but these borrowers have high transactions cost, and commercial lenders would incur low profit. The transactions cost come about as more effort is needed among commercial lenders, that is, monitoring costs to ensure frequent and constant payment of loans has to be done. As a result, there is a discontinuous marginal revenue curve for borrowers among the micro-borrowers or the entrepreneurial poor vis-à-vis borrowers from small and medium enterprises. This phenomenon partly explains the existence for a U-shaped supply curve, a downward sloping steep supply curve for low levels of borrowings, after which it reaches a minimum point, then the supply curve slopes upwards for higher levels of borrowings [3].

The microfinance industry has addressed or mitigated the occurrence of high transactions cost either by individual lending (rural banks) or group lending but with individual liability (NGOs). NGOs tend to have high information cost, thus, they seek other sources of funding, i.e. donors or investors [3], with transactions cost operationalized as governance cost, one can explain the institutional organization of MFIs, i.e. vertically integrated firm has to be the structure due to asset specific transactions [9], Skilled loan officers invest time and effort in order to understand the difficulties faced by micro-borrowers in achieving their weekly repayment of loans. This investment of time and effort may be viewed as a sunk cost for both NGOs and rural banks. Through time, there is an observed decrease in operational costs per borrower, reflecting the possibility of a downward sloping experience curve for the industry [2].

Frictions in the smooth flow of contractual arrangement in transactions give way to transactions cost. The economic counterpart of friction is transaction cost: for that subset of transactions where it is important to elicit cooperation, do the parties to the exchange operate harmoniously, or are there frequent misunderstandings and conflicts that lead to delays, breakdowns, and other malfunctions? Transaction cost analysis entails an examination of the comparative costs of planning, adapting, and monitoring task completion under alternative governance structures [10].

An application of the theory on governance costs on the microfinance industry shall now be discussed. The discussion centers on the reasons why credit does not reach the poor. First, it has been observed that there is a lack of available complementary inputs when lending to micro-entrepreneurs. For example, there is a lack of financial and accounting education, there is insufficient financial capital to invest and acquire human capital, land or entrepreneurial ability in order to improve the productivity of land or any foregoing business activity. Second, investment is not based on the marginal productivity of capital or the returns on capital, but on the risk-adjusted returns. The poor may promise higher returns but they also represent much higher risk [11,12]. An adverse selection problem usually happens. These problems have been reduced by monitoring but such activity lead to high cost due to the small scale of the loan made available to many borrowers. This aspect characterizes the asset specificity of negotiations for loans and the monitoring of loan payments. Third, is the transactions cost of loans. Partly, these are the costs of monitoring and of creating legal liens on whatever collateral the poor may have to offer. But besides these, the time the banker spent in helping an illiterate man fill out an application form (to have his particulars available), the time spent to process the loan and to take back cash in small installments and keep records, all have to be costed [13].

Empirical issues

Empirical findings based on various data sources show that there is a difference in performance when more years are covered per MFI. This may imply that the number of years of existence of an MFI is directly proportional to operational self-sufficiency (financial revenue over the sum of financial expense, impairment loss and operating expense), and, the capacity to sustain outreach targets with commercial funding and internally sourced equity [2,5], studied empirical outcomes first before any theoretical explanation is given; i.e. social performance, financial performance and the current phenomenon of mission drift [13], focused on the empirical assessment of microfinance performance in India, using indicators of transactions cost, especially with group lending, making use of [14], computation of information cost [13] stresses the importance of commercially operated MFIs, which allows the recognition of the role of transactions cost when examining the interest rates charged by MFIs. The results highlight the mistakes committed by the government of India in handling the MFIs in Andhra Pradesh. Microfinance activity was governed by state sponsored loans crowding-out private sector initiative and the needed financial discipline which arises through commercial or market-led operations in microfinance. Rural officials use microcredit as a way to increase patronage within the region of Andhra Pradesh. The government of India decided to stop microfinance activity in this state leading to client drop-out, access to funding froze, many MFIs in the area defaulted [1].

Transactions Cost for Microfinance Institutions

Hypotheses

The research hypothesis to be tested in the study is: higher experience or learning curve spillover effects lessens operating and transactions cost.

For the microfinance industry, regulation by the Bangko Sentral ng Pilipinas (BSP) plays an important role in monitoring operating costs and operational self-sufficiency. But only rural banks are regulated by the BSP. Thus, the study shall proceed with an analysis for rural banks and another analysis for NGOs.

Operating costs for rural banks may manifest higher experience or learning curve spillover effects and lesser transactions cost than NGOs. This phenomenon may be due to their longer commercial lending experience, their strict observance of industry standards for operational self-sufficiency, and the larger average loan portfolios, comparison to MFIs, handled by loan officers.

Operating costs for NGOs may manifest lower experience or learning curve spillover effects and may have higher transactions cost than rural banks. This phenomenon may be due to their shorter commercial lending experience, the non-regulated nature of their operations, and, smaller average loan portfolios in comparison to that handled by loan officers in rural banks.

Theoretical and conceptual framework

The theoretical approach to the study of the efficiency and productivity of MFIs focuses on the manner in which transactions between the micro-borrower and the loan officer are done. For group-lending MFIs, loans per borrower are radically of a smaller size than that of commercial banks, henceforth referred to as the traditional banking sector, with loans averaging to at most a tenth of loans given by the traditional banking sector to their borrowers. Also, borrowers of MFIs may operate their business in remote areas, far from the nearest MFI. As a consequence, loan officers of MFIs usually have to travel to these areas weekly so as to collect loan payments from a group of borrowers, usually numbering to 30-40 in the Philippines. Some loan officers of group lending borrowers collect more often than once a week. This process involves time and effort for loan officers as problems of repayment of loans have to be immediately resolved per collection period, i.e. 52 collection periods annually, so as to ensure that borrowers repay their loans.

Transactions of rural banks involved in MFI operations, henceforth referred to as simply rural banks, do not have to go to the area where their individual borrowers operate their business. The borrowers go to the most accessible rural bank in order to turn-in their weekly repayment. Given this background the theoretical approach most appropriate to the study of the efficiency and productivity of MFIs in the Philippines would be transactions cost economics.

These specific characteristics of microcredit can now be applied to the standard theory of average and marginal revenues. With asymmetric information explanation, marginal costs are much higher for the poorer people than for richer people. The economies of scale effect of the transactions cost explanation remains, as well as the ultimate increase in risks with over-indebtedness, and the supply curve becomes downward sloping as loan size increases for richer people. The final curve is U-shaped as in the standard literature because after some point over-borrowing by rich people increases their risks [3].

All the above reasons imply that even if there are no usury laws in a country, lending to the poor is not possible for the commercial sector, as illustrated in figures, which puts together the Marginal Revenue curve (MR) and supply curve for loans (based on the marginal cost curve). Although the simplistic model that is proposed suffers from many limitations as enumerated above, it is good for explaining the fundamentals. Although other authors may have said the same thing, the representation is new and may therefore lead to additional insights [3].

Figure 1 shows that the first portion of the MR curve does not have any equilibrium with the supply curve. As a result, the organized sector did not lend to the poor. The associated average revenue (AR) curve is consequently of little relevance to any monopolistic banker who decides to enter the market. The final equilibrium is at low rates of interest (r_o) but is available only to wealthy borrowers. Since this end of the market is more likely to be subject to (perfect) competition, interest rates are not going to be much higher than marginal cost, but we can associate a demand curve if for institutional reasons there is monopoly power. In this case, the demand curve would start at the same level as this portion of the discontinuous supply curve and (in the simple linear case) would slope downward at half the speed (the AR_{rich} curve would take twice as long as the MR_{rich} curve to reach the X-axis). Interest rates would then be higher at r_m [3].

The MR of capital curve is discontinuous at a point owing to effect of human capital available only to not so poor borrowers. The supply curve is U shaped owing to asymmetric information and transaction costs. As a result, poor people do not receive loans but wealthier people do, at a fairly low interest rate, r_o if there is competition and r_m if there is not solution [3],Why do money lenders lend at high interest rates? Figure 1 illustrates this graphically, using the discontinuous marginal revenue curve and U-shaped supply curve analysis developed above. The lower asymmetric information costs of moneylenders lower the supply curve of credit facing poorer borrowers. As a result, they also get loans, but at higher interest rates of $r_{ML,m}$, much higher than the

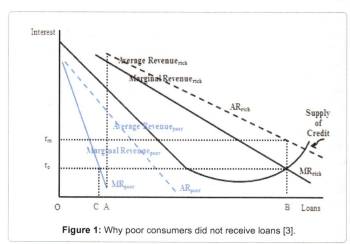

Figure 1: Why poor consumers did not receive loans [3].

rates charged by the organized sector of r_o to richer borrowers. Since moneylenders are monopolistic, they charge rates on the associated Average Revenue curve. The supply curve of moneylenders cannot fall lower because their costs are high for various reasons: no access to cheap deposits, little access to debt from the organized sector (they may get personal loans by pledging personal assets), making them reliant only on their own equity capital. This equity capital may also suffer from seasonal variations in demand, indicating that the moneylender may have to recover higher interest rates in the busy season [3].

Moneylenders have lower transaction costs and lower information asymmetry. As a result, they push down the supply curve for poorer borrowers to the dashed line shown in the diagram. They charge high interest rates r_{ML}, much higher than the interest rates r_o charged by the competitive organized sector to the wealthier borrowers [3].

Why do banks refuse to enter the market for microcredit? If moneylending is profitable, why don't new entrants like banks increase competition and drive down interest rates and profits? At the very least, they should drive these down to r_{MLc}. The suggested answers are several and are similar to reasons why banks don't come in reference [3].

The first is based on transaction cost or barriers to entry. A new entrant has high start-up costs: if he is not from the locality, he does not know the customers and does not have the case histories. These are developed by experience. Also, it is difficult, time consuming and expensive to market and monitor in isolated villages, driving up costs especially for small transaction sizes. As a result, a new entrant faces higher risks and higher costs than the local established moneylender (Figure 2) [3].

Also, the existence of more than one moneylender (competition as opposed to monopoly) breaks down the business model of the established moneylender. The borrower could shift from one moneylender to another. Greater competition will increase default rates to the first institution, drive down interest rates and reduce the total number of customers. As a result, moneylending would become a loss-making proposition, driving out competition. Therefore, increasing the number of moneylenders is not a solution [3].

Finally, more important, the market equilibrium in this segment would remain at OD in Figure 2 and interest rates would not fall below the MR curve. Thus, moneylending and other business would be competing only for lowering profits to the segment as a whole. This means that the market of DC for loans in this segment is still not being served and, in the face of excess labor available to people in the same segment, productive capacity is underutilized and economic development is suboptimal [3].

How can microcredit overcome information asymmetry and other barriers? One method to overcome problems linked with information asymmetry used by microcredit organizations is group lending. Although there are many different forms of group lending exercised by microfinance institutions (solidarity groups, village banking, branch banking, etc.), the essential method consists in lending to individuals in a group, and using group pressure to ensure repayment by individuals. This group pressure may come, for example, if other members of the group would get loans only if the first borrowers pay back. As a result of this, people would not like to form groups with others who are unlikely to pay back. Thus, the adverse selection problem is avoided without the bank getting information.

The second tool for overcoming asymmetric problems is the provision of incentives: to threaten to stop lending, on the individual level, is incremental loans or progressive lending. Thus, if the borrower's project can be divided into a series of projects, the MFI lends a small amount first for one project and the next loan is given only if the first one is repaid. Thus, the borrower is assured of funding for his project, if he can overcome the moral hazard issues of being capable of managing the project and be willing to repay. Another method used by MFIs is to collect repayments in public. Thus, an agent passes at a fixed time once a week and all the borrowers are present and repay him in front of everybody. This reduces collection costs as well as creates a social pressure to repay on time. In some MFIs, there are also medals given for a series of successful repayments, acting as further reinforcements both for the individual receiving the medal as well as the others watching him receive it.

The third tool mentioned above was frequent repayments. The fourth tool is non-traditional collateral. A fifth method used by MFIs is to focus on women. All of the above methods do not necessarily require information being transferred from the individual borrower to the bank, but they overcome the problems of asymmetric information. However, a sixth method is used to improve the information available to the MFI. This includes contacting neighbors to find out information about a potential borrower. Some MFIs also encourage cross reporting where borrowers are encouraged to be whistle blowers, in the interest of the larger group, if they think that some borrower is not going to repay.

The final result of all these factors is illustrated in Figure 3, For graphic simplicity the average revenue curve of the moneylender is taken off but we can see he is charging the higher monopolistic rate. Since no market is yet saturated, MFIs may also be in the position of monopolies. As a result they would charge interest rates somewhere between r_{MFIc} and r_{MFIm}, depending on whether their mission is purely social and purely for-profits.

These developments have led to money flowing from the MFIs to the poor to the extent of DD': with moneylenders, the market obtained OD, with MFIs, it obtains OD'.

If the supply curve only shifts downward in this range and not outward to the right, it would also affect the equilibrium solution for richer markets. As shown in Figure 3, the market of the poor now extends from OA earlier to OA' because these people now demand more loans since their productivity has gone up. The next segment therefore shifts to the right and the MR curve of the rich shifts to MR'_{RICH}.

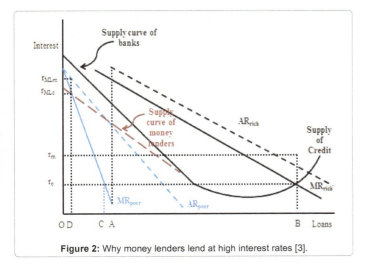

Figure 2: Why money lenders lend at high interest rates [3].

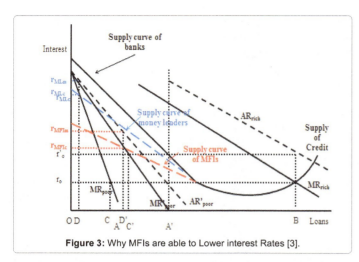

Figure 3: Why MFIs are able to Lower interest Rates [3].

Microfinance institutions have lower cost of capital and they overcome information asymmetry. As a result, they push down the supply curve for poorer borrowers further to the dotted line shown in the diagram. At the same time, group monitoring and involvement may actually boost the performance on projects and push the MR curve of the poor to MR'. The MFIs charge interest rates r_{MFIc}, or r_{MFIm}, depending on whether there is competition or monopoly in the local market, in either case much higher than the interest rates r_o charged by the organized sector to the wealthier borrowers, but much lower than the interest rates r_{ML} charged by money-lender.

The perfect competition equilibrium interest rate to the rich rises from r_o to r'_o. Some rich borrowers borrow less. Correspondingly, the unserved people in the poor market is D'C' since only those willing to pay interest rates above r'_o will be able to use the capital with their available labor, given the new human capital thanks to MFIs, other Non-Government Organizations and governmental dispositions. Although international flows may not affect the national markets of developing countries immediately, they would affect the relative availability of credit in developed countries and the raising of interest rates may occur [3].

Transactions cost economics can then be applied to the microfinance industry. The occurrence of a lowering of interest rates applied to borrowers with a satisfactory payment history would be possible only with the specialized effort applied by loan officers who have invested time and effort to provide information and education to micro-borrowers who may not have acquired the education necessary to carry-on and manage financial and business negotiations. The type of transactions cost proper to microfinance are relationship-specific assets: site specificity, physical asset specificity, dedicated specificity and human asset specificity [9,15]. Understanding the nature of behavioral characteristics in the monitoring of loan payments is not a question of understanding the statistical risks involved in the transactions, which often require a large number of instances, i.e. renegotiations. The bilateral business agreements are specific to the circumstances of the micro-borrower, and would require specific talents and communication capabilities on the part of the loan officers. These human-asset specific relationships enable the MFI to incur agency costs. The study focuses only on the asset specific causes of transactions cost, and specifically, on those which refer to human assets such as skills and capabilities which allow a longer term duration of negotiations between the micro-borrower and the loan officer.

As the scale of the transactions increase, the firm's demand for borrowings increase, and a vertically integrated firm can better exploit economies of scale and scope in production. Vertical integration is more likely to be the preferred mode of organizing the transaction for any given level of asset specificity. This process involves a learning phase for each firm involved in microfinance or micro-credit lending (Figure 4).

The experience of a firm at any given age may be measured in a number of ways including, inter alia, the age of the firm, the cumulative prior output of the firm, which for microfinance would mean average loan balance per borrower, and, number of active borrowers, the average tenure of its employees, or the average length of related work experience of its employees. The most popular implementation assumes that the current unit cost of a firm of age v, $c(v)$, is a decreasing function of its cumulative prior output, $y(v) = \int x(s)ds$, where $x(s)$ is the firm's output given its market share at age v. In most research, most especially in empirical and macroeconomic applications, a power rule, a functional form for cost, $c(v)$, using constant elasticity to scale, of the following form:

$$c(v) = c(0)\gamma(v)^{-\beta} = m + c_o e^{-\bar{y}} \quad (1)$$

is assumed [16,17] For Equation (1), c refers to cost, m refers to fixed costs, $\bar{y}$ is the cumulated industry output at the end of the period and λ refers to industry spillovers, i.e. organizational structures so as to improve repayment and other relevant experiences in dealing with micro-borrowers is made known to the entire industry. Note that the equation used to estimate the experience curve uses firm figures but the result will refer to the total industry as market shares per firm in the MFI industry are not significantly different from each other, i.e. the Hirshman-Herfindahl index is <0.15, indicating that market shares per firm in terms of number of borrowers and gross loan portfolio have a close to a perfectly competitive market structure[18,19]. This specification of the learning curve assumes that with a close to competitive market structure, cost structures are not significantly different and spillovers occur. Proprietary experience per firm due to the existence of patents is almost nil.

The differences in the cost curves will depend on the spillover parameter, λ, the mean of the assumed exponential function, which is also interpreted as a rate or speed of cost decrease. Lower levels of λ would indicate a faster learning time since the intercept at time = 0 would also be higher. Thus, from Figure 4, $|\lambda_3| < |\lambda_2| < |\lambda_1|$. Note that the spillover rate is the reciprocal of the coefficient of the variables indicating cumulative output, when a regression estimation is done on unit cost as dependent variable and a cumulative output indicator as repressor, it [18,19] would refer to experience or learning curve spillovers in order to incorporate the seminal concept of learning-by-doing [16].

Scale economies may be present for the commercial banking sector. However, such may not be the case for banks dealing with micro-entrepreneurs. The decrease in the cost of transactions within a specific level of borrowings among micro-entrepreneurs may not necessarily denote scale economies but may just be an indication that more experience in transacting with the unbanked poor enables microfinance institutions to acquire a higher level of learning, thereby, lessening the costs of monitoring. This phenomenon may be summarized by a downward sloping experience curve, which flattens rightwards. Passive learning, a phenomenon which gives rise to learning from experience, refers to the conventional economic characterization of organizational learning by doing as an incidental and costless byproduct of a firm's production activities [17]. A firm that increases productivity through

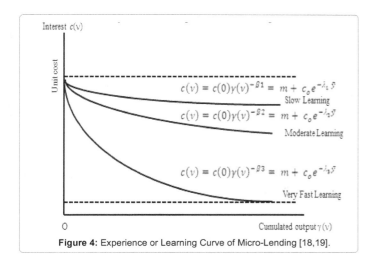

Figure 4: Experience or Learning Curve of Micro-Lending [18,19].

passive learning will be said to move along an experience curve [17].

The experience curve, also synonymously termed as the learning curve, is the curve that relates unit costs to accumulated volume [18,19]. The learning curve is believed to characterize the costs in some industrial markets, and can be an important determinant of competitive behavior in those markets (Spence, 1981). When there is a learning curve, the short-run output decision is a type of investment decision. It affects the cumulated output, a stock, and through it, future costs and market position [19]. When additions to output lower future costs, it is appropriate for the firm to go beyond the short-run profit maximizing level of output.

The occurrence of an experience curve or a learning curve spillover, that is, a decrease in operational and transactions cost in the case of the microfinance industry, with cumulated output, differs from economies of scale. Economies of scale refer to the ability to perform activities at a lower unit cost when those activities are performed on a larger scale at a given point in time. The behavior of the experience or learning curve spillover refers to reductions in unit costs due to cumulated experience over time. Economies of scale may be substantial even when learning or experience is minimal. This is likely to be the case in mature, capital-intensive production processes. Likewise, experience may be substantial even when economies of scale are minimal, as in such complex labor-intensive activities as the production of handmade watches [15]. In industries wherein asset specificity occurs due to the diversity of transactions handled by loan officers, initially high costs may happen in transactions and negotiations carried out even by skilled personnel. Through time, learning occurs on the part of bank personnel monitoring loan payments as well as micro-creditors, resulting to experience or learning curve spillovers.

Methodology

To be able to test the stated hypotheses, the empirical methodology shall proceed with two steps, which also pertain to the objectives of study. The study therefore attempts to empirically verify (1) a decreasing cost over cumulative output indicated by age, also called a learning or experience curve spillover, and (2) a U-shaped supply function, for the microfinance industry. Pooled least squares regression with cross-section random effects shall be performed for (1) and (2).

The coefficient of age upon establishment and average loan balance per borrower shall be the indicator for experience or learning curve spillovers. The greater the spill-over effects, the greater the capacity of the MFI to decrease transactions cost, assuming that the data covers a time period from zero output up to a planning period. The reciprocal of the coefficient of the cumulative output shall be the indicator for the spillover rate as the regression model to be performed will not be a logarithmic function. Experience in negotiations and transactions with micro-borrowers communicated within each MFI and to the whole MFI industry is likely to result to a trend towards lowering transactions cost.

Due to the unique nature of MFI operations, wherein, the human capital specificity of each transaction with borrowers is also a function of the average loan per borrower, a regression shall be performed for both rural banks and NGOs with human capital specificity as dependent variable. Human capital specificity, as indicated by personnel expense per average loan portfolio per borrower, accounts for more than 50% of operating expenses. Thus, the study would verify if MFIs undergo a learning curve as regards transactions with micro-borrowers. The data only extends to aggregates per firm and not by loan officer or employee per firm. Thus, the study shall use average loan per borrower and age upon establishment as the indicator for cumulative output, the operating expense ratio or cost per dollar of loan as the indicator for unit cost, and, personnel expense ratio or the personnel cost per dollar of loan as the indicator for human asset specificity, or the transactions cost indicator.

The functional form used for the learning or experience curve assumes spillovers, that is, rivals learn from each other's experience, i.e. organizational structures are made known to all in the industry, due to the presence of a regulatory body monitoring the financial viability of the players. If learning is neither too slow nor too rapid, no significant entry barriers arise.

Using the operating expense ratio as the cost indicator of MFI operations and dependent variable, a regression using operational self-sufficiency, average loan balance per borrower, number of active borrowers, capitalization, size, actual age (upon establishment), square of actual age, and, outreach as explanatory variables, can be done, answering objective 1. The regression model used is adapted from [20], who used the same independent variables to explain financial performance. In their empirical model, labor and capital costs were included as regressors. For the study, the operating expense ratio was been used, indicator for unit cost, as a dependent variable and cumulated output would be indicated by age upon establishment, and, average loan balance per borrower for objective 1. The estimated regression for Equations (2) and (3) shall be plotted with age upon establishment and operating expense ratio (unit cost indicator) and personnel expense ratio (asset specificity indicator).

The reciprocal of the coefficient of average loan balance per borrower and age upon establishment shall be the indicators for the experience or learning curve spillover rate. Through time, it has been observed, microfinance firms increase their average loan balance per borrower as they are more capable, with greater experience, to monitor and manage increasing amounts of credit made available to borrowers. To achieve an asymptotic curve, the square of age shall be included in the regression equation. The experience curve can be estimated using the following equation, with the operating expense ratio used as the indicator for unit cost:

Operating Cost per dollar of Loan$_{ijt}$ (Operating Expense Ratio) = α_{ij} + β_1 OSS$_{ijt}$ + β_2 Average Loan Balance per Borrower$_{ijt}$ + β_3 Number of Active Borrowers$_{ijt}$ + β_4 Capital Cost$_{ijt}$ + β_5 Gross Loan Portfolio per Asset$_{ijt}$ + β_6 Age upon Establishment$_{ijt}$ + β_7 Age upon

Establishment Squared$_{ijt}$ β$_8$ Scale$_{ijt}$ + β$_9$ Outreach$_{ijt}$ + β$_{10}$ Number of Women Borrowers$_{ijt}$ + β$_{10}$ Social Efficiency Index$_{ijt}$ + ε$_{it}$ (2)

Note that performance indicators have been used as regressors in the empirical model. This specification was used due to the need for MFIs to achieve the regulated or standard levels for operational self-sufficiency, which should be greater than 100%. This level of operational self-sufficiency has to be reached even while achieving its social outreach motives. The meaning of the above-mentioned explanatory variables and the expected signs from the regression are indicated in Table 1.

The downward sloping learning or experience curve happens as a result of a decreasing operating cost per dollar of loan across time, i.e. more years of experience by the micro-borrower in transacting with the MFIs and its personnel. As mentioned by Shankar [13], transactions costs do seem to decrease with time for the Philippines. In fact, there is much hope for interest rates charged to micro-borrowers due to an expectation that as micro-lenders acquire more experience they learn to lend more efficiently [2], thus, what is expected to be observed for operating costs must also be observed for transactions cost, the main cost driver for MFIs. This observation will be verified through the following regression, with the personnel expense ratio used as the indicator for transactions cost:

Personnel Cost per dollar of Loan$_{ijt}$ (Personnel Expense Ratio) = α$_{ij}$ + β$_1$ OSS$_{ijt}$ + β$_2$ Average Loan Balance per Borrower$_{ijt}$ + β$_3$ Number of Active Borrowers$_{ijt}$ + β$_4$ Capital Cost$_{ijt}$ + β$_5$ Gross Loan Portfolio per Asset$_{ijt}$ + β$_6$ Age upon Establishment$_{ijt}$ + β$_7$ Age upon Establishment Squared$_{ijt}$ β$_8$ Scale$_{ijt}$ + β$_9$ Outreach$_{ijt}$ + β$_{10}$ Number of Women Borrowers$_{ijt}$ + β$_{10}$ Social Efficiency Index$_{ijt}$ + ε$_{it}$ (3)

Neo-classical economic theory on competitive market structures points out that cost improvements happen as firms (or the whole industry in a given market) acquire more experience. Eventually, efficiency lessons are learned, and the experience curve flattens out. At this point efficiency improves slowly even in the absence of technological breakthroughs [2], In addition to the learning curve, there is hope that the pressure of competition will force lenders to find more efficient delivery systems. There seems to be, therefore, a global evidence for a flattening operating cost curve for the microfinance industry, as micro-lenders such as MFIs, gain more lending experience to micro-borrowers with time or age.

The study shall use high quality data reported in the Microfinance Information Exchange Portal (MIX). Profitability patterns can be observed across the two main institutional types, also denoted as lending types in the study, identified in the MIX are as follows:

1. Individual-based Rural Bank lenders: institutions that use standard bilateral lending contracts between a lender and a single borrower. Liability for repaying the loan rests with the individual borrower only, although in some cases another individual might serve as a guarantor;

2. NGO group lenders: institutions that employ contracts based on a group with either joint or individual liability implemented with solidarity groups (in the spirit of contracts used initially at the Grameen Bank in Bangladesh and at BancoSol in Bolivia). Loans are made to individuals within the group, which has between 30 to 40 members depending on the institution and location.

In a study by Morduch [20], it has been observed that village banks have the highest portfolio yields (indicator of financial self-sufficiency) and expense ratios (indicator of operating cost self-sufficiency), but at the same time has the lowest return on assets (indicator of profitability). The individual based lenders are observed to have the most financial and cost efficient mode of operations and are also the most profitable.

For RP, the MIX data can only specify the type of market, i.e. poor vis-à-vis better-off clients. Rural banks usually lend individually. Grameen type rural banks loan to groups, but liability is rendered to each individual member of the group. NGOs lend to groups but liability for loans can either be individual or by group. But accounting for liability cannot be observed from the MIX data. From Figure 5, it can be observed that rural banks have financial and cost efficient mode of operations and are also the most profitable [21-24].

This observation shows that the analysis of the operational efficiency by lending type i, referring to either individual-based lenders such as rural banks, or, group lenders or NGOs, across j firms and t years, from 2003 to 2011, would be affected by the level of operating and transactions cost, and vice versa. When costs per loan transaction are placed as dependent variable, the equation may be interpreted as a supply for loans function, obtaining the regression procedure to account for Objective 2 of the study. The basic regression model to be used, with the personnel expense ratio used an the indicator for human asset specificity, is as follows:

Transactions Cost$_{ijt}$ (Personnel Expense Ratio) = α$_{ij}$ + β$_1$ OSS$_{ijt}$ + β$_2$ Average Loan Balance per Borrower$_{ijt}$ + β$_3$ Average Loan Balance per Borrower Squared$_{ijt}$ + β$_4$ Number of Active Borrowers$_{ijt}$ + β$_5$ Capital Cost$_{ijt}$ + β$_6$ Gross Loan Portfolio per Asset$_{ijt}$ + β$_7$ Age upon Establishment$_{ijt}$ + β$_8$ Scale$_{ijt}$ + β$_9$ Outreach$_{ijt}$ + β$_{10}$ Number of Women Borrowers$_{ijt}$ + β$_{11}$ Social Efficiency Index$_{ijt}$ + ε$_{it}$ (4)

Due to the large percentage share of personnel expense per dollar of loan to operating expense per dollar of loan, the same set of explanatory variables in Equation (5) shall also be done with operating expense per dollar of loan, the indicator for unit cost for the supply curve equation, as dependent variable:

Operating Costs$_{ijt}$ (Operating Cost per Dollar of loan) = α$_{ij}$ + β$_1$ OSS$_{ijt}$ + β$_2$ Average Loan Balance per Borrower$_{ijt}$ + β$_3$ Average Loan Balance

Transactions Cost (Personnel Expense per US$100 of Loan) of Rural Banks (RB) and NGOs from 2000 to 2011 by Age							
Annual Transactions Cost (Personnel Expense per US$100 of Loan)	Age						Remarks on Outreach
	Young		Mature		Total		
	RB	NGOs	RB	NGOs	RB	NGOs	
Low: Less than $26	0	4	46	10	46	14	Narrow to moderate
Moderate: $26-$50	1	2	2	10	3	12	
High: $51-$100	0	0	0	3	0	3	Moderate to broad with several network affiliations
Total	1	6	48	23	49	29	

Note: Commercial sources of funds is the usual source of funding for all MFIs.

Table 1: Transactions Cost (Personnel Expense per US$100 of Loan) of Rural Banks (RB) and NGOs from 2000 to 2011 by Age.

per Borrower Squared$_{ijt}$ + β$_4$ Number of Active Borrowers$_{ijt}$ + β$_5$ Capital Cost$_{ijt}$ + β$_6$ Gross Loan Portfolio per Asset$_{ijt}$ + β$_7$ Age upon establishment$_{ijt}$ + β$_8$ Scale$_{ijt}$ + β$_9$ Outreach$_{ijt}$ + β$_{10}$ Number of Women Borrowers$_{ijt}$ + β$_{11}$ Social Efficiency Index$_{ijt}$ + ε$_{it}$ (5)

The dependent variable is transactions cost, indicated by personnel expense per average loan balance per borrower, the indicator used for human asset specificity. Transactions cost also signifies the personnel cost per dollar of loan. It shall be regressed on OSS (operational self-sufficiency by MFI institution, i.e. rural bank or NGO), average loan balance per borrower, the square of the average loan balance per borrower (to capture either an asymptotic behavior or a U-shaped curve, number of active borrowers). MFI History would refer to age and scale of the MFI, and, orientation would refer to the target market or outreach and type of outreach such as the number of women borrowers. The capital structure indicator shall not use the debt-to-equity ratio but shall use the gross loan portfolio over assets, as the debt-to-equity ratio for MFIs would need more information on funding sources. Note that the expected signs for Equations (4) and (5) are the same as the expected signs for Equations (2) and (3), and the explanatory variables are the same except for an additional variable which the square of the average loan balance per borrower which serves as the indicator for the behavior of costs.

If the supply curve is expected to be U-shaped, then the curve reaches a minimum level of costs then starts to increase as the amount of loans by micro-entrepreneurs increases. More loan officers and personnel have to be employed in order to process and assess the viability of bigger loan amounts, as well as assess the credit history and capacity to pay of the borrower. When the supply curve of MFIs starts to slope upwards, then one can say that the behavior of the loan officers and personnel would compare and follow the usual behavior of personnel employed in commercial banks. Note that Equations (4) and (5) incorporate the experience or learning curve spillover indicators. These regressors aim to capture the existence of a supply curve in the microfinance industry that is primarily denoting a downward-sloping experience or learning curve. When the learning curve spillovers are large enough as to influence players in the industry to achieve better monitoring of clients, then an industry-wide decrease in operating and transactions cost is expected to occur, prolonged, verified by an asymptotic marginal cost curve that flattens at a minimum point. It may start increasing as cumulated output increases, that is, when micro-borrowers are more capable of handling and managing larger loans for their micro-businesses.

MFIs listed in the Microfinance Information Exchange Portal (MIX), opt to be transparent with their data, and thus, their financial and operational viability. This attempt would imply that they observe the rules on the financial and operational self-sufficiency indicators imposed on all MFIs. However, the two main types of lenders studied: rural banks (mostly individual lenders) and NGOs (combination of individual and group lenders), would competitively behave differently, i.e. outreach vis-à-vis profitability. Thus, the NGOs will have to be analyzed separately from the rural banks. Some types of lenders try to attract the better-off borrowers (high profitability ratios) and/or sustainable borrowers (low operational costs). This may be true for rural banks. Other lenders, such as NGOs, target poorer borrowers.

Data Sources

Data for the study was obtained from the Microfinance Information Exchange Portal (MIX), which accounts for close to 60% of the total number of active borrowers around the world. MIX is the premier source, open access, incorporated since 2002, for relevant microfinance performance data and analysis. MIX provides performance information on microfinance institutions (MFIs), funders, networks and service providers dedicated to serving the financial sector needs for low-income clients. MIX fulfills its mission through a variety of platforms.

The MIX Market provides instant access to financial and social performance information covering approximately 2,000 MFIs around the world. MIX is a non-profit organization headquartered in Washington, DC with regional offices in Azerbaijan, India, Morocco, and Peru.

The current study uses the MIX portal for financial and social performance data for 104 MFIs, i.e. rural banks, NGOs and credit cooperatives. A total of only 50 MFIs: 18 Rural Banks and 32 NGOs, with historical data from 1998 to 2011, are included in the dataset. Not all MFIs have a complete set of financial and social performance indicator for all the years specified.

Analysis of Results

Descriptive analysis of the operational efficiency and social performance for MFIs

From the above-stated objective 1, that is, an evaluation of MFI performance based on financial viability and outreach, show the following results. A comparison of operational self-sufficiency, and outreach was done with rural banks and NGOs based on the MIX Portal database from 2000-2011 with a total of 50 rural banks and 32 NGO. It can be seen that more mature MFIs are able to achieve lower levels of personnel expense per dollar of loan, i.e. less than US$ 26.00. Due to the strict regulatory nature of the commercial banking system, most rural banks are able to control their transactions to less than US$ 26.00.

Not only are rural banks able to control their transactions cost, they are also able to strictly observe low risk and financially sustainable operations. NGOs, most of whom are not regulated, operate to sustain profits, decrease risk but increase outreach. Most rural banks are mature, whose client size mostly have a medium to large asset size. Also, rural banks have a market clientele or target market ranging from micro firms (better-off micro firms) to small and high end businesses. NGOs vary from young and new to mature firms. Client outreach is composed of small to large firms (by asset size). But NGOs primarily target low end (or poor) businesses as clients, indicated by a narrow to moderate level of outreach (Tables 1 and 2).

Rural banks are primarily focused on profitability as seen in the average profit margin, OSS and ROA's of the 50 listed rural banks in the MIX Portal. Cost per borrower is close to double that of NGOs but NGOs have more than double the number of active borrowers. Loans extended by rural banks are more than double that of NGOs (Table 3), for the specific MFIs).

Very little improvements in operational efficiency can be observed from 2000-2005 and 2006 to 2012. One can observe an increase in the average loan balance per borrower as the well an increase in the number of active borrowers for both rural banks and NGOs (Table 4).

Slight improvements in operational efficiency through the operational self-sufficiency indicator, can be observed with NGOs. However, their social efficiency index falls within poor levels, with

Transactions Cost (Personnel Expense per US$100 of Loan)	Age and Operational Self-Sufficiency (OSS)												Total		Remarks on Outreach
	Young						Mature								
	RB			NGOs			RB			NGOs			Rural Banks	NGOs	
	OSS <1	OSS ≥1	Total	OSS <1	OSS ≥1	Total	OSS <1	OSS ≥1	Total	OSS <1	OSS ≥1	Total			
Low: Less than $26			0		4	4	2	44	46	2	8	10	46	14	Narrow to moderate
Moderate: $26-$50	1		1	2		2	2		2	2	8	10	3	12	
High: $51-$100			0			0			0		3	3	0	3	Moderate to broad with several network affiliations
Total	0	1	1	0	6	6	4	44	48	7	16	23	49	29	

Note: The lowest level of operational self-sufficiency achieved by a bank from 2000 to 2011 is 0.48, and, 0.18 for NGOs for all samples. Commercial sources of funds is the usual source of funding for all MFIs.

Table 2: Transactions Cost (Personnel Expense per US$100 of Loan) of Rural Banks (RB) and NGOs (2000 to 2011) by Age and Operational Self-Sufficiency (OSS).

Relevant Information on Chosen Rural Banks and NGOs (2000-2011)				
Cost per Borrower (US$)	Number of Active Borrowers	Average Loan Balance per Borrower (US$)	Average Loan Balance per Borrower per capita Gross National Income (in %)	Total Operating Expenses over Total Loans (in %)
Rural Banks				
102	17,436	668	46	22
79	9,683	454	33	19
528	267,282	7,139	521	92
20	208	46	4	2
194	256	256	255	229
NGOs				
44	52,380	118	8	45
38	18,603	93	6	41
165	606,488	1,414	69	124
11	837	30	3	20
183	226	226	223	189

Table 3: Relevant Information on Chosen Rural Banks and NGOs (2000-2011).

a slight improvement to moderate level in 2006 to 2012. One can compare this with rural banks, whose social efficiency index improved in 2006-2012. The social efficiency index is computed as the cost per dollar of loan (or operating expense ratio) over cost per borrower and allows one to compare MFIs with different credit methodologies. NGOs seem to face several factors which make the cost of per dollar of loan more expensive. For example, MFIs in the Philippines provide complementary services such as health or training which will increase operating expenses but are not directly related to the cost of providing the loan. For NGOs, however, these complementary services allow them to fulfill their outreach mission.

Learning curve spillover and U-shaped supply curve analysis

All the regression results made use of a pooled least squares with cross-section random effects model. The estimation obtained a strong correlation between fixed and random effects, as the heterogeneity among rural banks and NGOs takes into account the varying intercepts, the indicator of fixed costs, of the regressions obtained per firm. The random effects model gave the correct signs for the explanatory variables, thereby giving sound theoretical results. The Durbin-Watson statistic obtained in all the regressions was less than 1.4, indicating problems of serial correlation. Problems of endogeneity among the explanatory variables are expected in the regression, as the other explanatory variables were meant to explain operational self-sufficiency, which was used as a regressor in the estimation procedure (Figure 6).

In spite of all the limitations of the regression model used, the study focuses on the level of significance that would be obtained from the coefficients of the cumulated output indicators. The levels of significance obtained from the regression with random effects and the regression without random effects did not differ significantly.

The regression on the learning curve and the U-shaped supply curve shall use the following variables with their corresponding significance and expected sign (Table 5). Specific indicators shall be observed in the regressions: (a) For the experience or learning curve spillover regression, the presence of spillovers among MFIs shall be captured through a learning curve that levels-off as the amount of cumulated output over time increases. These indicators shall be age and the square of age upon establishment, and average loan balance per borrower; (b) For a U-shaped supply curve, also known as the U-shaped marginal cost curve, the presence of a downward-sloping experience or learning curve is expected either to be asymptotic to the cumulated output indicator or that it reaches a minimum then increases as the supply of loans increases. The coefficients of the experience or learning curve spillovers are expected to be significant and negative.

From Table 6 we would observe a lower coefficient level, in absolute terms, for age upon establishment for rural banks than for NGOs, as a lower coefficient for age would refer to a higher experience or learning curve spillover rate, the reciprocal of the coefficient indicates the spillover rate. The square of age is positive and moderately significant for the regression for NGOs and rural banks, stating that the curve flattens as age increases. The slower learning process for NGOs may be due to the high social efficiency index as NGOs face high levels of operational expenses when training loan officers and personnel, following-up and educating micro-borrowers.

When the dependent variable is changed into the asset specificity indicator, which is the personnel expense ratio, it can be observed that the learning curve flattens out with age, but the regression result no longer holds age and the square of age as a significant explanatory variable for rural banks, only for NGOs (Figure 7).

The average loan balance per borrower for rural banks and NGOs continues to be negative and moderately significant with the regression on transactions cost. We can conclude that the experience or learning curve spillover phenomenon among MFIs is explained by increasing average loan balance per borrower and age for NGOs. For rural banks, age of the establishment no longer explains transactions cost (Table 7). Once the operational expense ratio has reached a low level of US$20, asset specificity no longer plays a significant role as micro-borrowers increase their average loan size. The goal of continuing efficient operations along with social performance requires a high level of capability among loan officers and personnel when dealing with higher average loan portfolios among micro-entrepreneurs. NGOs, on the other hand, are already on their way to achieving higher spillover effects. Both operating costs and transactions cost are not yet achieving an asymptotic level, but they are decreasing.

The succeeding regressions shall now combine the phenomenon of experience or learning curve spillovers with the presence of a U-shaped supply curve. This time, the other indicator for accumulated output, average loan balance per borrower, shall be used. This is also the indicator for output for the U-shaped supply curve (Figure 8).

When the personnel expense ratio, the indicator used for asset specificity is graphed using average loan balance per borrower on the abscissa, a steep downward sloping experience curve can be observed not only for NGOs but also for rural banks. While the evidence of a flattening experience can be observed with rural banks, the experience curve for NGOs seem to be reaching a low personnel cost per dollar of loan. The average loan balance per borrower, however, has not increased and thus a flattening experience curve cannot be observed (Figure 9).

From the regression results of Table 8, one can see the consistently negative sign of operational self-sufficiency and outreach for both NGOs and rural banks. The extent of outreach through the social efficiency index and the high level of operational self-sufficiency all seem to go hand-in-hand with a steeply downward sloping operating and personnel cost vis-à-vis age upon establishment and the average loan balance per borrower. Only rural banks seem to manifest a slightly increasing marginal cost curve, denoting the well-behaved portion of the supply curve for an individual firm.

Thus, in response to objective 2, the results from Table 9 seem to indicate that only rural banks are starting to manifest a well-behaved supply curve as they are no longer operating at the steep portion of the marginal cost curve (Figures 8 and 9). Operating costs are decreasing as the average amount of loan portfolio increase. The learning curve spillover effects among rural banks is already manifesting a marginal cost curve that has reached a minimum level, and is on its way towards an upward sloping marginal cost curve. On the other hand NGOs, most of whom have a narrow extent of outreach, i.e. only dealing

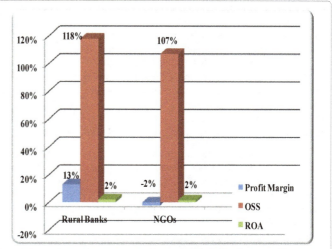

Figure 5: Profit margin, Operational Self-sufficiency and Return on Assets for Rural Banks and NGOs (MIXmark data).

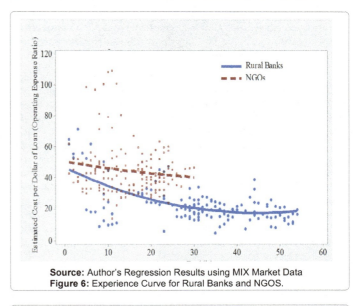

Source: Author's Regression Results using MIX Market Data
Figure 6: Experience Curve for Rural Banks and NGOS.

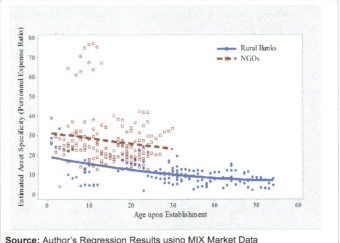

Source: Author's Regression Results using MIX Market Data
Figure 7: Experience Curve for Rural Banks and NGOs with Asset Specificity.

with small borrowers, and, with smaller average loan portfolios per borrower than rural banks, do not reflect an upward sloping marginal cost curve. In fact, most NGOs are not yet operating at the minimum level of operating costs, unlike that of rural banks. Average loan balance per borrower hardly reach US$500 (Figure 9). Transactions costs for NGOs, however, are approaching the minimum level reached by rural banks but over-all operating cost, that is, cost per dollar of loan, are still far from the minimum level of operating costs per dollar of loan achieved by rural banks. International regulatory bodies for MFIs put the standard to be within the range of US$10-US$26 per dollar of loan.

The results of the regressions may indicate that NGOs are devoting resources on operations which will enable them to extend loans to micro-borrowers. Efficient operations seem to be compromised by the need to monitor, educate and follow-up repayments done by micro-entrepreneurs. This phenomenon may explain why, in spite of a levelling-off of the cost per dollar of loan as well as transactions cost for rural banks, their social efficiency index is positively related to cost. This observation may be verified by the comparison of operational self-sufficiency and the social efficiency index. This result may suggest that NGOs have to re-think their organization and operations so as to achieve better levels of operational self-sufficiency and social performance efficiency, as their attempt to increase the outreach of their social projects might be comprised with less efficient operations and therefore sacrificing financial sustainability.

The extent of capitalization of the MFI may be indicated by the debt-to-equity ratio and the gross loan portfolio over assets. In principle, MFIs should not lend beyond their level of assets. Thus, more efficient operations may be indicated by a negative relationship of this indicator with costs. Both MFIs and rural banks seem to reflect this negative relationship. However, the structure of debt would be indicated by the debt-to-equity ratio. Efficiency would again be reflected by a negative relationship of this indicator with costs. However, this behavior can only be observed with rural banks as the debt-to-equity ratio has a positive relationship with costs for NGOs. This regression result may verify that NGOs have an extensive source of grants that help cover their outreach activities. However, such expenses do not seem to allow a healthy level of operational self-sufficiency and social efficiency index for NGOs (Figure 10).

It can be observed that a social efficiency index which is greater than 100 is likely to have an operational self-sufficiency that is lower than 1.0. This trend is most observed with NGOs. The social efficiency index for some rural banks, though, may fall within the moderate range but would report an operational self-sufficiency level which is lower than 1.0. Most of these rural banks loan more than 10%, the regulated level by the Bangko Sentral ng Pilipinas, of their credit line to MFIs.

The research hypotheses that were tested in the study led to the following results: Hypothesis for rural banks. Operating costs for rural banks have manifested higher experience or learning curve spillovers and lesser transactions cost than NGOs.

This phenomenon is observed to be explained by their longer commercial lending experience, and, their strict observance of industry standards for operational self-sufficiency. With efficiency gains, rural banks are operating at the low marginal cost levels in the supply curve attributed to the individual lending mode of transactions done among rural banks involved with MFI operations which follow the traditional or market-oriented manner of transacting with clients. Lower transactions cost among rural banks enable them to achieve high operational efficiency. Empirically, the presence of lower transactions

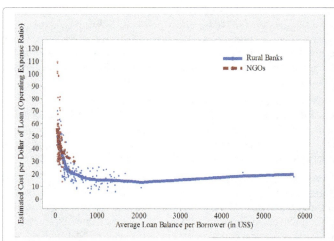

Source: Author's Regression Results using MIX Market Data
Figure 8: Estimated U-shaped Supply curve for Rural Banks and NGOs (2000-2001).

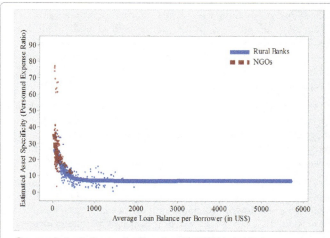

Source: Author's Regression Results using MIX Market Data.
Figure 9: Transactions cost with Experience or Learning Curve spillovers.

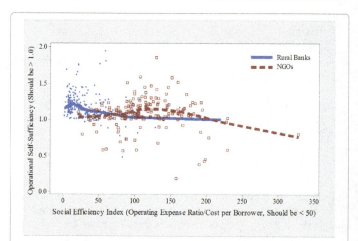

Source: MIX Data
Note: SEI<30 Excellent, 30<SEI<50 Good, 50 <SEI<100 Moderate, SEI >100 Poor
Figure 10: Operational and social outreach Effiency among Rural Banks and NGOs.

Annual Transaction Cost (in US$)	Age													Remarks
	Young						Mature						Total	
	Rural Banks			NGOs			Rural Banks			NGOs			Rural Banks / NGOs	
	OSS < 1	OSS > 1	Total	OSS < 1	OSS > 1	Total	OSS < 1	OSS > 1	Total	OSS < 1	OSS > 1	Total	Rural Banks / NGOs	
Low: Less than $26	0	0	0	0	FCBFI, JVOFI, HSPFI	3	RB Datu Paglas	Bangko Santiago de Libon, Bangko Kabayan, Bangko Luzon, Bangko Mabuhay, BCB Cantilan Bank, CBMO, FICO, First Macro Bank, GM Bank, Mallig Plains RB, New RB Victorias, PR Bank, RB Bagac, RB Cainta, RB Camalig, RB Cotabato, RB Dipolog, RB Digos, RB Guinobatan, RB Labason, RB Lebak, RB Liloy, RB Loon, RB Mabitac, RB Makiling, RB Oroquieta, RB Pagbilao, RB San Enrique, RB Solano, RB Sto. Tomas, RB Talisayan, RB Tangub City, Valiant RB	35	VEF, ASHI, ECLOF-Philippines, MEDF, PMDF, PALFSI	CMEDFI, Serviamus	8	35 / 11	Funding mainly via commercial sources, outreach is narrow to moderate
Moderate: $26-$50	0	0	0	0	0	0	0	1st Valley Bank, FAIR Bank, PBC, RB Montevista, Progressive Bank	5	CEVI	Kasagana-Ka, Kazama Grameen, KCCDFI, MILAMDEC	5	5 / 5	
High: $51-$100	0	RB San Jacinto	1	0	DSPI	1	OMB	K Bank, RB Katipunan	3	0	ABS-CBN, ARDCI, ASKI, DSPI, RSPI	5	4 / 6	Funding via commercial sources and grants, outreach is moderate to broad, several network affiliations
Very High: > $100	0	0	0	PAGASA	ASA Philippines, Life Bank	3	OK Bank	Card Bank, Green Bank	3	0	CARD-NGO, KMBI, NWTF, TSKI, TSPI	5	3 / 8	
Total	0	1	1	1	6	7	2	43	45	7	16	23	47 / 30	High information cost, possible via funding sources, especially for NGOs. Target varies from poor borrowers to SMEs.

Source: MIX Market Data

Note: The lowest level of operational self-sufficiency achieved by a bank from 2000 to 2011 is 0.48, and, 0.18 for NGOs for all samples. Rural Banks and NGOs in green have a positive ROS and ROE, those in red have a negative ROS and ROE averaged from 2000 to 2011.

Table 4: Transaction Cost per Borrower of Rural Banks and NGOs (2000 to 2011) by Age, Operational Self-Sufficiency (OSS) and Profitability (Return on Assets (ROS) and Return on Equity (ROE))

Selected Indicators for Operational Efficiency and Social Performance											
Descriptive Statistics		Average Loan Balance per Borrower		Operational Self-Sufficiency		Social Efficiency Index[2]		Personnel Productivity		Loan Officer Productivity	
		2000-2005	2006-2012	2000-2005	2006-2012	2000-2005	2006-2012	2000-2005	2006-2012	2000-2005	2006-2012
Rural Banks	Mean	490	769	1.19	1.16	39	27	103	104	72	86
	Median	375	495	1.16	1.13	23	19	96	98	60	50
	Maximum	2461	7139	1.95	1.91	219	163	195	1,040	490	871
	Minimum	46	62	0.66	0.48	9	2	41	11	6	1
NGOs	Mean	76	129	1.04	1.09	139	97	133	182	137	322
	Median	70	109	1.06	1.08	134	95	132	70	132	126
	Maximum	214	470	1.58	1.85	229	229	198	727	284	1,884
	Minimum	30	44	0.18	0.38	47	21	44	11	46	8
World Average[1]	East Asia				>1.0		11-14		110%-120%		200%-280%	
	Eastern Europe						26-45		60%-90%		155%-190%	
	Latin America						27-37		110%-140%		300%-310%	
	World						<10-47		High productivity, excellent asset quality			

Notes: [1]World Average uses 2009 to 2012 data
[2]Excellent < 30, Good 30-50, Moderate 50-100, Poor > 100

Table 5: Selected Indicators for Operational Efficiency and Social Performance

Variables Used for the Learning Curve and U-Shaped Supply Curve Regressions		
Variable Used	Relevance and Expected Sign for all Regressions	Computation and Commercial Bank or Traditional Banking Equivalent
Operational Expense Ratio also called Cost per Dollar of Loan.	• This ratio provides the best indicator of the overall efficiency of a lending institution. Also referred to as the Efficiency Ratio, measuring the institutional cost of delivering loan services compared to the average loan size of its portfolio. • Therefore, a general rule is the lower the Operating Expense Ratio, the higher the efficiency. • This variable is used as the dependent variable for the regression in the learning curve, indicator for cost per unit.	• Operating Expense over Average Loan Portfolio. • Goal is lower than 35% for urban MFIs but leading MFIs have 10% or lower. • Similar to the Efficiency Ratio or Cost/Income ratio used by the traditional banking sector to determine how efficiently the bank uses its assets and liabilities within internal operations related to the loan portfolio. This ratio measures the amount of non-interest expenses (operating expenses, excluding provisions of loan losses) needed to support operating revenues.
Personnel Expense Ratio	• Used as an indicator for asset specificity, or, human asset specificity. • Used as the dependent variable for the regression on transaction cost as asset specificity.	• Compensation or salaries over Average Loan Portfolio • No equivalent with the traditional banking sector
Operational Self-Sufficiency	• Indicator for Financial Self-Sufficiency, and, thus sustainability. • Used as an explanatory variable for the learning curve and transactions cost regression. • Expected to have a negative sign • MFIs operate with the goal of achieving sustainability. Thus, it acts as an explanatory variable for indicating efficiency of operations	• Financial Revenue over (Financial Expense + Impairment Loss + Operating Expense) • Financial revenues are revenues from the loan portfolio and from other financial assets and are broken out separately and by type of income (interest, fee). • Equal to or greater than 100% • No equivalent with the traditional banking sector
Average Loan Portfolio	• Gross loan portfolio over number of active borrowers. • Used as an indicator for supply of loans, also indicating cumulated output over time and is expected to have a negative sign for all regressions	
Square of Average Loan Portfolio	• Indicator for a U-shaped supply curve and is therefore expected to have a positive sign for all regressions	
Number of Active Borrowers	• The number of individuals or entities who currently have an outstanding loan balance with the MFI or are primarily responsible for repaying any portion of the Gross Loan Portfolio. Individuals who have multiple loans with an MFI are counted as a single borrower. • Used as an explanatory variable for the regression on the learning curve and U-shaped supply curve. • Expected to have a positive sign	
Debt to Equity Ratio	• The simplest and best-known measure of capital adequacy because it measures the over-all leverage of the institution. Hard to put a standard level as MFIs have various sources of local and international funding • It is of particular interest to lenders because it indicates how much of a safety cushion (in the form of equity) there is in the institution to absorb losses. • Expected to have either a positive or negative sign	• Computed as total liability over total equity as in the traditional banking sector • Reveals the extent to which the bank funds operations with debt rather than equity, allowing banks to monitor solvency and analyze their capital structure. • Varies considerably depending on the type of institution. NGOs typically have lower Debt/Equity (1:1 to 3:1) levels than regulated MFIs, such as rural banks, which even have lower levels than commercial banks. The only way to strengthen an NGO's equity is by reinvesting profits or through grants and donations.

Gross Loan Portfolio over Assets	• Indicator for all outstanding principals due for all outstanding client loans per dollar of assets, includes all outstanding client loans (current, delinquent and renegotiated, except those written-off) and includes interest receivables. • Expected to have either a positive or negative sign	
Age upon Establishment	• Age upon establishment as a rural bank or as an MFI. • Indicator for accumulated output over time • Used as explanatory variable for the learning curve regression and U-shaped supply curve regression • Expected to have a negative sign	
Square of Age upon Establishment	• Indicator for a learning curve that levels-off with a high level of accumulated output, due to the phenomenon of spill-overs. • Expected to have a positive sign	
Outreach	• Large Number of borrowers > 30,000 • Medium Number of borrowers 10,000 to 30,000 • Small Number of borrowers < 10,000 • Categorical variable: 1 refers to small, 2 refers to medium, 3 refers to large • Expected to have either a positive or negative sign	
Scale	• Large: Africa, Asia, ECA, MENA: >8 million; LAC: >15 million; • Medium: Africa, Asia, ECA, MENA: 2 million–8 million; LAC: 4 million–15 million; • Small: Africa, Asia, ECA, MENA: <2 million; LAC: <4 million • Categorical variable: 1 refers to small, 2 refers to medium, 3 refers to large • Expected to have either a positive or negative sign	
Percent of Women Borrowers	• Number of women over total number of active borrowers. An indicator of outreach as some NGOs focus on servicing women. • Used as an explanatory variable and may have a positive or negative sign	
Social Efficiency Index	• A proxy for how efficiently the institution is providing loans while neutralizing the effects of average loan size on efficiency (both operating expense ratio and cost per borrower are each heavily influenced by the loan size). • The Social Efficiency Index allows for a more direct comparison of different types of MFIs with different credit methodologies. • Used as an explanatory variable for the regression on the learning curve and transactions cost. • Expected to have either a positive or negative sign.	• Operating Expense Ratio over Cost per Borrower (Operating Expenses over Number of Active Borrowers). This is an index. • No equivalent with the traditional banking sector

Note: From Figure 1 it can be observed that rural banks do have higher experience or learning curve spillover rates than NGOs, when we use age upon establishment as the indicator for spillover effects.

Table 6: Variables Used for the Learning Curve and U-Shaped Supply Curve Regressions

Experience or Learning Curve Spillover Regression (For Rural Banks and NGOs) Method: Pooled Least Squares with Cross-Section Random Effects					
Explanatory Variables	**Expected Sign**	**Operating Expense per Average Loan Portfolio**			
		Rural Banks		NGOs	
C	+	69.52	***	122.69	***
		6.41		12.58	
Operational Self-Sufficiency (OSS)	−	−11.58	***	−22.70	***
		2.81		4.48	
Average Loan Balance per Borrower	−	−0.002	**	−0.04	**
		0.001		0.02	
Number of Active Borrowers	+	8.81E-05	***	1.74E-05	*
		1.72E-05		1.16E-05	
Debt-to-Equity Ratio	+ or −	−0.90	***	0.03	na
		0.29		0.12	
Gross Loan Portfolio over Total Assets	+ or −	−30.91	***	−56.29	***
		4.79		5.89	
Age upon Establishment	−	−0.40	**	−0.71	*
		0.22		0.62	
Age upon Establishment Squared	+	0.005	*	0.03	*
		0.004		0.02	
Scale (1 small, 2 medium, 3 large)	+ or −	−3.56	***	1.57	na
		1.03		1.40	

Outreach (1 small, 2 medium, 3 large)	+ or -	1.08	na	-0.95	na
		0.96		1.78	
Women Borrowers as a Percent of Total Borrowers	+ or -	3.59	**	-7.72	na
		1.77		6.26	
Social Efficiency Index	+ or -	0.07	***	0.01	na
		0.02		0.03	
Adjusted R-squared		0.53		0.39	
F-statistic		15.45		10.71	
Durbin-Watson Statistic		1.35		0.82	
Cross-Sections Included		45		29	
Total Unbalanced Panel Observations		140		165	
Years Covered		2001-2011		2000-2011	

Source: Author's Estimates, MIX Market Data
Note: Italicized numbers refer to the standard deviation. Regression uses White diagonal standard errors and covariance (degrees of freedom corrected). All p-values of the F-statistic are very significant or p less than 0.01.
p-values used are: *** p less than 0.01, ** p less than 0.05 and greater than 0.01, * p less than 0.15 and greater than 0.05. Swamy and Arora estimator of component variances.

Table 7: Experience or Learning Curve Spillover Regression (For Rural Banks and NGOs) Method: Pooled Least Squares with Cross-Section Random Effects

		Experience or Learning Curve Spillover Regression and Asset Specificity (For Rural Banks and NGOs) Method: Pooled Least Squares with Cross-Section Random Effects			
Explanatory Variables	**Expected Sign**	**Personnel Expense per Average Loan Portfolio**			
		Rural Banks		**NGOs**	
C	+	25.93	***	59.15	***
		3.47		8.09	
Operational Self-Sufficiency (OSS)	-	-6.46	***	-17.47	***
		1.69		2.71	
Average Loan Balance per Borrower	-	-0.0005	*	-0.03	**
		0.0004		0.02	
Number of Active Borrowers	+	4.66E-05	***	-3.01E-06	na
		6.71E-06		6.27E-06	
Debt-to-Equity Ratio	+ or -	-0.31	**	-0.04	na
		0.14		0.06	
Gross Loan Portfolio over Total Assets	+ or -	-7.48	***	-15.78	***
		2.29		3.93	
Age upon Establishment	-	0.10	na	-0.55	*
		0.11		0.43	
Age upon Establishment Squared	+	0.001	na	0.03	***
		0.002		0.01	
Scale (1 small, 2 medium, 3 large)	+ or -	-0.86	*	0.48	na
		0.51		0.90	
Outreach (1 small, 2 medium, 3 large)	+ or -	-0.65	*	0.59	na
		0.42		1.11	
Women Borrowers as a Percent of Total Borrowers	+ or -	1.12	*	-2.90	na
		0.77		3.32	
Social Efficiency Index	+ or -	0.08	***	0.04	*
		0.02		0.02	

Adjusted R-squared	0.58	0.33
F-statistic	13.51	7.07
Durbin-Watson Statistic	1.25	0.91
Cross-Sections Included	43	28
Total Unbalanced Panel Observations	102	136
Years Covered	2003-2010	2003-2011

Source: Author's Estimates, MIX Market Data
Note: Italicized numbers refer to the standard deviation. Regression uses White diagonal standard errors and covariance (degrees of freedom corrected). All p-values of the F-statistic are very significant or p less than 0.01.
p-values used are: *** p less than 0.01, ** p less than 0.05 and greater than 0.01, * p less than 0.15 and greater than 0.05. Swamy and Arora estimator of component variances.
Method: Pooled Least Squares with Cross-Section Random Effects
Table 8: Experience or Learning Curve Spillover Regression and Asset Specificity (For Rural Banks and NGOs).

U-Shaped Supply Curve Regression for Rural Banks and NGOs (With Transactions Cost and Experience or Learning Curve Spillovers) Method: Pooled Least Squares with Cross-Section Random Effects

Explanatory Variables	Expected Sign	Personnel Expense per Average Loan Portfolio				Operating Expense per Average Loan Portfolio			
		Rural Banks		NGOs		Rural Banks		NGOs	
C	+	26.10	***	49.94	***	68.23	***	113.69	***
		3.32		10.96		5.86		15.22	
Operational Self-Sufficiency (OSS)	-	-6.29	***	-17.24	***	-10.80	***	-22.04	***
		1.69		2.90		2.79		4.61	
Average Loan Balance per Borrower	-	-0.002	*	-0.01	na	-0.006	***	-0.03	na
		0.001		0.07		0.002		0.09	
Average Loan Balance per Borrower Squared	+	2.7E-07	*	-3.4E-05	na	9.3E-07	**	-2.3E-05	na
		2.2E-07		0.0001		3.7E-07		0.0002	
Number of Active Borrowers	+	4.7E-05	**	1.3E-06	na	8.0E-05	***	2.3E-05	**
		6.7E-06		6.3E-06		1.7E-05		1.1E-05	
Debt-to-Equity Ratio	+ or -	-0.32	**	-0.03	na	-1.00	***	-0.02	na
		0.14		0.06		0.28		0.12	
Gross Loan Portfolio over Total Assets	+ or -	-7.78	***	-15.02	***	-32.70	***	-56.01	***
		2.26		4.11		4.72		5.95	
Age upon Establishment	-	-0.04	*	0.42	**	-0.11	*	0.21	na
		0.04		0.22		0.07		0.29	
Scale (1 small, 2 medium, 3 large)	+ or -	-0.73	na	0.39	na	-2.93	***	1.16	na
		0.52		0.93		1.04		1.39	
Outreach (1 small, 2 medium, 3 large)	+ or -	-0.71	*	-0.20	na	0.68	na	-1.01	na
		0.43		1.11		1.00		1.79	
Number of Women Borrowers	+ or -	1.06	na	-2.50	na	3.94	**	-7.26	na
		0.77		3.49		1.75		6.32	
Social Efficiency Index	+ or -	0.06	***	0.05	*	0.06	***	0.02	na
		0.02		0.03		0.02		0.04	
Adjusted R-squared		0.58		0.30		0.55		0.39	
F-statistic		13.75		6.30		16.58		10.62	
Durbin-Watson Statistic		1.19		0.88		1.34		0.84	
Cross-Sections Included		43		28		45		29	
Total Unbalanced Panel Observations		102		136		140		165	

| Years Covered | 2003-2010 | 2003-2011 | 2001-2011 | 2000-2011 |

Source: Author's Estimates, MIX Market Data
Note: Italicized numbers refer to the standard deviation. Regression uses White diagonal standard errors and covariance (degrees of freedom corrected). All p-values of the F-statistic are very significant or p less than 0.01.
 p-values used are: *** p less than 0.01, ** p less than 0.05 and greater than 0.01, * p less than 0.15 and greater than 0.05. Swamy and Arora estimator of component variances.
Table 9: U-Shaped Supply Curve Regression for Rural Banks and NGOs (With Transactions Cost and Experience or Learning Curve Spillovers) Method: Pooled Least Squares with Cross-Section Random Effects.

cost denoting high learning or spillover effects have enabled rural banks to operate efficiently thereby allowing them to perform their outreach activities with more productivity and lesser cost. The satisfactory level of their social efficiency index indicates that financial and operational expenses are not compromised with extensive social outreach. All these indicators seem to precede the eventual occurrence of an upward sloping marginal cost curve, and thereby, allowing rural banks serving MFI clients to initiate operating at the well-behaved portion of the supply curve.

Hypothesis for NGOs Operating costs for NGOs have manifested lower experience or learning curve spillovers and have higher transactions cost than rural banks.

This phenomenon may be due to their shorter commercial lending experience, and, the non-regulated nature of their operations. Transactions cost among NGOs are high and are less likely to attain industry standards for operational self-sufficiency. With lesser efficiency gains, some NGOs may be experiencing disincentive effects, that is, being unable to increase their average loans credited to micro-borrowers, and, NGOs may not yet be operating at low marginal cost levels in the supply curve. This can be explained by the group lending with individual liability lending mode of transactions done among NGOs involved with MFI operations which do not follow the traditional or market-oriented manner of transacting with clients. Loan officers and personnel have to achieve a certain level or manner of negotiating capabilities to effectively deal with micro-borrowers. While still at the high level of transactions and operating costs, NGOs into microfinance are not yet in the capacity to operate at the well-behaved portion of the marginal cost curve, also known as the upward sloping supply curve. More efficient operations will have to be achieved while they attempt to accomplish their social outreach. Their social efficiency index seems to denote that financial resources are sacrificing operations thereby disallowing NGOs to operate more efficiently.

In terms of objectives of the study, the results are denoted (Table 10). The downward trend of cost per dollar of loan and transactions cost through time, indicated by age, establishes the presence of an experience or learning curve spillover for rural banks and NGOs. This is the result when the proxy variable in the scatterplot for cumulated output is time, that is, age upon establishment, per firm included in the data (Figures 6 and 7). When the proxy variable for cumulated output in the scatter plot is average loan balance per borrower, one can observe a very steep downward sloping marginal cost curve for NGOs and a U-shaped marginal cost curve for rural banks when the unit cost used is either cost per dollar of loan or transactions cost (Figures 8 and 9). This result establishes the need for a downward sloping with a levelling-off trend for cost per dollar of loan and transactions cost, before the marginal cost curve starts to increase. This phenomenon is observed only among rural banks, and denotes a U-shaped supply curve.

Efficient levels of operational self-sufficiency seems to coincide with the downward trend of transactions cost and cost per dollar of loan for both rural banks and NGOs. However, social outreach efficiency, indicated by a low social efficiency index, as of the moment, does not seem to coincide with the trend observed with costs as the social efficiency index has a positive relationship with costs [25-29].

Summary, Conclusion and Recommendation

The results of the study can be summarized by the combination of low operating and transactions costs, due to a fast learning environment due to high experience or learning curve spillovers, all seem to be positively related with a satisfactory or low social efficiency index. This combination of indicators allows the MFI to reach a minimum level of marginal costs, while at the same time allowing MFIs to operate efficiently and achieve an appropriate level of outreach. Higher levels of loans transacted by micro-entrepreneurs entail higher personnel and operational expenses in order to properly monitor larger loan portfolios. Only rural banks manifest this trend. On the other hand NGOs have to improve learning from the operations of other NGOs, thereby eventually achieving a higher level of spill-over effects. As of the moment, with a wide variety of micro-borrowers with very small loans, operational and transactions costs are still high, although showing a downward or decreasing trend through time.

The results lead to the following conclusion: high experience or learning curve spillovers in the microfinance industry allow lenders to learn from the experience of other lenders negotiating with micro-entrepreneurs. Learning from the experience of other MFIs allows the entire industry to reach a low level of operating and transactions costs. This level of costs, however, enables the MFI to appropriately reach its social outreach mission while at the same time achieve operational self-sufficiency, the indicator for financial viability used in the study [30,31]. This phenomenon, though, is being observed only among rural banks. NGOs are still operating at the steep portion of marginal costs but operating and transactions costs are showing a decreasing trend through time.

It is recommended that the observed relationships between the experience curve, operating costs, transactions costs and social efficiency be verified among a sample of MFIs so as to tract those costs which allow transactions and negotiations among micro-borrowers to be costly. Focusing the study on a few MFIs, who would represent a substantial proportion of active borrowers in the Philippines, would enable researchers to determine those costs, specifically costs related to human asset specificity, which explain why NGOs continue to operate at the steep portion of the marginal cost curve. With this intent, there seems to be a rationale behind the existence of a U-shaped supply curve for the microfinance industry of the Philippines, and for the microfinance industry, in general Verification of the existence of a U-shaped supply curve, through the presence of significant experience or learning curve spillovers before reaching the minimum level of marginal costs, may lead to the necessary conditions by which micro-lenders are able to reach an efficient level of costs and risks [32-34].

	Experience or Learning Curve Spillovers, Transactions Cost and a U-Shaped Supply Curve for Rural Banks and NGOs	
MFIs	Experience or Learning Curves (Objective 1)	Experience or Learning Curve Spillovers, Transactions Cost and a U-Shaped Supply Curve (Objective 2)
Rural Banks	Higher experience or learning curve spillovers translate to faster learning	1. Lower transactions cost, lower cost per dollar of loan, leading to a U-shaped supply curve 2. Excellent level of the social efficiency index but has a positive relationship to operating and transactions costs
NGOs	Lower experience or learning curve spillovers translate to slower to moderate learning	1. Higher transactions cost and operating expenses. NGOs still operate at the steep portion of the marginal cost curve 2. Poor level of the social efficiency index but has a positive relationship to operating and transactions cost

Source: Author's Regression Results.

Table 10: Experience or Learning Curve Spillovers, Transactions Cost and a U-Shaped Supply Curve for Rural Banks and NGOs

This efficient level of operations, which combine financial viability and social outreach, may be the starting point through which the microfinance industry, namely rural banks and NGOs, be included in the financial sector.

Refernces

1. Economic Intelligence Unit (EIU) (2013) Global Microscope on the Microfinance Business Environment. London, UK: Economic Intelligence Unit.
2. Richard R, Gaul S, Ford W, Tomilova O (2013) Microcredit Interest Rates and Their Determinants 2004-2011. Access to Finance Forum. Report by the Consultative Group to Assist the Poor (CGAP) and its Partners 69-104.
3. Arvind A (2009) Microcredit Capital Flows and Interest Rates: An Alternative Explanation Journal of EconomicIssues 661-683.
4. Microfinance Council (2006) Philippine Country Profile on Microfinance. Microfinance Information Exchange Portal 2011 Microfinance Report for the Philippines.
5. Beatriz A, Szafarz A (2011) On Mission Drift in Microfinance Institutions, in The Handbook of Microfinance: 341-366
6. James C (2007) Mainstreaming Microfinance: Social Performance Management or Mission Drift? World Development 35: 1721-1738.
7. Eduardo JC, Bernadette PR (2011) Case Study on Philippines Electronic Banking: Delivering Microfinance Services to the Poor in the Philippines".
8. Microfinance Information Exchange Portal (2011) Microfinance Report for the Philippines.
9. Oliver W (1989) Transaction Cost Economics in Handbook of Industrial Organization Volume 1: 150-159.
10. Oliver W (1975) Markets and Hierarchies:Analysis and Antitrust Implications.
11. George A (1970) The Market For 'Lemons': Quality Uncertainty and the Market Mechanism. Quarterly Journal of Economics 84: 488-500.
12. Stiglitz JE, Andrew W (1981) Credit Rationing in Markets with Imperfect Information American Economic Review 71: 393-410.
13. Svita S (2007) Transaction Costs in Group Microcredit in India.Management Decision 45: 1331-1342.
14. Richard R (2002) Microcredit Interest Rates.Consultative Group to Assist the Poor (CGAP) Washington DC.
15. Besanko, David D, Mark S, Scott S (2013) Economics of Strategy (6thedn), John Wiley and Sons 119-120
16. Kenneth AJ (1962) The economic implications of learning by doing. Review of Economic Studies 29: 155-173.
17. Peter T (2010) Learning by Doing in Handbook of the Economics of Innovation 1: 429-476.
18. Pankaj GA, Michael S (1985) Learning Curve Spillovers and Market Performance The Quarterly Journal of Economics 100: 839-852.
19. Spence A (1981) The Learning Curve and Competition. The Bell Journal of Economics 12: 49-70.
20. Cull R, Asli D, Jonathan M (2007) Financial Performance and Outreach: a Global Analysis of Leading Microbanks Economic Journal 117: F107-F133.
21. Balkenhol B, Hudon M (2011) Efficiency in The Handbook of Microfinance, Beatriz Armendáriz and Marc Labie. World Scientific Publishing, MA, USA 383-396
22. Bangko Sentral ng Pilipinas (2011) Financial Inclusion Initiatives Year-End Report.
23. Bazinzi N, Mangeni P, Nakabuye Z, Brendah A, Agasha E (2013) Transaction Costs and Outreach of Microfinance Institutions in Uganda. Issues in Business Management and Economics 1: 125-132.
24. Marvin B (1972) Perspectives on Experience. Boston, MA.
25. Jovi DC (2012) Can Outreach and Sustainability Co-Exist in the Microfinance Industry of the Philippines? An NGO and Rural Banks Performance Analysis 44.
26. Jovi DC (2014) Learning Curve Spillovers and Transactions Cost in the Microfinance Industry of the Philippines.
27. Dean KS, Jonathan M (2009) Handbook of Development Economics. Dani Rodrik and Mark Rosenzweig (eds). North Holland, Elsevier Science 5: 1-87.
28. Dean KS, Jonathan Z (2010) Expanding Credit Access: Using Randomized Supply Decisions to Estimate the Impacts Review of Financial Studies 23: 433-464.
29. Mcintosh C, Bruce W (2005) Competition and Microfinance Journal of Development Economics 78: 271-298.
30. Esubalew A, Niels H (2014) The Technical Guide: Performance and Social Indicators for Microfinance Institutions 23: 767-782.
31. Riordan HM, Oliver EW (1985) Asset Specificity and Economic Organization. International Journal of Industrial Organization 3: 365-378.
32. Saito KA, Villanueva DP (1981) Transaction Costs of Credit to the Small-Scale Sector in the Philippines Economic Development and Cultural Change 29: 631-640.
33. Louise TD (2012) Location and Performance of Microfinance Institutions Asian Research Publishing Network (ARPN). Journal of Science and Technology.
34. Tchamanbe DL (2009) bank failures in SSA.

Entrepreneurial Passion as Mediator of the Entrepreneurial Self Efficacy and Entrepreneurial Performance, Relationship: An Empirical Study in Small Medium Businesses

Muhammad Awais Siddiqui*

Management department, Allama Iqbal Open University, Pakistan

Abstract

On the Small Medium Enterprises, the paper aims to study the effects of entrepreneurial self- efficacy on entrepreneurial performance, while mediating the identity impact, that consider to be the important stimulating factor to drive passion in entrepreneurs for developing and founding new enterprises. From a source of self-efficacy and self-concordance theory perspective, the study assumes to apply exploratory factor analysis through direct oblimin rotation in order inspect discriminant validity concepts. Further, in order to analyze the causal relationship between entrepreneurial self-efficacy and entrepreneurial performance, while taking its mediating effect study apply hierarchical regression technique using SPSS. However, empirical findings allow us to understand the significant relationship between entrepreneurial self-efficacy and entrepreneurial performance. The study also suggests to explore the impact of identity in entrepreneurial passion further its relational impact on individual self-efficacy and performance through empirical findings. The study provides a mechanism that regularized passionate entrepreneur's self-efficacy and improves their individual performance.

Keywords: Entrepreneurship; Performance; Relationship; Small Medium Businesses; Mediator

Introduction

Performance required a great hardship, commitment and objectivity in order to attain the desired level among the competitors. Entrepreneurial commitment is a key indication that exerts consistent effort in the ups and downs of the enterprise [1]. In order to achieve desired enterprise goals, performance is a very important factor in entrepreneurship. For this it is very much important to understand which factors influence entrepreneurial performance.

The most influential factor that plays an important role to enhance performance in entrepreneurship is self-efficacy [2]. As Hallak et al. [3] in his study in the area of tourism management found self-efficacy as an important predictor of entrepreneurial performance and suggest that entrepreneurial self-efficacy as a strong predictor of high performance. Based on the self-efficacy theory [2] it is described as the individual confidence in his abilities that derive potential which stimulate him to ascertain enterprise performance. Self-efficacy is considered to be the critical factor in entrepreneurship because it continuously exerts a force to keep on performing even in the challenging situation [4]. When an individual believes that he can do it, then his confidence leads him to perform well in his entrepreneurial career.

It is observed that another critical factor that highly relate to entrepreneurial performance is identity impact, particularly in entrepreneurial passion [5]. Centered on the self-concordance model, self-identity includes connecting one's personality with certain behavior which encourage him to pursuit goals even when a person is getting sick of doing the same process [6].

Moreover, few researchers in different fields attempt to find out the association between entrepreneurial self-efficacy and performance [7] and also suggest that there is still need to examine how both of these constructs affect entrepreneurial performance in different field of study. So if our purpose mediating the relationship found, then this play a helping role in understanding the phenomena, with more clarity that, why self-efficacy is so impactful for entrepreneurial performance due to self-efficacy on entrepreneurial passion relationship.

However, our prime objective is to empirically examine the entrepreneurial role in view of its potential factors which have an impact on entrepreneurial performance. In past little attention is paid, particularly in an entrepreneurial role [8-14]. However Cardon et al. [5] shed a light on the passion as instinct factor that stimulate entrepreneurship role in a substantial way. Previously Cardon et al. [15] attempts to set, entrepreneurial passion as a criterion validity measure of entrepreneurial passion for founding and developing. Study results failed to find out the relationship of passion on developing, but found a unique relationship with entrepreneurial passion for founding. According to Cardon et al. [9] entrepreneurial passion for founding and developing are both the potential drivers of high performance, so that is why she suggests to find out their relationship because passion for developing is also a potential contributor to entrepreneurial performance [5]. Hence on the basis of his suggestion study aims to examine the relationship of both the potential drivers of passion on entrepreneurial performance because performance is a critical factor that advances the entrepreneurial career successfully. However, in the best of our information the relationship has not yet examined empirically between passion (developing and founding) and performance.

Secondly, the study aims to add to the work on self-efficacy and performance. On the other hand the relationship among self-efficacy and performance is well documented in small medium enterprises

---

*__*Corresponding author:__ Siddiqui MA, Management department, Allama Iqbal Open University, Pakistan, E-mail: Awaissiddiqui96@gmail.com*

[2]. The study aims to find out the relationship of entrepreneurial self-efficacy and performance while mediating the effect of passion in the model. We further suggest that inclusion of passion may diminish the importance of previous research results, but if research supports the study, then this may help to find out other potential factors which stimulate passion in order to achieve desired performance in entrepreneurship.

The research proceeded by reviewing the role of performance in entrepreneurship. Then we deliberate the potential effects of entrepreneurial self-efficacy on performance simultaneously through passion. Further study aims to find out the potential constructs passion for founding and developing impact by mediating its role. Then we aim to test the hypothesis at the end, we aim to discuss the results with implications.

Literature Review and Hypothesis

Performance in entrepreneurship

The performance requires objectivity to make the decision for specifications or goals [10]. Entrepreneurial Performance is the individual's ability to be effective in many careers (e.g., Medication, Store, Suppliers, Marketing, etc.) help to attain better outcomes in discussions [11], to obtain company success. Entrepreneurial performance is to promote primary company concepts, developing new products, identifying market opportunities, make a modern environment, building healthy investor relationships, and also ready to react upon amazing market patterns [12]. Entrepreneurial commitment level was a key indication of the best possible performance allowing entrepreneurs to keep continue to go on as they proceed against the opportunities and get over fatigue and pain to complete a procedure or meet a procedure [1]. For instance, the effective entrepreneurs might have or make excellent self-regulatory [13] systems that help them to notice, control, and improve their own performance, and that provide them with enhanced attention of their own perceptive highly effective factors [15,16]. Besides the many actions engaged further, acquiring a concept, financing the enterprise, purchasing the sources required, building a place of work, selecting staff, promotion the provider along with merchandise or more, one common business person requires many weeks to secure a completely new organization journey on the floor [16]. As a result of enormous cost effective dedication of time, attempt, along with investment into a completely new organization to have this started out, and the ongoing cost effective dedication connected with sources to take care of the business, up to the particular indicates useful overall performance is necessary during this process. However, performance is very much affected due to entrepreneurial functions, such as positive and negative effects [17], so on the reasons for that, many of us assimilate the outcomes in the discussion underneath involving two critical elements proposed inside materials do the job to get related to functionality, entrepreneurial self-efficacy [12] in addition to entrepreneurial passion [9].

Entrepreneurial self-efficacy and performance

Entrepreneurial self-efficacy is context specific valuate of self-efficacy. Based on "self-efficacy theory" [18] self-efficacy described as a person's perception in his abilities to proficiently accomplish the projects of business enterprise. It is usually approved that persons who regarded on their personal capability and sources will be effective in their initiatives and show greater performance level [19]. Self-efficacy is considered to be the best interpreter of an individual's performance in common [20]. Self-efficacy is usually a state such as characteristic that usually will increase together with encounter and is also extremely strongly related precise potential which influence the actual result [21]. For example, Cervone and Peake [22] discovered that the higher was the instated recognized self-efficacy, the longer people persevered on complicated and impossible problems before they quit. Therefore, people with a powerful sense of self efficacy will exert a higher level of attempt to get to know their responsibilities, and feature failing to things which are in their control, rather than accusing exterior aspects [23]. Thus, self-efficacy enables entrepreneurs to recover speedily via established facilitates, and at last will probably obtain their personalized objectives [18]. Conversely, people who have lower self-efficacy feel they cannot perform the job, and thus are generally less likely to make a critical, prolonged attempt as well as many consider complicated projects as risks that are to be prevented [24].

Self-efficacy specifically, is regarded the most immediate inspirational aspects of performance [25]. The link between self-efficacy and performance provided the emotional literary work that is the base for the individual self-efficacy scale. Procedures involved in small companies are due to the entrepreneurial techniques, actions, and abilities of the individuals. A lot of the business owners could be recognized via business owners depending on their own identity connected with entrepreneurial self-efficacy [26] the way it performs a crucial part in creating their entrepreneurial objectives which cause to accomplish great entrepreneurial performance [27]. Entrepreneurial self-efficacy impacts performance by impacting business owner passions, inspirations, and determination levels [26]. It is also favorably relevant to entrepreneurial performance [28]. For example, in a study of over 300 business supervisors, discovered a positive connection between entrepreneurial self-efficacy and entrepreneurial performance. They describe that when person have a question in his capability, then he is not able to execute well, hence self-efficacy performance relationship. Centered on prior self-efficacy research, we believe that entrepreneurial self-efficacy may positively relate to entrepreneurial performance even when they are experiencing complicated or uncertain difficulties in the company procedure. Thus, such powerful determining may cause to better results from the procedure. So, we hypothesize that:

Hypothesis 1: Entrepreneurial self-efficacy is positively related to entrepreneurial performance. Even though all of us predict making certain the company this link inside our exploration, all of us add to the literary functions by indicating that will enterprise awareness may mediate the hyperlink among entrepreneurial self-efficacy and performance. For this sort of mediation to occur, self-efficacy has to positively relate to passion and entrepreneurial passion should positively relate to entrepreneurial performance. We take the actual previous link first, then a second option.

Entrepreneurial self-efficacy and passion

Passion is determined as a different range of positive impacts, such as pleasure [29] really alike [30,31], understanding, along with happiness [32] which happen to include in the entrepreneurial process and gives a mental supply with regard to working with entrepreneurial difficulties. Appreciation has been related to travel, dedication, want to do the job expanded hours, bravery, fantastic stages associated with energy, along with dedication facing difficulties [29] in order to perform well [33]. For entrepreneurial passion, self-identity is regarded an essential element, and this can be deemed the "subjective perception of by yourself to be a person" [34]. Cardon et al. [5] boasts that will business passion likely be included quite possibly unique stages of desire to have distinct positions along with associated behavior that are frequent throughout entrepreneurship such as a desire to have creating possibilities, desire to have start brand-new firms, and also desire to have generating the organization. Therefore, to comprehend the passion of business owners, commitment along with self-efficacy and also performance, many of us consider just the identity-meaningfulness elements of the build by concentrating on the two particular factors associated with individual desire for founding and developing of business.

Passion is turned on not because some entrepreneurs are naturally getting rid of to such emotions, but rather, because they are involved in something that pertains to a significant self- identity for them [9]. Such as, acknowledgement notion shows that individuals will probably realize together with issues that they are confident throughout performing, so that you can safeguard their thoughts of self-efficacy [34]. Most entrepreneurs who are involved in identical role are more passionate toward creating and developing company. Therefore, identity identification is a fundamental piece of entrepreneurial passion, showing which self-efficacy must estimation your identity identification section of passion and individuals are generally fervent about the components of their identity that a lot of fulfill their particular self-esteem as well as self-efficacy needs [34]. This means that identity identification as a part of entrepreneurial passion and it may take place when self- efficacy is extremely good.

Entrepreneurial passion and performance

The other offered mediation is the relationship associated with entrepreneurial passion and performance. Individual passion, which include personality connected factor may perhaps enjoy an important aspect within enhancing upwards entrepreneurial efficiency. A good identity principle zoom lens, that supply helpful tips in wherever focus may well appear it affect performance [9].

Murnieks as well as Mosakowski [35] likewise create facts, in view of that enthusiasm is developed whenever a large entrepreneurial personality will be substantial. In the same way, the silent majority in a new start ups extremely involving in a certain identity, position (such seeing that "runner" "dieter" or "entrepreneur") are usually carried out nicely within the accomplishment with regards to affiliated objectives [6]. These kinds of self-meaning includes connecting one's personality using a certain behavior or strategy of accomplishing, individuals in the company effects just one defines [6]. That takes place while using self-concordance design [36,37], which will be based upon self-determination thought [38,39]. Within the self-concordance design, entities indulge in objectives extended after they experience extremely strategy for founding and for the purpose or after they discover with the uncovered with the goal [6]. They will accomplish their finest to keep efficiency because of the personality, by contribution in certain kinds of behavior, even though they do not possess "great knowledge, expertise, or sources in order to anticipate achievements" [6]. To ensure factors information on persona, identity provokes some sort of founder personality, in which the entrepreneur's focus involved within founding some sort of enterprise with regard to commercializing as well as choices and also get their self as a developer role, in which the entrepreneur's focus is good for proper behavior in order to grace with presence to, growing, as well as growing this enterprise as soon as it is often created [40]. Typically, particular person's energy with regard to identity, importance as well as consonance of their behavior [41], due to the fact "once the facts are usually built-into this self-concept, entrepreneurs are extremely enthusiastic to act in ways efficient with those facts [42,43] to have an entrepreneurial efficiency. Based on the above discussion, we hypothesize that:

Hypothesis 2: There is a positive relationship between entrepreneurial self-efficacy and performance when mediated by entrepreneurial passion for founding.

Hypothesis 3: There is a positive relationship between entrepreneurial self-efficacy and performance when mediated by entrepreneurial passion for developing (Figure 1).

Methodology

We test our hypothesis with a sample of entrepreneur's who are working in Lahore region. The sample is taken from small firms, which are profit base firm, privately owned and have worked with less than 15 employees. For newly started venture first six years is very critical from the development point of you [44]. The main aim of the research is to collect data from those entrepreneurs who are in search of identifying new market opportunities in order to expand their businesses as well as from those who are very much profound to develop their firms, so for this sake we aim to select those entrepreneur's whose experience to operate business is in between 7 to 10 years maximum. As our focus on small entrepreneur's, because they assume to be more vibrant in order to identify market opportunities and further develop their business, so that we come to know that the basic instinct factor which stimulate small business entrepreneurs to lead to entrepreneurial performance while others failed to achieve [45].

Survey design

The study assumes to collect data using previous validated scales. As developed and validated constructs or scales help to reduce social desirability biasedness [46]. The data aim to collect through questionnaire method from the entrepreneur's working in Lahore Region. For the convenience of entrepreneur study aim to separate

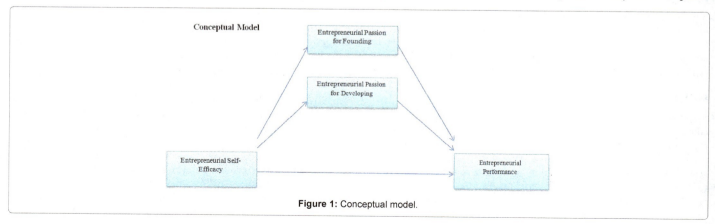

Figure 1: Conceptual model.

criterion and predictor variables in a survey so that it finds easy for the entrepreneur's to respond [46]. The anonymity factor is also assumed to be employed in the questionnaire so that the entrepreneurs respond honestly without feeling fear to leak out the personal information. Different scale end points may apply in the questionnaire so that respondent does not lose his interest.

Measures

A survey assumes to collect on a five point scale from strongly agree to disagree.

Entrepreneurial performance: To measure the performance individuals are considered as the unit of analysis. To measure the entrepreneurial performance personal self-assessment of entrepreneur's is required, so that it draws a clear picture in order to understand how they rate business performance according to their abilities. In this regard, a scale developed by Kropp et al. [47] is assumed to be used in our study. The subjective measure of performance is not unusual in small businesses. However, for this sake five-point Likert scale from strongly disagree to strongly agree is used to collect the entrepreneurial subjective business performance which is used to validate entrepreneurial business performance. Scale is previously used and validated by the Hallak et al. [17] in his study.

Entrepreneurial passion: The scale which assumes to apply for entrepreneurial passion is derived from Cardon et al. [48] study. For entrepreneurial passion separate measures are to be chosen for entrepreneurial passion for founding and development and one sub scale item for each category is to be used which is identity centrality and the same was adopted from the study of Cardon et al. [48]. Four items assume to be used for entrepreneurial passion for founding and three items scale assume to be used for entrepreneurial passion for developing. The scale has previously used and proof to be valid by Cardon et al. [48].

Self-efficacy. In order to assess the entrepreneurial self-efficacy four items Scale designed is used. The scale is used and validated previously by Zhao et al. [49]. Respondents were asks to indicate their self-confidence being an entrepreneur (e.g., identifying new business opportunities, creating new products or services, thinking creatively, and commercializing an idea). They were asked to indicate their confidence on a five-point scale (1=not very confident, 5=very confident).

Control variables: Firms age, and number of employees are assumed to consider as control variables.

Results and Discussion

We assume to employed exploratory factor analysis through direct oblimin rotation in order to inspect the discriminant validity of the concepts, because the oblimin rotation factor allows examining the accurate impact of all influences [49]. Further, we assume to apply hierarchial regression analysis using SPSS because for small sample size this technique is very much valid, especially in entrepreneurial research studies [50,51]. For large sample size exploratory and confirmatory analysis are generally used to reduce the sampling error, researchers notes that sample size more than 50 respondents provides adequate reliability for exploratory factor analysis [52]. Exploratory factor analysis with direct oblimin rotation was conducted to examine the discriminant validity of the constructs, and found items were above 0.40 and retain for the study which results are shown in Table 1. Confirmatory factor analyses were further conducting using AMOS

	1	2	3	4
a3	0.712			
b3	0.714			
v3	0.58			
d3	0.655			
f3	0.64			
a4	0.558	0.667		
b4		0.725		
c4		0.697		
d4			0.592	
a5			0.674	
b5			0.657	
c5				0.786
a7				0.739
b7				0.727
c7				0.488

Effect of entrepreneurial self-efficacy on each type of passion-passion for founding, and developing—and each effect was positive and significant at p<0.001.

Table 1: Confirmatory analysis in SPSS.

18.0 (IBM, Armonk, NY, USA) to determine cross factors loading and found measures were fit for the model (Table 1).

Table 2 provides the means, standard deviations, and correlations for variables used in the study. All measures have Cronbach's alpha reliabilities greater than .7, which is considered acceptable [53]. The conceptual model and hypotheses were tested using hierarchical regression analysis using SPSS (18.0, IBM). Studies with smaller sample sizes are common in entrepreneurial research [51], and use of regression analysis avoids issues of model fit that can become problematic with use of structural equation modeling in small data sets [54,55]. In the first step, control variables were entered with performance as the outcome variable. In the second step, entrepreneurial self-efficacy was entered. In the third step, each type of passion was entered individually, resulting in the two models to test hypothesis 2, and hypothesis 3. Results of these regressions are displayed in Table 3. In hypothesis 1, we argued that greater entrepreneurial self- efficacy would lead to greater entrepreneurial performance, which was supported (ß=0.458, p<0.01). In the remaining hypotheses, we argued that entrepreneurial passion mediates the effect of entrepreneurial self-efficacy on entrepreneurial performance, and these hypotheses were first tested following procedures recommended by Baron and Kenney. If mediation is present, we would expect the effect of self-efficacy on each type of passion to be significant, and would expect the effect of self-efficacy on performance to be reduced with the addition of passion in the model. In addition to the models described above, regression analyses were run to determine (Tables 2-4).

Hypothesis 2 states that entrepreneurial passion for founding mediates the effect of entrepreneurial self-efficacy on entrepreneurial performance, and it is supported (p<0.01). Further, the coefficient for self-efficacy becomes insignificant when passion for founding is entered into the regression analysis (Table 3), indicating full mediation. Hypothesis 3, stating that passion for developing mediates the effect of entrepreneurial self-efficacy on performance, is also supported (p<0.05). However, the fact that the coefficient for entrepreneurial self-efficacy remains significant at p<0.05 (Table 3) suggests partial rather than full mediation (Table 4).

We examined whether the two types of passion mediate the effect of entrepreneurial self-efficacy on performance when examined simultaneously. Using multiple hierarchical regression analysis with

	Mean	SD	1	2	3	4	5	6	7	8	9	10	11	12
1. Gender	1.41	0.49	-											
2. Mstatus	1.62	0.48	-0.09	-										
3. Age	2.32	1.02	0.02	0.465**	-									
4. HEDegree	3.28	1.21	0.1	0.04	0.06	-								
5. Tindustry	1.57	0.49	-0.002	0.275*	0.07	.274*	-							
6. Fage	2.07	0.77	0.07	0.255*	0.27*	0	0.07	-						
7. NEmployes	1.41	0.52	0.03	-0.027	0.06	0.087	0	0.05	-					
8. Estatus	1.8	0.4	0.006	0.02	0.157	0.259*	-0.23	0.13	.272*	-				
9. ESE	3.9	0.72	0.03	-0.09	-0.185	0.218	0.18	-0.11	-0.18	0.15	-			
10. PFounding	3.96	0.46	0.018	-0.16	-0.112	0.367**	0.17	0.09	0.09	0.19	0.52**	-		
11. PDeveloping	3.99	0.56	0.032	-0.07	-0.197	0.304**	0.18	-0.03	-0.12	0.12	0.65**	0.79*	-	
12. EFP	3.8	0.73	0.15	0.07	-0.064	0.229	0.21	0.08	0.328**	0.251*	0.44**	0.46*	0.40**	-

**p ≤ 0.01 *p ≤ 0.05 Regression results (standardized coefficients)

Table 2: Descriptive statistics, scale reliabilities, and correlation table.

DV EP	Model 1	Model 2	Model 3	Model 4	Model 5
Gender	0.12	0.122	0.147	0.124	
Mstatus	0.1	0.127	0.181	0.129	
Age	-0.19	-0.114	0.081	-0.091	
Hedegree	0.86	0.041	0.07	0.009	
Tindustry	0.22	0.109	0.173	0.1	
Fage	0.04	0.09	0.104	0.079	
Nemployees	0.26	0.392	0.151	0.399	
Estatus	0.23	0.087	0.215	0.083	
Epfounding			.201**		0.391
EPDeveloping				0.183*	-0.098
Adjusted R Square	0.16	0.332	0.36	0.342	0.244
R Square		0.418	0.451	0.436	0.275
F	2.664	4.87	4.933	4.643	8.84

*p ≤ 0.05; **p ≤ 0.01 Regression Results (standardize coefficients)

Table 3: The effect of entrepreneurial self-efficacy and entrepreneurial passion on entrepreneurial performance.

	Passion for founding	Passion for Developing
Gender	-0.074	-0.009
Marital status	-0.228	-0.008
Age	-0.004	-0.12
HE Degree	0.28	0.177
T industry	0.057	0.048
F age	0.222	0.063
N employees	0.16	-0.036
E status	0.160	0.22
ESE	-0.019	0.57
Adj R square	0.35	0.38
F	5.192	5.77

Table 4: The effect of entrepreneurial self-efficacy on entrepreneurial passion.

performance as the dependent variable, we entered entrepreneurial self-efficacy alone in the first step, adding the three types of passion simultaneously in the second step. While the effects of passion for founding on performance is positive and significant (p<0.01 and p<0.05, respectively; see Table 3, Model 5), while the effect of passion for developing is insignificant (p<0.01 and p<0.05 respectively). Arguing that inclusion of passion item will reduce the impact of relationship between entrepreneurial self-efficacy and performance.

We found that passion for founding reduces the self-efficacy impact on performance. However, passion for developing is not significantly support our argument hence, proved non-significant.

Conclusion

This research examined the relationship between ESE and entrepreneurial performance by mediating passion for founding and developing new enterprises among entrepreneurs serving in services or manufacturing businesses. It focused on the individual entrepreneurs as the unit of analysis as he or she has a dominant influence on the business activities. Focusing on entrepreneurs in Upper Punjab region of Pakistan, we find that contrary to previous studies conducted in other industries, entrepreneur's passion fuel self-efficacy and increase the entrepreneurial performance.

The purpose of our study was to examine two espoused drivers of performance in entrepreneurship, specifically looking at the relationship between entrepreneurial self-efficacy and performance, both directly and as mediated by entrepreneurial passion for founding and developing. Prior research has found evidence that self-efficacy has a strong relationship with entrepreneurial performance [7] but given that entrepreneurial passion has also been suggested to have an influence on engaged goal pursuit [5], and previous work that has suggested that passion rather than self-efficacy is a key driver to regulate entrepreneurial behavior [48], we sought to examine how these variables work together in their influence on entrepreneurial performance. However, results confirms that passion immensely effect the entrepreneurial self-efficacy. Contrary to this we assume passion for development new enterprises invigorate the individual performance, but result differs this argument which is in confirmatory with the previous study conducted by Cardon et al. [5]. Study confirms that identity centrality plays a driving role in pursuing entrepreneurial journey.

The conceptualization of entrepreneurial passion is based on an individual identifying with active "do-er" identities of founder, and developer, all associated with doing things, with engaging with activities [9]. Because of this, entrepreneurial passion may be more relevant to individual performance especially in the face of failures. Overall results suggests that it is passion that derive entrepreneurial self-efficacy and improve individual performance. Feelings of self-confidence in pursuing entrepreneurship may make entrepreneurs more passionate because people tend to identify with activities they are good at. When their self-efficacy leads to passion for an activity, their passion in turn appears to drive entrepreneurial pursuits, for founding and developing new enterprises.

References

1. Schindehutte M, Morris M, Allen J (2006) Beyond achievement: Entrepreneurship as extreme experience. Small Business Economics 27: 349-368.
2. Bandura A (1977) Social learning theory. Englewood Cliffs, NJ: Prentice Hall.
3. Hallak R, Assaker G, O'Cornnor P (2012) Are Family and Nonfamily Tourism Business Different? An Examination of the Entrepreneurial Self-Efficacy-Entrepreneurial Performance Relationship. Journal of Hospitality & Tourism Research 38: 388-413.
4. Shane S, Locke EA, Collins CJ (2003) Entrepreneurial motivation. Human Resource Management Review 13: 257-279.
5. Cardon MS, Kirk CP (2013) Entrepreneurial Passion as Mediator of the Self-Efficacy to Persistence Relationship. Entrepreneurship Theory and Practice 39: 1027–1050.
6. Houser-Marko L, Sheldon KM (2006) Motivating behavioral persistence: The self-as-doer construct. Personality and Social Psychology Bulletin 32: 1037-1049.
7. Hallak R, Brown G, Lindsay NJ (2012) The place identity-performance relationship among tourism entrepreneurs: A structural equation modelling analysis. Tourism Management 33: 143-153.
8. Murnieks CY (2007) Who am I? The quest for an entrepreneurial identity and an investigation of its relationship to entrepreneurial passion and goal-setting. Unpublished doctoral dissertation. University of Colorado-Boulder.
9. Cardon MS, Wincent J, Singh J, Drnovsek M (2009) The nature and experience of entrepreneurial passion. Academy of Management Review 34: 511-532.
10. Dransfield R (2000) Human Resource Management (3rdedn) Guildford, Heinemann, Great Britian.
11. Lewicki RJ, Barry B, Saunders DM, Minton J (2003) Essentials of Negotiation (3rdedn) McGraw Hill, New York.
12. DeNoble A, Jung D, Ehrlich S (1999) Entrepreneurial self-efficacy: The development of a measure and its relationship to entrepreneurial action. In Reynolds RD, Bygrave WD, Manigart S, Mason CM (Eds), Frontiers of entrepreneurship research. Waltham, MA: P&R Publications.
13. Ericsson KA, Charness N, Feltovich PJ, Hoffman R (2006) The Cambridge Handbook of Expertise and Expert Performance. Cambridge University Press: New York 41-67.
14. Zimmerman BJ (2006) Development and adaptation of expertise: The role of self-regulatory processes and beliefs. In The Cambridge Handbook of Expertise and Expert Performance, Ericsson KA, Charness, N, Feltovich, P. J, & Hoffman, R (eds) Cambridge University Press: New York; 705-722.
15. Kanfer R (1990) Motivation theory and industrial and organizational psychology. In Handbook of Industrial and Organizational Psychology (2ndedn) Dunnette M, Hough G (eds) Consulting Psychologists Press: Palo Alto CA; 76-170.
16. Carter NM, Gartner WB, Reynolds P (1996) Exploring start-up event sequences. Journal of Business Venturing 11: 151-166.
17. Foo MD, Uy M, Baron RA (2009) How do feelings influence effort? An empirical study of entrepreneurs' affect and venture effort. The Journal of Applied Psychology 94: 1086-1094.
18. Bandura A (1997) Self efficacy: The exercise of control. Freeman, New York.
19. Bandura A (1989) Social cognitive theory. In R. Vasta (Ed.), Annals of child development: Six theories of child development 6: 1-60.
20. Locke EA, Latham GP (2002) Building a practically useful theory of goal setting and task motivation. American Psychologist 57: 705-717.
21. Phillips JM, Gully SM (1997) Role of goal orientation, ability, need for achievement, and locus of control in the self-efficacy and goal-setting process. Journal of Applied Psychology.
22. Cervone D, Peake PK (1986) Anchoring, efficacy, and action: The influence of judgmental heuristics on self- efficacy judgments and behavior. Journal of Personality and Social Psychology 50: 492-501.
23. Bandura A (1994) Self-efficacy. In Ramachaudran VS (Edn) Encyclopedia of human behavior. New York: Academic (Reprinted in H. Friedman (Ed.), Encyclopedia of mental health. San Diego: Academic 4: 71-81.
24. Margolis H, McCabe P (2006) Improving self-efficacy and motivation: What to do, what to say. Intervention in School and Clinic 41: 218-227.
25. Latham PG, Pinder CC (2005) Work motivation theory and research at the dawn of the Twenty-first century. Annual Review of Psychology 56: 485-516.
26. Chen CC, Greene PG, Crick A (1998) Does entrepreneurial self-efficacy distinguish entrepreneurs from managers? Journal of Business Venturing 13: 295-316.
27. Boyd NG, Vozikis GS (1994) The influence of self-efficacy on the development of entrepreneurial intentions and actions. Entrepreneurship: Theory & Practice 18: 63-77.
28. Lindsay NJ, Balan P (2005) Entrepreneurial self-efficacy, reasons for venture startup, and perceived success. In Proceedings of the AGSE regional entrepreneurship research exchange forum. Melbourne: Swinburne University of Technology.
29. Bierly PE, Kessler EH, Christensen EW (2000) Organizational learning, knowledge, and wisdom. Journal of Organizational Change Management 13: 595-618.
30. Baum JR, Locke EA (2004) The relationship of entrepreneurial traits, skill, and motivation to subsequent venture growth. Journal of Applied Psychology 89: 587-598.
31. Cardon MS, Zietsma C, Saparito P, Matherne B, Davis C (2005) A tale of passion: New insights into entrepreneurship from a parenthood metaphor. Journal of Business Venturing 20: 23-45.
32. Smilor RW (1997) Entrepreneurship: Reflections on a subversive activity. Journal of Business Venturing 12: 341-346
33. Brannback M, Carsrud A, Elfving J, Krueger NK (2006) Sex, drugs, and entrepreneurial passion? An exploratory study. Paper presented at the Babson College Entrepreneurship Research Conference Bloomington.
34. Vignoles VL, Jen G, Regalia C, Manzi C, Scabini E (2006) Beyond selfesteem: Influence of multiple motives on identity construction. Journal of Personality and Social Psychology 90: 308-333.
35. Murnieks, C, Mosokowski, E (2006) Entrepreneurial Passion: An identity theory perspective. Paper presented at the annual meeting of the Academy of Management Atlanta.
36. Sheldon KM, Elliot AJ (1999) Goal striving, need satisfaction, and longitudinal well-being: The self-concordance model. Journal of Personality and Social Psychology 76: 482-497.
37. Sheldon KM, Houser-Marko L (2001) Self-concordance, goal attainment, and the pursuit of happiness: Can there be an upward spiral? Journal of Personality and Social Psychology 80: 152-165.
38. Deci EL, Ryan RM (1985) Intrinsic motivation and self-determination in human behavior. Plenum, New York.
39. Deci EL, Ryan RM (2000) The "what" and "why" of goal pursuits: Human needs and the self-determination of behavior. Psychological Inquiry 11: 227-268.
40. Gartner WB, Starr JA, Bhat S (1999) Predicting new venture survival: An analysis of "anatomy of a startup" cases from Inc. magazine. Journal of Business Venturing 14: 215-232.
41. Hogg MA, Terry DJ, White KM (1995) A tale of two theories: A critical comparison of identity theory with social identity theory. Social Psychology Quarterly 58: 255-269.
42. Burke PJ, Reitzes DC (1981) The link between identity and role performance. Social Psychology Quarterly 44: 83-92.
43. McCall GJ, Simmons JL (1966) Identities and interactions. The Free Press, New York.
44. Shrader RC, Oviatt BM, McDougall PP (2000) How new ventures exploit trade-offs among international risk factors: Lessons for the accelerated internationalization of the 21st century. Academy of Management Journal 43: 1227-1247.
45. Morse EA, Fowler SW, Lawrence TB (2007) The impact of virtual

embeddedness on new venture survival: Overcoming the liabilities of newness. Entrepreneurship Theory and Practice 31: 139-159.

46. Podsakoff PM, MacKenzie SB, Lee JY, Podsakoff NP (2003) Common method biases in behavioral research: A critical review of the literature and recommended remedies. The Journal of Applied Psychology 88: 879-903.

47. Kropp F, Lindsay NJ, Shoham A (2006) Entrepreneurial, market, and learning orientations and international entrepreneurial business venture performance in South African firms. International Marketing Review 23: 504-523.

48. Murnieks CY, Mosakowski E, Cardon MS (2014) Pathways of Passion: Identity Centrality, Passion and Behavior Among Entrepreneurs. Journal of Management 40: 1583-1606.

49. Zhao H, Seibert SE, Hills GE (2005) The mediating role of self-efficacy in the development of entrepreneurial intentions. Journal of Applied Psychology 90: 1265-1272.

50. Samiee S, Chabowski B (2012) Knowledge structure in international marketing: A multi-method bibliometric analysis. Journal of the Academy of Marketing Science 40: 364-386.

51. Short JC, Ketchen DJJ, Combs JG, Ireland RD (2010) Research methods in entrepreneurship. Organizational Research Methods 13: 6-15.

52. De Winter J, Dodou D, Wieringa P (2009) Exploratory factor analysis with small sample sizes. Multivariate Behavioral Research 44: 147-181.

53. Crook TR, Shook CL, Morris ML, Madden TM (2010) Are we there yet? An assessment of research design and construct measurement practices in entrepreneurship research. Organizational Research Methods 13: 192-206.

54. Kline RB (2005) Principles and practices of structural equation modeling. Guilford, New York.

55. Baron RM, Kenney DA (1986) The moderator-mediator variable distinction in social psychological research: Conceptual, strategic, and statistical considerations. Journal of Personality and Social Psychology 51: 1173-1182.

Compare the Characteristics of Male and Female Entrepreneurs as Explorative Study

Abdulwahab Bin Shmailan*
Jubail Industrial College, Jubail Industrial, KSA

> **Abstract**
> The purpose of this literature review is to examine the characteristics of male and female entrepreneurs globally. This document will compare and contrast the similarities and differences between the two regarding on risk tolerance, financing, management, motivation and network. The literature review will explain what entrepreneurship is, who are the entrepreneurship and entrepreneurship traits. There also may be consistency in the barriers they face as well as their global counterparts.

Keywords: Male; Female; Entrepreneurship; Characteristics; Traits

What is Entrepreneurship?

The word entrepreneur comes from the French word "entreprendre" which means to "undertake" [1]. The word entrepreneur was first used by Cantillon in the early 1700's to describe someone who takes a risk by purchasing certain things at one price and by selling another unknown price. The French further defined an entrepreneur as someone who had certain personal traits that made them produce more [2]. Entrepreneurs identify opportunities and then found organisations that capitalise on them [3]. Mintzberg believes that entrepreneurship is taking the vision of the entrepreneur and realizing it. Growth is an essential quality of any entrepreneurial venture and growth represents success [4].

Entrepreneurship is a key element of the success of any economy. Every day entrepreneur's generate economic growth, create new jobs, form new businesses, increase exports, reduce imports, and foster creativity and innovation. In Poland, entrepreneurship has been essential to the renewal and development of the economy. Entrepreneurs are able to take risks, introduce innovation, adapt to change and work in a highly-competitive environment. They are very important in an unstable and transformational economy. Entrepreneurs in India are helping to reduce poverty and growing the new middle class in India. Everyday individuals with a little money, resourcefulness and a drive to succeed are becoming entrepreneurs [5]. In an article by Lee and Venkataraman [6] they defined entrepreneurship as: "the search process of alternative or new opportunities". Entrepreneurism is not an alternative to employment. It is starting a new venture that requires a person's time, energy, and financial resources.

According to GEMS (2004) there are two ways to measure entrepreneurial activity. The first is to compare self-employment and total employment in an economy. The second is to examine the different levels of entrepreneurial activities from start-up to mature enterprise. GEMS (2004) has identified four types of entrepreneurial enterprises. The first is the Nascent enterprise, a relatively new venture that was started within the last year. The second are the Baby Enterprises that have been operating for between 4 and 42 months. The third types are Established Enterprises that have been operating for more than 42 months.

There are many factors that influence a person's decision to become an entrepreneur. Some become entrepreneurs because they are unemployed, others are downsized and others their jobs may be outsourced. They become entrepreneurs for more economic stability and to help stimulate the economy. These individuals can be driven to become entrepreneurs for the sense of independence, a family tradition of entrepreneurialism, to gain status, and because they want to create new products and services. Discrimination based on gender and race can also contribute to the desire to become an entrepreneur. These groups may not have the career opportunities that others have. They may also not receive the same pay. Being an entrepreneur provides them with the opportunity to earn more money [7]. In some countries, like the UK being an entrepreneur may be the only way to make a living [8].

One emerging sector of entrepreneurism is social entrepreneurship. In this model social or community goals play a part in the starting of a new organisation. These organisations are said to be trading in the social economy. According to Mort the main objective of social entrepreneurship is to "create superior social value for their clients". The concept of social entrepreneurship according to Brinckerhoff is a key ingredient to the success of a not for profit organisation. Social Entrepreneurship is a vital part of the economy. In Europe employment in this sector can range from 3.3 to 16.6%. Social entrepreneurship can be for profit businesses and businesses with a social conscience. Two examples of the latter are Timberland and the Body Shop. Both of these organisations donate profits to charity and support social programs throughout the world.

Not all entrepreneurs are managers of their businesses. Entrepreneurs can have different roles on their businesses depending on how their business is set up .An entrepreneur can operate on three basic levels. The may have started their own enterprises. They may work for other entrepreneurs. And thirdly, they may be an entrepreneur who is part of a larger enterprise. The third classification can be called intrapreneurship [9].

The following section talks about who are entrepreneurs and what factors influence their decisions to become entrepreneurs. They are

---

*****Corresponding author:** Abdulwahab Bin Shmailan, Associate Professor, Jubail Industrial College, Jubail Industrial, KSA, E-mail: asns2010@gmail.com

different from employees and recognize opportunities and then exploit them.

Who are the Entrepreneurs?

Entrepreneurs are people who can take information and find new opportunities that other people do not have to capacity to do so [10]. Entrepreneurs are visionaries who identify opportunities, act on them and start new businesses [11]. Entrepreneurs are opportunists who must be always aware of the ever-changing environment around them [11]. They then take those new opportunities, evaluate them and exploit in the marketplace. This can be done by introducing new products and services, expanding into new markets, inventing new processes and acquiring raw materials in a new way [12]. Entrepreneurs are self-employed and they create and run new businesses [13]. According to Gartner, an entrepreneur is someone "who started a new business where there was not before". Entrepreneurs use a wide range of tools to accomplish their visions including creating, adapting, founding and managing.

Entrepreneurs are people who start and manage a small business. They do not have organisational constraints like managers do. They are highly motivated to achieve and can readily accept a challenge. An entrepreneur is also willing to take on a risk a traditional manager would not be willing to take on. Entrepreneurs choose owning their own businesses because it suits their personality and likewise managers choose to work in organisations because that suits their personality.

Family can influence someone's decision to become an entrepreneur. In the early stages of development parents may serve as a role model to the budding entrepreneur. Research suggests that there is a connection between a parent being an entrepreneur and their children becoming entrepreneurs. Their parents' attitude and actions becomes a strong role model for the child. They often are the inspiration for the child to follow in their footsteps. Many women entrepreneurs come from a family who has an entrepreneurial background.

Entrepreneurs come from all age groups. Most make the decision to start their own enterprise between the age of 25 and 40. By this time they will have gained enough work experience and have enough knowledge. They will have enough background to make the decision to start their own business, be more confident in their own abilities and to understand the potential of the business they want to start. Many entrepreneurs also have served an "apprenticeship" in a SME that also gives them the skills they need [14].

Education can play a role in the decision to become an entrepreneur. Many become entrepreneurs because they do not have the formal qualifications that managers have in corporations. They can be passed over when it comes time for promotions because of their limited education. This can be the impetus to start a new business and leave the corporate environment. Most entrepreneurs are better educated than the general public.

Research has shown that there are distinct differences between entrepreneurs and small business owners [15]. The research has shown that entrepreneurs are more interested in maximising profits, generating growth, fostering innovation and exploiting opportunities rather than resources. Small business owners are more interested furthering there personal goals, spending most of their time in the business and linking business with family needs and desires. People may own a business simply to generate a living for their families [15].

The next section will examine whether or not there are certain traits or characteristics that are common to entrepreneurs. It will also discuss how these traits influence their decisions to become entrepreneurs.

Entrepreneurial traits

Research suggests that there are certain traits that are common in entrepreneurs. The process of becoming an entrepreneur may be due to the inherent nature of these characteristics rather than a rational process [1]. Entrepreneurs may look at the risk of becoming an entrepreneur vs. the financial return they will get from the traditional workforce [10].

Entrepreneurs have certain natural characteristics that make them successful [11]. They have more energy than the normal person. According to Ang and Chang entrepreneurs are hard workers and have the ability to overcome obstacles. They seek opportunities and solutions. Entrepreneurs are self-reliant and good internal self-control. They are also very perceptive and can easily identify new business ideas, new products or new markets and determine whether or not the new venture is viable [16]. In general entrepreneurs like to be the dominant person in the business and are driven to influence others. They like to get people to do what they want and like to direct the activities of those below them [9].

Entrepreneurs are people who believe that they can control their destiny and are much focused. This ability to concentrate on the new venture and confidence in their abilities is very necessary for the entrepreneur. In order to undertake the risk of starting a new business a person must be confident that it will succeed. Without this confidence a person may not take the risk. They may not be able to handle the obstacles and challenge of starting up a new business. A person with strong inner control and focus will be able to shoulder the burdens easier. Individuals with this focus will be able to keep up the energy and drive necessary to successfully launch the new business.

Some would argue that entrepreneurs are born and not made [17]. One such opinion was expressed by psychologist Alan Jacobwitz. In a study that was conducted using interviews of over 500 entrepreneurs Jacobwitz found that there were certain common character traits that entrepreneurs had. Entrepreneurs strive for independence. They can be loners. Most are restless and looking for new challenges. And most have very high self-confidence [17]. There has been additional research conducted to suggest that there may be other factors that foster entrepreneurship. Entreprenuers may be influenced by a number of factors like differing perceptions, personal characteristics, values, background and environment [18]. The choice to be an entrepreneur may be influenced by an individual's characteristics, the environment they are operating in, the business environment, their goals and whether or not they have a valid business idea [18].

Entrepreneurs are also risk takers. Risk is based on the interpretation of external events and circumstances. Entrepreneurs differ on their perception of risk [19]. Research show that entrepreneurs are better at determining risk potential, what the reward will be and are able to manage the uncertainties associated with risk. The ability to take risks is a primary characteristic of the entrepreneur [14]. Entrepreneurs often take advantage of untapped opportunities and in doing so they must manage risk effectively. Entrepreneurs have to be flexible and have keen insight [20].

Sexton [21] found that entrepreneurs are visionaries who form an image of their business that helps guide them to success. To grow an entrepreneur must effectively communicate their vision to their employees and stakeholders. The entrepreneur must have clear intentions of where they want to go. The inspiration that an entrepreneur has for a business must be followed up with consistent attention and intention. Entrepreneurs are goal oriented and focus to achieve their goals [22].

Entrepreneurs have certain traits that help them to become entrepreneurs. They are risk takers, have high energy, are visionaries, can exploit opportunities, are confident and hard workers. The following section Female Entrepreneurship will be discussed including the traits of female entrepreneurs. It will also discuss their contribution to the economy, why they started their businesses, and their management styles.

Differentiating Between Male and Female Entrepreneurs

There are successful male and female entrepreneurs all over the world. Research has found that there are some characteristics that are found in both men and women. There are some distinct differences that do exist between the two. The basic themes are their decision making styles, risk tolerance, goals for the business, financing of the business, management styles, networking ability, motivations.

General characteristics of female and male entrepreneurs

Contemporary research has shown that there are some differences between men and women when it comes to entrepreneurship. Male and female entrepreneurs may be similar demographically and psychologically. They tend to be married and be the first born child. First born children are more likely to achieve according to a study conducted by Harvard and Columbia universities. Female entrepreneurs tend to pursue degrees in liberal arts rather fields like engineering or more technical disciplines [23]. It is a much more difficult decision for a woman to become an entrepreneur than men. Women are more sensitive to men when it comes to non-financial issues [23]. Both men and women have experience prior to starting a business. They also may have role models and mentors who help them make their decision to become entrepreneurs.

Table 1 shows that male and female entrepreneurs make decisions differently. Men tend to make them quicker and women need more time. Male entrepreneurs focus on making sure costs are under control and are more profit driven. Women seek to make a social contribution and want to insure their quality. The table also shows that men and women tend to start different kinds of enterprises. When it comes to financial risk, men are more willing to undertake the risk than women. Men and women also differ in how they manage their businesses. Men tend to be more task oriented than women. Good relationships with employees are more important to women. The table indicated that male and female entrepreneurs have differing characteristics.

Female entrepreneurs have goals that drive them to achieve that may be different than those of males. The next section discusses the business goals for male and female entrepreneurs.

Business goals for male and female entrepreneurs

There are differences between men and women when it comes to business goals and management styles [23]. Male and female entrepreneurs often start a business to have more autonomy and control. They also want the income and the personal satisfaction a business can give them. Men tend to focus on the economic reasons for business ownership whereas women also seek to make some kind of social contribution [24]. Women also may become entrepreneurs to achieve their own or their spouses dream.

There may be more inherent reasons for women to start up a business. There goals are not just financial, the have a deeper meaning [23]. In a study by Moore and Buttner [25] they found the most important reason women become entrepreneurs is that they want to feel self-fulfilled. Women care about their clients and feel some sort of societal responsibility a well.

In a study by [26] they found that female entrepreneurs were more likely to close their businesses, had fewer resources to start their businesses. The study also revealed that women used innovative strategies to overcome the shortages they faced. Women focused more on product quality than men who focused more on customize and be cost efficient. In managing women empowered their employees and focused on relationships, team building, and perseverance [27]. Women often chose to have a smaller retail operation or service business instead of construction, technology or manufacturing operation.

All entrepreneurs are risk takers. Men have different attitudes toward risk than women. The following section outlines the differences regarding risk between male and female entrepreneurs.

Risk tolerance

Entrepreneurs are often seen as people who are willing to take a risk. Research has shown that men are much more willing to take a financial risk than women. Women have a different attitude toward risk and are less risk tolerant. Jianakoplos and Bernasek [28] found that men were less concerned about hazards than women. Men are more willing to take a risk and fail than women. Sexton [21] determined that women and men process information differently. Women are more detailed oriented and are more aware of the cues that indicate risk. Male and female entrepreneurs may have similar characteristics however when it comes to risk there is a difference.

All entrepreneurs have set of social and human capital [29]. The social structures of women are different than men and this creates a different context for women than for their male counterparts. These differences influence their attitudes toward risk [29]. Women try to insure that they have the proper social support before they start their business [30]. Many women start up their business with the support of their families and friends who may have helped them in the past [19].

This unwillingness to fail may contribute to the fact that growth of female entrepreneurs [31]. Banks when evaluating women for financing often score women lower on the risk taking scale than men. The women are perceived to be less entrepreneurial than their male counterparts [21]. The scale takes into account four facets of risk including financial, physical, social and ethical. Monetary risk is

Male Entrepreneurs	Female Entrepreneurs
Decision Making Easy	Difficulty in Making Decisions
Business focused on Economy and Cost	Business Focused on Making Social Contribution and Quality
Willing to Take Financial Risk	More Conservative When it Comes to Financial Risk
Task Oriented Managers	Focus on Good Relationships with Employees
Business manufacturing and construction	Business small retail and service orientation

Table 1: General characteristics of male and female entrepreneurs.

however the most important. Through the research by Sexton [21] they have concluded that women are much less likely to take a risk when there is an uncertainty of a monetary outcome.

Table 2 examines the risk tolerance of male and female entrepreneurs. Men are more willing to take risks when it comes to business. Women are more conservative, particularly when it comes to financial risk. Men require less information when making decisions than women do. Women need to have more information prior to making decisions. Women require much more social support prior to starting up a business than men. They need the support to help minimize the risks of being an entrepreneur. Men are also more willing to fail in business than women. This allows men to take greater risks when it comes to growing the business. Female entrepreneurs may not grow their businesses as quickly because they do not want to risk failure. In general, men are much more willing to take risks than their female counterparts.

Finance is crucial to the success of any new business. The next section discusses the differences between male and female entrepreneurs when it comes to financing.

Financing

There are some differences between men and women regarding the financing of the business. Women usually start up their business with less capital than men and their businesses tend to be smaller [29]. This can put women at a significant disadvantage when starting up their business [32]. This lack of start-up capital can affect the survival rates of female owned businesses and their ability to grow.

A study in Holland confirmed that women are different than men in business because they start up their businesses with far less money [33]. Women have lower capitalisation and lower debt than male owned businesses. Banks may be less willing to provide capital to women because they tend to have less industrial experience than men [26]. Women may also have a lack of track record for financing and lack of assets for collateral. Their skills in financial planning, accounting and marketing may make them less credible to banks [34]. Bank workers tend to view women as less entrepreneurial than men [35].

In a study conducted in Canada by Shrag, Yacuk and Glass they found that female entrepreneurs face obstacles including limited business experience and training, access to capital, unreceptive atmosphere, and the unconstructive effect business can have on the family. The research found though that the major obstacle was the negative self-image the woman had about their abilities. Research from Canada indicates that there are no differences between men and women when it comes to lending. Banks in Canada tend not to discriminate. In New Zealand research suggests that some banks discriminate against female entrepreneurs. For university graduates, education is more important to female applicants than male applicants. However women with high school educations were more likely to get a loan than their male counterparts.

Most women start up their businesses with personal assets and have minimal if any external funding [23]. They tend to start up with half the capital that men have. Women also have less access to informal financial networks that can provide funding [23].

Expanding a business may be more of a challenge to women because banks have more strict requirements for them when it comes to collateral for loans. This can affect their ability to grow. Women are more likely to get access to capital once their business has a track record [29]. A study in Asia did find that 43% of women who got financing from the bank were not discriminated against.

Financing is crucial to business growth. In study by Carter et al. [26] they found that having access to financial resources was more important than the intention to grow. Women found that getting start-up capital was much easier than getting capital for growth [29]. Even though the women had a good track record in business they were still viewed as more of a risk than men [36]. For women to be successful at growth strategies research found that women did excellent planning, focused on market and technology expansion, were more committed to their businesses and were willing to get additional capital for growth [36]. They had formal organisational structures, planned for growth, and used more financial resources. An important factor for Canadian women to expand their business was the effect it would have on their personal life. These women also adopted a slower growth strategy and were less risk adverse (Table 3).

Motivations

There are some differences in what motivates female and male entrepreneurs. Brush CG [23] concluded that there may be differences in their personal and business profiles. Men and women start their businesses in different sectors. They may also develop different types of products. Women may have differing goals like to be autonomous whereas a man may have purely profit goals. There also may be differences in the way they structure their business [23]. According to Schiller and Crewson, women tend to have more positive business traits than men including strong initiative, good common sense, the ability to think critically and they are skilled in decision making. They

Male Entrepreneurs	Female Entrepreneurs
Less Concerned About Hazards in Business Ownership	More Concerned about Hazards in Business Ownership
Feel Have Enough Information	Require More Detailed Information
Require Less Social Support to Start Business	Require Social Support to Start Business
Willing to Fail in Business	Less Willing to Fail in Business
Propensity for Risk in General	Risk Adverse Generally

Table 2: Risk tolerance.

Male Entrepreneurs	Female Entrepreneurs
More capital	Less capital
More debt	Low debt
	A lack of track record for financing
Bank trust male	Bank not trust female
Easy to access to capital	Not easy to access to capital

Table 3: Financing.

can be very aggressive in achieving their goals and have strong resolve to be successful [23].

In research conducted by Buttner and Moore [32] women and men were found to have differing reasons for starting a business. For men the reasons are more externally focused. They see an opportunity and then act on it. Women are motivated by more internal reasons like the opportunity to be their own boss. Men are more focused on earning more money while women want to be more fulfilled and achieve a sense of accomplishment.

In America women often make the decision to become entrepreneurs because of the high demands and inflexibility of the workplace. Their experience working in corporate America does not satisfy their personal goals and they feel that personal circumstances are not important. In Asia women have to move beyond there informal networks and move to other sources for financing their businesses [7]. This means they may have to go to lending institutions rather than family.

Research on male and female entrepreneurs in Sweden indicated that women usually start a business because of family priorities. The men in Sweden usually founded a business that they had previous experience in. Being able to make decisions on their own and also the fulfilment of having one's own business motivated both sexes in Sweden [36] (Table 4).

Management

Female entrepreneurs tend to manage differently than their male counterparts. Management is how the entrepreneur manages the business. The most pronounced differences between men and women as entrepreneurs are in their management styles [23]. Women claim to manage using more "feminine" strategies than men. An example of this would be that women tend to value the relationships with their employees more than the task at hand. Men and woman also may think differently. Male entrepreneurs are more logical thinkers. Female entrepreneurs are more intuitive thinkers. Women exhibit more social leadership styles that focus on communicative and expressive behaviours. Men tend to be more task oriented leaders [37]. Men and women also may differ in the way the think regarding the business. Women tend to be more intuitive and men more logical. Women's communications skills are excellent. They tend to be better listeners and can understand the needs of their employees [23].

Both male and female entrepreneurs want to grow their businesses. They do differ in how they want to grow the business. Women tend to be more cautious and conservative about expansion than men. They want to have a more controlled and manageable growth rate. Men are much more aggressive when it comes to expansion. According to Brush [23] some women do not pursue aggressive expansion goals because of family concerns. Women expressed more concern over external factors such as economic conditions than men. They believe these conditions contributed to their lack of growth whereas men did not.

Buttner [32] found that men and women do have some differing leadership traits. Most women run their businesses democratically. When it comes to professional growth it is important for the women to consider the growth of others as well. Buttner [32] also contends that women tend to share in the decision making process and are very much team oriented. There is a sharing of knowledge between the women business owner and their staff. Success for them is associated with having strong relationships.

They need to determine what existing resources can be used and those that they will need. Research conducted by Timmons [14] suggest that there are four types: human capital, financial resources, assets and a business plan. In most cases the entrepreneur will have some of these resources and they may help in making the decision to become an entrepreneur. Entrepreneurs like to have control over their new enterprise and will find the necessary resources with this in mind (Table 5).

Networking

Networking is very crucial to the success of any business. Buttner [32] indicates that networking may be more critical than having financial resources. Women and men can be excellent networkers, however men usually have larger networks, that are stronger, with more depth and strength. Women's networks are often smaller, and have less density. Their networks tend to be collaborative external relationships and are not as prone to use clubs, business associations and networks. Their networks include their family, staff, society and other business relationships [32]. These networks are valuable sources of information and can help during the start-up phase of the business. Family can be a very helpful network when it comes to decision making [30].

Women have to grow their networks in business because they are newer to the business world [38]. Women are however sometimes "excluded" from networks like the 'old boy's network', networks that have school ties and social organisations [38]. Women who are working from home have even less access to networks because they are not a visible in the business community. The networks for women tend to be more formally organised and help provide role models, assist in problem solving and sharing of information. The failure to develop good networks can hinder a woman's chance at becoming a successful entrepreneur and finding new business opportunities. This may suggest that networking can be more crucial to the female entrepreneur than their male counterparts [39]. Networks that are not well developed can lead to poor performance. Women sometimes find the time required and costs associated with networking make it difficult to participate in fully.

For all entrepreneurs, it is important to have networks that are based on trust. Networks help entrepreneurs with business information, advice, exchanging resources and helping to reduce

Male Entrepreneurs	Female Entrepreneurs
Externally focused	Autonomous
Strong initiative	More positive
	Good common sense
	Think critically
	Very aggressive
	Own boss
Earning more money	Achieve a sense of accomplishment
Previous experience	

Table 4: Motivation.

Male Entrepreneurs	Female Entrepreneurs
Logical thinkers	Intuitive thinkers
Oriented leaders	Communicative and expressive behaviours
	Communications skills are excellent
	Understand the needs of their employees
Grow their businesses	Grow their businesses
More aggressive when it comes to expansion	Cautious and conservative about expansion

Table 5: Management.

the risk an entrepreneur encounters. Thrust in the network helps determine the viability of the information and resources provided. A good network usually has a good flow of information, support and trust that guides the behaviour of the network [40]. In many networks there is an informal process to determine who is credible and who is not. For women it is important to determine who to trust so they know what information they can share.

In Israel research was conducted on the importance of networking for business women. They determined that there was a direct connection between being part of a business women's network and profitability.

Chan and Foster concluded in a study in Hong Kong that networking was more important for female entrepreneurs than their male counterparts. Research in Northern Ireland concluded that networks for both were similar however female entrepreneurs relied on their male counterparts and then often switched to their female associates. Men tend to focus on men for advice (Table 6).

Conclusion

The purpose of the literature review was to examine the characteristics of female and male entrepreneurs around the world. In order to do this the first section began with a definition of what entrepreneurship is. Entrepreneurship is the process of identifying opportunities and turning those opportunities into a viable business proposition. Throughout the world Entrepreneurship contributes to economic growth, creates new jobs, form new businesses, increase exports, decrease exports and innovation. Entrepreneurs are the people who uncover new opportunities and exploit them. They are highly motivated and are willing to take risks. Many become entrepreneurs because they do not like to work in traditional work environments.

There are a number traits have been identified as common to men and women of become an entrepreneur. They usually have more energy than other people and are more willing to take risks. Entrepreneurs' are self-sufficient and have good internal self-control. They are people who believe they can control their own destiny. And all entrepreneurs are visionaries. Female entrepreneurs have many of these characteristics and more. They are good net workers, they tend to have an open mind, are full of energy, and can share the power.

There are differences between male and female entrepreneurs. In general entrepreneurs may be similar demographically. They are mostly married and are first born children. Men are much more willing to take risks than women and also have an easier time making decisions. Women are much more conservative especially when it comes to financial risk. Men are more cost and profit driven than women who tend to focus on making a contribution to society and maintaining quality. Management styles differ between men and women. Men are more task focused and women are more relationship oriented. In starting up their businesses men and women also have different goals. Women are more socially focused when it comes to goals and men are more financially focused. When it comes to financing the business men are much more willing to take risks and get outside financing than women.

All entrepreneurs face obstacles and barriers when starting their enterprises. For women there are some additional barriers. Women may not have received the experience and training to make them successful that their male counterparts have had. Access to sufficient capital is also a challenge for female entrepreneurs. Some banks may not have the confidence in female entrepreneurs that they have in males. It is also difficult for women to balance work and home. Women may not have access to some of the networks that men have. These networks may provide more financial assistance and mentoring. There are also cultural barriers that can prevent women from starting a business and ultimately being successful. In some cultures women are not viewed as equal to men and are not given access to the resources they need for their enterprises.

Male Entrepreneurs	Female Entrepreneurs
Large network	Small network
Organizations	Family and friend
More access to network	Less access to network

Table 6: Networking.

References

1. Cunningham JB, Lischeron P (1991) Defining entrepreneurship. Journal of Business Management 25: 22-29.
2. Stevenson HH, Jarillo JC (1990) A perspective of entrepreneurship: Entrepreneurial management. Strategic Management Journal 11: 17-27.
3. Bygrave W, Hoffer C (1991) Theorizing about entrepreneurship. Entrepreneurship: Theory and Practice 16: 13-22.
4. Mintzberg H (1998) Covert leadership: Notes on managing professionals. Harvard business review 76: 140-148.
5. Gupte M (2004) Participation in a Gendered Environment: The Case of Community Forestry in India. Human Ecology 32: 365-382.
6. Lee H, Venkataraman S (2006) Aspirations, market offerings, and the pursuit of entrepreneurial opportunities. Journal of Business Venturing 21: 1.
7. Basu A, Altinay E (2002) The interaction between culture and entrepreneurship in London's immigrant businesses. International Small Business Journal 20: 371-394.
8. Herron L (1994) Do Skills Predict Profits? A Study of Successful Entrepreneurship. Garland Publishing, New York.
9. Neider L (1987) A Preliminary Investigation of Female Entrepreneurs in Florida. Journal of Small Business Management 25: 22-29.
10. Campbell CA (1992) A decision theory model for entrepreneurial acts. Entrepreneurship Theory and Practice 17: 21-27.
11. Bolton B, Thompson J (2000) Entrepreneurs: Talent, Temperament, Technique. Butterworth-Heinemann, Oxford.
12. Shane S, Venkataraman S (2000) The promise of entrepreneurship as a field of Small Business Owners: A Conceptualization. Academy of Management Review 9: 354-359.
13. Reynolds P, Elkin E, Scalf R, Von Behren J, Neutra RR (2001) A case-control pilot study of traffic exposures and early childhood leukemia using a geographic information system. Bioelectromagnetics Suppl 5: 58-68.
14. Timmons JA (1994) New Venture Creation; Entrepreneurship for the 21st Century.
15. Wennekers S, Lorraine M, Uhlaner A, Thurik R (2002) Entrepreneurship and its conditions: A macroperspective. International Journal of Entrepreneurship Education 1: 25-64.
16. Learned K (1992) What happened before the organization? A model of organization formation. Entrepreneur. Theory Pract 17: 39-48.
17. Cohen AP (1980) Effectiveness of student-rating feedback for improving college instruction: A meta-analysis of findings. Research in Higher Education 13: 321-341.
18. Krueger NF, Brazil DV (1994) Entrepreneurial Potential and Potential Entrepreneurs. Entrepreneurship Theory and Practice 18: 91-103.
19. Brindley C (2005) Barriers to women achieving their entrepreneurial growth: women and risk. International Journal of Entrepreneurial Behaviour and Research 11: 144-161.
20. Cox C, Jennings R (1995) The foundations of success: The development and characteristics of British entrepreneurs and entrepreneurs. Leadership and Organisation Development Journal 16: 4-9.

21. Sexton DL (1990) Research on women-owned businesses: Current status and future directions. In: Hagen O, Rivchum C, Sexton DL (eds.) Women-owned Businesses, Praeger, New York, NY, 183-193.

22. Bird B (1988) Implementing Entrepreneurial Ideas: The Case for Intention. Academy of Management Review 13: 442-453.

23. Brush CG (1992) Research on women business owners: Past trends, a new perspective and future directions. Entrepreneurship Theory and Practice 16: 5-30.

24. Orhan M, Scott D (2001) Why Women Enter Into Entrepreneurship: an Explanatory Model. Women in Management Review 16: 232-243.

25. Moore DP, Buttner EH (1997) Women Entrepreneurs: Moving Beyond the Glass Ceiling. Sage Publications. Thousand Oaks, USA.

26. Rosa P, Carter S, Hamilton D (1996) Gender as a Determinant of Small Business Performance. Small Business Economics 8: 463-478.

27. Buttner EH, Moore D (1997) Women's organisational exodus to entrepreneurship: self-reported motivations and correlates with success. Journal of Small Business Management 35: 34-46.

28. Jianakoplos NA, Bernasek A (1998) Are women more risk averse? Economic Inquiry 36: 620-630.

29. Brush CG (1997) Women-owned businesses: obstacles and opportunities. Journal of Developmental Entrepreneurship 2: 1-25.

30. Ljunggren C (1996) Medborgarpubliken och det offentliga rummet. Om utbildning, medier och demokrati. Uppsala Studies in Education, Uppsala p. 68.

31. Johnson JEV, Powell PB (1994) Decision making, risk and gender: Are managers different? British Journal of Management 5: 123-138.

32. Buttner H (2001) Examining female entrepreneurs management style: An application of a case of Pakistan. Journal of Business Venturing 11: 507-529.

33. Verheul IA, Thurik R (2001) Start-up capital: Differences between male and female entrepreneurs; Does gender matter? Small Business Economics.

34. Hirsh W (1984) Career Management in the Organisation. Institute of Management Studies. Brighton.

35. Buttner EH, Rosen B (1989) Funding new business ventures: Are decision makers biased against women entrepreneurs? Journal of Business Venturing 4: 249-261.

36. Holmquist C (1997) The other side of the coin or another coin? Women entrepreneurship as a complement or an alternative. Entrepreneurship and Regional Development 9: 179-182.

37. Eagly AH, Karau SJ (1991) Gender and the emergence of leaders: Ameta-analysis. Journal of Personality and Social Psychology 60: 685-710.

38. Davis SEM, Long DD (1999) Women entrepreneurs: What do they need? Business and Economic Review 45: 25-26.

39. Deakins D, Whittam C (2000) Business start-up: theory, practice and policy. In: Carter S (ed.) Jones-Evans D Pearson Education, London pp. 115-131.

40. BarNir A, Smith KA (2002) Interfirm alliances in the small business: the role of social networks. Journal of Small Business Management 40: 219-233.

Impact of MBA on Entrepreneurial Success: Do Entrepreneurs Acquire Capacity through the Program or Does MBA Only Signal Gifted Talent and Experience?

Matsuda N[1]* and Matsuo Y[2]

[1]*Ministry of Economy, Trade and Industry, Japan*
[2]*Faculty of Engineering, University of Tokyo, Japan*

Abstract

When people obtains MBA degree, can he/she performs better in founding a firm than ones without it? If so, is it because of prestigious signal of MBA degree or because of acquired capability thorough the MBA program? In order to answer this question, we originally collected a survey of 1503 entrepreneurs in Japan via internet. We divide MBA degree effect on entrepreneurial activity into three effects; gifted talent, occupational experience and acquirement thorough MBA program. Gifted talent and occupational experiences of an individual enable him/he to entry a MBA program while this talent also enhance possibility to be a successful entrepreneur. When only these two effects matter on entrepreneurship, it leads that an MBA program signals that the entrepreneur is talented in nature and occupationally experienced but her/his capability acquired through the program do not matter on entrepreneurship. In our data, however, it is clarified that after controlling the effects of gifted talent and occupational experience, MBA still impacts entrepreneurship. This result implies that acquirement through MBA program positively affects on success of start-ups. This insight is useful for candidates of MBA program, who are also targeting to be entrepreneurs in the future and certificates that the program is worth to be invested for them.

Keywords: MBA; Entrepreneurship; Gifted talent; Experience JEL Classification L25; L26; J24

Introduction

MBA (Master degree of Business Administration) programs have attracted millions of business focusing students for decades in the world. Among varieties of appealing points of business schools for recruiting candidates as providers of MBA programs, advantage of starting-up own business has been always a major point. However, in academics, there are few studies examining the impact of MBA degree on entrepreneurship. We approach a question whether MBA programs itself impact an entrepreneurial activity.

In this thesis, using original survey of entrepreneurs and non-entrepreneurs, we gauged the impact of MBA on entrepreneurship. The survey is collected online and covers 7023 people, including 1,503 entrepreneurs, within Japan. Do MBA holders perform better than the ones without it? If the answer is yes, the next question is whether the better performance origins from MBA program or not. Even when it superficially boosts entrepreneurs' success, it is possibly because of gifted talent, which helps them enter MBA programs or because of occupational experience, which also helps the entrance. In these cases, MBA degrees just certificate the talent and/or experience of MBA holders but not accomplishment in the program for two years. Harmon et al. [1] explains that if it is true, the degree is only a signaling of productive potentials of entrepreneurs, which is not what they acquire through the MBA program.

As above, we divided the impact of the degree into three aspects. The one is MBA as signals of gifted talent which is mainly explained with academic scores, the second is occupational experience of holders and the third is acquired skills thorough MBA program. We carefully analyzed the data by excluding the effects of talent and experience, and discuss the value of acquiring the degree. The verification of the true value of the program will attract potential MBA candidates and encourage them to spend two years in the program at the cost of other occupational choices.

This thesis is structured as follows. The Chapter Two reviews the previous literature of entrepreneurial skills and effects of MBA. There are not few literatures for both of the issues but the relationships of the two are scarcely discussed through data. One of the reason of the rarity of the relationships discussion is lack of data connecting the two. It is not easy to follow the MBA degree alumni until they start-up and even after they started up. The Chapter Three explains our survey of entrepreneurs and statistical methodology as well. The Chapter Four follows the estimation results and verifies the effect of MBA on start-ups and we conclude in the Chapter Five.

Literature Review

MBA effects on entrepreneurship

Regarding being a successful entrepreneur, Charney and Libecap [2] collected data from alumni of Business school of Arizona state university. Analyzing the data of sales and size of start-ups of alumni entrepreneurs, they empirically showed that MBA alumni performs better than those of other master degree programs. However, their analysis do not identify the impacts of MBA program effect with other latent effect of such as talents and skills.

As Lange et al. [3] discuss the effect of MBA on entrepreneurship, although obtaining MBA degree and an entry into ventures are positively

---

*Corresponding author: Matsuda N, Ministry of Economy, Trade and Industry 1-3-1, Kasumigaseki, Chiyoda, Tokyo, Japan
E-mail: naomatsuda@weblab.t.u-tokyo.ac.jp

correlated as a whole, why and how the program effect on students bear various ways of interpretations. Simpson et al. [4] suggests that while leaving previous position and replacing professional identity, Chinese MBA alumni who obtained the degree in the United Kingdom earned creativity thorough the program. While Lerner and Ulrike [5] focus on peer effects among classmates, Krishnan et al. [6] is on self-monitoring which enables an entrepreneur to be more self-monitoring; managing one's internal states, impulses and emotions.

In application process, a MBA candidate is usually selected with academic talent and occupational experiences. They are both effective to entrepreneurial success as many previous literature mention. By differentiating with effects of these personal propensities from effect of accomplishment of MBA program, we contribute to the why and how issues as above.

Entrepreneurial success factors

Previous literature, such as Davidsson and Honig [7] commonly reassembly the factors of an entrepreneur's performance into four parts; human capital, social capital and financial capital of an entrepreneur and the firm's character. Each factors are proxied by entrepreneurs'/firm's indicators. We utilize this framework of three kinds of capitals of an entrepreneur in the following chapters.

Rich human capital affects positively on his/her entrepreneurial performance as well as other two entrepreneur's capitals do Shane [8], Bosma et al. [9], Colombo et al. [10], Parker and Van Praag [11]. Entrepreneurs' talents and experience we mentioned is included in these proxies of human capital. Van Der Sluis et al. [12] reveal that there is positive relationships between academic performance and entrepreneurial outcomes. Previous work experience such as management professional experience in a previous firm is essential. Brush et al. [13] indicates that by exercising management skills before start-up an entrepreneur's own business enhance the possibility of success. Also, duration of service as an ordinary employee, not as a manager, positively affects the performance of a start-up Davidsson and Gordon [14] Bosma et al. [9] indicate that skills and experience of particular industry in which he/she starts-up is advantage for an entrepreneur. This suggests that investor experience as an angel investor or a venture capitalist and starting up in the same industry in which he/she was employed before can positively affect the entrepreneurial performance.

Secondly as for social capital, Nahapiet and Ghoshal [15] and Adler and Kwon [16] define it is linkage with friends or acquaintances which bring us information and/or knowledge thorough communication with them. Adler and Kwon [16] explain that thorough social capital, we can access variety of information, enhance credibility of information and shorten the duration until we get necessary information. Ostgaard and Birley [17] verified that social capital of an entrepreneur positively impact on sales, profit and size of employee of the start-up. Honig [18] also verified that social capital positively impact on revenue of an entrepreneur.

Thirdly an entrepreneur needs financial capital when he/she starts the business and invests thereafter. When a founder obtained richer financial capital, the performance of the start-up becomes better Cooper et al. Hsu [19,20]. The financial capital can be owned by an entrepreneur her/himself or by his/her family, and can be invested by venture capital or loaned by commercial banks.

Lastly, firm characteristics are not surprisingly critical to firm performance as much as three capitals of an entrepreneur. Kaplan et al. [21] furthermore suggest that firm characteristics affects more than the others even when the firm has just founded.

Survey Data and Methodology

Survey data

This thesis utilizes the "Internet Survey on Entrepreneurship at Start-ups" jointly conducted in 2012 by the Research Institute of Economy, Trade and Industry (RIETI) and Kazuyuki Motohashi, professor in the Faculty of Engineering, University of Tokyo. The survey questionnaire was sent to 135,059 individuals, out of whom a total of 85,007 people aged 22 to 60 and who are graduates from 14 universities[1] were selected for statistical analysis. A total of 7,023 valid responses were obtained, including 1,501 respondents[2] with experience in starting a business.

The average age of the respondents is 44.5, the median is 45.0, and the standard deviation is 9.0. As Figure 1 shows, their ages range from 22 to 60, and are concentrated between 35 and 55, while there are a few below age 35. The 1,501 respondents with entrepreneurial experience, as Figure 2 shows, have an average age of 46.2 years, the median is 47.0, and the standard deviation is 8.8; there are fewer respondents aged below 35 compared to the entire sample, and more aged 45 or older. As Figure 3 shows, the average age of starting up is 34.8, while the median is 34, and the standard deviation is 8.6. For serial entrepreneurs who had started multiple businesses, the age at which the first business was started was considered to be the age at which they started their business. The oldest age is 60, while the lowest is 13. Some of the entrepreneurs are responding regarding the currently running business while others are responding retrospectively 3.

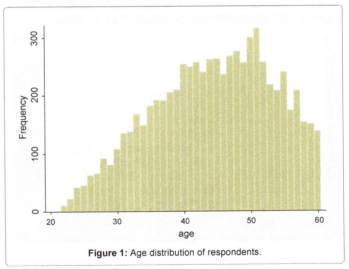

Figure 1: Age distribution of respondents.

---

[1]The 14 universities include The University of Tokyo, Keio University, Waseda University, Kyoto University, Osaka University, Hitotsubashi University, Tokyo Institute of Technology, Doshisha University, Sophia University, Chuo University, Aoyama Gakuin University, Tohoku University, Meiji University and Tokyo University of Science. Japan Venture Research Co., the biggest entrepreneurial data base company in Japan, compiled data of domestic entrepreneurs. It sorted entrepreneurs by alma maters and selected these 14 universities as above, from which more than 10 entrepreneurs graduated and not from other universities. Since we analyze effects of MBA which is hardly gained by other universities' alumni, we focused on these universities.

[2]The 1,501 entrepreneurs among the 7,023 valid responses is an excessively high ratio compared to the average ratio of entrepreneurs in Japan. This is because Transcosmos Inc., which was commissioned to conduct the survey, allowed less time for respondents with no entrepreneurial experience compared to those with experience, since the focus of the survey is on collecting data of entrepreneurs.

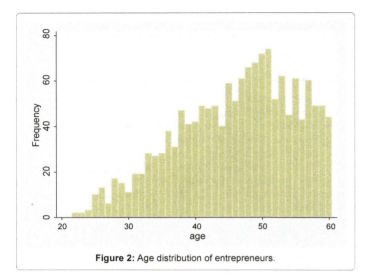

Figure 2: Age distribution of entrepreneurs.

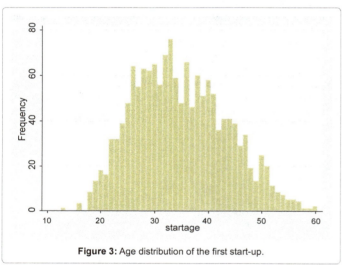

Figure 3: Age distribution of the first start-up.

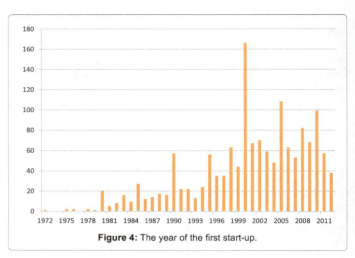

Figure 4: The year of the first start-up.

Industries	Number of firms
Material	27
Electoral Precision	55
Transportation	8
Food	43
Automobile	12
Living ware	30
Financial	105
Real Estate, Construction	152
Energy	20
Leisure, Entertainment	63
Service	377
Distribution	67
Media	25
Local Governments Related	9
ICT, Telecommunication	252
Others	360

Table 1: Industries of start-ups in our survey.

Among the 7,023 who gave valid responses, 5,694 have a bachelor's degree, while 1,329 have either a graduate or doctorate degree including MBA. MBA holders count 90. The survey subjects had a higher academic background compared to the average entrepreneur in Japan since we focused on MBA effects.

Figure 4 shows the distribution of the timing at which the respondents started a business. The earliest is 1972, while the latest is 2012. The number of instances increased around the year of 2000. The distribution of the industry sectors for their first start-up is shown in Table 1. There are more start-ups in the Service industries and Information and Communication Technology (ICT) industries compared to other industries. The distribution of the industry sectors for their first start-up is shown in Table 1. There are more start-ups in the service and IT industries compared to other industries.

As a whole, out of the sample of 7,023 respondents, 1,501 started a business, 962 made a profit.

Models

In this thesis we decompose the effect of MBA into gifted talent effect, occupational experience effect and acquired skills thorough MBA program. Model 1 examines whether MBA impact on entrepreneur's performance as whole. Model 2 and 3 estimates the impact after excluding effects of occupational experiences. In Model 4 and 5, by controlling gifted talent and occupational experiences, we test whether MBA still affect entrepreneurial success. Model 3 checks the robustness of Model 2 and Model 5 does Model 4 by replacing the dependent variable.

In Models 1, 2 and 4, the probability function $\pi(y_i = 1 | x_i)$ of being profitable for an entrepreneur i is defined as below. x_i describes attributes of an entrepreneur i, which consist from human capital, social capital and financial capital in this thesis. Firm characteristics is included in the control factors.

$$\pi(y_i = 1 | x_i) = \ln\left(\frac{\pi(y_i = 1 | x_i)}{1 - \pi(y_i = 1 | x_i)}\right) + \varepsilon_i$$

$= f(\text{human capital}_i, \text{social capital}_i, \text{control variables}_i) + \varepsilon_i$

An index whether an entrepreneur holds MBA or not is categorized in human capital. In Model 1,2 and 4, the profitability here is defined that if an entrepreneur realized operating profit so far, that becomes $y_i = 1$ and if not so far at all, equals 0. The dependent variable is described as "profit". In Model 1, we only used control variables, foundation year dummies and an industry dummy to see simply the effect of MBA. In Model 2, we add human capital and social capital related to occupational experiences, and dummy variables. Then in Model 4, we adopt a variable of an entrepreneur's gifted talent which is proxied by academic scores in the universities where he/she graduated from prior entering MBA curriculum. Also we adopt a variable whether an entrepreneur obtains a family member who is also an entrepreneur as the other proxy of his/her gifted status for being a successful entrepreneur. We adopted binary probit regression for these estimations.

These three models divide the sample into the 886 respondents whose startup is successful and 421 respondents whose startup is not successful. In order to prevent our study from failing to capture business with future potentiality only because a profit had not yet been procured Davidsson and Gordon [14] respondents who launched two or more businesses were given the dependent variable of 1 if they made a profit in their first company and excluded 95 respondents who started their first business in 2011 or later.

Models 3 and Model 5 use ordinary least squares regressions in order to test robustness of Model 2 and Model 4 for each by replacing a binary dependent variable into an integer dependent variable (rating), which is based on ten scaled rating of performance of a start-up by an entrepreneur him/herself. In these regressions, too, first start-ups created in 2011 and later were excluded. Respondents who launched two or more businesses were given the dependent variable of the first start-up.

Independent variables

For the configuration of the independent variables, we used Davidsson and Honig [7] and Honig B and Karlsson [22], Hsu [20] and Ostgaard and Birley [14] in Table 2. All of these studies used questionnaire survey results. Our all variables are described in Table 3.

Regarding independent variables we use whether the respondent have a MBA degree (mba) in order to estimate whether a MBA degree matters on success of entrepreneurship. We use three categorical variables of academic scores (score) in university to gauge gifted academic talent. By adding this variable to estimations, we can exclude the effect of what is gifted to entrepreneurs regardless of MBA program from what is acquired in the program. An index of whether an entrepreneur's family member is also an entrepreneur (familyentre) is included to the effect of gifted as well.

As for other variables related to human capital, we used the years of employed (yrsexp), years in managerial positions during the years employed (yrsmanager), experience in investing venture capital funds (investor exp). We also added parameters asking whether the respondent had started a business in the same industry he/she was in during the employed period (preexp). These four variables are all categorized to explain the effect of occupational experience of an entrepreneur. We mention chronological order of these experience variables later in this chapter. Except for the categorical variable of academic score, ten scaled rating and the number of years, all the other variables are binary. As Van der Sluis et al. [12] suggest, years of education is also worth considered as an independent variable to verify the relationship between the human capital of an entrepreneur and his/her performance, however, since in our survey, respondents are all graduated from universities, we do not adopt it as a variable.

As for social capital, we used binary independent variables for the answers "yes" (=1) and "no" (=0) to questions asking whether the respondents had friends/acquaintances (friends-entre) who are founders/CEOs when respondents started a firm. The variable of "family-entre" we described above is also included in social capital. As Davidsson and Honig [7] explain, family members provide daily management advice to an entrepreneur while friends provide more fresh information and knowledge which is not ever heard before, since they don't see often compare to family members.

As much as human capital and social capital, financial capital is also an important factor in entrepreneurship. While Davidsson and Honig [7] and Ostgaard and Birley [14] did not use variables related to financial capital, Hsu [20] set two binomial control variables on whether the respondent 1) received funds from "angel" investors and 2) received written offers for funds in the past. The survey does not

	Ostgaard & Birley 1996	Davidsson & Honig 2003	Hsu 2007
Dependent Variables	· Sales, growth of sales · Profit, growth of profit · Employment, growth of employment	· Foundation of a firm · Sales & profit within 18 months after foundation · Progress of gestation process · Progress of gestation process within 18 months after foundation	· Valuation of a firm · Investment from VC
Human Capital	**Firm level** · Pre-college level education · Years since foundation · Numbers of employer at the foundation	**Entrepreneur level** · Years of education · Management class enrollment · Years of employer · Years of manager · Previous entrepreneurial experiences	**Entrepreneurial team level** · MBA · Ph.D. · Years since foundation · Number of firms to raise in the past
Social Capital	**Entrepreneur level** · Numbers of affiliated export association and industry association · Numbers of consultees in recent 6 months · What to consult (acquisition of new sellers, investors and customers) · Time spent on networking · Numbers of acquaintances who are engineers or experts (diversity)	**Entrepreneur level** · Parents who are founders/CEOs · Mental support from friends and family members · Neighbors and close friends who are founders/CEOs · Close communication with start-up support association · Affiliated a start-up team in the past · Affiliated a social club or a chamber of commerce married	**Entrepreneurial team level** · Among the board members in post foundation, the ratio of persons who have acquainted to the original founding team members
Result	· Pre-college level education is positive on scale of profit and growth of sales. · Information for acquisition of investment and customers are positive on growth of profit. · Longer time spent of networking are positive on numbers of employers.	· Human capital is positive on a start of a business. · Social capital, especially being affiliated to a social club or a chamber of commerce is positive on a profit and sales.	· Number of business to start in the past and social capital of a founding team are positive on valuation of a firm. · In a sector of internet business, founding team members' doctoral degrees are positive on valuation of a firm.
Data	Questionnaire survey	Questionnaire survey	Questionnaire survey

Table 2: Explanatory Variables of Previous Research.

reveal if the respondents had financial capital, but it asked whether they had "made a request to raise funds (=1)". We assigned it as a proxy of the availability of financial capital and used it as a control variable (finance).

As for gender control, Brush et al. [13] and Rietz et al. [23,24] suggest that performance of entrepreneur is heterogenetic between male and female. The assigned dummy variables, dummy70, dummy80 and dummy90, are for every 10 years in order to control longitudinal changes in the number of business foundations. The baseline is foundation in 2000-2009. As we mentioned earlier, we dropped respondents who started up after in 2010 to avoid truncated bias that they can be successful given enough time. We also adopted industry dummy (ict) to control gap between ICT industries and the others as Colombo et al. [10] suggested.

In this study, we assume a sequence in which entrepreneurs first go universities and then succeeded with their entrepreneurial activity. Respondents who were employed for the first time after they found firms are not few, 116 among the 1,501. This means that when these respondents started their firms, they had not experienced being employed or working in managerial positions, and also did not have investment experience or being employed in the same industry. Therefore, we drop these respondents from our estimations. Similarly, we drop respondents who launched at an early age such as 13 or 16, because they did not have a bachelor's degree or higher, including an MBA, and it is impossible to see the effect of MBA on entrepreneurial activity.

Some of the correlations of independent variables in Table 4 are worth considering. Because when applying MBA program, academic scores in university is always screened. This fact possibly leads that the variable "score" and "mba" be correlated each other. Also human capital and social capital, human capital and financial capital, and social capital and financial capital can be correlated each other according to previous literature[3]. Albeit with these concern, there are no high correlation coefficients between these variables and these statistics lead us to treat them as independent of each other, just as assumed by Davidsson and Honig [7].

Estimation Results

Effects of MBA on entrepreneurial success

The results of estimation are shown in Table 5. First of all, it is verified that a MBA degree matters on entrepreneurial success. The

Variables	Definition
Profit	If a respondent achieved operational profit so far, it equals 1 and if not, equals 0
Rating	Ten scaled self-rating by an entrepreneur regarding his/her start-up
MBA	If a respondent holds MBA degree, it equals 1 and if not, equals 0
score	Three categorized academic scores in undergraduate The higher, the better
Yrs exp	Years of work experience as an employee
Yrs manager	Years of work experience as an employed manager
Investor exp	If a respondent obtains work experience as an investor or venture capitalist
Pre exp	If a respondent obtains work experience in the same industry where a respondent started-up, it equals 1 and if not, equals 0
Friends entre	If a respondent have friends who are entrepreneurs, it equals 1 and if not 0
Family entre	If a respondent have family member who are entrepreneurs, it equals 1 and if not 0
Finance	If a respondent made a request to raise funds, it equals 1 and if not 0.
Gender	If a respondent is male, it equals 1 and if female, it equals 0
Dummy70	If an entrepreneur's start-up is founded in 70's, it equals 1 and if not 0
Dummy80	If an entrepreneur's start-up is founded in 70's, it equals 1 and if not 0
Dummy90	If an entrepreneur's start-up is founded in 70's, it equals 1 and if not 0

Table 3: Description of Variables.

	Obs	Mean	Std. Dev	Min	Max	Profit	Rating	MBA	Score	Yrs exp	Yrs manager	Investor exp	Pre exp	Friends entre	Family entre	Finance	Gender	Dummy 70	Dummy 80	Dummy 90
Profit	1307	0.0678	0.467	0	1															
Rating	1307	5.679	2.337	1	10	0.405														
MBA	1307	0.035	0.184	0	1	0.061	0.119													
Score	1307	2.082	0.692	1	3	0.07	0.176	0.133												
Yrs exp	1307	7.9	8.372	0	37	-0.019	0.024	0.007	0.045											
Yrs manager	1307	4.936	7.421	0	40	0.089	0.082	0.009	0.025	0.425										
Investor exp	1307	0.144	0.351	0	1	-0.053	0.061	0.229	0.074	-0.024	-0.007									
Pre exp	1307	0.314	0.464	0	1	0.089	0.019	-0.004	-0.028	0.164	0.183	0.024								
Friends entre	1307	0.487	0.5	0	1	0.132	0.026	0.021	0.031	0.077	0.106	-0.012	0.07							
Family entre	1307	0.286	0.452	0	1	0.063	0.067	0.044	0.006	-0.069	-0.007	0.035	-0.016	0.185						
Finance	1307	0.147	0.354	0	1	0.059	0.095	0.05	0.042	0.044	0.037	0.058	0.013	0.088	0.024					
Gender	1307	0.871	0.335	0	1	0.019	-0.058	0.011	-0.13	0.14	0.114	0.008	0.092	0.073	0	0.043				
Dummy70	1307	0.006	0.078	0	1	-0.009	0.036	-0.015	-0.009	-0.032	0.021	-0.004	-0.053	0.041	0.015	-0.033	-0.029			
Dummy80	1307	0.11	0.313	0	1	0.122	0.073	-0.054	-0.028	-0.099	0.022	-0.068	-0.022	0.082	0.134	0.054	0.026	-0.028		
Dummy90	1307	0.284	0.451	0	1	0.093	0.012	-0.019	-0.016	0.004	0.116	-0.05	0.028	0.018	-0.016	0.026	0.049	-0.049	-0.0222	
Ict	1307	0.174	0.38	0	1	0.058	0.043	0.076	0.056	-0.028	-0.045	0.053	0.185	0.04	-0.019	-0.009	0.038	-0.036	-0.027	-0.044

Table 4: Fundamental Statistics and Correlation Matrix.

[3]For example, (Bosma et al. 2004) and (Glaeser, Laibson, and Sacerdote 2002) suggest that people who have excellent human capital tend to spend more time obtaining social capital.

	Model 1	Model 2	Model 3	Model 4	Model 5
Dependent variable	Profit	Profit	Rating	Profit	Rating
MBA2	0.556*	0.635**	1.37***	0.559*	1.126**
Score	-	-	-	0.135*	0.510***
Yrs exp	-	-0.011**	0.002	-0.011*	-0.055
Yrs manager	-	0.016**	.024**	0.016*	0.265
Investor exp	-	-0.239**	0.252	-0.256*	0.515**
Pre exp	-	0.210**	0.018	0.218*	1.314
Friends entre	-	0.283***	0.550***	0.266***	0.626**
Family entre	-	-	-	0.078	0.167
Finance	-	0.169	0.011	0.16	0.23
Gender	0.02	-0.034	-0.541***	0.008	0.001
Dummy70	0.088	-0.009	1.28	0.001	0.023*
Dummy80	0.728***	0.645***	.654***	0.641***	0.194
Dummy90	0.389***	0.323***	0.163	0.325***	0.053
Ict	0.224*	0.177	0.276	0.164	-0.388*
_Cons	0.215*	0.123	5.66***	-0.195	4.460***
Observations	1,307	1,307	1,307	1,307	1,307
-2LL (Degree of Freedom)	54.18 (6)	93.23 (13)	-	100.13 (14)	-
Adjusted R^2	-	-	0.036	-	0.076

*p < 0.05, **p < 0.01, ***p < 0.001

Table 5: Estimation results.

coefficients of a MBA degree (mba) on profitability and self-evaluation of a start-up are all positive. MBA holders more likely to success in start-ups than ones without it.

After controlling the effect of occupational experiences in Model 2 and Model 3, the coefficients of a MBA degree are still positively significant. Furthermore we exclude the effects of what is gifted, the effects of MBA are still positively significant in Model 4 and Model 5.

Since the MBA effects are divided into gifted, experience and acquirement through a MBA program, these estimation results mean that acquirement thorough MBA program positively boost entrepreneurial success.

Other variables effects

As for human capital, length of employment in years (yrsexp) has negative impact on success of start-ups mainly in Models 2 and Model 5. By contrast, the length of experience as a manager (yrsmanager) and vocational experience in the same industry (pre-exp) has a positive impact. Experience as an investor (investor-exp) differs between dependent variables.

Having friends who are entrepreneurs/CEOs (friends-entre) positively affect profitability meanwhile having a family who are entrepreneurs/CEOs (family-entre) has no bearing on the profitability and scale of performance. As for financial capital (finance), effects are insignificant in our estimations.

As for dummy variables, females are slightly less successful than males. Entrepreneurs who started up in 80s and 90s compared to 70s and 2000s are more positive on performance. Starting up in ICT industries only shows vague effects.

We mention the fitness of models for the last, as Table 5 shows, a chi-squared test confirms that null hypothesis that all the coefficients equal to zero is rejected in each estimation model of Models 1, 2 and 4. In Model 3 and Model 5, p-value associated with the F value confirms that the independent variables over all reliably predict the dependent variable in each estimation.

Conclusion

From five estimations of performance, we verified that MBA holders have advantage on staring up a new business. The reasons is not that MBA holders are privileged with gifted talent or occupational experience but that MBA holders gain resource through the MBA program. There are some arguments that being an alumna is the all you should do with the degree. It implicates that MBA degree is certification that you have talent of being good entrepreneur and enough experience to be so even without schooling the program very ironically. However instead this thesis completely denies this argument. MBA program is worth completion because even when we controlled the gifted talent and experience, it still heightens performance of an entrepreneur.

This conclusion encourages potential applicants of MBA program by explaining that MBA program is worthwhile of investing their two years as students. Meanwhile it does not always guarantee that MBA education is effective. Since we mentioned in the Chapter Two, the mechanism of MBA program impacts on entrepreneurial activity is still vague. MBA programs are possibly effective because the education gives a student creativity, leadership or other essential sense as an entrepreneur whereas, they are possibly effective because of peer network encompassed through classmates. Further empirical research is expected in this mechanism discussion.

Acknowledgements

This research is granted by Research Institute of Economy, Trade and Industry (RIETI). We thank thoughtful comments and suggestions from participants at the Discussion Paper Seminar held in RIETI and at workshops in Matsuo Laboratory in University of Tokyo.

References

1. Harmon C, Oosterbeck H, Walker I (2003) The returns to education: Microeconomics. Journal of Economic Surveys 17: 115-155.
2. Charney AH, Libecap GD (2003) The Contribution of Entrepreneur Education: An Analysis of the Berger Program. International Journal of Entrepreneruship Education 1: 385-418.
3. Lange JE, Marram E, Jawahar AS, Yong W, Bygrave W (2011) Does an entrepreneurship education have lasting value? A study of careers of 4,000 alumni. Frontiers of Entrepreneurship Research 31: 209-224.
4. Simpson R, Sturges J, Weigh P (2010) Transient, unsettling and creative space: Experiences of liminality through the accounts of Chinese students on a UK-based MBA. Management Learning 41: 53-70.
5. Lerner J, Ulrike M (2013) With a little help from my (random) friends: Success and failure in post-business school entrepreneurship. National Bureau of Economic Research Working Paper Series 26: 2411-2452.
6. Krishnan VR (2008) Impact of MBA education on students' values: Two longitudinal studies. Journal of Business Ethics 83: 233-246.
7. Davidsson P, Honig B (2003). The role of social and human capital among nascent entrepreneurs. Journal of Business Venturing 18: 301-331.
8. Shane S (2000) Prior Knowledge and the Discovery of Entrepreneurial Opportunities. Organization Science 11: 448-469.
9. Bosma N, Van Praag M, Thurik R, De Wit G (2004) The Value of Human and Social Capital Investments for the Business Performance of Startups. Small Business Economics 23: 227-236.
10. Colombo MG, Delmastro M, Grilli L (2004) Entrepreneurs' Human Capital and The Start-Up Size of New Technology-Based Firms. International Journal of Industrial Organization 22: 1183-1221.
11. Parker SC, Van Praag M (2006) Schooling, Capital Constraints and Entrepreneurial Performance: The Endogenous Triangle. Journal of Business and Economic Statistics 24: 416-431.

12. Van Der Sluis J, Van Praag M, Vijverberg W (2008) Education and entrepreneurship selection and performance: A review of the empirical literature. Journal of Economic Surveys 22: 795-841.
13. Brush C, Manolova TS, Edelman LF (2008) Properties of emerging organizations: An empirical test. Journal of Business Venturing 23: 547-566.
14. Davidsson P, Gordon SR (2011) Panel studies of new venture creation: a methods-focused review and suggestions for future research. Small Business Economics 39: 853-876.
15. Nahapiet J, Ghoshal S (1998) Social capital, intellectual capital, and the organizational advantage. Academy of Management Review 23: 242-266.
16. Adler SP, Kwon SW (2009) Social Capital: Prospects for a New Concept. Academy of Management Review 27: 17-40.
17. Ostgaard TA, Birley S (1996) New Venture Growth and Personal Networks. Journal of Business Research 36: 37-50.
18. Honig B (1998) What determines success? Examining the human, financial, and social capital of Jamaican microentrepreneurs. Journal of Business Venturing 13: 371-394.
19. Cooper AC, Folta TB, Woo C (1995) Entrepreneurial information search. Journal of Business Venturing 10: 107-120.
20. Hsu DH (2007) Experienced entrepreneurial founders, organizational capital, and venture capital funding. Research Policy 36: 722-741.
21. Kaplan SN, Sensoy BA, Stromberg P (2009) Should Investors Bet on The Jockey or The Horse? Evidence from The Evolution of Firms from Early Business Plans to Public Companies. Journal of Finance, LXIV: 75-115.
22. Honig B, Karlsson T (2004) Institutional forces and the written business plan. Journal of Management 30: 29-48.
23. Rietz AD, Henrekson M, Small S, Economics B, Feb N, et al. (2000) Testing the Female Underperformance Hypothesis. Small Business Economics 14: 1-10.
24. Glaeser EL, Laibson D, Sacerdote B (2002) An Economic Approach to Social Capital. The Economic Journal 112: 437-458.

Effects of Leadership Behavior on the Organizational Commitment and Job Satisfaction: A Public Sector Research

Mehmet Sahin G[1]* and Büşra K[2]

[1]*Faculty of Business Administration, Gebze Technical University, Kocaeli, Turkey*
[2]*Department of Administrative Science, Beykent University, Istanbul, Turkey*

Abstract

This study arisen from the basic hypothesis that employees with high job satisfaction also have high organizational commitment analyzed the importance of leadership behavior for institutions through different sub-dimensions. For that purpose, while analyzing the effects of leadership behavior upon organizational commitment and job satisfaction, effects of commitment level upon employee satisfaction were also evaluated. Within the scope of the study, 234 valid questionnaires were collected from different public institutions, and the data obtained from these questionnaires were evaluated through multiple regression analyses. The analysis results indicated that leadership behaviors had a significant effect upon organizational commitment and job satisfaction; however, this effect was lower than expected. Practicing this research to the public sector where employees have been accepted as a mechanical factor of the state both provided a contribution upon the relevant literature and offered important suggestions for the practitioners.

Keywords: Job satisfaction; Organizational commitment; Leadership; Institutional commitment

Introduction

In dynamic socio-economic structure of today's world competition has rapidly increased, the importance of job satisfaction has improved for employees and organizations. It can be observed that when employees feel themselves happier and more peaceful in their individual and organizational life, their job satisfaction increases directly proportional [1], in this sense, job satisfaction means that as long as individuals are happy and peaceful in their job, the positive feeling they have towards their job increases.

On the other hand, the concept of organizational commitment in firms has an important place in industrial psychology, and whether it has a relationship with job satisfaction has been discussed [2]. Upon "*leadership*," definition and roles of the manager, managerial levels and skills, efficient leadership, reflections of leadership and leadership theories in terms of the current entities affect job satisfaction and organizational commitment directly [3].

With reference to this, this study had the main purpose of analyzing organizational commitment and job satisfaction levels of individuals as result of leadership behavior presented in organizations under the titles of "*Job Satisfaction, Organizational Commitment, and Leadership,*" and examining the reflections of possible effects upon institutional performance. Within the scope of the study, the mutual relationships between organizational commitment, leadership and job satisfaction and their effects upon the institutional performance were analyzed. From this point forth, results of job satisfaction, and performance, productivity, and job dissatisfaction in relation with job satisfaction were discussed in theoretical background section. The concept of organizational commitment, its classification, the factors affecting the organizational commitment of employees and the relation between leadership behavior and job satisfaction were also analyzed within the scope of this section.

Theoretical Background

In today's conditions, majority of employees' time is observed to be spent in their workplaces. This made the subjects of understanding job satisfaction and increasing the level of satisfaction more important.

Bullock [4] explained job satisfaction as "the total of several experiences desired and not related to job". Vroom discussed job satisfaction as "a criteria of various-dimension job attitudes related to the perceptions, feelings, and behaviors of employees" [5,6]. In this sense, job satisfaction is a function of values, and desire of an employee related to obtain –actualize- anything whether consciously or not determines the level of job satisfaction [7-9]. In other words, job satisfaction means meeting the values of an individual related to job at work, adaptation of these values with the needs of individuals, and emotional satisfaction achieved by an employee while evaluating the job or work life [10].

Priorities of employees related to their work can vary. For that reason, employees in different positions can achieve different satisfactions from a specific situation. Job satisfaction is a balance created from the salary and people individuals get happy from working together. If someone is materially and morally satisfied with the senior-junior relationships, working conditions, relations in team works, and get happy due to this environment, his/her achieving job satisfaction will facilitate. Moreover, personal characteristics of employees affect job satisfaction differently. Individual factors affecting the job satisfaction are age, education, gender, status, personality, experience, level of intelligence, working conditions, wage, and sociocultural environment [11].

On the other hand, there is a remarkable relationship between job satisfaction and performance. The reason for this is the thought that employees should be both productive and happy. Job satisfaction and performance relationship has been tried to be explained through two different viewpoints. According to the first approach, job satisfaction

**Corresponding author: Mehmet Sahin G, Assistant Professor, Faculty of Business Administration, Gebze Technical University, Kocaeli, Turkey
E-mail: sahingok@gtu.edu.tr*

affects performance, and employees should be provided to be happy for a higher productivity in production [9]. In other approach, it is argued that high performance brings about job satisfaction. The common point of both approaches is the necessity of satisfying the employees and necessity of creating a reward system depending upon the performance [10].

According to modern management understanding, success of organizations and their performance should not be evaluated according to the variables depending upon profitability, market share, tax pay, but according to human dimension. Job satisfaction in terms of organizations should be an ethical necessity and social responsibility before anything else and its effects upon the institutional performance should be considered [12].

In this sense, economic, social, and psychological satisfaction of employees should be provided at work they carry on. When the manager of an entity provides these using different kinds of methods, creating the commitment and trust of employees to the workplace and increasing the motivation will be easier. When people are in compliant with the organization they work for, they will adapt the targets and instruments of the organization and this will contribute upon sharing the common purposes [13]. Accordingly, increasing the level of organizational commitment becomes prominent as a prior issue in terms of entities.

Three different approaches can be mentioned upon commitment of employees. Whereas organizational behavior researchers prefer to emphasize attitudinal commitment heavily, social psychologists emphasize behavioral commitment and multi-dimensional commitment more [14]. Attitudinal commitment can be defined as "the desire of an individual to identify with the value judgments and targets of the institution, and the desire to maintain organization membership in order to facilitate reaching these targets." In other words, attitudinal commitment means individuals' adaptation and integrating with the organization [15]. According to this viewpoint, behavioral commitment discusses organizational commitment as a behavior. It defines organizational commitment explaining the difference between behaviors and attitudes. This type of behavior can be defined as individuals' creating reasons to commit themselves into their workplace reducing the desires, expectations and dissatisfaction in order not to leave the place they work.

Multiple commitment approach as another view assumes that individuals present different commitment to their profession, customers, managers, and colleagues, total commitment individuals feel towards the organization is the total of commitment felt towards the different dimensions of organization. The groups in the organization and their targets create the center of individuals' multiple commitments. This unity and solidarity in nature of the organization creates multiple-dimension commitment approach [16]. In all three approaches, it is concluded that employee commitment has a multi-dimensional and complex structure and has a direct effect upon the firm performance; and in this sense, role of manager, leadership approaches in other words, becomes prominent in order to provide organizational commitment.

Leadership is defined as the process of individuals' affecting and directing the other employees in order to provide individuals or group reach their targets under specific conditions [17]. Accordingly, the leader means the one who has followers, and there is a relationship depending upon trust between the leader and followers. In this sense, leader is defined as the person who can most efficiently direct the group upon determining the targets of a group and achieving these targets [18]. In another approach, leader is the person who is followed by a group of people for achieving their own or group targets, and they behave in accordance with the instructions and orders of that person. The common points of these definitions that show similarity in the literature are leader's directing individuals using a more efficient power rather than the legal one an organization accords for himself/herself related to one or more purposes and providing to present behaviors that will create positive values for the targets, purposes and strategies of the entity [19].

The roles of the leader appear in two different dimensions including the emotional roles and mission oriented roles. Mission oriented roles include a series of roles related to creating, prompting, and managing a group in order to actualize specific purposes. And emotional roles include the leadership roles related to meeting the social and psychological needs of employees. It can be defined as the role of internalizing limitless diversities of people in terms of their styles, abilities and interests, and prompting these properties in a way that will provide advantages for the firm [19].

The studies carried out upon basic behaviors of leadership, acquisition of leadership competences and various sides of leadership process have generally been categorized into two main groups as classical and modern leadership theories. Classical leadership theories include three main sub-titles as Personal Traits Approach, Situational Reaction Approach, and Leader's Followers' Approach that emerge as result of the reactions caused by attitudes and behaviors of people. The fundamental philosophy in personal traits approach is established upon the fact that successful leaders have more specific traits and qualities rather than the unsuccessful leaders. According to the situational reaction theory, specific situations and conditions cause the result that people with specific qualities should be leaders. Leader's followers' theory does not ignore the importance and specific qualities of a situation or conditions, but argues that leaders should be evaluated with the followers around them. In this sense, it argues that behaviors of leaders take form under the effect of people and groups around themselves [19].

Modern leadership theories are explained in two dimensions as the approach based upon behavior data and situational modern approach. Behaviorist theory regards behaviors of leaders rather than their properties. Success and efficiency of leaders does not depend upon their properties, but depends upon the behaviors they show while leading. In these behaviors, the behaviors such as communication skills of the leaders with followers, view and practice towards transfer of authority, approach towards the planning process, and way of determining the targets, etc. are evaluated as the basic factors determining the efficiency of a leader. Accordingly, followers as well as the characteristic traits affect the success of a leader [20]. According to the contingency approach, integrity of an efficient leader does not have only one property, and there is no leadership style presenting an efficient leadership property in all situations. Because the factors affecting the efficiency of leadership style vary in any situations, they have been tried to be determined separately [6,7]. These factors are personality, experience and expectations of the leader, expectations and behaviors of senior managers, requirements of assignment, organization culture and policies, and expectations and behaviors of employees. According to another modern approach evaluating the leadership properties, 6 types of leadership approaches can be mentioned [21].

These approaches are grouped as (i) Charismatic leadership, (ii) Transformational leadership, (iii) Democratic leadership, (iv)

Authoritarian leadership, (v) Transformational leadership, and (vi) Laissez faire leadership. To sum up, leadership is a process and reality in any environments where people, groups and organizations exist. Upon the unity of employees with the framework of company's common targets, their level of satisfaction and emergence of organizational commitment and job satisfaction in the big picture, leadership can be mentioned to have a prominent importance.

Research Design

In this study Research analysis of leadership upon job satisfaction and organizational commitment, and research on its effect upon the public personnel were carried out. In the research, questionnaire was used as the data collection tool. The questionnaire used in the research included three sections. Job satisfaction scale was used in the first section of the questionnaire, organizational commitment scale was used in the second section, and leadership scale was used in the final section. The questionnaire performed related to job satisfaction in the first section [22], included seven questions from the study of Keleş. Organizational commitment scale used in the second section was developed by John [23], and included 26 questions separated in four different types of commitment. These organizational commitment types included the sub-factors of (i) Emotional commitment, (ii) Conscientious commitment, (iii) Normative commitment, and (iv) Institutional commitment. In the third and final section, leadership items were created collecting from current transformational and interactive leadership questionnaires. These scale items were on 7-point Likert type in questionnaire form, and limited as (1) I totally disagree (2) I mostly disagree (3) I partly disagree (4) Neither agree nor disagree (5) I partly agree (6) I mostly agree (7) I totally agree.

The results of 234 questionnaires were included into the analyses. In this study carried out in public sector, private permission was obtained from managers, and security of the obtained data was confirmed. Considering the sensitivity and ethical principles of managers, an environment of confidence was created mentioning that no name was used in questionnaires, and the research had totally a scientific purpose.

The relationships between job satisfaction, organizational commitment, and leadership analyzed within the scope of the research were presented as in below through the study model. Those were also listed in items in hypotheses (Figure 1).

Analysis and Results

The study analyses were actualized using SPSS 17.0 package program. Firstly, a reliability analysis was performed in a way covering the whole questionnaire. Cronbach Alpha coefficient was determined as 0.867 in analyses in which totally 40 questions were discussed. In order to secure scientific validity of research results, reliability analysis was performed to each factor separately. According to these results, job satisfaction scale including 7 questions had the value of 0.656; job satisfaction including 5 questions had the value of 0.835; and organizational commitment including 26 questions had the value of 0.851. Although job satisfaction scale seemed below the threshold value, it increased the general reliability of the scale because it became significant when evaluated together with all scales.

After the reliability analyses, factor analyses were performed. According to the factor analysis results, leadership and job satisfaction were loaded to their own factors. And organizational commitment was grouped into four different sub-factors within itself. In order to analyze the mutual relationship between the variables, Pearson correlation analysis was carried out. Obtained results were presented in Table 1.

According to above correlation analysis table, a statistically significant relationship was found between job satisfaction and emotional commitment, conscientious commitment and leadership. Whereas emotional commitment had the highest (0.474) correlation coefficient among these variables, conscientious commitment (0.400) was on the second rank, and leadership (0.176) had the third relationship level. On the other hand, no significant relationship was

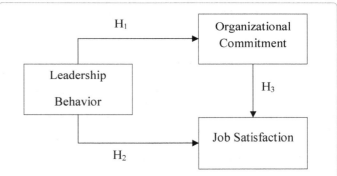

H_1: Leadership behavior positively affects organizational commitment.
H_2: Leadership behavior positively affects job satisfaction.
H_3: Organizational commitment positively affects job satisfaction.

Figure 1: Research Model.

		Emotional Commitment	Conscientious Commitment	Institutional Commitment	Normative Commitment	Leadership	Satisfaction
Emotional Commitment	Pearson	1	0.606**	0.183**	0.198**	0.197**	0.474**
	Sig.		0.000	0.005	0.002	0.002	0.000
Conscientious Commitment	Pearson		1	0.180**	0.355**	0.350**	0.400**
	Sig.			0.006	0.000	0.000	0.000
Institutional Commitment	Pearson			1	0.185**	-0.027	0.116
	Sig.				0.005	0.679	0.076
Normative Commitment	Pearson				1	0.203**	0.077
	Sig.					0.002	0.243
Leadership	Pearson					1	0.176**
	Sig.						0.007
Satisfaction	Pearson						1
	Sig.						

** Significant at 0.01 level
N=234

Table 1: Correlation Analysis Results.

found between job satisfaction and institutional commitment and normative commitment. Furthermore, there is a significant relationship between leadership and institutional commitment; however, it had no statistically significant relationship with the other types of commitment. According to analysis results, as well, organizational commitment variables had significant relationship among themselves as expected.

In subsequent stage of the study, regression analyses were performed in order to analyze the effect of organizational commitment sub-factors and leadership upon employee satisfaction, and analysis results were presented in Table 2. In established multiple regression model, 4 sub-factors of the organizational commitment and leadership factor were included into the process as independent variables. Especially emotional commitment (β=0.361) and conscientious commitment (β=0.183) had a determinant strength upon job satisfaction; and they affected job satisfaction positively. Effecting percentage of these two factors upon job satisfaction was 25.2% (R^2=0.252); in other words, 25.2% of the changes in job satisfaction were explained with these commitment sub-factors (Table 2).

On the other hand, according to regression analysis results, leadership had no significant effect upon job satisfaction. The basic reason for this was organizational commitment factors' shading the leadership factor. The reason for this was that leadership was noticed to be in a mutual interaction with job satisfaction though at a low level in correlation analysis. In order to analyze in more details, regression analysis was actualized in the second stage. In this analysis model, the variables of conscientious commitment and normative commitment that had significant effect upon job satisfaction were excluded from the model. The analysis results were presented in Table 3.

Institutional commitment, normative commitment and leadership factors were included into the regression analysis explained in terms of the results in Table 3. The analysis results indicated that leadership factor had effect upon job satisfaction with 0.175 coefficients. So that it was revealed that leadership factor was shaded by emotional commitment and conscientious commitment. Accordingly, it can be stated that leadership qualities partly lost their importance in an entity where organizational commitment is intense.

Conclusion

The study results revealed that employees that can establish strong ties with their organizations could maintain their permanence in organization. As known, permanent commitment is related to employees' being aware of the cost for leaving the organization and its results. Moreover, it was determined in analysis results that employees experiencing high level of job satisfaction in their organization presented higher commitment towards their organization. In this sense, if environments that will provide job satisfaction are created for employees, commitment towards organization can be mentioned to increase.

On the other hand, according to the study results, leadership was noticed to affect organizational commitment and job satisfaction positively. Furthermore, it was also concluded that this effect was lower than expected in public sector. The reason for this could be considered as that managers in public sector do not regard leadership much. This caused the reality that there is a need for developing leadership methods and behaviors in public institutions, and studies that will be carried upon this can have positive effects.

A leader should be the Pearson who unifies prompts and efficiently manages employees in order to provide them actualizes determined targets. Leaders should encourage people for working through their broad vision, and provide employees to reveal all their abilities determining interpersonal group strategies among the people who will efficiently work. Accordingly, administrative leaders who do not accept public employees as a mechanical factor of the state will not only increase the organizational commitment of employees but also provide positive effects upon institutional performance increase.

Refrences

1. Steyrer J, Schiffinger M, Lang R (2008) "Organizational commitment - A missing link between leadership behavior and organizational performance?". Scandinavian Journal of Management 24: 364-374.
2. Baek YM, Jung CS (2014) "Focusing the mediating role of institutional trust: How does interpersonal trust promote organizational commitment?". The Social Science Journal.
3. Kim WG, Brymer RA (2011) "The effects of ethical leadership on manager job satisfaction, commitment, behavioral outcomes, and firm performance". International Journal of Hospitality Management 30: 1020-1026.
4. Bullock RP (1953) Position, Function, and Job Satisfaction of Nurses in the Social System of a Modern Hospital. Nursing Research 2: 4-14.
5. Vroom VH (1962) "Ego-Involvement, Job Satisfaction, and Job Performance". Personnel Psychology 15: 159-177.
6. Simsek, Levent (1995) Job Satisfaction Efficiency Magazine (MPM Publishing).
7. Lightning, Sharif Tahir A, Adnan C (2003) Introduction to Behavioral Sciences and Organizational Behavior Science.
8. Neal M, Ashkanasy WJ, Barutcugil (2002) Management of emotions in organizations.
9. Barry AC (2004) The Complex Resource-Based View: Implications for Theory and Practice in Strategic Human Resource Management Strategic Human Resource Management.
10. Izgi, Hussein (2011) "Definitions Related to Job Satisfaction." Industrial and Organizational Psychology in, by: Konya Training Academy Press.
11. Fatih V (2010) Organizational commitment and Job Satisfaction the effect your intentions to quit.
12. Beryl A (2001) Corporate Culture.
13. Ejike D, Sevda (2011) Organizational Trust, organizational commitment and Job Satisfaction in terms of the perception of Employees, Kahramanmaras Textile Industry Research.
14. Banai M, Reisel WD, Probst TM (2004) "A managerial and personal control model: predictions of work alienation and organizational commitment in Hungary". Journal of International Management 10: 375-392.

	β	T	Sig.
Constant	2,354	5,520	0.000**
Emotional Commitment	0.361	4,981	0.000**
Conscientious Commitment	0.183	2,337	0.020*
Institutional Commitment	0.033	0,558	0.578
Normative Commitment	-0.078	-1,246	0.214
Leadership	0.058	0.934	0.351

** Significant at 0.01 level; * Significant at 0.05 level,
R^2=0.252, F=15.380

Table 2: Regression Analysis Results.

	β	T	Sig.
Constant	3,597	8,219	0.000**
Institutional Commitment	0.117	1,786	0.075
Normative Commitment	0.019	0.290	0.772
Leadership	0.175	2,662	0.008**

** Significant at 0.01 level
R^2=0.046, F=3.700

Table 3: Second Stage Regression Analysis Results.

15. Podsakoff PM, MacKenzie SB, Bommer WH (1996) "Transformational leader behaviors and substitutes for leadership as determinants of employee satisfaction, commitment, trust, and organizational citizen". Journal of Management 22: 259-298.

16. Emine C (1999) On the Relationship Between Organizational Commitment Organizational Trust With An Instance of The Event.

17. Tamer K (2005) Business Fundamentals. Istanbul, Turkey: Ankara publishing.

18. Ballard (2004) Ayse can Behavioral Sciences. Istanbul: Avciol publishing.

19. Canan C (2008) Administrators leadership Styles, change management and team work assessment as Multi-directional Relationships Between.

20. Dean T (2005) Features of public and private Sector Organizations. A field for the identification of Leadership Behavior Works English Social 1-16.

21. Ozsahin M, Zehir C, Acar ZA (2011) "Linking leadership style to firm performance: the mediating effect of the learning orientation". Procedia - Social and Behavioral Sciences 24: 1546-1559.

22. Khan S, Hatice N (2006) Job Satisfaction Impact on organizational commitment related to pharmaceutical manufacturing and Distribution Firms a study.

23. John M, Natalie A (1991) A three-Component Conceptualization of Organizational Commitment. Humman Resource Managment Review 1: 61-89.

Medical Value as a New Strategy to Increase Corporate Viability: Market Chances and Limitations in the Diagnostic Industry

Schäfer H Hendrik, Filser Ludwig[2], Rohr Ulrich P[1], Laubender Ruediger P[2], Dieterle Thomas[1], Maitland Roger[3] and Zaugg Christian E[4]

[1]Divisional Medical and Scientific Affairs, F. Hoffmann-La Roche Ltd, 4070 Basel, Switzerland
[2]Roche Professional Diagnostics, Biostatistics and Data Management, 82377 Penzberg, Germany
[3]Graduate School of Business, University of Cape Town, 8002 Cape Town, South Africa
[4]Roche Professional Diagnostics, Global Medical and Scientific Affairs, 6343 Rotkreuz, Switzerland

Abstract

Study background: While the strategic advantage of Medical Value (MV) products is widely accepted in developed markets, it remains unclear if varying societal wealth influences the perception of customers on MV products.

Methods: 231 of 240 Internal Medicine physicians from 8 countries participated in a survey with 5 multiple choice questions on MV. Responses from countries have been allocated to income levels according to world-bank data. Three groups have been defined (high-income countries: Canada, Norway and Switzerland=developed markets, upper-mid income markets: Argentina, China, Mexico and Turkey, lower-mid income counties: India=emerging markets). Answers have been statistically analyzed in subgroups (emerging markets vs. developed markets).

Results: The majority of physicians believed that reliable and clinically validated treatment algorithms should accompany a product qualifying for MV. Algorithms should be created, predominantly for existing markers. Emphasis has been given to the discovery of better markers for well-known diseases in developed markets. Physicians' answers on pivotal factors for MV products yielded highest emphasis for generalizability (global technical standardization and data comparability). Technical excellence was given lower priority in developed markets comparing to emerging markets. Cost control was emphasized mainly in high-income markets.

Conclusion: Both developed and emerging markets demand more clinical trials to establish algorithms for diagnostic tests. The prove of clinical utility is a pivotal factor for sustainable business success.

Keywords: Medical value; Diagnostic industry; Corporate viability; Societal value; Health care; Cost-control

Introduction

Innovation requires non-transferrable solutions

In the last five years the diagnostic industry is facing stricter regulatory hurdles for product approval [1]. In addition, the competition for customers, and market segments has grown remarkably. Because competition leads to product substitutability and to price erosion [2] diagnostic vendors try to outperform competitors with high-throughput volume of diagnostic devices, technical improvement of their assays and high-level customer support.

Although, environmental factors force businesses to constantly innovate [3], related costs are high and executives become increasingly risk averse [4]. Current management literature describes a negative relationship between competition and innovation [5]. Other authors state an inverse U-curve relationship between these two determinants [6]. Competitive pressure seems to result in an initial increase in innovation, but a decline can be observed in the long run. Facing competition, the inclining part of the inverse U-shape can be explained by the attempt of companies to explore alternative business models [7]. This "escape phenomenon" creates a momentum for companies to innovate and to develop non-transferrable solutions, which allow them to quickly gain high market shares.

A changing environment requires new value-based thinking

In recent years diagnostic companies have realized that the simple service provision based on high volume test devices, that target testing efficiency and accuracy, might not be sufficient anymore to maintain annual growth rates. This is based on a changing landscape of payer policies resulting from monetary constraints in developed markets (DM) and emerging markets (EM) [8]. Especially notable is a tendency of health care systems to change from service-based towards value-based reimbursement, which emphasizes the payer's need for more effective patient management (Figure 1).

Multiple theoretical articles elucidate the related concept of "customer value" in service delivery [9]. While this concept certainly holds true for pharmaceutical agents, the reimbursement of diagnostic tests is still driven by the technology used and not by the value it creates [10].

Different to this, for pharmaceutical agents, the National Institute for Health Care Excellence (NICE) has targeted the cost-intensive approach of service reward several years ago by introducing strict evidence-based medicine and outcome-based reimbursement of physicians, e.g. in hypertension [11]. Also in Germany, in 2011 the AMNOG (Act on the Restructuring of the pharmaceutical market) has changed the landscape of reimbursement. The legislation became necessary as the expenditure for drugs have increased dramatically by 1.5 billion € in 2009 (5.3%). AMNOG was created to sustain a new balance between innovation and affordable medicines [12].

---

*Corresponding author: Schäfer H Hendrik, Divisional Medical and Scientific Affairs, F. Hoffmann-La Roche Ltd, 4070 Basel, Switzerland
E-mail: Hendrik.Schaefer@roche.com

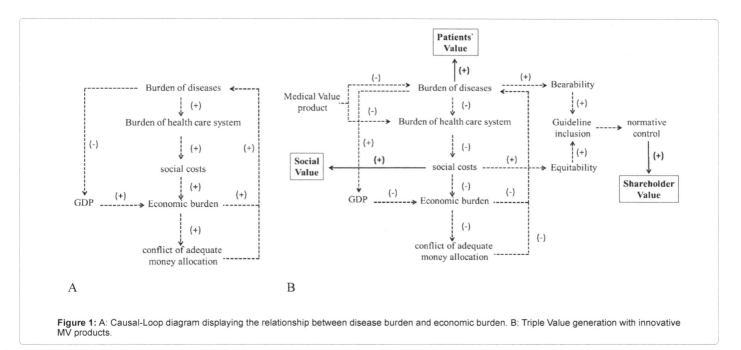

Figure 1: A: Causal-Loop diagram displaying the relationship between disease burden and economic burden. B: Triple Value generation with innovative MV products.

According to the new legislation the manufacturer now is required to submit evidence of the added value for the patient. The Federal Joint Committee decides whether and what additional benefits a new drug has and how this will be reflected in the pricing. For medical products, prices are negotiated on the basis of the evaluation of the added value. For drugs with no additional benefit a fixed amount is set. The new law aims to create savings of about 2 billion € per year. AMNOG is planned to be extended to medical devices. More systems are likely to change and will prospectively base their policies on reliable cost-effectiveness data [13] to lower economic and social costs. Figure 1 displays how Medical Value products reduce social costs. Their contribution to the society may result into Guideline inclusion and increase bearability and equitability. Normative control yields profit for shareholders Figure 1.

The effectiveness of health systems differs

Interestingly, healthcare spending and Disability Adjusted Life Years (DALYs) follow an exponential function. Figure 2 displays the different effectiveness of the 8 health care systems, which are in focus in this paper. Whilst Norway, for example, at the steep part of the DALY-healthcare spending grid, has one of the highest expenditures in the world, their accumulated DALYs in 2012 are only marginally higher than those of Canada, whose per capita healthcare spending is 3000 USD lower. Vice versa, in the middle part of the curve a moderate increase in healthcare spending translates into a considerable decline of DALYs [14].

Interventions that prove to reduce DALYs have a high potential to preserve or even release financial resources. Such resources can be reinvested in the health care system to stabilize it further and to improve patient`s lives. Figure 2 implicates that higher cost per capita do not necessarily translate to better healthcare. Theoretically, health care systems that may range at the right upper corner of the pictogram are likely to profit most from diagnostic tests that release financial resources.

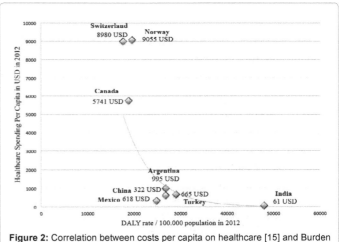

Figure 2: Correlation between costs per capita on healthcare [15] and Burden of Disease (in DALY).

Targeting social costs becomes an important argument for payers

Social costs express the expense to an entire society resulting from a defined event, an activity or a change in policy. More tangibly, they reflect the amount of Years Life Lost (YLL) and Years Lived with Disability (YLD). On the other side, economic costs portray productivity losses (which were first introduced in the "Value of lost output model" [16] by the WHO) as well as direct health care costs, impacting a society`s total GDP.

While pharmaceutical companies have implemented a dual concept of targeting a) physicians and b) payers simultaneously by running both, clinical and health economic trials, the diagnostic industry has only marginally adopted this thinking in their market access approaches.

For many years the registration of diagnostic tests in the

European Union only required the CE label, however in the light of financial shortcuts, more and more health authorities request a proof, that diagnostic tests not only have reasonable pricing but also add considerable value to the society [17]. With the CE marking, the manufacturer declares "that the product meets the applicable requirements according to EU Regulation 765/2008 for its affixing."

Medical value

Since more than a decade the question how Value in Health care can be measured has been discussed controversially; however there is agreement on the overarching concept of assessing health outcomes achieved per dollar spent [18]. Thus, the "value"- term arises around patients and payers simultaneously describing a framework for performance improvement in health care [19].

Roche Diagnostics has introduced the term Medical Value in their corporate language to differentiate products of the mature product portfolio from products with innovative character. Novel products with MV follow a stringent definition and must:

1) Improved patient outcome that is derived through diagnostic tests and algorithms, validated in clinical utility studies.

2) Deliver actionable and medically relevant information enabling support and guidance in decision-making and justifying the change of the current disease management by addressing a currently unmet medical need.

Diagnostic tests with MV can help to improve patient management and reduce direct and indirect health care costs. However, to prove a potential benefit for payers, clinical evidence must be created [20]. In this respect, randomized controlled trials and meta-analyses are credible tools to validate a diagnostic concept [21] while providing the highest levels of evidence. MV is added, when e.g. a test allows patient stratification into responders/non-responders for a given medical treatment or allows a more efficient/more effective allocation of patients to a certain treatment or disease management.

Medical value translates to societal value

MV creates benefits for patients, the society and ultimately for shareholders (Figure 1B). Hitherto the separation of product development and evidence generation for product utility was a well-accepted axiom in the diagnostic industry. Often it took a considerable amount of years until the medical community had accepted and incorporated a diagnostic test into the clinical practice. Creatinine for example, discovered by Max von Pettenkofer (1818-1901), developed its value as a marker for impaired kidney function only over time and required more than 160 years until its use has been recommended in clinical guidelines. While "outsourcing" of clinical studies to the society was a "low-cost" approach for vendors, it often implied increased social costs (AUC [Area under the curve] Figure 3A). Social costs arise due to false clinical decision making and have to be carried by all stakeholders involved in healthcare (patients, payers, physicians, society).

Technical product improvement not always translate into medical value, for patients or physicians

When the first high sensitivity troponin T assay had been introduced, the technical improvement created a high level of confusion amongst the medical community. Suddenly more patients without myocardial infarction turned out to be troponin-positive on the basis of conditions other than myocardial infarction [22]. Thus, experts have created the term "troponitis" referring to a limited usefulness of positive test-results. In the absence of harmonized recommendations that clearly indicated under which conditions a patient could be sent home safely, more confirmatory tests had to be performed and, physicians' triage decisions got more individualized, guided by risk perception [23] or fear of malpractice [24]. The troponin example demonstrates the risk for over-utilizing health care costs [25], caused by unnecessary interventions through more false-positive results [26].

While the financial attractiveness for vendors to leave "evidence creation" to the society has been clearly outlined, this traditional approach also yields downsides for companies:

Patent protection often expires until the value of a diagnostic parameter has been completely understood by physicians and until a given marker has made its way in clinical guidelines. This leads to lower revenue creation and slow market uptakes until the level of knowledge and the limitations are assessed [27]. Figure 3 displays the classical device development (A) and the development of a MV product (B).

In the described troponin example, the reluctance of physicians to use the test forced companies to readjust and to establish algorithms allowing early rule out of patient without myocardial infarction [28]. The acceptance of the assay remarkably increased, along with customer`s trust in the innovation.

The "MV approach" (Figure 3B) provides a "product" and a "product`s manual" but clearly creates more costs for the vendor. Nevertheless, early evidence creation implies advantages for patients, the society (AUC Figure 3B < AUC Figure 3A) and, in the long-run for shareholders. (Figure 1). However, in diagnostics, appropriate reimbursement does not follow the magnitude of innovation yet [10].

Is medical value a concept applicable in all markets?

While the concept of reducing societal costs is desirable in developed markets, it remains elusive if a MV strategy is appropriate for emerging markets and to what extend customers will base their purchase decision on clinically validated diagnostic algorithms. This study has been undertaken to better understand customer-perception of MV depending on the socio-economic context. Uncertainty remains, particularly in EM, whether financial aspects and general access to diagnostics is more important than the improvement of the current medical "gold standard".

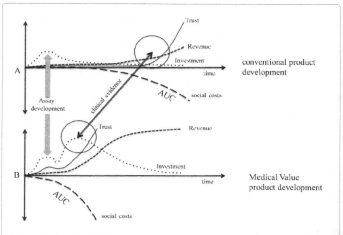

Figure 3: Creation of clinical evidence and its consequence regarding revenue, investment, customer`s trust and social costs.

In this light, it needs to be investigated whether restrained access to treatment options or their total absence limits the value or even governs the rejection of such products. Ultimately it needs to be understood if the perception of higher net-benefit for society justifies higher prices for MV products in these markets

Methods

Five key-questions have been designed in a multiple-choice manner. These questions target the view of physicians (N=240) on the development of the health system (Q1, Table 1) and on the definition and how the term "gold standard" is conceptualized in different health care systems (Q2, Table 1). We investigated what the customer associates with the term "Medical Value" in the context of their health care environment, targeting prospective product features that could potentially perceived as "value adding" (Q3, Table 1). Based on this we assessed which aspect of a MV product is seen as the most pivotal factor that would guide a purchase decision (Q4, Table 1). To understand customer's expectations we finally investigated which areas the diagnostic industry should invest more, targeting prospective product strategies (Q5, Table 1).

The survey has been executed by Genentech, California, USA using an anonymized internet-based crowd-sourcing tool (SERMO), hosted by World One, Boston, USA. SERMO is a shared service, allowing multiple companies to gain quick and comprehensive insights on conceptual questions. Invitations to participate in this cross-sectional survey have been sent out to 240 Internal Medicine physicians in 8 different countries (Figure 4). A monetary compensation has been paid to attending physicians.

To assess differences in customer expectations, responses from countries have been allocated to income levels according to world-bank data (atlas method) 2013.

Three groups have been defined as follows: Canada, Norway and Switzerland [N=77] qualified as high-income countries with a

Survey Questions
From your country/region perspective what do you think will be the future of the health system in the next 10-15 years? Select the most appropriate answer.
• A 2-class Medicine (or a private-public sector) scenario is most likely. Products will be successful, that continue to improve the standard of treatment in the private sector regardless of the price. In the public sector price matters. Cheap products will succeed that meet the current gold standard.
• The whole society must profit from solutions that are better than the current gold standard. Reimbursement will continue for new innovative test. To compensate for higher costs, governments will ask for flat pricing of standard tests.
• There will be no regulation and mandatory health insurance.
• Government will shift the focus on primary prevention and will foster the reimbursement of screening, vaccination and risk-stratification rather than treatment, where all people will receive the standard care.
• Stricter monitoring of citizens and their health behavior is the solution for cost control. Reimbursement will be performed according to patient s compliance/behavior.
Depending on your particular context (regional/cultural) what do you think is the most appropriate interpretation of the term "gold standard"? Select the most appropriate answer.
• Gold standard is a well-defined term without room for interpretation and refers to a guideline-based and generally accepted standard that is defined to treat/diagnose a disease.
• For me (in my view) "gold standard" refers to the highest standard (regarding treatment/cure) that my health system is able to afford.
• For me (in my view) "gold standard" is the equitable access of all patients to basic but well-performing diagnostic tools all over the world regardless of their social heritage.
What do you associate with the term „Medical Value" in diagnostics? Select the most appropriate answer.
• Providing cheapest diagnostic/therapeutic option according to gold-standard **(Emphasis on cost-control)**
• Providing diagnostic/therapeutic solutions, better than current gold-standard at the monetary expenses required for innovation **(Emphasis on innovation)**
• Providing a specific service that accompanies a diagnostic/therapeutic option (reliable treatment and diagnostic algorithms, validated in clinical trials that may shorten time to diagnosis and or treatment and simplify diagnosis/treatment **(Emphasis on service)**
• Maximize technical preciseness **(Emphasis on technical excellence)**
• Providing highest quantity of diagnostic tests **(Emphasis on variety)**
When creating a "medical value product" multiple factors must be taken into consideration. It is unlikely that a product will be able to meet all aspects. What do you think is the most pivotal factor?
• Generalizability (global technical standardization and data compatibility)
• Non/Minimal-Invasiveness
• Release of health-care resources (through faster processes/algorithms)
• Price of test/equipment
• General accessibility/Mobility of the device
What do you think is the area in which the diagnostic industry should invest more? Select the most appropriate answer.
• Establishment of treatment algorithms that help to maximize the diagnostic value of existing markers to reliably guide physicians in the diagnosis of patients in their daily practice.
• Discovery of new/better diagnostic markers for well-known diseases.
• Discovery of new markers for orphan/neglected disease areas.
• Development of electronic devices to improve processing/distribution of data (Apps, handhelds, devices for self-management).
• Investment in companion-diagnostics (development of diagnostic markers and corresponding drugs) that allow a reliable tracking of therapy success.

Table 1: Survey Questions.

gross national income per capita of 12,746 USD or more. The US has been purposely excluded from this investigation due to the ongoing implementation of the Patient Protection and Affordable Care Act. Current structural change implies the possibility of biased answers. Argentina, China, Mexico and Turkey [N=74] were allocated to the group of upper-mid income countries with a gross national income per capita between 4,126 to 12,745 USD.

India [N=80] has been chosen for a representative for lower-mid income countries with a gross national income per capita between 1,046 to 4,125 USD. Low-income countries have not been included due to the unavailability in SERMO.

High-income countries have been defined as DM while lower-mid income countries and upper-mid income countries have been allocated to the group of EM.

Answers have been collected by SERMO and were statistically analyzed using R 3.0.1 (R Foundation for Statistical Computing, Vienna, Austria) by Roche Professional Diagnostics, Biostatistics and Data Management in Penzberg, Germany. For each question, the physician could only pick one response option. Thus, for each question, a table with response options stratified by EM and SM were constructed. For such a table, frequencies for each response option and corresponding proportions (frequencies divided by the corresponding numbers of doctors) have been calculated.

The difference (Δ) of the proportions between the two groups (EM and DM) was assessed for each response option and a p-value based on a two-sided z-test for that difference of proportions has been established. P-values as a measure of evidence against the null hypothesis were simply reported from these tests instead of performing statistical hypothesis tests at a multiplicity-adjusted, predetermined level of statistical significance.

Results

231 out of possible 240 Internal Medicine physicians responded to the survey, of which N=77 physicians originated from high-income countries (developed Markets), N=74 from upper-mid income countries and N=80 from lower-mid income countries thus N=154 physicians originated from emerging Markets.

The future of the health care systems

33.8% (N=78 out of 231) of all doctors foresaw a two-class Medicine scenario with high prices for innovative products accompanied with premium prices in the private (first class) sector and cost centered products according to gold standard in the public (second-class) sector.

Similar proportions in EM (32.5%, N=50 out of 154) and DM (36.4%, N=28 out of 77) could be observed. Physicians in the EM (14.3%, N=22 out of 154) rather predict a future health care system without regulation and mandatory health insurance than their colleagues in DM (2.6%, N=2 out of 77) with Δ = 11.7% (p = 0.0005).

The second most frequently chosen answer in both markets was that a whole society should profit from more expensive but innovative markers. More physicians from DM compared to EM (30%, N=23 and 24%, N=37 in EM, Δ=5.8%, p=0.35) believed that the whole society must profit from solutions exceeding the current gold-standard and that the health care system will continue to reimburse new innovative tests. However, to compensate for higher costs, governments will ask for flat pricing of standard tests.

Fairly comparative results for both markets have been gathered for the future focus on primary prevention (14.3% for both markets). This also held true (EM 14.9%, N=23 out of 154, SM 16.9%, N=13 out of 77) for a stricter monitoring of citizens and their health behavior (as a solution for cost control in a sense that reimbursement for treatment will be performed according to patient`s compliance and behavior). In this scenario diagnostics will play a pivotal role for monitoring disease prevention and cost-control.

Conclusion: Physicians anticipate either a future 2-class medicine in which innovative products are affordable only in the private (first class) sector or a health care system in which the costs of innovative products are hedged by flat pricing of non-MV products.

"Gold-standard" is subjective to the environment

Overall, 55.0% (N=127 out of 231) of physicians relate to the generally accepted definition of "guideline-based standards in treating and diagnosing a disease", however, differences were observed between the markets. 63.6% (N=49 out of 77) of DM-physicians, but only 50.6% (N=78 out of 154) of physicians in the EM agreed on this. About 25% of all physicians believe that "Gold Standard" refers to the highest standard that a health system is able to afford. Surprisingly there was only a marginal difference between DM and EM (22.1%, N=17 out of 77 in SM, 26.6%, N=41 out of 154 in EM). 8.4% (p=0.11) more physicians from EM (22.7%, N=35 out of 154) than from SM (14.3%, N=11 out of 77) believed that the term "Gold Standard" refers to the equitable access of all patients to basic but well-performing tools regardless of their social heritage.

Conclusion: The term Gold standard is interpreted differently in EM and DM.

Both markets mainly adhere to the believe that "gold standard" is a term used to describe a method/procedure that is widely recognized as the best available. A main concern of EM is the equitable access of all patients to well-performing diagnostic tools, which seems less relevant in DM.

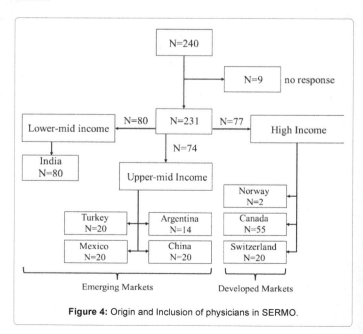

Figure 4: Origin and Inclusion of physicians in SERMO.

Cost-control and reduced emphasis on technical excellence indicates a paradigm change in the health care system of saturated with developed markets

37.2% of all physicians (N=86 out of 231) believed that diagnostic tests should be accompanied by reliable and validated treatment algorithms to qualify for a Medical Value product (Figure 5). This was true for both, DM (42.9%, N=33 out of 77) and EM (34.4%, N=53 out of 154).

Low emphasis has been given to technical excellence and maximal technical accuracy in DM (2.6%, N=2 out of 77) comparing to 13.0%, N=20 out of 154 in EM with Δ=10.4% (p=0.001).

Providing the most cost-effective diagnostic/therapeutic option according to the level of the current gold standard in the light of cost control was surprisingly more strongly emphasized in DM (29.9%, N=23 out of 77). Fewer physicians (16.2%, N=25 out of 154) were concerned about this aspect in EM (Δ = 13.6% with p=0.023) (Figure 5).

Conclusion: Treatment algorithms is highly desirable in both markets. Fewer physicians are concerned about technical excellence in DM comparing to EM. In DM more emphasis was given to cost control comparing to EM. Both findings indicate a need for high-volume solutions in EM and for more cost-effective MV solutions in DM.

Data generalizability and comparability as a feature of medical value products

The majority (N=85) of all surveyed physicians believed that global technical standardization and data comparability is an important additional factor for a MV product (N=27; 35% in SM, N=58; 38% in EM). The release of heath care resources appeared less relevant. The difference between DM and EM was statistically not significant (N=18; 23% in SM, N=28; 18% in DM). This also held true for the remaining factors, general accessibility/mobility of the device, and minimal invasiveness.

Key message: There is a high demand for inter-assay comparability and technical standardization in both, DM and EM. Of note, the impact of MV products on the society (release of health care resources) has given rather low emphasis in both markets.

Emerging and developed Markets demand clinical evidence through validated treatment algorithms

Regarding future product strategy, the majority of all physicians believe that treatment algorithms should be created, predominantly for existing markers (33.8%, N=78 out of 231). A fairly comparable amount of physicians supported this strategy in DM (35.1%, N=27 out of 77) and EM (33.1%, N=51 out of 154). Major differences between both markets could be identified regarding the need for better diagnostic markers for well-known diseases.

33.8% (N=26 out of 77) of physicians in DM saw a high unmet need for such development, while only 17.5% (N=27 out of 154) of the medical community in EM agreed with this statement (Δ=16.2% with p=0.009). Completely contrary answers were derived for the question of whether investment should be increased for the development of markers for orphan/neglected diseases. Here, 14.9% (N=23 out of 154) of physicians in EM indicated a strong interest for a more focused approach in the diagnostic industry, whereas only 3.9% (N=3 out of 77) of physicians in DM saw this as a medical necessity (Δ = 11.0% with p=0.002) (Figure 6).

Regarding the development of electronic devices to improve processing and distribution of data (such as Apps and devices for self-management), comparable interest has been indicated by both markets (EM: 7.8%, N=12 out of 154, DM: 7.8%, N=6 out of 77).

Slightly more (Δ = 7.1% with p = 0.21) relevance for the development of companion diagnostics has been stated from physicians of EM (26.6%, N=41 out of 154) than from DM-physicians (19.5%, N=15 out of 77). This product strategy, however, remained the second most frequently chosen option; particularly in the low-mid income economy India.

Key message: Physicians of both markets expressed their belief for the necessity to develop treatment algorithms for existing markers. Physicians in DM demand better markers for well known-diseases.

Discussion

This paper addresses the current world-view of a small randomly selected group of physicians from eight different countries and three different economic prosperities on the Medical Value strategy. The survey had a high return rate of 96.3% (N=231 out of 240). Because the origin of the questions was blinded for participating physicians, a bias of answers concerning the vendor's reputation could be excluded. The current investigation at least provides 4 important results.

1. There is a large demand in all markets for reliable treatment algorithms that accompany new product developments. Clinical trials have a strong potential to enhance the confidence of physicians to apply assays in their clinical practice. Confidence for application of diagnostic assays may erode when the consequence of a test result

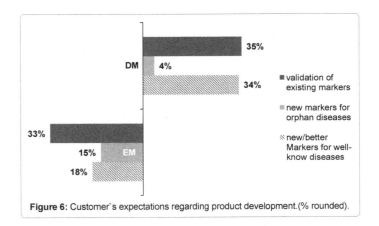

Figure 6: Customer's expectations regarding product development.(% rounded).

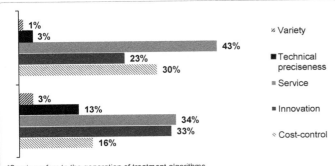

*Service refers to the generation of treatment algorithms

Figure 5: Comparison of answers from Saturated and Emerging Markets regarding future product strategy.

cannot confidently be translated into clinical decisions or actions. Potentially this concern is an explanation why technical excellence and preciseness is not ranked as the most critical parameter for future product development in both markets. Sensitivity improvements (e.g. in cardiac troponins or increasing the sensitivity of HIV detection) without providing the means for a better patient management may limit the value of assays only to "technical innovation". This finding highlights the importance of understanding the connection between the psychological concept of "confidence" concerning a given product/procedure and the willingness to apply it.

2. The MV concept is not limited to novel markers. A high number of physicians believed that the focus for development should be shifted towards exploiting the diagnostic potential of existing markers in both DM and EM. Given different economic prosperities physicians from DM saw a higher need to develop better diagnostic markers for well-known diseases. This result displays the gap between the medical care standard of SM and EM, where the potential of existing markers has not been utilized yet.

3. The level of economic prosperity has an impact on the willingness to pay for medical innovation. In the light of increasing financial pressure, the most cost-effective diagnostic/therapeutic option has given higher priority in DM compared to EM. This is rooted in different market environments. Based on global scenarios the health economic outlook of the OECD [29] predicts that the majority of EM will create health care costs that positively correlate with their GDP development [29] and therefore, are likely to accept also costly innovations that add value to an individualized treatment approach. DM, on the other hand, is likely to experience financial cutbacks on their health care systems and will navigate towards society-focused, rather than individually focused systems. This theory is in line with the answers from the current survey, in which the majority of DM physicians believed that the whole society must profit from solutions exceeding current gold-standards.

4. There is a different perception of the term "Gold Standard", which can be fundamentally different depending on the economic environment. This might be rooted in the fact that the term, historically taken over from economists, has no clear definition. Occuring 1955 for the first time and used in its current sense by Rudd since 1979 [30] "Gold Standard" describes a method/procedure that is widely recognized as the best available. With more than 10.000 publications since 1995 [31[the term is now widely accepted in the medical literature [32]. Even though, in our investigation the majority of physicians comprehend "Gold standard" as previously defined, a main concern of EM was the equitable access of all patients to well-performing diagnostic tools. This can be seen as a "Gold Standard" of a higher abstraction level. Like in Maslow`s hierarchy of needs [33] a primary unmet need has to be met before the next higher need emerges. Equitable access to diagnostic tools speaks to the primary need of cost efficient high-volume testing efficiency.

In DM the situation is different as the primary need is generally met and the current "Gold Standard" can be challenged. This finding displays how differently the term "Gold Standard" is used. It is important to acknowledge that a "Gold Standard" is subjective and, despite oriented on contemporary guideline recommendation, not generalizable.

Limitations of MV and Further Research

The "added MV component" in terms of a biomarker algorithm is unique and product-specific. Proposals for clinical decision-making have to be established in derivation cohorts of clinical trials, and tested in validation cohorts. Thus, biomarker algorithms, leading to clinical decisions are not interchangeable and thus unique to the investigated biomarker (e.g. Troponin T, Troponin I). This fact cannot accommodate the request of customers for global data comparability but naturally prevents "product substitution" through "aut-idem" products and services. Product uniqueness is a "condition sine qua non" to remain a competitive advantage. The contradiction between customers` demand and entrepreneurial necessity displays the limits of the MV concept and should be investigated in further studies. Especially more research is required to assess how the concern about data-comparability can be addressed to increase social value without destroying shareholder value.

Conclusions

Added value, based on an improvement of patient flows (diagnostic algorithms) is a valuable product strategy in DM but less applicable in EM. While customers in EM still see technical refinement of test systems as important, customers of DM emphasize the value component of accompanying algorithms. Especially in DM, attention must be paid not to destroy value through exclusive focus on technical improvement while neglecting the applicability and utility of refinement. Our results also show that the impact of MV on society (release of health care resources) has not been fully understood by customers yet.

More cost-effectiveness studies are needed, whose current lack increases the risk of uninformed decision making by policy makers, government officials and payers as important stakeholder groups [34].

Our results emphasize a likelihood of revenue decline for the diagnostic industry, when the MV concept is not given attention. The high desire for the "value" component in both markets is particularly emphasized through the demand for the validation of existing diagnostic tests.

Diagnostics must support physicians towards more straightforward decision-making. If this requirement is fulfilled, not only MV but also societal value is created. MV is a design strategy to insure the long-term stability of Roche`s competitive advantage through organizational innovation by addressing the needs of society and patients.

References

1. Smith KM, Kates JA (1996) Regulatory hurdles in bringing an in vitro diagnostic device to market. Clinical Chemistry 42: 1556-1557.

2. Salop SC (1979) Monopolistic Competition with Outside Goods. Bell Journal of Economics 10: 141-156.

3. Koberg CS (2003) An empirical test of environmental, organizational and process factors affecting incremental and radical innovation. The Journal of High Technology Management Research 14: 21–45.

4. Singh JV (1986) Performance, Slack, and Risk Taking In Organizational Decision Making. Academy of Management Journal Academy of Management Journal 29: 562-585.

5. Schumpeter JA (1976) Capitalism, Socialism and Democracy. George Allen and Unwin Publishers, Australia.

6. Dixit AKS, Joseph E (1977) Monopolistic Competition and Optimum Product Diversity. American Economic Review 67: 297-308.

7. Aghion P, Bloom N, Blundell R, Griffith R, Howitt P (2005) Competition and Innovation: an Inverted-U Relationship. The Quarterly Journal of Economics 120: 701-728.

8. Travis P, Bennett S, Haines A, Pang T, Bhutta Z, et al. (2004) Overcoming

health-systems constraints to achieve the Millennium Development Goals. Lancet. Public Health 364: 900-906.

9. Ruyter KD, Wetzels M, Lemmink J, Mattason J (1997) The dynamics of the service delivery process: a value-based approach. International Journal of Research in Marketing 14: 231-243.

10. Desiere F, Gutjahr TS, Rohr UP (2013) Developing companion diagnostics for delivering personalised medicine: opportunities and challenges. Drug Discovery Today: Therapeutic Strategies.

11. Jaques H (2013) NICE guideline on hypertension. European Heart Journal 34: 406-408.

12. Fischer KE, Stargardt T (2014) Early Benefit Assessment of Pharmaceuticals in Germany: Manufacturers' Expectations versus the Federal Joint Committee's Decisions. Med Decis Making 34: 1030-1047.

13. Eichler HG, Kong SX, Gerth WC, Mavros P, Jonsson B (2004) Use of cost-effectiveness analysis in health-care resource allocation decision-making: how are cost-effectiveness thresholds expected to emerge? Value in health. The Journal of the International Society for Pharmacoeconomics and Outcomes Research 7: 518-528.

14. WHO (World Health Organization) Burden of Disease.

15. The World Bank: Health expenditure per capita, 2014.

16. Harvard School of Public Health: The Global Economic Burden of Non-Communicable Diseases: A report by theWorld Economic Forum and the Harvard School of Public Health.

17. Miller I, Ashton-Chess J, Spolders H, Fert V, Ferrara J, et al. (2011) Market access challenges in the EU for high medical value diagnostic tests. Personalized Medicine 8: 137-148.

18. Porter ME (2010) What is value in health care? N Engl J Med 363: 2477-81.

19. Porter ME, Teisberg EO (2006) Redefining Health Care: Creating Value-Based Competition on Results. Harvard Business School Press, Boston.

20. Deverka PA (2009) Pharmacogenomics, evidence, and the role of payers. Public Health Genomics 12: 149-157.

21. Woolf SH, Grol R, Hutchinson A, Eccles M, Grimshaw J (1999) Clinical guidelines: potential benefits, limitations, and harms of clinical guidelines. BMJ 318: 527-530.

22. Jeremias A, Gibson CM (2005) Narrative review: alternative causes for elevated cardiac troponin levels when acute coronary syndromes are excluded. Annals of Internal Medicine 142: 786-791.

23. Pearson SD, Goldman L, Orav EJ, Guadagnoli E, Garcia TB, et al. (1995) Triage decisions for emergency department patients with chest pain: do physicians' risk attitudes make the difference?. Journal of general Internal Medicine 10: 557-564.

24. Katz DA, Williams GC, Brown RL, Aufderheide TP, Bogner M, et al. (2005) Emergency physicians' fear of malpractice in evaluating patients with possible acute cardiac ischemia. Annals of Emergency Medicine 46: 525-533.

25. Hwang U, Baumlin K, Berman J, Chawla NK, Handel DA, et al. (2010) Emergency department patient volume and troponin laboratory turnaround time. Academic Emergency Medicine 17: 501-507.

26. Tubaro M (2011) Use of high-sensitivity troponins in clinical practice: is it a solution or or a problem? Troponin sensitivity results in safety and timeliness. G Ital Cardiol (Rome) 12: 492-496.

27. Pai NP, Marina K (2008) Are we Ready for Home-based, Self-testing for HIV?. Future HIV Therapy 2: 515-520.

28. Mueller M, Biener M, Vafaie M, Doerr S, Keller T, et al. (2012) Absolute and relative kinetic changes of high-sensitivity cardiac troponin T in acute coronary syndrome and in patients with increased troponin in the absence of acute coronary syndrome. Clinical Chemistry 58: 209-218.

29. What future for health spending? OECD (2013) OECD Economics Department Policy Notes.

30. Rudd P (1979) In search of the gold standard for compliance measurement. Arch Intern Med 139: 627-628.

31. Claassen JA (2005) Gold standard, not golden standard. Ned Tijdschr Geneeskd 149: 2937.

32. Versi E (1992) Gold standard is an appropriate term. BMJ 305: 187.

33. Rakowski N (2008) Maslow's Hierarchy of Needs Model - the Difference of the Chinese and the Western Pyramid on the Example of Purchasing Luxurious Products. GRIN Verlag, Germany.

34. Parkinson DR, Ziegler J (2009) Educating for personalized medicine: a perspective from oncology. Clinical Pharmacology and Therapeutics 86: 23-25.

The Effect of Supervisor Support on Employee Voice Behavior based on the Self-Determination Theory: The Moderating Effect of Impression Management Motive

Jui-Chih Ho*

National Changhua University of Education, Graduate Institute of Human Resource Management, Taiwan

Abstract

Although numerous studies have adopted social exchange theory to investigate the mechanism through which leadership influences employee voice behavior, few studies have placed their focus on the mediation of employees' basic psychological needs. To address this research gap, this study adopted self-determination theory to explore how supervisor support encourages subordinates to engage in voice behavior. Furthermore, the moderating effect of impression management motive was clarified. This study adopted structural equation modeling and hierarchical regression approach to analyze 268 sets of data of a pair of supervisor and subordinate. The results revealed that basic psychological needs mediated the relationship between supervisor support and self-determined prosocial motivation, which, in turn, was positively related to voice behavior. In addition, subordinates' impression management motive weakens the positive relationship between self-determined prosocial motivation and voice behavior.

Keywords: Supervisor support; Basic psychological needs; Self-determined prosocial motivation; Voice behavior; Impression management motives

Introduction

Morrison [1] proposed a theoretical model of voice behavior, suggesting that voice is an intentional concept and that the perceived efficacy and perceived safety are two crucial factors of consideration influencing voice motivation and voice behavior. In other words, voice behavior is a type of "planned behavior" [2], in which the judgments of behavioral control or the perceived ease of performing a behavior are influenced by the chance to perform the behavior successfully and the belief regarding the accessibility of necessary resources [3]. Generally, employees engage in voice behavior only when they believe that speaking up is safe and would yield effective outcomes. To date, numerous studies have based their research on this perspective when examining the predictors and mechanisms of voice behavior. In particular, most studies have focused on the relationship between leadership and voice behavior, using the social exchange theory as the theoretical framework and reciprocity as the foundation for inducing voice behavior [4-9]. In fact, when determining whether to speak up, people cannot undergo a risky decision-making process entirely on the basis of social exchange. Some people are unwilling to express constructive opinions with regard to their respective unit's operations, even though they get along well with their supervisors and have established a relationship of trust with them. However, there are some people who have the courage to speak up even if they are situated in an unfavorable voice environment. Therefore, using the social exchange theory is insufficient for explaining the mechanism through which voice behavior is motivated. To answer this question, we must start with the process of individual intrinsic motivation because speaking up is an extra-role behavior in which employees proactively and voluntarily engage. People have the freedom to decide whether to speak up or not; they not only consider whether they should and whether they can, but also evaluate whether they are capable of speaking up. The present study asserts that when employees proactively decide to engage in voice behavior, and they perceive their ability to accomplish the task and have a strong sense of belongingness to their group [10], then these employees are intrinsically motivated to engage in voice behavior. Therefore, we propose that the perspective of self-determination should be adopted to extensively explore the "black box" involved in the relationship between individuals and their voice behavior.

Self-determination theory concentrates on the extent to which human behavior is voluntary or self-determined. The theory asserts that motivation is the underlying reason behind a behavior and that behavioral motivation is dependent on social factors. Specifically, if social factors can facilitate building a supportive environment in which basic psychological needs are met, then self-determined motivation is induced and in turn improves behavioral performance [11,12]. According to theoretical perspectives, voice behavior is a form of self-regulation and self-determination because it is a self-initiated behavior [1] in which an individual consciously deliberates on the positive and negative consequences of a decision [13,14]. Consequently, the support provided in a working environment is the key factor motivating employees to become self-determined to engage in voice behavior. In a workplace, supervisors are highly influential, and employees generally regard supervisor support as an indicator of organizational support [15]. Therefore, supervisor support is crucial for employee interaction in a working environment. However, few studies have examined voice behavior from the perspective of self-determination. To bridge this research gap, the present study adopted a self-determination perspective centering on subordinates to explore the effect of supervisor support on employee voice behavior in an organizational setting.

Regarding voice motivation, past studies have confirmed the relationship between prosocial motivation and voice behavior [16,17]. Prosocially motivated employees hold a strong sense of

---

*Corresponding author: Jui-Chih Ho, National Changhua University of Education, Graduate Institute of Human Resource Management 2, Shi-da Rd, Changhua, 500, Taiwan, E-mail: mandy@nutc.edu.tw

responsibility toward enhancing the well-being of their colleagues and the organization, which in turn increases their probability to commit to engaging in voice behavior. SDT posits that motivation can be classified according to the level of autonomy and they are autonomous motivation and controlled motivation. Controlled motivation is stimulated by external incentives, whereas autonomous motivation is induced internally making it equivalent to an intrinsic motivation. Autonomous motivation exhibits higher quality compared with controlled motivation [18]. Previous studies on voice behavior have focused primarily on the level or quantity of prosocial motivation, rarely discussing the quality of motivation. Specifically, the autonomous motivation proposed in SDT is often neglected in voice behavior studies or mistakenly integrated with controlled motivation. We therefore calculated the level of self-regulation in the present study by using the relative autonomy index (RAI) to score the self-regulation level (total scale score=intrinsic motivation identified motivation introjected motivation extrinsic motivation) [19]. This approach can manifest employees' self-regulated autonomy in demonstrating prosocial motivation. The present study referred to this type of prosocial motivation as self-determined prosocial motivation (SDPM).

In addition, recent studies have also suggested adopting a mixed-motive perspective in investigations on citizenship behavior [16,20]. Because humans by nature tend to prioritize their personal interests before anything else; they inherently act for the sake of protecting and improving their personal interests [21]. When people wish to maximize their personal benefits or protect their image, impression management is generally the measures they adopt [16,17]. Therefore, we assert that when employees are aware of others' impression of themselves (personal interest), they are likely to perceive that engaging in voice behavior, which has potential costs and risks, will jeopardize their own image, which weakens the predictive effects of prosocial motivation on voice behavior. Moreover, research results regarding the interactive relationship of these two types of motivation remain inconclusive [16,20]. In addition, Takeuchi et al. [20] emphasized that impression management motive exerts differing moderating effects in different social cultures. We therefore assert that the moderating effect of impression management motive on prosocial motivation and voice behavior merits further investigation.

This study provides several contributions to existing literature on voice behavior. First, in contrast to previous studies, the present study adopted SDT to examine the effects of supervisor support on subordinates' voice behavior and to propose the process through which supervisor support influences voice behavior through basic psychological needs and prosocial motivation, in order to manifest the relationship among social environment, psychology, motivation, and behavior. Second, the present study not only stressed the factors that influence autonomous motivation (basic psychological needs), but also employed the Relative Autonomy Index (RAI) to measure self-regulation of motivation at the individual level, which truly reflects employees' level of self-determination in engaging in voice behavior. Third, the present study adopted the multiple motives (prosocial and impression management motives) perspective to extend the motivation model of SDT and investigate the effects that the interaction between other-oriented and self-oriented motives have on employees' voice behavior, thereby bridging the research gap in this field of study. Figure 1 illustrates the hypothetical relationship model.

Theoretical Background and Hypotheses Development

Supervisor support and voice behavior

Although voice behavior involves offering constructive advice, it is ultimately aimed at changing the current state. Therefore, voice behavior is often deemed as an act of challenging the current state and management authorities [13]. Because supervisors are the main entity receiving employees' voiced opinions, and holding the authority to evaluate employee performance, supervisors are often the main reason why employees are afraid of engaging in voice behavior [1]. Enabling employees to perceive supervisors' affirmation of their work [22] is extremely important for motivating employees to proactively engage in voice behavior. Perceived supervisor support refers to employees' perception of how much their supervisors value their efforts, are concerned about their welfare [22,23], and give them the support they need. Previous studies have verified that when employees perceive a high level of support and assistance from their supervisor, such perception facilitates improving employees' attitude toward work, which encourages employee to devote greater effort to their work and in turn motivates employees to do things that are beyond the scope of their duties [24]. Based on the aforementioned discussions, the present study proposed the following hypothesis:

Hypothesis 1. Perceived supervisor support significantly and positively influences employees' voice behavior

The mediating effect of basic psychological needs and self-determined prosocial motivation

SDT accentuates the level of self-determination in people's behavior, positing that the social environment can boost intrinsic motivation and promote the internalization of extrinsic motivation through satisfying the three basic psychological needs of autonomy, competence, and relatedness [18]. Individual work-related behavior and psychological health are in turn enhanced. The need for autonomy can be satisfied when an individual experiences a choice in the initiation, maintenance, and regulation of a behavior. The need for competence is satisfied when an individual succeeds optimally in challenging tasks and is able to attain desired outcomes. The need for relatedness is fulfilled when an individual is able to establish a sense of connectedness with significant people in his/her life [25]. The satisfaction of these three needs promotes optimal motivation [26]. According to SDT, if an organization wishes to motivate employees' active devotion and contribution by effectively satisfying their three basic psychological

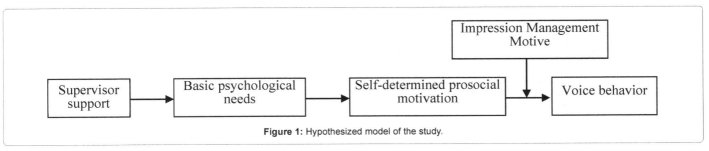

Figure 1: Hypothesized model of the study.

needs, then building a supportive working environment appears to be extremely important.

In an organization, workplace support is closely related to employees, and this type of support includes organizational support, supervisory support, and co-worker support [27]. In particular, supervisory support is the most direct and most important source of workplace support for employees because supervisors can provide tangible tools and intangible social emotional support, which can assist employees in integrating work-related and non-work-related needs, thereby alleviating the work stress employees experience [28]. When employees feel that their supervisor values their contributions and care about their well-being [22], this is equivalent to their supervisor affirming their job performance, which in turn makes employees feel a sense of achievement and recognize their value of existence. May et al. [29] indicated that supervisor support enables employees to feel that they are situated in an environment where they can work at ease and obtain feedback. Such perception boosts employees' confidence in completing a job, enhances employees' perception toward mutual support, increases their courage to take risks or even make mistakes and also encourages them to show agentic behavior. Furthermore, a supportive supervisor generally prefers to establish a high-quality leader–member exchange (LMX) relationship, which elevates employees' sense of belongingness and heightens their perception that they are capable of influencing the environment and hold greater control over their actions [30]. Based on the above illustration, the support from supervisor can indeed satisfy the basic psychological needs of the employees.

According to SDT, satisfaction of psychological needs is positively related to optimal individual operations, including intrinsic autonomous work motivation and willingness to volunteer spending time on work [31], intrinsic motivation, as well as positive attitudes and behaviors (e.g., being energetic and contributive; La Guardia et al. [32]; Vansteenkiste et al. [33]). This phenomenon reveals that when supervisor support satisfies employees' need for autonomy, this satisfaction can elicit employees' autonomous potentials, which then promotes them to actively engage in helping behaviors. When their need for competence is satisfied, they will be more confident in proposing a solution or solving the problems of others. When employees' need for a relationship is satisfied, stronger group identification and commitment are produced, increasing employees' desire to help others for the sake of others. Overall, satisfying employees' basic psychological needs prompts employees to freely, confidently identify with demonstrating prosocial motivation, with hopes of helping others. La Guardia et al. [32] indicated that people are inherently prosocial animals because adequate nourishment (e.g., an autonomy-supportive environment) guides people to pay attention to others, elicits their prosocial motivation, and entices people to engage in others-oriented behavior [31].

Some scholars view supervisor support as a critical work-related resource for employees [34,35], emphasizing that supervisor support at work facilitates enhancing work engagement [29,34]. Because a resourceful working environment provides a greater possibility for employees to experience psychological freedom (i.e., autonomy), interpersonal connection (i.e., relatedness), and effectiveness (i.e., competence) so that they could feel less exhausted and more energetic when working [36] and in turn demonstrate more extra-role behavior (e.g., voice). May et al. [29] maintained that supervisors who cultivate a supportive work environment generally display concern for employees' needs and feelings, provide positive feedback, and encourage employees to express their concerns, develop new skills, and solve work-related problems. Such supportive behavior enhances employees' level of self-determination and interest in work, thereby elevating their work engagement. Work engagement represents a person's intrinsic motivation [32], suggesting that complete dedication and engagement in work naturally motivate employees to engage in voice behavior. Therefore, the following hypotheses are proposed:

Hypothesis 2. Supervisor support promotes the satisfaction of basic psychological needs.

Hypothesis 3. Satisfaction of basic psychological needs mediates the relationship between supervisor support and employees' SDPM.

Hypothesis 4. Satisfaction of employees' basic needs and, in turn, SDPM, mediates the relationship between supervisor support and voice behavior.

Moderating effect of impression management motive

Impression management motive refers to the motivation of a person to raise and protect his or her image as perceived by others (in the organization). Therefore, when people practice impression management to realize their own goals, they will endeavor to avoid demonstrating negative responses and criticisms, while refining their behavior in order to satisfy the requirement of a social context and the behavioral norms expected by others. Grant and Mayer [16] determined that impression management motive strengthens the positive relationship between prosocial motivation and affiliative citizenship. Employees express citizenship in ways that both "do good" and "look good." However, Takeuchi et al. [20] recently re-examined the interaction between various types of motivation. Their results showed that impression management motive weakens the positive relationship between prosocial value and organizational citizenship behaviors toward individuals or groups (OCBI). They believed that such inconsistency in the moderating effect of impression management motive is attributed to cultural differences in the research context. In a collectivist culture, workplaces often exhibit "a bird in the lead is always shot down" phenomenon, and peers sometimes believe that people who present overly exceptional performance or who attract attention are not as devoted to their job, causing impression management motive to inhibit proactive behavior.

In addition, although voice behavior is a prosocial behavior, such challenging behavior that attempts to alter the current situation also has risks. To prevent damaging their interpersonal relationship and personal image (to be regarded as a troublemaker or complainer), which may influence their career development, employees are likely to engage in self-protective behavior and reduce constructive voice behavior. Grant and Mayer [16] verified that a strong impression management motive does not steer employees toward a riskier citizenship behavior (e.g., voice behavior). Instead, it guides employees toward affiliative citizenship behavior, such as helping, being courteous, and taking initiatives, that supports the current state. For this reason, the present study proposes the following hypothesis:

Hypothesis 5. Employees' impression management motive will moderate the relationship between SDPM and voice, such that its positive relationship will be weaker when impression management motive is high.

Methods

Sample and procedure

Participants of the study involve subordinates and their immediate supervisors in multiple companies located in Taichung, Taiwan. Each subordinate completed an assessment of the immediate supervisor's support, self-reported basic psychological needs, self-determined prosocial motivation, impression management motive and personal information. Supervisors rated subordinates' voice behavior. A total of 400 subordinate questionnaires and 85 supervisor questionnaires were distributed, among which 323 subordinate questionnaires and 78 supervisor questionnaires were returned. The overall response rate was 81%. Excluding unpaired questionnaires and incomplete questionnaires (missing answers and questions that were carelessly answered such as selecting the same answers for all questions or not providing a reverse answer to reverse-worded questions), we obtained 268 valid, paired questionnaires for a valid response rate of 67%. As a show of gratitude for their participation, a voucher worth NT$50 was gifted to the respondents along with the questionnaire. Reminder emails and troubleshooting (e.g., problems related to not receiving the pre-stamped envelope) were administered two and four weeks after questionnaire distribution.

The research participants were mostly involved in the manufacturing industry (53.4%), followed by the service industry (21.3%) and information industry (12.7%). By nature of work, the participants were primarily working in the marketing/sales (20%) and research and development/design (19%) departments, followed by manufacturing (18%) and human resource (16%) departments. Among the samples, 50.7% of the participants were women; 48.5% had attained a bachelor's degree; 53.4% were married; the average age was 35.24; and their average years of service were 6.22.

Measures

Voice behavior: The present study adopted the Voice Behavior Scale, which was developed by Liang et al. [2]. For this scale, the supervisor assesses employees' performance in voicing innovative and constructive advices. The scale contains five items (e.g., the employee provides active and constructive advice for problems that may influence the department). A 5-point Likert scale was adopted (1=*never* to 5=*always*). The Cronbach's α was .93.

Supervisor support: Supervisor support was measured using the Supervisor Support Scale proposed by Kottke and Sharafinski [22]. The scale has four items (e.g., my direct supervisor is very concerned about my welfare) and adopts a 6-point Likert scale (1=*strongly disagree* to 6=*strongly agree*). One of the items was a reverse-worded item, which was scored in reverse. The Cronbach's α was 0.89.

Basic psychological needs: Satisfaction of basic psychological needs was measured using the Basic psychological needs scale proposed by La Guardia et al. [32]. This scale is used to measure the satisfaction of employees' psychological needs, including autonomy, competence, and relatedness. Each dimension has three items, with a total of nine items (e.g., measure of autonomy: I feel free to be myself; measure of competence: I think I am a capable person; measure of relatedness: I feel loved and cared for). The sum of the scores for each item under a specific dimension is the score for that dimension; the sum of the scores for the three dimensions represents the total basic psychological needs score. A 7-point Likert scale was adopted (1=*strongly disagree* to 7=*strongly agree*). One of the questions for each dimension is a reverse-worded item. The Cronbach's α of the overall scale was 0.92.

Self-determined prosocial motivation: The operational measures for motivation to prosocial behavior were adopted based on several validated Self-Regulation scales selected from Deci and Ryan [12], which measures the level of self-determination employees exhibit in engaging in actions beneficial or helpful to others. According to the SDT continuum for manifesting the different patterns of motivation in an individual behavior, motivation can be classified into external, introjected, identified, and internal motivation depending on the levels of autonomy. Twenty-three items of this scale were selected and revised (e.g., extrinsic motivation: I will be rewarded; introjected motivation: If I don't behave as such, I will feel ashamed of myself; identified motivation: Behaving as such is important to me; intrinsic motivation: Behaving as such is a happy thing). A 7-point Likert scale was adopted (1=*strongly disagree* to 7=*strongly agree*).

To display the level of self-determination in self-regulation, this study adopted RAI to score the scale. The total scale score internal motivation identified motivation-introjected motivation-external motivation [19]. When RAI is a negative value, a large absolute value represents a tendency of controlled motivation; when RAI is a positive value, a large absolute value represents a tendency of autonomous motivation. The Cronbach's α of the overall scale and the four sub-scales was 0.89, 0.81, 0.86, 0.92, and 0.95, respectively.

Impression management motive: The "Impression Management Motive Scale" in the Citizenship Motives Scale developed by Rioux and Penner [17] was employed to measure impression management motive. The scale has six items (e.g., I will avoid being punished by my supervisor) and adopts a 7-point Likert scale. The Cronbach's α was 0.77.

Control variables: According to a review of related literature [13,37,38], the variables of gender, educational attainment, department tenure, marital status, and age were controlled.

Research Results

Scale reliability and validity

Regarding content validity, this study asked three Level-1 and Level-2 supervisors with more than 5 years of work experience to examine the preliminarily drafted scale items, including the semantics in both Mandarin and English, semantic appropriateness, and readability. After the contexts were revised according to the supervisors' suggestions, the preliminary questionnaire was developed. Therefore, the scales used in this study should exhibit a certain degree of content validity. This study constructed a hypothesized five-factor model (i.e., supervisor support, basic psychological needs, SDPM, voice behavior, and impression management motive). Subsequently, a chi-square different test was conducted on the proposed model and three competing models. As shown in Table 1, the fit indices support that the hypothesized 5-factor model, $\chi^2=320.08$; $df=143$;

Model	χ^2	df	$\Delta\chi^2$	CFI	TLI	RMSEA
1- Factor (all items load on a single factor)	1973.15	152	1653.07*	0.42	0.35	0.21
3-Factor (SDPM, IMV and BPN merged)	627.95	149	307.87*	0.85	0.83	0.11
4-Factor (SDPM & IMV merged)	362.33	146	42.25*	0.93	0.92	0.074
5-Factor (expected model)	320.08	143		0.94	0.93	0.068

Note: N=268; The χ^2 difference was compared with the value of the five-factor model (our proposed model); SS=Supervisor Support; BPN=Basic Psychological Needs; SDPM=Self-Determined Prosocial Motivation; IMV=Impression Management Motive; *p<0.001.

Table 1: Alternative model test results for the study variables.

RMSEA=0.068; CFI=0.94 and TLI=0.93, yielded a better fit to the data than the four-factor, three-factor and one-factor models. These CFA results also provide support for the distinctiveness of the five study variables for subsequent analyses. Except for the average variance extracted (AVE) for the impression management motive, which was slightly low but still acceptable (0.46), the AVE values of other research variables were satisfactory with a maximum of 0.72 and minimum of 0.60. Regarding composite reliability, the maximum value was 0.93 and minimum value was 0.83, both of which were higher than the recommended value (0.60); concerning the construct reliability, the maximum value was 0.93 and minimum value was 0.83, both exceeding the recommended value of 0.50 [39]. These results indicate that the five research variables examined in the present study exhibited construct reliability, discriminant validity, and composite reliability.

Correlation coefficient matrix

Table 2 lists the mean, standard deviation, and correlation coefficients of each research variable, showing that the coefficients did not exceed the 0.7 standard. This result indicated low to moderate correlation.

Hypothesis Testing

This study adopted the most streamlined path relationship (i.e., full mediation) as the basic model, proposing two alternative models (Table 3). First, Alternative Model 1 incorporated the path of supervisor support to voice behavior into the basic model, whereas Alternative Model 2 incorporated the path of supervisor support to SDPM into Alternative Model 1. Table 3 reveals that the three models exhibited good fit, and Alternative Model 2 has better relative appropriateness. Table 4 shows the path coefficients of the variables in Alternative Model 2. Table 4 reveals that the effect of supervisor support on voice behavior achieved a significant level (β=0.28, p<0.001). Therefore, H1 was supported. The effect of supervisor support on basic psychological needs achieved a significant level (β=0.74, p<0.001). Therefore, H2 was supported.

Finally, this study adopted two types of mediation test analysis (lower half of Table 4). First, concerning the mediating effects of basic psychological needs on supervisor support and SDPM, the Z value of total effects was 5.269 (>1.96); therefore, the mediating effect was significant. The Z value of indirect effects was 2.266 (>1.96); therefore, the indirect effect was significant. The Z value of direct effects was 1.540 (<1.96); according to the bootstrap results, the lower and upper direct effects for the bias-corrected and percentile methods contained zero, suggesting a full mediation. Regarding the mediating effects of basic psychological needs and SDPM on supervisor support and voice behavior, the products of coefficients were all greater than 1.96 for each effect, and the lower and upper values for both bias-corrected and percentile methods contained no zero. Therefore, mediating effect was exerted. In other words, both H3 and H4 were supported.

Table 5 presents the verification of the moderating effective. The control variables, SDPM and impression management motive, and the cross-multiply items of SDPM and impression management motive were inputted into the regression equation. The cross-multiply items exhibited significant negative predictive effect on voice behavior (β=-0.12, R^2=0.13, p <0.05). To ascertain the direction of the moderating effect, an interaction diagram was plotted. Figure 2 shows that a high impression management motive weakens the positive relationship between SDPM and voice behavior. This result indicates that in a context involving high impression management motive, employees' SDPM negatively influence their voice behavior. Therefore, H5 was supported.

Discussion and Implications

This study was aimed at using SDT to investigate the effects of supervisor support on employee voice behavior and to determine the moderating effect of impression management motives on the relationship between SPDM and voice behavior. As we hypothesized, basic psychological needs and SPDM sequentially mediated the relationship between supervisor support and voice behavior. In

Variables	Mean	SD	`	2	3	4	5	6	7	8	9
Supervisor support	4.43	0.93	-0.89								
Basic Psychological Needs	4.87	1.11	0.67*	-0.92							
SDPM	3.99	2.27	0.33*	0.33*	-0.89						
Voice behavior	3.15	0.97	0.32*	0.31*	0.23*	-0.93					
Impression Management Motive	5.46	0.82	0.12*	0.15*	-0.05	0.03	-0.83				
Gender	0.49	0.5	-0.04	0.02	-0.05	0.12	0.01				
Marital status	0.47	0.5	-0.04	-0.15**	-0.1	-0.18**	-0.02	-0.01			
Age	35.24	8.12	-0.11	0.01	0.13*	0.12*	-0.06	0.1	-0.49**		
Education	15.35	1.75	0.13*	0.02	0.01	0.11	0.15*	0.01	0.13*	-0.35*	
Departmental tenure	6.22	6.2	-0.11	0.05	0.04	0.1	-0.09	0.04	-0.40**	0.63**	-0.36**

Note: N=268; Value in parenthesis indicates the Cronbach's α of the scale; In terms of gender, 1 represents male and 0 represents female; Education in ascending order was represented by 9 years for junior high school or below; 12 years for senior high or vocational school; 14 years for college; 16 years for university and 18 years for graduate or above; SDPM=Self-Determined Prosocial Motivation; *p<0.05; **p<0.01.

Table 2: Mean, Standard deviation, reliabilities, and correlations among study variables.

Model	χ^2 (df)	GFI	CFI	AGFI	RMSEA	$\Delta\chi^2$ (Δdf)
Basic model	102.56 (59)**	0.946	0.983	0.916	0.053	Baseline
Alternative Model 1[a]	84.17 (58)*	0.954	0.99	0.928	0.041	18.39 (1)
Alternative Model 2[b]	81.41 (57)*	0.955	0.99	0.928	0.04	2.76 (1)

Note: N=268; [a]. Alternative Model 1 incorporated a path of supervisor support to voice behavior into the basic model; [b]. Alternative Model 2 incorporated the path of supervisor support to self-determined prosocial motivation (SDPM) into Alternative Model 1; *p<0.05; **p< 0.001.

Table 3: Model comparison results.

Relationship	Direct Effect	Indirect Effect	Total Effect
Supervisor support → Basic psychological needs	0.736***		0.736***
Supervisor support → SDPM	0.174	0.179*	0.353**
Supervisor support → Voice behavior	0.285***	0.061*	0.346**
Basic psychological needs → SDPM	0.243*		0.243*
Basic psychological needs → Voice behavior		0.042*	0.042*
SDPM → Voice behavior	0.173*		0.173*

	Variable	Estimates	Product of Coefficient		Bootstrapping			
			SE	Z	Bias-Corrected 95%CI		Percentile 95%	
					Lower	Upper	Lower	Upper
X-M1-M2	Total Effects	0.353	0.067	5.269	0.254	0.472	0.218	0.477
	Indirect Effects	0.179	0.079	2.266	0.058	0.319	0.025	0.34
	Direct Effects	0.174	0.113	1.540	-0.025	0.361	-0.06	0.395
X-M1-M2-Y	Total Effects	0.346	0.059	5.864	0.241	0.435	0.22	0.458
	Indirect Effects	0.061	0.029	2.103	0.019	0.118	0.008	0.126
	Direct Effects	0.285	0.066	4.318	0.173	0.39	0.151	0.412

Note: N = 268; SDPM = Self-determined prosocial motivation; *p<0.05; **p<0.01; ***p<0.001.

Table 4: Path coefficient and result of mediation effect analysis.

Variable	Voice behavior
Step 1 (Control variables)	
Gender	0.12*
Age	0.02
Marital status	-0.12
Education	0.15*
Departmental tenure	0.08
R^2	0.07
$F_{(5,262)}$	3.96**
Step 2 (Main effects)	
SDPM	0.21**
Impression management motive	0.04
R^2	0.12
$F_{(7,260)}$	4.93**
Step 3 (Interaction effects)	
SDPM×Impression management motive	-0.12*
R^2	0.13
$F_{(8,259)}$	4.90**

Note: N=268; Numbers in the table are standardized β coefficients; SDPM=Self-determined prosocial motivation. *p<0.05; **p<0.01.

Table 5: Results of moderated regression analysis of Self-determined prosocial motivation and impression management motive on voice behavior.

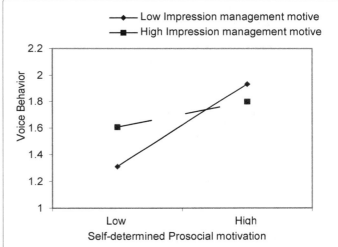

Figure 2: Moderating effect of impression management motive on the relationship between SDPM and Voice behavior.

addition, impressive management motive exhibited a weakening moderating effect on the relationship between SPDM and voice behavior.

Theoretical contribution

The findings of our study contribute to existing knowledge in the following ways. First, previous studies have adopted the social exchange theory, asserting that "supervisors and employees establish their relationship on the principle of reciprocity and that when supervisors treat employees with a positive attitude and behavior, employees tend to return the favor with a positive approach (e.g., voice behavior)." However, reciprocity involves an exchange of satisfaction, and it is also deemed as a sense of obligation to return favors to others [23]. Such behavior is likely to be passive rather than voluntarily. The present study is one of the few studies to adopt an SDT perspective to investigate employee's level of self-determination in exhibiting voice behavior by constructing the process of influence of supervisor support [10,18] and found that supervisor support can effectively satisfy subordinates' basic psychological needs, which in turn nurture SPDM, thereby encouraging employees to demonstrate voice behavior. However, previous studies have not examined the relationship between supervisor support and voice behavior from an SDT perspective. In addition to gaining empirical support, the present study also applied the self-determination theory in an organizational context, as recommended by Greguras and Diefendorff [40].

Furthermore, previous studies primarily examined the effects of prosocial motivation (quantity) on voice behavior, whereas we focused on the effects of the quality of prosocial motivation on voice behavior. To demonstrate employee's level of autonomy in showing prosocial motivation, we adopted RAI to measure prosocial motivation. The findings indicated that when employees are prosocially and autonomously motivated, they are more likely to demonstrate voice behavior. Such finding not only reveals the importance of autonomous motivation, but also unveils the underlying motivation of voice behavior [41].

Finally, this study explored the effect that the interaction between impression management motive (self-oriented) and prosocial motivation (other-oriented) has on employee voice behavior. As expected, subordinates' impression management motive weakens the positive relationship between SDPM and voice behavior. This result verifies the viewpoints of Grant and Mayer [16] that impression management motive guides employees toward affiliative citizenship behavior (supporting the current state) rather than toward challenging citizenship behavior (simulating change). Moreover, the result also resonates with the assertion of Takeuchi et al. [20] that in a collectivist culture, employees with a high degree of other-oriented motives are likely to feel conflicted about engaging in Organizational citizenship behavior (OCB) because of impression management (self-oriented) motives. In other words, high impression management motive weakens, rather than strengthens, the positive effect of other-oriented motives and voice behavior. In theory, the aforementioned findings provide an insight into the mechanisms of mixed-motives under different cultural contexts [Appendix].

Implications for practice

From SDT perspective, this study verified that supervisor support can effectively satisfy employees' basic psychological needs, inducing a high level of SDPM, which in turn encourages them to demonstrate extra-role voice behavior that is beneficial to their organization. Meanwhile, this study verified the moderating effect of impression management motive on the relationship between SDPM and voice behavior. This study provides the following four managerial implications.

First, organizations can create a supportive environment and climate to nurture employees' basic needs, specifically supervisor support for employees' work and emotions. Second, the need for autonomy and competence can evoke intrinsic motivation, whereas the need for relatedness is crucial for internalization of a behavior [18]. Therefore, an organization should ensure the satisfaction of all three basic psychological needs because a higher degree of need satisfaction is more likely to elicit individual autonomy and promote the motivation to increase collective benefits or benefits for others. Third, the human resource department should ascertain employees' self-regulation or state of work motivation regulation by adopting the Self-Regulation Scale to design a more accurate Basic Psychological Needs Satisfaction Plan for employees. Fourth, because a high level of impression management motive weakens the positive relationship between SDPM and voice behavior, supervisors hoping that their subordinates would demonstrate more voice behavior should not only stimulate employees' prosocial motivation, but also discourage their employees from having overly high impression management motive. In other words, in employee management and performance evaluation, supervisors should make employees aware and believe that being a "good soldier who seeks to help others and the organization" is better than being a "good actor who attempts to create favorable images in the eyes of others."

Research Limitations and Future Research

This research involved a cross-sectional study, in which the data of all variables were collected at the same time point. Future studies can adopt a longitudinal research approach to conduct measurements at different time points. In addition, this study included only supervisor support as the variable representing social support. We recommend future studies to incorporate colleague support and organizational support to elucidate the differences in employees' basic psychological needs, motivation, and voice behavior when employees perceive different sources of support provided to them.

References

1. Morrison EW (2011) Employee voice behavior: Integration and directions for future research. The Academy of Management Annals 5: 373-412.
2. Liang J, Farh CIC, Farh JL (2012) Psychological antecedents of promotive and prohibitive voice behavior: A two-wave longitudinal examination. Academy of Management Journal 55: 71-92.
3. Ajzen I (1991) The theory of planned behavior. Organizational Behavior and Human Decision Processes 50: 179-211.
4. Hsiung HH (2012) Authentic leadership and employee voice behavior: A multi-level psychological process. Journal of Business Ethics 107: 349-361.
5. Bhal KT, Ansari MA (2007) Leader-member exchange-subordinate outcomes relationship: role of voice and justice. Leadership Organization Development Journal 28: 20-35.
6. Burris ER (2012) The risks and rewards of speaking up: Managerial responses to employee voice. Academy of Management Journal 55: 851-875.
7. Walumbwa FO, Schaubroeck J (2009) Leader personality traits and employee voice behavior: Mediating roles of ethical leadership and work group psychological safety. Journal of Applied Psychology 94: 1275-1286.
8. Wang D, Gan C, Wu C (2016) LMX and employee voice: A moderated mediation model of psychological empowerment and role clarity. Personnel Review 45: 605-615.
9. Zhang Y, Huai MY, Xie YH (2015) Paternalistic leadership and employee voice in China: A dual process mode. Leadership Quarterly 26: 25-36.
10. Deci EL, Ryan MR (2000) The "what" and "why" of goal pursuits: Human needs and the self-determination of behavior. Psychological Inquiry 11: 227-268.
11. Deci EL, Ryan MR (1985) Intrinsic motivation and self-determination in human behavior. New York: Plenum Press.
12. Deci EL, Ryan RM (2008) Self-Determination Theory. An approach to human motivation personality. The Self-Regulation Questionnaires 49: 186-193.
13. Detert JR, Burris ER (2007) Leadership behavior and employee voice: Is the door really open? Academy of Management Journal 50: 869-884.
14. Morrison E, Milliken F (2000) Organizational silence: a barrier to change and development in a pluralistic world. Academy of Management Review 25: 706-725.
15. Eisenberger R, Huntington R, Hutchison S, Sowa D (1986) Perceived organizational support. Journal of Applied Psychology 71: 500-507.
16. Grant AM, Mayer DM (2009) Good soldiers and good actors: Prosocial and impression management motives as interactive predictors of affiliative citizenship behaviors. Journal of Applied Psychology 94: 900-912.
17. Rioux SM, Penner LA (2001) The causes of organizational citizenship behavior: A motivational analysis. Journal of Applied Psychology 86: 1306-1314.
18. Gagné M, Deci EL (2005) Self-determination theory and work motivation. Journal of Organizational Behavior 26: 331-362.
19. Ong AD, Phinney JS (2002) Personal goals and depression among Vietnamese American and European American young adults: A mediational analysis. The Journal of Social Psychology 142: 97-108.
20. Takeuchi R, Bolino MC, Lin C (2015) Too many motives? The interactive effects of multiple motives on organizational citizenship behavior. Journal of Applied psychology 100: 1239-1248.
21. De Dreu CKW, Nauta A (2009) Self-interest and other-orientation in organizational behavior: Implications for job performance, prosocial behavior, and personal initiative. Journal of Applied Psychology 94: 913-926.
22. Kottke JL, Sharafinski CE (1988) Measuring perceived supervisory and organizational support. Educational and Psychological Measurement 48: 1075-1079.
23. Eisenberger E, Stinglhamber F, Vandenberghe C, Rhoades L (2002) Perceived supervisor support: Contributions to perceived organizational support and employee retention. Journal of Applied Psychology 87: 565-573.
24. Shanock LR, Eisenberger R (2006) When supervisors feel supported:

24. (continued) Relationships with subordinates' perceived supervisor support, perceived organizational support, and performance. Journal of Applied psychology 91: 689-695.

25. Luyckx K, Vansteenkiste M, Goossens L, Duriez B (2009) Basic need satisfaction and identity formation: Bridging self-determination theory and process oriented identity research. Journal of Counseling Psychology 56: 276-288.

26. Ryan RM, Deci EL (2000) Self-determination theory and the facilitation of intrinsic motivation, social development, and well-being. American Psychologist 55: 68-78.

27. Lin CC, Shiaw SY (2005) Relationship among Social Support, Trust, Organizational Relationship and Knowledge Sharing Behaviors Based on the Perspective of Social Exchange Theory. Commerce Management Quarterly I6: 373-400.

28. Halbesleben JRB (2006) Sources of social support and burnout: A meta-analytic test of the conservation of resources model. Journal of Applied Psychology 91: 1134-1145.

29. May DR, Gilson RL, Harter LM (2004) The psychological conditions of meaningfulness, safety and availability and the engagement of the human spirit at work. Journal of Occupational Organizational Psychology 77: 11-37.

30. Fox S, Spector PE (2006) The many roles of control in a stressor-emotion theory of counterproductive work behavior. Research in Occupational Stress and Well Being I5: 171-201.

31. Gagné M (2003) The Role of Autonomy Support and Autonomy Orientation in Prosocial Behavior Engagement. Motivation and Emotion 27: 199-223.

32. La Guardia JG, Ryan RM, Couchman CE, Deci EL (2000) Within-person variation in security of attachment: A self-determination theory perspective on attachment, need fulfillment, and well-being. Journal of Personality and Social Psychology 79: 367-384.

33. Vansteenkiste M, Neyrinck B, Niemiec CP, Soenens B, De Witte H, et al. (2007) On the Relations among Work Value Orientations, Psychological Need Satisfaction and Job Outcomes: A Self-Determination Theory Approach. Journal of Occupational Organizational Psychology 80: 251-277.

34. Demerouti E, Bakker AB, Nachreiner F, Schaufeli W B (2001) The job demands–resources model of burnout. Journal of Applied Psychology 86: 499-512.

35. Janssen PPM, Peeters MCW, Jonge J, Houkes I, Tummers GER (2004) Specific relationships between job demands, job resources and psychological outcomes and the mediating role of negative work-home interference. Journal of Vocational Behavior 65: 411-429.

36. Van den Broeck A, Vansteenkiste M, De Witte H, Lens W (2008) Explaining the relationships between job characteristics, burnout, and engagement: The role of basic psychological need satisfaction. Work Stress 22: 277-294.

37. Frese M, Teng E, Wijnen CJD (1999) Helping to improve suggestion systems: Predictors of giving suggestions in companies. Journal of Organizational Behavior 20: 1139-1155.

38. Stamper CL, Van Dyne L (2001) Work status and organizational citizenship behavior: A field study of restaurant employees. Journal of Organizational Behavior 22: 517-536.

39. Fornell C, Larcker DF (1981) Evaluating structural equation models with unbervables and measurement error. Journal of Marketing Research I8: 39-50.

40. Greguras GJ Diefendorff JM (2009) Different fits satisfy different needs: Linking person-environment fit to employee commitment and performance using self-determination theory. Journal of Applied Psychology 94: 465-477.

41. Liden RC, Wayne SJ, Sparrowe RT (2000) An examination of the mediating role of psychological empowerment on the relations between the job, interpersonal relationships, and work outcomes. Journal of Applied Psychology 85: 407-416.

Role of Relational Capital and Firm Performance: Analysis of a Cluster of Bell-metal Enterprises in a Rural Region in West Bengal, India

Soumyendra Kishore Datta* and Tanushree De

Department of Economics Burdwan University West Bengal, India

Abstract

This paper has tried to assess the impact of relational capital components on the performance of bell-metal clustered firms in Dharmada region of Nadia district in the State of West Bengal in India. The issue of relational capital has been considered in relation to the notion of intangible asset. Eight components of relational capital indicators were considered and they were combined into a single overall index by using principal component method. A study was conducted on a sample of sixty firms in the cluster. Cronbach's alpha has been used to assess the reliability or internal consistency of the set of individual relational capital indicators. The overall index of relational capital is found strongly associated with profitability performance. The overall regression of profitability figures on individual relational capital indicators has been observed to be significant and some of the indicators are also found to significantly influence firm performance level. The analysis identifies and provides suggestion regarding upgrading and maintaining relational capital components in which the firms may have some advantage. This can make substantial contribution to the performance of firms.

Keywords: Relational capital; Cronbach's alpha; Entrepreneurship; Regression

Introduction

While earning, sustained profit serves as an important driver of a firm's action, maintaining the market share, maximizing sales or even retaining or increasing the customer base often supersedes the profit motive on the part of a firm's conduct. In fact, in this globalized world when spirits of both perfect and imperfect competition, dominate the market economy, apart from usual market conduct, firms try to survive the market uncertainties by taking recourse to subtle behavioral actions that provide competitive edge compared to others. Hence alongside putting efforts towards possible expansion in the scale of production, undertaking investment for maintaining the tempo of expansion, spending on advertisement or innovative works, in order to flourish business firms often feel concerned in maintaining cordial relation with all the stakeholders who may be directly or indirectly linked with its process of production and disposal of final output. Maintaining a sociable and affable relation with all the related stakeholders leads to smoothening of the production channel, enhancement of the market base, and arresting the attention of the potential customers. Enhancing the bonding and good trust relationship with input suppliers, laborer's, customers or even clustered firms in the locality usually proves very effective for the firm to improve the quality of its product, market its output and/or lower the prices in order to remain competitive in the market.

According to Adeeco [1], in the backdrop of a flourishing knowledge economy, it has become easier for competitors to gain access to same technology, develop a similar product, enter the same market by strengthening the access to credit base etc. This enhances the importance of sources of capital for better competitive edge, that are difficult to emulate and replicate and relational capital falls in this category. Relational capital encompasses all the intangible assets generated by developing, maintaining, and nurturing high quality relationships with the external partners that could enhance the firm's performance [2]. Kijek and Kijek [3], emphasized two-fold impacts of relational capital on firms performance namely: cost reduction and increased market value. They opined that knowledge embedded in relationship among employees, customers and suppliers may lead to cost reduction. This may be achieved through process innovations, increased outputs that results in economies of scale.

Carlucci [4] observes that, enhanced investment in relationships with internal and external stakeholder groups for improving performance, usually have multiple effects in the production network. Internal source of relational capital refers to informal bonding with members of the family, relation with business partners or the laborer's who deal with inputs. While external networks in the form of linkages with customers and suppliers, informal relation with firms in a cluster and mutual trust or coordination of their efforts, linkages with external bodies such as local/state Govt., location of the firm as well as reputation or goodwill of the firm-all constitute the external source of relational capital. Young and Snell [5] observed that with enhanced level of relational capital, there emerges greater likelihood of increased production and better efficiency in service delivery.

Andriessen [6], opine that not all businesses can set up relation with their environment and this is mostly the case for newer business ventures which do not have any history and so cannot recognize and manage the relational assets. On the other hand, established firms/entrepreneurs, do not usually falter in comprehending the strength of relational capital due to their long experience in business dealings. In the context of an industrial cluster however, the relatively new firms because of close proximity and coordination with established older firms, are likely to realize early the importance of relational capital. For successful handling of relational capital, firms should recognize that it is a very important component of intangible asset apart from financial and physical assets.

---

*__Corresponding author:__ Datta SK, Professor, Department of Economics, Burdwan University, Golapbag, Burdwan-713104, West Bengal, India
E-mail: soumyendra_d@rediffmail.com

According to Ogundipe [7], Cluster competitive advantage can be enhanced if relational capital concept can be embraced and developed both within the organization and the cluster as an entity. Value creation based on mutual trust and cooperation within the cluster should be encouraged. This can be achieved through employees share value and togetherness built on trust and open culture within the cluster. Barney et al. [8] state that common values and shared visions among firms in a cluster, promote the bonding based on mutual faith and trust relationships, thus lessening the possibility of cheating and opportunistic behaviors. In case of small and medium scale firms particularly in case of developing economies, relational capital is directly linked to business performance, without this capital the organizational competitiveness and higher performance level can hardly be achieved [9]. In the context of the importance of relational capital as an intangible asset for flourishing of firm performance in a cluster, it seems imperative to focus on the impact of relational capital on a set of clustered firms in a rural region in a developing country like India. For this purpose this paper focuses on the following objectives (a) to derive an overall index of relational capital in case of some small scale clustered firms in a rural region in India and find the degree of correlation of this index with that of firm performance level (b) test the reliability of the relational capital items and (c) analyses the influence of individual relational capital components on the level of firm performance.

Relational Capital and its Link to Intangible Asset

Relational capital as an intangible asset has in recent years captured more focused interest of organizations than that of physical and financial capital. In the era of globalized uncertainties regarding use of financial assets and stringent imposition of environmental norms regarding use of physical capital, firms have tended to get inclined to more efficiently nurture the intangible relational capital as an adjunct of intellectual capital. According to Martín de Castro, López and Navas [10], the basic foundation of intangible assets rests on information and knowledge sharing, cordial business relationship and mutual trust and sympathetic behavior with all stakeholder groups, and hence these assets are hardly detectable, mostly inimitable, irreplaceable and nontransferable in the markets This type of intangible asset is broadly categorized as a form of manifestation of intellectual capital, which have a bearing on the performance of the firms. Several authors declare that firms with an adequate intellectual capital have a better chance of survival [11]. Swart [12] opines that intellectual capital is broadly divided into four categories: human capital, customer capital, social capital and organizational capital. Edvinsson and Malone [13] argue that, intellectual capital covers the relationship between customers and other stakeholder groups.

Extending the definition of Edvinsson and Malone [13], relational capital is reflected as a form of intellectual capital which can be viewed in terms of three layers. The first layer covers the importance of networks, collaborations and associations in knowledge spillover and sharing, The second focuses on the relationships with customers, input suppliers, business partners and all stakeholder groups both internal and external, while the third takes care of mutual bonding based on trust, faith and reputation. Relational capital serves as a reservoir wherefrom the firms can get enriched through external outsourcing of information and knowledge and channelizing that knowledge into developing improvised technique. It may be noted that pertinent to the knowledge based view of the firm, there has been an evolution in usage of terms associated with intellectual capital. Since now-a-days knowledge economy pervade the environment in which organizations have to operate, there is an increasing realization towards developing a strong relation with their environment in order to acquire and share essential knowledge for the promotion of their business. The present business tune is to move towards a knowledge-based economy where intangible assets and investments are seen as essential elements for value creation in companies and, consequently, to economic wealth [14].

In the era of increased competition when the threat of being superseded is high, there is a need for quick adjustment in internal organization for surviving in the competitive ambience. In order to adjust with changes of competitive forces, the need is to have an ability to understand and quickly adopt new knowledge. The ability to read the signals provided by the market and then to decode the signals to adjust it to the needs of the customers and to enhance the competence of the organization, holds as a competitive advantage. This necessitates the maintenance of good relationship with all stakeholders who might be party in promoting the competitive strength of the firm. There is a tendency towards a closer focus on the core-competencies, as firms tend to outsource activities that do not hold the potential to differentiate the firm from its competitors. As a sequel the focus is on developing closer relationship with customers, suppliers, knowledge institutions and universities [15].

Fitzpatrick [16] analyzed the importance of business relationships in recession. According to him, business relationships can be viewed as the businessmen's relational capital that has an intrinsic value. According to him business flourishes on the basis of dynamic forces which are powered by twin drivers like people and relationships.

The capital aspect of the relationships is now widely recognized as it is seriously believed that there exists strong connection of relational capital to firm performance level and relationship capital is now considered as a major source of competitive advantage [17,18]

Components of Relational Capital and Relevant Hypotheses

Relational capital is composed of several interlinked components. The individual components and relevant hypothesis with regard to link with firm level performance are outlined below.

Relation with customers

In the event of growing competition in the business world and era of advertisement, maintaining good customer relation is deemed as an important form of external intangible asset by a firm. Strong bonding with customers leads to sustained value addition to a firm and better prospects of gaining strategic information that might help into capturing the share of rival firms. Contacts, reactions and responses from customers send signals about drift of market demand, change in consumer preferences, substitute products and likely price movement. Consumers are deemed as sovereigns in the market and hence their expectation attitude, emotions and tastes needs to be systematically taken care of in order to retain the customer base. Better dealings with them, ready reciprocation, satisfaction of their expectation and tastes and keeping an overall healthy relation with customers puts the level of firm performance on a higher platform. So it is reasonably expected that good customer capital embedded in the form of maintenance of good customer relation has a direct association with the level of firm performance.

Relation with input suppliers

Constant liaising with input suppliers in order to have timely and adequate flow of quality inputs involves an important component of relational capital. Timely payment of input cost, placing demand for inputs at predictable time sequence, gentle bargaining for rebate on input price, firm reputation in the market place involve strong points for keeping good relation with input suppliers. Sometimes survey undertaken by firms regarding satisfaction of suppliers from whom products/services are purchased, reflect upon the concern of firms to maintain good relation with them for continued support in future. It is highly expected that external capital of this type would have a positive impact in sustaining the tempo of firm performance.

Sharing of technological knowledge

Mutual interaction and reciprocation across the cluster of firms enhance the quality of relational capital in the form of increased scope of knowledge spillover, information sharing and improved technological competence. This creates scope of mutually better value addition for the stakeholders. Interflow of knowledge, mutual technological support and stream of information, enhance prospects of improving the quality of running product and better marketing arrangements. This is likely to be mirrored in terms of higher profitability.

Bonding with external groups

Maintaining links with external organization often help in promoting firm level performance. Thus connections with Govt. organizations, credit agencies, import/export companies, NGOs as well as common people residing in the neighborhood help in gathering valuable information, knowledge, credit, better access to marketing channels or strategic information about the market environment. External linkage of this sort is expected to positively influence the level of firm performance.

Informal relation with firms in cluster

Amiable informal interaction and absence of conflict amongst firms in a cluster can have a positive impact on perceived congeniality of social environment, agreeable ambience for continued production and an atmosphere of steady cooperation and healthy rivalry. This is deemed as an intangible asset and enhances productive zeal of an entrepreneur that is supposed to be conducive to enhanced firm performance

Location

Location of a firm linked with good transport facility to input and product market, opportunities of having the local support base in the form of technology, skilled labor and steady electricity as well as availability of large work space, engender a congenial atmosphere for better firm performance that may be reflected in higher profitability.

Reputation

Sociable way of dealing and transacting with all stakeholder groups helps enhance the level of reputation of an entrepreneurial firm and this creates avenues for further growth. Reputation serves to entice new customers, facilitates access to credit, eases the availability of raw material and other resources [19]. It enhances sort of credence amongst customers about the unassailable quality and durability of the product and hence an assured market share. Thus a reputed firm is supposed to have comparative advantage with regard to production, distribution and marketing opportunities and this brings in prospect of better marketability and profitability.

Trust and good faith relationship

Better reputation of a firm is likely to be reflected in the form of mutual trust and faith. It strengthens the tie across input suppliers, customers, retailers, credit providers and enhances the likelihood of obtaining uninterrupted supply of inputs, maintaining the time bound production order in subcontracting frame and enables the production process to run on smooth and sustained basis with assured or even rising trend in market demand. This is likely to have a direct link with firm performance indexed by profitability.

Data and Method

The data were collected from the clustered firms producing bell metal items in Dharmada region of Nadia district in the state of West Bengal in India. A sample of 60 firms were covered in the study on the basis of face to face interview with the owner of the firms, based on a pre-structured questionnaire. The owners were favored as respondents to the questions, since they shouldered the day to day management responsibility and actively participated in overall decision making process.

Derivation of an overall index of relational capital on the basis of principal component method is based on the consideration of diverse individual indicators of relational capital. The overall index is considered as a latent or unobserved variable. Here the problem is the weight assignment to the individual indicators which is critical to maximize the information from a data set included in an index. A good composite index should comprise important information from all the indicators, but not strongly biased towards one or more of these indicators. Here it needs to be stressed that the individual indicators of relational capital are measured in terms of 5-point Likert type scaling ranging from 1=extremely unfavorable to 5=extremely favorable.

We consider the overall index of relational capital linearly determined by eight relevant components. The indicators are sharing of technological knowledge, relations with customers, relations with suppliers of inputs, informal relations with firms in the cluster, linkage with external bodies, locational advantage, trust and good faith relationship as well as reputation. These are denoted as X_{1i}, X_{2i}, X_{3i}, X_{4i}, X_{5i}, X_{6i}, X_{7i} and X_{8i} respectively. In latent form the relational capital index can be expressed as

$$R_i = \delta_1 X_{1i} + \delta_2 X_{2i} + \delta_3 X_{3i} + \delta_4 X_{4i} + \delta_5 X_{5i} + \delta_6 X_{6i} + \delta_7 X_{7i} + \delta_8 X_{8i} + w_i$$

(Where $i = 1$ to 60).

We denote λ_j (j=1, 2, 3, 4, 5, 6, 7, 8) as the jth Eigen value. Subscript j refers to the number of Principal Components that also coincides with the number of corresponding indicators. Noting that the values of gradually falls as the suffix increases, we denote P_j (j = 1, 2......7, 8) as the jth Principal Component. We get the corresponding relational capital index according to the following weighted average:

$$D_i = \frac{\sum_{j=1}^{8} \lambda_j P_j}{\sum_{j=1}^{8} \lambda_j}$$

Although usually the whole set of causal variables is replaced by a few principal components, which account for a substantial percentage of the total variation in all the sample variables, here we consider as many components as the number of explanatory variables. This is due to our concern in order to avoid discarding information that could affect the estimates. Thus this procedure accounts for 100 percent of the total variation in the data.

Cronbach's alpha is used to assess the reliability or internal consistency of the set of individual relational capital indicators.

It is computed by correlating the score for each item with the total score for each observation and then comparing that to the variance for all individual indicator scores.

Where $a = \left(\dfrac{k}{k-1}\right)\left(1 - \sum \sigma_{yi}^2 / \sigma_x^2\right)$

Where k refers to the number of relational capital items

σ_{yi}^2 indicates to the variance associated with indicator/item i

σ_x^2 implies the variance associated with the observed total scores.

The following multiple regression is set to assess the impact of the individual indicators on firm performance level,

$LnY = \alpha + \beta_1 X_1 + \beta_2 X_2 + \beta_3 X_3 + \beta_4 X_4 + \beta_5 X_5 + \beta_6 X_6 + \beta_7 X_7 + \beta_8 X_8$

Where X_1 = technological knowledge sharing, X_2 = relation with customers, X_3 = relationship with input suppliers, X_4 = informal relation with firms in cluster, X_5 = Linkage with external bodies, X_6 = location, X_7 = trust and good faith relation, X_8 = Reputation and LnY refers to log value of per capita profit in the enterprise.

Empirical Results and Discussion

Principal component method has been applied to derive the relational capital index for sixty entrepreneurs based on eight relational capital items. For this purpose all the possible eight principal components have been used in order to fully utilize the available data and not to leave any information wasted. The following Table 1 provides the values of coefficients linked with the eight items of normalized values of relational capital for each of eight principal components. The corresponding Eigen values are tabulated at the bottom of the table (Table 1).

The corresponding relational capital index values for sixty entrepreneurs are computed by using the method

Further log values of per capita profitability of the enterprise families are also calculated. It is found that there exists highly significant correlation between these two series. The correlation coefficient is 0.765 which is significant at 1% level (p value being 0.00), Further if we regress the log values of profit on relational capital index, the coefficient is found to significantly positive as expected.

The reliability of the instrument used for measuring relational capital indicators is provided by the Cronbach's alpha coefficient which reflects the level of internal consistency of the indicators. Alpha coefficient value ranges from 0 to 1 and proves useful in describing the reliability of factors extracted from multi-point formatted questionnaires or scales (i.e., rating scale: 1=most unfavorable, 5=most favorable). Higher value of the score indicates better reliability level. According to Nunnaly, 0.7 can be considered as an acceptable reliability coefficient. However in specific cases lower thresholds are not uncommon in the literature. In the present case the value of alpha, based on eight relational items, emerges as 0.715 which is indicative of reasonably good reliability of the instrument used for measuring relational capital indicators. However alpha if some item is deleted, as depicted in Table 2 is also an important element in this context. It is representative of Cronbach's alpha reliability coefficient for internal consistency if some individual item is removed from the scale. Thus as shown in Table 2, if item 5 (Linkage with external bodies) were removed the reliability of instrument used for firms" relational capital would somewhat rise in terms of value 0.751. Other variables are important as their omission decrease the value of the alpha coefficient (Table 2).

The following Table 3 indicates the mean value of the relational capital items, variation in perception level of entrepreneurs regarding relational capital components and the rank of the perceived status of the items. It is observed that as expected in a performing cluster, trust and good faith relationship achieve rank 1, reputation attain rank 2, while location of the cluster of firms is considered in a position of rank

Relational Capital Item	Coefficients							
	PC 1	PC 2	PC 3	PC 4	PC 5	PC 6	PC 7	PC 8
X1	0.371416	0.01194	0.057849	-0.30994	0.799616	0.17476	-0.29863	0.058281
X2	0.473534	-0.35103	-0.14192	0.079903	-0.05099	-0.02055	0.1905	-0.76597
X3	0.441702	-0.348	-0.0751	0.141028	-0.06287	-0.27069	0.480141	0.592037
X4	0.304974	0.516903	0.267075	-0.26517	-0.4052	-0.56851	-0.04373	-0.09415
X5	0.044526	-0.17714	0.939027	0.229857	0.059206	0.156681	0.051325	-0.03667
X6	0.268171	0.674638	-0.06898	0.34552	0.23448	0.369711	0.395817	-0.02165
X7	0.382081	0.000614	-0.10644	0.536943	-0.21265	0.084802	-0.69213	0.151403
X8	0.360308	-0.04276	0.041054	-0.58892	-0.29355	0.635721	-0.06111	0.160594
Eigen value	2.953575	1.03256	1.017932	0.843751	0.683888	0.623917	0.568405	0.275973

Source: Author Calculation based on Field Survey data 2016.

Table 1: Coefficients and eigen values based on normalized value of relational capital items.

Relational Capital Variables	Scale Mean if Item Deleted	Scale Variance if Item Deleted	Corrected Item-Total Correlation	Cronbach's Alpha if Item Deleted
Sharing of technology knowledge	27.6667	8.395	0.467	0.677
Relations with customers	27.5333	9.202	0.61	0.645
Relations with suppliers of inputs	27.5333	9.711	0.562	0.66
Informal relations with firms in the cluster	27.5333	9.779	0.398	0.688
Linkage with external bodies	28.0667	11.555	0.051	0.751
Location	27.4833	10.22	0.325	0.703
Trust good faith relationship	27.3667	9.524	0.471	0.673
Reputation	27.4333	9.945	0.447	0.679

Source: Author Calculation based on Field Survey data 2016

Table 2: Item-total statistics.

3. Being close to Calcutta the firms do not have to face great problems in marketing their product. The roads being in good condition, the entrepreneurs also have relatively easy access to mahajans. However linkage with external bodies is given least importance in their perception. This is probably because the enterprise owners are mostly linked with respective mahajans with respect to their subcontracting relationship. Hence they hardly have to bother about the conduct and relation of external agencies that might exist. Further the work being mostly of stereotyped fashion, the owners do not attach much importance to it. However sometimes it is found that some long term workers in a particular enterprise leave laboring job and engage in some other enterprise or launch individual enterprise on his own effort or by hiring some labor. This provides some scope of knowledge percolation or sharing (Table 3).

The regression equation is fit to assess the impact of the chosen components of relational capital on the firm performance level measured in terms of profitability. The results of regression equation are given in Table 4. It is observed that the sign of the coefficient of variable "shared knowledge" is expectedly positive, its value being 0.026 and it makes significant impact on the variation of log value of profitability. This is indicated by its t value and level of significance ($t=2.174$, $p<0.05$). Similarly sign of coefficient of the variable "customer capital" is also in the desired positive direction, with a value of 0.045, it is also significant ($t=1.846$, $p<0.10$). Again there is expected positive sign associated with the variable, "relation with supplier of inputs", which is however insignificant. The sign of the coefficients of the variables "Informal relation with other firms" is as expected positive and also significant ($t=2.573$, $p<0.05$). Again, the sign of the coefficient of the variable "location" is found to be in the expected direction which is also significant ($t=2.969$, $p<0.01$). Reputation has also direct significant impact on performance level as indicated by $t=2.04$, with $p<0.05$. The overall regression is found to be good fit with R^2 value as 0.634, and F value being 11.041 which is significant at 1% level (Table 4).

Further the regression coefficient of firm performance on overall index of relational capital appears to be 0.58 which is significant at 1% level (the corresponding R^2 value being 0.586 and F being equal to 82.09). The correlation coefficient between log value of firm profitability figures and that of relational capital indices turns out to be 0.765 which is significant at 1% level. The implication is that relational capital has significant influence in shaping firm performance.

Concluding Remarks

The above analysis reveals that there is reasonably good internal consistency of relational capital indicators. Again it is important to note that if the indicator like "Linkage with external bodies" is deleted, the value of Cronbach's alpha increases. This reflects the relative incoherence of this indicator. From the analysis of the value of perception about the relational capital variables and the regression results, it may be noted that reputation, location of the firms in the cluster, customer relationships, informal relationships with firms in the cluster have relatively high mean values and significant impact on the per capita profitability. This finding is completely in the desired direction. However while mean value of trust and good faith relation has rank 1, this is found to be insignificant and while that of technological knowledge sharing has rank 7, it is observed to be significant in influencing firm level performance. Trust and good faith are considered to be a cornerstone for long persistence of activity in a cluster based enterprises.

However mere mutual trust may not be reflected in productive activity of the firms leading to profitability. Knowledge sharing here is perceived to be relatively unimportant. Since almost all the firms produce articles of the same type/use same type of technology, there is neither attached great importance nor it is perceived necessary for sharing of knowledge. However, evenness of knowledge leads to competitive spirit and better quality that is reflected in significantly better profitability performance. Again the bell metal firms in this region have a long tradition of enterprise based production. The supply of their output in the market through the chain link of mahajans, clustering of a number of skilled enterprise owners in a small neighborhood and their earlier link with Moradabad group of firms and inclination to excel their production quality have helped spread their reputation. There has therefore been a favorable perception about the informal relation across the firms in the cluster. Because of geographical proximity to metropolitan market at Calcutta, the locational advantage of the cluster is also considerable.

It is however heartening for the firms to maintain good relation with customers. Maintaining customer repeat rates, stable prices along with good product quality as well as uninterrupted supply of output are some of the factors that contribute to the fostering of good relation with customers. The enterprise owners however do not have to bother much about maintaining good relation with the suppliers of inputs. The input suppliers are mostly mahajans and for their own interest, they subcontract production orders with partial/full scale supply of necessary inputs.

Overall, the analysis suggests that relational capital is connected with the competitive performance level of small enterprises operating in the bell metal sector in the study region, through the positive relationship of its subcomponents. Moreover, higher the level of relational capital

Relational Capital Variables	Mean	Standard Deviation	Rank of Mean
Sharing of technology knowledge	3.85	1.03	7
Relations with customers	3.98	0.7	4
Relations with suppliers of inputs	3.95	0.62	6
Informal relations with firms in the cluster	3.96	0.76	5
Linkage with external bodies	3.45	0.69	8
Location	4.03	0.73	3
Trust good faith relationship	4.15	0.75	1
Reputation	4.08	0.67	2

Source: Author Calculation based on Field Survey data 2016

Table 3: Perceived status of relational capital items.

Independent Variables	Coefficients	t	Sig.
(Constant)	7.041*	63.49	0
Sharing of technology knowledge	0.026*	2.174	0.034
Relations with customers	0.045*	1.846	0.071
Relations with suppliers of inputs	0.004	0.176	0.861
Informal relations with firms in the cluster	0.041*	2.573	0.013
Linkage with external bodies	0.025	1.577	0.121
Location	0.048*	2.969	0.005
Trust good faith relationship	0.001	0.066	0.948
Reputation	0.038*	2.04	0.047
R^2	0.634		
F	11.041*		
Durbin-Watson	1.01		

Source: Author Calculation based on Field Survey data 2016 *Indicates 1% level of significance

Table 4: Regression results of firm performance.

and its associated spillover, better is likely the result in problem solving, planning and management quality of a firm, which over the long run can enhance competitive efficiency and reduce organizational cost.

Acknowledgement

The field work for this paper has been funded by a Major Research Project funded by UGC.

References

1. Adeeco (2007) The intrinsic link between human and relational capital: A key differentiator for today's leading knowledge economy companies. Adecco pp: 1-6.
2. Carson E, Ranzijn R, Winefield A, Marsden H (2004) Intellectual capital: Mapping employee and work group attributes. Journal of Intellectual Capital 5: 443-463.
3. Kijek T, Kijek A (2007) Relational Capital and its Impact on Firms Performance: The Case of Polish Enterprises. Economics and Competition Policy 4: 78-84.
4. Carlucci D, Marr B, Schiuma G (2004) The knowledge value chain: how intellectual capital impacts on business performance. International Journal Technology Management 27: 575-579.
5. Young MA, Snell SA (2004) Intellectual Capital Profiles: An Examination of Investments and Returns. Journal of Management Studies 41: 235-361.
6. Andriessen D (2004) Capital Valuation and Measurement: Classifying the State of the Art. Journal of Intellectual Capital 5: 230-242.
7. Ogundipe, Emmanuel S (2012) Business Relational Capital and Firm Performance in South, Western Nigerian Small Scale Enterprise Clusters. European Journal of Business and Management 4: 2222-2839.
8. Barney JB, Hansen MH (1994) Trustworthiness as a source of competitive advantage. Strategic Management Journal 15: 175-190.
9. Bontis N (2001) Assessing knowledge assets: A review of the models used to measure Intellectual Capital. International Journal of Management Reviews 3: 41-60.
10. Castro de M, Saez LP, Navas NJ (2004) The Roll of corporate reputation in developing relational capital. Journal of Intellectual Capital 5: 575-585
11. Hormiga E, Batista-Canino MR, Medina A (2011) The Impact of Relational Capital on the Success of New Business Start-Ups. Journal of Small Business Management 49: 617-638.
12. Swart J (2005) Identifying the Sub-Components of Intellectual Capital: a literature Review and Development of Measures. University of Bath School of Management.
13. Edvinsson L, Malone MS (1999) El capital intelectual. Cómo identificar y calcular el valor de los recursos intangibles de su empresa. Barcelona: Gestión 2000.
14. Cañibano L, García-Ayuso M, Sánchez MP (2000) Accounting for Intangibles: A Literature Review. Journal of Accounting Literature 19: 102-130.
15. Nyholm J, Normann L, Frelle-Petersen C, Riis M, Torstensen P (2001) Innovation policy in the knowledge-based economy: can theory guide policy making. The globalizing learning economy pp: 253-272.
16. Fitzpatrick K (2009) Relational Capital, Job Retention Vital in Recession. Central Penn Business Journal 25: 10.
17. Teece DJ (2000) Strategies for Knowledge Assets: The Role of the Firm Structure and Industrial Context. Long Range Planning 33: 35-54.
18. Mu J, Di Benedetto A (2012) Networking capability and new product development. IEEE Transactions on Engineering Management 59: 4.
19. Shane S, Cable D (2002) Network Ties, Reputation, and the Financing of New Ventures. Management Science 18: 364-381.

Technology Innovation and Global Competition-evidence from Global 500 Strong Construction Enterprise

Lai Xiao-Dong*

School of Tourism and Urban Management, Jiangxi University of Finance and Economics, Nanchang, China

Abstract

Technology innovation plays a key role in strengthening the competitiveness of the enterprises. It is a good method for the company to win the market within background of global economy and fierce competition. Based on the literature review of the enterprise innovation and technology development status, choosing the construction enterprise listed in top 500 companies of 2015 as an example, this paper firstly analyzed the enterprises' basic ranking status and overall competitiveness. From the perspective of technology innovation management, then explored the differences among the construction enterprises from five aspects of technology innovation: (1) R and D human resources, (2) capital investment, (3) organization management, (4) incentives mechanism, and (5) innovation cooperative mechanism. The comparison between Chinese construction companies and international construction companies are presented as well with the root cause analysis of the difference on innovation management. Research found that Chinese construction enterprises are dominated the global leading position, but the technology innovation management mode and internationality is not strong. Finally, the paper put forward corresponding countermeasures and suggestions on how to improve the innovation performance for Chinese construction enterprises. It pointed out that the Chinese construction enterprises should strengthen technological innovation management, establish a professional technological innovation system and incentives mechanism to maintain international competitiveness and achieve sustainable development goals.

Keywords: Construction enterprises; Technological innovation; Innovation management; Top 500

Introduction

FORTUNE announced the latest top 500 companies of 2015 on May 18th, which includes eight construction enterprises. It has three companies decrease compared with eleven companies engaged in 2014. There are five construction companies from China, two companies from France and one from Spain. The famous American construction company Fluor and other international company are no longer within the top 500 strong companies due to the grim competitive market. Under the background of international economic depression, how these eight companies could keep leading position in construction industry and why the Chinese construction companies can dominate their realm in such fierce international competition background? From the perspective of technology innovation, this article firstly analyzes the companies' international performance, then explores the companies experience on innovation management from five elements of technology innovation like "R and D human resources, capital investment, organization management, incentives mechanism, and innovation cooperation mode to find the innovative or creative capabilities differences between the Chinese construction enterprises and other international corporate. This will help the related construction enterprises to figure out the potential opportunities for the future development and aid the sustainable development for the construction enterprises with a benchmark and experiences reference for domestic and foreign corporate.

Literature Review on Technological Innovation

The concept of innovation was initiated by economist Schumpeter in 1912 in his *Introduction to Economic Development*, he defined that innovation is a "new combination" to introduce new production elements and production conditions into production system [1]. Enterprises are the main participants of technology innovation. Michael Spence and Heather A Hazard [2] believed that enterprise competitiveness is the ability of one country's enterprises to do business internationally. Therefore, it is critical for the enterprise to form the competitive advantages by means of reform through the well distribution of various resources, through which the enterprises can cultivate its survival ability in the process of products service period. Competitive analysis is one of the best methods for enterprises to know the competitive environment and get self-awareness against their own strengths and environmental opportunities. It is also a path for enterprises to verify their ability of technology innovation through the whole cycle of technology market demand analysis, conception formulation, planning, decision-making, R and D, engineering, mess production and market adoption.

Kharbanda [3] thought that, under the background of business trade freedom, globalization and fierce international competition, The establishment of strategic development plan on technology management could help the enterprises (especially for those in developing countries) to strengthen their corporate technical competency and enhance their international competitiveness. Barnett [4] introduced a model called Red Queen evidenced from some big hard drive manufacturers and verified the importance of enterprise organizational strategy plan, then concluded that the large enterprises can lead the technological competition in the market but cannot win the competition with other small-scale companies.

There are some scholars studied the influence of R and D activities to corporate competitiveness like Kumar and Aggarwal [5], Belderbos Rene [6]. Based on the case study of laser disc player industry

---

*Corresponding author: Lai Xiao-dong, School of Tourism and Urban Management, Jiangxi University of Finance and Economics, Nanchang, China
E-mail: tylerlai@126.com

development in China, Lu Feng and Mu Ling [7] studied the engine of enterprise's innovation and its competitive advantages, and found that the product innovation with market demand orientation, the efforts on technology learning and the development of capability are the reasons why the enterprises in technology backward countries can gain the competitive advantages in open market. Xie Wei [8] thought that innovation can be divided into system innovation, core technology innovation and external innovation, he pointed that most innovation strength of Chinese enterprises performed are external innovation.

Wei Xin-ya and Lin Zhi-yan [9] pointed that the innovation ability of Chinese construction enterprises is weak with limited value-adding. It should focus on the development of science and technology to really confirm the pillar position of construction industry. The development strategy for construction industry China lies in conception reform and enhancement on innovation measures. Based on the main problems of the development construction market, Wang Tong-zhou put forward a reform path for the large construction enterprise to develop through the resources integration and system reform, then enhance the core competitiveness of enterprises [10]. Some scholars have studied the organization form of technology innovation in construction industry Wang Bo and Liu Hua, [11], enterprise innovation motivation and capability Chen Jian-guo and Cai Wen-lu [12,13], innovation system and regulation Jin Wei-xin et al. [14], innovation mechanism Guo Hui-feng et al.[15]. Moreover, the research on enterprise technology innovation for construction industry is relatively scarce. Most of the themes discussed are just the advance technology introduction from abroad brand companies instead of management reviews Chen and Xie [16].

About the evaluation of technology innovation, the initial indexes released by European Union(EU) in 2001 only covered with human resource, knowledge production, knowledge dissemination and application, financial innovation, innovation output and innovation market. Late on in the year of 2008~2010, EU put the innovation assessment indicator like "innovation-drive, enterprise innovation behavior and innovation output" as the first-level indexes, the indicators like "enterprise human capital investment, enterprise investment, entrepreneurship, productivity and innovation effectiveness" are put in the second level system [17,18].

While Chinese scholar Zhang [19] argued that the assessment of enterprises' competition need to be evaluated from seven aspects, like "social influence, technical ability, ability of financing, financial status, marketing ability, project management capability and resource management capabilities". Then Pu Xiang-ping [20] made a comparison of enterprise competitiveness indexes for constructions industry and abroad, and pointed that the indicators selected lies in the perspectives of assessment, the evaluation dimension may different is different assessment purpose.

Based on the study of Japanese construction enterprises, Kangari and Miyatake [21] found that the development success of construction technology innovation is attributed to four aspects, namely, strategic alliance, effective information collection, innovation reputation and technology diffusion.

Yeung JFY et al. [22] proposed eight key indicators to evaluate the success of construction enterprises, namely, customer satisfaction, cost, quality, time, communication, security, trust and respect, and improvement on innovation, etc.

Radujkovic et al. [23] studied nearly 37 innovation evaluating indicators based on more than 30 construction companies in southeast Europe and found that the top ten key assessment indicators could affect the enterprise competitiveness, they are including quality, cost, number of investors, sustaining reform on project, time increase, customer satisfaction, employee satisfaction, innovation and learning ability, efficiency and identification of customer requirements, etc.

Shang Mei, Du Yan-yan [24] found that the output of technological innovation and its major affecting factors has a long-term integration relationship in construction industry; enterprises need to define the technological assessment indexes together with the tasks of the projects.

From the above literatures review, we found that the research on enterprise innovation and technology development has been relatively mature, but most of the contributions are based on the empirical study and technology introduction. For the research of technology innovation management from construction industry, most of them China just stay at the level of macro perspective and qualitative analysis. The themes about technology management and analysis of technological competitiveness are relatively short.

Herein, this paper selects the construction corporate from Fortune Global 500 strong companies of 2015 as the sample to study their innovation effectiveness from five aspects, namely, R and D human resources investment, capital investment, organization management, incentives mechanism, and innovation cooperative mechanism. Based on the construction enterprises performance in global market and the comparison analysis on technological innovation management among those global construction enterprises, this paper is trying to put forward the corresponding countermeasures for construction industries on technology management to enhance the enterprises' competiveness ability.

Global Construction Corporate Competiveness Analysis

There are eight strong construction enterprises engaged in the global 500 companies in 2015 (Table 1). Five constructions corporate are from China, namely China State Construction Engineering (CSCE), China Communications Construction (CCC), China Railway Group (CRG), China Railway Construction (CRC) and China Metallurgical Group (CMG). These five Chinese corporate are enlisted in global 500 strong companies for more than 10 years (CCC and CMG only enjoys eight years history) and dominated the leading position since 2005,

Item	Company	6	7	8	9	10	11	12	13	14	15
1	China State Construction Engineering (CSCE)	v	v	v	v	v	v	v	v	v	v
2	China Communications Construction (CCC)	**	**	v	v	v	v	v	v	v	v
3	China Railway Group (CRG)	v	v	v	v	v	v	v	v	v	v
4	Vinci Group (Vinci)	v	v	v	v	v	v	v	v	v	v
5	China Railway Construction (CRC)	v	v	v	v	v	v	v	v	v	v
6	Bouygues Group (Bouygues)	v	v	v	v	v	v	v	v	v	v
7	ACS Group (ACS)	v	**	v	v	v	v	v	v	v	v
8	China Metallurgical Group (CMG)	**	**	v	v	v	v	v	v	v	v
9	Fluor Company (Fluor)	**	**	**	v	v	v	v	v	v	**

Note: "**"means the enterprise is not in top 500 companies in this year or the enterprise hasn't joined the assessment, "v" means the enterprise are listed in top 500 companies in the year.

Table 1: Top 500 construction industries list in 2015.

which indicates that Chinese construction enterprise are getting more internationally and stable. The rest three international constructions companies are Vinci Group and Bouygues Group from France, ACS Group from US. Vinci and Bouygues have been ranked in global 500 strong companies for more than 10 years since 2006. While another famous construction enterprises, Fluor Company in US, has no longer within global 500 strong companies list due to the violent competition. Fluor ranked in top 500 more than 6 years from 2009 to 2010 (Table 1).

Per the enterprise's business turnover and profit record within the decade 2006 to 2015. Chinese construction companies dominated their leadership position, since 2010, CSCE caught up and outstripped Vinci Group with average annual growth rate of 23.4%. The average turnover growth rate from the enlisted eight global construction enterprises in 2015 is 13%. The highest growth rate in CCC is 40%. In terms of profitability, the annual average growth rate increased with 1.35% against the dada in 2014. But two of them have negative profit growth, which reflects a limited growth trend compared to the other global foreign corporate.

Anyway, as the members of global 500 strong companies, their competitive strength cannot be ignored. Considering the enterprises' operation stability and enterprises history, we modestly take nine global construction companies enlisted in Fortune 500 strong companies with terms of stable business turnover and at least with five consecutive years in the list. Based on the companies' annual reports and enterprise's website information, the author decided to study the competitive strength and the rule of the technological innovation in construction industry from five technical innovation elements mentioned above.

R and D human resource investment

Technological innovation is an important production outcome of R and D activities. The R and D human resources investment is the most original engine anchored the technological innovation performance. The R and D human resources here refer to personnel engaged in the technological innovation. The numbers of R and D personnel in enterprise engaged in technology development activity will directly determine the benefit output of technology innovation. Herein, the investment on R and D personnel of technology innovation is a critical indicator. In fairness, this article only takes the data in the year of 2014[1] to have a transverse comparison of each construction company and explore the R and D personnel distribution including their education level. The information or data is mainly

Collected from the companies' annual report or the company's website. A detail comparison on R and D human resources investment is shown in Table 2.

From above data we can see that the rate of technology development personnel in Chinese construction enterprise is accounted for more than 10% against the company's total quantity of employees. The highest one is 46.8% in CSCE, the lowest one is 12.64% in CMG. While the rate of the other four global foreign construction companies is relatively different, Bouygues group shows 1.5%, Fluor Company reflects 1.44%, ACS is 2.2%, Vinci group shares 0.13%. We understand it may have some difference on the statistic and the definition of R and D personnel in different companies. The number of R and D personnel of the foreign construction companies (Bouygues, ACS, Vinci and Flour) only counted their professional R and D personnel. While for the construction company in their statistics is including engineers, technicians and technical support personnel.

Moreover, during the review process, we found that the Chinese construction enterprises have a high proportion with highly educated[2] workers, like in CCC, the high educational portion is 47.5%, and the lowest one is 21.7% in CRG. This shows that the investment of Chinese construction companies in science and technology human resources gets more and more attention[3].

Capital investment

Most countries in the world pay great attention on the investment for the development of science and technology and create related science and technology development strategy to ensure the investment funds in all fields. There is no exception for in enterprise' development, because the science and technology innovation investment is one of the key measurements for the enterprise sustainable development. The engineering projects long duration industry characteristics in construction industry requests the company must have a certain sustaining capital investment to enhance the enterprise's innovation strength on workmanship, technology, construction and service management to save the cost and improve the efficiency. From the comparison of those eight construction companies, we found that science and technology innovation investment in every construction company has received high attention, and the investment strength is increased year by year.

In 2014, the average investment growth rate of those eight corporate is 12.8%. The investment strength from China's corporate is very big, such as CRG invested $1.447 million in 2014 on innovation, 13.8% increase compared in 2013. This is due to the rapid growth of overseas business for Chinese construction companies in recent decade. Compared to the other global construction companies, like Bouygues, ACS, the investment degree is relatively slow and flat hovering between 5%~10%.

R and D investment percent of sales turnover in Chinese construction companies also shows a strong strength, like China Railway Group (CRG) and China Railway Construction (CRC), the investment portion in 2013 is 0.7% and 1.5% respectively. It is much higher than the average level of 0.7% internationally. But for the other four construction companies, namely, Vinci, Flour and ACS, their investment rate is just within 0.1% ~ 0.3% of the yearly sales turnover.

Above data reflects an obvious difference among the global

Item	Company	R and D personnel (%)
1	China State Construction Engineering (CSCE)	46.8%
2	China Communications Construction (CCC)	30.8%
3	China Railway Group (CRG)	33%
4	Vinci Group(Vinci)	0.13%
5	China Railway Construction (CRC)	19.5%
6	Bouygues Group	1.5%
7	ACS Group	2.2%
8	China Metallurgical Group (CMG)	12.64%
9	Fluor Company	1.44%

Table 2: R and D humane resources investment rate of global nine construction companies.

[1]Some listed company annual report is not officially published till June-10 as the authors drafted this paper.

[2]Per the practice China, high educational level works refer to the employees with at least bachelor education degree or above.

[3]Due to statistic dimension problems, the authors cannot get the educational structure data or frame from the foreign construction (Bouygues, ACS, Vinci and Flour), herein, above analysis only discussed the state we can get to indicate the investment on human resource.

#	Corporate	Technological innovation organization management mode
1	China State Construction Engineering(CSCE)	Have sound science and technology R and D system from decision-making mechanism, implementation, consultancy, to capital investment, process management, performance assessment and incentive mechanism(Figure1)
4	China Communications Construction(CCC)	Have the plan of "core talent height" and "Four-Five-Five" core talents system. It is formed a science and technology management system of "one system, five standard, ten ways" and set up a three level science and technology R and D system (namely, headquarter, branch company and subsidiary factory) with a feature of "up and down interaction, three-level linkage, reasonable structure and high efficient" innovation operation.
2	China Railway Group(CRG)	Have particular department of science and technology (technology center) belongs to the group managers of board
3	China Railway Construction (CRC)	Have a strong enterprise technology innovation system with perfect network, it is formed a four-level innovation system of "general headquarters, group companies, engineering companies and project department. It has an own characteristics of technological innovation organization structure to promote technological innovation.
5	Vinci Group	Have a special R and D department belongs to the chief executive of science and technology development and is responsible to the director of the commission. The core task is to carry out R and D innovation and internal information exchange to support and coordinate the innovation work among the various departments. The company has innovation City factories and regional R and D club to have a regular technology innovation theme discussion or case analysis timely
6	Bouygues Group	Has a sustainable development department lead by acting CEO who should response for the supervision and coordination with all internal affairs including low carbon strategy, green IT, R and D management, quality assurance and global procurement according to the priorities of each project and the R and D progress of each branches.
7	ACS Group	Equipped with specialized technical development committee to carry out R and D activities cooperating with the related scientific research institutions, colleges or universities
8	Fluor Company	No particular introduction on the company's technology management mode

Table 3: Global construction corporate technology innovation management mode (portion).

construction companies. The investment percentage of sales amount from Chinese enterprises seems a little big but with dramatic shaken during the decades. While the other four international construction companies show a robust investment trend on technology innovation. It indicates that the investment maturities of Chinese construction enterprises need to be strengthened.

Organization management

Effective organization management can ensure the implementation of technical innovation activity. The author summarized the technological innovation organization management mode states of above mentioned construction enterprises based on the review of the companies' annual report in 2014 and website information or other public report collection shown in Table 3.

From above summary shown in Table 3, it indicates that the organization structure of technology innovation in construction companies is core organization for the enterprise's sustainable development, below is the main difference analysis form the management mode perspective.

(1) Organization structure: Chinese construction companies are all state-owned company, not private enterprises, the company's organizational structure of innovation system is formed based on the national and corporate strategic. Most of them are adopted with three-level innovation system, namely, the technical innovation organization management form level of national, provincial, and enterprises of special projects perspective. Like CSCE, CCCC and CMG (Figures 1-3). While the organization in CRC is different, it is a new innovation mode with four linkage pattern of technological innovation including headquarter administration, group companies, engineering companies and project department. The foreign large-scale construction enterprise adopts three-level innovation management system as well, like Vinci Group, its innovation organization is designed within the enterprise development based on the market demand instead of being assigned from the administration. The enterprise will set up a specific development company based on the project demand and directly report to the managing director.

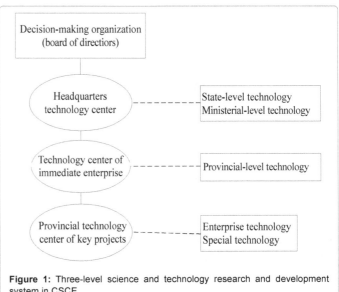

Figure 1: Three-level science and technology research and development system in CSCE.

(2) Technology innovation driving factors: technology innovation drive of foreign enterprise mainly comes from enterprise inner drive and market demands, most of innovation behaviors are market oriented. While for the innovation drive in Chinese construction industry, the dominated one is from the national development strategy, such as the national science and technology research plan, some of the drives are from market demand. The organization of R and D team or innovative projects is mainly structured based on the governmental strategy. But government function in the global international construction enterprise is not so obvious; the investments in R and D innovation are financed based on the market demand.

(3) Innovation organization management mode: the management mode in Chinese construction enterprise is similar with the traditional management mode. It has strict innovation organization chart, namely, the top level of policy making, management level of process control

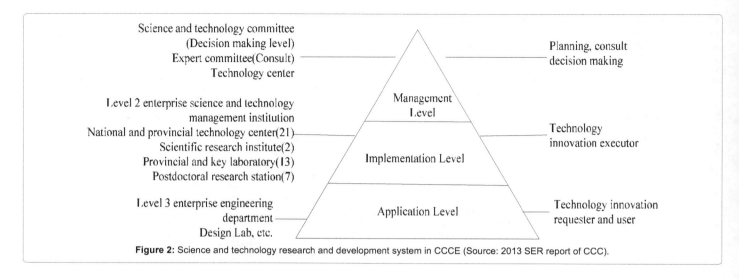

Figure 2: Science and technology research and development system in CCCE (Source: 2013 SER report of CCC).

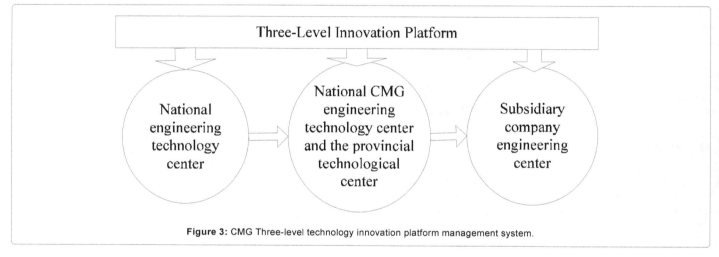

Figure 3: CMG Three-level technology innovation platform management system.

and implementation level. Each level system has a clear command system. While the technology innovation management mode in the foreign construction enterprises are loosen and flexible. Such as the organization management mode in Vinci Group is very flexible, their management mission is to provide employees with good innovation environment by means of providing innovative city factory, regional innovation club and innovation forum like BBS, etc. to provide a free communication innovation platform and learning organization environment within the enterprises.

Incentive mechanism

Science and technology personnel is the key element of technology innovation, the effective incentive mechanism is the guarantee for the success of enterprise technology innovation. Enterprises are required to establish a set of mechanism of talents cultivation, employment, and evaluation and incentive instruments to ensure the technology innovation benefit and R and D personal interest, which is good to arouse their innovation enthusiasm in maxim. According to the technological innovation of the bidirectional interaction and incentives Lv Zhen-yong, Dang Xinhua [25], we compared the construction companies' incentive mechanism and found that:

(1) For the incentive method: The global foreign construction companies not only provide employees with good welfare, comfortable office environment and generous bonuses, but also provide equity to the contracted staff of company. The company will publish their staff incentive data timely in their annual report. For insistence, Fluor conducted an "Executive Performance Incentive Plan" to reward the personnel with outstanding performance on innovation or management. Some enterprises will set up special enterprise awards to encourage the innovative staff, such as Vinci announced Vinci Innovation Award to encourage the innovation contribution in all fields (e.g. the innovation of technology, management and service, etc.). While the employee innovation incentive policy of construction enterprises China focuses on short-term, direct material rewards, or encourage the employees to attend the contest, like National Science and Technology Progress Prize, Zhan Tian-yu Award, Lu Ban Prize, etc., then the company award the money according to the contribution. The incentives of employee stock ownership or equity just depends on the company actual situation. Some construction companies will consider the dividend for the outstanding talent.

(2) Company culture of innovation: both Chinese and foreign construction companies pay much attention on the cultivation of innovative culture. Like, CRG conducted a "five same" management mode in the company, namely, "leaning together, work together,

item	Company	Research institution or cooperative partnership
1	China State Construction Engineering(CSCE)	Set the company's direct operation design group with specialized technical center and experiment center
4	China Communications Construction(CCC)	With ten large design institute, two state-level technology center, seven provincial technology center, six key laboratory and post-doctoral scientific research workstation
2	China Railway Group(CRG)	With seven large design institute, two state-level technology center, seventeen provincial technology center, two national key laboratories, fourteen testing experiment center certificated by the national laboratory accreditation committee and four post-doctoral scientific research workstation
3	China Railway Construction (CRC)	With fourteen high and new technology enterprise, twenty provincial technology center, one provincial key engineering laboratory and four post-doctoral scientific research workstation
5	Vinci Group	Establish city factory innovation laboratory, Vinci-Paris technology R and D cooperative institution like Mines Paris Technology, école des Ponts ParisTech and Agro - Paris Tech engineering schools, regional R and D club, etc.
6	Bouygues Group	With particular enterprise innovation center, innovation laboratory, technology center and enterprise library
7	China Communications Construction(CCC)	With ten large design institute, five state-level technology center, twelve provincial technology center, five key laboratory, two post-doctoral scientific research workstation
8	ACS Group	With nearly fifty-nine research center in China and abroad, have cooperative relations with ninety-six universities and forty-two technology center; With seventeen institute, eighteen R and D centers and fifteen technology development center
9	Fluor Company	With several experimental research center, supply chain research center, project (safety) testing center and regional innovation factory or workshop in worldwide

Table 4: Global construction enterprises R and D institute and innovation cooperation mode summary (portion).

manage together, live together and same reward". Fluor established an incentive system with the basis of creating value to replace its original incentive system. CCC hold the view of difference acknowledgement and fairness to form a culture of cooperation, collaboration, comfortable workplace and harmonious environment by implementation of management innovation and value concept through human resources, strategic planning, evaluation and control process(Dominic Barton and Clayton Deutsch [26].

Generally speaking, technology innovation incentive mechanism in above mentioned construction companies shows a diversification, the measures on the material incentive or spiritual are different. The construction companies from China emphasize the cultivation of the collective innovation and self-innovation spirit. While the foreign construction companies encourage the individual innovation, or offer motivation with flexible platform and work ambience.

Innovation cooperative mechanism

According to the endogenous economic growth theory, technological innovation is the source of economic growth [27]. It is a kind of activity with risks, the investment behavior on technological innovation enhances the risks [28]. With the business expansion in each of the construction company, the technological innovation mode is different as well. The innovation focus of construction companies may different because of the business scale. But for the construction engineering, infrastructure construction, the enterprise pays more attention on the elements of innovation, production technology and equipment. But for the innovation on products and equipment, it is better to implement the technical innovation with market and cost oriented.

Both Chinese construction enterprises and foreign international enterprises have the characters with independent innovation and external cooperation innovation. As the summary shown in Table 4, the investment from these enterprises in technology development realm is very big. Most of companies have their own technical design center and laboratory. But it still has slightly difference in the following two aspects:

(1)Besides the enterprise itself R and D tasks for company development, Chinese construction companies still need to undertake their national technology research assignment. It is rare to see in the foreign construction enterprise whose business is operated with market based. The technology innovation demand for these enterprises is mainly determined by customers and market demand.

(2)Though both the Chinese construction enterprises and the foreign construction go the way with the university-enterprise joint innovation mode, their management mode is different. Chinese construction companies emphasized the joint technology development together with the institution or universities. They run the cooperation by establishing the doctoral research station or signing cooperative program with the school, but don't involve their institution administration. The foreign construction companies is different, they not only associate with the institution, but also directly engage in the construction of institution or universities. Such as, Vinci group directly invested the construction of Mines Paris Tech, écoledes Ponts Paris Tech and Agro-Paris Tech engineering schools. ACS group is similar with Chinese enterprise. It widely sets up different level of cooperation relations with professional universities, worldwide research institutions and technology centers so as to meet the need of enterprise technical innovation demand or make up the lack of technology innovation team.

From above exploration, the technology innovation mode in construction enterprises are different, some of them even are complicated and overlapping. A flexible and suitable cooperative innovation mode is very important to the company's development.

Difference Between Chinese Enterprises and International Companies

Although Chinese construction enterprises hold an absolute predominance among the construction enterprises in Fortune global 500 strong companies, based on the above exploration, particularly the contrastive analysis with the foreign construction company, the author found that Chinese construction enterprises still have certain gap in technological innovation management. Below is the key difference between Chinese construction companies and foreign construction companies.

(1) Technology innovation in Chinese construction enterprises has

big potential policy risk: The innovation within Chinese construction enterprise is mainly relies on the support of national key research projects or large scale engineering; the ability of independent research and development is not strong and lack of related market mechanism support. The enterprise's scientific and technological innovation needs a strong support from local government. It exist a big potential policy risk. While the science and technology innovation in the foreign international construction companies have just been oriented by the market demand, it has a stronger market operation mechanism on risks prevention.

(2) Rigid cooperation mode: the major technical research of Chinese construction enterprises takes a path of institution-enterprise joint or university joint mechanism, the conversion ratio of technological achievement is very low. While the foreign construction enterprises go with multi-level cooperation mode like university-enterprise cooperation or research institutions-enterprise mode. Meanwhile, they can directly invest the money to establish their own institute of technology to solve the enterprise's technology problem and cultivate the R and D talent.

(3) Low rate of R and D investment: The modern architecture enterprise has a strong consciousness of technology innovation. Most of the enterprises have set up the specialized R and D institution or technology development center, but the investment budget on science and technology development is still low compared to the other expense. The highest rate on R and D activity in CRCC just accounted for 2% of sales turnover, the lowest one is only 0.5% of sales turnover in CSCE. It has not exceeded 5% rate of sales turnover of Japan's construction companies, which is considered as a normal R and D investment rate internationally [29].

(4) Lack of technology innovation talents and with low internationalization degree: From the above comparative analysis, the technical personnel of construction enterprises in China sounds like share a big percentage of the total number of employees compared with foreign construction companies, but the real personnel engaged in scientific and technological innovation is still not enough. The foreign construction companies have a strictly definition of R and D personnel or experts from different regions. Moreover, the internationalization of foreign international company is very high, e.g. Vinci group, its foreign employees accounted for 96% of total staff, the employee of Fluor are from nearly 66 countries or regions worldwide, which account for 1.44% of the total employees.

(5) Bother Chinese construction enterprise and foreign companies have the three-level innovation management system of organization structure but with difference. Chinese construction enterprises organization generally adopts the "pyramid" mode from the top to the bottom. While the foreign enterprise organization usually employs with a division or specialized project management mode, it has great flexibility among the innovation teams. Some enterprises even have the development in the project workshop, or arrange the innovation activities through the R and D innovation committee. Vinci is a typical example going through innovation workshop or committee method.

(6) Finally, from the perspective of technology innovation incentive mechanism, both the Chinese construction and foreign construction enterprises have emphasized the incentive and training to the technical personnel. The foreign construction enterprises pay more attention to the long-term training and motivation of the employees. But the Chinese construction just focuses on the short-term honor to incentive to the employee.

To sum up, the technology innovation management construction industry still has certain gaps compared to the international construction enterprises, which limits its sustainability. Based on the analysis of above five innovation elements, below is the main reasons causing above differences:

(1) In accordance with the common three-level innovative system. The construction enterprises should response for their own innovation risk and cost in their own value-added chain respectively, which limits the technology innovation output in construction industry. The building product is a system with multi-technology integration but have different regional characters. It is in the discrete state in space; herein the implementation of technology innovation in construction industry is not replicable. It cannot enjoy the advantage economies scale like the general manufacturing industry. Besides the lack of enough and stabile information exchange among the enterprises (such as the general contractor and the subcontractor), it leads the slow technology diffusion or produces "bullwhip effect", which restricts the overall technology enhancement in construction industry.

(2) The complexity of the engineering project in construction industry restricts the development of enterprise innovation ability, such as the complexity and durability of building materials, long period of construction. Plus the long technology diffusion cycle, it restricts the technology innovation as well in the whole industry.

(3) Due to most of Chinese construction companies are the "state" enterprises. The government's administrative control could influence the efficiency of technology innovation. For example, the bidding system of tendering and bidding process, and the provisions to the contractor and subcontractors, they seem have protected the rights and interests of the owners but ignored the rights and interests of the contractor who are the main participants of technological innovation. In the process of technological innovation, the contractor has to bear the most responsibility and innovation risks. This greatly limits their innovation enthusiasm. Moreover, the government regulation leads the more cost paid for the construction material supplier chain, which limits the development of the technology innovation.

(4) It has an information communication obstruction in the technical innovation organization management. The existing innovation system in construction industry is independent. The technical communication within the construction industry system is inadequate and unobstructed. Current construction industry technical communication is mainly arranged through the form of BBS or meeting assignment, but the real technical communication is often not enough and comprehensive, it need more channel to communicate with modern information technology.

(5) Finally, the internationalization of the Chinese construction industry also caused the expansion of technological innovation. Due to the system and management pattern is different. The innovation tasks in Chinese construction enterprise have been completed by the local Chinese engineers or researchers. They conduct the independent innovation strategy but with technology import as a complement. The thinking of "going out" has not been extended, which restricts the technology innovation achievements for construction industry.

Technology Innovation Management Improvement for Construction Industry

Through the review of the top 500 construction enterprises on technological innovation management, we found that, although the Chinese construction enterprise dominated the leading position in the international construction industry, the technology innovation in Chinese construction companies has got much improvement, the engineering project complex characteristic and management mode difference restricts the further development of construction technology, it is imperative to continue the strength on technology innovation management China's construction industry thought below measurement to keep the enterprises sustainability:

(1) Accelerate the system innovation with market orientation. Because of the complexity and particularity of construction product in building industry, the industry admittance threshold is high; the investment of technology innovation can be solved through market mechanism. Through the enterprise system reform and innovation, accelerate the introduction of advanced technology and narrow the gap between the international construction companies based on the market economy orientation.

(2) Enhance the current three-level innovation management mode for Chinese construction enterprises and improve the relevant supporting facilities. It required to have a more flexible technology innovation management organization structure, such as to set up the particular agencies specialized in researches on innovation theory to improve the existing management mode and clear necessary institutional obstacles for technology innovation.

(3) Increase technological innovation investment continuously. The contribution brought by the scientific and technological innovation is obvious. The investment rate of enterprises' sales turnover in science and technology from Chinese construction companies is gradually increased, but the complexity of construction market causes some disorganizes business behavior, such as the phenomenon of undercut engineering price and embezzlement of public funds to undertake engineering task is often happened Ming Liang Yang [30], which caused the problem of capital returning and seriously impacted the normal investment in science and technology innovation. So the basic guarantee is to earmark a fund for the implementation on technological innovation

(4) Strengthen the personnel and incentive mechanism of technology innovation. In order to cope with the international standards of technological innovation for Chinese construction, it needs to strengthen the cultivation of technology innovation talents in construction industry. The personnel introduction of professional engineers with solid theory knowledge and rich practice is helpful to keep the enterprise international competitiveness. At the same time, it should increase the training for the staffs to improve their working quality as the whole.

(5) Deepen the integration of production, education and research, and establish technology innovation center in large scale construction enterprises. The existing cooperation between building enterprises and research institutes or universities has roughly formed a scale of China right now, the various enterprises has cooperative relations with domestic and international universities in different level. But the technology center of enterprises relatively weak. It needs to improve the abilities of research and development. To deepen the integration of production, education and research on technology innovation cooperation mode, and use the platform combined with the enterprise practice can close to the actual market demand for the enterprise R and D center.

Research Limits and Expectation

From the perspective of technology innovation management, this paper selected the top eight construction enterprises enlisted in Fortune global 500 companies of 2015 as an example and discussed their technology innovation status from five technology innovation elements like scientific research personnel, capital investment, organization management, incentive mechanism and cooperation mode of technology innovation management. A detailed comparison has been made between the Chinese construction enterprises and foreign construction companies. The study found that construction enterprises in the investment of technology innovation and management has some certain limitation and insufficiency. Based on the root-cause analysis for such difference, this paper puts forward the corresponding countermeasures on the improvement of technology management for construction enterprises.

Due to construction companies' information or data is not open enough, or the report emphasis each construction company is different for the public data. The dada or analysis in this paper has leaves some limits and incomplete. This will encourage the author to continue the further research with a method of tracing study. Modestly, we think above exploration still can basically reflect the current management status of construction enterprises in technological innovation management. Especial for the Chinese construction enterprise, it could provide some management reference for the practitioners and enhance the international competitiveness of construction companies.

Acknowledgement

This research is supported by the Soft Science Research Project of Jiangxi Province in 2015 (Code: 20151BBA0033) and the Humanities and Social Science Research Project of Colleges and Universities in Jiangxi Province (Code: JC1403).

References

1. Schumpeter JA (2003) The theory of economic development. The European Heritage in Economics and the Social Sciences 1: 61-116.
2. Spence M, Hazard HA (1998) International competitiveness. Florida: Ballinger Publishing Company.
3. Kharbanda VP (2001) Strategic Technology Management and International Competition in Developing Countries-The Need for a Dynamic Approach. Journal of Scientific and Industrial Research 60: 291-297.
4. Barnett WP, McKendrick DG (2004) Why Are Some Organizations More Competitive Than Others? Evidence from a Changing Global Market. Administrative Science Quarterly 49: 535-571.
5. Kumar N, Aggarwal A (2005) Liberalization, outward orientation and in-house R and D activity of multinational and local Firms: A quantitative exploration for Indian manufacturing. Research Policy 34: 441-460.
6. Rene B, Elissavet L, Reinhilde V (2008) Strategic R and D Location in European Manufacturing Industries. Review of World Economics 144: 183-206.
7. Feng L, Ling M (2003) Product Creation Based on Local Market, Ability Development and Competitive Advantage. World Management 12: 57-82.
8. Wei X (2006) The Distribution of Technical Innovation and Competitive Strategies in China's Firms. World Management 2: 50-62.
9. Xin-ya W, Zhiyan L (2004) Present status and development of construction in China. Journal of Harbin Institute of Technology 36: 124-128.
10. Tong-zhou W (2009) Building the core competitiveness of state-owned construction enterprise. World management 15: 64-65.
11. Bo W, Hua L (2009) Research on technological innovation organization model of construction industry research. Industrial Technology and Economy 28: 57-79.
12. Jiang-uo C, Wen-lu C (2001) Accession to the WTO to strengthen technology innovation ability of construction. Construction Economy 223:16-19.
13. Yun-ning Z, Jun Y (2014) Technological innovation capability evaluation of

construction enterprises based on rough set theory. Journal of Engineering Management 28: 138-142.

14. Wei-xin J, Zhang-Jianru TX (2004) Research of construction industry technological innovation system China. Construction Economy 9: 17-22.

15. Hui-feng G, Shao-gang L, Qi-ming L (2008) China's technology innovation dynamic mechanism research on construction industry in China. Construction Economy 6: 31-34.

16. Fan C, Hong-tao X (2014) Comparison and classification study on construction industry regional technical innovation ability. Science and Technology and Economy 27: 34-38.

17. Wei-jun C (2009) The research progress of European Union's innovation index. Forum on Science and Technology in China 125-128.

18. Wei-jun C, Wei Z (2012) International Comparison on Innovation Capacity between China and other Major Innovation Economies: An Analysis based on European Innovation Scoreboard. China Soft Science 42-51.

19. Shao-jun Z, Wei-ya C (2007) Foundation and evaluation of competitive indicator system for construction enterprise. Journal of Wuhan Institute of Technology 29: 13-15.

20. Xiang-ping B, Yin-fei Y (2007) The review on corporate competitiveness of Both Native and Foreign Enterprises. Commercial Research 11-16.

21. Kangari R, Miyatake Y (1997) Developing and Managing Innovative Construction Technologies in Japan. Journal of Construction Engineering and Management 123: 72-78.

22. Yeung J, Chan A, Chan D (2009) Developing a Performance Index for Relationship-Based Construction Projects in Australia: Delphi Study. Journal of Management in Engineering 25: 59-68.

23. Radujkovic M, Vukomanovic M, Dunovic IB (2010) Application of key performance indicators in South-Eastern European construction. Journal of Civil Engineering and Management 16: 521-530.

24. Mei S, Yan-yan D (2013) China's construction of technology innovation research regional differences. Techno-economics and Management Research, 45-48.

25. Zhen-yong L, Xing-hua D (2002) Research on incentive mechanism of enterprise technology innovation. Economic Management 44-47.

26. Barton D, Deutsch CG (2008) Transforming a South Korean chaebol: An interview with Doosan's Yongmaan Park. The Mckinsey Quarterly 1-9.

27. Grossman GM, Helpman E (1991) Innovation and growth in the global economy. Cambridge: MIT Press.

28. Demarzo P (2007) Technological innovation and real investment booms and busts. Journal of Financial Economics 85: 735-754.

29. Chang-hong J (2007) The main problems that the technology innovation for construction industry is confronted with and counter measures China. Optimization of Capital Construction 28: 54-57.

30. Ming-liang Y (2010) Practice of process audit on construction engineering project. China Modern Economics Publishing House.

The Effects of Non-interest Banking on Entrepreneurship in Nigeria

Larry Anifowose*

Department of Entrepreneurship Management Technology, The Federal University of Technology, Akure, Ondo State, Nigeria

Abstract

For long, there has been controversy as to the banking system which involves no interest. The non-interest banking system has raised huge controversy and argument as to its relevance to the banking sector. It has also raised argument as to whether this type of banking system is relevant to entrepreneurs.

This paper tends to look at the relevance of non-interest banking on entrepreneurs. It would show to the reader that non-interest banking is very relevant to entrepreneurs. It would also show to the reader that non-interest banking helps entrepreneurs in raising capital and funds.

Keywords: Non-Interest banking; Entrepreneurship; Nigeria; Business opportunity; Economic resources

Introduction

Non-interest banking otherwise or also known as Islamic Banking is one which raised a lot of fumes in Nigeria and in the world over. Its usefulness as well as its religiosity raised a lot of controversy. Some have seen it as a good way of banking while others have given it a dismissal attitude.

If this is so, we would like to know what this system of banking entails and whether it is useful to the society and to entrepreneurs. In doing so, it raises a question in our mind. That is, "What is Non-Interest Banking?"

Non-interest banking or Islamic banking is banking or banking activity that is consistent with the principles of sharia and its practical application through the development of Islamic economics. Also, according to Charles M. Hudwick, in his book Banking Evolution, 2008, pg. 205, Islamic banking refers to a banking activity or a system of banking that is in consonance with the basic principles of Islamic Shraiah (Rules and values set by Islam).

Furthermore, as defined by Abdul Gafoor in his book titled "Interest-free Commercial Banking", 1995, Islamic banking is a banking system which is based and propelled by the sharia. That is, all workings of Islamic banking must be in line with the sharia. Nothing is done by a non-interest bank without reference to the sharia and the Quran.

Having seen all the definitions above, I can stand on the authorities above and describe non-interest banking as a banking system which entails the banking in accordance and in cognisance with the sharia and the Quran.

Definitions

Entrepreneur: According to McConnell Brue, in his book titled microeconomics 1999, entrepreneurs are individuals who recognize or operate a business or businesses. He saw entrepreneurs as individuals who view and identify a business opportunity in the society and ensures that this opportunity is transformed to an enterprise.

According to Webster's dictionary and thesaurus, 2004 [1], entrepreneur is an individual who engages in the process of launching or managing a business venture. It viewed entrepreneurs as the individual who engage in the process of handling a business venture.

Also, Ricky Griffin in his book titled 'management' [2] described entrepreneurs as a person who directs the process of planning, organizing, operating and assuming the risk of a business venture. He further described entrepreneurs as all the events which are geared by individuals towards operating a business through risk taking.

Furthermore, Oxford dictionary, 5th edition defined entrepreneurs as the activities employed in the organization and risk taking in a business by an individual.

Also, in the year 1734, Richard Cantillon viewed entrepreneurs as non-fixed income earners who pay certain cost of production and earn uncertain incomes. He saw entrepreneurs as persons who pay a known amount of money for the production of a particular product and is likely to have an uncertain return from the goods.

In the year 1803, Jean-Baptiste Say defined an entrepreneur as an economic agent who unites all the means of production- land of one, the labour of another and the capital of yet another and thus produces a product. By selling the product in the market, he pays rent of land; wages to labour, interest on capital and what remains is his profit. He also saw entrepreneurs as one that shifts economic resources out of an area of lower and into an area of higher productivity and greater yield.

Furthermore, Horngren in his book titled Accounting defines an entrepreneur as an individual who employs all the needed resources (land, labour and capital) having identified an opportunity and taken the needed risks so as to attain and procure profit through the production of desired products which will satisfy the needs of consumers

Having seen all these, I can say that entrepreneurs are individuals, persons, group of persons or even a firm that employ all the needed resources and taking the risks involved so as to set up a business enterprise.

For the purpose of understanding this research work better, some

---

*****Corresponding author:** Larry Anifowose, Department of Entrepreneurship Management Technology, The Federal University of Technology, Akure, Ondo state, Nigeria, E-mail: anifowosedotun@yahoo.com

terms which would be used are defined as follows:

Islam: A monotheistic faith regarded as revealed through Mohammed as the prophet of Allah. A religion characterized by the acceptance of the doctrine of submission to the will of Allah.

Sharia: The body of doctrines that regulates the life of those who profess Islam. The moral code and religious laws of Islam.

Quran: The sacred writings of Islam revealed by God to the prophet Mohammed during his life at Mecca and Medina. A sacred book divided into 1145 chapters, or suras: revered as the word of God, dictated by the prophet Mohammed.

Entrepreneur: A person who organizes and operates a business or businesses, taking on financial risk to do so. A person who, rather than working as an employee, runs a small business and assumes all the risk and reward of a given business venture, idea, goods or service offered for sale.

Interest: Mathematically, interest is the money paid for using someone else's money whether for personal or business use. It is normally calculated in percentage. It is referred to as "Riba" in Islamic terms.

Having analyzed all these words, we should have a clearer perspective as to this research.

History of Islamic banking

The origin of Islamic banking system can be traced back to the advent of Islam when the Prophet himself carried out trading operations for his wife. The "Mudarbah" or Islamic partnerships has been widely appreciated by the Muslim business community for centuries but the concept of "Riba" or interest has gained very little diligence in regular or day-to-day transactions.

The first model of Islamic banking system came into picture in 1963 in Egypt. Ahmad Al Najjar was the chief founder of this bank and the key features are profit sharing on the non interest based philosophy of the Islamic Shariah. These banks were actually more than financial institutions rather than commercial banks as they pay or charge interest on transactions. In 1974, the Organization of Islamic Countries (OIC) had established the first Islamic bank called the Islamic Development Bank or IDB. The basic business model of this bank was to provide financial assistance and support on profit sharing.

By the end of 1970, several Islamic banking systems have been established throughout the Muslim world, including the first private commercial bank in Dubai(1975), the Bahrain Islamic bank(1979) and the Faisal Islamic bank of Sudan (1977) [3,4].

History of Islamic banking in Nigeria

The history of Islamic banking in Nigeria is very short and not most individuals regard Islamic banking in Nigeria as having a history due to its young age. However, for the purpose of understanding this research, we would give a brief history about the history of Islamic banking in Nigeria.

Islamic banking was first introduced in Nigeria by the Central Bank of Nigeria (CBN) governor, Sanusi Lamido Sanusi as an alternative to the other forms of banking in Nigeria in the year 2010. He introduced this banking system so as to ensure that the excesses of the commercial banks where checkmated.

The first Islamic bank to be formed in Nigeria is the Jaiz Bank in the year 2003. Although it had been in existence before the official introduction of Islamic banking, it was until the formal introduction that this bank widened its operations.

Thus, we can say that the history of Islamic banking in Nigeria begins from 2010 and was propelled by the CBN governor [5].

Literature Review

Non-interest banking also known as Islamic banking can be portrayed as the youngest and most controversial banking system. This is because of its religious nature. Due to the fact that it is deeply rooted in Islam, it has had mixed reactions from several people.

However, this does not mean that this banking system is useless. In fact, it is very useful to individuals especially entrepreneurs. This is because it offers loans and assistance without collecting interest on these loans, thereby, facilitating entrepreneurship [6].

As we all know, the greatest problem of any and every entrepreneur is the problem of acquiring fund for the formation and management of the business. Thus, this banking system serves as a means of breaking this barrier and ensuring that entrepreneurs have adequate funding for their business.

If this is true, then, Islamic banking plays a vital role to every entrepreneur. Thus, it is useful. We would look in-depth as to the relevance of non- interest banking to entrepreneurs in the paragraphs below

Relevance of non-interest banking to Entrepreneurs

Islamic banking and the finance industry is growing at an annual rate of 20%. Many international as well as local institutions have stepped into this multi-billion dollar booming industry by establishing its Islamic wings and units. International giant banks such as HSBC (HSBC Amanah), Citi Bank (Citi Islamic) and Standard Chartered have already established their Islamic units and functioning in the Middle East region.

In Sri Lanka, despite the Muslim population being just 8% of the total population, a considerable growth is reported in the past few years with the establishment of Amana, Ceylinco Profit Sharing, First Global and a new comer ABC Barakah. Recently it is reported that the largest state owned commercial bank, Bank of Ceylon intends to commence its Islamic banking unit in early 2008. All these new entries imply that this alternative banking system has drawn the attention of Muslims as well as non-Muslims due to its unique developmental characteristics.

The underlying principle of Islamic banks is the principle of justice which is an essential requirement for all kinds of Islamic financing. In profit sharing of a financed project, the financier and the beneficiary share the actual or net profit/loss rather than throwing the risk burden only to the entrepreneur. The principle of fairness and justice requires that the actual output of such a project should be fairly distributed among the two parties. If a financier is expecting a claim on profits of a project, he should also carry a proportional share of the loss of that project.

In contrast with conventional finance methods, Islamic financing is not centered only on credit worthiness and ability to repay the loans and interest by entrepreneurs; instead the worthiness and profitability of a project are the most important criteria of Islamic financing while the ability to repay the loan is sub-segmented under profitability.

One of the unique and salient characteristics of Islamic banks is that the integration of ethical and moral values with its banking operation. The ethical and moral consideration of Islamic banks cannot be detached and their behaviour should be consistent with the moral and ethical standards laid down by the Islamic Shari'ah. Thus, any entrepreneurial venture must be ethically sound.

Unlike the conventional banks, the financing of Islamic banks are restricted to useful goods and services and refrain from financing alcoholic beverages and tobacco or morally unacceptable services such as casinos and pornography, irrespective of whether or not such goods and services are legal or not in a given country, hence, ensuring that the entrepreneur does not become a criminal or engage in criminal activities.

In contrast with conventional banks, Islamic banks do not consider only the credit worthiness and interest rate as standards; instead they must apply Islamic moral/ethical criteria in their provision of financing. This adds another merit for Islamic banks since there is a beneficial impact on the productivity in the economy as it reduces the social and economic cost of such harmful products and activities [7].

Another important relevance which forms the basis for the development of Islamic banks is the relationship with depositors. They deal with their customers on investment grounds rather than a pre-determined fixed interest rate. They invest the money of their depositors on high profitable projects after going through a strategic analysis in order to give a substantial return to their depositors. In other words, the entrepreneur relates with the bank on the grounds of investment and not on the grounds of interest.

Thus in Islamic banking industry, each bank will attempt to out-perform other banks if it wants to attract funds from investors. And the ultimate result is that a high return on investments for the entrepreneur, which is unlikely in a conventional bank where it deals with entrepreneurs on a pre-determined fixed interest rate.

Furthermore Islamic banks eliminate the barrier between those who save and those who invest, and bring them closer to the real market. That is, it eliminates the barrier between individuals and entrepreneurs. The nature of the financial intermediation of Islamic banks significantly defers from conventional banks and it is in harmony with real market and developmental changes in it.

Having seen all these, let us look at the relevance of non- interest banking in a scholarly way with Nigeria as a case study.

Importance of non-interest banking to entrepreneurs in Nigeria

As already said, non-interest banking is very important to entrepreneurs. This is no different to the entrepreneurs in Nigeria. Non- interest banks serve very important use to the entrepreneurs in the following ways:

Capital formation: non- interest banking serves a major function of providing funds to the entrepreneurs. They do this by ensuring that anyone with a good business idea is supported and given fund to start and manage their businesses. This becomes one of the motivators that propel entrepreneurs to greater participation in the economy.

No interest loans: Non-interest banks otherwise known as Islamic banks give no interest loans to their customer. That is, their loans do not attract any interest. This is because the Holy Quran condemns the collection of interest. Thus, entrepreneurs enjoy the freedom of collecting loans without bothering about interest. This makes life a lot easier for entrepreneurs.

Equal opportunities: Non-interest banks give equal opportunities to all entrepreneurs. Unlike in the conventional banking system where loans are given according to credit worthiness and amount of money in one's account, Islamic banking grants loans on the profitability of one's idea. That is, one might not have so much money in his account but because he has a good idea, he can be able to secure a good loan from an Islamic banking.

Creation of better relationship amongst entrepreneurs: Non-interest banks creates better relationship between their customers. As the main aim of Islamic banking is to create a universal brotherhood amongst its customers and Muslims, it ensures that entrepreneurs have a good relationship existing between them. Thus, it enables them to be able to exchange ideas which would aid them in their innovation.

Summary

This research work centers on the relevance of Islamic Banking or otherwise called Non- interest banking on entrepreneurs. It studied briefly the history of Islamic banking system in chapter two, looking at it from the two aspects- the history of Islamic banking in the world and the history of Islamic banking in Nigeria.

It also studied the relevance of Islamic banking on entrepreneurs, explaining the reasons why this banking system is advantageous to entrepreneurs.

It finally came into conclusion about the relevance of Islamic banking on entrepreneurs drawing into attention about its usefulness in capital formation.

Conclusion

In conclusion, Islamic banking is very relevant to entrepreneurs. As the most difficult factor to every entrepreneur is the sourcing of capital, Islamic banking has now come into existence to break this barrier and ensure that entrepreneurs are no longer affected by capital.

Recommendations

In consideration of everything said above, we can recommend the following as recommendations so as to promote Islamic banking and its relevance to entrepreneurs.

Government should encourage entrepreneurs to undertake in Islamic banking as a source of securing loans and aids.

Government should make provisions and also invest in Islamic banking so that individuals and entrepreneurs may invest. Government should educate entrepreneurs and the entire public so that they may see this banking system as helpful to them and their business and not as a religious thing.

Refernces

1. Acs Z, Storey D (2004) Introduction: Entrepreneurship and Economic Development. Regional Studies 38: 871-877.
2. Griffin R (2005) Management. 8th edn. Dreamtech Press, New Delhi, India.
3. Business Environment and Enterprise Performance Surveys (2007) Problems and Challenges of Small Medium Enterprises.
4. Ariyo D (2005) Small firms are the backbone of the Nigerian economy. Africa economic analysis.
5. Alao O (2005) Principles of Economics: Macro. Darkol Press and Publishers, Isolo, Lagos.

Personal Variables and Perception of Customers on Service Quality of Commercial in Madurai

Selvaraj N*

Saraswathi Narayanan College, Madurai, Tamilnadu, India

Abstract

Customers have come to gauge the 'technical factors' of services such as core and systematization of the service delivery as the yardstick in differentiating good and bad performance. Customer service is an important adjunct in any undertaking especially in business and service organizations like banks. Day in and day out banks deal with customers, be it the depositors or borrowers or anyone who walks into its portals for transacting any financial business. Now a days, a stiff competition between commercial banks has arisen in providing world class financial services to customers by using information technology, reducing costs, increasing profits and compete with international banks. To explore the relationship between personal variables and the perception of customers on dimensions, the Kruskal Wallis one way ANOVA test was applied. The Kruskal Wallis test was administered to verify that the null hypothesis that there is no significant difference in the perception scores of dimensions among different groups of customers classified according to age, gender, education, occupation, income, type of accounts and customers' duration.

Keywords: Perceptions; Banks; Customer and service

Introduction

Customers have come to gauge the 'technical factors' of services such as core and systematization of the service delivery as the yardstick in differentiating good and bad performance. Researches had also shown that organizations in the service sector are more susceptible to brand loyalty erosions due to falling customer perception of the service.

Customer service is an important adjunct in any undertaking especially in business and service organizations like banks. Day in and day out banks deal with customers, be it the depositors or borrowers or anyone who walks into its portals for transacting any financial business. They now offer a basketful of services to their customers. They are trying to make their customer a "pleased customer" and above all a "satisfied customer" by offering more services than the ingenuity of a customer can demand [1-3].

Now a days, a stiff competition between commercial banks has arisen in providing world class financial services to customers by using information technology, reducing costs, increasing profits and compete with international banks. In the era of technologically backed competition, the awareness level of customers is raising every day. Expectations of customers from banks are mounting to have a wide choice of products and services. The concept of generation to generation banking has also undergone changes [4]. Customer's loyalty is now conditioned by the quality of products of service and their delivery mechanism. All these have necessitated the banks to render warm and excellent customer service [4-6].

Methodology

The present study is based on both primary and secondary sources. The primary data was collected from the customers of commercial banks by sample survey through structural interview schedule. The secondary data were collected from books, journals, newspapers, periodicals, reports, Internet and the like.

Period of the study

The study covers a period of ten years from 2005-2006 to 2014-2015.

Sample Design

The study entitled customer perception to the services of commercial banks in Madurai city is carried out in the Temple city which is the second largest one in Tamil Nadu. Twenty four public sector banks and fifteen private sector banks function in Madurai district. On the whole twenty branches were selected from public and private sector banks respectively [7].

Field work and collection of data

Field work for this study was carried out by the researcher himself. The researcher had used the interview schedule for collecting data from bank customers. After collecting the information through the interview schedule the data were verified and edited. The survey was conducted during the period from January 2015 to June 2015.

To explore the relationship between personal variables and the perception of customers on dimensions, the Kruskal Wallis one way ANOVA test was applied.

Relationship between age and perception scores

The Kruskal Wallis test was administered to verify that the null hypothesis that there is no significant difference in the perception scores of dimensions among different groups of customers classified according to age. The results of the test are presented vide Table 1.

There was a significant difference in the perception scores of the customers on all the dimensions in public sector as well as private

---

*Corresponding author: Selvaraj N, Assistant Professor of Commerce, Saraswathi Narayanan College, Madurai, Tamilnadu, India
E-mail: profgsk2007@yahoo.co.in

Sl. No	Various Dimensions	Public Sector Banks			Private Sector Banks		
		Critical Value	Level of Significance	Result	Critical Value	Level of Significance	Result
1	Tangibility	44.362	0.000	**	81.309	0.000	**
2	Reliability	13.713	0.008	**	170.572	0.000	**
3	Responsiveness	51.029	0.000	**	122.867	0.000	**
4	Assurance	54.792	0.000	**	134.961	0.000	**
5	Accessibility	60.544	0.000	**	38.730	0.000	**
6	Empathy	58.528	0.000	**	91.594	0.000	**
7	Financial	31.875	0.000	**	36.880	0.000	**
8	Technology	22.798	0.000	**	174.644	0.000	**
9	Agency	17.973	0.001	**	103.622	0.000	**
10	Miscellaneous	14.808	0.005	**	76.131	0.000	**
11	Overall	22.301	0.000	**	143.272	0.000	**

Source: Computed from primary data.
Degree of freedom: 4, **Significant at 5 per cent level.

Table 1: Relationship between age and perception scores - Kruskal Wallis test.

Sl. No	Various Dimensions	Public Sector Banks			Private Sector Banks		
		Critical Value	Level of Significance	Result	Critical Value	Level of Significance	Result
1	Tangibility	4.605	0.032	**	4.694	0.030	**
2	Reliability	2.408	0.121	NS	2.039	0.153	NS
3	Responsiveness	2.186	0.139	NS	11.046	0.001	**
4	Assurance	2.033	0.154	NS	5.626	0.018	**
5	Accessibility	0.051	0.822	NS	0.197	0.657	NS
6	Empathy	0.976	0.323	NS	5.304	0.021	**
7	Financial	0.224	0.636	NS	1.049	0.306	NS
8	Technology	0.951	0.329	NS	81.869	0.000	**
9	Agency	8.568	0.003	**	19.256	0.000	**
10	Miscellaneous	7.374	0.007	**	1.323	0.250	NS
11	Overall	0.936	0.333	NS	17.806	0.000	**

Source: Computed from primary data.
Degree of freedom: 1, **Significant at 5 per cent level, NS - Not Significant.

Table 2: Relationship between gender and perception scores - Kruskal Wallis test.

sector banks. It indicated that age factor influenced the dimensions in both public and private sector banks [8].

With regard to the overall score, the value of the level of significance was less than 0.05 (5 percent level), and hence the null hypothesis is rejected. It is seen that age factor influenced the perception score of both public and private sector banks.

Relationship between gender and perception scores

To test whether there is any relationship between the gender and the perception scores of dimensions the following null hypothesis has been framed [9].

There is no significant difference in perception scores among different dimensions based on the gender of the customers. The result of the Kruskal Wallis test is shown vide Table 2.

There was no significant differences in the perception scores of all dimensions expect the tangibility, agency and miscellaneous dimensions in public sector banks. It indicates that the factor gender influenced the tangibility, agency and miscellaneous dimensions. It also showed that the overall perception score, the value of the level of significance was more than the 0.05 (5 percent level) and the null hypothesis is accepted. Hence it is concluded that the gender had no influence on the perception score of public sector banks.

As regards private sector banks, there was a significant relationship between the gender and the perception scores of all dimensions except the reliability, accessibility, financial and miscellaneous dimensions. It indicated that gender had no influence on the reliability, accessibility, financial and miscellaneous dimensions. It is also seen that there was significant difference in the overall perception score and hence the null hypothesis is rejected. It is concluded that the gender had influenced the perception score of private sector banks.

Relationship between education and perception scores

To test whether there is any relationship between the education and the perception scores of dimension the following null hypothesis has been framed.

There is no significant difference in perception scores among different groups of customers based on the education. The results of the Kruskal Wallis test are presented in Table 3.

There was a significant difference in the perception scores of the customers of all dimensions except the agency dimension in public sector banks. It indicated that education had not influenced the agency dimension. It is also seen that there was significant difference in the overall perception score and hence the null hypothesis is rejected. It is concluded that the education had influenced the perception of respondents in public sector banks [10].

In the case of private sector banks, it could be observed that there was a significant difference in the perception score among different customers according to their level of education for all categories. It

Sl. No	Various Dimensions	Public Sector Banks			Private Sector Banks		
		Critical Value	Level of Significance	Result	Critical Value	Level of Significance	Result
1	Tangibility	25.050	0.000	**	75.218	0.000	**
2	Reliability	14.466	0.002	**	84.189	0.000	**
3	Responsiveness	12.515	0.006	**	51.312	0.000	**
4	Assurance	51.682	0.000	**	42.082	0.000	**
5	Accessibility	15.654	0.001	**	14.927	0.002	**
6	Empathy	15.332	0.002	**	73.657	0.000	**
7	Financial	36.536	0.000	**	36.501	0.000	**
8	Technology	28.849	0.000	**	99.119	0.000	**
9	Agency	03.219	0.359	NS	57.230	0.000	**
10	Miscellaneous	16.301	0.001	**	69.386	0.000	**
11	Overall	14.638	0.002	**	95.681	0.000	**

Source: Computed from primary data.
Degree of freedom: 3, **Significant at 5 per cent level, NS - Not Significant.

Table 3: Relationship between education and perception scores - Kruskal Wallis test.

Sl. No	Various Dimensions	Public Sector Banks			Private Sector Banks		
		Critical Value	Level of Significance	Result	Critical Value	Level of Significance	Result
1	Tangibility	94.792	0.000	**	39.712	0.000	**
2	Reliability	131.751	0.000	**	83.550	0.000	**
3	Responsiveness	114.069	0.000	**	53.483	0.000	**
4	Assurance	92.337	0.000	**	48.514	0.000	**
5	Accessibility	92.036	0.000	**	46.615	0.000	**
6	Empathy	102.107	0.000	**	92.140	0.000	**
7	Financial	92.654	0.000	**	65.737	0.000	**
8	Technology	133.208	0.000	**	96.169	0.000	**
9	Agency	95.159	0.000	**	61.419	0.000	**
10	Miscellaneous	100.804	0.000	**	82.394	0.000	**
11	Overall	124.192	0.000	**	90.071	0.000	**

Source: Computed from primary data.
Degree of freedom: 5, **Significant at 5 per cent level, NS - Not Significant.

Table 4: Relationship between occupation pattern and perception scores - Kruskal Wallis test.

also shows that for the overall perception score, the value of level of significance was less than the 0.05 (5 percent level). Therefore the null hypothesis has been rejected. It is concluded that the education had influenced the perception of customers in private sector banks.

Relationship between occupation pattern and perception scores

In order to test whether there is any relationship between the occupation pattern and the perception score of dimensions, the Kruskal Wallis test has been applied to the following null hypothesis.

There is no significant difference in perception scores of the dimensions among different groups of customers based on occupation pattern. The results are presented vide Table 4.

It could be understood that there was a significant relationship between the occupation pattern and the perception scores of all the dimensions in both public and private sector banks. It is also shown that for the overall perception score, the value of level of significance was less than 0.05 (5 percent level). Therefore the null hypothesis had been rejected. It is concluded that the occupation pattern had influence on the perception score of public as well as private sector banks.

Relationship between income and perception scores

In order to test the null hypothesis that there is no significant difference in the perception scores of customers among different groups based on their income, the Kruskal Wallis test has been applied. The results are given vide Table 5.

It could be seen that there was a significant difference in perception scores among different customers of public sector banks according to income for all categories except tangibility and miscellaneous dimensions [11]. It is also observed that for the overall perception scores, the value of level of significance was less than the 0.05 (5 percent level) and therefore the null hypothesis is rejected. It is observed that the factor income had influenced the perception score of public sector banks.

There was a significant difference in the perception scores of all categories of dimensions. The table also shows that for the overall perception scores, the value of level of significance was less than 0.05 (5 percent level) and so the null hypothesis has been rejected. It is determined that the income had influence on the perception scores of private sector banks.

Relationship between type of accounts and perception scores

In order to test whether there is any relationship between type of accounts and perception scores the following hypothesis has been framed. A Kruskal Wallis test has been used to test the hypothesis.

It was seen that there was no significant difference in the perception scores of dimensions among the different groups based on the type of accounts. The result of the Kruskal Wallis test is shown in Table 6.

There was no significant difference in the perception scores of

Sl. No	Various Dimensions	Public Sector Banks			Private Sector Banks		
		Critical Value	Level of Significance	Result	Critical Value	Level of Significance	Result
1	Tangibility	03.316	0.506	NS	63.872	0.000	**
2	Reliability	30.155	0.000	**	40.753	0.000	**
3	Responsiveness	20.871	0.000	**	25.605	0.000	**
4	Assurance	25.480	0.000	**	27.800	0.000	**
5	Accessibility	40.439	0.000	**	22.629	0.000	**
6	Empathy	57.910	0.000	**	19.997	0.001	**
7	Financial	30.323	0.000	**	22.645	0.000	**
8	Technology	12.024	0.017	**	22.755	0.000	**
9	Agency	20.352	0.000	**	39.538	0.000	**
10	Miscellaneous	80.821	0.066	NS	22.502	0.000	**
11	Overall	20.283	0.000	**	33.270	0.000	**

Source: Computed from primary data.
Degree of freedom: 4, **Significant at 5 per cent level, NS - Not Significant.

Table 5: Relationship between income and perception scores - Kruskal Wallis test.

Sl. No	Various Dimensions	Public Sector Banks			Private Sector Banks		
		Critical Value	Level of Significance	Result	Critical Value	Level of Significance	Result
1	Tangibility	2.964	0.397	NS	3.424	0.331	NS
2	Reliability	5.313	0.150	NS	3.398	0.334	NS
3	Responsiveness	15.993	0.001	**	1.595	0.661	NS
4	Assurance	3.565	0.312	NS	1.912	0.591	NS
5	Accessibility	4.539	0.209	NS	1.804	0.614	NS
6	Empathy	10.362	0.016	**	1.615	0.656	NS
7	Financial	8.144	0.043	**	1.262	0.738	NS
8	Technology	4.383	0.223	NS	1.577	0.665	NS
9	Agency	18.684	0.000	**	4.046	0.257	NS
10	Miscellaneous	2.092	0.553	NS	3.521	0.318	NS
11	Overall	6.452	0.092	NS	3.297	0.348	NS

Source: Computed from primary data.
Degree of freedom: 3, **Significant at 5 per cent level, NS - Not Significant.

Table 6: Relationship between type of accounts and perception scores - Kruskal Wallis test.

all categories of dimensions except in the cases of responsiveness, empathy, financial and agency dimensions in public sector banks. It is also seen that for the overall perception score, the value of level of significance was more than 0.05 (5 percent level). Therefore, the null hypothesis has been accepted. It is concluded that the type of accounts had no influence on the perception score of public sector banks.

It could be observed that there is no significant relationship between the type of account and the perception scores of all dimensions in private sector banks. The value of level of significance was more than 0.05 (5 percent level). Therefore the null hypothesis is accepted. It is concluded that the type of account had no influence on the perception score of private sector banks.

Relationship between customer duration and perception scores

In order to test the null hypothesis that there is no significant difference in the perception scores among different groups based on customers' duration, the Kruskal Wallis test has been applied. The results can be found vide Table 7.

There was a significant difference in the perception scores of the customers of all categories of dimensions in both public and private sector banks in this regard. It is also observed that for the overall perception score, the value of level of significance was less than 0.05 (5 percent level). Therefore the null hypothesis is rejected. It is concluded that the customer duration had influenced the perception scores in public as well as private sector banks.

Findings

Public sector banks

❖ There was a significant difference between age and the perception scores of the customers on all the dimensions and the hypothesis indicated that age influences all the dimensions. There was a significant relationship between age and the overall perception of the services.

❖ There was no significant differences in the perception scores of all dimensions expect the tangibility, agency and miscellaneous dimensions and the hypothesis showed that the factor gender influenced the tangibility, agency and miscellaneous dimensions. There was no significant relationship found between gender and the overall perception of the services.

❖ There was a significant difference between education and perception scores of the customers of all dimensions except the agency and the hypothesis pointed out that education did not influence the agency dimension. There was a significant difference between education and the overall perception score of the services.

❖ There was a significant relationship between the occupation pattern and the perception scores of all the dimensions and hypothesis indicated that occupation pattern influenced all the dimensions. There was a significant relationship noticed between occupation pattern and the overall perception score of the services.

❖ There was a significant difference in perception scores

Sl. No	Various Dimensions	Public Sector Banks			Private Sector Banks		
		Critical Value	Level of Significance	Result	Critical Value	Level of Significance	Result
1	Tangibility	30.679	0.000	**	58.277	0.000	**
2	Reliability	20.071	0.000	**	42.213	0.000	**
3	Responsiveness	21.615	0.001	**	51.014	0.000	**
4	Assurance	34.680	0.000	**	44.206	0.000	**
5	Accessibility	24.392	0.000	**	41.875	0.000	**
6	Empathy	39.434	0.000	**	48.351	0.000	**
7	Financial	36.646	0.000	**	88.336	0.000	**
8	Technology	51.582	0.000	**	25.924	0.000	**
9	Agency	61.916	0.000	**	47.771	0.000	**
10	Miscellaneous	78.298	0.000	**	63.170	0.000	**
11	Overall	32.066	0.000	**	52.812	0.000	**

Source: Computed from primary data.
Degree of freedom: 5, **Significant at 5 per cent level, NS - Not Significant.

Table 7: Relationship between customer duration and perception scores - Kruskal Wallis test.

among different customers according to income for all categories of dimensions except tangibility and miscellaneous dimensions and the hypothesis showed that income did not influence the tangibility and miscellaneous dimensions. There was a significant difference between income and the overall perception score of the services.

❖ There was no significant difference between the type of account and the perception scores of all categories of dimensions except the responsiveness, empathy, financial and agency dimensions and the hypothesis pointed out that the type of account influenced the responsiveness, empathy, financial and agency dimensions. There was no significant relationship between type of account and the overall perception score of the services.

❖ There was a significant difference between customer duration in the banks and the perception scores of the customers of all categories of dimensions and the hypothesis indicated that the customer duration influenced all the dimensions. There was a significant relationship between customer duration and the overall perception score of the services.

Private sector banks

❖ There was a significant difference between age and the perception scores of the customers on all the dimensions and the hypothesis showed that the age influenced all the dimensions. There was a significant relationship between age and the overall perception of the services.

❖ There was a significant relationship between the gender and the perception scores of all dimensions except the reliability, accessibility, financial and miscellaneous dimensions and the hypothesis pointed out that the gender had did not influence the reliability, accessibility, financial and miscellaneous dimension. There was a significant difference between gender and the overall perception of the services.

❖ There was significant difference in the perception score among different customers according to their education for all categories and the hypothesis indicated that the education influenced all the dimensions. There was a significant relationship between education and the overall perception score of the services.

❖ There was a significant relationship between the occupation pattern and the perception scores of all the dimensions and the hypothesis showed that the occupation pattern influenced the all the dimensions. There was a significant relationship between occupation pattern and the overall perception score of the services.

❖ There was a significant difference between income and the perception scores of all categories of dimensions and the hypothesis pointed out that income influenced all the dimensions. There was a significant difference between income and the overall perception score of the services.

❖ There was no significant relationship between the type of account and the perception scores of all dimensions and the hypothesis indicated that the type of account did not influence all the dimensions. There was no significant relationship between the type of account and the overall perception score of the services.

❖ There was a significant difference between the customer duration and the perception scores of the customers of all categories of dimensions and the hypothesis showed that the customer duration influenced all the dimensions. There was a significant relationship between the customer duration and the overall perception score of the services.

Suggestions

1. The customers of both public as well as private sector banks got the ATM facility within one year. The waiting time for getting ATM facility must be minimized. Efforts should be taken up to provide ATM facility at the time of opening the account itself.

The public sector banks should improve the services which come under the accessibility dimension. In the case of private sector banks, the dimension on miscellaneous factor must be augmented by banks.

References

1. Abraham P (2011) Emerging role of india's banking sector in promoting inclusive growth: A highlight. Banking sector in global scenario, Sri maruthi publishers, India.
2. Natarajan S, Parameswaran R (2010) Indian Banking. S. Chand & Company Ltd, New Delhi.
3. www.expressindia.com.
4. RBI Annual Reports 2014-2015.
5. RBI Report on Trend and Progress of Banking in India, 2014-2015.
6. www.banknetindia.com.
7. Ananth A, Ramesh R, Prabaharan B (2011) Service quality gap analysis in private sector banks a customer perspective. Indian Journal of Commerce and Management Studies 2: 245-252.
8. Krishnaswami OR, Ranganatham M (2007) Methodology of research in social science. Himalaya Publishing House, Mumbai.

9. AbdulKalam APJ (2006) Be Leader, Friend and Philosopher. Industrial Herald.

10. Anderson EW, Fornell C, Lehmann DR (1994) Customer satisfaction, market share, and profitability: Findings from Sweden. The Journal of Marketing pp: 53-66.

11. Afsar B, Rehman ZU, Qureshi JA, Shahjehan A (2010) Determinants of customer loyalty in the banking sector: The case of Pakistan. African Journal of Business Management 4: 1040.

Transnational Entrepreneurship and Ghanaians Abroad: What are the Motives?

Elvis Asiedu* and Patrick Dede Nyarkoh

Servicio Nacional De Aprendizaje (SENA), Neiva, Huila, Colombia

Abstract

Business Creation is something that does not come into being on its own; but it emerges from people who see a need for service or product in a society, with that desire to be self-employed and rise above, and use that opportunity. These individuals are dedicated people who are willing to absorb all their time, passion, and money in the work they have created to ensure business growth and success. Though these entrepreneurs operate in a condition where costs may be known but rewards are uncertain, yet they are motivated and the question here is; what really drives the performance to engage in such entrepreneurial activities?

The general results show that though individuals motives for seeking self-employment are diverse and numerous; and differ on certain points. However, there are some basic motives common to all and that is majority of the respondents with the average score of 63.3% supported that Economic Mobility, Financial Independence, Success Perspective, and Social Factor, are the most driven factors for the engagement in transnational entrepreneurship. It was also discovered that the success of these entrepreneurs are based on attitudinal, the degree of embededdness in the home country, personal and the institutional regulations of the destination countries. The results found that Ghana Transnational Entrepreneurs are more into Merchandising Business with (59.21%) as compared to Service Business (34.21%) and Manufacturing Business (10.53%). The results also disclosed that, in Ghana, transnational entrepreneurs businesses are managed and run mostly by their families (59.21%). Ashanti Region of Ghana was spotted to be more involved in doing business with 52.63%.

The research employed both deductive and exploratory approach and the methods were both primary and secondary. The study focused on small-scale entrepreneurs who run their businesses through personal social connections. The research is subjected to the bias of the respondents, therefore, 100% accuracy cannot be guaranteed.

Keywords: Transnational entrepreneurship; Ghana; Migration; Entrepreneurial ventures; Social relationship; Economic mobility; Financial independence

Abbreviations: TE: Transnational Entrepreneurship; GSA: Ghana Statistical Authority

Introduction

Ghana is considered one of the more stable countries in West Africa since its transition to multi-party democracy in 1992 [1]. Formerly known as the Gold Coast, the country gained independence from Great Britain on 6th March, 1957 under the leadership of Kwame Nkrumah, thereby becoming the first country in sub-Saharan Africa to break the chains of colonialism. Ghana is ranked as the 86th country with unemployment rate of 11% as of June, 30, 2015 as compared to 5.7% in the final quarter of 2013 [2]. Cocoa, Gold, Bauxite, Timber, and more recently Oil form the cornerstone of Ghana's economy and have helped fuel an economic growth. Ghana is the 9th largest economy in Africa and 2nd largest in West Africa, with 27 million populations [1].

It is argued that, a country's economic development, employment, innovation and productivity are driven by entrepreneurial activities. Hisrich [3] supported that economic progress of a country is significantly advanced by pragmatic individuals who are innovative with entrepreneurial skills, and willing to take risk in order to exploit opportunities that may be uncertain. Daniel and Mead [4] argued that such enterprises play a major role in poverty alleviation for households and can be significant contributors to economic development of a country. In Ghana, the majority of the working populations are employed in small-scale enterprises. These small-medium enterprises employ 15% of the working population with a high rate of growth than any other companies and contributing 6% to the country's GDP [5]. In simply put, the establishment of micro, small and medium enterprises contribute immensely to a country's economic growth. This has made the topic "transnational entrepreneurship", a popular area of research within the international business, ethnic and immigrant entrepreneurship.

Though transnational entrepreneurs are seen as the catalyst of these small-medium business establishments in Africa and within the context of Ghana, many of us have not sought to ask about their motive towards this establishment. Many of us are aware that establishing and managing business from a far distance can be very hectic and difficult and as a matter of fact, these entrepreneurs operate in a condition where cost may be known but rewards are uncertain, yet they are motivated. Do you know that this kind of business creation requires someone who is hardworking, information seeking, independent-minded, and willing to take risk and personal initiative? Are you also aware that exploiting opportunities that may be uncertain could be the biggest risk to take as a transnational entrepreneur? So if that is the case, then the question is; what really drives them to engage in such entrepreneurial activities?

*****Corresponding author:** Elvis Asiedu, Servicio Nacional De Aprendizaje (SENA), Centro de la Industria, la Empresa y los Servicios Carrera 5 Avenida la Toma, Neiva, Huila, Colombia
E-mail: akwasiasiedu63@yahoo.com; padeny4u@yahoo.com

It is based on this assumption that the study focused on the factors that drive the performance of small-medium entrepreneurs (SMEs) from Ghana, who run their businesses across international boundaries and borders, developing activities in socio-economic field at home and abroad through personal social connections; by answering the following research questions:

- What is transnational entrepreneurship? Is there any link between Migration and Entrepreneurial Ventures?
- What kind of influence do social relations, family and ethnic background have on transnational entrepreneurial success?
- What kind of businesses and industries are in the focus of Ghanaian transnational entrepreneurs?
- What are the motives for the performance of transnational entrepreneurship and why such businesses normally fail?

This study will go a long way to help the youth who wants to enter entrepreneurship to know the risk, and the motives behind such establishment. It will also assist them to identify the factors that make such businesses fail sometimes. It focuses on Ghanaians abroad and their ties through personal social connections and the factors that drive the spirit of entrepreneurial activities as well as the kind of mobility involves in doing such businesses. Though, not all the entrepreneurs the researcher met and interviewed were mobile, most of them used to travel to Ghana at least once a year to work for their businesses and maintain their relationship with their representatives.

Literature Review

The migration history of Ghanaians

Many Ghanaians most especially; the youth constituting 33% of the country's population with 5.5% unemployment rate have sought to look for different means of employment; lo and behold, migration has been the alternative. Ghanaians have a history of migrating to Europe and America due to the country's cultural, socio-economic, colonial and political climate. Black and Castaldo [6] advocated that Ghanaians are traditionally found of travelling to the United Kingdom and more recently to the United State of America. To buttress their point, they said "it was reflected in the sample with 40% of Ghanaian returnees interviewed coming from UK, and 21% from the United State of America". However, Ghana in recent years has experienced a diversification of migration destination just like other African countries [7]. They have created a social diaspora across the world and they keep increasing in their numbers and their contributions to the individual household and the country's economy cannot be over emphasized.

In 2010, a total number of 250,624 Ghanaians whose age ranges from 15 years and above were found living abroad. Out of the total population of 250, 624 Ghanaian abroad, 2/3rd representing 6% were male and 1/3rd representing 36% were females [2]. According to GSA, 78.5% of them between the ages of 20 years and 40 years were males and 77.5% were female. Statistical analysis show that, migrants from Ghana hail from all the ten regions in the country but the majority of them representing 52.8% are from Ashanti and Greater Accra Region respectively. Table 1 shows the regions in Ghana with their migration percentage rate (Table 1);

Among many countries in the world, Europe and America remain the most preferable destination for Ghanaian migrants with a total percentage of 61.3% respectively. According to Ghana Statistical Authority, 37.7% of Ghanaian migrants are believed to be in Europe, 23.6% are in America, 30.1% in Cote d'Ivoire and 26.8% in Anarfi [8] argued that the cultural and historical affinity can explain the reasons and importance behind these migration streams. Records also reveal that these migrants who are male are higher than females [2] and this is the breakdown; 33.2% male migrants and 24.4% female migrants reside in ECOWAS countries such as Nigeria, Cote d'Ivoire, and Togo.

Similarly, 13.2% male and 5.5% female migrants were spotted living in other parts of Africa. In the words of Anarfi [8], Cote d'Ivoire has been a major destination for most Ghanaian female migrants and their activities in that country has attracted the attention of both academia and media. It has also been disclosed that each region in Ghana has its preferred destination and Figure 1 shows the regions and their preferred country of destination.

When it comes to employment demarcation, over 76.2% of Ghanaians living abroad are employed, 6% are unemployed and 14% are students. The proportion employed according to Ghana Statistical Authority grows from 42.8% (at age 15-19 years) to a peak of 85.4% (at age 50-54 years) before it declines again at the older age. Most of these people abroad are working as officials of Government and Special Interest Organisations, Professionals, Technicians and Associate Professionals, clerks, sales/service workers, farmers, fishermen and forestry workers, trade related workers, plant and machine operators, labourers and unskilled workers and special occupations. All these working groups contribute immensely to the total remittances sent to the country, Ghana (Table 2).

Though there are several factors of Ghanaian migration, conditions in the country serve as the major inspirations in sacrificing time spent in one's comfort zone to strive for greener pastures abroad. Lucas and Morris [9] argued that wage differences seldom become the deciding factor to migrate. Among the numerous factors aforementioned, migration is mainly driven by individual's desire to rise higher and change. Surely, there are corresponding costs and gains when it comes to migration. However, since many people see migration as both risk and as a form of investment, migrants continue to find their ways to grow unlimited income outside employment through engaging in

S/No	Region	Migrants %
1.	Ashanti	27.6%
2.	Greater Accra	25.2%
2.	Brong Ahafo	13.4%
3.	Western	8.7%
4.	Others	25.1%

Source: Ghana Statistical Authority, Population and Housing Census [2].

Table 1: Regions with high migration rate in Ghana.

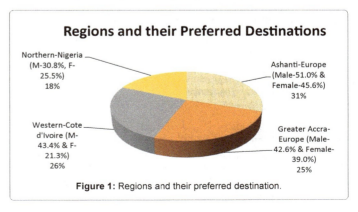

Figure 1: Regions and their preferred destination.

Age	Total	Employed	Unemployed	Students	Other
15-19	100.0	42.8	9.0	43.3	4.8
20-24	100.0	58.7	9.0	27.8	4.5
25-29	100.0	70.0	7.8	18.8	3.4
30-34	100.0	78.1	6.0	12.8	3.2
35-39	100.0	81.4	5.4	10.1	3.1
40-44	100.0	84.2	4.6	8.2	3.0
45-49	100.0	85.3	4.0	7.8	2.9
50-54	100.0	85.4	4.1	7.0	3.5
55-59	100.0	84.8	4.8	7.2	3.2
60-64	100.0	81.8	6.2	6.4	5.7
65-69	100.0	76.1	8.6	6.1	9.1
70-74	100.0	68.1	12.9	7.0	12.1
75+	100.0	70.8	10.2	8.6	10.4
Total	100.0	76.2	6.1	14.0	3.6

Table 2: Employment status of Ghanaians abroad from 15 years and above.

transnational entrepreneurial activities. So, the question is what is transnational entrepreneurship?

Transnational entrepreneurship (TE)

The term "transnational entrepreneurship (TE)" was first used in the immigration literature as a web of contacts between Diasporas and their home countries. It was established as a form of engaging in a practice of to-and-fro movements across different borders in search of political voice and economic advantage [10,11]. According to Bridge [12], these entrepreneurs are people with the confidence and foresight to operate in conditions where costs may be known but rewards are uncertain. Through leveraging resources from both locations, enterprising immigrants serve as agents of international business in the facilitation and promotion of bilateral investment and trade.

Transnational entrepreneurs are individuals with the ability to search the environment both in their country of origin and country of destination to mobilise resources, identify opportunities and execute actions to maximise such opportunities. They do this by maintaining a strong relationship between their destination country and country of origin. Drori [13] argued that these entrepreneurs simultaneously engage in different environments they are socially embedded to maintain global relations that improve their ability to dynamically, logistically and creatively maximise their resource base. They take risk to innovate, provide services, employ people and through their experiences and combination of materials; create new products for the market.

Cronje [14] argued that transnational entrepreneurs play an important role in economic development of every country by reducing unemployment rate through their small-scale business creations. According to Fuller [15], transnational entrepreneurs have investment components located in different countries and their mode of operations is spelled by the optimization of two contexts in which they are placed. This implies that transnational entrepreneurship requires flexible, hardworking and open-minded people who can seek for information and capitalise on every opportunity to spread their entrepreneurial activities.

Min [16] and Light [17] preached that transnationalism is crucial to a foreign land so long as the number of foreign children grows in that country. To them, this will go a long way to influence that country's international trade. Portes [11], viewed transnational entrepreneurs as self-employed immigrants whose business activities demand frequent travel abroad and who depend for the success of their firms through contacts and associates in another country, primarily their home of origin. These entrepreneurs always leverage their resources and networks from their home country and create links with their destination country to exploit opportunities that might not be recognised [13].

Contrary to the above assessment, Wong and Ng [18] opined that transnational entrepreneurship is a "business in the ethnic economy which entails separate components of the enterprise being located in different countries and the transmigration of the owners in order to operate it". This really explains transnational entrepreneurship as a culturally derived, reliant and oriented on peculiar community and link of immigrant embeddedness [19]. Migrant entrepreneurs are always engaged in one or two socially embedded environment trying to maintain global relations, maximising resource base and enhancing creativity. This activity is what Mazzucato defined as a "double engagement".

From the print views of Portes [11] and Mazzucato [20], the unique aspect of these transnational entrepreneurs is their ability of social embeddedness both in their home of origins and destination countries. Leung [21] argued that immigrants involved in transnational embeddedness, engaged in cross border practices and relations, always create spaces that are used as a "point of anchorage" for their social networks to engage in information, capital and movement. This point of anchorage as stated by Leung [21] allows convenient and frequent access to resources and networks which enable in initiation of business ventures and opportunity recognition. Hatton and Williamson [22] added that transnational entrepreneurship refers to the business activities created and operated by returned migrants. However, transnational entrepreneurs are different from returnee entrepreneurs who focus largely on their home country to guide their business strategy [15].

While most research on transnational entrepreneurship among Ghanaians abroad focus on economic impacts and remittances, this study focuses on the factors that drives the performance of T.E. Though several studies have shown that this kind of business is difficult and can be stressful sometimes, yet these entrepreneurs are motivated and the question is; what are the factors that drives the performance of these transnational entrepreneurships?

Migration and Entrepreneurial Ventures

Migration in this context is defined as the movement of people from one country to another country with the aim of searching for greener pasture. It normally takes place between countries with similar economic, historic, colonial and cultural ties. Ghanaians migrate to Europe and the USA due to the similar connection that exist between them; in terms of economic, social, history and culture. Littunen [23] proposed that there are numerous factors that determine entrepreneurial activities but life situations, changes and experiences are very crucial and that is where migration comes to play part.

A study investigated the effect of labour market institution on immigration from 221 countries of origin to 15 OECD countries during the 1980 to 2006 disclosed that the difference in wages between immigrants' home of origin and foreign country is one of the deciding factors for migration [24]. What this means is that migration in most at times is driven by either the desire for individual to change his/her social status, life situation or gain experiences and skills, though some see it as a risk; it is also an investment.

In Ghana, employment and economic opportunities since 1957 has been major challenge to many individuals most especially the youth. This has made travelling abroad the most lucrative business for most Ghanaian youth. Valencia argued that there are pull and push factors that compel individuals to migrate and those factors can be financial, family, personal opportunistic and economical. This shows that conditions in the country of origin coerce or as, someone might say, motivate individuals to seek for greener pastures. Research has revealed that most Ghanaians migrate with the aim of coming back home to establish jobs so that there will be no need to search for jobs abroad [23]. This ambition of many Ghanaians shows there is a positive correlation between migration and entrepreneurial ventures [25].

Besides, scholars such as Beauchemin and Schoumaker [26], Hatton and Williamson [22] stressed that migration is a growing phenomenon on the African continent due to lack of development among the countries on the continent. Is this true or false? Interestingly, these scholars are not far from the truth because migration or travelling abroad has become the only means for Africans, most especially Ghanaians to better their lives and that of their families. It is of no surprise that many Ghanaians abroad including the researcher; have sought to invest in new entrepreneurial activities to enter into economic independence. If that is the case, then how large is immigrant companies? Lucas and Morris [9] opined that immigrants companies most at times are inconsequential, small and most at times, focused on the small-medium enterprises. However, scholars such as Min and Bozorgmehr [27], Wong and Ng [18] disagreed with Lucas and Morris [9] and argued that it is impossible to consider all immigrants businesses as the same.

Another point to be noted when digesting about the correlation between migration and entrepreneurial venture is that many people migrate with aim of getting capital, gaining experiences and skills to venture into business in order to enter into economic independence. One of the interviewees: Agyakoo Shipping Company (Oxford-UK) emphatically said that *"there is a link between migration and business establishment because through migration, we have been able to accumulate capital, and develop experience to establish our businesses"*. McComick and Wahba [28], Black and Cotalno [6] agreed that there is a positive correlation between the accumulation of savings and investment in entrepreneurial activities.

Contrary to the above, Portes and Sensenbrenner [29] identified some basic factors that can influence immigrants to enter into transnational economic activities. They argued that married status, high level of education, male gender, professional experience, certain scope and size of social relations and years of spent abroad, are influential factors for immigrant to venturing into transnational economic activities. Faist [30], Faist and Siereking [31] supported that historical context of these migrants flow and the features of the immigrants' communities can influence the tendency toward transnational entrepreneurships. In 2010, Xiaohua and Chrysostome [32] argued that the intersection between entrepreneurship (business) and immigration (social) is the immigrant entrepreneurship.

Kivisto and Granovetter [33-35] based their argument on the significance conditions of incorporation in the immigrants for the development of transnational relations. These scholars exposed that difficult conditions of incorporation like discrimination sometimes influence the creation of self-employment through transnational economic activities. Zhhou and Kim [36] arguably stressed that the job creation positively affects the social dimension of the people through recognition of immigrants, provision of role models for immigrants, development of vibrant ethnic communities and building of entrepreneurial spirit among the people. According to Nijkamp [37], high internal locus control, achievement of motivation, participation in social networks and risk-taking tendency are some of the factors that drives Ghanaian migrants to venture into entrepreneurship.

Social Relations in Small-Scale Enterprises and Entrepreneurial Success?

In transnational entrepreneurship, social relations (networks) are crucial in terms of establishing the business, circulating goods and services, providing accommodation and psychological support as well as continuous improvement of socio-economic information of the two countries. Cassini [38] stressed that financial capital is not enough to develop a small-firm but issues such as trust and social responsibility are important in developing a small-scale enterprise. However, she noted that members of the migrants' social network can undermine the success of the entrepreneurial activities. Buane [39] continued that family and social relations disadvantage entrepreneurs, by increasing unrealistic demands on their resources.

Contrary to the above assessment, Steel and Becky believed that such relations provide the individual entrepreneur the intellectual, economic, emotional and spiritual support to do their business. Mitchell [40] opined that the contents of the links in an individual entrepreneur's social relations may compose of kingship obligation, economic assistance, religious cooperation or it may be simply friendship. Transnational entrepreneurs use these social ties to acquire or pass on information, achieve some objects as well as to influence some other people in a desired direction. The significant of social relations in maintaining and promoting small-business activities in Ghana has been noted by scholars such as Mazzucato [20] and Ley [41]. Lewis [42] cited how firms in Nigeria have used social ties to respond to structural adjustment by retreating to 'rental havens' protected by key allies in the state.

Kloosterman and Rath [43] based his argument on socio-economic embeddedness as a key element when it comes to the interaction between the demand and supply sides of business initiation and its successes. To him embeddedness is an umbrella of social networks, socio-economic and politico-institutional settings. Granovetter [35] argued that embeddednesss of socio-economic relations can be grouped into structural embeddedness and relational embeddedness.

The structural embeddedness typology consists of relationship in a broader network and social relations of several individuals [31].

Scholars such as Granovetter [35] and Portes; and Sensenbrenner [29] observed that, in order to sustain and maintain these two kinds of relationships, solidarity must be built between the two partners. This will go a long way to help the transnational entrepreneurs to utilise certain sanctions to enforce trust among them to keep the relationship moving all the time. "Solidarity" in this context refers to the foundation of a collective identity which is based on rules, symbolic bonds, and shared ideas [31]. The entrepreneurs need to have a well-structured connections built on solidarity to define their collective identity. This identity allows the members of the community to advocate for one another without necessarily knowing each other personally [31]. Many of the interviewees declared that they have developed a very strong and well-structured relationship with people back in Ghana and they are guided by solidarity.

The second category-relational embeddedness involves an entrepreneur's social relationship with two or more entrepreneurs [31]. To them, this relational embeddedness is identified by mutual reciprocity and normative expectation in interaction. Entrepreneurs through relational embeddedness can help one another and share their experiences and skills. Faist [30] stressed that 'what one receives from the other-in this kind of social relationship-requires something in return-to make it reciprocal'. The experiences and skills shared among them marks the beginning of their reciprocal interaction [29]. "*Personal trust*" plays an important role in this kind of social relations. There is nothing that motivates and excites people like a "trust" to accomplish something special. Personal trust strengthens entrepreneurs' social relations between individuals who are part of their businesses. Faist and Siereking [31] supported that trust is more important for small-scale business due to the risk of losing significant resources through sometimes misconduct.

Trust in an entrepreneur's social relations brings about cooperation between the business partners. The "business partner" in this context could be the representative (manager) in-charge of the parent company and subsidiaries back home in your absent. When there is trust, there will be cooperation. Through trust, the cooperation partners would be able to understand their counterpart actions. However, both partners are supposed to follow their independent business objectives to make each one autonomous. Faist and Siereking [31] argued that cooperation is shaped by the need of the partners to create mutual obligation as well as to ensure that both partners are dependent on each other. Semlinger referred to this cooperation as "bounded autonomy". Faist and Siereking [31] concluded that if these cooperation partners are able to dispose of the amount of autonomy and the opportunity to control one another, then there would be a symmetric dependency between the cooperating entrepreneurs.

Notwithstanding that, transnational entrepreneurs also have social relations with others who are not part of their business. Many at times, economic actions are determined by social expectations and ties. If that is the case, then how can transnational entrepreneurs protect themselves from private issues which are not supposed to be closed to their rational business activities? Evers opined that embeddedness in a person's social relations/ties needs enterprises to find a balance between social obligation on one side as well as economic survival and efficiency on the other. Besides, maintaining a balance between the creation of culture or geographic distance is crucial when it comes to embeddedness in social relations. This is because it prevents "*decoupling*" as Granovetter [35] put it and thereby creating sufficient social cohesion and restricting claims to implement common values and norms to ensure a "*coupling process*".

In business, either local or international, knowing one another at the upper levels of management is important. It is argued that knowing the person, being able to trust this person and sharing the same values are important aspect of business which is given by the image of common family origin. This becomes more important when the firm want to expand into a foreign country. Trust between the manager of the parent company and the subsidiaries are very important and can influence the actions of the various parties. Trust in a person's social relations is crucial when it comes to embeddedness in transnational entrepreneurship. In a small-scale business, where most often do not have the needed managerial capabilities to engage in corporation, trust can be used to avoid loses that might come as a result of someone's misconduct.

To amass everything on this part, social relations allow entrepreneurs to get access to the contacts and information they need to know to enhance their idea sharing and take necessary steps. Social relations in this type of business guide the entrepreneurs through specific network of inter-personal ties. Many Ghanaian transnational entrepreneurs rely on social ties back home to have a business in a particular town or city. From the discussion above, it could be seen that social relation in pre-migration networks are linked to the factors such as the reasons for the migration, the means of migration, the destination and future for both occupational and physical mobility. In a small-scale business, this social network differs and it is sometimes based on the national conditions and the history of migration. Transnational entrepreneurs in Ghana mostly rely on family or colleagues networks to do their businesses.

The Conceptual Framework

The ideas of this research was organised based on Financial Independence; Economic Mobility, Success Perspective and Social Factors (FESS) to achieve the study purpose which is to find out the motives that drive the performance of transnational entrepreneurship among Ghanaians Abroad. Though individuals motives for seeking self-employment are diverse and numerous and might differ on certain points, there are some basic motives common all and they are Economic Mobility, Financial Independence, Success Perspective and Social Factor.

This conceptual framework was chosen because the study adopted both deductive and explanatory approach which focuses on "why or what caused" a phenomenon to occur. Figure 1 depicts the conceptual framework; (Figure 2).

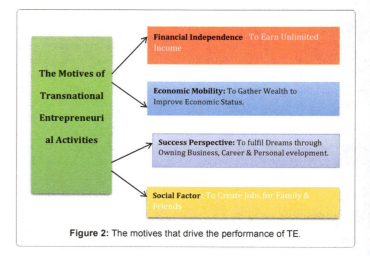

Figure 2: The motives that drive the performance of TE.

What is Economic Mobility? Economic Mobility in this study is viewed as the desire, the passion and the ability to change and rise higher in the economic ladder in terms of wealth and income.

Financial Independence is defined as the state of having the desire to earn unlimited income in order to have sufficient personal wealth to live, without necessarily having to work actively for basic needs and necessities in future.

Success Perspective in this context is defined as the desire, the passion and ability to complete and fulfil the original intent or purpose for your existence or why you were created. From the definition, we could see that success is not only making a lot of money, owning a big car or a big house; but it is also about dream fulfilment, career and personal development and exploitation of endless business opportunities.

Lastly, Social Factor is the desire to perform a community or social responsibilities as a citizen in terms of creating jobs for the family, friends and the general public.

Research Approach

Though there are different empirical and theoretical insights into transnational entrepreneurship, I decided to approach this topic in a way that would allow me to discover the factors that drive the performance of transnational entrepreneurship among Ghanaians abroad.

The paper adopted both deductive and exploratory approach. As a Ghanaian transnational businessman, consultant, lecturer and researcher in this field, this approach was guided by my personal experience. The approach was appropriate for gaining an insight and understanding of the kind of motives, reasons, and drivers for transnational entrepreneurship. Smith [44] argued that an exploratory approach to transnational entrepreneurship is appropriate, most especially for research that focuses on African country like Ghana.

The researcher also used a survey strategy to collect data from Ghanaian transnational entrepreneurs who were engaging continuously in cross-border economic transaction between United Kingdom, USA and Ghana. The aim was to figure out the various motives, reasons, and drivers that pushed these people into this kind of business and the kind of mobility involved.

Methodology

Using data collected from Ghanaians living in the United Kingdom, and the USA; this research examined the motives that drive the performance of transnational entrepreneurship, the mobility involved and why such businesses normally fail.

In 2012, I carried-out a field research by interviewing Ghanaians living in Europe; more precisely, United Kingdom on their motives for the involvement in transnational entrepreneurial activities. At the start of the studies, I made use of the exploratory and open character of semi-structured interviews. Those I interviewed were the entrepreneurs who were active in a myriad of economic sectors (Table 3). Most of the interviewees were mobile in different ways and had created different ways of administering their businesses. In view of this, I primarily obtained an overview of their fields, its diversity and complexity. The Population of the study included;

Data collection was done based on questionnaires and interviews. These two instruments were selected because they are cheap, quick and provide moderately high measurement validity. The questionnaires were designed based on the extensive fieldwork and existing literature

Sector	Sample Size	Percentage (%)
Restaurant Operators	30	25
Car Dealers	5	4
Others like Beer Bar Operators	15	13
Second Hand Clothing Dealers	60	50
Micro-Finance Operators	5	4
Educational Operators	5	4
TOTAL	**120**	**100**

Table 3: Population of respondents.

and were grouped into demographic; personal and work experiences in abroad dimension; general perception about Ghana's business environment; family lives and transnational experience. There was pre-test on a few individuals and the pre-test revealed that many Ghanaians abroad were not comfortable with the filling of surveys like placing numbers in likert scales. In view of that, the researcher adopted many closed-ended questions with fixed response groups.

The interviews on the other-hand were done in London and Oxford in the United Kingdom respectively. The one which was done in London was done in three public forums in a Ghanaian community in London, while the one in Oxford was done on Sundays after church services in 2012-2013. The interview continued in 2015-2016 through Social Network Sites such as Facebook, Twitter, Google+ and Whatsapp with friends who were into transnational entrepreneurships. The interviews were done with four people due to their proximity to the researcher. Out of the four people interviewed, three (3) of them were living in the UK and One (1) lives in the USA.

In an attempt to ensure respondents understanding of the topic, the researcher explained transnational entrepreneurship in both English and Akan language in the questionnaire as "those who reside in Europe and America; and frequently move between their home country and the various countries of destination for the success of their businesses". In Akan "W)n a)te akwantuo w) Englesi-Bronikurom ne America, na) di ak)neaba w) Ghana ne aburokyirman so; esan se won ndwuma bek) so nti".

Findings and Discussions

Characteristics of the Respondents

The Table 4 shows the demographic variables and descriptions of the 76 respondents who took part in the study. The aim of this table was to answer the research questions on demographical variables of the respondents based on gender; age, education, ethnic background, business location in Ghana, employment status, the kind of business they are involved and the person who manages their businesses in Ghana.

A total of 76 questionnaires were returned out of 120 distributed questionnaires; giving a response rate of 63.3%. The majority of the respondents were males representing 65.79% and the least were female representing 34.21%. The results demonstrate that most of the respondents came from the age groups of 45-60 years representing 46.05%. The least were the young respondents with then age groups of 18-30 representing 14.47% of the respondents. Other respondents came from age groups of 30-45 representing (23.68%) and over 60 years were 15.79%. The findings also indicated that majority of the respondents in this study held bachelor's degrees (39.47%), followed by Master's degrees (30.26%), followed by Ph.D. (11.84%) and those held professional diploma qualifications in the field of specialization represented 10.53%. The other respondents that took part in the study were high school certificates holders (7.89%).

Variables	Descriptions	Frequency/Percentage
Are You Transnational Entrepreneur? (N=120)	(1) Yes	76 (63.3%)
	(2) No /	42 (35%)
	(3) No Answer	2 (1.67%)
If you answered yes, then continue please. (n=76)		
Gender	(1) Male	50 (65.79%)
	(2) Female	26 (34.21%)
How old are you? (Age)	(1) 18-30	11 (14.47%)
	(2) 30-45	18 (23.68%)
	(3) 45-60	35 (46.05%)
	(4) 60-65+	12 (15.79%)
Education	(1) Ph.D.	9 (11.84%)
	(2) MBA/MSc/MA,	23 (30.26%)
	(3) BA/Bed.	30 (39.47%)
	(4) Diploma	8 (10.53%)
	(5) High School/below	6 (7.89%)
Ethnic Background	(1) Ashanti,	40 (52.63%)
	(2) Greater Accra,	21 (27.63%)
	(3) Brong Ahafo,	6 (7.89%)
	(4) Others	9 (11.84%)
Parent Business Location in Ghana	(1) Kumasi,	30 (39.47%)
	(2) Accra,	33 (43.42%)
	(3) Sunyani,	3 (3.95%)
	(4) Others	10 (13.16%)
Employment Status	(1) Full Time	15 (19.74.%)
	(2) Part-Time	17 (22.37%)
	(3) Self-Employed	25 (32.89%)
	(4) Not Working	19 (25%)
What kind of business are you into?	(1) Service Business	26 (34.21%)
	(2) Merchandising Business	45 (59.21%)
	(3) Manufacturing Business	8 (10.53%)
Who Manages Your Business in Ghana?	(1) Family	45 (59.21%)
	(2) Old School Friend	13 (17.11%)
	(3) Church Member/Pastor	14 (18.42%)
	(4) Other	4 (5.26%)

Table 4: Demographic variables and descriptions.

The results show that most of the respondents came from Ashanti region with a frequency rate of 40 (52.63%); followed by the Greater Accra region (27.65%), Brong-Ahafo region came third with 7.89% and 11.84% represented the other seven regions in Ghana. This explains that Ashanti Region population in Ghana are more into transnational entrepreneurial activities than any other region in Ghana-West Africa.

"One of the interviewees, Mr. Lawrence Opoku-a family business-providing a service for transnational exchange told me "I am the owner of a cargo business, called Agyakoo shipping logistic. I offer the service of shipping goods from here in UK to Ghana. I have a brother back home who manages the business. I have three branches in Ghana; Kumasi, Accra and Sunyani but my main office is in Kumasi. Why did you enter into transnational entrepreneurship? He laughed and said-You know I am an Ashanti guy and doing business is my hobby" (Interview with Mr. Opoku, August, 2013)".

The results also demonstrate that majority of the respondents were self-employed (32.89%); followed by 22.37% of part time workers, 19.74% full-time workers and 25% represented the respondents who were not working and only concentrating on their businesses.

When it comes to the kind of businesses they were involved; the results show that, the majority of the respondents 45 (59.21%) were into merchandising businesses. Merchandising business in this context refers to the kind of business in which entrepreneurs buy products at wholesale price and sells the same at retail price. These entrepreneurs make profit by selling the products at prices higher than the purchase costs. This system is called "buy and sell" businesses. In Ghana it is called "*t)-na-t)n*" in Akan language. They purchase goods such as second-hand clothes, tvs, computers, cars, spare parts, phones and accessories, and send them to Ghana where their representatives help to sell them. "According to Nana Kwaku, a spare parts dealer in Oxford told me that "I make lots of profit by selling these products at prices higher than their purchase costs (Interview with Nana Kwaku, August, 2013". A merchandising business sells a product without changing its form. Notable examples are convenience stores, grocery stores, distributors and other sellers.

The second majority of the respondents were into service business with a frequency rate of 26 (34.21%). A service business is another type of business which provides intangible products (that's products with no physical form). This type of business offers professional expertise, skills and other similar products. Notable examples of such businesses include hair salons, banks, micro finance, accounting firms, law firms, repair shops, schools, and many more. The least of the respondents (10.53%) were involved in manufacturing businesses. In manufacturing businesses, the business owner purchases products in a form of raw materials with the intention of using them to make or produce a new product. A manufacturing business combines raw materials, labour, and factory overheads in its production process. The manufactured goods will then be sold to customers.

In a quest to answer "who manages their businesses?" the majority of the respondents (59.21%) agreed that family members run their businesses in their absence. In a transnational business structure, the entrepreneurs achieve integration by appointing specific type of managers. The country or regional managers act as a focal point for customers and oversee all products and functions performed their area. Conversely, the managers oversee the activities of a particular function such as marketing, technology, or manufacturing. The remainder of the respondents were drawn from church members/pastors (18.42%); old-school friends (17.11%); and others (5.26%), all in the name of trust.

One of the interviewees, Juliana Amoakowaa explained that upon establishment of the business, she was required to identify a reliable person who could be trusted and administer the daily affairs of the business in her absence. This activity is what Mazzucato defined as a "double engagement". It is double engagement because she is engaged in economic activities of two countries. See the conversation that went on between the researcher and Miss Juliana Amoakowaa;

"For me (Juliana Amoakowaa Speaks) "I purchase goods in this country and send them to Ghana where my representatives (my mum & siblings) help to sell them. Though engaging in this kind of business can be frustrating and difficult, yet I am motivated to do it. Amoakowaa lives in London (Waterloo). According to her "I am the head of Amoakowaa second-hand clothing's in Ashtown-Kumasi. How did you get this entrepreneurial idea? I got the idea of establishing this business in Ghana from my mum, Maame Amoakowaa. Oh so your mum helped you! She replied, Yes! My mum helped me to set the business in Kumasi. What do you do? I buy second-hand clothes here in UK and send them to Ghana. I distribute the "fos bail" as in Akan to over 20 people within Kumasi metropolis. What do you do to keep the business moving since you are here in London? I am constantly on telephone conversation with my mum and siblings to keep myself informed about the business. Though I am in London, I still take responsibilities for certain things that cannot be handled by my old mum. I also fly to Ghana every year to see the welfare of the business".

Wow! This proves that social relations are very important in this type of business. But wait! Look at how difficult this kind of business could be: always on phone and to the extent of travelling to Ghana every year, all because of her business. Hmmmm! If that is the case, then what really drives them to engage in this kind of entrepreneurial activities? This set the grounds for the main objective of this study "*What are the motives that drive the performance of transnational entrepreneurship?*"

Motives that Drives the Performance of Transnational Entrepreneurship

This research is aimed at assessing the motives behind the performance of transnational entrepreneurship among Ghanaians abroad on the basis of financial independence, economic mobility, social factors, and success perspective. The respondents were asked to measure the motives for the performance of transnational entrepreneurship based on a scale of 1-4, with average scores less than 2 means "it doesn't form part of the motives that drive the performance of transnational entrepreneurship". The results were tabulated in Table 5 below.

The results show that the overall mean score for the respondents on economic mobility was 2.4. Economic mobility in this study refers to the individual's ability to gather wealth to improve their economic status through business creation or any other legal means and it is usually measured in income. Though the overall rating was 2.4, there was a consensus among the respondents on economic mobility because the range of perspective among the participants was small from 2.2 to 2.8. Statistically, however, there was a significant difference when ANOVA Analysis was conducted and that's $F_{(4, 30)}=0.74$, $P<0.05$. Interestingly, the respondents from Auto-Mobile Industries (2.8) rated the performance of economic mobility higher than Restaurant Operators (2.2) and that shows extreme side of range. To amass everything, we can easily see from the table that economic mobility is one of the motives that drive the performance of transnational entrepreneurship among Ghanaians abroad since the figures were all above 2.0 with exception of "Others" that did not rate it at all.

On the Financial Independence perspective, the overall means score was 2.9 which shows that the respondents viewed financial independence as one of the main reasons that drives the performance of transnational entrepreneurship among Ghanaians abroad. From the figures in the table, it is obvious that though, the overall rating was 2.9; there is a huge gap of perspective among the respondents from 2.4 to 3.3. Interestingly, the Auto-Mobile Dealers rated the performance of financial independence higher (3.3) than the Micro-Finance Operators and these differences are not statistically significant, $F_{(5, 69)} =4.99$, $P>.0.5$. In general, the overall rating on financial independence was very convincing signifying that most Ghanaians entered into transnational entrepreneurship with the potential aim of earning unlimited income.

The overall mean score for the respondents on the Success Factors was 2.8. This means that the respondents viewed Success Factors as one of the significant motives that drives the performance of the transnational entrepreneurial ventures. This means many migrants venture into transnational entrepreneurship because they want society to see their success in life through owning a business (that's "be their own bosses"), manage their own time as part of fulfilling their dreams. The respondents declared that entering into transnational entrepreneurship was an avenue to fulfil their dreams. Though the overall rating was 2.8, there was a wide range of perspective among the respondents from 2.4 to 3.2. Based on the table stats, Restaurant Operators (3.2) rated the Success factors higher Auto-Mobile Dealers (2.4) and Educational Operators (2.4). More so, these differences are statistically significant since $F_{(5, 70)}=1.86$, $p<0.5$. The rating 2.8 on success factors was not a surprise figure from the respondents because the respondents have made it clear that they want to have unlimited income by rating financial independence 2.9.

Many of the interviewees who also filled the questionnaires explained that they were tired of the corporate set-up and the early morning wake-up all in the name of beating time to work. They also argued that they ventured into transnational entrepreneurship in order to manage their own time and this has made them more flexible to work on their businesses and other ventures. According to them, they had busy schedules when they were working for someone but now they have been able to turn their hobbies into business opportunities. Success has been the main motive that drives the performance to explore endless business opportunities.

The results also show that the overall mean score for the 73 respondents under the social factors was 2.2 out of 4.0 grading point. This means that the 73 respondents viewed the social factors as one of the motives that drive the performance of transnational entrepreneurship among Ghanaians abroad. Though the overall rating was 2.2, there was a wide range of perspective among the respondents from 1.6 to 2.9. Respondents operating restaurants interestingly rated social factors higher (2.9) than Second-Hand Clothes Dealers (1.6). Based on ANOVA analysis results, these differences are statistically significant, $F_{(4, 30)}=1.88$, $p<0.5$. One of the restaurant operators who rated social factors higher than any others explained that one of the motives of going into business was to create jobs for the 5.5% unemployment rate in Ghana. To them entering into transnational entrepreneurship has helped them to create more jobs for their families and friends back home. Entering into transnational entrepreneurship is an avenue to help society and people and the entire Ghanaian economy to thrive.

Summary and Conclusion

The study assessed the motives that drive the performance of transnational entrepreneurship among Ghanaians abroad. The study began with a brief history of Ghana its economy and employment status. The study further reviewed and discussed the meaning of transnational entrepreneurship, and the link between migration and

Perspectives	Restaurant Operators	Auto-Mobile Dealers	Second-Hand clothes Dealers	Educational Operators	Micro-Finance Operators	Others e.g. Beer Stations Operators	Mean Score
Economic Mobility	2.2	2.8	2.3	2.4	2.4	n/a	2.4
Financial Independence	2.6	3.3	2.6	2.5	2.4	3.1	2.9
Success Factors	3.2	2.4	2.8	2.4	2.7	2.8	2.8
Social Factors	2.9	2.6	1.6	2.1	2.1	n/a	2.2
Mean Score	2.5	3	2.3	2.4	2.4	3	2.6

Table 5: Results from respondent's survey.

entrepreneurial ventures. It discussed the kind of influence social relations such as family, friends and ethnic background have on such entrepreneurial activities. The study also talked about the kind of business and the industry these entrepreneurs are engaged in and the mobility involved. The motives that drive the performance of transnational entrepreneurial activities among Ghanaians were also discussed on the basis of Economic Mobility; Financial Independence; Success Perspective and Social Factors.

The study has proven that most of the transnational entrepreneurs from Ghana are into small-medium business establishment as referred in the literature review earlier. It was discovered that operating in two different countries can increase their ability to discover opportunities, develop experience and make connections. The study also revealed that migration exposes individuals to some important information which can help them to build upon their skills and knowledge. These are the reasons why most entrepreneurs extend their businesses beyond ethnic boundaries and operate within the corridors of two countries simultaneously [45].

The study revealed that the successes of transnational entrepreneurial activities depend on individual characteristics, institutional regulations, firm organisation, and the external environment. The findings showed that, in Ghana, most successful transnational entrepreneurs are male, educated and middle aged. Kiggundu explained that education, work experience, training, overseas visits, apprenticeship and other human development initiatives are influential factors for entrepreneurial failure or success. The study disclosed that social relations provide the individual entrepreneur the intellectual, economic, emotional and spiritual support to do their business. We learnt that the majority of the respondents agreed that their family members run their businesses in their absence.

Recommendation

Based on the above findings, it is recommended that transnational entrepreneurs should adopt the various points below on the "Factors to Ensure Successful Entrepreneurial Economic Activities" written by Drori [45]. There are five theoretical factors that can help transnational entrepreneurs to enjoy successful entrepreneurial economic activities. They continued that this framework influences individual entrepreneur's capabilities and resources.

➢ According to Drori [45], agency approach is very crucial and should be outlined when talking about the embeddedness of transnational entrepreneurs in the context of both foreign country and their country of origin. The agency in this context needs special attention to handle both political and socio-economic resources like class, state, family and network on multiple levels, assessing simultaneous operations in at least two social contexts.

➢ Secondly, it is argued that transnational entrepreneurship needs three (3) domains for their network formation and they are: network of industry, network of destination and network of home of origin (national & ethnic). They believe that acquiring this information from both host country and home of origin can influence their capability of exploiting certain chances differently. This is what they referred to as social capital and network perspective. Another factor is based on cultural perspective. Culture repertoires that deals with the entire range of skills used in occupation also influences transnational entrepreneurs' entrepreneurial actions. The skills and aptitudes acquired through multi-culture encountered, entrepreneurs are able to adapt, modify or elaborate the rules to new circumstances.

➢ More so, power-relations perspective is very important when it comes to factors that influence transnational entrepreneurs' individual capabilities and resources. Inherently, the business strategies of these entrepreneurs bear political consequences and meanings. Drori [45] pinpointed that power-relations underlines the strategic position these entrepreneurs can obtain through leveraging the political atmosphere in the two countries. This implies that the dimension of this perspective shape the meaning and the choice attached to a specific form of transnational entrepreneurs.

➢ The last factor Drori [45] talked about was based on institutional perspective. According them, the institutional perspective can be differentiated based on emerging market and developed economies. From the institutional perspective, transnational entrepreneurs should bear in mind that since different market economy demands different strategy to operate, it would only takes those who understands the rules of the game to perform better in their business ventures. Every transnational entrepreneur needs to study these carefully because it will help them to understand the actions and logics, rules and practices that coordinate and govern human and organisational activities in certain national context.

Limitation and Future Research

While interpreting the findings of the research, it is necessary to know the limitations of this study. The first deals with the sample for the study which was drawn from immigrant entrepreneurs from Ghana. Also the research was designed cross-sectional; therefore, it is subject to hindrances of cross-sectional studies. The study is subjected to the bias of the respondents, therefore, 100% accuracy cannot be guaranteed.

In future, other researchers can also research on the following questions: what is the role diaspora and immigration in transnational entrepreneurship? Does transnational entrepreneurship concentrate on particular markets or location? What kinds of international resource flows are associated with transnational entrepreneurship?

References

1. BBC News (2017) Ghana Country Profile.
2. Anarfi JK, Kpakpa M (2013) Migration Urbanization (Chapter 10) in the 2010 Population and Housing Census, Ghana Statistical Service. National Analytical Report.
3. Hisrich RD (2005) Entrepreneurship (7th edn). Boston.
4. Daniels L, Mead DC (1998) The Contribution of Small Enterprises to Household and National Income in Kenya. Economic Development and Cultural Change 47: 45-71.
5. Kayanula D, Quartey P (2000) The Policy Environment for Promoting Small and Medium-Sized Enterprises in Ghana and Malawi. IDPM Finance and Development Research Programme Working Paper Series 15.
6. Black R, Castaldo A (2009) Return migration and entrepreneurship in Ghana and Côte d'Ivoire: the role of capital transfers. Tijdschrift voor economische en sociale geografie 100: 44-58.
7. Black R (2004) Migration Pro-poor Policy in Africa.
8. Anarfi JK (2000) Push and Pull Factors of International Migration. Country Report: Ghana. Eurostat Working Papers.
9. Lucas D, Morris M (2007) Towards a Synthesis. A Model of Immigrant and Ethnic Entrepreneurship. In: Dana L ed., Handbook of research on the ethnic minority entrepreneurship. A Co-Evolutionary View on Resource Management, Cheltenham, UK pp: 803-811
10. Saxenian A (2002) Transnational Communities and the Evolution of Global Production Networks. The Cases of Taiwan, China India. Industry and Innovation 9: 183-202.

11. Portes A (2002) Transnational Entrepreneurs: An Alternative Form of Immigrant Economic Adaptation. American Sociological Review 67: 278-298.

12. Bridge S (1998) Understanding enterprise: entrepreneurship and small business. Palgrave, New York.

13. Drori I (2009) Transnational Entrepreneurship. An Emergent Field of Study. Entrepreneurship Theory and Practice 33: 1001-1022.

14. Cronje GJ (1996) Introduction to Business Management. International Thompson Publishing, Johannesburg.

15. Fuller DB (2010) Networks Nations: The Interplay of Transnational Networks Domestic Institutions in China's Chip Design Industry. Int J Technol Manag 51: 239-257.

16. Min PG (1990) Problems of Korean Immigrant Entrepreneurs. International Migration Review 24: 436-455.

17. Light I (2002) Transnational and American Exports in an English-Speaking World. International Migration Review 36: 702-725.

18. Wong LL, Ng M (2000) The Emergence of Small Transnational Enterprise in Vancouver. The Case of Chinese Enterpreneur Immigrants. International Journal of Urban and Regional Research 26: 508-530.

19. Sequeira JM (2009) Transnational Entrepreneurship: Determinants of firm type and owner attributions of Success. Entrepreneurship: Theory and Practice 33: 1023-1044.

20. Mazzucato V (2006) Transnational Migration the Economy of Funerals: Changing Practices in Ghana. Development Change 37: 1047-1072.

21. Leung MWH (2004) Chinese Migration in Germany: Making Home in Transnational Space. Frankfurtiko Verlag.

22. Hatton TJ, Williamson JG (2003) What Fundamentals Drive World Migration. Wider Discussion Paper pp: 15-38.

23. Littunen H (2000) Entrepreneurship the Characteristics of the Entrepreneurial Personality. International Journal of Entrepreneurial Behaviour and Research 6: 295-3009.

24. Cicagna C, Sulis G (2006) On the Potential Interaction between Labour Market Institutions and Immigration Policies. International Journal of Manpower 36: 441-468.

25. Sam GA (2013) Remittances from Abroad. The Ghanaian Household Perspective. International Journal of Business Services 4: 1-7.

26. Beauchemin C, Schoumaker B (2005) Migration to Cities in Burkina Faso. Does the Level of Development in Sending Areas Matter? World Development 33: 1129-1152.

27. Min PG, Bozorgmehr M (2003) United States: Entrepreneurial Cutting Edge. Immigrant entrepreneurs: Venturing abroad in the age of globalization, pp: 17-37.

28. McComick B, Wahba J (2003) Return International Migration and Geographical Inequality. The Case of Egypt. Journal of African Economies 12: 500-532.

29. Portes A, Sensenbrenner J (1993) Embeddedness Immigration. Notes on the Social Determinants of Economic Action. American Journal of Sociology 98: 1320-1350.

30. Faist T (2000) The Volume and Dynamics of International Migration and Transnational Social Spaces. Oxford, Clarendon Press, UK.

31. Faist T, Siereking N (2011) Unravelling Migrants as Transnational Agents of Development: Social Spaces in Between Ghana Germany. Munster: Lit-Verlag.

32. Chrrysostome E, Xiaohua L (2010) Immigrant Entrepreneurship: Scrutinising a Promosing Type of Business Venture. Thunderbird International Business Review 52: 77-82.

33. Kivisto P (2001) Theorizing Transnational Immigration: A Critical Review of Current Efforts. Ethn Racial Stus 24: 549-577.

34. Granovetter M (1985) Economic Action Social Structure: The Problem of Embeddedness. American Journal of Sociology 91: 481-510.

35. Granovetter M (1995) The Economic Sociology of Firms Entrepreneurs, pp. in Portes, A. (ED), The Economic Sociology of Immigrant Essays on Networks, Ethnicity Entrepreneurship. Russel Sage Foundation, New York pp: 128-165.

36. Kim S, Zhou M (2006) Community Forces, Social Capital Educational Achievement: The Case of Supplementary Education in the Chinese Korean Migrant Communities. Harvard Educational Review 76: 1-29.

37. Nijkamp P (2009) Cultural Diversity and Urban Innovativeness. Personal Business Characteristics of Urban Migrant Entrepreneurs Innovation: The European Journal of Social Sciences 22: 251-281.

38. Cassini S (2005) Negotiating Personal Success and Social Responsibility: Assessing the Developmental Impact of Ghanaian Migrants' Business Enterprises in Ghana. International School of Humanities and Social Sciences.

39. Buane SK (1996) Entrepreneurship: A Contextual Perspective. Lund Universty Press, Lund.

40. Mitchell JC (1969) Social Networks in Urban Situations. Analysis of Personal Relationships in Central Africa Towns. Manchester University Press, Manchester.

41. Ley D (2006) Explaining Variations in Business Performance Among Immigrant Entre preneurs in Canada. J Ethn Migr Stud 32: 743-764.

42. Lewis P (1994) Economic Statism. Private Capital and the Dilemmas of Accumulation in Nigeria. World Development 22: 437-451.

43. Kloosterman R, Rath J (2003) Immigrant Entrepreneurs. Venturing Abroad in the Age of Globalization. Oxford, New York.

44. Smith RC (2003) Diasporic Membership in Historical Perspective: Comparative Insights from the Mexican, Italian, Polish Cases. Int Migr Rev 37: 722-759.

45. Drori I (2006) Transnational Entrepreneurship: Toward a Unifying Theoretical Framework. Academy of Management Proceedings 1: Q1-Q6.

The Influence of Decision Making in Organizational Leadership and Management Activities

Nichodemus Obioma Ejimabo*
Wayland Baptist University Fairbanks, Alaska, USA

Abstract

This study explores the influence of decision making in organizational leadership and management activities that impact creativity, growth and effectiveness, success, and goal accomplishments in current organizations. The purpose of this qualitative critical ethnographic study was focused on identifying the factors influencing success in decision making among organizational leaders and managers in organizations' practices. The qualitative paradigm was used in order to gain in-depth knowledge and understanding of the issues and challenges influencing effectiveness, and success among organizational leadership and managements in business practices. The author being committed and determined to discovering a pattern of meaning through experience, systemic thinking, assessment, and creative analysis used the Kurt Lewin leadership philosophical underpinning approaches of leadership namely: autocratic, democratic, and laissez-faire methods of leadership decision making processes in the context of this study, with the aim of discovering the main factors rather than specific variables and outcomes affecting decision making among business leaders. Approximately, four hundred past and current business executives and managements participated in this study. Data was collected through structured interviews and surveys. The results that emerged from the data indicated that there is a great need for change and improvement in decision making among organizational executives while accommodating technology, diversity, globalization, policy, teamwork, and leadership effectiveness.

Keywords: Teamwork; Leadership; Management; Decision-making; Policy; Communication; Organizational growth; Ethics and leadership activities

Introduction

In general, leadership decision making (LDM) among other qualities and functions of a leader offers an ongoing creativity and important new insights into leadership and management activities in all organizational operations. The purpose of this study was focused on identifying the factors influencing success in decision making among organizational executives, leaders, mangers, and supervisors in organizations' practices. Organization is undoubtedly a systemic network that is both complex and dynamic in nature. In organizations, tough quality and sound decision making are the major element and essence of leadership. The other goal of this work is to discover a scientific break-through which is based on the experience, knowledge, and the skills of the selected participants of this study with the aim of improving quality decision making among leaders and overall accomplishment of organizational goals, objectives, and performance. In this regard and for effectiveness, a leader must have self confidence in order to gather and process information and solve problems. For them a person riddled with self-doubt would never be able to take the necessary actions nor command the respect of others. Leaders must know what decisions to make and keep the interest of all stakeholders involved. Followers will be less committed to the team if the leader doubts their decisions. They must show followers that they are able to acknowledge when they are wrong and move forward to a better solution. In discussing the statement of the problem; bad policy and inconsistence in decisions making are among the major challenges in organizational systems and have created many unresolved problems among leaders and their employees in our current workplace and entire society. The inabilities of some leaders in developing good policy standards, knowledge, basis, protocols, environments, and skill that incorporate support and optimal decision design for their organizations is troubling and have caused the closure of many business in the country due to either law suit or mismanagement. Another significant problem that encouraged this work is the lack of knowledge on how to design positive decision environment, healthy communication skills, and essential tools for leadership decision making in the entire organization. Many leadership practitioners and scholars believed that any organization faced with negative policy and decisions by its leadership and management will continue to fail, their people will be often left to ponder the cause, and that organization would be unproductive in their business while giving way to employees to break the circle for both job performance and goal accomplishment. For instance [1], said, "Authentic leaders exemplify high moral standards, integrity, honesty, and authentic leaders acknowledge their personal limitations and shortcomings, and are therefore less likely to adopt a defensive attitude about organizational problems". Furthermore, creative policy development and decision making among organizational leaders and management are of vital importance to the growth, development, and success of any business establishments. For instance, choosing the best alternative from many alternatives and making a good decision in critical matters and challenging situations is always a good strategy of solving problems in most organizations. Thus, the problem in most organizations is that problems tend to present themselves in non-associated symptoms. And the tendency of organizational members and business executives is often to address symptoms of the problem irrespective of the facts that members may "know" that the problem they are addressing is just a mere symptom. This point contributes among other factors, one of the major loopholes in decision making by managements and organizational leaders. However, being able to see problems from a

---

***Corresponding author:** Nichodemus Obioma Ejimabo, Wayland Baptist University Fairbanks, Alaska, USA, E-mail: nickejimsmith@yahoo.com

variety of other perspectives from within the organization allows for a better understanding of the problem [2].

There is a plethora of studies on different topics on organizational leadership and decision making. However, there is a gap in literature particularly on leadership decision making and the variations that exist on the manner, perceptions, skills, and processes used in making decisions.

This qualitative ethnography study was centered on identifying the factors influencing success in decision making among organizational executives, leaders, mangers, and supervisors in organizations' practices and effectiveness. This method allowed the researcher to see and work with the participants from both their natural environment and cultural individual settings. By using this method, the researcher did not seek to conduct full contextual description but rather looked for patterns in meaning as well as similarities and differences that lead to contextualization, categorization and eventual theoretical codes and relationship among concepts that explained this variation. He also examined some leaders' attributes while being determined to provide a framework for helping organizational leaders and executive managers the ability to choose who should make distinct decisions in various critical and challenging situations. This work was designed to discover a concrete, effective, efficient, unambiguous, and useful means to know and use to implement each leadership decision processes that the situation deems fitting well in the company's problems. It was also the hope of the researcher to find a distinct, precise, and concise (separating oranges and apples) way to tailor solutions to fit the needs of the individual employees and employers based on their leadership and learning styles; mission and vision; strategic objectives, and goal accomplishment. A nationwide study of four hundred past and current business executives, leaders, and managements participated in this study and they identified some factors that influenced their decision making in their respective organizations.

This work was also aimed at showing that the establishment and implementation of a proper policy and decisions that will influence the organizational leadership and management must include a review of the existing policies, strategies, and standards to ensure that leaders, managers, supervisors, and employees will continue to achieve an efficient and effective role in both performance management and goals accomplishment in the system. The best approach to lead, and manage an organization effectively is to understand the organization in all its entity, and its growth, success, and goal accomplishments will be based solely on the policy, mission, and vision of the organization. A good understanding and the establishment of sound decisions and policies are very important for organizational leadership activities and reform [3]. Sound decision making in every organization must be for leaders and managers the direct result of knowing their criteria for success, the scope of their choices, and the inherent risk of each alternative [4].

Meaning and Definition of Leadership and Decision Making

According to [5], the term leadership is a word taken from the common vocabulary and incorporated into the technical vocabulary of a scientific discipline without being precisely redefined. Both leadership and decision making are terms that are seriously considered to be of vital in the operations of any organization, society, and country. These terms have been a major topic of research in both psychology, social sciences, and other disciplines for almost a century and has spawned thousands of empirical and conceptual studies. They have gained the attention of researchers worldwide and are expensive terms with many (different) meanings, definitions, and applications in which case one size does not necessarily fit all. There are almost as many definitions of leadership (and decision making) as there are persons who have attempted to define the concept [6]. Because of their importance, usefulness, and value; many people have tried to define them differently to suit their situation, individual or group interests, positions, perspectives, and circumstances while creating a pattern of meaning as well as maintaining their effectiveness in any organizational activities and practices. While the term "leadership" is associated with influence and the ability to empower, encourage, support, and help others by an individual or group of individuals to accomplish a goal; decision making as a theory is focused exclusively choice and the ability of the leader to select the best alternative from the many options [7]. How to integrate the two processes has emerged as a complex and important issue in the organizational literature [8].

Below are some the ways different scholars had defined the above terms:

• Leadership is a process whereby an individual influences a group of individuals to achieve a common goal [9].

• Leadership is the process of making sense of what people are doing together so that people will understand and be committed [10].

• Leadership is the process of influencing others to understand and agree about what needs to be done and how to do it, and the process of facilitating individual and collective efforts to accomplish shared objectives [5].

• "Leadership is a process of giving purpose (meaningful direction) to collective effort, and causing willing effort to be expended to achieve purpose" [11].

• Decision making is a deliberative and decisive social action, concerned with choosing what to do in the face of a problem [12,13].

• Decision making is a choice from among two or more alternative courses of action, or objects, giving due regard to the advantages and disadvantages of supporting information about each" (http://www.merriam-webster.com/dictionary/decision).

• Leadership decision making is an intendedly rational human choice leading to human action embodying the logic of consequence (March, 1991).

• Decision making is a commitment to action, a discrete and concrete phenomenon driven by rationality [13].

In this study, leadership decision making (LDM) is defined as a dynamic process of choosing from the best different alternatives and associated with the systemic act of making a choice. In organizational worldview, decision making has been a serious educational and organizational issue for many years and had continued to baffle many researchers as they look for creative and effective solution for this profound societal and organizational challenge. Therefore, to understand organizational decision making process, leadership must define what the future should look like, aligns with that vision, and inspire them to make it happen despite the challenges and obstacles involved. Leaders must know how to lead as well as manage, otherwise, without leading as well as managing effectively, today's organizations will face the threat of extinction [14]. Thus, leaders and workers in every organization should be influenced by their policy and decisions while working together to attain strategic goals and objectives. Complexity and other factors or challenges had shown that there is a great need for the development and implementation of proper policy by organizational leaders. Basically, some recent studies have shown that decision making has a central role to play in developing and influencing organizational activities. These activities include healthy working environment and trust that helps in developing effective communication and openness in the relationship between employees and management; between superiors and subordinates; between trade union and management; and among workers in the workplace [15].

The Theoretical Framework of Kurt Lewin

The author used the theoretical framework of psychologist Kurt Lewin methods of leadership behavioral styles and decision making processes in the context of this study, with the aim of using them in discovering the main factors rather than specific variables and outcomes affecting decision making among business leaders. Lewin 's theories of " leadership styles and their effects" in collaboration with colleagues Lippitt and White carried out research relating to the effects of three different leadership styles on active boys' activity group in Iowa-1939. His thinking was changing to emphasize social psychological problems. These school-children were assigned to one of three groups with an authoritarian, democratic or laissez-fair leader. The children were then led in an arts and crafts project while researchers observed the behavior of children in response to the different styles of leadership. He is well known for his term "life space" and work on group dynamics, as well as T-groups. Lewin's commitment to applying psychology to the problems of society led to the development of the M.I.T. Research Center for Group Dynamics - "He wanted to reach beyond the mere description of group life and to investigate the conditions and forces which bring about change or resist it" [16].

The Kurt Lewin's three leadership styles or behaviors, described below, influence the leader-follower relationship, group success, group risk-taking, group problem-solving strategies, group morale, and group. The three different leadership styles which are namely; autocratic (authoritative), participative (democratic), and delegative (laissez-faire) are described in (Figure 1).

Although everyone makes decisions on a daily and regular basis, but the clear understanding of the role that authoritarian, democratic, and laissez-faire leadership styles play in groups is vital background for all those interested in leadership, management, and the sociology of social interaction in groups and organizations. While these decisions are made in our personal and professional lives; various factors influence leaders and managers' decisions in their individual workplace. Leaders choose their paths based on their style of decision-making. The above Lewin 's three major leadership styles in Figure 1 was designed to show that it is possible for both leaders and manager of any organization to change their styles, and to be trained to improve their leadership and adopt appropriate management styles for their situation and context [17]. Lewin is now mainly remembered as the originator of the 3-Step model of change [18], and this tends often to be dismissed as outdated [19-24] yet many researchers and leaders still agree that his contribution to our understanding of individual and group behavior and the role these play in organizations and society was enormous and is still relevant in leadership and management practices.

Over the years, the study of organizational behavior has led to a number of useful models for decision making in many businesses. As with decision making and all other organizational issues and challenges, overcoming any kind of small deficiency can help leaders and managers become more dynamic, efficient, and successful in their organizations as well as the society. All groups (employees and employers) must be educated about the relevant needs and concerns of their company in order to produce visionary and dedicated leaders to lead their businesses. For example: a business owner should start out by examining all possible alternatives when making decisions, including the option of doing nothing. Coherent awareness and knowledge in this matter should be established in order to maintain appropriate contingency model that identifies styles of leadership decision making that is useful to the different situations in any working organization [25]. People associated with administration and management in companies must know that decision making process in any organization is somehow complicated and complex in nature.

Major Factors that Influence Leadership Decision Making in Organizations

This work continues to explore the major factors that influence decision making among organizational leaders. Studies designed to examine the positive challenges of good leadership decision making as an ongoing leadership process [9] may have application to any organizational success and goal attainment in the future. Many studies by different professions had shown that there are several important factors that may influence leadership decision making in organizations. These factors include: past experience [26], cognitive biases [27], age and individual differences belief in personal relevance [28], and an escalation of commitment as well as the influence what choices people make.

People make decisions about many things differently and under different circumstance or situation. For example, a decision about a new product may rest with those in product management, manufacturers, marketing research and finance. They make political decisions; personal decisions, including medical choices, romantic decisions, and career decisions; and financial decisions, which may also include some of the other kinds of decisions and judgments. Quite often, the decision making process is fairly specific to the decision being made. Some choices are simple and seem straight forward, while others are complex and require a multi-step approach to making the decisions [29].

Leaders and managers in any organization should weigh all necessary options and the outcomes of their decisions while being aware that each of the decisions made may either affect the organization as a whole, shareholders or any member of the organization. For a sound and comprehensive decision making, leaders should understand that all rational decision making processes requires a great deal of time and a valid sharing or knowledge of information. They should be able to use the best type of leadership decision making style described in Figure 1 to determine the systemic process to apply in any given situation as well as the people or group to be involved in the decision making

Autocratic	Participative	Delegative
• Autocratic leadership, otherwise known as authoritative, is a leadership style by which leaders have absolute control over a group, make choices and all decisions in the organization based on their own ideas and judgments and rarely accept any advice from followers.	• Participative, which is also known as democratic is a leadership style that allows and encourages members of the group to share, express their ideas, and take a more participative role in the decision-making process of the organization.	• Laissez-faire leadership, also known as delegative, also known as laissez-faire is a type of leadership style in which leaders by providing the tools and resources needed (with little guidance) are hands-off and allow group members to make the decisions in their organizations.

Figure 1: Kurt Lewin's three major leadership decision making styles.

process. Since leadership and management activities in organizations involve change, inspiration, motivation, and influence, management and effective leadership, both leaders and managers must then strive to focus on the process of setting and achieving the goals of their businesses through the functions of management, with reference to strategic planning, organizing, directing, controlling, and goal accomplishments.

Despite the factors mentioned above as well as the ones shown in Figure 2 sometimes, some individual differences may also influence decision making. Research as postulated earlier has indicated that age, socioeconomic status, and cognitive abilities influences decision making [30]. For instance, anger, hatred, divorce, death, and other individual challenges and crises may add to the factors that influence leadership decision making in the workplace and other environments.

However, there are many elements and unavoidable factors that influence the leadership decision making process in many organizations in the society, including who makes the decision and the type of leadership styles (Autocratic, participative, or delegative leadership style) used in making the decision. In this study, the most important factor influencing leaderships in their decision making is the systematic process behind decision-making as well as the ongoing complexities associated with it. These factors are mentioned in Figure 2. These identified major factors are affecting the decisions leaders make in their organizations as well as increasing the wave of challenges and inconsistency among the employees in the workplace. Every organization has the chance of being great and successful when all of the employees work toward achieving its goals. Poor leadership decision making is always associated with chaos and conflicts among working people in organizations. Since leadership is focused on the ability to influence others to accomplish a goal, the researcher believed that the quality of decisions exhibited by organizational leaders is a critical determinant of organizational success. Therefore a good leader must be the one who sees the whole picture rather the particular. He/she must be the one who organizes the experience of the group, offers a vision of the future, as well as train followers to become leaders [25]. Thus, the understanding of these factors will empower and enable leaders to be creative and effective in choosing from the best alternatives when making decisions for their businesses as well as the establishment of a healthy working environment for everyone in the their companies.

Although some studies have provided significant insight into the factors, constraints, and obstacles influencing decision making among

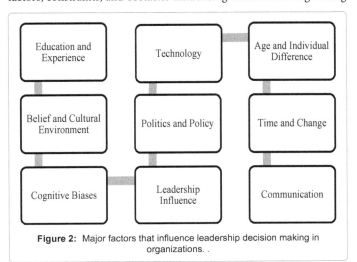

Figure 2: Major factors that influence leadership decision making in organizations.

organizational leadership and management in our society, there is still a need for more studies regarding effective leadership decision making, systemic thinking, creativity, dedication, managerial communication, and accountability to enable improvements and leadership capabilities on business leaders and managers. For instance, Sunstein and Thaler [31] stated that a new general strategy for improving biased decision making has been proposed that leverages our automatic cognitive processes and turns them to our advantage [31]. According to Moore and Loewenstein, some research on joint-versus-separate decision making highlights the fact that our first impulses tend to be more emotional than logical. Shiv and Fedorkihn indicated that some additional suggestive results in this domain include the findings that willpower is weakened when people are placed under extreme cognitive load and when they are inexperienced in a choice domain [32].

In like manner, some recent research have shown that some leaders still lack the education, knowledge, quality, and leadership styles associated with sound decision making in their organizations. They either neglect or ignore decision making processes that are aimed at improving the standard of the strategic plans, mission, vision, and goal attainment of their companies. This work is designed to enable leaders and managers to make good decisions for their business as well as to accomplish their organizational goals while remedying the lack of clarity surrounding the construct of some employees and employers participation in the decision making processes. In order to help our current leaders, educate, and train future leaders, the need has been recognized for integrative research which explicitly considers the impact of context on strategic processes [33].

Support of Literature

The study was aimed at understanding the major factors that influence leadership decision making in organizations. It shows that forms of participation are functional, when a leader has the authority to make decision; when a decision can be made without stringent time limitation; when the subordinate have the relevant knowledge to discuss and implement the decision; as well as when a leader is skilled in the use of participative techniques [34]. To help identify what makes for efficient leadership decision making, a nationwide study of four hundred past and current business executives, leaders, and managements in the United States, participated and identified some factors that influenced their decision making in their respective organizations. This work was based on the perceptions and views of the above selected leaders in discovering the major factors that influence organizational decision making in most businesses across the nation. Making decisions is what leaders and managers do every day in their individual workplace. Thus, apart from individual or group outcomes, leadership decision making is at the heart of virtually all management work and a key driver of organizational outcomes [35-37]. The review of related literatures in this study reveals that leadership decision making in organizations has emerged as one of the most challenging, complex, and active areas of leadership and management future research. Studies of complex social systems suggest that the major reason for (organizational) failure lies in the way decision makers think about and execute the change process [38].

The literature review consists of six main sections, namely: (1) the role of a leader in organizational decision making, (2) understanding the importance of decision-making process, (3) factors influencing leadership decision making, (4) ethics and decision making models, and (5) Communication in decision making.

The literature review enabled the author to identify a resemblance, what has been done and what needs to be investigated with regard to the topic. Understanding the process by which leaders and managers make decisions is important to understanding the decisions they make in organization. Effective leaders and managers often provide an encouraging atmosphere to perk up the performance and efficiency of their followers Leiter and Maslach. As already stated, making decisions in organizations is what leaders and managers do every day in their respective business endeavors. While some choices in decision making process may be seen as being simple and easy in thinking, most of the organizational decisions are complex, challenging, time consuming and often require a multi-step approach to making the right needed decisions by leaders. Although many researchers had argued that the size of organizations can be a factor in the decisions their leaders make. For example: Fredrickson and Iaquinto agreed that larger size is associated with comprehensiveness in organizational strategic decision making. More importantly, Dean and Sharfman as well as the Bradford studies [39] found no differences in strategic decision making process that could be attributed to organizational size.

For this researcher, regardless of the nature and size of the organization, leadership decision making is always of vital importance and special significance because they affect the fate of all employees and the entire system in the organization in one way or the other. For instance, identifying critical situations and making quality leadership decisions on that regard, on behalf of the entire organization has been recognized by both organizational and academic investigators as a defining aspect of effective leadership and management processes in businesses. In his opinion, Yukl [5], identified good decision making as one of the key components of leadership strategies in organizational management. All Leaders and other decision makers in companies should understand that a leader is one who can lead a group of people to accomplish common goals in the right direction, with cost efficiency, within the time frame, and achieving the desired outcomes [40].

The Role of a Leader in Organizational Decision Making

Everyday leaders make decisions. Decision making is the key role of leadership and people always associate leadership in business and politics with making good decisions and a great emphasis on being the head of a group. Leaders must be effective in their organizational decision making by pulling rather than pushing; by inspiring their subordinates rather than ordering them; by enabling people to use their own initiative and experiences rather than by denying their efforts or constraining their experiences and actions in the organization. It of vital importance to know that functional leadership is not usually defined by a specific set of behaviors but instead by generic responses that is prescribed for and will vary by different problem, issues, challenges, circumstances, and different situations. In their views, Hackman and Walton maintained that: the emphasis switches from "what leaders "should do" to "what needs to be done for effective performance" (p. 77). Every organization is a systemic whole and network that is dynamic, challenging, complex in nature, and established for the purpose of serving the common good, and goal accomplishments. While no leader exists and operates outside the organization, all organizations need leaders to exist, and survive in all its operations. According to [14], leaders must know how to lead as well as manage. Otherwise, without leading as well as managing effectively, today's organizations face the threat of extinction.

In the view of Glanz [41], the crux of good leadership is the ability to make thoughtful, reasoned decisions. In order to be the best judge, a leader should have critical thinking skills. They must respond quickly to situations. They must also reflect and be able to point out areas that need improvement. Good judgment in the context of educational leadership requires that the leader have a firm grounding in the educational enterprise, combined with a keen sense of awareness of the complex factors that impinge on school practice. According to Northouse [9] leadership is defined as: "a process where by an individual influences a group of individuals to achieve a common goal" (p. 3). For him, a leader must be willing to take responsibility and tasks, pursue goals, self-confident, exercises initiative in social situations, and willing to accept consequences in all organizational decisions. The paradigm of Northouse, which states that leadership is a process whereby an individual influences a group of individuals to achieve a common goal, clearly focused on the leadership decision making in organizations. It conceptualizes and identifies the five basic elements common to the phenomenon of leadership. These five components include the following elements, and themes that form the core "consensus" components of how leadership is currently conceptualized in the views of Northouse: *1. leadership is a process, 2. leadership emerges out of a reciprocal relationship of influence, 3. leadership occurs in a community or group context, 4. leadership involves goal attainment around shared visions, purposes, and values, 5. leadership is intentional about making real or concrete change* [9].

A greater attention to the above paradigm and five components of organizational leadership and management decisions should provide distinct insight into effective decision making process in all situations. Both employers and employees should know that sometimes mistakes may happen and the important decisions made by intelligent, responsible people with the best information and intentions may go wrong. For instance: the Iraq war and the meltdown of the financial markets in 2008. In such situations, effective leaders are required to acknowledge their mistakes and take the necessary steps to either repair, correct, or amend the situation. For in every organizational activity, constant, clear, and quality leadership is necessary for success [42,43]. The way leaders behave and what they choose to do will be judged ultimately by the purpose or motivation of those actions and the values that guide their leadership decisions and behaviors. Leana [44] has found that leader behavior strongly influences the number of alternative solutions proposed and discussed by groups and the actual final decisions made by them. Due to the complexities associated with many organizations, leaders and managers should through sound decision making be able to influence the growth and development of their businesses by bringing in new strategic techniques, technologies, training and development of employees, updating of policies, as well as keeping to the moral standards while maintaining the mission and vision of the organization.

Every business and institutional leader should be held to common standards, with rules and procedures that are clear, firm, fair, and consistent while treating all involved in their company with dignity, prudent, and respect irrespective of their differences. In making good decisions and working effectively well among workers in the organizations, it is necessary that leaders should be deemed as a strategic aim of the organization [45]. However, leaders must have self-confidence, plan ahead, listen, seek correct information, be analytical, and where necessary get their subordinates involved in the decision making process while avoiding not to act in a hurry. There must be a set of steps to incorporate the above elements into a sound decision making process. These elements allow business leaders ability to translate intentions into reality by aligning the energies to the organization behind an attractive goal. As a leader you are expected to make decisions that are in the best interest of the whole organization.

In affirmation and support of the above statement; Jacobs and Jaques [46] stated:

Executive leaders "add value" to their organizations in large part by giving a sense of understanding and purpose to the overall activities of the organization. In excellent organizations, there almost always is a feeling that the "boss" knows what he is doing, that he has shared this information downward, that it makes sense, and that it is going to work.

Understanding the importance of decision-making process

A good understanding and the establishment of sound decisions and policies are very important for leadership in all businesses. Leadership is a functional one, meaning that leadership is at the service of collective effectiveness [47-49]. People in leadership positions, be it in institutions, businesses, government, or nonprofit organizations are challenged every day with a myriad of leadership decision making in their individual company. These business leaders and managers are always making decisions that are associated with their subordinates, policy, planning, controlling, methods, training, and compensations do so often in a critical, complex, and challenging situations. Leadership decision-making is an integral part of any organization. It involves a sequence of activities that involves leadership's courage, and evaluation, as well as "gathering, interpreting and exchanging information, creating and identifying alternative courses of action, choosing among alternatives by integrating the often differing perspectives and opinions of team members; and implementing a choice and monitoring its consequences" [50]. As a process of selecting from the many different alternatives, organizational leaders must consider, analyze, and evaluate the best of all different alternatives from which advantages and disadvantages are known. This particular process will help them to make good decisions and enhance the successful operation of their business.

The more skilled leaders are, the more likely they will feel confident in their abilities and competent to make good decisions. For it is only the leader that understands the nature and principles of decision making will be able cope with complex and challenging situations more effectively than the leader who does not possess any of the ideas. For example: the leader who had the knowledge and have studied the qualities and characteristics of organizational diversity stands a better chance of making decision on team building when compared with a leader who have not. Decision making is of vital importance in organization because it permeates through all managerial functions and all areas of business including; recruitment, selection, job description, organizing, planning, training, marketing, policy, and compensation among others. Simply put, it is the act of carrying out managerial tasks and responsibilities. According to Mumford, Zaccaro and Harding [51], problem-solving skills refer to a leader's creative ability to solve new and unusual, ill-defined organizational problems. Nahavandi [40] claims that a leader is anyone who influences individuals or groups within an organization, helps them in the establishment of goals, and guides them toward achievement of those goals, thereby enabling them to be effective.

Factors influencing leadership decision making

Organizational leadership is the plan the leaders have in place for the organization. They organize a plan in place to establish success and accomplish goals of a company. Decisions are made in organizations daily. These decisions, no matter how big or small, impact organization in a major way. It's important for leaders to evaluate the situation before making a decision. As earlier indicated, many studies by different professions had shown that there are several important factors that may influence leadership decision making in organizations. These factors include: *past experience* [26], *cognitive biases* [27], *age and individual differences belief in personal relevance* [28], and an escalation of commitment as well as the influence what choices people make. Understanding the factors that influence decision making process is important to understanding what decisions are made. That is, the factors that influence the process may impact the outcomes [29]. In like manner, the other major factors that can influence decision making include: leadership style influence, a variety of cognitive biases, change, technology, politics, communication, economic status, market cost, and social responsibility among other factors. The above mentioned factors can affect any organization in one way or the other. Dietrich in discussing leadership decision making strongly agrees that age, environment, socioeconomic status, biases, past experiences are among the relevant factors that influences decision making among organizational leaders and managers.

As mentioned in Figure 1 the three major leadership behavioral styles Kurt Lewin can influence decision making in any organization. There are namely: autocratic, participative, and delegate leadership style. The autocratic also known as authoritative decision making is associated with a leader having a total control and ownership in making decisions in the organization. Here the leader makes decisions with no consultation or suggestion of ideas from his subordinates. This style works well when decisions have to be made quickly and in emergency situations. The participative or democratic style is more inclusive of the group. This is a leadership style that allows and encourages members of the group to express their ideas, and be involved in the decision-making process of the organization. The Laissez-faire otherwise known as delegate style allows the leader to delegate the decision-making responsibility to an individual or group. This style works well if the leader is surrounded by motivated, skilled and talented group of employees.

The understanding of the culture of the people of any group by a leader is an authentic way of knowing them. Morgan [52] describes culture as an active living phenomenon, through which people jointly create and recreate the world in which they live. The lack of the culture and knowledge of the people in your organization may affect your decision making in your business. The people's culture is very important and what they think ought to be done in their society [53]. Previous experiences can greatly affect future decisions. Juliusson, Karlsson, and Garling [26] also indicated that past decisions may influence the decisions people make in the future.

More recently, some researchers have stressed the importance of environmental, social, and emotional influences on decision-making [54-56]. Fischhoff [54] emphasizes the effect that context and interpretation can have on decision-making, and Loewenstern [55] stresses that visceral factors, such as sexual arousal or hunger, can greatly affect decision-making processes. Today, teams and organizations face rapid change like never before. Globalization and technology have increased the markets and opportunities for more growth and revenue. Leadership is human communication which modifies the attitudes and behaviors of others in order to meet shared goals and needs.

Ethics and decision making models

Ethical codes in organizations are tool for clarifying acceptable behavior and provide guidance to managers when dealing with ethical dilemmas [57]. Ethics is very important in business and each leader has an important role to play in ethical decision making in their organizations. Since ethics is defined as the philosophical study of moral behavior, of moral decision making or of how to live the good life. The expectation and common theme for any organizational leader and manager to play in ethical decision making process is dedication, trust, fairness, acting in good faith, and transparency. It is an essential configuration of organizational leadership and management. For instance, it will be of vital importance to have a valid framework in place that would encourage leaders to analyze and make ethical decisions while helping them avoid some complexities and ethical dilemmas in the system that cannot be resolved through the application and implementation of codes of ethics. In this regard, Corey [58] suggested the following ethical decision making model to keep both leaders and decision makers informed in decision making process as well as in the resolution of ethical dilemmas. The model is as follows:

Step 1: Identify the problem.

Step 2: Identify the potential issues involved.

Step 3: Review relevant ethical guidelines.

Step 4: Know relevant laws and regulations.

Step 5: Obtain Consultation.

Step 6: Consider possible and probable courses of action.

Step 7: List the consequences of the probable courses of action.

Step 8: Decide on what appears to be the best course of action [58].

The author strongly believed that the above model is of great significant and also maintains that there are some other ethical values that leaders can use to help them better make their decision and serve the value that is most important to them in any given situation. These ethical standards include; integrity, respect, compassion, justice, prudence, temperance, and common good among other things. In order to make a decision in leadership, a thorough explanation requires appealing to a rule, using a theory, and applying a value. This value simply defined is a single word or phrase that identifies something as being desirable for human beings. Values are those goods that our theories, rules, and decisions work to bring about in the world. They (values) are acted on and applied on by theories and then rules [59]. In simple terms, values are not a high-minded code based on personal or company ethics, they are a proposal for creating a work environment that drives accomplishment. Values offer people a framework for their decision, broad limitations for their ideas, and more independence to make a change. In his perspective, Despain [60] postulated that values is defined as shared beliefs with standards for behavior in the workplace, are the key to succeeding in changing and challenging times.

Leaders and managers must have guidelines about what decisions are moral because we have identified certain things as being good, which these decisions seek to uphold. Organizational leaders must possess the following qualities both in leading and decision making in their business:

- Being true to one's basic moral values.

- Involves: honesty, promise keeping, loyalty, dependability and consistency.

- Uphold the dignity of persons; treating them as an ends and not as the means.

- Have concern for the suffering of others and be willing to help out.

- Act on one's professional duties and obligations.

- Able to perform good for people and avoiding harm.

The above principles suggest that leaders must endeavor to do the right thing in their decisions because their subordinates depends to an extraordinary degree on the expressed values of the leader and believe to success by following their leadership decisions. Adherence to ethical standards both in leadership and decision making process must be a foundation of all organizational rules and policies. Macintyre [61] affirmed that virtue is an acquired human quality, the possession and exercise of which enables us to achieve those goods which are internal to practices, and the lack of which prevents us from achieving any such goods. Leadership decision making is about others and not about self. It is about trust and not about power. It is about creating results by generating cultures where people know it is okay to be unique and unlike others, so they freely take off their fronts, express themselves, and do great things. Looking within ourselves and modeling how we think through our own personal and professional ethical code helps shape our teaching and reconfirms what we are teaching in the classroom [62].

Communication in decision making

A good understanding and the establishment of a valid communication and decision-making are of such significance to leaders and managers in the creation of clear policies in all their individual organizations and businesses. While leadership is a functional one, meaning that leadership is at the service of collective effectiveness [47-49] communication in the other hand is arguably one of the single most important aspects of organizational management tool. Communication is the primary function of any effective leader in an organization. In any business operations, valid, effective, and share communication are of great importance to the leaders and manager of every organization. Although organizational leadership has become increasingly complex in both purpose and structure and therefore requires suitable methods of leadership decision systemic styles to address this challenge. One of these suitable methods centers on effective communication and the provision of good working environment.

Communication is one most essential skill that contributes to any successful business. While some of the importance roles of effective leadership in present-day business improvement have been stressed, there is a continuing global debate about the leadership decision making approaches that are most beneficial to maintainable major organizational improvement. It is also useful to be aware that, in today's society, organizational leadership, decision-making, growth, effective management, and organizational success are based on the quality of the decisions policy makers or leaders make Ejimabo [3]. Thus, the establishment of appropriate approach, ways of improving communication, and quality of decision making in any organizations must include the following elements by organizational leaders:

- Appropriate channel for all communications

- Awareness of how perception, culture, channel, and language can create

- Provide a valid working relationship and climate

- Encourage feedback

- Mutual respect and trust

- Promote dialogue and group consensus

- Listen effectively

• Be clear with words used as intended meaning may be misinterpreted

• Be aware of the culture and diverse nature of the employees

Leadership is all about getting people to work together to make things happen that might not otherwise occur or prevent that which ordinarily would take place. Leaders must cultivate a meaningful relationship in all businesses that requires clear, honest, and reciprocal communication. Leadership position involves motivating others and one way to accomplish this is through a process of sharing information in the system decision making. It is believed that in organizations, leaders have a moral responsibility to take care of their followers and help them develop their personal cares, to be a consultant for followers' personal problems [63]. They must decide on their values and set goals to insure a fruitful decision-making process. Therefore, before making a final decision or taking any course of action, leaders must discover or create a set of alternative courses of action and gather information about each. Having gathered the information with which to make a decision, they must apply information for each course of action to predict the outcomes of each possible alternative and make a decision for implementation [64].

Communication is both complex, irreversible (it is difficult to take back messages that have been sent), and it involves more than just one person sending a message to another. Instead, communication can be seen as the primary defining characteristic of every leader that involves the negotiation of shared interpretations and understanding in the entire organization. Leaders need followers and followers need leaders in order to accomplish the desired goals and outcomes [65-68] in their individual organizations.

Research Questions

The purpose of this study was aimed at understanding the major factors that influence leadership decision making in organizations. It was focused on identifying what makes for efficient leadership decision making in businesses from the perceptions and views of a nationwide study of four hundred past and current business executives, leaders, and managements in the United States. Decision-making is about facing a question, to be the one you want to be or not to be. The research questions were:

1. *How can quality and sound leadership decision making process be improved in major organizational operations?*

2. *What factors facilitate the implementation of a successful decision making process among leaders in organization?*

3. *What are the best processes of uncovering strategies to fend off decision-making errors in any organization?*

The researcher believed that the answers generated from the above and other related questions that have emerged in the course of this study may provide meaningful and useful insights to organizational leaders and managers in their decision making processes. Organizational decisions are at the heart of leader triumph, and at times there are critical moments when they can be difficult, confounding, and terrifying. However, the bravest decisions are the safest.

Methodology

The author used the qualitative critical ethnography paradigm in this study to understand the major factors that influence leadership decision making in organizations. The qualitative method places emphasis on understanding through observation, careful documentation, and thoughtful analysis of people's words, actions, and records Creswell [69]. This methodology was based on the experiences of the researcher and the selected participants with the aim of identifying what makes for efficient leadership decision making in organizations. Although the design of a particular business program in San Antonio, Texas and the background and experiences of the investigator set the context of this research. It is important to note that the design and some of the organizational activities in Texas offered the researcher a unique opportunity to effectively examine the role of leader's behavioral styles with reference to leadership activities and decision making in these sittings.

The principal concern in all aspects of this study was to reach some relevant understanding of the major factors that influence sound decision making among leadership and management in businesses as well as to discover an avenue of better solutions to the challenges and complexities associated with decision making in organizations. In this regard, a nationwide data was randomly collected from four hundred past and current business executives, leaders, and managements in some cities and states of the United States. This study was confined to full time organizational leaders, managers with at least seven years' experience in leadership decision making and other leadership activities. With this process, the author was able to gather, not only useful, relevant, and meaningful information, but more importantly, the ability to employ a distinct and analytical techniques in his effort of discovering the major factors that influence leadership decision making in organizations. These made interpretation and understanding of the phenomenon in its context and even beyond, more viable [70].

In this study, the researcher resorted to a critical ethnographic design in this study in order to gain in-depth knowledge and authentic understanding of the issues and problems associated with leadership decision making in businesses. The author was disposed to discovering a pattern of meaning the natural and cultural setting, was interested in the process rather than outcomes, in the context rather the specific variables, and in discovering rather than confirmation [71]. In the views of Denzin and Lincoln a research design is defined as "a basic set of beliefs that guide action' dealing with first principles, ultimate or the researcher's worldviews. The critical ethnographic design was selected in this study because it is seen by many scholars as one of the most effective means of doing comprehensive, systemic, and authentic research. It is also a research method that is located in the practice of both sociologist and anthropologists, and which should be regarded as the product of a cocktail of methodologies that share the assumption that personal engagement with the subject is the key to understanding a particular culture or social setting. Participants' observation is the most common component of this cocktail, but interviews, conversational and discourse analysis, documentary analysis, film and photography, life histories all have their place in the ethnographer's repertoire. Description resides at the core of ethnography, and however that description is constructed it is the intense meaning of social life from the everyday perspective of groups members that is sought [72].

Based on the researcher's judgment and the purpose of the research Babbie, Greig and Schwandt [73-75] and in looking for those who "have had experiences relating to the phenomenon to be researched" Kruger [76], the key participants were limited to the perceptions, experiences and views of 400 hundred past and current business executives, leaders, and managements from some cities and states in the United States. The participants were randomly selected from different cities and states in the country. They consist of 400 hundred full time organizational leaders and managers with at least seven years' experience in leadership decision making and other leadership activities, three hundred men, and one hundred women, with an average age of 55. They also had bachelor degree as their minimum education level, although 55% of them have master's degree in their professions. The informed consent agreement form and the purpose of the research study were explained to the participants at the beginning of each interview [3].

To achieve these objectives, this study was based upon a qualitative method, duplicating the self-designed survey questionnaire developed from the research questions and discussions from the focus group interviews. The (quantitative) survey data were collected only as a response to the questionnaire and used to support the qualitative data only in the study. It took about 17 months of intensive fieldwork to be designed and executed and can be characterized as a multi-method, in-depth research [77]. The data collection include: (1) individual and semi-structured interview with the selected participants forming twelve groups of different individual leaders, (2) selected leaders and managers useful responses to the research questions, (3) survey data which was collected as a response to the questionnaire and used to support the qualitative data, (4) examining the leadership literatures over the past 12 years, (5) supplementary information from archives with reference to internal documents and reports. All selected individuals and each group participated in two separate interviews to avoid responses being filtered only in the single ideas of a particular interviewee. Here, the investigator chose the researcher's role as an active listener and collaborator "to tell the story from the participants' view rather than as 'expert' who passes judgment on the participants" [78].

According to Creswell, data analysis employed a concurrent nested model. The study followed a sequence of distinct steps in order to secure the reliability of the data based on participant's recall. The qualitative data analysis, which is primarily inductive and recursive process, were analyzed and organized into categories in order to identify themes or patterns as these facilitated a deeper knowledge and understanding of the major factors that influence leadership decision making in businesses. The questionnaire and final survey revisions were made to support and improve the content and process of the data collections, both incorporated qualitative and survey (quantitative) items. Thus, the survey (quantitative) data was systematically organized, analyzed and given a basic descriptive statistical treatment in the study. A follow-up research was conducted by implementing focused interviews of both the selected past and current leaders and managers in different organizations to corroborate the data from the final survey and identify additional variables. The author allowed the selected participants to serve as a check to the study to ensure immediate validation as to the accuracy and credibility of the narratives in the data. The constant communication between the researcher and the selected participants added to the confidence and validity of the interview transcripts [3].

Findings

The findings are based upon the purpose, objectives, and research questions of this study as well as examined in multiple levels Creswell that include three major sources: (a) open-ended questions posed through interviews, (b) demographics and observation, (c) the survey questionnaire. Based on the research questions, the interview questions were developed thematically. The interview questions helped to provide the structure for data gathering and also served as a means for recording information that was used in this study.

Demographics

The key participants were limited to the perceptions, experiences and views of 400 hundred past and current business executives, leaders, and managements from some cities and states in the United States. The participants were randomly selected from different cities and states in the country. They consist of 400 hundred full time organizational leaders and managers with at least seven years' experience in leadership decision making and other leadership activities, three hundred men, and one hundred women, with and average age of 55. While 22% (91) were associated with bachelor degree, 55% (180) of them had master's degree as their minimum education level, 17% (68) of them have Ph.D. degree, and 15% (61) of them had some technical skill (certifications) in their professions. Among these selected participants, 45 of them are the founder of their organizations. All the eligible participants completed the survey and the demographic questions. A general description of the participants shows that they were primarily (75%) male and (25%) women with the mean age of 48.25 years old, the mean years of education was 82.75, and the mean years of work was 46.35. The position or title of the participants ranged from "President General" (PG) to the "Founder": 130 participants had the leadership rank of president general (32.5%), 90 of them were "Executive Presidents" (22.5%), 70 of them had the title of CEO (17.5%), 65 of them had director positions (16.3%), and 45 of them were the founder of their organizations (11.3%). There was no data on either race or ethnicity collected. More information on the demographic of the selected participants is shown below in Table 1. Table 2 shows that majority of the participants (228) used the democratic leadership decision making behavioral style in their businesses. Both men and women tend to use the democratic style when compared to other leadership decision making style. While some leaders (157) associated themselves with autocratic decision making style, only very few leaders (115)

	Number	Percentage
Gender		
Male	300	75%
Female	100	25%
Age		
25–35	91	22.7%
36–44	84	21.5%
45–55	81	20.3%
56–64	76	19%
65–75	68	17.%
Level of Education		
Bachelor degree	91	22%
Technical Skill	61	15%
Master's degree	220	55%
Doctoral degree	68	17%
Years of Experience		
1–5	115	28.8%
6–10	87	21.7%
11–15	75	18.7%
16–20	64	16.5%
21–26	59	14.8%
Position/Title		
President General	130	32.5%
Executive President	90	22.5%
CEO	70	17.5%
Director	65	16.3%
Founder	45	11.3%

Table 1: The demographics of the participants in the study.

Gender	Autocratic	Democratic	Delegative
Male	131	173	96
Female	26	55	19
Total	157	228	115

Table 2: Leadership decision making style used among participants.

prefer using the delegative decision making style in their organizations. Table 3 shows the minimum score, maximum score, and means for leadership effectiveness level: Overall, the survey completers seemed to have a good opinion of them based on the survey results. Only one of the result items mean scores was below 4.00 on a 5-point scale – item 14, "Able to demonstrate patience when the group cannot reach mutually acceptable decisions," which had a mean score of 4.00 ($SD = 1.02$). The four lowest scored items according the above survey results seem to relate to each other thematically. They include the following items: "Able to cope with the ever changing priorities in our organization" ($M = 4.31$, $SD = 1.10$); "Show tolerance for diverse opinion" ($M = 4.031$, $SD = 0.61$); "Able to effect career planning and counseling" ($M = 4.33$, $SD = 1.03$): "Demonstrate appropriate interpersonal relations with team decision making decision making" ($M = 4.38$, $SD = 1.10$). These items together showed that there are several of the outcomes that may result from a decision are regret or satisfaction; both of which may influence leadership decisions in one way (positive) or the other (negative) in any organizational structure.

In like manner, below are the results of leadership effective items with the four highest scores. These items suggest that the leaders take their roles in organizational decision making seriously in order to achieve their organizational goals and objectives. These items are: "Communicate with the group and individuals appropriately in decision making" ($M = 4.85$, $SD = 0.96$); "Help the group understand the need to work as a group" ($M = 4.77$, $SD = 0.94$); "Influence others to achieve their goals" ($M = 4.62$, $SD = 1.08$); and "Maintain an appropriate knowledge base" ($M = 4.54$, $SD = 1.09$). In order of vital importance, the following are the major factors the participants in the survey said were both most significant and most frequently relied upon in order to be effective as well as to achieve good decisions in their individual businesses:

1. Demonstrate appropriate interpersonal relations with team decision making decision making.

2. Communicate with the group and individuals appropriately in decision making.

Leadership effectiveness level	Minimum	Maximum	Mean	SD
Able to effect career planning and counseling	10	5	4.33	1.03
Influence others to achieve their goals	17	5	4.62	1.08
Able to understand people and treat them with respect	14	5	4.46	0.61
Maintain an appropriate knowledge base	16	5	4.54	1.09
Help the group understand the need to work as a group	19	5	4.77	1.26
Able to appropriately assign tasks and work-loads	10	5	4.46	0.79
Show tolerance for diverse opinion	9	5	4.31	0.61
Demonstrate patience when the group cannot reach mutually acceptable decisions	5	5	4.00	1.02
Able to explain things to all in a clear way	16	5	4.54	1.18
Able to cope with the ever changing priorities in our organization	9	5	4.31	1.10
Appreciates the groups confidence in me and take my leadership position seriously	16	5	4.54	1.07
Communicate with the group and individuals appropriately in decision making	21	5	4.85	0.91
Demonstrate appropriate interpersonal relations with team decision making decision making.	11	5	4.38	1.10
*Note: The above table was designed by the author.				

Table 3: The survey results on leadership effectiveness.

Behavioral Skill	Average Likert-scale scores		
	Priorities for achievement	Frequently used	Level of concerns
Demonstrate an understanding of what is important and what is not	4.6	4.5	4.8
Introduce new ideas and approaches to problems.	4.5	4.1	4.6
Take my assigned position in the organization seriously	4.4	4.2	4.3
Maintain a confident professional image	4.4	4.3	4.3
Keep people interested in finishing their assigned tasks	4.3	3.9	4.0
Being a change agent in the organization	3.8	3.7	3.9
Present new and unique ways of solving problems	3.6	3.6	3.3
Appreciates the groups confidence in me and take my leadership position seriously	3.2	3.0	2.7

*Note: The researcher used the Likert-scale values which were as follows:
• The priorities for leaders to achieve their goals in organizational decision making: 1=not important; 2=less important; 3=important; 4; very important; 5=most important
• The frequency used by leaders to perform their individual activity in the organization: 1=not applicable; 2=less applicable; 3=applicable; 4=very applicable; 5=most applicable
The level of concerns of leaders in applying their skills and expertise in organization: 1=not concerned; 2=less concerned; 3=concerned; 4=very concerned; most concerned

Table 4: Behavioral styles of organizational leaders.

3. Maintain an appropriate knowledge base

4. Help the group understand the need to work as a group.

The findings indicate support for the factors influencing decision making in the organization. However, the results above (Table 4) really showed how committed and concerned most organizational leaders are in making sure that they make sound decisions in their businesses. For good decisions will always lead to the establishment of good organization. Great leaders always engage in influencing individuals to attain their goals. Individuals are able to contemplate through difficult issues and submit ideas without being swayed by individuals in leadership positions [79]. For him, every leader must make a choice (choosing from among the options), process (electing to make the decision independently or involving others), and purpose (achieving the desired outcome). Thus, the choice a leader makes should be to minimize the negative consequences and maximize the positive outcomes in his/her individual organization. In like manner, the findings in this study were in line with existing research and ideas of Green [79] who believes that individuals and/or groups should be involved in the decision making process when their involvement will enhance the quality and/or acceptance of the decision.

Discussions

The purpose of this study was aimed at understanding the major factors that influence leadership decision making in organizations. This part of work presents the discussion of results and incorporates related literature in identifying a pattern of meaning in this study. There are four main themes that emerged in this research, namely: *(1) listening skills, (2) good communication, (3) interpersonal relation with teams, and (4) trust and dialogue*. The discussion of these themes was meant to enable the organizational leaders to better understand the process of decision making as it affects the employees in their organizations. The stories and experiences of the focus group were the tools and elements used in order to discover a pattern of meaning and achieve result. In the views of the participants, most of them commented on the need to consider the complexities and unpredictability that are associated with decision making in organizations. Evidently, the roles of the participants could be seen in most of what some of them shared with the researcher. For instance, one of the Participants stated that:

Leaders make decisions based on data, experience and influence. In my 22 years leadership experience, I do sincerely think that creative leaders must be willing to listen to their subordinates in order to make the best decision …. For me, valid communication is always the key to success. Having a two way communication will enhance the team's effectiveness in positive leadership decision making in any business (Participant XXX142, February, 2014).

In the present challenging world, the leadership decision making process can be complicated and overwhelming in almost all businesses. As a result, it is valuable for organizational leaders to be educated in technology, cultural diversity, ethical standards to enable them learn the best model to follow, that may be applied to everyday decisions, as well as life changing choices in their individual businesses. Leadership needs to be looked at as an exercise rather than as a role. Most of them also agree to the usefulness of the Lewin leadership approaches namely: autocratic, democratic, and laissez-faire methods of leadership decision making processes in the context of this study.

For others, in sharing their knowledge, stories, and experiences as leaders and decision makers in their businesses expressed great concerns about the factors that influence leadership decision making and leaders' behavioral styles. They all agree that leadership and management activities in organizations involve change, inspiration, motivation, influence, management and effective leadership. They also, suggested that both leaders and managers must strive to focus on the process of setting and achieving the goals of their businesses through the functions of management, sharing of valid information among groups, and maintaining a positive status quo with the aim of accomplishing a goal. In that regard, one of the participants said:

…. You gain strength, courage, and confidence by every experience in which you really stop to look fear in the face. Wherever you see a successful business, someone once made a brave decision. The struggle in life is the choice … and then we make our real decision for which we are responsible. … (Participant XXX095, July, 3013).

The interviews and discussions with some of the participants in this study revealed that most of them are highly educated in their individual profession but fail to appreciate their groups' confidence and effort in their positions as executive leaders in the organization. Furthermore, some of them think only about their positional power and not what they can achieve by working as a team with their subordinates. They impose their power (authority) on their subjects while dictating to them what to do in the organization without involving them in any decision making. This study argues that group dynamics and participative leadership behavioral style in decision making is of vital relevance and significance in any organizational decision making. Most employees are more comfortable when included or allowed to participate in the organization decisions. According to Participant XXX 023 (March, 2013) he stated:

…openness to dialogue and positive sharing of meaningful ideas and experiences in making organizational decision is useful. It allows creative and more experienced workers to contribute their rich ideas and valuable knowledge … to the decision making process.

While decision making is at the root of all we do, it is useful for leaders and manager to develop effective decision making skills and strategies in their organizations. More importantly, openness of communication and the ability to allow creative shared information at workplace can always encourage worker's job satisfaction. Problem solving strategies include, but are not limited to brain storming, cost benefit analysis, written remediation plans, and an examination of possible choices [80].

Conclusion

The purpose of this qualitative critical ethnographic study was focused on identifying the factors influencing success in decision making among organizational leaders and managers in organizations' practices. This study examined the influence of decision making in organizational leadership and management activities that impact creativity, growth and effectiveness, success, and goal accomplishments in current organizations. The author being committed and determined to discovering a pattern of meaning focused on identifying the major factors that influence success in decision making process among organizational leaders through the views and experience of the selected participants in this study. They indicated the importance and urgent need towards the understanding of how leaders arrive at their choices in their leadership decision making process.

In the views of the participants, they all agreed that leadership decision making are one of the most dynamic, challenging, and ongoing concept in every organization. They affirmed that leaders and managers of all levels should consider the general interest of the people they are serving in their decisions while encouraging effectiveness. Findings indicated that there is a great need for change and improvement in decision making among organizational executives while accommodating technology, diversity, globalization, policy, teamwork, and leadership effectiveness. The answers generated from both the research and the interview questions really contributed, provided a meaningful and useful insights to this study. Finally, decision making in organization is an ongoing process. In that regard, there is need for future research on leadership decision making. Thus, the leadership ability to understand the factors that influence decision making process in their business is important and a major key to understanding what decisions are made for the progress of the organization.

Recommendations

1. It is valuable for leaders to be educated in technology, cultural diversity, and ethical standards to enable them learn the best model to follow in their leadership decision making process.

2. Leaders must cultivate a meaningful relationship in all businesses that requires clear, honest, and reciprocal communication.

3. Leaders must have self-confidence, plan ahead, listen, seek correct information, be analytical, and where necessary get their subordinates involved in the decision making process while avoiding not to act in a hurry.

4. Leaders must know what decisions to make and keep the interest of all stakeholders involved.

5. They must show followers that they are able to acknowledge when they are wrong and move forward to a better solution.

6. There is a great need for future research on this matter "Leadership decision making process.

References

1. Hsiung H (2012) Authentic Leadership and Employee Voice Behavior: A Multi-Level Psychological Process. Journal of Business Ethics 107: 349-361.
2. Olsen EE, Eoyang GH (2001) Facilitating organization change: lessons from complexity science. Jossey Bass, San Francisco, CA.
3. Ejimabo NO (2013) Understanding the impact of leadership in Nigeria: its reality, challenges, and perspectives. Sage Open 1-14
4. Nelson D, Quick J (2003) Organizational behavior: Foundation, realities, and challenges. Mason OH: Thomson Southwestern.
5. Yukl G (2010) Leadership in Organizations (7thedn.) Prentice Hall.
6. Stogdill RM (1974) Handbook of leadership: A survey of theory and research. Free Press, New York.
7. Glaholt MG, Wu MC, Reingold EM (2010) Evidence for top-down control of eye movements during visual decision making. Journal of Vision 10.
8. Yukl G, Lepsinger R (2005) Why integrating the leading and managing roles is essential for organizational effectiveness. Organizational Dynamics 34: 361-375.
9. Northouse PG (2004) Leadership: Theory and practice (3rdedn.) Sage, Thousand Oaks, CA.
10. Drath W, Palus CJ (1994) Making common sense: Leadership as meaning-making in a community of practice. Center for Creative Leadership, Greensboro, NC.
11. Jacobs TO, Jaques E (1990) Military executive leadership. In: Clark KE, Clark MB (eds.) Measures of leadership. Leadership Library of America, West Orange, New Jersey pp: 281-295.
12. Pomerol JC, Adam F (2004) Practical decision making-From the legacy of Herbert Simon to Decision Support Systems. In: Decision Support in an Uncertain and Complex World: The IFIP TC8/WG8.3 International Conference 2004. Symposium conducted at The IFIP TC8/ WG8.3 International Conference, Monash University.
13. Langley A, Mintzberg H, Pitcher P, Posad E, Saint-Macary J (1995) Opening up decision making: The view from the black stool. Organization Science 6: 260-279.
14. Kotter JP (1990) A Force for Change: How leadership differs from management. The Free Press, New York, USA.
15. Thomas GF, Zolin R, Hartman J (2009) The Central Role of Communication In Developing Trust and its Effect on Employee Involvement. Journal Of Business Communication 46: 287-310
16. Marrow AJ (1969) The Practical Theorist: The Life and Work of Kurt Lewin. Basic Books Inc., New York.
17. Likert R (1947) Kurt Lewin: a pioneer in human relation research. Human Relations 1: 131-140.
18. Cummings TG, Huse EF (1989) Organization Development and Change (4thedn.) West Publishing, St. Paul MN.
19. Burnes B (2000) Managing Change (3rdedn.) FT/Pearson Educational, Harlow.
20. Dawson P (1994) Organizational Change: A Processual Approach. Paul Chapman Publishing, London.
21. Dent EB, Goldberg SG (1999) Challenging resistance to change. Journal of Applied Behavioral Science 35: 25-41.
22. Hatch MJ (1997) Organization Theory: Modern, Symbolic and Postmodern Perspectives. Oxford University Press, Oxford.
23. Kanter RM, Stein BA, Jick TD (1992) The Challenge of Organizational Change. Free Press, New York.
24. Marshak RJ (1993) Lewin meets Confucius: a re-view of the OD model of change. The Journal of Applied Behavioral Science 29: 393-415.
25. Boone, Bowen D (1987) The great writing in management and organizational behavior. Random House Inc., New York.
26. Juliusson EA, Karlsson N, Gärling T (2005) weighing the past and the future in decision making. European Journal of Cognitive Psychology 17: 561-575.
27. Stanovich KE, West RF (2008) On the relative independence of thinking biases and cognitive ability. Journal of Personality and Social Psychology 94: 672-695.
28. Acevedo M, Krueger JI (2004) Two egocentric sources of the decision to vote: The voter's illusion and the belief in personal relevance. Political Psychology 25: 115-134.
29. Dietrich M (2010) Efficiency and profitability: a panel data analysis of UK manufacturing firms 1993-2007.
30. Finucane ML, Mertz CK, Slovic P, Schmidt ES (2005) Task complexity and older adults' decision-making competence. Psychology and Aging 20: 71-84.
31. Sunstein CR, Thaler RH (2003) Libertarian paternalism is not an oxymoron. University of Chicago Law Review 70: 1159-1199.
32. Milkman KL, Rogers T, Bazerman M (2008) Harnessing your inner angels and demons: What we have learned about want/should conflict and how that knowledge can help us reduce short-sighted decision making. Perspectives on Psychological Science.
33. Bateman TS, Zeithami CP (1989) The psychological context of strategic decisions: A model and convergent experimental findings. Strategic Management Journal 10: 59-74.
34. Kerr J, Slocum JW Jr (1987). Managing corporate culture through reward systems. Academy of Management Executive 1: 99-108.
35. Barnard CI (1968) The functions of the executive. Harvard University Press, Cambridge MA.
36. Donaldson G (1983) Decision making at the top: The shaping of strategic direction. Basic Books, NewYork.
37. Finkelstein S, Hambrick D (1996) Top management team tenure and organizational outcomes: The moderating role of managerial discretion. Administrative Science Quarterly 35: 484-503.
38. Smith LT (1999) Decolonizing methodologies: Research and indigenous peoples. University of Otago Press, Dunedin, New Zealand.
39. Hickson CJ (1986) Quaternary volcanics of the Wells Gray-Clearwater area. East central British Columbia: Ph.D. Thesis, University of British Columbia, Vancouver.
40. Nahavandi A (2004) The art and science of leadership (4thedn.) Pearson Education, Upper Saddle River, NJ.
41. Glanz J (2002) Finding your leadership style: A Guide for Educators. Association for Supervision and Curriculum Development, Alexandria VA.
42. Everett C (2002) Penn States commitment to quality improvement. Quality Progress 35: 44-49.
43. Buch K, Rivers D (2002) Sustaining a quality initiative. Strategic Direction. 18: 15-17.
44. Leana CR (1985) A partial test of Janis' groupthink model: Effects of group cohesiveness and leader behavior on defective decision-making. Journal of Management 11: 5-17.
45. Feigenbaum A (1991) Total quality control (3rdedn.) McGraw-Hill, NY.
46. Jacobs TO, Jaques E (1991) Executive leadership. In: Gal R, Manglesdorff AD (eds.) Handbook of military psychology, Wiley, New York.
47. Fleishman EA, Mumford MD, Zaccaro SJ, Levin KY, Korotkin, AL, et al. (1991) Taxonomic efforts in the description of leader behavior: A synthesis and functional interpretation. Leadership Quarterly 2: 245-287.
48. Hackman JR, Walton RE (1986) Leading groups in organizations. In Goodman PS (ed.) Designing effective work groups. Jossey-Bass, San Francisco.
49. Lord RG (1977) Functional leadership behavior: Measurement and relation to social power and leadership perceptions. Administrative Science Quarterly 22: 114-133.
50. Thompson LL (2008) Making the Team: A guide for Managers (3rdedn.) Prentice, NJ.
51. Mumford MD, Zaccaro SJ, Harding EA (2009) The leadership. Quarterly Newsletter 11: 155-170.
52. Morgan G (1997) Images of Organization. Sage Publications, Thousand Oaks, CA.
53. Hofstede GH (2001) Culture's consequences: Comparing values, behaviors, institutions, and organization across nations (2ndedn.) Sage, Thousand Oaks, CA.

54. Fischhoff B (1996) The real world: what good is it? Organizational Behavior and Human Process 65: 232-248.

55. Moore D, Lowenstein G (2004) Self-interest, automaticity, and the psychology of conflict of interest. Social Justice Research 17: 189-202.

56. Strack F, Neumann R (1996) "The spirit is willing, but the flesh is weak": beyond mind-body interactions in human decision-making. Organizational Behavior and Human Process 65: 272-292.

57. Lewis CW (1991) The ethics challenge in public service--A problem solving guide. Jossey-Bass, SanFrancisco, CA.

58. Corey G, Corey M, Haynes R (1998) Student workbook for Ethics in Action. Brooks, Pacific Grove, CA.

59. Brincat CA, Wike VS (2000) Morality and the Professional Life: Values at Work. Prentice Hall Inc.

60. Despain JE (2003) And dignity for all: unlocking greatness through values-based leadership. Upper Saddle River: Pearson Education.

61. Macintyre AC (1981) After virtue. University of Notre Dame Press, San Francisco, CA.

62. Shapiro JP (2005) Ethical leadership and decision making in education: applying theoretical perspectives to complex dilemmas. Lawrence, Mahwah.

63. Bass BM (1995) Theory of transformational leadership redux. Leadership Quarterly 6: 463-478.

64. Deutsch M, Coleman PT (2000) The Handbook of Conflict Resolution Theory and Practice (eds.) Jossey-Bass Publishers, San Francisco.

65. Burns JM (1978) Leadership. Harper and Row, New York, NY.

66. Heller T, Van Til J (1983) Leadership and followership: Some summary propositions. Journal of Applied Behavioral Science Volume 18: 405-414.

67. Hollander EP (1992) Leadership, followership, self, and others. Leadership Quarterly 3: 43-54.

68. Jago AG (1982) Leadership: Perspectives in theory and research. Management Science 28: 315-336.

69. Creswell JW (2003) Research design: Qualitative and quantitative, and mixed method approaches. Sage, Thousand Oaks, CA.

70. Mertens DM (1998) Research methods in education and psychology: Integrating diversity with quantitative and qualitative approaches. Sage, Thousand Oaks, CA.

71. Unknown Author (2015) The meaning of leadership decision making. Retrieved from (http://www.merriam-webster.com/dictionary/decision).

72. Hobbs D (2006) Ethnography. In: Jupp V (ed.) The Sage Dictionary of Social, Research Method. Sage, Oxford, UK, pp. 25-38.

73. Babbie E (1995) The practice of social research (7thedn.) Wadsworth, Belmont, CA.

74. Greig A, Taylor J (1999) Doing research with children. Sage, London, UK.

75. Schwandt TA (1997) Qualitative inquiry: A dictionary of terms. Sage, Thousand Oaks, CA.

76. Kruger D (1988) An introduction to phenomenological psychology (2ndedn.) Juta, Cape Town, South Africa.

77. Snow CC, Thomas JB (1994) 'Field Research Methods in Strategic Management: Contributions to Theory Building and Testing'. Journal of Management Studies 31: 457-448.

78. Creswell JW (1998) Qualitative research and design: Choosing among five traditions. Sage, Thousand Oaks, CA.

79. Green LR (2013) Practicing the art of leadership. Pearson education Inc., Upper Saddle River, NJ.

80. Wester SR, Christianson HF, Fouad NA, Santiago-Rivera AL (2008). Information processing as problem solving: A collaborative approach to dealing with students exhibiting insufficient competence. Training and Education in Professional Psychology 2: 193-201.

The Consequences of Entrepreneurial Outlook on Business Initiatives: The Case of Restaurant Operators

Yeboah AM* and Alhaji A

Department Liberal Studies, Cape Coast Polytechnic, Cape Coast, Ghana

Abstract

This study examined the linkages between entrepreurial outlook and business initiatives of restaurant operators. The five multidimensional constructs of entrepreneurial orientation were adapted to measure the entrepreneurial outlook, while the business initiatives were measured based on the frequent development of new products, new services and new business venturing.

The study employed census approach and self-administered questionnaires in collecting data from 41 registered restaurant operators located in the Cape Coast Metropolis. Descriptive, correlation and Chi-Square were the statistical tools used. The findings indicate that the restaurant operators demonstrated a somewhat high entrepreneurial outlook. However, they do not develop business initiatives regularly. Again, significant association existed between the dimensions of entrepreneurial outlook and business initiatives. The study therefore concludes that a high entrepreneurial inclination will propel the frequent development of business initiatives. The restaurant operators must therefore attend periodic workshops to be abreast of current knowledge, they must be involved with every aspect of the restaurant business with complete professionalism. They must create an encouraging work environment, care for customers and must get to know their regular customers by their names, favourite dishes and drinks.

Keywords: Entrepreneurial outlook; Business initiative; Restaurant firms

Introduction

Entrepreneurship is key to an economy because all business ventures are started by individuals conversant with entrepreneurship. People exposed to entrepreneurship commonly submit that they have extra opportunity to use ingenious freedoms to create new products. These assertions imply that fostering a robust entrepreneurship culture will positively maximize individual and collective economics, social success on a local, national, and global scale. Kuratko [1], posits that entrepreneurship entails essential ingredients such as the willingness to take calculated risks, and formulate an effective venture team. Besides, it marshals needed resources, builds a solid business plan, and finally provides the vision to recognize opportunities where others see contradiction and confusion. Business owners or managers that want to engage in successful and effective business operations need to have an entrepreneurial orientation mindset. Dess and Lumpkin [2] define entrepreneurial orientation as a collectively five dimensions of entrepreneurial practices, namely innovativeness, pro-activeness, risk-taking, competitive aggressiveness and autonomy that permeate the decision-making styles and practice of members of a firm. As increasing number of consumers want to dine out or take prepared food home, the number of food-service operations has skyrocketed, hence the need for restaurant operators to be entrepreneurially conscious. Restaurants have always played an essential role in the business, social, intellectual and artistic life of a thriving society. The majority of events of life, personal and professional, are celebrated in restaurants. Acquaintances become friends around a table in the safe and controlled environment of a restaurant. Individuals become lovers across a restaurant table. Restaurants are more important than ever and as such the restaurant industry across the world is evolving rapidly into providing a range of products and services. Andaleeb and Conway [3], intimate the restaurant industry is lucrative in size, fiercely competitive, and very important to the public palate.

In Ghana, the restaurant industry is growing fast due to the ever-increasing new local and international restaurant outlets across the country, providing a variety of goods and services that are of immense benefit to the citizens and the economy. Local restaurants in Ghana commonly referred as "Chop bars", help you get acquainted with local food. Here, a seat may be nothing more than a simple wooden stool, or a shared bench. The main traditional dishes sold include "kenkey" with pepper and fried fish, "banku", with fried fish and pepper or with okro or groundnut soup, fried ripped plantain with bean stew. Others are "omo tuo" (cooked rice rolled into balls) served with palm or groundnut soup, fried yam with turkey tail with hot spicy pepper. In recent times, international chains have sprung up in Ghana; hence the menu is predominantly chicken and fried rice, burger, and pizza. Also, these international restaurants are housed in plush buildings or part of a hotel facility. International brands like Kentucky Fried Chicken (KFC) and Barcelos are operational in Ghana. Andaleeb and Conway [3], alluded that people, specifically women, are limited by time to plan and prepare food for their dependents, hence the high preference for food prepared at restaurants. In line with these changes in the Ghanaian demographics with increased urbanization and more career women working outside the home, Ashitey [4], saw that the restaurant sector is expected to continue growing rapidly. Considering the booming nature of the hospitality industry in Ghana, which is inseparably interwoven with the restaurant sector, entrepreneurial outlook of restaurant operators is an imperative management principle, which is the objective of this study. The paper commences with a brief review of the literature that relates to entrepreneurial orientation and restaurant

---

*Corresponding author: Yeboah AM, Department Liberal Studies, Cape Coast Polytechnic, Ghana, E-mail: ahomkakofi@yahoo.com; aspicious@yahoo.co.uk

industry, followed by the research method used. The paper proceeds with a detailed analysis of demographic and business information of the restaurant operators and restaurant firms respectively. Also, the relationship between the entrepreneurial dimensions and business initiatives is analyzed. A set of tentative recommendations conclude the paper.

Literature Review

Entrepreneurial outlook

Entrepreneurs might not necessarily be the smartest people on earth, but certainly they are people with dreams, ideas and passion coupled with basic business plan to get off the unemployment treadmill onto a way of life that offers independence. People with entrepreneurial outlook are generally described as persons who have an enterprise, venture or idea and assume significant accountability for the inherent risks and the outcome of these ventures. Again, having entrepreneurial outlook means looking at the world a bit differently. It is an attitude and an approach to thinking that actively seeks out change, rather than waiting to adapt to change. It is a mindset that embraces critical questioning, innovation, service and continuous improvement. McGrath RG and MacMillan IC [5], show that strategists/firms should adopt an entrepreneurial mindset to sense opportunities mobilize resources and exploit opportunities. Also, Senges [6], submits that an entrepreneurial mindset describes the innovative and energetic pursuit of opportunities and it facilitates action aimed at exploiting these opportunities. Entrepreneurial firms tend to have a more innovative approach to thinking about their products or service, new directions to take the company in, or new ways of doing old tasks. To have an entrepreneurial outlook in an organization, employees must think that anything is possible and have tenacity to accomplish it. Moreover, all employees regardless of their status have a voice that needs to be nurtured, not criticized, in order to continue bringing innovative ideas forward. The entrepreneurial spirit of a firm gets more challenging as firms grow and mature because of the tendency to gravitate towards more complacency, increased hierarchy and entrenched bureaucratic procedures. This causes companies to become more risk-adverse and protective of the business establishment. Owners or managers of such big companies feel they have more to lose than when they started out. But it is imperative that employers and employees keep their entrepreneurial spirit alive as the organization grows.

Entrepreneurial orientation

The extent to which a firm is entrepreneurial is commonly referred to as its entrepreneurial orientation. Miller [7], pioneered the definition of entrepreneurial orientation which was developed further by Covin and Slevin [8] and many other researchers, notably [9]. The widely accepted dimensions of entrepreneurial orientation are innovativeness, proactiveness, risk-taking, competitive aggressiveness and autonomy. The following paragraphs briefly discuss each of these dimensions.

Innovation is generally defined as incremental and revolutionary changes in thinking, processes, products or organizations. Today, innovation and entrepreneurship have changed. The empirical reality is they are not all systematic and manifested the same in an international market as concluded by Drucker [10], there are varied ways of practicing those concepts around the world. For instance, the US and China have incubators with divergent methods of breeding innovation and entrepreneurship.

Proactiveness described the distinctiveness of business managers to anticipate future opportunities, both in terms of products or technologies, markets and consumer demand [11,12]. Define proactiveness as firm's response to market opportunities and this implies opportunity-seeking perspective, introducing new product and services ahead in order to increase the competitive positioning in relation to other firms. Risk-taking is making decisions and taking actions without certain knowledge of probable outcomes. Risk has various interpretations and different meanings depending on the contexts in which the conception is used. Risk-taking can be studied through the lenses of preference or aversion, perception, propensity and behavior [13]. Additionally [14], considered risk-taking as the capacity of the entrepreneur to perceive risk at its inception and to find avenues to mitigate transfer or share the risk. Non-entrepreneurs and entrepreneurs differ in taking the risk where the later take more. Lumpkin and Dess [9], put forward autonomy and competitive aggressiveness as two additional dimensions. They define autonomy as independent action undertaken by entrepreneurial leaders or teams in bringing forth an idea or a vision and carrying it through to completion. Competitive aggressiveness is the intense effort to outperform industry rivals. It is characterized by a combative posture or an aggressive response aimed at improving position or overcoming a threat in a competitive marketplace. These five dimensions of entrepreneurial orientation show high inter correlation with one another ranging from r=0.39 to r=0.75 [15,16]. But, the dimensionality of entrepreneurial orientation is exposed to divergent agreement. Some scholars considered the entrepreneurial construct as unidimensional concept and this consequently influence business performance in the same ways [8,17]. In recent time, scholars suggest the dimensions of entrepreneurial orientation are multi-dimensional and as such impact performance differently [12,18]. Regardless of the preceding disagreement among scholars, entrepreneurial orientation is often mentioned as an antecedent of business growth, competitive advantage and superior performance. Prior empirical studies have repeatedly shown a positive influence of entrepreneurial orientation on business performance. The paragraphs that follow will discuss the restaurant industry from the global and Ghanaian perspectives. Discussed below is history of the restaurant industry cited from the internet blog of Lorri Mealey [19], a Restauranting Expert.

Restaurant industry 02

A restaurant is a place people visit to eat, drink and socialize with other people. Every country in the world can boast of restaurants which are operated along the cultural orientation of that country. The origin of restaurant operation can be credited to the French Revolution. This happened toward the end of the eighteenth century. The French still play a major role in the restaurant's development. The first restaurant proprietor is believed to have been one A. Boulanger, a soup vendor, who opened his business in Paris in 1765. The business motive of selling food for profit has existed during the earliest civilization. The earliest forms of restaurants were the roadside inns located in the middle of the countryside. Inns served meals at a common table to travelers and also served as central social place that brought people together. Notable European countries had a stint with the revolution of restaurant operation in the Middle Ages. In Germany and Austria, alsace brauwin and weisteben were served while, bodegas-serving tapas was the popular meal in Spain. The British preferred sausage and shepherd's pie and the French opted for stews and soups. The major breakthrough in the restaurant industry during the 20th century is attributed to McDonalds. The McDonald brothers operated their restaurant business prudently by offering food efficiently and inexpensively, but had a setback in franchising. Ray Kroc, a restaurant equipment salesman, bought the McDonald brothers out in 1954 and pioneered an apt formula for franchising, therefore, changing the landscape of dining in America and the world at large. The restaurant industry has metamorphosed over the years. Beyond the basic purpose to provide food and drink, restaurants today play a vital component in the business, social, intellectual and artistic life of a striving society. For example, millions of people are employed either to wait on tables, cook, or wash dishes for their livelihood. Experts in the restaurant sector stress that urbanization; digitization and globalization are the three dynamic and interactive forces reshaping the restaurant industry. In recent times, restaurant operators must be customer focused in order to stay in business in that people are very conscious of health and nutrition, and so carefully select what foods they patronize at restaurants.

The Restaurant industry in Ghana

Ghanaians are recognized for their warm hospitality. However, this is not reflected in the current hospitality industry. Holmes [20], asserts that vast majority of hotels and restaurants fail to offer quality of services needed to promote the sector. This could be due to the absence of adequate technical and vocational institutions mandated to train and instill technical skills in employees of the industry, hence the general lack of international service standards. At present, restaurant operators are trying to mitigate the challenge by conducting in-house training, which is obviously not working by the evidence of the prevailing standards. The option of importing expatriates is very expensive and unsustainable. Currently, the African Institute of Hospitality (AIH) is the only institution in Ghana that deals exclusively with vocational training in the hospitality sector. The underperformance of the restaurant sector could be attributed to the repeal of legislation titled LI 1817. Prior to the repeal of the LI 1817, the said LI empowered the Ghana investment promotion centre (GIPC) to grant incentives in the form of tax exemptions to operators in the hotel and hospitality industry. Such operators enjoyed tax exemptions on imported materials such as refrigerators, air conditioners, carpets, kitchen equipment, one vehicle among others, required for their establishment and smooth operations. Unfortunately, some beneficiaries abused the facility and used it to import luxury cars, furniture and other goods which they sold on the open market and avoided tax payment on them. This attitude necessitated the repeal of the LI 1817. Regrettably, reliable data on how much contribution the restaurant sector makes to the economic development of Ghana is not available. This could be partly due to the fact that the majority of these restaurant firms are in the informal sector. So, economic statistics on this sector is added jointly to the hospitality industry. The Ghana Statistical Service reported that hotels and restaurants accounted for 4.3% and 3, 877 million Ghana cedis contribution to the gross domestic product (GDP) of Ghana in 2013. In all, the service sector recorded the highest contribution of 49.5% to the GDP of Ghana in 2013 [21].

Business initiatives in the restaurant industry

Every business entity is established to achieve a purpose. Undoubtedly, the ultimate goal of every business organisation is to satisfy its clients at a profit. A business initiative explains how a business minded individual is able to turn ideas into fruitful action. One must have the urge to perform and reach the set goals. Initiative is very essential to run a business. Success in a business venture can be achieved if all employees show much initiative in performing well. In the domain of entrepreneurship discourse, the outcomes of business initiatives are product, service or process innovations and new market segments. Morris and Sexton [22], assert that entrepreneurial firms are capable of multiple entrepreneurial initiatives over time. This implies that a single initiative does not constitute a high entrepreneurial outlook. In line with this argument [23], considered firms frequently developing new products, new business ventures and additional services as very entrepreneurially oriented. Conversely put, some firms may have a greater tendency to behave entrepreneurially than others [24].

Building a customer base for a restaurant is more complicated than simply cooking meals. The main activities of a restaurant business are cooking and serving it to the public. In recent times, most restaurants have added additional services such as organizing events, playing live music and providing entertainment facilities. For the purpose of this study, the business initiatives of the restaurant operators are the frequency of new products [meals and drinks], services [working hours, live music and entertaining facilities] and business venture [new outlets].

Research Methodology

The study involved restaurant firms located in the Cape Coast Metropolis. Cape Coast is the capital town of the Central Region of Ghana and is situated on the south to the Gulf of Guinea. The list as well as the location of registered restaurant firms in the Cape Coast Metropolis was obtained from the Cape Coast Metropolitan Assembly. The number of restaurant firms was 46, located unevenly at the various suburbs. All the 46 restaurant firms formed part of the study, hence a census approach was used. However, 41 responded positively representing 89.13% response rate. The entrepreneurial outlook was measured using the five multidimensional constructs of entrepreneurial orientation [innovativeness, proactiveness, risk-taking, autonomy and competitive aggressiveness] propounded by Dess and Lumpkin [9]. The Entrepreneurial Orientation Questionnaire (EOQ) developed by Covin and Slevin [25], was adapted to develop the questionnaire. The original items were fine-tuned to suit the restaurant sector as well as new items were added to exhaustively cover all the five dimensions. Information from extant literature enabled the development of the new items. The business initiative variables [new products, new services and new business ventures] were measured using an adapted version of the Entrepreneurial Performance Instrument (EPI) questionnaire developed by Morris and Sexton [22]. The restaurant operators were asked to rank the degree of the business initiative improvements over the immediate past three years. Both the entrepreneurial outlook and business initiative variables were measured on a 5-point Likert scale with 1 being 'strongly disagree' and 5 being 'strongly agree'. Data was analysed using the Statistical Product and Service Solutions (SPSS 20.0 version). The entrepreneurial outlook and business initiatives of restaurant operators are depicted using the mean, standard deviation and coefficient of variation statistics. Moreover, chi-square was employed to test the two hypotheses. Correlation analysis was employed to describe the associations between the various dimensions of entrepreneurial outlook and business initiatives. The reliability of the various dimensions is depicted in Table 1.

The results in Table 1 show that each dimension of entrepreneurial orientation and business initiatives recorded a Cronbach's alpha greater than 0.7. According to Fraenkel and Wallen this implies that all the constructs were reliable and could be used in this study

Results

This section describes the demographic and business profile of the restaurant operators and firm correspondingly. Next is descriptive

Dimensions	Number of items	Cronbach's Alpha
Entrepreneurial Orientation		
Innovativeness	6	0.778
Proactiveness	6	0.815
Risk-taking	4	0.789
Autonomy	6	0.788
Competitiveness aggressiveness	5	0.880
Business Initiatives		
Product	2	0.865
Service	3	0.891
Business venture	2	0.865

Table 1: Cronbach's alpha coefficients.

statistics of the entrepreneurial outlook and business initiative dimensions. The two hypotheses are tested. It concludes by examining the associations between these dimensions.

Demographic profile of restaurant operators

Findings show that the majority of the restaurant operators were females with 76.2% while their male counterparts were 23.8%. The respondents' ages ranged from 20 to 44. The greater part was in the 35 to 40 age group and accounted for 44%. A majority representing 42.9% had Commercial/Vocational/Technical education, while 28.6% and 16.7% had Bachelor's Degree and post graduate education respectively. Another 7.1% had post secondary diploma and 4.8% had senior high school education. This implies that all the restaurant operators had at least senior high school education. Moreover, 61.9% of the respondents had not worked in a previous restaurant firm but, 38.1% were previously engaged by a restaurant firm.

Business profile of restaurant firms

The majority (64.3%) of the restaurant operators doubles as owners and managers. 21.4% and 14.3% were managers and owners respectively. Besides, 61.9% of the restaurant firms had existed at least 6 years; 38.1% had operated not more than 5 years. With regard to how the restaurant firm started, 52.4% established the business from that start, 31.0% inherited and 16.7% purchased it from another person. Sole proprietorship is the highest (66.7%) form of business ownership followed by partnership with 19.7%. Company form recorded 13.7%. The majority (83.3%) of the restaurants operators sell both Ghanaian and foreign dishes, and 16.7% sell Ghanaian meals only.

Entrepreneurial outlook and business initiatives of restaurant operators

This section uses the mean, standard deviation and coefficient of variation to describe the entrepreneurial inclination and business initiatives of the restaurant operators. A mean score of 1-2.9 and 3-5 depicted low and high entrepreneurial outlook respectively. Table 2 illustrated the Entrepreneurial Outlook and Business Initiatives of the Restaurant Operators.

Entrepreneurial outlook

The findings as shown in Table 2 indicate that the restaurant operators have high entrepreneurial outlook with the mean score of 3.11. Specifically, autonomy recorded the highest followed by proactiveness. But, risk-taking, innovativeness and competitive aggressiveness recorded low entrepreneurial outlook. This outcome implies the restaurant operators crave for absolute control over their business. This desire is confirmed by 64.3% of them operating as owners and managers at the same time. Also, 66.7% preferred sole proprietorship form of business ownership. The high score in proactiveness could mean the restaurant operators take the initiative to provide new food, experiences to customers ahead of their competitors. Nonetheless, the general impression is that the restaurant operators are risk averse in being the first to be innovative and aggressively competitive.

Business initiative

The overall propensity of business initiatives engaged by the restaurant operators was high (mean score of 3.03, Table 2). Specifically, new product development scored high. But, the development of new services and new business ventures recorded low mean score. This suggests the restaurant operators seldom introduce novel services or expand their operation by establishing new outlets. The reason could be that most restaurant operators have limited resources and also due to the small geographical space inhabiting the Cape Coast Metropolis. It does not make business sense to create more outlets. The Metropolis covers an area of 122 square kilometres and is the smallest metropolis in Ghana.

Relationship between restaurant establishment modes and entrepreneurial outlook

H0: Mode of establishing a restaurant firm has no significant effect on entrepreneurial outlook of the restaurant operators.

This part considers whether the mode of establishing the restaurant firm can influence the entrepreneurial outlook of the restaurant operators. The mode of establishment were categorized into three; started by myself, inherited and purchased. The Chi-square was used to examine the relationship. The results are presented in Table 3 at the appendix. The Pearson Chi-Square recorded x (1)=10.167, p=0.253. This shows that there is no statistically significant association between the establishment mode of a restaurant and entrepreneurial outlook. Hence, the study failed to reject the null hypothesis. The inference is that restaurant operators can be entrepreneurially minded regardless of how that restaurant firm was established.

Relationship between gender and business initiatives

H0: Gender will have no significant effect on business initiatives.

This sought to find out whether the gender of the restaurant operator has any connection with how frequent the restaurant operators churn out business initiative. The Chi-square was used to achieve this objective. The findings are captured in Table 4 at the appendix. The association between gender of the restaurant operator and business initiatives recorded a Pearson Chi-Square of 2.6479 and a corresponding p value of 0.266. Therefore, the study failed to reject

Dimension	Mean	Standard deviation	Coefficient of variation
Entrepreneurial Orientation	3.11	1.11	1.19
Innovativeness	2.67	1.22	1.51
Proactiveness	3.54	0.94	0.98
Risk-taking	2.84	1.11	1.25
Autonomy	3.70	0.96	0.92
Competitiveness aggressiveness	2.78	1.12	1.28
Business Initiatives	3.03	1.14	1.03
Product	3.73	1.06	0.30
Service	2.87	1.18	1.40
Business venture	2.50	1.17	1.17

Table 2: Entrepreneurial outlook and business initiatives of restaurant operators.

the null hypothesis. The conclusion is that the propensity of restaurant operators to develop business initiatives is not gender specific. Hence, both male and female restaurant operators can increase their scope of business initiatives.

The results in Table 5 reveal that all the five dimensions of entrepreneurial outlook associated significantly with new products and new business ventures. Autonomy had less significant relationship with new services. This outcome implies that the restaurant operators will come out with frequent business initiatives if their entrepreneurial outlook is high. In other words, an entrepreneurial inclination will enable the restaurant operators to habitually develop new products, new services and establish more restaurant outlets.

Discussion

The results indicated the restaurant firms in the Cape Coast Metropolis were largely by females and the common age group was 20 to 44 years. Most of them had Commercial/Vocational/Technical education. A good number of restaurant operators established their business from the start and also run the dual roles of being the owner and manager. Sole proprietorship is the preferred form of business ownership, while the menu is commonly both Ghanaian and foreign dishes. The restaurant operators demonstrated a somewhat high entrepreneurial outlook with autonomy been the most practiced dimension. Innovativeness recorded the least practiced dimension. This outcome is not surprising since thorough observation of the restaurants business activities suggests that they all operators use the same business model. Moreover, it seems they benchmark their business activities against each other rather than on international best practices. Their risk averse posturing could explain this behaviour. The restaurant operators are not frequent with churning out business initiatives because they scored a marginal high mean value. They focus primarily on the meals and drinks on sale and not enthused over by providing quality services. The low mean score for new business venturing confirms why all the restaurants studied have only one place of business. The mode for establishing a restaurant business has no significant influence on the entrepreneurial outlook of the operator, just as the gender of the restaurant operator does not determine the desire to champion business initiatives. Both male and female restaurant operators can engage in frequent business initiatives. The dimensions of the entrepreneurial

	Products		Services		New business Venture	
	R	P	R	P	R	P
Innovativeness	0.699**	0.000	0.821**	0.000	0.632**	0.000
Proactiveness	0.848**	0.000	0.553**	0.000	0.731**	0.000
Risk-taking	0.823**	0.000	0.539**	0.000	0.895**	0.000
Autonomy	0.390*	0.011	0.288	0.064	0.755**	0.000
Competitive Aggressiveness	0.825**	0.000	0.539**	0.000	0.864**	0.000

Table 3: Relationship between the dimensions of entrepreneurial outlook.

Chi-Square Tests

	Value	df	Asymp. Sig. (2-sided)
Pearson Chi-Square	10.167a	8	0.253
Likelihood Ratio	11.296	8	0.185
Linear-by-Linear Association	0.003	1	0.960
No of Valid Cases	42		

a. 14 cells (93.3%) have expected count less than 5. The minimum expected count is 0.50.

Symmetric Measures

		Value	Approx. Sig.
Nominal by Nominal	Phi	0.492	0.253
	Cramer's V	0.348	0.253
	N of Valid Cases	42	

Business establishment mode * Preferred entrepreneurial dimension Cross tabulation

			Preferred entrepreneurial dimension					Total
			Innovativeness	Proactiveness	Risk-taking	Autonomy	Competitive aggressiveness	
Business establishment mode	Started by myself	Count	6	3	0	9	4	22
		% within Business establishment mode	27.3%	13.6%	0%	40.9%	18.2%	100.0%
		% within Preferred entrepreneurial dimension	66.7%	33.3%	0%	64.3%	57.1%	52.4%
		% of Total	14.3%	7.1%	0%	21.4%	9.5%	52.4%
	Inherited	Count	3	4	1	3	2	13
		% within Business establishment mode	23.1%	30.8%	7.7%	23.1%	15.4%	100.0%
		% within Preferred entrepreneurial dimension	33.3%	44.4%	33.3%	21.4%	28.6%	31.0%
		% of Total	7.1%	9.5%	2.4%	7.1%	4.8%	31.0%
	Purchased from another person	Count	0	2	2	2	1	7
		% within Business establishment mode	0.0%	28.6%	28.6%	28.6%	14.3%	100.0%
		% within Preferred entrepreneurial dimension	0.0%	22.2%	66.7%	14.3%	14.3%	16.7%
		% of Total	0.0%	4.8%	4.8%	4.8%	2.4%	16.7%
	Total	Count	9	9	3	14	7	42
		% within Business establishment mode	21.4%	21.4%	7.1%	33.3%	16.7%	100.0%
		% within Prefered entrepreneurial dimension	100.0%	100.0%	100.0%	100.0%	100.0%	100.0%
		% of Total	21.4%	21.4%	7.1%	33.3%	16.7%	100.0%

Table 4: Relationship between restaurant establishment mode and entrepreneurial outlook.

Gender * Frequent business initiative Crosstabulation						
			Frequent business initiative			
			Products	Services	Business ventures	Total
Gender	Gender	Count	3	5	2	10
		% within Gender	30.0%	50.0%	20.0%	100.0%
		% within Frequent business initiative	13.6%	35.7%	33.3%	23.8%
		% of Total	7.1%	11.9%	4.8%	23.8%
	Female	Count	19	9	4	32
		% within Gender	59.4%	28.1%	12.5%	100.0%
		% within Frequent business initiative	86.4%	64.3%	66.7%	76.2%
		% of Total	45.2%	21.4%	9.5%	76.2%
	Total	Count	22	14	6	42
		% within Gender	52.4%	33.3%	14.3%	100.0%
		% within Frequent business initiative	100.0%	100.0%	100.0%	100.0%
		% of Total	52.4%	33.3%	14.3%	100.0%

Chi-Square Tests			
	Value	df	Asymp. Sig. (2-sided)
Pearson Chi-Square	2.649a	2	0.266
Likelihood Ratio	2.693	2	0.260
Linear-by-Linear Association	1.939	1	0.164
No of Valid Cases	42		

a. 3 cells (50.0%) have expected count less than 5. The minimum expected count is 1.43.

Symmetric Measures			
		Value	Approx. Sig.
Nominal by Nominal	Phi	0.251	0.266
	Cramer's V	0.251	0.266
	N of Valid Cases	42	

Table 5: Relationship between gender of restaurant operators.

outlook had a significant positive association with business initiatives apart from autonomy that recoded insignificant influence on services. Consequently, this study contends that entrepreneurial mindset is imperative for developing and promoting business initiatives in the restaurant business.

Recommendations and Conclusions

Based on its findings, this study concluded that the restaurant operators in the Cape Coast Metropolis have a somewhat entrepreneurial outlook as well as the urge to develop business initiatives. The following suggestions will improve their entrepreneurial outlook and business initiatives. The restaurant operators must be abreast of current knowledge in order to utilize new technology in the restaurant industry by attending seminars and workshops. They must be involved with every aspect of the restaurant with complete professionalism. Employees must be treated professionally and not means to an end. This will enable employees to offer constructive ideas and criticisms. With regard to customer service, every restaurant must have a trendy menu and star chef. Restaurant managers must get to know their regular customers by their names, favourite dishes and drinks. In summary, restaurant operators must plan ahead, communicate expectations to staff, care for customers and carry out all these in a consistent and an up-beat manner.

Refernces

1. Kuratko DF (2007) The Corporate Entrepreneurship Process: A Research Model Foundations and Trends. Entrepreneurship Journal 3: 62-182.
2. Dess GG, Lumpkin GT (2005) The role of entrepreneurial orientation in stimulating effective corporate entrepreneurship. Academy of Management Executive 19: 47-56.
3. Andaleeb SS, Conway C (2006) Customer satisfaction in the restaurant industry: an examination of the transaction-specific model. Journal of Services Marketing 20: 3-11.
4. Ashitey E (2008) Ghana's Food Service Sector. GAIN Report, USDA Foreign Agricultural Service. Number: GH8008.
5. McGrath RG, MacMillan IC (2000) Assessing technology projects using Real Options Reasoning. Research-Technology Management 43: 5-49.
6. Senges M (2007) Knowledge entrepreneurship in universities: Practice and strategy of Internet based innovation appropriation
7. Miller D (1983) The correlates of entrepreneurship in three types of firms. Management Science 29: 770-791.
8. Covin JG, Slevin DP (1989) Strategic Management of Small Firms in Hostile and Benign Environment. Strategic Management Journal 10: 5-87.
9. Lumpkin GT, Dess GG (1996) Clarifying the Entrepreneurial Orientation Construct and Linking it to Performance. The Academy Management Review 21: 35.
10. Drucker PF (1985) Innovation and Entrepreneurship: Practice and Principles.
11. Schillo S (2011) Entrepreneurial Orientation What is it and how can it be Useful for Policy and Program Development? Innovation and Entrepreneurship.
12. Lumpkin GT, Dess GG (2001) Understanding and Measuring Autonomy: An Entrepreneurial Orientation Perspective. Entrepreneurship Theory and Practice, 47-69.
13. Fayolle A, Basso O, Legrain T (2008) Corporate culture and values: Genesis and sources of L'Oreal's entrepreneurial orientation. Journal of Small Business and Entrepreneurship 21: 215-230.
14. Ogunsiji AS, Ladanu WK (2010) Entrepreneurial Orientation as a Panacea for the Ebbing Productivity in Nigerian Small and Medium Enterprises: A Theoretical Perspective. International Business Research 3: 92-199.
15. Tan J, Tan D (2005) Environment-strategy Coevolution and Coalignment: A staged-model of Chinese SOEs under transition. Strategy Management Journal 26: 41-157.
16. Bhuian SN, Menguc B, Bell SJ (2005) Just Entrepreneurial Enough the Moderating effect of entrepreneurial on the relationship between market orientation and performance. Journal of Business research 58: 9-17.
17. Knight GA (1997) Cross-cultural reliability and validity of a scale to measure firm entrepreneurial orientation. Journal of Business Venturing 12: 3-225.
18. George BA (2006) Entrepreneurial Orientation: A theoretical and Empirical Examination of the consequences of differing Construct Representations.

19. Mealey L (2015) A History of the Restaurant.

20. Holmes G (2012) A Solution to the hospitality Challenge of Ghana. Modern Ghana, Business Blog.

21. Ghana Statistical Service (2014) Gross Domestic Product, National Account Statistics.

22. Morris MH, Sexton DL (1996) The concept of entrepreneurial intensity: Implications for company performance. Journal of Business Research 36: 5-13.

23. Mariono L, Strandholm K, Steensma HK, Weaver KM (2000) The Moderating Effect of national Culture on the relationship between entrepreneurial orientation and strategic alliance portfolio extensiveness. Entrepreneurship theory and practice 26: 45-160.

24. Scheepers MJ, Marlese B, Eric W, Herrington M (2005) How innovative are South African firms? Global entrepreneurship monitor: South African report 2005.

25. Covin JG, Slevin DP (1991) A conceptual entrepreneurship as firm behaviour. Entrepreneurship Theory and Practice 16: 7-25.

Stimulating Innovation within Social Sector Organizations: The Application of Design Thinking

Berzin SC[1]* and Catsouphes MP[2]

[1]Associate Professor, Boston College Graduate School of Social Work, 140 Commonwealth Avenue, Chestnut Hill, MA 02467, USA
[2]Associate Professor, GSSW and the Carroll School of Management, 140 Commonwealth Avenue, Chestnut Hill, MA 02467, USA

Abstract

In an era of diminishing resources available to social service agencies and increasingly complex social problems, it has become almost imperative that the leaders of nonprofit organizations search for new strategies and solutions. This article discusses a pilot project which utilized experiential learning about design thinking to stimulate innovation in social sector organizations. Results suggest that even limited exposure to design thinking can lead to changes in individual capacity for innovation and increased work engagement. Implications for nonprofit management and the potential for intrapreneurial paths to innovation are discussed.

Keywords: Social innovation; Design thinking; Intrapreneurship; Social entrepreneurship; Innovation

Introduction

Leaders of organizations in the social sector today face some challenging realities. Social problems are increasingly complex [1] public support for social services continue to decline [2,3] and there is pressure to establish cross-sector partnerships despite the difficulty of these collaborations [4,5]. The social innovation framework offers options for addressing these challenges. Social innovation is widely understood as the development and application of new solutions to social problems – solutions that are either more efficient and/or more effective than those which have been tried [6]. Nonprofit managers who want to strengthen their organizations' capacities to engage in social innovation need to ensure that their staffs develop competencies for social innovation. Competencies relate to ideation, solution generation, pilot testing, implementation, and assessment of the innovative approaches to social problems. It therefore becomes a priority to train staff and integrate the principles and practices into daily operations [7].

Design thinking is an approach developed over the past twenty years that fosters the specification of solutions which have not emerged through traditional planning practices [8]. At its core, design thinking elevates the importance of using expanded strategies for 1) understanding the problem to be addressed, 2) generating alternative solution-focused ideas, and 3) engaging in serial pilot testing. While design thinking has been applied to a range of business settings for some time, the adoption of design thinking by nonprofits is just emerging. However, there are indications that design thinking is a promising approach for social innovation.

In this article, we discuss the findings from an exploratory assessment of the outcomes associated with a training project developed to enhance the design thinking skills of social sector leaders. The project, the Social Innovation Lab (the Lab), engaged individuals from multiple organizations in action learning projects so that they could develop design thinking competencies and use these skills to address a social issue.

Literature Review

Social innovation within existing organizations

There are two primary paths for social innovation projects: social entrepreneurship and social intrapreneurship. Although there are different definitions in the academic literature, social entrepreneurship often refers to the projects and initiatives that emerge from solutions developed by individuals. In most cases, social entrepreneurs create new organizations which implement the innovations.[1] In contrast, the origins of social intrapreneurship are different because the social innovation projects begin in the context of an existing organization.

While the work of individual social entrepreneurs has the potential to produce significant social impact [9,10] there are some challenges associated with entrepreneurship approaches that rely on the establishment of new organizations. As discussed by the authors (XX), these challenges include difficulties with scalability (i.e., the need to devote time and resources to establishing the infrastructure needed to serve large numbers of people), sustainability (i.e., the importance of investing in financial and non-financial resources to ensure that the new initiatives survive), and leadership transition (i.e., taking the steps so that the founder develops the management capacities needed to sustain the organization or passes the leadership to a different person who possess management competencies).

In contrast to social entrepreneurship, social intrapreneurship emerges within an existing organizational structure [11]. This context offers unique opportunities as well as challenges to social innovation initiatives. As conceptualized by Pinchot and Pellman [12], intrapreneurs are those who, on behalf of their organizations, take responsibility and risk for developing an idea so that it can become a new product or service. Existing organizations typically

---

[1]It should be noted that some writers, such as Paul Light (2011), take a broad view of social entrepreneurship that include many kinds of innovative activities in addition to the creation of new organizations.

*Corresponding author: Berzin SC, Boston College Graduate School of Social Work, 140 Commonwealth Avenue, Chestnut Hill, MA 02467, USA
E-mail: Berzin@bc.edu

bring extensive competencies and expertise to the opportunity for innovation. Furthermore, they can engage stakeholders' intellectual and experiential capital in a new venture. Social service organizations may also be able to leverage the relationships they have to launch social innovations. Furthermore, the organizational infrastructures already developed at existing organizations could help support sustainability.

The scholarly literature has identified some of the difficulties associated with intrapreneurial efforts. Organizational resistance to change, competing priorities already established by existing organizations, and the need to address the politics of change have been discussed as challenges (authors, XX). Training experiences can help organizations address some of the challenges associated with intrapreneurial efforts. The XX School (edited out for blind review) developed the Social Innovation Lab to expose social service agencies to some core activities associated with design thinking and guide them through the initial stages of a social innovation initiative.

Design thinking

Design thinking, an approach that is often associated with model-building activities used by design, engineers, architects, and urban planners, has been used as one way to unleash creativity so that innovative solutions can emerge [13]. Although people have described design thinking in different ways [14], a key characteristic of this approach is that it is "human-centered." Human-centered design puts the experiences of the people experiencing particular problems (individuals who might become the "users" of new solutions) at the center of all discussions about possible solutions.

Brown contends that design thinking is best understood as a continuum of overlapping "spaces" rather than a linear process where one step follows the next [13]. He indicates that the three spaces of innovation are *inspiration* (the problem or opportunity that motivates the work), *ideation* (a series of activities related to generating, elaborating, and testing solutions), and *implementation* (the path from the design phase to real-world application) [13]. Cross, who links design thinking research with experience and exposure, describes practices that support building conclusions from incomplete information, using visual modeling, learning by doing, and conjecturing solutions to deepen the understanding of problems [15]. Similarly, Brown (2009) identifies visual thinking, prototyping, and brainstorming as key design thinking activities [13].

Other experts in design thinking emphasize the importance of activities needed to develop a clear understanding of users' perspectives of problems. When the nuances of problems experienced are detailed, it becomes possible for innovators to move to a deeper understanding of the problem. In turn, it becomes possible to generate the broadest range of solutions. The steps might include observing users' interface with the problem, seeking user input, and defining the problems from multiple perspectives [16].

Design thinking has been used to create new products and services, and to support organizational change and growth in industry [17]. Its use has expanded considerably over the past twenty years [18]. There are opportunities to translate the design thinking skill set to address social problems [8]. Some design firms, like IDEO, have begun to take their work into the nonprofit sector. To date, however, there has been no focus in the literature about the possibilities for building organizations' capacity so that they are able to engage in independent design thinking rather than relying on consultants or design firms.

Creating organizational capacity for social innovation

Before designing the Lab, we reviewed the literature to identify organizational factors related to innovation. Research suggests that leadership, a culture of innovation, and team process are important predictors of innovation [19,20].

Leadership has long been considered a critical factor in stimulating and sustaining innovation at the workplace [21,22]. Leaders can be catalysts for innovation, mobilizing relevant stakeholder groups to engage in innovation activities [23]. Jaskyte suggests that leaders spur innovation when they challenge traditional processes and the status quo [24]. Other leadership practices, including those that support creativity, risk taking, the consideration of innovative ideas, and experimentation, are also linked to workplace innovation [21]. Leaders also impact the organizational culture which shapes the contours of a culture of innovation [25,26].

A vibrant culture of innovation requires that people at all levels of the organization share expectations that everyone will contribute to innovation [12,25]. Innovation culture is also rooted in a belief that agency staff will value diverse perspectives which can lead to creative thought and action [27]. Innovation is supported when people perceive that the organization values creativity, embraces experimentation, and has a tolerance of risk and failure [28].

The engagement of teams in innovation projects is a third success factor noted in the literature. When teams rather than individuals articulate new ideas, it can become easier to generate a broader range of solutions. These solutions are more likely to reflect the experiences of diverse stakeholder groups. Additionally, a team approach supports the diffusion of the innovation across the organization [29]. Strong innovation teams welcome individuals with different skills, and celebrate individuals who drive excellence [20].

While the Social Innovation Lab was not structured as a culture change initiative, it was designed to leverage two of these factors for social innovation: leadership and team process. Our study examined whether the Lab could effectively train agency staff to use design thinking for sparking ideation and rapid prototyping that would lead to new solutions. The study considered whether Lab participation was associated with changes in innovation capacity and work engagement.

Methods

Design thinking and the social innovation lab

The Lab was developed to bring design thinking to organizations in the social sector. Each participating organization identified 2-4 project Champions and 6-10 members to form an Innovation Team. Informed by the principles of action learning [30,31]. The Lab activities were organized into six stages.

1. Orientation: The Champions from all of the agencies were invited to an orientation session. Orientations for the Innovation Teams were held at each agency, giving the Teams an opportunity to consider Lab activities in the context of their own organization.

2. Problem Definition: The Champions began to specify their perspectives of the problem during discovery interviews. During team orientation sessions, the teams added new perspectives to the definition of the problem and underlying factors.

3. Design Thinking Training: Using a simulation, each Team was introduced to design thinking approaches.

4. Ideation and Prototyping: A full day was devoted to ideation, the development of a preliminary prototype, feedback sessions, and re-prototyping.

5. Pilot testing and Iteration: Each agency selected at least one component of their prototypes to pilot test for three months.

6. Celebrating Success and Transitioning to Full Implementation: The final activity was an event during which each of the participating organizations made a presentation about their prototype, the accomplishments made during pilot testing, and plans for the implementation of the full prototype.

Participants

The Lab engaged eight social sector organizations from Massachusetts and one national membership group (N=99 participants) in three Lab "classes." All of the agencies had social service missions, though their target populations and social issues varied. A majority of the agencies (n=7) are nonprofits, with one being a for-profit. The ninth group is a membership group which had not yet incorporated at the time of its participation in the Lab. Executive directors from each agency/group were recruited and made the decision about their group's participation in the Lab.

The agencies brought a range of projects to the Lab, summarized in Table 1. Agencies had an average of 11 participants per organization, including 2-4 Champions, and 7-9 Team members. Of the 99 participants in the Lab, 91 responded to the surveys, for a response rate of 92%. Respondents were primarily female (71%), White (78%), and had a Master's degree or higher (66%). Respondents worked at the participating organizations an average of 6.7 years (SD=7.7).

Measures

For this study, we examined possible changes in three of the measures included in the Time 1 survey (data collected at the beginning of the Lab) and the Time 3 survey (data collected after the Lab had ended). In addition, at Time 3, we asked the participants about their perceptions of the impact of the Lab.

Individual Innovation. Five items were used to measure innovation at the individual level, each of which was measured on a 4-point scale. The questions asked respondents to rate their ability to: 1) consider diverse sources of information to generate new ideas, 2) look for connections with alternative solutions, 3) generate alternative solutions before selecting a response, 4) generate solutions that are different from established ways of doing, and 5) model innovative behaviors. These items were adapted from Zhang [32-34]. For the purpose of analysis, we examined change in the individual items as well as change in a scale that combined the responses from all five items (∞=.65). The scale at Time 1 had a mean score of 3.3 (SD=.62).

Work Engagement. Nine items from the Utrecht Work Engagement Scale were used to measure employee engagement and satisfaction [35]. Each of the questions was measured on a 7-point scale and is related either to dedication, vigor, and absorption at work. We examined change in individual items as well as changes in the combined scale (∞=.94), which had at a Time 1 had a mean score of 5.9 (SD=.81). The

Pseudonym	Description	Project Focus/Foci
Care in Your Community	An agency with adult day health centers in three cities, offering comprehensive services during the day to elders, many of whom have memory disorders.	1. Responding to the needs of individuals (families) receiving diagnoses of dementia before symptoms begin to emerge. 2. Providing supports to employed family caregivers. 3. Continuing relationships with family caregivers whose family member is now deceased.
Charter School	An independent school providing challenging educational experiences to youth who have been unsuccessful in public school settings so that they can become scholars who attend college.	1. Anticipating the challenges that students typically encounter which cause them to dis-engaged. 2. Maintaining consistently high levels of student engagement with their education.
Mental Health Provider	Large agency providing a comprehensive range of mental health services to children, families, and adults.	1. Anticipating the transitions associated with the enactment of the Affordable Care Act, becoming the primary port of entry for people with persistent mental health problems.
School for Children with Special Needs	An organization providing educational and therapeutic services (residential as well as non-residential) to students with emotional and behavioral problems.	1. Increasing the recruitment and retention of diverse staff.
Community Multi-Service Center	A multi-service organization with sites in several cities. Programs include housing, job training, and sports and wellness opportunities.	1. Increasing the efficiency of space utilization. 2. Leveraging agency assets to expand programming offered to community residents.
Health Care in Your Home	A for-profit agency providing home care and home health services to elders and people with disabilities.	1. Improving the quality of the work experiences for individuals providing direct care to the clients. 2. Strengthening clients' understanding of the expertise that employees can offer.
Home for Homeless Youth	An organization that provides a range of health and services to youth who are homeless.	1. Improving youth access to and use of preventive and primary health care services.
Foster Care Organization	An organization providing comprehensive health, education, and social services to children in foster care.	1. Responding to the challenges faced by young adults who will transition out of the foster care system due to age.
Membership for You	A membership organization for individuals with disabilities.	1. Creating a funding stream. 2. Promoting a stronger sense of community among members. 3. Developing resources to help people with disabilities make choices about the type of care that they prefer.

Table 1: Highlights of participating organizations.

level of work engagement at Time 1 was also used as a predictor to examine its association with the participants' perception of change in organizational capacity for innovation.

Organizational Capacity for Innovation. – We used six items (6-point scale) to measure innovation at the organizational level. The items included questions about the perceived acceptance of new ideas, the organization's ability to respond when change is indicated, managers' ability to recognize when change is needed, organizational flexibility, the availability of assistance for developing new ideas, and norms related to new ways to address problems. Items were adapted from measures developed by Patterson [36]. Our analyses used these items individually and as a scale (∞=.93) which had a mean score=4.6 (SD=.98).

Impact of Lab. Eight questions were developed by the authors to measure the Lab's impact on the organization and the project's potential impact, each of which was measured on a 6-point scale. These items were combined into a scale (∞=.86), with a mean of 5.1 (SD=.59).

Job Characteristics. Two items were included on the survey to assess their association with the dependent variables. One variable was included to indicate whether the respondent currently worked as a supervisor (69%). We also measured the respondents' tenure at their current organizations as a continuous variable (mean=6.7 years; SD=7.7).

Data collection and analysis

The Lab participants were surveyed at three time points, the beginning, middle and end of the Lab. Most of the respondents accessed the survey using a secured website; although some decided to answer surveys using pencil and paper (researchers entered these responses into the dataset). For this article, we used paired t-tests to analyze change over time, from Time 1 to Time 3. All comparisons were also run using the nonparametric test, Wilcoxon Signed Rank Test; results were the same when using this test. Additional analysis explored associations between job characteristics and outcome variables.

Results

Building individual capacity for innovation

The respondents indicated that they perceived a change in their own capacity for innovation, with scores on this innovation scale rising from 3.34 to 3.53 (p<.05) over the course of the study period (Table 2). The response to two items, in particular, showed significant improvement: "the ability to look for connections with solutions used in diverse areas" (mean difference=.23, p<.05) and "generating a significant number of solutions to a particular problem" (mean difference=.33, p<.05). We did not find statistically significant relationships between the respondents' tenure or their status as a supervisor and changes in perceptions of the participants' capacity for innovation.

Design thinking processes and work engagement

Participants reported increase in two of the work engagement items as shown in Table 3. Specifically, there were increases in scores on "happiness while working intensely" (mean difference=.42, p<.05) and "feeling strong and vigorous at one's job" (mean difference=.39, P<.05). However, we did not find a change in the overall levels of work engagement as indicated by the overall scale or on other individual items.

Organizational capacity for innovation

While the Lab focused on building the capacity of leaders and team members to engage in design thinking, we were interested in whether the participants would report changes in the extent to which they felt their organizations were innovative. Examining both the organizational innovation scale (overall) as well as the individual items that comprise this scale yielded no significant results, even when examining results by organization (Table 4).

We did, however, find relationships between the respondents' perception of change of their organizations' capacity for innovation and levels of engagement as well as their status as supervisors. People who were less engaged in their workplace at the beginning of the study perceived greater increases in their organizations' innovation capacity (r=-.42, p<.05). Individuals with supervisory roles saw a greater increase in their own organization's innovation capacity than those individuals without supervisory responsibility (t=2.1, p<.05). Tenure was not associated with perceptions of change in organizational capacity for innovation.

Impact of the Lab

A clear majority of the participants (93.3%) agreed the Lab helped them develop a better understanding of how to innovate at their organization (Table 5). Almost all participants (96.6%) would recommend that their organization use this approach to innovation for another project. These measures suggest participants felt that the design thinking process improved their innovation capacity.

Discussion

Building the innovation capacities of individuals within nonprofit organizations opens the door for promoting intrapreneurship. The Lab was established to train the members of nonprofits in design thinking as a way to strengthen their capacities to engage in social innovation initiatives. Engaging individuals in opportunities to build their own innovation capacity may also serve the purpose of strengthening organizational capacity. Preliminary results from the Lab indicate that participation in the Lab was associated with a strengthening of the participants' assessment of their own capacity for innovation. Results also suggest that the Lab experience can have a positive effect

	Time 1 Mean (SD)	Time 3 Mean (SD)	t
Innovation and You Scale	3.34 (.62)	3.53 (.54)	-2.24*
I consider diverse sources of information for generating new ideas.	3.45 (.51)	3.62 (.49)	-1.54
I look for connections with solutions used in seemingly diverse areas.	3.27 (.52)	3.50 (.57)	-1.76*
I generate a significant number of alternatives to the same problem before I choose the final solution.	3.00 (.53)	3.33 (.71)	-2.4 *
I try to devise potential solutions that move away from the established ways of doing things.	2.97 (.49)	3.17 (.65)	-1.4
I model innovative behaviors, such as exploring opportunities, generating ideas, and putting effort into developing innovative approaches.	4.00 (.93)	4.00 (.54)	.000

Note. *p<.05

Table 2: Comparing means for innovation and the individual at time 1 and time 2.

	Time 1 Mean (SD)	Time 3 Mean (SD)	t
Work Engagement Scale	5.90 (.81)	6.01 (.73)	-1.08
At work, I feel bursting with energy.	5.37 (1.11)	5.56 (.97)	-.87
I am enthusiastic about my job.	6.14 (.99)	6.24 (.74)	-.52
I feel happy when I am working intensely.	6.03 (.98)	6.45 (.78)	-2.12*
My job inspires me.	5.89 (.96)	6.00 (.98)	-.52
I am proud of the work that I do.	6.57 (.74)	6.64 (.56)	-.40
I get carried away when I am working.	5.55 (1.21)	5.83 (1.26)	-1.00
At my job, I feel strong and vigorous.	5.52 (1.06)	5.93 (.99)	-1.89*
When I get up in the morning, I feel like going to work.	5.69 (1.11)	5.83 (1.23)	-.55
I am immersed in my work.	6.36 (.78)	6.32 (.91)	.189

Note. *p<.05

Table 3: Comparing means for work engagement at time 1 and time 2.

	Time 1 Mean (SD)	Time 3 Mean (SD)	t
Innovation and Your Organization Scale	4.60 (.98)	4.67 (.84)	-.37
Assistance in developing new ideas is readily available at this organization.	4.41 (1.24)	4.62 (.94)	-.84
New ideas are readily accepted at this organization.	4.96 (.94)	5.07 (.99)	-.59
This organization is very flexible; it can change quickly.	4.45 (1.30)	4.41 (1.10)	.14
Managers here are quick to respond when changes need to be made.	4.67 (1.14)	4.41 (1.05)	.98
This organization is quick to respond when changes need to be made.	4.45 (1.09)	4.62 (1.05)	-.78
People in this organization are always searching for new ways of looking at problems.	4.66 (1.23)	4.76 (.95)	-.43

Note. p<.05

Table 4: Comparing means for innovation and the organization at time 1 and time 2.

Item	Somewhat disagree	Somewhat agree	Agree	Strongly Agree
The LAB helped you develop a better understanding of how to innovate in your organization.	6.7	13.3	56.7	23.3
You would recommend that your organization adopt a similar approach to innovation for some other programs	3.3	13.3	40.0	43.3
If implemented, your team's innovation will provide real benefits to your organization.	0	10.0	36.7	53.3
The innovation is a breakthrough at your organization.	10.0	30.0	46.7	13.3
If implemented, the innovation would provide a good return on investment.	0	13.3	40.0	46.7
Our prototype is very innovative.	10.0	36.7	43.3	10.0
If implemented, there is a high likelihood that our organization could find a way to sustain the innovation	0	13.3	30.0	56.7
If implemented, the project would have a positive impact on our organization's goals for social justice	0	13.3	30.0	56.7

Table 5: Frequencies for lab impact items (% are shown).

on the level of work engagement which, in turn, may augment job performance [37].

The results did not indicate any changes in the participants' perception their organizations' capacity for innovation. The Lab was not an intensive, on-site engagement process, but instead relied heavily on a few primary touch points. While this was the most efficient way to have an impact on as many organizations as possible, it may have muted our ability to have an impact on change in perceptions of organizational innovativeness. Recognizing that organizations tend to remain in stasis, may make it more difficult to affect change at the organizational level [38,39]. It seems possible that more intensive contact with the participating organizations would be necessary to measurably expand organizations' capacity for innovation. Study results do suggest, however, that even minor engagement in design thinking does have considerable impacts on individual capacity.

Study Limitations

The study is exploratory in nature and provided some early indications of the potential for the use of design thinking in this context. However, data should be interpreted cautiously due to study limitations. The study suffers from a selection bias given the organizations chose to participate in the Lab activities. Further, the individual participants, while not required to participate, were asked by their organizations and agreed. The study is not representative of all social service organizations nor can the findings be generalized to all employees working in the social service sector.

The study findings are also constrained because we relied on self-reported measures of innovation capacity at the individual and organizational level. People's perceptions of their own innovativeness may be different than assessments connected to objective behavioral indicators. Further, the organizational perspectives were taken from only the Lab participants, not from other organizational stakeholders.

Finally, the study was exploratory in nature. It was not possible to structure the study as an experimental design with comparison groups. We also were not able to systematically document factors exogenous to the Lab that may have influenced the change in innovation capacity.

Implications for Management

Despite the study limitations, this research provides early insight into the applicability of design thinking for nonprofit organizations. Leaders and team members expressed high levels of satisfaction with the Lab outcomes, and the potential to use design thinking in other situations. Importantly, participation in the Lab prepared a cadre of innovation experts who could bring this learning back to their organizations. This in turn, could support the organization's ability to engage in social innovation again and again.

This study offers insights about new ways that leaders of organizations in the social service sector can support creativity [40] and innovation at their organizations [41]. Nonprofit managers interested in promoting their staffs' capacity for innovation can consider how to help employees incorporate design thinking skills into their repertoire of assessment and program planning capabilities.

Stimulating individual capacity for innovation may also have an indirect impact on organizations' culture of innovation. Buono *et al.* suggest that the willingness of organizational members to assume responsibilities for implementing and sustaining change are one of the five factors associated with organizational capacity for change [28]. When individuals embrace a mindset of experimentation, they are free to consider bold, new solutions. Developing and nurturing the innovation competencies of individual employees may embolden nonprofit organizations to be more innovative.

Leadership is a critical success factor for social intrapreneurship [42]. The project leaders sanctioned the organizations' participation in the Lab, articulated the issue, selected the team members, and (in most cases) provided informal coaching to team members [12]. Importantly, the leaders modeled design thinking behaviors [43]. Effective leaders also communicate the importance of their organizations' social innovation work, both internally and externally [28,44].

Our preliminary assessment of the pilot Social Innovation Lab suggests that design thinking can help stimulate changes in perceptions, behaviors, and attitudes for individuals working for non-profit organization. As organizations face the challenge of continuous innovation [45], design thinking may become an important planning strategy. Future research will need to further explore this potential and the conditions under which it can be most effective.

Refernces

1. Johansen B (2009) Leaders make the future. Ten new leadership skills for an uncertain world. San Francisco, CA: Berrett-Kohler Publishers Inc.
2. Husch B (2011) The Fiscal Survey of States: National Governors Association and the National Association of State Budget Officers.
3. Salamon LM, Geller SL, Spence KL (2009) Impact of the 2007-2009 economic recession on nonprofit organizations. (No.14). Baltimore, MD: Center for Civil Studies, Institute for Policy Studies: The John Hopkins Listening Post Project.
4. Le Ber MJ, Branzei O (2010) (Re) Forming strategic cross-sector partnerships: Relational processes of social innovation. Business and Society 49: 140-172.
5. Sabeti H (2009) The emerging fourth sector. Washington D.C: The Aspin Institute.
6. Phills Jr, Deiglmeier K, Miller TD (2008) Rediscovering social innovation. Stanford Social Innovation Review 6: 34-43.
7. Dart R (2004) Being business-like in a nonprofit organization: A grounded and inductive typology. Nonprofit and Voluntary Sector Quarterly 33: 290-310.
8. Brown T, Wyatt J (2010) Design thinking for social innovation. Development Outreach 12: 29-43.
9. Bornstein D (2007) How to change the world: Social entrepreneurs and the power of new ideas. Oxford, England: Oxford University Press.
10. Galinsky L (2011) Work on purpose. New York: Echoing Green.
11. Antoncic B, Hisrich RD (2003) Clarifying the intrapreneurship concept. Journal of Small Business and Enterprise Development 10: 7-24.
12. Pinchot G, Pellman R (1999) Intrapreneuring in action. A handbook for business innovation. San Francisco, CA: Barrett-Koehler Publishers, Inc.
13. Brown T (2009) Change by design: How design thinking transforms organizations and inspires innovation. New York: Harper Collins Publisher.
14. Rylander A (2009) Design thinking as knowledge work: Epistemological foundations and practical implications. Journal of Design Management 14: 7-19.
15. Cross N (2011) Design thinking: Understanding how designers think and work. Oxford, England: Berg Publishers.
16. Ratcliffe J (2009) Steps in a design thinking process. Stanford Design School. Stanford, CA.
17. Sato S, Lucente S, Meyer D, Mrazek D (2010) Design thinking to make organization change and development more responsive. Design Management Review 21: 44-52.
18. Martin RL (2009) The design of business: Why design thinking is the next competitive edge. Cambridge, MA: Harvard Business Press.
19. Arrata P, Despierre A, Kumra G (2007) Building an effective change agent team. The McKinsey Quarterly 4: 39-43.
20. Boynton A, Fisher B (2005) Virtuoso teams: Lessons from teams that changed their worlds. Boston, MA: Prentice Hall Financial Times.
21. Shin J, Mc Clomb G (1998) Top executive leadership and organizational innovation: An empirical investigation of nonprofit human service organizations. Administration in Social Work 22:19-33.
22. Cangemi J, Miller R (2007) Breaking-out-of-the-box in organizations: Structuring a positive climate for the development of creativity in the workplace. Journal of Management Development 26: 401-410.
23. Reeves M, Deimler M (2011) Adaptability: The new competitive advantage. Harvard Business Review 135-141.
24. Jaskyte K (2004) Transformational leadership, organizational culture and innovativeness in nonprofit organizations. Nonprofit Management and Leadership 15: 153-168.
25. Schein EH (2010) Organizational culture and leadership. San Francisco, CA: John Wiley and Sons.
26. Un CA, Montoro-Sanchez A (2010) Innovative capability development for entrepreneurship. A theoretical framework. Journal of Organizational Change Management 23: 413-434.
27. Jaskyte K, Dressler WW (2005) Organizational culture and innovation in nonprofit human service organizations. Administration in Social Work 20: 23-41.
28. Buono AF, Kerber KW (2010). Intervention and organizational change: Building organizational change capacity. EBS Review 27: 9-21.
29. Greenhalgh T, Robert G, MacGarlane F, Bate P, Kyriakidou O (2004) Diffusion of innovations in service organizations: Systematic review and recommendations. The Millbank Quarterly 82: 581-629.
30. Forrest SP III, Peterson TO (2006) It's called andragogy. Academy of Management Learning and Education 5: 112-122.
31. Marquardt M, Waddill D (2004) The power of learning in action learning: A conceptual analysis of how the five schools of adult learning theories are incorporated within the practice of action learning. Research and Practice 1: 185-202.
32. Zhang X, Bartol K (2010) Linking empowering leadership and employee creativity: The influence of psychological empowerment, intrinsic motivation, and creative process engagement. Academy of Management Journal 53: 107-128.
33. Reiter-Palmon R, Illies JJ (2004) Leadership and creativity: Understanding leadership from a creative problem solving perspective. Leadership Quarterly 15: 55-77.

34. Amabile TM (1983) The social psychology of creativity: A componential conceptualization. Journal of Personality and Social Psychology 45: 357-377.

35. Schaufeli WB, Bakker AB (2003) Test manual for the Utrecht Work Engagement Scale.

36. Patterson M, West M, Shackleton V, Dawson J, Lawtham R, et al. (2005) Validating the organizational climate measure. Journal of Organizational Behavior 26: 379-408.

37. Bakker AB (2009) Building engagement in the workplace. In Burke RJ, Cooper CL(Eds.). Oxon, UK: Routledge. The peak performing organization: 50-72.

38. Van de Ven AH, Sun, Kongyong S (2011) Breakdowns in implementing models of organization change. Academy of Management Perspectives 25: 58-74.

39. Gilley A, Godek M, Giley JW (2009) Change, resistance, and the organizational immune system. *SAM* Advanced Management Journal 74: 4-10.

40. Amabile TM, Schatzel EA, Moneta GB, Kramer SJ (2004) Leader behaviors and the work environment for creativity: Perceived leader support. The Leadership Quarterly 15: 5-32.

41. McMurray AJ, Islam MdM, Sarros JC, Pirola-Merlo A (2013) Workplace innovation in a nonprofit organization. Nonprofit Management and Leadership 23: 367-388.

42. Orridge M (2009) Change leadership. Developing a change adept organization. Ashgate Publishing Company: Burlington, VT.

43. Gardner JW (1990) On leadership. NY: The Free Press.

44. Rogers EM (2003) The diffusion of innovation. New York, NY: The Free Press.

45. Light PC (2011) Driving social change: How to solve the world's toughest problems. Chichester, United Kingdom: John Wiley and Sons Ltd.

Performance of Entrepreneurs' Involvement of Industrial Estates in Southern Districts of Tamilnadu - A Study

Selvaraj N*

Department of Commerce, Saraswathi Narayanan College, Madurai, Tamilnadu, India

Abstract

The promotion of indigenous entrepreneurship is a major objective in any developing country and industrial estates are recognized as one of the most promising ways of achieving this objective. One of the important objectives of the Government in its industrialization process are decentralization of industries and the balanced regional development. Government policies are aimed at diverting the industries from large concentration centers to relatively less developed or depressed areas and facilitating the establishment of industries in these areas. The small-scale industrial sector which plays a pivotal role in the Indian economy in terms of employment and growth has recorded a high rate of growth since independent in spite of stiff competition from the large scale sector and not so encouraging support from the Government. The enterprise involvement indicates the level of participation by the respondents in the enterprising. The enterprise involvement by the respondents is assessed by ten important aspects, namely source of inspiration, help during setting up stage, managing various function, major decision, time spent towards unit related work, satisfaction, training, pride in being an entrepreneur, membership and future plans.

Keywords: Performers; Entrepreneurship; Industries; Involvement and personal traits

Introduction

The principal objective of industrial estate programme is to achieve the promotion of small scale industries by providing facilities, assistance and guidance at every stage of establishment, operation and management. It aids in the expansion, diversification and modernization of existing small industries sector. It enables the small industry to become a sector of industrial activity. Finally the simulation of local entrepreneurship is possible through the development of small industries in concentrated location such as industrial estates.

The availability of standard factory on rent or hire purchase, common service facilities such a tool room maintenance and repair workshops and testing laboratories are major inducements to ensure industrial operation.

Industrial estates make possible the expansion; diversification and modernization of the existing small scale industries. Expansion is possible as this provides organized and well developed space for the existing industry, the provision of technical and managerial counseling in the estates, evaluation diversification and modernization.

The promotion of indigenous entrepreneurship is a major objective in any developing country and industrial estates are recognised as one of the most promising ways of achieving this objective. It is a major inducement to small entrepreneurs with the limited financial means since it provides factories on hire purchase basis or rental basis. Their existence is an another adjunct to entrepreneurship, since industrial extension services without assistance to people with little or no technical and managerial knowledge will not motivate people to take up an industrial occupation.

In this sense an industrial estate is a promotional instrument and not a real estate operation. Further, it is not a substitute or an overall development programme for small scale industries.

One of the important objectives of the Government in its industrialization process are decentralization of industries and the balanced regional development. Government policies are aimed at diverting the industries from large concentration centres to relatively less developed or depressed areas and facilitating the establishment of industries in these areas. Government carries out these policies through programmes of incentives of which the establishment of an industrial estate is an important one. Industrial estates are constructed in backward and rural areas based on these objectives. The programme thus enables the community development through employment opportunities, with the help of local entrepreneurship etc [1,2].

Involvement

The small-scale industrial sector which plays a pivotal role in the Indian economy in terms of employment and growth has recorded a high rate of growth since independent in spite of stiff competition from the large scale sector and not so encouraging support from the Government. This is evident by the number of registered units which went up from 16,000 in 1950 to 36,000 units in 1961 and 58.57 lakhs units in 2006-07. During the last decade alone, the small-scale sector has progressed from the production of simple consumer goods to the manufacture of many sophisticated and precision products like electronic control systems, micro-wave components, electro-medical equipment, T.V. sets and the like. But not this is really a tough period for the entrepreneurs to survive because of uncontrollable variables causing unforeseen situations like changing roles of Government, threats from multinational corporations and other internal variables.

In Tamil Nadu, Tamilnadu Small Industries Development Corporation Ltd., (TNSIDCO) has established a large number of industrial estates throughout the district. However, despite these

---

*Corresponding author: Selvaraj N, Assistant Professor of Commerce, Saraswathi Narayanan College, Madurai, Tamilnadu, India
E-mail: selvaraj_narayanan@yahoo.com

efforts, many units in these estates are not functioning well. Hence, an attempt has been made to survey the operational performance of industrial estates in selected districts of Tamil Nadu. This study aims at identifying the factors influencing the operational performance of industrial estates and the perception of entrepreneurs towards the functions of the industrial estates for its development in the concerned district [3].

The enterprise involvement indicates the level of participation by the respondents in the enterprising. The enterprise involvement by the respondents is assessed by ten important aspects, namely source of inspiration, help during setting up stage, managing various function, major decision, time spent towards unit related work, satisfaction, training, pride in being an entrepreneur, membership and future plans developed by Kalyani and Chandralekha [4]. The variables are rated on a five-point scale. The scores of each enterprise involvement variable are used to prepare the Enterprise Involvement Index.

Data Source

The study is based on both primary data. Primary data have been collected from the selected entrepreneurs in the southern districts (Madurai, Theni, Dindigul, Virudhunagar, Ramanathapuram and Sivaganga) of Tamil Nadu with the help of an interview schedule. Secondary data have been obtained from the books, journals, web sites and unpublished records.

Period of the study

The primary data relating to the entrepreneurs of has been collected during 2014–2015.

Framework of analysis

The 't' test is applied to find out the significant difference between two means of any variables in the study.

The F-test is applied in the present study to find out the significant difference among the samples regarding the particular variable and when the variables are in interval and the number of sample is more than two groups.

The entrepreneurs are classified into good and poor performers on the basis of their average return on involvement as 8.62 per cent. The involvement is highly essential for the performance of the entrepreneurs and the performance also acts as a motivation to involvement among the entrepreneurs. There is a cyclical relationship between these two aspects. In order to analyses the association between the performance of the entrepreneurs and their involvement, the mean score of each involvement variables is calculated. The 'F' statistics is computed to find out the significant difference among the different group of entrepreneurs. The resultant mean score of the variables and their respective 'F' statistics are presented in Table 1.

From Table 1, it has been inferred that the most involved aspects among the good and poor performance are future plans and membership since their mean scores are 3.7121 and 3.1115 respectively. The mean scores of overall involvement among them are 3.1345 and 2.4510 respectively. The significant difference among the good and poor entrepreneurs are noticed in few enterprise involvement variables namely sources of inspiration, helping during setting up stage, managing various functions, time spent towards unit related work, pride in being an entrepreneur and future plans since their respective 'F' statistics are significant at 5 per cent level. The higher mean differences regarding the involvement variables among the good and poor performers are

Enterprise involvement variables	Average score		F-Statistics
	Good performer	Poor performer	
Sources of Inspiration	3.0124	1.8212	2.6075*
Help during setting up stage	2.5624	3.0514	1.2025*
Managing various functions	3.2121	1.6812	2.0079*
Major decisions	2.7016	1.8861	1.4072
Time spent towards unit related work	3.3517	2.5681	1.7096*
Satisfaction	3.4217	3.0527	0.8011
Training	2.5082	2.5151	0.6091
Pride in being an Entrepreneur	3.5011	2.0517	1.6227*
Membership	3.5012	3.1115	0.4121
Future plans	3.7121	1.8654	2.2416*
Overall Involvement	3.1345	2.4510	1.8011*

*Significant at 5 percent level

Table 1: Involvement among the entrepreneurs.

Enterprise Involvement Index	No. of Respondents		Total
	Good Performer	Poor Performer	
Up to 20	10 (8.07)	32 (31.68)	42 (18.67)
21-40	31 (25.00)	30 (29.70)	61 (27.12)
41-60	39 (31.45)	16 (15.84)	55 (24.44)
61-80	30 (24.19)	17 (16.84)	47 (20.88)
Above 80	14 (11.29)	6 (5.94)	20 (8.89)
Total	124 (100.00)	101 (100.00)	225 (100)

Table 2: Distribution of entrepreneurs according to involvement index.

source of inspiration and future plans, whereas the mean difference is 1.1603 and 1.8467 respectively. It reveals that the good performer has more source of inspiration and excellence in future plans whereas the poor performers are very weak in the above said two aspects.

Distribution of entrepreneurs according to involvement index

The distribution of entrepreneurs regarding their involvement index is shown in Table 2. From Table 2 it has been inferred that around 27.12 per cent of the total entrepreneurs have a high involvement index of 21-40. It is followed by 24.44 per cent of them who have an involvement index of 41-60. Only 8.89 per cent of entrepreneurs have an involvement index of above 80. Among the good performers (124), who have involvement index of less than 40 constitute 33.07 per cent. While among the poor performers (101) it is 61.38 per cent. At the same time the number of good performers who have involvement index of above 60 constitute 35.48 percent whereas among the poor performer, it is 22.78 per cent.

Correlation between profile of the entrepreneurs and their involvement

The correlation between the profile variables of the entrepreneurs and their involvement is analyzed with the help of Karl Pearson coefficient. The included profile variables are age, education, sex, caste, nature of family, marital status, family size, earning members per family, occupational background, material possession, monthly income, family income and personal traits. The score on the above said variables along with involvement index of the entrepreneurs is taken into account. The correlation between these variables is calculated separately among the good and poor performers and also among total entrepreneurs. The calculated correlation coefficient with its statistical significance is shown in Table 3.

From Table 3, it is evident that there is significant relationship

Profile variables	Correlation Coefficient		Pooled Performer
	Good Performer	Poor Performer	
Age	-0.3110*	-0.1292	-2.2172*
Education	0.3512*	0.0189	0.1761*
Sex	0.1017	0.1235*	0.1141
Caste	0.0821	0.0524	0.0619
Nature of Family	0.1117	0.0189	0.0789
Marital Status	0.0192	-0.0817	0.0821
Family Size	-0.2172*	-0.1821*	-0.2131*
Earning members per family	0.1931	0.0813	0.1325*
Occupational background	0.2795*	0.1019	0.1893*
Material Possession	0.0715	-0.0773	0.0123
Monthly Income	0.0196	-0.0721	0.0381
Family Income	0.2134*	0.1208*	0.1939*
Personal Traits	0.3017*	0.2019*	0.1837*

*Significant at 5 percent level

Table 3: Correlation between enterprise involvement index and profile variables.

between the profile variables and involvement index is noticed with respect to age, education, family size, earning members per family, occupational background, family income and personal traits of the good performers since the related correlation coefficients are significant at 5 percent level. Among the correlation coefficients the age and family size are negatively correlated with the involvement index. It shows that the increase in the age and family size is related with a fall in involvement. Among the poor performers the significantly correlated profile variables with the involvement index are sex, family size, family income and personal traits since the correlation coefficients are significant at 5 percent level. The correlation analysis for the pooled entrepreneurs reveals that there is a significant relationship between involvement and the profile variables namely age, education, family size, earning members per family, occupational background, family income and personal traits. The only variables namely age and family sizes are negatively correlated.

Impact of Profile Variables on Involvement

The impact study is essential for some policy implication to enrich involvement among the entrepreneurs. The score of independent (profile variables) and dependent variables (involvement index) is included for the analysis. The multiple regression analysis is used to find out the impact of profile variables on involvement. The fitted regression model is:

$$Y = a X_1^{b1} X_2^{b2} X_3^{b3} X_4^{b4} X_5^{b5} X_6^{b6} X_7^{b7} X_8^{b8} X_9^{b9} X_{10}^{b10} X_{11}^{b11} X_{12}^{b12} X_{13}^{b13} \cdot e$$

This is converted into log form:

$$\text{Log } Y = \log a + b_1 \log X_1 + b_2 \log X_2 + b_3 \log X_3 + b_4 \log X_4 + b_5 \log X_5 + b_6 \log X_6 + b_7 \log X_7 + b_8 \log X_8 + b_9 \log X_9 + b_{10} \log X_{10} + b_{11} \log X_{11} + b_{12} \log X_{12} + b_{13} \log X_{13} + e$$

Where,

Y=Entrepreneurship index of the respondents,

X_1=Age of the respondents,

X_2=Education of the respondents,

X_3=Sex of the respondents,

X_4=Caste of the respondents,

X_5=Nature of family belonged by the respondents,

X_6=Marital status of the respondents,

X_7=Family size of the respondents,

X_8=Earning member per family of the respondents,

X_9=Occupational background of the respondents,

X_{10}=Material Possession of the respondents,

X_{11}=Monthly income of the respondents,

X_{12}=Family income of the respondents,

X_{13}=Personal index of the respondents,

a=Intercept,

e=Error term.

b_1 to b_{13} Regression coefficients of the independent variables.

The regression analysis is carried out among the good performers, poor performers and for both. The resultant regression coefficients of profile variables on involvement are shown in Table 4.

From Table 4, it has been observed that the significantly influencing profile variables on involvement among the good performers are age, education, earning members per family, occupational background and personal traits. That is an unit of increase in education, earning members per family, occupational background and personal traits of the good performers enhances the involvement by 0.0709, 0.1134, 0.1888 and 0.2089 units respectively. At the same time, an unit of increase in age and family size of the good performers leads to a decline in involvement by 0.1851 and 0.1234 unit respectively.

Among the poor performers, the significantly influencing variables are age, sex, family size, material possession and personal traits. The given independent of variables that explain the change in involvement among the poor performers is to the extent of 45.32 per cent only.

The regression analysis for the pooled performer reveals that an unit of increase in education, earning members per family, occupational background and personal traits of the entrepreneurs enhances their involvement by 0.0734, 0.0453, 0.1109 and 0.1405 unit respectively.

An unit of increase in age and family size results in the decrease

Profile Variables	Regression Coefficient		Pooled Performer
	Good Performer	Poor Performer	
Age	-0.1851*	-0.1251*	-0.1134*
Education	0.0709*	0.0721	0.0734*
Sex	0.0134	0.0296*	0.0543
Caste	0.0771	0.0054	-0.0335
Nature of Family	-0.0863	0.0712	0.0121
Marital Status	-0.1143	-0.0241	-0.0818
Family Size	-0.1234*	-0.2124*	-0.1405*
Earning members per family	0.1134*	0.0913	0.0453*
Occupational background	0.1888*	0.0911	0.1109*
Material Possession	0.0208	-0.0561*	0.0099
Monthly Income	0.0718	0.0921	0.0609
Family Income	0.0431	0.0523	0.0283
Personal Traits	0.2089*	0.1151*	0.1405*
Constant	2.6598	1.8451	2.7124
R^2	0.4878	0.4532	0.6341
F-Statistic	18.6121*	16.0891	18.1411*

*Significant at 5 percent level

Table 4: Impact of profile variables on enterprise involvement index.

of involvement by 0.1134 and 0.1405 unit respectively. The coefficient of determination conveys that the independent variables influence involvement to the extent of 63.41 per cent. The fitted regression model is viable since its 'F' statistics is significant at 5 per cent level.

Factors Discriminating Good and Poor Performers

The entrepreneurs are classified into good and poor performers on the basis of their mean returns on investment. Fourteen profile variables including the involvement index are taken into account to identify the most important factors to discriminate between the good and poor performers among the entrepreneurs. The scale value of the discriminate values is taken and the discriminant function analysis test was applied. The Mahanobolis D^2 statistics was calculated to measure the variation between two groups of entrepreneurs.

From Table 5, it has been observed that the value of D^2 and F ratio calculated are 2.0012 and 8.7543 respectively. The F ratio was found to be significant at 5 per cent level. Hence the variation between good and poor performers is significant. This implies that fourteen variables together are useful in discriminating good and poor performer. Of the mean difference obtained in among the fourteen variables, the significant difference is found in case of thirteen variables.

The calculated discriminant scores Z_1 and Z_2 for good performers are 2.854 and 1.127 respectively. The critical values of discriminate score (2) for these two groups were 2.1. Based on these scores, the discriminate function can be used to predict whether the entrepreneur belongs to poor performer or good performer. If the value of the discriminant score is more than 2.1, it indicates a good performer while a score less than 2.1 indicates a poor performer.

Constraints faced by the Entrepreneurs in the Industrial Estates

Perception towards problems in industrial estates

Management of resources both human and non-human is a crucial factor in enterprising. The successful entrepreneur has to take into consideration the family circumstances, and environmental constraints in order to establish their hold in the field of enterprise which they choose to enter. The problems encountered by the entrepreneurs are at multidimensional. The mindset of the entrepreneurs' influences them to have varied perception of the problems in industrial estates.

Variables	Mean Difference	Discriminant Function Coefficient	Product	Percentage
Enterprise Involvement Index	3.84* (6.3211)	2.0321	8.3085	53.68
Personal Traits	2.28* (9.251)	1.2871	3.1818	19.37
Education	3.07* (8.381)	0.6543	2.2125	13.62
Earning Members per family	2.06* (6.5121)	1.0062	2.0850	12.07
Occupational Background	1.83* (8.012)	0.8241	1.7108	10.29
Family Income	1.56* (6.2916)	0.2471	0.4928	2.70
Sex	0.31* (1.589)	0.1321	0.0809	0.49
Material Possession	1.38 (0.721)	0.0085	0.0043	0.090
Monthly Income	1.18* (5.229)	0.0006	0.0803	0.46
Nature of Family	0.31* (1.5800)	-0.0805	-0.0281	-0.14
Marital Status	1.15* (3.132)	-0.2211	-0.3046	-1.4240
Caste	1.55* (4.8127)	-0.1088	-0.4218	-2.10
Family Size	2.49* (7.8537)	-0.1388	-0.5111	-2.77
Age	2.08* (5.266)	-0.3868	-1.0275	-5.58

Significant at 5 per cent level. D^2=2.0012, F=8.7543.

Table 5: Factors discriminating good and poor performers.

Perception in Enterprises	Number	Percentage
Highly Problematic	56	24.88
Problematic	42	18.67
Moderate	48	21.33
Interesting	45	20.00
Challenging	34	15.12
Total	225	100.00

Table 6: Perception towards problems in enterprising among the entrepreneurs.

The profile of entrepreneurs may have significant impact on individual perception. The views of entrepreneurs on different angles are summarised in Table 6.

From Table 6, it has been observed that a majority (24.88 per cent) of the entrepreneurs viewed that enterprising is highly problematic, followed by 21.33 per cent who viewed it as moderate. However 20.00 per cent of the entrepreneurs felt that the enterprising is interesting. Further 15.12 per cent found it challenging.

The entrepreneurs viewed as either problematic or highly problematic are considered as problem perceived entrepreneurs whereas the others who viewed it as moderate, interesting and challenging are considered as non-problem perceived entrepreneurs for further analysis.

Problems encountered by the entrepreneurs

For the study, the problems encountered by the entrepreneurs are confined to thirteen problems namely poor infrastructure, shortage of finance, acute competition, lack of collateral security, lack of time, lack of family support, lack of network, limited demand, poor information flow, higher credit sales, lack of innovations, defective marketing arrangement and high cost of capital.

The above said problems rated by the entrepreneurs on a five point-scale namely highly serious, serious, moderate, not serious and not at all serious. They have the score value of 5,4,3,2 and 1 respectively. The average score of each problem in enterprising was separately calculated among the problem perceived and non-problem perceived entrepreneurs are shown in Table 7.

Table 7 reveals that among the entrepreneurs of non-problem perceived outlook the most seriously viewed problems are lack of innovation and lack of network since the mean scores are 3.1007 and 3.0511 respectively. The less non-problem perceived problems are higher credit sales and poor infrastructure since the mean scores are 0.8220 and 1.0714 respectively. Among the problem perceived entrepreneurs, the highly perceived problems are shortage of finance and acute competition since the mean scores are 4.1525 and 4.0607 respectively whereas the less problem perceived problems are limited demand and lack of network since the mean scores are 1.7254 and 2.0518 respectively. In aggregate, the important problems perceived by the entrepreneurs are high cost of capital, lack of innovation and shortage of finance since the average scores are 3.9142, 3.0652 and 3.0468 respectively.

The significant difference between the non-problem perceived and problem perceived entrepreneurs regarding different aspects of problems in enterprising was analyses by the 't' statistic and the results are shown in Table 8.

From Table 8, it has been observed that the significant difference among two groups of entrepreneurs (non-problem perceived and problem perceived) is noticed in a few problems namely shortage of

Nature of Problems	Average Score		
	Non-Problem Perceived	Problem Perceived	Pooled
Poor infrastructure	1.0714	2.7131	1.7215
Shortage of finance	2.2015	4.1525	3.0468
Acute competition	2.6158	4.0607	2.8071
Lack of collateral security	1.1214	3.7071	2.2492
Lack of time	1.3456	2.8559	2.0063
Lack of family support	2.2017	3.0071	2.5050
Lack of net work	3.0511	2.0518	2.5227
Limited demand	1.8135	1.7254	1.7740
Poor information flow	2.6018	2.3045	2.4653
Higher credit sales	0.8220	2.6534	1.6123
Lack of innovation	3.1007	2.8034	3.0652
Defective Marketing Arrangement	1.1121	4.0551	2.3241
High cost of capital	1.1032	4.0550	3.9142
Overall Average	2.0098	2.8546	2.3152

Table 7: Problems encountered by the entrepreneurs.

Problems in Enterprising	Average Score		't' Value
	Non-Problem Perceived	Problem Perceived	
Poor infrastructure	1.0714	2.7131	1.4207
Shortage of finance	2.2015	4.1525	1.8561*
Acute competition	2.6158	4.0607	0.7064
Lack of collateral security	1.1214	3.7071	2.0161*
Lack of time	1.3456	2.8559	1.7172*
Lack of family support	2.2017	3.0071	1.3321
Lack of net work	3.0511	2.0518	1.4172
Limited demand	1.8135	1.7254	0.3031
Poor information flow	2.6018	2.3045	0.5071
Higher credit sales	0.8220	2.6534	2.0513*
Lack of innovation	3.1007	2.8034	0.6064
Defective Marketing Arrangement	1.1121	4.0551	0.3104
High cost of capital	1.1032	4.0550	2.2934*
Overall Average	2.0098	2.8546	1.6041*

*Significant at 5 per cent level.

Table 8: Significant difference of problems perceptions among entrepreneurs.

finance, lack of collateral security, lack of time, higher credit sales and higher cost of capital since the respective 't' values are 1.8561, 2.0161, 1.7172, 2.0513 and 2.2934 respectively. The mean of overall perception towards all problems together among the non-problem perceived entrepreneurs and problem perceived entrepreneurs are 2.0179 and 2.8541 respectively. The 't' statistic indicates that there is a significant difference among the above said group of entrepreneurs regarding their problems perceptions.

Problem perception among their good and poor performer

The problems in enterprising may be perceived by entrepreneurs (good and poor performer) in different ways. In order to analyze the perception on the various problems perceived by the entrepreneurs in industrial estates, the mean score on the perception of each problem in enterprising among the good and poor performers is analyzed separately. The 't' test is applied to know the significant difference between two means in each aspect of the problems in enterprising. The results are summarized in Table 9.

Table 9 reveals that the highly perceived problems among the good performers in enterprising are lack of innovation and higher credit sales since the mean scores are 2.7081 and 2.6111 respectively, whereas among the poor performers the problems are shortage of finance and high cost of capital since the mean scores are 4.0735 and 4.0135 respectively. The less perceived problems among the good performers are limited demand and lack of network since the mean scores are 0.6321 and 0.7558 respectively. Among the poor performers, they are limited demand and lack of family support since the mean scores are 1.2076 and 1.7031 respectively. The mean scores on the perception of overall problems among the good and poor performers are 1.5703 and 2.8695 respectively. There is significant difference between good and poor performers regarding poor infrastructure, shortage of finance, acute competition, lack of collateral security, lack of networking, poor information flow, defective marketing arrangements and high cost of capital since the 't' statistic are significant at 5 per cent level. The 't' statistic on the problem perception on all items together also reveals that there is a significant difference among the good and poor performers.

Correlation between profile of the entrepreneurs and problem perception

The relationship between the profile variables of the entrepreneurs and their overall problem perception is analyzed with the help of Karl Pearson coefficient of correlation. The overall score on problem perception among the entrepreneurs and their score on profile variables are included for the correlation analysis. The resultant correlated coefficient is shown in Table 10.

From Table 10, it has been inferred that among the good performers, negatively correlated profile variables with the overall problem perception are education, earning members per family, occupational background, monthly income, family income, personal traits and enterprise involvement index since the correlation coefficients are significant at 5 per cent level whereas in poor performer it is increase in education, occupational background, monthly income, family income, personal traits and enterprise involvement index . The correlation analysis for the pooled data reveals that there is a significant negative correlation between problem perception and the profile variables namely education, earning members per family, occupational background, family income, personal traits and enterprise involvement index among the entrepreneurs.

Problems in Enterprising	Average Score		't' Value
	Good Performer	Poor Performer	
Poor infrastructure	1.1132	3.2015	2.3091*
Shortage of finance	1.5083	4.0735	3.0186*
Acute competition	2.0124	3.8512	1.7071*
Lack of collateral security	1.7531	3.7121	2.5242*
Lack of time	2.2051	2.5024	0.7150
Lack of family support	1.1011	1.7031	0.5217
Lack of net work	0.7558	2.2004	1.7046*
Limited demand	0.6321	1.2076	0.8293
Poor information flow	1.0768	2.8117	2.1017*
Higher credit sales	2.6111	2.3041	0.5071
Lack of innovation	2.7081	3.3057	0.6081
Defective Marketing Arrangement	1.2192	2.3018	1.6138*
High cost of capital	2.0114	4.0135	3.0708*
Overall Average	1.5703	2.8695	2.1338*

*Significant at 5 per cent level.

Table 9: Significant difference of problems and perceptions among good and poor performers.

Profile Variables	Coefficient of Correlation		
	Good Performer	Poor Performer	Pooled
Age	0.0371	0.1374*	0.0607
Education	-0.3124*	-0.2082*	-0.2153*
Sex	0.1081	0.1107	0.0179
Caste	0.0174	0.1076	0.0117
Nature of Family	0.2118	0.1029	0.0174
Marital Status	0.0174	0.0611	0.0883
Family Size	0.0603	0.1204	0.1087
Earning members per family	-0.3078*	0.1072	-0.2162*
Occupational background	-0.2515*	-0.2118*	-0.1007*
Material Possession	0.0161	0.0104	0.0753
Monthly Income	-0.1805*	-0.1807*	-0.0124
Family Income	-0.2056*	-0.0822	-0.1623*
Personal Traits	-0.2306*	-0.0814	-0.1508*
Enterprise involvement index	-0.3030	-0.1042*	-0.2072*

*Significant at 5 per cent level.

Table 10: Correlation between profile and perception of problems among the entrepreneurs.

Impact of profile variables on problem perception

An attempt has been made to analyze the impact of profile variables on perceptions of problem in enterprising with the help of multiple regression analysis. The dependent variables in the analysis is the sum of the score on the problem perceptions on various aspects of problems in enterprising. The score on profile variables is taken as the score of independent variables.

The regression analysis is done among good performer, poor performer also for the pooled entrepreneurs. The resultant regression coefficient of the profile variables on problem perception is presented in Table 11.

Table 11 reveals that among the good performers the significantly influencing variables on the problem perception are family size, earning members per family, family income, personality traits and enterprise involvement index. A unit increase in the family size results in an increase in problem perception by 0.1514 units. At the same time, the one unit increase in the earning members per family, family income, personal traits and enterprise involvement index among the entrepreneurs decreases the problem perception by 0.0041, 0.1524, 0.1332 and 0.2151 respectively. The regression analysis for the pooled entrepreneurs reveals that the significantly influencing variables are age, education, family-size, occupational background, personal traits and enterprise involvement. The profile variables influence the change in problem perception to the extent of 69.27 per cent.

Factors discriminating the non-problem perceived and problem perceived entrepreneurs

An attempt has been made to identify the variables discriminating the non-problem perceived entrepreneurs and problem perceived entrepreneurs. Fourteen profile variables were considered to analyze their effect on problem perception among the entrepreneurs. The score of independent variables was used in the discriminant analysis for the purpose of finding relative importance of fourteen variables with regard to their power to discriminate between non-problem perceived and problem perceived entrepreneurs. Fisher's discriminant function analysis test was applied. In total, 275 entrepreneurs are treated, as non-problem perceived entrepreneurs and the remaining 175 are treated as problem perceived entrepreneurs. The mahanobolis D^2 statistic was calculated to measure the distance between the two groups of entrepreneurs. The 'F' statistic was used and the two groups were different from each other. The resultant discriminant function coefficient, mean difference of the discriminant variables and their relative importance in discriminant function are computed and shown in Table 12.

From Table 12, it has been observed that the values of D^2 and F-ratio calculated were 2.5718 and 11.5259 respectively. The F-ratio is found to be significant at 5 per cent level. Hence the distance between two groups of entrepreneurs is significant. This implies that fourteen variables together were useful in discriminating the two groups of entrepreneurs. Among the mean differences obtained in fourteen variables, the significant difference was found in the case of twelve variables. The ranking of the percentage distance measured by important factor revealed that the first three ranks compared personal traits 20.89 per cent, enterprise involvement index 17.82 per cent and education 14.81 per cent were found individually contributing more than the average distance in terms of discrimination as compared to other variables in discriminating two group of entrepreneurs. The calculated discriminant score 'Z' and 'Z²' for non-problem perceived and problem

Profile Variables	Regression Coefficient		
	Good Performer	Poor Performer	Pooled
Constant	0.7381	0.1318	0.0331
Age	0.0127	0.1237*	0.0412*
Education	-0.0613	-0.1081*	-0.0517*
Sex	0.0121	0.0312	0.0407
Caste	0.0856	0.0112	0.0321
Nature of Family	0.0082	0.0146	0.0654
Marital Status	0.0527	0.0627	0.0304
Family Size	0.1514*	0.0812	0.0119*
Earning members per family	-0.0041*	0.0127	-0.0145
Occupational background	-0.0184	-0.2811*	-0.1267*
Material Possession	0.0318	0.0139	0.0207
Monthly Income	-0.0257	-0.0309*	-0.0128
Family Income	-0.1524*	-0.0128	0.0829
Personal Traits	-0.1332*	-0.0914	-0.0835*
Enterprise involvement index	-0.2151*	-0.2187	-0.1028*
R^2	0.4227	-0.1058	0.6927
F-Statistics	13.4049*	16.2518*	18.6420*

*Significant at 5 per cent level

Table 11: Impact of profile variables on perception of problem in enterprise.

Variables	Mean Difference di	Discriminant Function Coefficient Li	Product	Percentage
Personal traits	2.39* (6.458)	1.6128	4.1745	20.89
Enterprise involvement index	2.47* (4.207)	1.3027	3.5371	17.82
Education	3.02* (7.0017)	0.8592	3.0177	14.81
Occupational background	3.18* (4.295)	0.7077	2.5077	12.78
Family Income	2.01* (8.103)	1.1027	2.3829	12.00
Earning members per family	2.11* (6.511)	1.0729	2.2609	11.68
Age	1.75* (4.027)	0.8057	1.5534	8.10
Material Possession	1.58 (1.567)	0.6172	1.1086	6.01
Monthly Income	2.33* (5.217)	0.2366	0.7268	4.03
Family size	2.10* (7.712)	0.1078	0.3301	2.16
Nature of Family	1.85* (5.819)	-0.0257	-0.0557	-0.23
Sex	0.38* (6.027)	-0.8197	-0.2685	-1.77
Caste	1.68 (1.107)	-0.3241	-0.6442	-3.62
Marital Status	2.02* (4.812)	-0.4082	-1.0357	-5.06

D2=2.5718; F=11.5259 *Significant at 5 per cent level.

Table 12: Factors that discriminant the problem perception.

perceived entrepreneurs were 1.1724 and 3.0703 respectively. The critical values of discriminant score (Z) for these groups were 2.0653. Based on these scores, the discriminant function can be used to predict whether an entrepreneur would belong to non-problem perceived and problem perceived entrepreneurs. If the value of discriminant score of a given entrepreneurs is less than 2.0653, it could be predicted that they would be non-problem perceived entrepreneurs and greater than 2.0653 would indicate a problem perceived entrepreneur.

Summary

The principal objective of industrial estate programme is to achieve the promotion of small scale industries by providing facilities, assistance and guidance at every stage of establishment, operation and management. There is significant relationship between the profile variables and involvement index is noticed with respect to age, education, family size, earning members per family, occupational background, family income and personal traits of the good performers since the related correlation coefficients are significant at 5 percent level. Among the correlation coefficients the age and family size are negatively correlated with the involvement index. The regression analysis for the pooled performer reveals that an unit of increase in education, earning members per family, occupational background and personal traits of the entrepreneurs enhances their involvement by 0.0734, 0.0453, 0.1109 and 0.1405 unit respectively. The calculated discriminant scores Z_1 and Z_2 for good performers are 2.854 and 1.127 respectively. The critical values of discriminate score (2) for these two groups were 2.1. Based on these scores, the discriminate function can be used to predict whether the entrepreneur belongs to poor performer or good performer. If the value of the discriminant score is more than 2.1, it indicates a good performer while a score less than 2.1 indicates a poor performer.

Suggestions

The essence of the study is that entrepreneur's background. i.e., nativity, father's profession and his experience, have little to do with his success. It is the inner drive, need for achievement (nurtured and developed through child rearing practices), and the conductive entrepreneurial climate, which will ultimately lead to the promotion, development and success of the entrepreneur. The study reveals that entrepreneurs are not born but they are made through different and arduous training.

In order to raise the performance level, there is a need to cultivate managerial skills besides entrepreneurial skills, keeping in line with the increased growth in the size of the organization.

An entrepreneurs club may be organized in each region with the following objectives. a) to interact with other members, b) to get technical knowledge, c) people from draft trade, d) to develop entrepreneurial culture, and e) to promote professional, industrial, economical, financial, technical and co-operative members.

The major aspects of improvement as far as the study area is concerned are that security in the estate premises should be beefed up. The erratic power supply should be regulated to have uninterrupted flow of electricity for the units to work. The water supply for industrial use should be augmented. Proper upkeep and maintenance of the industrial estates should be adopted. A canteen should be established and subsidized food items should be supplied to labourer. The harassment of the entrepreneurs by petty bureaucracy on trivial issues should be done away with. The road facility inside the industrial estate premises should be taken care of.

References

1. Padaki R (1994) Women and her Enterprise-A study in Karnataka state, KSFC, the P and Pamp Bangalore.
2. Murchison (1935) Hand Book of Social Psychology.
3. Krech D (1948) Theory and Problem of Social Psychology.
4. Kalyani W, Chandralkha K (2002) Associations between socio–economic demographic profile and Involvement of women Entrepreneurs in their Enterprise Management. The Journal of Entrepreneurship 11: 222-223

Psychological Need Satisfaction as a Pre-determinant of Entrepreneurial Intentionality

Francoise U*, Donghong D and Janviere N

University of Science and Technology of China Hefei, Anhui, China

Abstract

Drawing from self-determination theory, this study investigated the influence of psychological need satisfaction as a determinant of entrepreneurship personality profile, thereafter a pre-determinant of entrepreneurial intentionality. Data was collected on a sample of 407 Chinese undergraduate students from four universities in Hefei-Anhui China. The results of structural equation modeling revealed that the satisfaction of each three psychological needs: autonomy, competence and relatedness was a significant positive predictor of entrepreneurship personality profile and altogether contributed to its variance. Entrepreneurship personality profile was a significant positive predictor of entrepreneurial intention at 67% variance. The study concludes with some theoretical and practical recommendations.

Keywords: Psychological need satisfaction; Proactive personality; Entrepreneurial intention; Personal development; Career development

Introduction

The role of entrepreneurs in making the world economically dynamic is no longer deniable [1-4]. Consequently, societies are desperately eager to produce even more entrepreneurs. Several countries have established some major policies to increase revenue based entrepreneurship. China for instance, in 1980 has set up some mechanisms through which ventures based technology were financed, either from the government directly or through universities and state-owned companies [5]. Among other policies, many universities have included entrepreneurship modules in their curriculum. America, for example, had more than 1600 schools offering more than 2200 courses in entrepreneurship education by 2003 [6]. Obviously, financial funding could be among key stimulus of start-ups. Also, entrepreneurship curriculum introduces individuals to a number of important skills needed in entrepreneurship careers, including negotiation, leadership, new product development, creative thinking, exposure to technological innovation, sources of venture capital, idea protection [7]. Yet, the courage to embark on entrepreneurship career journey takes more than financial capitals and entrepreneurship modules.

Since the evolution of entrepreneurship research, studies have been carried out about the most significant personal characteristics influencing entrepreneurial behavior in people. Studies have found that some psychological characteristics including need for achievement, ambiguity tolerance [8] locus of control, self-esteem propensity to take risk [9], innovativeness and self-esteem [10,11] are associated with entrepreneurial behavior and altogether define what is often referred as an individual's "entrepreneurship personality profile". The latter has been also evidenced to have a significant link with entrepreneurs' success [12]. Moreover, employees with high to moderate entrepreneurship profile are believed to behave entrepreneurially in their organizations and hence have high probability to attain high job performance [13]. When and how these referred characteristics come to develop within people is yet a subject of academic debates and scientific researches. Although scholars have argued that these psychological traits can be acquired and developed within people throughout their lifespan [14-16] there is still scarce about the mechanisms through which those so called entrepreneurial psychological traits develop. In this study, we applied self-determination theory (SDT) and tested psychological need satisfaction (competence satisfaction, autonomy satisfaction and relatedness satisfaction) as determinant of entrepreneurship personality profile and pre-determinant of entrepreneurial intention. According to STD human beings are born with some psychological needs, competence, Autonomy and Relatedness. The theory argues that when these three needs are satisfied, individuals have an enthusiastic view about the world and are intrinsically motivated to pursue life at its fullest [17]. Our study is guided by the assumption that: "as the more people perceive psychological need satisfaction the higher the likelihood to develop psychological characteristics of entrepreneurship and thus lead to entrepreneurial intentions".

Psychological characteristics of entrepreneurship personality profile

1) Need for Achievement: need for achievement has been identified at the very beginning of entrepreneurship research as a significant predictor of entrepreneurial behavior. People with higher need for achievement are goal-oriented and have strong desire for success [18,19]. Therefore, they are more likely to behave entrepreneurially. (2) Internal Locus of Control: refers to the extent to which people believe in their abilities to control things/events that happen in their lives as opposed to those who put blame on external forces or fate [20]. People who score high on internal locus of control are likely to have a higher performance than those who do not [21]. (3) Propensity to Take Risk: has to do with making decisions in uncertain situations. Risk propensity is positively associated with entrepreneurship character because people who score high on it are likely to dare and hence their chances of discovering opportunities are very high [22,23] (4) Tolerance of Ambiguity: refers to emotional reactions an individual would express when faced with unfamiliar situations. People with a low tolerance of ambiguity have a tendency to avoid ambiguous situations and are likely to experience stress when they occur. On the other hand, people with a high tolerance of ambiguity tend to desire

---

*Corresponding author: Francoise U, University of Science and Technology of China Hefei, Anhui China, E-mail: bakaeri1@gmail.com

ambiguous situations, finding them challenging but interesting [24]. (5) Self-esteem: refers to a person's belief of self-worth. In psychology, people with high self-esteem are identified as feeling happier about life [14,25] and likely to have better performance [14,26]. Whereas, people with low self-esteemed are doomed to negative feelings and have high tendency to display detrimental behavior [27]. Innovativeness: can mean an individual's spirit which drives them to find new and better ways of doing things. In the Entrepreneurship world and in other related fields the concept comes from "innovation". The latter has been defined as the art of improving business processes, products and market distributions [1], in organizations, innovation refers to the development and implementation of new ideas [28]. However, this concise definition by Jackson and Manual [29]. "A tendency to be creative in thought and action" seems even more appropriate to this study.

It should be noted that not all people who score high on the above discussed characteristics would become entrepreneurs, nor all people who become entrepreneurs necessarily score high on them. However, entrepreneurs with high/moderate levels of psychological entrepreneurial characteristics are likely to be successful [12]. Likewise, employees who possess those characteristics are believed to behave entrepreneurially in their organizations and hence have high probability to attain high performance [13]. Thus, we suggest that entrepreneurial characteristics are worth being developed and encouraged in people (especially young ones) regardless of the career path they may take in life. To emphasize, young people tend to learn new skills or acquire new behavior easier than old people.

Psychological need satisfaction theoretical framework

According to SDT, human beings are born with three psychological needs namely competence, Autonomy and Relatedness that once they are satisfied, catalyze people to be intrinsically motivated and goal-oriented [30]. Need for autonomy: feeling of self-initiation as opposed to pressured or coerced feeling [31], need for competence: competence need satisfaction refers to the feeling of self-effectiveness as opposed to the feeling of passiveness and helplessness; need for relatedness: has to do with the extent to which a person perceive the love and care from people close to her/him [25]. The satisfaction of the mentioned three needs has positive effect to individual's self-growth and well-being whereas lack or insufficient of them result into low motivation feeling and may even lead to mental illness [30]. Consequently, people who live in need supportive environment experience need satisfaction and hence, benefit growth and wellness whereas people who live in need thwarting environment experience need frustration and hence likely to experience malfunction and & ill-being [32].

The connection between psychological need satisfaction and entrepreneurship

Although there seem to be no many studies where self-determination theory has been directly applied in the field of entrepreneurship, this theory has considerable contribution in behavioral disciplines which directly or indirectly could be linked to entrepreneurship behavior. In education for instance, studies have revealed that the concept of psychological need satisfaction plays a paramount role in students' motivation for learning and academic performance [33]. Students who felt controlled and pressured by their teachers tended to be less intrinsically motivated in classroom and were likely to perform less on their subjects [34], whereas, those who perceived high level of autonomy were intrinsically motivated and performed well on their school activities [35]. Furrer and Skinner [36] investigated the influence of perceived relatedness on 3rd to 6th grade students and its impact on their academic engagement and performance. They found that the high perception of relatedness was associated with positive attitudes towards school activities, less negative emotions and good academic performance, whereas the low perception scores was associated with negative emotions (including a sense of rejection, frustration, boredom and alienation) and poor performance. Also, the satisfaction of the psychological basic needs has been demonstrated to have a positive effect to employees' motivation for work performance [17] and their job satisfaction [37].

Arguably, there are limited studies concerning the direct impact of psychological needs satisfaction on the development of entrepreneurial behavior and entrepreneurship actions. However, some studies have investigated the topic indirectly. For instance, some traits of entrepreneurship personality profile like need for achievement [38], self-confidence and locus of control [39] have been found to be linked with authoritative parenting. The latter refers to the parenting style where parents support and set rules for their children but at the same time accord them a certain level of autonomy [40] and such parenting has been evidenced to have a positive impact on development of entrepreneurial early competencies [41]. Conversely, people feel less self-esteem under need thwarting social context [30]. Consequently, they tend to pursue extrinsic goals which are mostly as result of need frustration and rarely give inner satisfaction [42]. Arguably, it would be rather difficult to develop psychological entrepreneurship characteristics under need frustration. Thus, we hypothesize that "for psychological traits of entrepreneurship to develop within a person, at least moderate satisfaction of competence, autonomy and relatedness should be attained".

H1a: Autonomy satisfaction is positively associated with entrepreneurship personality profile

H1b: Competence satisfaction is positively associated with entrepreneurship personality profile

H1c: Relatedness satisfaction is positively associated with entrepreneurship personality profile

The relevance of self-determination theory to entrepreneurship behavior and entrepreneurial intentions is rooted into the concept of intrinsic motivation. According to SDT, an individual's intrinsic motivation results from the satisfaction of three important human psychological needs: autonomy, competence and relatedness [30]. Therefore, since entrepreneurship is embedded from perceived desirability and perceived behavior control [20], psychological need satisfaction especially high perception of competence and autonomy would increase entrepreneurial self-efficacy and hence, entrepreneurial intention.

H2a: Autonomy satisfaction is positively associated with entrepreneurial intention

H2b: Competence satisfaction is positively associated with entrepreneurial intention

H2c: Relatedness satisfaction is positively associated with entrepreneurial intention

H3: Entrepreneurship profile is positively associated with entrepreneurship intention.

Methodology

Data was collected through questionnaire survey. A questionnaire was translated into Chinese and was emailed to several teachers in four universities in Hefei, China. Separate letters were emailed to the teachers asking their assistance in motivating the students to fill out the questionnaire. Some of these teachers were doing PhD program in the same university with the researcher, which made it easier to approach them. Students were given 20 minutes to fill the questionnaires in their classrooms and later teachers collected the filled-out questionnaires and mailed to the author respectively. Participants were third and fourth year undergraduate students from technology and engineering majors. The reason to choose this sample is based on researcher observation. China is an emerging market where entrepreneurship in high-tech industry is advancing and a big number of young adults are obsessive to venture in high-tech industry either through joining big companies or starting their own business. To succeed in this sector requires strong entrepreneurship personality because of tremendous increase of competition in the market.

Measurement

Unless indicated otherwise, variables were measured on 5-likert scale, 1 standing for total disagreement and 5 for total agreement. Dependent variable 1: Entrepreneurship personality profile: An entrepreneurship personality profile was defined as the average of six psychological characteristics (namely, innovativeness, need for achievement, internal locus of control, self-esteem, propensity to take risk and ambiguity tolerance,) that are assumed to predict an individual's entrepreneurial behavior and entrepreneurship career inclination. We hypothesized that the likelihood of behaving entrepreneurially will depend on the individual's score on these six characteristics. That is, on a 5-likert scale, a person with high entrepreneurship profile would score 5 points whereas a person with tendency to behave less entrepreneurially would score 1. Psychological characteristics of entrepreneurship were assessed using a questionnaire developed and validated by Chye Koh [10]. We removed six items which show low consistency to our study and we used the remaining 30 items. Innovativeness was measured on 4 items, internal locus of control on 7 items, need for achievement on 5 items, risk taking on 5 items, self-confidence on 3 items, and ambiguity tolerance on 6 items. Then, all the six constructs were averaged to form a single variable, namely entrepreneurship personality profile.

Dependent variable 2: Entrepreneurship Intentionality: Entrepreneurship intentionality was measured using 5 items taken from entrepreneurship intention questionnaire developed by Liñán et al. [43]. Respondents were asked to what extent they were convinced that they will create their own business in future. Those who have a dream of being self-employed somewhere in their life were considered to have high entrepreneurial intention whereas those who did not consider self-employment as their dream career were considered to have lower entrepreneurial intention.

Independent variables

Competence satisfaction, autonomy satisfaction and relatedness satisfaction were measured using a Chinese version of a questionnaire instrument directly taken from: (http://selfdeterminationtheory.org/basic-psychological-needs-scale/) as it was developed and validated by Chen et al. [44]. The scale has been translated in various languages including Chinese. The whole scale is composed 24 items, 12 intended to measure need satisfaction and other 12 to measure need frustration. However, considering the high number of items in measuring our dependent variables, we decided to only use 12 items intended to measure need satisfaction in our study. Thereby, 4 items to test the satisfaction of each psychological need: autonomy, competence and relatedness.

Results

Respondents were composed of 304 males and 103 females. 98.50% of respondents were between 18-24 years old and only 1.50% of respondents were above 24 years old. Data analysis was firstly approached by calculating bivariate correlation among all variables involved in the study (Table 1). As shown in inter-correlation among variables (Table 1), all three components of psychological need satisfaction positively correlated with entrepreneurship personality profile as predicted; notably autonomy satisfaction (r=0.57, p<0.01); competence satisfaction (r=0.53, p<0.01) and relatedness satisfaction (r=0. 53, <0.01). Also, entrepreneurship personality profile highly correlated with entrepreneurial intentionality as predicted (r=0.81, <0.01). The correlation between gender and relatedness satisfaction was significantly negative (r=-0.11, p<0.05). Age did not show any significant correlation.

We run independent t-test to find the explanation behind the negative correlation found between gender and relatedness satisfaction. The results of equal variances not assumed t-test statistic showed that there was a significant difference between female and male in their satisfaction of relatedness, t (df=241)=2.56, p<0.05. The mean values indicates that relatedness satisfaction was higher among females (M=4.23) than in males (M=3.89)

N: 407 students, all coefficients are significant at p<0.001 level. R^2 is shown in blue color.

Then, we conducted a structural equation modeling using AMOS software to test our hypotheses. The first path analysis predicted the influence of three psychological need satisfactions: autonomy, competence and relatedness on entrepreneurship personality profile of participants. The second path analysis predicted the direct influence of the three psychological needs on entrepreneurial intention. The last path analysis predicted the effect of entrepreneurship personality profile on entrepreneurial intention

The results are presented in Figure 1. As hypothesized, we found that all the three independent variables were significant predictors of entrepreneurship personality profile. Both autonomy satisfaction and competence satisfaction had same standardized coefficients: β=0.38,

Variable name	M	SD	1	2	3	4	5
Gender	1.75	0.44	-				
Autonomy satisfaction	4.07	1.53	-0.002	-			
Competence satisfaction	4.23	1.35	-0.016	0.208**	-		
Relatedness satisfaction	3.96	1.45	-.109*	0.378**	0.245**	-	
Entrepreneurship personality	4.21	0.73	-0.032	0.573**	0.532**	0.529**	-
Entrepreneurial intention	3.78	1.6	-0.027	0.572**	0.442**	0.423**	0.810**

* Correlation is significant at the 0.05 level (2-tailed).
**Correlation is significant at the 0.01 level (2-tailed).

Table 1: Correlations among variables. N=407.

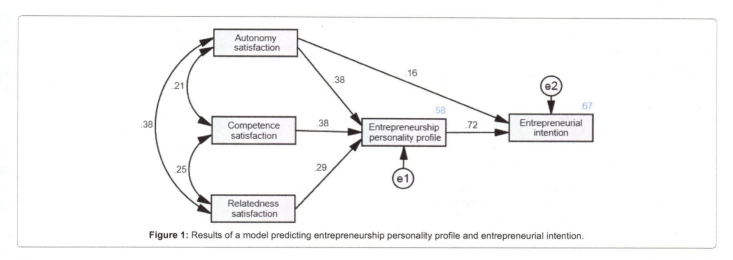

Figure 1: Results of a model predicting entrepreneurship personality profile and entrepreneurial intention.

$p<0.001$; relatedness satisfaction: $\beta=0.29$, $p<0.001$. The covariances between the three predictors are positively significant (0.38 between autonomy satisfaction and relatedness satisfaction; 0.21 between autonomy satisfaction and competence satisfaction and 0.25 between relatedness satisfaction and competence satisfaction). Entrepreneurship personality profile highly predicted entrepreneurial intention among respondents $\beta=0.72$, $p<0.001$. The modification indices suggested the changes in the model and those changes were taken into account. The arrows from competence and relatedness to entrepreneurial intention were removed and the model was re-estimated (Figure 1). The overall model was a good fit with $\chi^2=(N=407, d\ f=2)=1.838$, $p=0.399$ normed fit index (NFI)=0.998; RFI=0.990; comparative fit index (CFI)=1.00; root mean square error of approximation (RAMSEA)=0.000. While autonomy satisfaction was positively correlated with entrepreneurial intention $\beta=0.16$, $p<0.001$, respectively, competence and relatedness satisfaction did not have a significant direct effect on entrepreneurial intention. This result partly confirms our second hypothesis. The squared multiple correlations show that 58% variance of entrepreneurship personality profile was explained by its predictors: autonomy satisfaction, competence satisfaction and relatedness satisfaction, whereas, 67% of entrepreneurial intention variance was explained by entrepreneurship personality profile.

Discussion

This study aimed at investigating the effect of psychological need satisfaction (competence, autonomy and relatedness) in predicting personality profile of entrepreneurship and how the latter in return, affect the entrepreneurial intentionality among young adults. The results revealed that higher perception of competence; autonomy and relatedness have a significant direct positive impact on development of entrepreneurship personality profile, those supported 1a-1c hypotheses. Autonomy satisfaction was the only psychological need which had a direct effect on entrepreneurial intention ($\beta=0.16$, $p<0.001$) and hence partially supported 2a hypothesis. Hypotheses 2b and 2c were not supported with the results where competence satisfaction and relatedness satisfaction did not show direct significant effect in prediction of entrepreneurial intention. The third hypothesis was substantially supported; high perception of entrepreneurial intention was to high extend explained by higher score on entrepreneurship personality profile ($\beta=0.72$, $p<0.001$).

To the best of authors' knowledge, this was the first study investigating psychological need satisfaction as a pre-determinant of entrepreneurial intentionality. Previous studies on predictors of entrepreneurial behavior and entrepreneurial intentions had mainly limited their attention to social context as a source of behavior direction based on perceived social norms [20], entrepreneurship education [45] and role modeling [46]. Besides, the motivation to become entrepreneur has been mostly attached to drive outcomes like money [47] and independence [48]. This study proposes another perspective of research as far as the role of society in cultivating entrepreneurial behavior and stimulating entrepreneurial intentions is concerned. The role social context has in developing potential entrepreneurs through nurturing and catalyzing autonomy, competence and relatedness deserve further investigations. This is in consistency with what Holland identified as a second source through which people acquire entrepreneurial traits [49]. Apart from inborn characteristics (e.g., big five personality), people acquire other important traits associated with entrepreneurship as a result of their surrounding's reinforcement and support [49]. The latter has been identified by previous studies as a promising factor of potential entrepreneurship [41].

Therefore, we hope that this study will contribute on entrepreneurship researches, provoke discussions among scholars and stimulate more studies on the relationship between psychological need satisfaction and various aspects of entrepreneurship. For instance, future research could explore in depth the impact of psychological need satisfaction in stimulating individuals' entrepreneurial behavior and entrepreneurial intentions in different cultures. Also, longitudinal studies could investigate how psychological need satisfaction during childhood would affect individual's entrepreneurial behavior tendency during adulthood and the likelihood of becoming entrepreneurially oriented. Furthermore, it would be interesting to investigate how the satisfaction of autonomy, competence and relatedness as basic psychological needs influence entrepreneur's decisions during the whole venturing journey. Several questions rose from this research and need yet to be answered. Do some potential entrepreneurs fail to act on their entrepreneurial dreams due to psychological need frustration? Does need satisfaction moderate entrepreneur's level of commitment and persistence? More importantly, further studies using different samples are needed before this study findings can be generalized to the larger population. We note also that the number of male respondents was triple the number of female in our sample; we did not however explore all possible effects of gender differences in this study, future researches are encouraged to overcome that shortcoming.

This study raises some important implications in entrepreneurship practice. Given its irreplaceable role in generating economic revenues and creating employment, entrepreneurship is to be encouraged. However, in order to remarkably benefit from the change it brings, entrepreneurship has to be valued in its quality rather than quantity. For sustainable quality entrepreneurship to take place within a society there is a need for entrepreneurial culture cultivation [15]. This study suggests that psychological need satisfaction constitutes a major input in entrepreneurial behavior development which is the foundation of qualitative type of entrepreneurship that should be advocated. Instead of pushing people to pursue entrepreneurship out of necessity, countries especially developing ones, should empower its citizens to think and act entrepreneurially and for that to happen, the satisfaction of autonomy, competence and relatedness should be attained at least at moderate level. For psychological need satisfaction to take its course within individual, it should be invested at a very young age. Therefore, the concerned stakeholders including educationalists, policy makers and parents could work together to set up mechanisms through which children are accorded some level of autonomy, facilitated to excel at their competencies and at the same time feel related. For example, students could be encouraged to choose subjects related to their abilities and their own career dreams. By doing so, young people could excel in the subjects they like and therefore, the more chance to have entrepreneurship based interest, the one that would last. Parents could also be educated about the importance of supporting their children to pursue their dreams at a very young age.

Besides, since the so called psychological characteristics of entrepreneurship, notably locus of control, innovation, need for achievement, self-esteem, propensity to take risk and tolerance of ambiguity are not only beneficial to entrepreneurship career, but also to other careers, they should be encouraged and nurtured in young people regardless the career path. When people feel reasonably satisfied with their psychological needs, they are likely to explore their interests [30]. Thus, the more autonomous, competitive and related individuals feel the more likely they would act on their entrepreneurial intentions. Social context where psychological need satisfaction is valued, people especially young adults would be likely to develop entrepreneurship personality profile and hence high chance to have entrepreneurial intentionality.

References

1. Schumpeter JA (2013) Capitalism, socialism and democracy: Routledge.
2. Acs Z (2006) How is entrepreneurship good for economic growth? Innovations 1: 97-107.
3. Wennekers S, Thurik R (1999) Linking entrepreneurship and economic growth. Small business economics 13: 27-56.
4. Holcombe RG (1998) Entrepreneurship and economic growth. Quarterly Journal of Austrian Economics 1: 45-62.
5. Saxenian A (2005) From brain drain to brain circulation: Transnational communities and regional upgrading in India and China. Studies in comparative international development 40: 35-61.
6. Kuratko DF (2003) Entrepreneurship education: Emerging trends and challenges for the 21st century. White Paper, US Association of Small Business Education.
7. Vesper KH, McMullan WE (1987) Entrepreneurship: Today courses, tomorrow degrees: University of Calgary, Faculty of Management.
8. Begley TM, Boyd DP (1987) Psychological characteristics associated with performance in entrepreneurial firms and smaller businesses. Journal of Business Venturing 2: 79-93.
9. Brockhaus RH (1982) The psychology of the entrepreneur. Encyclopedia of entrepreneurship 39-57.
10. Chye Koh H (1996) Testing hypotheses of entrepreneurial characteristics: A study of Hong Kong MBA students. Journal of managerial Psychology 11: 12-25.
11. Gürol Y, Atsan N (2006) Entrepreneurial characteristics amongst university students: Some insights for entrepreneurship education and training in Turkey. Education Training 48: 25-38.
12. McClelland DC (1987) Characteristics of successful entrepreneurs. The journal of creative behavior 21: 219-233.
13. Chung LH, Gibbons PT (1997) Corporate Entrepreneurship, The Roles of Ideology and Social Capital. Group & Organization Management 22: 10-30.
14. Baumeister RF, Campbell JD, Krueger JI, Vohs KD (2003) Does high self-esteem cause better performance, interpersonal success, happiness, or healthier lifestyles? Psychological science in the public interest 4: 1-44.
15. Mueller SL, Thomas AS (2001) Culture and entrepreneurial potential: A nine country study of locus of control and innovativeness. Journal of Business Venturing 16: 51-75.
16. Krueger NF, Brazeal DV (1994) Entrepreneurial potential and potential entrepreneurs. Entrepreneurship Theory and Practice 18: 91-104.
17. Baard PP, Deci EL, Ryan RM (2004) Intrinsic Need Satisfaction: A Motivational Basis of Performance and Well-Being in Two Work Settings1. Journal of applied social psychology 34: 2045-2068.
18. McClelland DC, Atkinson JW, Clark RA, Lowell EL (1976) The achievement motive.
19. Harackiewicz JM, Barron KE, Pintrich PR, Elliot AJ, Thrash TM (2002) Revision of achievement goal theory: Necessary and illuminating 94: 638-645.
20. Ajzen I (1991) The theory of planned behavior. Organizational Behavior and Human Decision Processes 50: 179-211.
21. Bono JE, Judge TA (2003) Core self-evaluations: A review of the trait and its role in job satisfaction and job performance. European Journal of Personality 17: S5-S18.
22. Gnyawali DR, Fogel DS (1994) Environments for entrepreneurship development: key dimensions and research implications. Entrepreneurship Theory and Practice 18: 43-62.
23. Shook CL, Priem RL, McGee JE (2003) Venture creation and the enterprising individual: A review and synthesis. Journal of Management 29: 379-399.
24. Furnham A, Ribchester T (1995) Tolerance of ambiguity: A review of the concept, its measurement and applications. Current psychology 14: 179-199.
25. Baumeister RF, Leary MR (1995) The need to belong: desire for interpersonal attachments as a fundamental human motivation. Psychological bulletin 117: 497-529.
26. Marsh HW (1990) Causal ordering of academic self-concept and academic achievement: A multiwave, longitudinal panel analysis. Journal of educational psychology 82: 646-656.
27. McGee R, Williams S (2000) Does low self-esteem predict health compromising behaviours among adolescents? Journal of adolescence 23: 569-582.
28. Van de Ven AH, Polley DE, Garud R, Venkataraman S (1999) The innovation journey.
29. Jackson D, Manual JPIR (1994) Port Huron. MI: Sigma Assessment Systems.
30. Deci EL, Ryan RM (2000) The" what" and" why" of goal pursuits: Human needs and the self-determination of behavior. Psychological inquiry 11: 227-268.
31. Ryan RM, Deci EL (2006) Self-regulation and the problem of human autonomy: does psychology need choice, self-determination, and will? Journal of personality 74: 1557-1585.
32. Vansteenkiste M, Ryan RM (2013) On psychological growth and vulnerability: Basic psychological need satisfaction and need frustration as a unifying principle. Journal of Psychotherapy Integration 23: 263.
33. Niemiec CP, Ryan RM (2009) Autonomy, competence, and relatedness in the classroom Applying self-determination theory to educational practice. Theory and research in Education 7: 133-144.
34. Roth G, Assor A, Kanat-Maymon Y, Kaplan H (2007) Autonomous motivation for teaching: How self-determined teaching may lead to self-determined learning. Journal of educational psychology 99: 761-774.

35. Pelletier LG, Séguin-Lévesque C, Legault L (2002) Pressure from above and pressure from below as determinants of teachers' motivation and teaching behaviors. Journal of educational psychology 94: 186-196.

36. Furrer C, Skinner E (2003) Sense of relatedness as a factor in children's academic engagement and performance. Journal of educational psychology 95: 148-162.

37. Broeck AVD, Vansteenkiste M, Witte HD, Soenens B, Lens W (2010) Capturing autonomy, competence, and relatedness at work: Construction and initial validation of the Work-related Basic Need Satisfaction scale. Journal of Occupational and Organizational Psychology 83: 981-1002.

38. Aunola K, Stattin H, Nurmi JE (2000) Parenting styles and adolescents' achievement strategies. Journal of adolescence 23: 205-222.

39. Schneewind KA, Pfeiffer P (1995) Impact of family processes on control beliefs. Self-efficacy in changing societies 114-148.

40. Baumrind D (1991) The influence of parenting style on adolescent competence and substance use. The Journal of Early Adolescence 11: 56-95.

41. Schmitt-Rodermund E (2004) Pathways to successful entrepreneurship: Parenting, personality, early entrepreneurial competence, and interests. Journal of Vocational Behavior 65: 498-518.

42. Deci EL, Ryan RM (2008) Self-determination theory: A macrotheory of human motivation, development, and health. Canadian psychology/Psychologie canadienne 49: 182-185.

43. Liñán F, Rodríguez-Cohard JC, Rueda-Cantuche, JM (2011) Factors affecting entrepreneurial intention levels: a role for education. International entrepreneurship and management Journal 7: 195-218.

44. Chen B, Vansteenkiste M, Beyers W, Boone L, Deci EL et al. (2015) Basic psychological need satisfaction, need frustration, and need strength across four cultures. Motivation and Emotion 39: 216-236.

45. Peterman NE, Kennedy J (2003) Enterprise education: Influencing students' perceptions of entrepreneurship. Entrepreneurship Theory and Practice 28: 129-144.

46. Bosma N, Hessels J, Schutjens V, Van Praag M, Verheul I (2012) Entrepreneurship and role models. Journal of Economic Psychology 33: 410-424.

47. Eckhardt JT, Shane SA (2003) Opportunities and entrepreneurship. Journal of Management 29: 333-349.

48. Francoise U, Janviere N, Ding D (2016) African S&T Professionals Trained in Chinese Universities: Orientations towards Entrepreneurship. Science Technology & Society.

49. Holland JL, Odessa FL (1997) Making vocational choices: A theory of vocational personalities and work environments: Psychological Assessment Resources (3rdedn).

Study on the Bank Finances to Small Scale Industries in Theni District in Tamil Nadu

Selvaraj N[1]* and Balajikumar P[2]

[1]Assistant Professor of Commerce, Saraswathi Narayanan College, Madurai, Tamil Nadu, India
[2]Assistant Professor of Management, Saraswathi Narayanan College, Madurai, Tamil Nadu, India

Abstract

Finance is an important input for an industry. For a small scale industry the need for finance is very essential due to its limited resources. The sources of finance for small scale industries are of two types-internal and external. The role of commercial banks in the process of economic development is well recognized. The year 1969 was a major turning point in Indian financial systems when 14 major banks were nationalized. Different national and state level institutions operating in the country for meeting the credit requirements of the SSIs sector include Small Industries Development Bank of India, Commercial Banks, Regional Rural Banks, Co-operative Banks (State, Central and Primary), State Financial Corporations/ State Industrial Investment Corporations, State Small Industries Development Corporation, National Bank for Agriculture and Rural Development, statutory bodies (KVIC, COIR Board, Handloom Board and Handicraft Boards), National Small Industries Corporations Limited and the like. The State bank of India lending to the small-scale industries in Theni district, compared to the public sector and the priority sector lending. The trend values showed that the target has increased faster than the actual amount of advances. The recovery rate of the SSI advances is a maximum of 69% in Theni district.

Keywords: Banks; Small-scale industries; Lending, Recovery; Economic development; Sources of Finance and trend values

Introduction

Finance is an important input for an industry. For a small scale industry the need for finance is very essential due to its limited resources. The sources of finance for small scale industries are of two types-internal and external. The internal sources consist of initial capital and profits reinvested. The external sources consist of loans and other assistance from the institutional and the non-institutional sources. This paper attempts to study the extent of bank finance made available to small-scale industries at National level, Tamil Nadu level and Theni district.

In spite of the thrust accorded through the administrative machinery of the government and financial assistance extended by financial institutions and commercial banks, the growth of the SSIs sector has been much below the expected level. At the end of the Tenth Plan, (March 2007), the small-scale industries produced goods worth Rs. 790759 crore against the target of Rs. 880805 crores. They exported goods valued at Rs. 202017 crore against the Tenth Plan target of Rs.233079 crores [1]. Though the SSIs sector contributed significantly to the economy of the country, it has not emerged as an engine of exponential growth and rapid economic transformation of the semi-urban, rural and backward areas. The liberalization and reform process initiated in India since, 1991 has enlarged the problem areas of the SSIs sector. While notable advances were made in exports and use of high technologies the general state of many small units continues to be critical. The role of commercial banks in the process of economic development is well recognized. The year 1969 was a major turning point in Indian financial systems when 14 major banks were nationalized. Thereafter there was re-orientation of credit flows, so as to benefit the till then neglected sectors such as agriculture, small-scale industries and small borrowers. The Government has constituted several committees from time to time to improve the credit delivery system of commercial banks towards SSIs. Accordingly, at present SSIs have been recognized as a priority sector by commercial banks and they lend liberally to SSIs units.

Statement of the Problem

Different national and state level institutions operating in the country for meeting the credit requirements of the SSIs sector include Small Industries Development Bank of India, Commercial Banks, Regional Rural Banks, Co-operative Banks (State, Central and Primary), State Financial Corporations/State Industrial Investment Corporations, State Small Industries Development Corporation, National Bank for Agriculture and Rural Development, statutory bodies (KVIC, COIR Board, Handloom Board and Handicraft Boards), National Small Industries Corporations Limited and the like In Theni district there are several financial institutions and commercial banks which provide all sorts of financial assistance to the SSI units. Of these the State bank of India, a leading government owned bank is playing a predominant role. Hence the present study, "Bank Credit to Small-Scale Industries in Theni district– A study with reference to State bank of India".

Review of Literature

Inderjit singh and Gupta [2] in their book on "Financing of small industry" also pointed out the inadequacy of institutional credit. They concluded that only 5.1% of the borrowers were financed by institutional finance. Kopardekar [3] attributes excess capacity remaining unutilized in small firms was due to the lack of adequate finance. The lack of adequate finance especially in meeting working

---

*Corresponding author: Selvaraj Narayanan, Assistant Professor of Commerce, Saraswathi Narayanan College, Madurai 625022, Tamilnadu, India
E-mail: selvaraj_narayanan@yahoo.com

capital requirement leads to inefficient utilization of the installed capacity, which in turn leads to inconsistent operation of the units. Many units are not in a position to apportion funds to fix and working capitals. Moorthy [4] focused his attention on the financing of the small-scale industries in the rayalaseema region of Andhra Pradesh. His emphasis was on the role of the government agencies, financial institutions and the commercial banks in augmenting adequate finance for the small-scale sector. Chaudhary [5] in his article entitled "Success in Urban Small Entrepreneurship", pointed out that creation of political awareness among the present day entrepreneurs was desirable, though not essential. This would help to carry out their entrepreneurial activity successfully since business and politics had inter-acting relationship. Natarajan [6] in his study entitled, "A Study of Utilization of Incentives by Small-Scale Industrial Units in Madurai District", measured the extent of utilization of incentives by small-scale industrial units in Madurai district. The study also highlighted the factors influencing the utilization and the impact of incentives on the industrial units. George Verghese [7] in his paper "Leading Issues in Credit flow to SSIs Sector is Finance for Small Enterprise in India" stated that focus on the limited impact of polices on the SSIs sector in India was mainly due to the isolated treatment accorded to the SSIs sector, the SSIs sector needs a renewed thrust enhancing credit flow by drastically improving the problem areas of administration personal, entrepreneurial development and infrastructure in dispensation of credit. Harinath Reddy's [8] Study on Working Capital Management in Small-Scale Industries, indicating improper controls on the working capital funding. The preparation of periodical working capital reports at least once a month, better planning to overcome shortages and over trading are some of the steps suggested and above all banks to monitor working capital utilization to detect early signs of sickness. Jyotirmayee khar [9] in his article "Credit Repayment by the Small-Scale Industries", highlighted that lending program to the small-scale sector was fraught with two primary problems: administered rate of interest, insufficient to meet the cost and risk of small business lending, had forced the financing institutions to channelize their resources towards the large corporate sector considered less risky. Uma Rani [10] argued that by its less capital intensive and high labour absorption nature, the SSIs sector had made significant contributions to employment generation and also to rural industrialization. This sector is ideally suited to build on the strength of our traditional skills and knowledge by infusion of technologies, capital and innovative marketing practices. Small scale sector has emerged as a dynamic and vibrant sector of the economy due to the new reforms. In the years to come, the SSIs would be exploited of its fullest export potential. Karthihaselvi et al. [11] desorbed that small-scale industries were dreams of Mahatma Gandhi come true. He supported the growth of small-scale industries in India, because he had the vision that it would help the poor people of India to come up. Small-scale and micro industries are not capital based, but the talent and effort based business. So even a middle class person can own and run this. According to new international poverty line of $1.25, around 40% of Indian population is under poverty line. As it is hard to provide employment to all, at least we can encourage the self employment through small-scale industries. Fortunately the country is endowed with adequate natural resources. So it is a propitious time for the growth of small-scale industries, government can come up with the loan facility and proper training for these industries. This may encourage unemployed people to start their career in this sector. With the government's scheme and succor, the dream of Mahatma Gandhi can come true.

Objectives of the Study

To analyze the extent of the financial assistance given by the State bank of India to the SSI units in Theni district. To conclude and suggest measures to ensure more flow of credit to the SSI units on the basis of findings of the study.

Framework of Analysis

In order to examine the growth of credit extended by State bank of India during the period under study, the Arithmetic mean (X) and the Coefficient of Variation (C.V) of the following formula were used

$$\text{Coefficient of Variation } (\%) \, (C.V) = \times 100 \, \frac{S.D}{X}$$

Where, S.D=Standard Deviation.

The trend and compound growth rates are computed for the advances to SSI by State bank of India by adopting the semi-log trend model as given below;

Log y=a + bt Where,

y=Amount of loans

t=Time Variable.

a and b are the parameters to be estimated.

The above model was estimated by the method of least squares. The compound growth rate was calculated by using the formula,

Compound Growth Rate (%)=(anti log b−1) × 100

Period of the Study

The secondary data relating to advances in India and Tamil Nadu were obtained for a period of 12 years from 1998-99 to 20010-2011. The same data for Theni district was collected for the period of 13 years from 1998-99 to 2010-2011.

Profile of the SBI in Theni District

The Theni district State bank of India in the Madurai Zonal office (Regional office) started its operation on 2nd August 1979. This region consists of nine districts namely, Madurai, Theni, Dindigul, Virudhunagar, Sivagangai, Ramnad, Tirunelvelli, Tutitcorin and Kanniyakumari. The branches of the State bank of India in Theni are claSSIfied under three heads namely rural, semi-urban, and urban. There are about 135 branches in the region, of which 28 are in the urban area, 48 in the rural and 59 in semi-urban areas. The total strength of the number of staff of this region is 3243, of which 791 are officers, 1579 are clerks and 873 are messengers. There are one Personal Banking Branch and four Agricultural Development Branches (ADBs) in the Madurai region. The deputy general managers directly control the entire 135 branches. For administrative purpose, this region is divided into three sub regions. The head office of the region is located in Madurai which controls the branches in Madurai and Theni districts. The region II consists of four districts, namely Dindigul, Sivagangai, Ramnad and Virudhunagar districts, and its head office is in Dindigul which has about 46 branches. Tirunevelli, Tutitcorin and Kanniyakumari are in region III. Its head office is in Nagarcoil which controls 41 branches [12].

Historical Development of the Presidency Banks

The SBI has about 200 years of experience in banking business. The Bank of Calcutta began its operation in 1806, the Bank of Bombay in

1840 and the Bank of Madras in 1843. All these banks were formed at the initiative of the British in the three presidency towns, Calcutta, Bombay and Madras. The names of the presidency towns were changed into Kolkata, Mumbai and Chennai respectively in recent times. The modern type of banking however was developed by the agency houses of Calcutta and Bombay after the establishment of rule by the East India Company in the 18th and the 19th centuries [13]. One-fifth of its total initial capital of Rs. 50 lakhs, was subscribed by the state government, which also appointed three out of the total nine directors. In 1840, the Bank of Bombay and in 1843 the State Bank of Madras also set up their capital of Rs. 52 lakhs and Rs. 30 lakhs respectively. Moreover, East India Company contributed Rs. 3 lakhs in respect of each bank [14]. The banks came into existence either as the result of the compulsions of the imperial finance or by the felt needs of the local European commerce. Their evolution was however, shaped by ideas on the analogy of similar developments in Europe and England. This was influenced by changes occurring in the structure of both the local trading environment and those developments in the Indian economy and the economy of Europe. The position of the presidency banks was thus "similar to the ladies of the Janana of the India prince. They had high status, they were protected, but they were not allowed out of the boundaries of their Janana walls [15]. Although these three banks performed banking functions, they have been termed as 'apex' banking in India. But India did not have a portal banking till 1935. Before the formation of the Imperial Bank of India in 1921, there was a need for amalgamating the three presidency banks.

SSI Advances by the State Bank of India in India

In this section, an attempt is made to analyze the advances to the small-scale industrial sector by the State bank of India in comparison to public sector banks.

Share of public sector banks and the state bank of India in the SSI finance

The SSIs are financed by all banks. It is logical at this stage to analyze the share of the State bank of India to the total credit extended to the SSI units by the public sector banks. Hence, the relevant information is furnished in Table 1.

Year	State Bank of India	Public Sector Banks	% of Credit by SBI to Public Sector Banks
1998-99	43690	105838	41.28
1999-00	46045	127477	36.12
2000-01	48400	149116	32.45
2001-02	49743	171185	29.06
2002-03	52988	203097	26.08
2003-04	58278	245582	23.74
2004-05	67634	310670	21.77
2005-06	82492	409791	20.13
2006-07	104703	521181	20.08
2007-08	148651	610450	24.35
2008-09	185208	720083	25.72
2009-10	221765	864564	25.65

Table 1: Bank credit to small scale industries by public sector banks and the state bank of India from 1998-1999 TO 2009-2010 (Rs. In Crores).

Sources: 1. Reserve Bank of India, Annual Report 1998 to 2010.
2. Banking Finance, January, 2010.
3. Money and Banking Centre for Monitoring Indian Economy, August–November 2006–10.

Particular	Mean	Standard Deviation	Co-efficient of Variation (Percentage)
Public Sector Banks	347836.46	256458.97	73.72
State Bank of India	88533.23	59710.15	67.44

Table 2: Average and Stability of credit to the SSI units by public sector banks and state bank of India.
Source: Computed data

Particular	Trend Co-Efficient A	Trend Co-Efficient B	R^2	Compound Growth Rate (Per cent)
Public Sector Banks	11.118	0.197 (48.939)	0.99	21.8
State Bank of India	10.236	0.140 (9.567)	0.893	15.1

Table 3: Trend and Growth rate of bank credit to Small scale industries.
Source: Computed data, Figures in brackets are t – values, Significant at 5 per cent Level

It is observed from Table 1 that the amount of financing to SSI's by public sector banks and State bank of India are increasing year by year. Amount of financing to SSI's by public sector banks has been steadily increased from Rs. 105838 crores in 1998-1999 to Rs. 864564 crores in 2009-2010. Mean while amount of financing by State bank of India's to SSI's also increasing from Rs. 43690 crores in 1998-99 to Rs. 221765 crores in 2009-10. However, it is also inferred that the share of SBI financing to total amount financed by the public sector banks is decreasing year by year. It is concluded from above Table that State bank of India reduced their share of financing to SSI's compared with all public sector banks during the study period.

The average and stability of credit to the SSI units by the public sector banks and State bank of India are calculated and presented in Table 2. It could be observed from Table 2 that the average amount of lending to the SSI units by State bank of India was Rs. 347836.46 crores which was Rs. 88533.23 for public sector banks. The above Table also reveals that the co-efficient of variations is high (73.12%) in case of public sector banks, but it was slightly low (67.44 %) in State bank of India Banks. The trend and growth in lending by the public sector banks and State bank of India to the SSI units were calculated and are presented in Table 3. The above Table 3 shows that the trend co-efficient of credit to SSI by the public sector banks and the State bank of India were statistically significant at 5% level. The Table also reveals that the rate of growth in lending to SSI was increasing at the rate of 19.7% and 14.0 % per annum, by public sector banks and the State bank of India respectively. The compound growth rate was high in public sector banks comparing to State bank of India during the study period.

Share of SSI in priority sector credit by the SBI

The credit to the priority sector and the SSI units by the State bank of India from 1998-1999 to 2009-2010, are presented in the Table 4.

Table 4 shows the total credit extended to the priority sector and the SSI units by the State bank of India at all India level. It is observed that the total credit increased from Rs. 80200 crores in 1998-99 to Rs. 437317crores in 2009-10. The credit extended to the priority sector other than SSI has been increased from Rs. 36510 crores in 1998-99 to Rs. 215552 crores in 2009-10. The percentage share of the priority sector other than SSI to the total credit ranged from 45.52% in 1998-99 to 60.89% in 2005-06. The credit to the SSIs alone also increased from Rs. 43690 crores in 1998–99 to Rs. 221765 crores in 2009-10. Even though amount of financing to SSIs by State bank of India has shown increasing trend the share of SSI credit to total credit showed

Year	Total Credit	Priority Sector Credit	Percentage of Priority Sector Credit to Total credit	SSI Credit	Percentage of SSI Credit to Total Credit
1998-99	80200	36510	45.52	43690	54.48
1999-00	90523	44478	49.13	46045	50.86
2000-01	100846	52446	52.00	48400	47.99
2001-02	108406	58663	54.11	49743	45.88
2002-03	117535	64548	54.92	52988	45.08
2003-04	136229	77919	57.20	58278	42.80
2004-05	164065	96431	58.78	67634	41.22
2005-06	210961	128469	60.89	82492	39.10
2006-07	249252	144549	57.99	104703	42.00
2007-08	312719	164068	52.46	148651	47.53
2008-09	375415	190207	50.66	185208	49.33
2009-10	437317	215552	49.28	221765	50.71

Table 4: Share of SSI in priority sector credit by the state bank of India from 1998-1999 TO 2009-2010 (Rs. In Crores).
Sources: 1. Annual Report of the Reserve Bank of India, 2000 to 2010
2. Money and Banking, Center For Monitoring India Economy-Nove, 2005 to 2010
3. Statistical Tables Relating To Banks of India, RBI. (Various Issues)
4. Economic Statistics, 2008 – 2010

Particular	Mean	Standard Deviation	Co-efficient of Variation (Percentage)
Total Credit	205875.58	132775.32	64.49
Priority Sector	106153.33	60884.36	57.35
SSI Credit	92466.41	60580.76	65.51

Table 5: Average and Stability of credit to priority sector and the SSI units by the State bank of India.
Source: Computed data

Particular	Trend Co-Efficient A	Trend Co-Efficient B	R^2	Compound Growth Rate (Per cent)
Total Credit	10.982	0.166 (18.013)	0.970	18.0
Priority Sector	10.337	0.166 (35.554)	0.922	18.0
SSI Credit	10.281	0.152 (9.804)	0.906	16.4

Table 6: Trend and growth rate of credit to priority sector and Small scale industrial sector.
Source: Computed data, Figures in brackets are t – values, Significant at 5 per cent Level

decreasing trend till the year 2005-06 and thereafter started increasing to 50.71% in 2009-2010. Table 5 gives the average and stability of the total credit to priority sector and the credit to SSI sector during period under study. From Table 5, it is seen that the average lending by State bank of India was Rs.205875.58 crore, and the average lending amount to priority sectors other than SSI was Rs. 106153.33 crore and the average lending amount to SSI alone was Rs. 92466.41 crores during study period. The computed results of the trend and the growth rate of credit to the priority sector and the SSI credit by the State bank of India are given in Table 6. It is understood from Table 6 that the trend co-efficient of the total credit to priority sector and the SSI credit were statistically significant at 5% level. The Table further shows that on an average the total credit to priority sector and the SSI credit have been increasing at the rate of 16.6%, 15.2% and 10.9% per annum respectively. The compound growth rate was found high in priority sector (18.0%) followed by the total credit (18.0%) and the SSI credit (16.4%) in India.

Advances to SSI by the SBI in Tamil Nadu

This section attempts to analyze the advances made to SSI units sector by SBI in Tamil Nadu. The share of SSI credit in overall priority sector credit extended by the bank during the study period was also analyses.

Share of the SBI lending to SSI in the public sector banks in Tamil Nadu

The lending by the State bank of India and the public sector banks to the small-scale industries in Tamil Nadu is presented in Table 7.

Table 7 shows the total lending to the SSI units by the public sector banks which increased from Rs. 1754.69 crores in 1998-99 to Rs. 6032.16 crores in 2009-10. The lending to the SSI by the State bank of India alone ranged from Rs. 696 crores in 1998-99 to Rs. 1155 crores in 2009-10. The share of the State Bank lending to SSIs in comparison to lending by public sector banks ranged between 19.15% and 39.66% during the study period. The average and stability of lending to the SSIs by the public sector banks and the State Bank are computed and are presented in Table 8. From Table 8, it can be observed that the average lending by public sector bank and the State bank of India to the SSI sector in Tamil Nadu were Rs. 3424.66 crores and Rs. 826.66 crores respectively during the study period. It is inferred from the analysis of co-efficient of variation that high fluctuations were found in SSIs credit by public sector bank compared to the State bank of India. The computed trend and growth rate of lending to the SSI units by the public sector banks and the State bank of India are given in Table 9. It is inferred from Table 9, that the trend coefficient of the public sector banks and the State Bank lending to the SSI sector are positive and statistically significant at 5% level. It is found that the public sector banks lending to the SSI sector has been increasing at the rate of 10.9% per annum which is 4.6% for the SBI. The compound growth rate of lending was found high in public sector banks (11.5%) compared to the

Year	Public Sector Banks (Rs. in Crores)	State Bank of India (Rs. in Crores)	Percentage of SBI Credit Public Sector Banks
1998-99	1754.69	696	39.66
1999-00	2013.50	704	34.96
2000-01	2355.62	707	30.01
2001-02	2540.23	711	27.99
2002-03	2502.42	719	28.73
2003-04	2889.16	713	24.68
2004-05	2981.31	735	24.65
2005-06	3591.48	846	23.55
2006-07	4201.65	912	21.71
2007-08	4811.82	978	20.32
2008-09	5421.99	1044	19.25
2009-10	6032.16	1155	19.15

Table 7: State bank of India and public scetor banks lending to SSI units in Tamilnadu during 1998-1999 TO 2009-2010.
Sources: 1. Indian Overseas Bank, Lead Bank Department, Chennai
2. Money and Banking, Center for Monitoring India Economy, November 2006 to 2010

Particular	Mean	Standard Deviation	Co-efficient of Variation (Percentage)
Public Sector Bank	3424.66	1394.24	40.71
State Bank of India	826.66	159.06	19.24

Table 8: Average and stability of lending to small scale industries by public sector banks and the sbi.
Source: Computed data

Particular	Trend Co-Efficient A	Trend Co-Efficient B	R^2	Compound Growth Rate (Per cent)
Public Sector Bank	7.358	0.109 (21.088)	0.978	11.5
State Bank of India	6.403	0.046 (7.273)	0.841	4.7

Table 9: Trend and growth rate of lending to the SSI units by the public sector banks and the State bank of India.
Source: Computed data
Figures in brackets are t – values, Significant at 5 per cent Level

Year	Target (Rs. In Crores)	Disbursements (Rs. In Crores)	Percentage of Disbursements to Target
1998-99	410.34	421.46	102.71
1999-00	452.76	510.59	112.77
2000-01	562.96	606.46	107.73
2001-02	638.66	640.34	100.26
2002-03	673.28	674.44	100.17
2003-04	712.61	776.92	109.02
2004-05	761.25	740.90	97.33
2005-06	918.07	906.30	98.72
2006-07	1074.89	1071.70	99.70
2007-08	1230.17	1237.10	100.56
2008-09	1386.99	1392.50	100.39
2009-10	1542.02	1558.24	101.05

Table 10: Target and disbursement of advances by state bank of India to SSI units in Tamilnadu during 1998-1999 to 2010-2011.
Sources: 1. Indian Overseas Bank, Lead Bank Department, Chennai.
2. Money and Banking, Center For Monitoring India Economy, Nov-2006 to 2010.

Particular	Mean	Standard Deviation	Co-efficient of Variation Percentage
Target Fixed	863.66	369.38	42.77
Disbursed Credit	878.07	361.66	41.18

Table 11: Average and stability of credit target and disbursed credit to small-scale industries.
Source: Computed data

State bank of India (4.7%) in Tamil Nadu, during the study period. The State banks of India target credit and sanctioned credit to SSI units in Tamil Nadu during the period of study are presented in Table 10.

Table 10 clearly shows that the credit target of State bank of India to SSI has been increasing year by year from the amount of Rs. 410.34 crore in 1998-99 to Rs. 1542.02 crore in 2009-2010. Moreover almost in all the years (except 2004-2007) the bank has been disbursed credit more than their targeted credit amount. The average and stability of credit targeted and disbursed to SSI's are presented in Table 11. It is inferred from the Table 11 that the average credit target and disbursed amount of credit to the SSI in Tamil Nadu were Rs. 863.66 crores and Rs. 878.07 crores respectively. It was also inferred that high fluctuation in credit target amount was found comparing with disbursed credit amount to SSI units. The trend and growth rate of the State bank of India bank credit target and disbursed amount of credit to the SSI units in Tamil Nadu were computed and are presented in the Table 12.

From Table 12, it can be observed that the trend coefficient of the State bank of India, credit target and disbursed amount of credit to SSI's were statistically significant at 5% level. It implies that the credit target amount and disbursed have been increasing at the rate of 11.8% and 11.1% respectively. Moreover the compound growth rate of SBI credit target amount to SSI were (12.5%) which is the highest compared to the credit disbursed to SSI units.

Advances to the SSI units by the State Bank of India in the study area

In this section, an attempt is made to analyze the advances made to the SSI, outstanding credit amount from SSI units and recovery performance of the SBI in the study area. For this required data were collected from the year of 1998-1999 to 2010-2011.

Bank credit to small-scale industries

Table 13 exhibits the details of lending by the State bank of India and by the public sector banks to SSI units in Theni district during the period of 1998-1999 to 2010-2011. It is observed from Table 13 that the State bank of India lending amount have been increasing from year to year during the study period. It is evident from Table 13 that lending amount was Rs. 8034 thousand in 1998-99 and it increased to Rs. 286615 thousands in the year of 2010-11. In the total amount disbursed to SSI by all the public sector banks, SBI's contribution has increased from 6.16% to 46.21% during the study period. The average and stability of lending to the SSI units by the State bank of India and public sector banks are computed and presented in Table 14. From Table 14 it is seen that the average amount of financing to the SSI units

Particular	Trend Co-Efficient a	Trend Co-Efficient B	R^2	Compound Growth Rate (Per cent)
Target Credit	5.912	0.118 (27.013)	0.986	12.5
Disbursed Amount of Credit to SSI	5.979	0.111 (20.084)	0.976	11.8

Table 12: Trend and growth rate of credit target disbursed amount of credit
Source: Computed Data
Figures in brackets are t – values, Significant at 5 per cent Level

Year	Advances to SSI by Public Sector Banks (Rs. In Thousands)	Advances to SSI by SBI (Rs. In Thousands)	Share of State Bank of India in Public Sector Banks
1998-99	130409	8034	6.16
1999-00	135229	6767	5.00
2000-01	155445	17760	11.42
2001-02	150625	48523	32.21
2002-03	147101	59516	40.46
2003-04	138753	67501	48.65
2004-05	176789	76467	43.25
2005-06	185133	96073	51.89
2006-07	256417	107074	41.76
2007-08	317539	171940	54.15
2008-09	468562	230924	49.28
2009-10	544362	268034	49.24
2010-11	620162	286615	46.21

Table 13: Advances to SSI units by public sector banks and state bank of India in Theni district from 1998–1999 to 2010–2011.
Sources: 1. Annual Credit Plan for Theni District from 1998-99 to 2010-11
2. Lead Bank Section of State Bank of India, Theni

SSI Finance	Mean	Standard Deviation	Co-efficient of Variation Percentage
By Public Sector Banks	263578.92	171383.10	65.02
By State Bank of India	111171.38	97310.70	87.53

Table 14: Average and stability of the SSI units finance by public sector banks and state bank of lending.
Source: Computed data

by public sector banks and the State bank of India were Rs. 263578.92 thousands and Rs. 111171.38 thousands respectively during the study period. Moreover the State bank of India's lending amount had the high fluctuation comparing to that of public sector financing. The computed results of trend and growth rates of the SSI units finance by the public sector banks and by the State bank of India are given in Table 15. It is understood from Table 15 that the trend coefficient of the public sector banks and the State bank of India's disbursement of credit to the SSI units are statistically significant at 5% level. It is also observed that the amount of financing to the SSI units by public sector banks and the State bank of India were increasing at the rate of 13.4% and 30.5% per annum respectively. Further the compound growth rate of the SBI lending to SSI was 35.6%, which is comparatively higher to public sector banks lending to the SSI (14.3%).

Share of SSI credit amount to total priority sectors advances by SBI

Table 16 gives the details of priority sector advances and SSI advances by SBI form 1998–1999 to 2010-2011 in study area. It is understood from Table 16 that the priority sector advances made by the State bank of India ranged from Rs. 198792 thousand in 1998-99 to Rs. 2348337 thousand in 2010-11. The share of the SSI advances in the priority sector advances made by the State bank of India in Theni district increased from 4.04% in 1998-99 to 13.46% in 2009-2010. A fluctuating trend in the share of the SSI advances in the priority sector advances was observed during the study period. Table 17, gives the average and stability of SSI advances and priority sector advances by the SBI during the period. From Table 17, it is observed that the average advances to the SSI units and priority sector was Rs. 111171.38

SSI Finance	Trend Co-Efficient		R^2	Compound Growth Rate (Percentage)
	a	B		
By Public Sector Bank	11.382	0.134 (7.840)	0.848	14.3
By State Bank of India	8.967	0.305 (10.857)	0.915	35.6

Table 15: Trend and growth rate of SSI units finance by public sector banks and state bank of India.
Source: Computed data
Figures in brackets are t – values, Significant at 5 per cent level

Year	Priority Sector Advances (Rs. In Thousands)	SSI Advances (Rs. In Thousands)	Share of SSI Advances in Priority Sector
1998-99	198792	8034	4.04
1999-00	281272	6767	2.40
2000-01	354062	17760	5.02
2001-02	364807	48523	13.30
2002-03	437597	59516	13.60
2003-04	497180	67501	13.58
2004-05	638209	76467	11.98
2005-06	915601	96073	10.49
2006-07	1254099	107074	8.54
2007-08	1416358	171940	12.14
2008-09	1748328	230924	13.21
2009-10	1990734	268034	13.46
2010-11	2348337	286615	12.20

Table 16: Priority sector and SSI units advances by state bank of India in Theni district from 1998–1999 to 2010-2011.
Sources: 1. Annual Credit Plan for Theni District from 1998-99 to 2010-11
2. Lead Bank Section of SBI, Theni

Particular	Mean	Standard Deviation	Co-efficient of Variation Percentage
Priority Sector Advances by SBI	957336.61	722274.80	75.44
SSI Advances by State Banks of India	111171.38	97310.70	87.53

Table 17: Average and stability of SSI units advances made by state bank of India.
Source: Computed data

Particular	Trend Co-Efficient		R^2	Compound Growth Rate (Percentage)
	A	B		
Priority Sector Advances by SBI	12.031	0.208 (28.258)	0.986	23.1
SSI Advances by the State Bank of India	8.966	0.305 (10.857)	0.915	35.6

Table 18: Trend and growth rate of advances to the SSI units in Theni district.
Source: Computed data
Figures in brackets are t – values, Significant at 5 per cent level

and Rs. 957336.61 thousands respectively. A high fluctuation was found (87.53 %) in the SBI advances to the SSI units during the study period, whereas in case of State bank of India advances to priority sector a low fluctuations was found (75.44%). The computed results of the trend and growth rate of advances to the SSI units made by State bank of India are given in Table 18. It is understood from Table 18, that the trend co-efficient of the advances to the SSI units made by the State bank of India were statistically significant at 5% level. It implied that on an average advances to the SSI units made by the State bank of India and priority sector advances were increasing at the rate of 30.5% and 20.8% per annum respectively. The compound growth rate of advances to SSI units and priority sector was 35.6% and 23.1% respectively. The compound growth rate of SSI units advances show high value comparing to other priority sector. So it is evident that the SBI the increases its amount of credit year by year.

Actual amount of advances to the SSI

Table 19 gives the details of the actual amount of advances to the SSI against commitment made by the State bank of India during the period from 1998-1999 to 2010 -2011. It is observed from Table 19 that the State bank of India gave more advances to the SSI than the targeted amount in all the years except 2000-01 during the study period. The targeted amount of advances by the State bank of India to the SSI units in Theni district has fluctuated during the period. The targeted amount ranged from Rs. 14442 thousands in 1998-99 to Rs. 285031 thousand in 2010-11, while the actual advances to the SSI units ranged from Rs. 8034 thousands in 1998-99 to Rs. 286615 thousands in 2010-2011. A steady increase was found in the actual amount advances to SSI units during the period. The average and stability in target amount advances and the actual amount of advances to the SSI units by State bank of India in Theni district are given in Table 20. From Table 20 it is revealed that the average target and the average actual amount to SSI of advances by State bank of India in Theni district were Rs. 109977.69 thousand and Rs. 122285.00 thousand respectively. It is inferred from the analysis that high fluctuation is found in the credit target to SSI units compared to the actual amount of advances as indicated by the coefficient of variations. The computed results of trend and growth rate of target and actual amount of advances by the State bank of India in Theni district are given in Table 21. It is understood from Table 21 that the trend co-efficient of the target of the SSI units advances made by the State Bank is statistically significant at 5% level and positive. It also implies that on an average the target of the SSI units advances

Year	Target of SSI Advance by SBI	Percentage Increase/ Decreases	Disbursed Amount of Advance by the SBI	Percent age Increase/ Decreases
1998-99	14442	-	8034	-
1999-00	23385	61.92	6767	-15.77
2000-01	32186	37.63	29027	-57.10
2001-02	41180	27.94	48523	67.16
2002-03	57466	39.55	59516	22.65
2003-04	66734	16.13	67501	13.42
2004-05	75535	13.19	76467	13.28
2005-06	85360	13.00	96073	25.64
2006-07	89721	5.11	107074	11.45
2007-08	168915	88.27	171940	60.58
2008-09	227544	34.71	230924	34.30
2009-10	262211	15.23	268034	16.07
2010-11	285031	8.70	286615	6.93

Table 19: Target and disbursed amount to SSI units in Theni district during 1998-1999 to 2010–2011 (Rs. In Thousands).
Sources: 1. Annual Credit Plan for Theni District from 1998-1999 to 2010-2011
2. Lead Bank Section of SBI, Theni

Particular	Mean	Standard Deviation	Co-efficient of Variation Percentage
Target of the SSI Advance by SBI	109977.69	93699.10	85.20
Actual Amount of Advance made by the SBI	122285.00	87251.59	71.35

Table 20: Average and stability of target and actual amount of credit to the state bank of India.
Source: Computed data

Particular	Trend Co-Efficient a	Trend Co-Efficient B	R^2	Compound Growth Rate (Percentage)
Target of SSI Advance made by SBI	9.579	0.237 (20.207)	0.976	26.8
Actual Amount of Advance made by SBI	10.408	0.155 (5.695)	0.747	16.7

Table 21: Trend and growth rate of target and actual disbursed amount to small-scale industries
Source: Computed data
Figures in brackets are t – values, Significant at 5 per cent level

made by the State Bank has been increasing at the rate of 23.7% per annum. The compound growth rate was found high in target of the SSI units advances made by the State bank of India (26.8%) during the period followed by the actual amount of advances (16.7%) in Theni district. The actual amount of advances by the SBI to SSI units has been increasing at the rate of 15.5% during the study period in Theni district.

Loan outstanding to state bank of India by SSI and priority sectors

Table 22 explains the loan outstanding of SSI and priority sectors to the State bank of India during the period from 1998-1999 to 2010-2011. It is clear from Table 22 that the total advance of the State Bank increased form Rs. 453373 thousand in 1998-99 to Rs. 8902600 thousands in 2010-11. In the total advances made by the SBI priority sector outstanding amount has increased from Rs. 63109 thousand in 1998-99 to Rs. 2281428 thousands in 2010-11. The amount of outstanding from priority sector to total advances was the lowest (7.57%) in the year of 2005-06 and it was the highest (28.58%) in the year 2002-03. Outstanding credit from the SSI units increased from Rs. 99932 thousands in 1998-99 to Rs. 352630 thousands in 2010-11. The total credit outstanding of the SSI units increased from 22.04% in 1998-99 to 3.96 % in 2010-2011. From the Table, it can be concluded that the outstanding position for the SSIs is only marginal and hence it is hoped that the lending institution will pay more attention to the SSI units among the other segments of the priority sector. The average and stability of the total advances, priority sector and the SSI advances over the priority are given in Table 23.

Table 23 shows that the average total advances to priority sector and the SSI units credit by the State bank of India Theni district were Rs. 3508973.53 thousands, Rs. 686399.23 thousands and Rs. 170539.69 thousands respectively from 1998–99 to 2010–11. It is also inferred that from the analysis high fluctuation was found in the SSI units credit compared to the total advances as indicated by the co-efficient of variation. The computed result of trend and growth rate of the total advances, priority sector and the SSI unit's credit by the State bank of India in Theni district are given in Table 24. From Table 24, it could be identified that the trend coefficients of the total advances, priority sector and the SSI credit were statistically significant at 5% level and positive. It implies that on an average the total advances, priority sector and the SSI credit have been increasing at the rate of 26.8%, 28.3%

Year	Total Advances	Priority Sector Outstanding	Percentage of Priority Sector Outstanding to Total Credit	SSI Sector Outstanding	Percentage of SSIs Credit to Total Credit
1998-99	453373	63109	13.92	99932	22.04
1999-00	648809	96045	14.80	108208	16.68
2000-01	842321	159154	18.89	115637	13.73
2001-02	937757	247791	26.42	124005	13.22
2002-03	1080525	308856	28.58	107537	9.95
2003-04	1275961	204823	16.05	99169	7.77
2004-05	1832634	167142	9.12	132281	7.22
2005-06	3390192	256680	7.57	149685	4.41
2006-07	4572684	798334	17.46	169902	3.71
2007-08	5880000	1029200	17.58	202700	3.45
2008-09	7370000	1298300	17.62	250000	3.39
2009-10	8429800	2012328	23.87	305330	3.62
2010-11	8902600	2281428	25.62	352630	3.96

Table 22: Outstanding loan amount of priority and SSI sector to the state bank of India in Theni district (Rs. in Thousands).
Sources: 1. Annual Credit Plan for Theni District from 1998 to 2011
2. Lead Bank Section of State Bank of India, Theni

Particular	Mean	Standard Deviation	Co-efficient of Variation Percentage
SBI Advances	3508973.53	3161142.56	90.08
Priority Sector	686399.23	755137.01	110.01
SSI Credit	170539.69	83509.56	48.96

Table 23: Average and stability of outstanding in priority sector and small scale industries advances.
Source: Computed data

Particular	Trend Co-Efficient a	Trend Co-Efficient B	R^2	Compound Growth Rate (Percentage)
SBI Advances	12.733	0.268 (20.836)	0.975	30.7
Priority Sector	10.860	0.283 (9.542)	0.892	32.7
SSI Credit	11.236	0.102 (7.716)	0.844	10.8

Table 24: Trend and growth rate of outstanding advances in total priority sector and the SSI credit.
Source: Computed data
Figures in brackets are t – values, Significant at 5 per cent level.

Year	Demand	Collection	Balance	Percentage of Recovery
1998	176868	110278	99932	62
1999	101100	653000	108208	64
2000	203300	123900	115637	61
2001	129500	712000	124005	55
2002	219634	135860	107537	60
2003	201220	124075	99169	61
2004	125300	703000	132281	56
2005	423100	274900	149685	65
2006	592058	392096	169902	65
2007	199200	137400	202700	69
2008	220500	143300	250000	65
2009	234800	167200	291430	66
2010	254000	199900	-	66

Table 25: Recovery performance of state bank of India towards SSI units lending in Theni district during 1998 to 2010 (Rs. in Thousands).
Sources: 1. Annual Credit Plan for Theni District from 1998 to 2010
2. Lead Bank Section of SBI, Theni

and 10.2% per annum respectively. The compound growth rate was found high in the total advances (32.7%) followed by the priority sector (30.7%) of the SSI credit (10.8%) in Theni district.

Recovery of outstanding loan of SSI sector position by the SBI in Theni

The details about the demand, collection and balance percentage of recovery are presented in Table 25. It is understood from Table 25 that the demand has ranged from Rs. 176868 thousands to Rs. 2540000 thousands in 1998 to 2010, whereas in collection it has ranged from Rs. 110278 thousands in 1998 to Rs. 199900 thousands in 2010. The balance amount in the SSI unit's credit ranged from Rs. 99932 thousands in 1998 and Rs. 291430 thousands in 2009. It is inferred that the steady increase in the balance amount was found during the period under study. The rate of recovery ranged from 62% in 1998 to 66% in 2010. The rate of recovery is more than 65% in six years out of the 13 years. It shows that debt recovery rate is moderate in the case of SSI units lending by the State bank of India in the study area. The average and stability in the demand, collection and balance over the period are given in Table 26.

Particular	Mean	Standard Deviation	Co-efficient of Variation Percentage
Demand	236967.69	132768.46	56.02
Collection	298223.76	236181.31	79.19
Balance	154207.16	63083.14	40.90

Table 26: Average and stability demand, collection and balance of the State bank of India in Theni district.
Source: Computed data

Particular	Trend Co-Efficient a	Trend Co-Efficient b	R^2	Compound Growth Rate (Percentage)
Demand	11.850	0.059 (1.840)	0.235	6.1
Collection	12.530	-0.027 (-0.470)	0.020	-2.5
Balance	11.287	0.091 (6.593)	0.813	9.6

Table 27: Trend and growth rate of demand, collection and balance in the state bank of India in Theni district.
Source: Computed data
Figures in brackets are t – values, Significant at 5 per cent level

Table 26, exhibits that the average demand, collection and balance of the State bank of India in SSIs lending in Theni district were Rs.236967.69 thousands, Rs.298223.76 thousands and Rs.154207.16 thousand respectively from 1998 to 2010. It is inferred from the analysis that high fluctuations were found in the collection compared to the demands as indicated by the co-efficient of variation. The computed result of trend and growth rate of the demand, collection and balance by the State bank of India in Theni district are given in Table 27.

Table 27 shows that the trend coefficient of demand and balance were statistically significant at 5% level and positive. It implies that on an average the demand and balance in the State bank of India in Theni district have been increasing at the rate of 05.9% and 09.1% per annum respectively. Whereas the trend value of collection on an average is decreasing at a rate of 02.7% per annum. The compound growth rate was found high in balance (9.6%) during the period under study followed by demand (6.1%) in Theni district.

Summary

The share of the small scale industries advances made by the State bank of India to the public sector banks ranged between 25.65% and 41.28% in India. It is found that the share of the SSI units advances to the total priority sector advances varied from 39.10% to 54.48% during the period under study. In Tamil Nadu, the share of the State bank of India, lending in public sector banks is around 19.15% to 39.66% and in the priority sector, it is nearly 47.97%. In Theni district the share of the State bank of India lending to small-scale industries in the public sector bank and the priority sector ranged between 6.16% and 54.15% and 2.40% to 13.60% respectively. But fluctuation was observed in the State bank of India lending to the small-scale industries in Theni district, compared to the public sector and the priority sector lending. The trend values showed that the target has increased faster than the actual amount of advances. The recovery rate of the SSI advances is a maximum of 69% in Theni district.

Suggestions

1. The Bank under study may have specialized branches in each district to the loan requirements of the small-scale industries.

2. If the State bank of India does not have exclusive branches

for SSI units, the bank may provide separate cells in all branches to deal exclusively with small-scale industries. Such cells could monitor the disbursement and utilization of loans to SSI units.

3. Adequate delegation of power at the branch level may be given so as to avoid several layers of hierarchy in granting loans to SSI units.

4. The regular repayment of loans by SSI units may be rewarded by the bank under study with increase in the loan amount and reduction in the rate of interest for further loans.

5. The lead banks in all districts may have periodical meetings with the DICs and the Association of the SSI units to assess the nature, type and amount of loans required by SSI units.

6. A monthly newsletter on the SSI sector may be circulated among the staff at the specialized branches. The newsletter should project the latest developments in the SSI sector which will sensitize the bank staff and reorient them regarding the working of the SSI sector.

References

1. Laghu Udyog Samachar (2002) Government of India.
2. Singh I, Gupta NS (1977) Financing of Small Industry. Chand S & Co Ltd, New Delhi.
3. Kopardekar, Sharad D (1974) Financing of Working Capital in Small-Scale Industries. S.Chand and Co. Ltd, New Delhi.
4. Moorthy GK (1980) Financing of Small-Scale Industries in Rayalaseema Region. Ph.D. Thesis submitted to Sri Venkateshwara University, Thirupathi.
5. Chaudhary KVR (1986) Success in Urban Small Entrepreneurship. Khadi Gramodyog 32: 10-473.
6. Natarajan K (1988) A Study of Utilization of Incentives by Small-Scale Industrial Units. Ph.D. Thesis of Madurai Kamaraj University, Tamilnadu, India.
7. Verghese GK (1998) Leading Issues in Credit Flow to SSI Sector in Finance for Small Enterprise in India. ISED Cochin.
8. Reddy H (2000) Working Capital Management in Small-Scale Industries. Thesis Submitted to Sri Venkateswara University, Thirupathi, AP, India.
9. Khar J (2000) Credit Repayment by Small-Scale industries. Prajnan 18: 33-41.
10. UmaRani N (2007) Export Potential of SSIs in India: A Study. Southern Economist 46:10-12.
11. Karthihaselvi V, Neelamegam R, Magesan AA (2010) Significance of Small-Scale Industries. Southern Economist, Tamilnadu, INDIA.
12. Pamphlets from the SBI, Madurai Regional Office, Madurai.
13. Bagchi AK (2003) The Era of Imperial Bank of India. Sage Publication, New Delhi, India.
14. Ibid page No. 17.
15. Bagchi A K Op cit page No. 15.

Prospects and Challenges for Small-Scale Mining Entrepreneurs in South Africa

Zandisile Mkubukeli* and Robertson Tengeh

Faculty of Business and Management Sciences, Cape Peninsula, University of Technology, South Africa

Abstract

Small-scale mining entrepreneurs are confronted with a variety of challenges during both the start-up and growth phase of their businesses not only in South Africa, but all over the world. Therefore, losing prospects available to them. The aim of this paper was to explore prospects and challenges faced by small scale mining entrepreneurs in South Africa (SA). To attain this end, a qualitative research paradigm was instituted for both data collection and analysis. The findings of this study concur with the literature, that there are indeed plenty of prospects available to small scale mining entrepreneurs. However, the most outstanding prospects was free training and funding. Nonetheless, the receptiveness of these prospects is somehow conditional.

Keywords: Prospects; Challenges; Small scale mining; Entrepreneurs

JEL Classification

M00, M1, M10, M130

Introduction and Background

Unemployment and poverty facts are painful, yet these are some of South Africa's vital statistics that cannot be put aside. According to Statistics South Africa the current unemployment rate is 25.5% of the workforce, with approximately 10 million people subject to high levels of poverty. On the flipside, it is believed that the mining sector has the potential to mitigate South Africa's unemployment and poverty crisis [1].

In this paper we answered the following questions: what are the prospects for small-scale mining entrepreneurs in SA? What are the challenges facing small-scale mining entrepreneurs in SA? We wanted to know two things. Firstly, what prospects are there for small scale mining entrepreneurs in South Africa that can help small scale miners grow their small scale mining operation? Secondly, what are the impediments preventing the latter in establishing sustainable businesses.

Traditionally, the efficacy of small scale mining has been gauged from different perspectives, for instance, Hilson and McQuilken [2] investigated the availability of support structures for small scale mining entrepreneurs and found that, public perception on small scale mining remains consistent, lack of support. Mkubukeli and Tengeh [3] explored the support structures and success factors relevant to small-scale mining and the results of the study and the results affirmed the availability of a comprehensive support structure for aspiring small-scale mining entrepreneurs. Appiah [4] scrutinized the organisation of small scale mining activities and revealed that there are monetary rewards sustained from operating a small scale mine. On the one hand, Dondeyne and Ndunguru [5] investigated small scale mining from a rural developmental perspective; the study found that; mining entrepreneurs fail to fulfil their financial obligations. On the other hand, Childs [6] explored new approaches for governing mining activities and proposed that, small-scale mining to be administered with trading channels for their minerals.

Notwithstanding the prevalence on small scale mining, scholarship on prospects and challenges for small scale mining entrepreneurs in SA is reasonably scanty. Therefore, the research problem under investigation is a remarkably partisan mining sector that favours more established companies, with small scale mining entrepreneurs sidelined. Despite being a significant source of revenue for SA, the current state of the mining sector is one that does not directly benefit previously disadvantaged people. Notwithstanding government interventions, small-scale mining entrepreneurs face numerous challenges during both the business start-up and growth phase of their businesses. This translates to the significant prospects lost. Against the just mentioned backdrop, this paper aimed to: explore prospects and challenges to small-scale mining entrepreneurs in SA.

In view of the foregoing, many would argue that most small-scale mining entrepreneurs lack the capacity to take advantage of the opportunities that are available to them and this is reflected in the sluggish growth of their businesses. On a different note, there is growing evidence that small-scale mining entrepreneurs are growing in numbers and young men and women entrepreneurs are being drawn into small-scale mining all over the world [7]. Despite this seeming contradiction, small-scale mining entrepreneurs, like other entrepreneurs in SA, are confronted by daunting challenges during both the start-up phase and next phases of their businesses.

Given the impediments they face, small-scale mining entrepreneurs are compelled to use rudimentary methods and often conduct small-scale mining operations individually and illegally [8-11]. The use of unorthodox business methods of extracting gold or other mineral resources are deleterious to the environment and human health [11-13]. According to Drasch et al. [13] small-scale mining entrepreneurs extract gold from the ore using mercury (a highly toxic chemical), thus creating a gold-amalgamation. Additionally, to separate the gold from the amalgamation, the gold-amalgamation is heated in the open,

---

*Corresponding author: Mkubukeli Z, PhD candidate and CEO of Zandisile Holdings, Faculty of Business and Management Sciences, Cape Peninsula University of Technology, South Africa, E-mail: zmkubza@gmail.com

thus contributing to air pollution. It seems that small-scale mining represents an environmental threat.

Regardless of the challenges small scale mining entrepreneurs face it seems that small scale mining entrepreneurs can exploit a set of prospects. For instance, Anon asserted that mining entrepreneurs in South Africa are likely to exploit the following prospects: direct ownership of mines or either contracting mining services to established mines. Heemskerk and van der Kooye [8] are convinced that given the increased number of prospects for small-scale mining entrepreneurs, small-scale mining entrepreneurs can exploit more of these prospects. In their view this would involve direct ownership of mines, contracting mining services, outsourcing new services and more effective marketing and trading. At present both national and international governments are considering formalising small-scale mining so that the sector can continue to contribute to the development of the rural economy [5]. Some governments have recognised what small-scale mining could offer and are establishing bilateral arrangements. For instance, Mothomogolo [14] acknowledges that Brazil, Russia, India, China and SA (BRICS) have opened up participation in their economies to South African entrepreneurs by means of bilateral agreements.

Despite the significance of small scale mining in rural communities, it seems as if a considerable pool of small scale mining entrepreneurs are limited by capital; geological information and the business know how [7,8,15,16]. As a result Mutemeri and Petersen [15] avowed that small scale mining operations are forever inconsistent due to their limitations. Phiri [11] notes that, the limitation of capital and business know how amongst small scale mining entrepreneurs has instead propelled a lack of recognition for the sector. Mutemeri et al. [7] are of the opinion that due to a lack of recognition: small scale mining often consists of informal and illegal activities. Hence, financial institutions are reluctant towards small scale mining.

The Problem Statement

Traditionally, the efficacy of small scale mining has been gauged from different perspectives, for instance, Hilson and McQuilken [15] investigated the availability of support structures for small scale mining entrepreneurs and found that, public perception on small scale mining remains consistent, lack of support. Mkubukeli and Tengeh [3] explored the support structures and success factors relevant to small-scale mining and the results of the study and the results affirmed the availability of a comprehensive support structure for aspiring small-scale mining entrepreneurs. Appiah [4] scrutinized the organisation of small scale mining activities and revealed that there are monetary rewards sustained from operating a small scale mine. On the one hand, Dondeyne and Ndunguru [5] investigated small scale mining from a rural developmental perspective, the study found that; mining entrepreneurs fail to fulfil their financial obligations. On the other hand, Childs [6] explored new approaches for governing mining activities and proposed that, small-scale mining to be administered with trading channels for their minerals.

Notwithstanding the prevalence on small scale mining, scholarship on prospects and challenges to small scale mining entrepreneurs in SA is reasonably scanty. Therefore, the research problem under investigation is a remarkably partisan mining sector that favours more established companies, with small scale mining entrepreneurs side-lined. Despite being a significant source of revenue for SA, the current state of the mining sector is one that does not directly benefit previously disadvantaged people. Notwithstanding government interventions, small-scale mining entrepreneurs face numerous challenges during both the business start-up and growth phase of their businesses. This translates to the significant prospects lost. Against the just mentioned backdrop, this paper aimed to: explore prospects and challenges to small-scale mining entrepreneurs in SA.

The following section consists of the following: literature survey on small scale mining; prospects and challenges to small scale mining entrepreneurs in SA. Subsequent to that, the research design and strategy will be explained. This is followed with the findings and discussion. Thereafter, the conclusions and limitations are addressed.

Literature Survey

Although there has been dominate scholarship on small scale mining gauged from different perspectives [3,9-11], limited attention has been paid to the prospects and challenges for small scale mining entrepreneurs. The literature survey is therefore, structured accordingly firstly; an entrepreneur is contextualised. Secondly small scale mining is defined. Thirdly, small scale mining entrepreneurs; and the theoretical framework underpinning this study is presented. Fourthly, prospects and challenges for small scale mining entrepreneurs are discussed. Lastly, a conceptual model is presented as a lens to view the challenges faced by small scale mining entrepreneurs.

Entrepreneur

According to Bolton and Thompson, an entrepreneur is any person who either creates or innovates a business thus adding value to the consumer. A similar perspective is held by Hisrich et al. asserts that, an entrepreneur is a person that combines resources innovatively in such a manner that new products or services are created in spite of the risk associated thereto. Barringer and Ireland agrees that an entrepreneur assembles the following resources; money, people, business model, the strategy, and transforms these resources into a feasible business start-up. Although many would agree that a true definition of entrepreneur is someone who habitually starts a business. However, in the context of this study an entrepreneur is any person that has at least started and operated a small scale mining business, but has not been successful in growing the business to appoint where it is sustainable.

Small-scale mining

Small-scale mining varies from country to country. Researching this field presents a daunting challenge to researchers throughout the world [10,11,13,17,18]. It seems that there is not yet consensus on a single definition of small-scale mining. Phiri [11], for instance, attempts to define small-scale mining by using benchmarking. The determinants he uses are the size of the mine, legality (law abiding or not) of operations, and mining paradigm. Another notable attempt was made by Hentschel et al. [18]. They argue that small-scale mining refers to mining operations with limited mechanisation, conducted by poor individuals or families and young children throughout the world. It can also be said that small-scale mining is defined as a process of mining involving both extracting and commercialising of minerals. However, what the literature neglects to mention is that, small scale miners are not the ones benefiting mostly from the minerals they mine but the syndicate they sell their minerals to. Furthermore, there mere fact that there is not a common understanding of what small scale mining is, may be a mammoth concern policy makers because they do not know what they are dealing with.

This study uses the above definition and confines itself to the prospects and challenges to small-scale mining entrepreneurs; it does not include junior to large scale mining. The following section explores the difference between small-scale miners and mining entrepreneurs. It poses the question: Are we dealing with small-scale miners or mining entrepreneurs?

Small-scale mining entrepreneurs

The evolution of diamond mining in SA saw mine workers making use of shovels and picks as their means of extracting minerals. According to Pegg, small-scale mining entrepreneurs are people driven by poverty to conduct informal and often illegal mining operations. Werthmann contends that small-scale miners are indigenous people in pursuit of financial benefits and social independence. This statement is supported by the views of [19]. Small-scale mining entrepreneurs in Southern Africa employ whoever is available in the host community, thus making it the leading employer in Southern African rural communities [2012]. As a rule, those who start a business are seen as entrepreneurs, regardless of their reasons for starting or running the business. However, in the event of small-scale mining, most small-scale miners are not entrepreneurially orientated, but are poverty driven. Therefore, do not reflect any entrepreneurial characteristics as opposed to large scale mining entrepreneurs.

What most scholars fail to comprehend regarding small scale mining is the fact that there is a clear distinction between a small-scale miner and entrepreneurs in general. This can be illustrated using the work of Nieman and Nieuwenhuizen [20]. Small-scale miners are regarded as survival entrepreneurs; the fact that they operate in isolation and are not educated, means they are not eligible for funding [20]. Although current literature criminalises small scale mining and suggests that small scale miners are illegal miners, the premise has no ground. The reason for that is because small scale miners are more concerned with providing food for their families. Therefore, according to them they are not breaking any law. Hence they are predominately seen as survival entrepreneurs throughout the world. Hence, the challenges they face are inevitable.

It seems as if that scholarship on whether small scale miners are entrepreneurs or not, is by far limited, given that the literature fails to address small scale miners as entrepreneurs rather addresses them as people who are poverty driven and are engaging in small scale mining for the purpose of alleviating poverty.

Theoretical framework underpinning this study

This section focuses on the push and pull factors of entrepreneurship, these factors are mere reasons behind new venture creation. All things being the same the "pushed" entrepreneurs are more likely to experience challenges therefore losing prospects available to them. This theory is widely utilised to bring to the core factors behind the reason of becoming an entrepreneur. On the one hand, the theory notes that, in most instances, people are forced into entrepreneurship by their circumstance. On the other hand, people can also be enticed to entrepreneurship by opportunities. Nonetheless, in the context of this study, the theory is used to determine whether small scale mining entrepreneurs are pushed or pulled into entrepreneurship, given the correlation between the former, opportunities and challenges.

Push and pull factors of small scale mining entrepreneurs: Currently, there are a number of theories on why people decide to become entrepreneurs. For instance the, the push-pull theories propound that people are pushed into entrepreneurship by their circumstances while others are pulled into entrepreneurship by opportunities [20]. This theory is adopted in this paper to understand the factors that push or entices people to become small-scale mining entrepreneurs.

It is believed that people are often pulled into entrepreneurship by the need for independence or for financial rewards [21]. Shane, Kolvereid and Westhead [22] argue that the vast majority of people are pulled into entrepreneurship by their passion to become entrepreneurs and a need for independence. In similar vein to Shane et al. [22], Barringer and Ireland [17] contend that the factors enticing people into entrepreneurship are the need for independence and pursuit of financial rewards.

In the case of small-scale mining, many consider that small-scale mining entrepreneurs are pushed into entrepreneurship rather than enticed into it, given that small scale miners are people who are pushed into entrepreneurship through poverty, as stated earlier in the argument. The latter view is supported by Kirkwood [23] who contends that most people are pulled into entrepreneurship by their difficult circumstances. This strengthens the call that further exploration is necessary to determine whether small-scale mining entrepreneurs are pushed into entrepreneurship and not pulled into it. Figure 1 illustrates push and pull factors of entrepreneurship in the context of small-scale mining entrepreneurs.

Figure 1 illustrates driving factors towards being an entrepreneur. On the left hand side are the favourable drivers to wards being an entrepreneur and on the right hand side are unfavourable conditions that drives people to become entrepreneurs. Bellow the drivers are explained more in-depth.

Push factors to entrepreneurship: The following are factors that push people to become entrepreneurs. The factors include unemployment, job insecurity, disagreement with management, an inability to fit in with the organisation, or no alternative.

Table 1 illustrates push factors to entrepreneurship. On the left are the factors and on the right is the explanation of the factors. The following table illustrates pull factors to entrepreneurship.

Pull factors to entrepreneurship: There are several factors that

Push factors to entrepreneurship	
Factors	Explanation
Unemployment	Small scale miners are pushed into small-scale mining by poverty and unemployment [12,18,19,24-27].
Job security	Small-scale mining entrepreneurs do not seem to have started up their enterprises because they were affected by job insecurity. The reasons are more likely to be retrenchment, unemployment and employment that is seasonal only, as well as previous experience as a mine workers.
Disagreement with management	It is a fair assumption that few of those in small-scale mining were pushed into entrepreneurial enterprises because of a disagreement with management.
Does not fit with the organisation	Understandably, people's views may often conflict with that of the organisation that employs them. It seems that small-scale mining entrepreneurs did not leave an organisation to start their own business. They started a small-scale mine to put food on the table for their family.
No other alternative	Due to limited alternatives, small-scale mining entrepreneurs may be said to be pushed into entrepreneurship.

Table 1: Push factors of entrepreneurship.

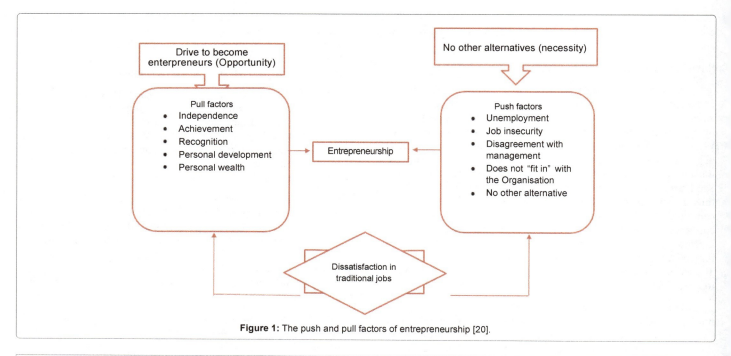

Figure 1: The push and pull factors of entrepreneurship [20].

Pull factors to entrepreneurship	
Factors	Explanation
Independence	Hentschel et al. [18] point out that small scale mining entrepreneurs are poverty-alleviation. Hence, it is fair to say that small scale mining entrepreneurs are not pulled into entrepreneurship.
Achievement	Small-scale miner's main achievement is to put food on the table for their families rather than an establishing entrepreneurial business.
Recognition	Given that there is no evidence that small-scale mining entrepreneurs are driven by a desire for recognition or achievement, many would agree that small-scale mining entrepreneurs are driven into entrepreneurship.
Personal development	Small-scale mining entrepreneurs are more likely to exercise their freedom and ability to pursue their own business ideas for financial gain.
Personal wealth	Small scale mining entrepreneurs do not start an enterprise due to pursuit of wealth but rather start businesses to be able to provide food for their families.

Table 2: Pull factors of entrepreneurship.

entice people to become entrepreneurs. A few of these are discussed below: independence, achievement, recognition, personal development and personal wealth.

Table 2 illustrates pull factors to entrepreneurship. Factors are located on the left column and on the right column is the explanation of the factors.

The push and pull factor theory highlights the factors that push and entice people to become entrepreneurs. One may thus argue that small scale mining entrepreneurs that are pushed into entrepreneurship are bound to experience more complex challenges than those pulled into entrepreneurship. It seems pulled entrepreneurs are bound to reap the benefits from the prospects available in the mining industry.

Prospects for small scale mining entrepreneurs in SA

South Africa is one of the countries blessed with considerable mineral resources. Actually many would contend that South Africa is a world leader in mining. The country is renowned for its plethora of mineral resources, accounting for a substantial proportion of world production and reserves, and South African mining companies are essential players in the global industry.

Estimated at R20.3-trillion ($2.5-trillion), South Africa's total reserves remain some of the world's most valuable and the world's fifth-largest mining sector in terms of GDP value [28]. Despite the SA's total mineral reserves estimated at $ 2.5 trillion, the South African mining sector favours most the minority of the country. It is believed that there is considerable potential for the discovery of other world-class deposits in areas yet to be exhaustively explored. South Africa's prolific mineral reserves include precious metals and minerals, energy minerals, non-ferrous metals and minerals, ferrous minerals, and industrial minerals [28].

Bilateral agreements signed between South Africa and countries, such as Brazil, Russia, India and China (all members of BRICS) open up opportunities for small-scale mining sector entrepreneurs and those in the rural areas in South Africa [14]. Small-scale mining entrepreneurs can create joint ventures with international companies and share synergies in order to increase their business efficiency. Heemskerk and van der Kooye [8] argue that these opportunities mean that small-scale mining entrepreneurs have the prospect of: direct ownership of mines, contracting mining services, outsourcing new services and marketing and trading.

Progressive policy changes in the mining sector in South Africa has created a number of opportunities for small scale mining entrepreneurs. The mining charter is a case in point. The objective of the mining charter includes but not limited to:

- Promoting equitable access to mineral resources
- Expansion opportunities for previously disadvantaged people:

- Empower previously disadvantaged people
- And to promote beneficiation of SA's mineral resources [29].

Small-scale mining has been documented from different perspectives. For instance Hilson and McQuilken [2] have examined support for small-scale mining entrepreneurs and found that despite small-scale mining being critical to rural economic growth, policy makers' perceptions of this sector have not changed. On the one hand, Appiah's [4] investigated the organisation of small-scale mining activities in Ghana and found that there are financial gains from operating a small-scale mine. On the other hand, Dondeyne and Ndunguru [5], however, take a different view. Their analysis of small-scale mining from a rural developmental perspective found that without government support, small-scale mining entrepreneurs cannot start-up businesses. Drawing from the foregoing, it became imperative to note that small scale mining as a sector is not a priority to policy makers and thus propels a lack of recognition all around the world.

Challenges to small scale mining entrepreneurs in SA

Challenges facing small scale mining entrepreneurs in South African and those outside SA are no different to one another. However, a common challenge is whether they participate in the economy or not. It is believed that most small scale mining entrepreneurs are operating informally and illegally. In some instances, they tend to operate in abundant mining sites. As a result of this, small scale mining entrepreneurs lack effective participation in the mainstream economy partly due to the wide-ranging challenges they face [15,16]. On a different note, Mutemeri, Sellick and Mtegha [7] contend that small-scale mining entrepreneurs are growing in numbers and young men and women entrepreneurs are being drawn into small-scale mining all over the world. Despite this seeming contradiction, small-scale mining entrepreneurs like other entrepreneurs in SA are confronted by daunting challenges during both the start-up phase and next phases of their businesses. Although several studies have confirmed similar challenges, it seems there is quite scantly studies focusing on addressing the various challenges identified as a handicap for small scale miners.

Given the impediments they face, small-scale mining entrepreneurs are compelled to use rudimentary methods and often conduct small-scale mining operations individually and illegally [8-11]. As a direct result of the impediments to small-scale mining entrepreneurs, their use of unorthodox business methods of extracting gold or other minerals are increasingly becoming deleterious to the environment and human health [12,13]. Supporting the foregoing premise, Drasch et al. [13], small-scale mining entrepreneurs extract gold from the ore using mercury (a highly toxic chemical), thus creating a gold-amalgamation. Additionally, in order to separate the gold from the amalgamation, the gold-amalgamation is heated in the open, thus contributing to air pollution. Scale-scale mining represents an environmental threat.

Conceptualising the challenges to small-scale mining entrepreneurs in SA

The problem underpinning this study can be best described using the conceptual model which is based on the literature as a lens to view challenges to and prospects for small-scale mining entrepreneurs in both starting and growing their businesses. Figure 2 is a proposed conceptual model. The model suggests that there are factors (challenges) hindering a small-scale mining business from being sustainable in terms of raising finance and utilising appropriate equipment for business success. The model is categorised into four stages. Colour was therefore, used to distinguish the different stages. The first stage is where small-scale mining entrepreneurs are faced with factors hindering small-scale mining entrepreneurs. The next (second) stage is the Small to Medium Enterprise (SME) business start-up. The third stage is SME growth stage. The fourth (last) stage is the SME sustainability phase. The relationship and meaning of these stages are explained underneath the figure.

The four circles marked with F1, F2, F3 and F4 in the first element of Figure 2, are the challenges that prevent small-scale mining entrepreneurs from establishing successful businesses. These include a lack of geological information, access to markets, and lack of human and financial capital. The start-up, growth and sustainability layers

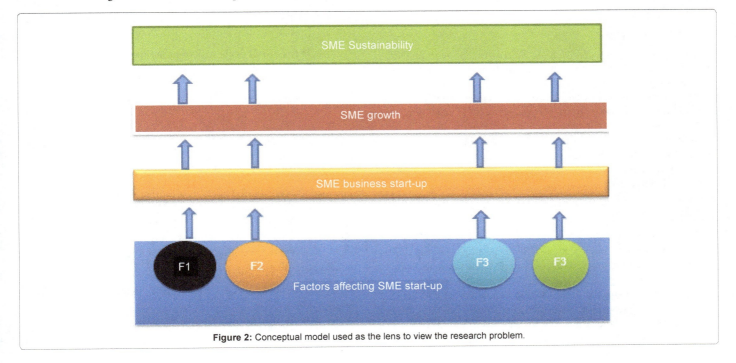

Figure 2: Conceptual model used as the lens to view the research problem.

of the figure indicate the resources available to small-scale mining entrepreneurs to build sustainable businesses. The relationship between the challenges and start-up, growth and sustainability factors suggests that these businesses would be sustainable if the challenges are mitigated. Furthermore, if each of these phases is successfully achieved, the next phase will follow and the venture will be a successful mining business. However, if the entrepreneurs do not overcome the challenges, the mining business will fail. The trajectory is thus that when those challenges are met, a business start-up will successfully emerge, followed by growth and sustainability. If these challenges are poorly managed, sustainable growth will not be possible. In short, the mining business will not be successful. Therefore, small-scale mining entrepreneurs will have no prospect of building successful businesses (Figure 2).

Research Methodology

Glaser and Strauss [30] believe that the grounded theory methodology is fated for exploring " grey " areas in order to gain a fresher perspective. Accordingly, the research question in this paper was examined from the grounded theory perspective. This study was conducted in four of the nine provinces of SA. The provinces: included; the Free State; KwaZulu-Natal; Limpopo and Mpumalanga. The prevalence of mining activities laid behind the reason for selecting the aforementioned provinces. Other aspects of the research design and methodology follow.

Research design

A qualitative research paradigm anchored the methodology of this study, in which face to face interviews were conducted to arrive at an in-depth understanding of this particular phenomenon [31-33].

Research population

The population of this research constituted of small scale mining entrepreneurs meeting the following requirements: mining entrepreneurs had to be registered with Mintek: mining entrepreneurs had to be in business for more than five years and mining entrepreneurs had to hold a mining permit.

The sampling design

Owing to the absence of reliable statistics on the status and activities of small scale mining entrepreneurs in South Africa [7], a cohort of mining entrepreneurs was drawn from those registered the database of Mintek. Mintek is a research and development (RandD) organisation that specialises on mineral processing, extractive metallurgy and related technology. The database, provided impetus for the application of random sampling. In support of this approach, Blumberg et al. [34] asserts that sampling can either be done randomly or purposefully. Furthermore, Anderson [35] concurs that in quantitative survey studies, it is important to select probability samples so that statistics can be used to provide generalizations to the population from which the sample was drawn.

In terms of sample size selection, there appears to be no "one size fits all" in qualitative studies. Reports describe single-person studies and yet other commentators suggest sample sizes ranging from to 30 [36]. In all 21, respondents were selected and it was felt that this number of respondents should be able to supply varied and detailed accounts for the purposes of this study. The twenty– one (21) mining entrepreneurs selected for this study were drawn from four provinces, namely: Free State; KZN; Limpopo and Mpumalanga. However, upon confirmation of appointments, it became apparent that ten (10) mining entrepreneurs were no longer in business. Therefore, reducing the sample size to eleven (11) entrepreneurs: Free States compromised of two (2) entrepreneurs: KZN comprised of three (3) entrepreneurs; Limpopo compromised of four (4) entrepreneurs while Mpumalanga had two (2) small scale mining entrepreneurs.

Data collection and analysis

The data collection approach is anchored to describe the prospects and challenges for small-scale mining entrepreneurs. Therefore, data were collected through face to face interviews with small scale mining entrepreneurs. The mining entrepreneurs were preferred due to the probability of them being in possession of the most comprehensive and accurate information about the activities of the business. Following Weerawardena and Mort [37], open-ended questions, followed by prompts used to elaborate on the discussion and to elicit the views and opinions of the participants were utilized. Each interview lasted for approximately 30 minutes. The interviews were of paramount importance as they helped to validate what the literature postulates regarding small-scale mining. In total, eleven (11) interviews were conducted with small-scale mining entrepreneurs from four different provinces.

The interviews were audio recorded while in progress the researcher also took notes to supplement the audio record. The interviews and observed data were cross checked for consistency and included for further analysis. Content analysis was utilized to categorize the participant's feedback into themes. The transcribed data were then categorized into themes in accordance with the research questions. The emerging themes are reported in-depth in the following section [34].

Findings and Discussions

In this section the findings and discussion of this research are reported under the verbatim responses and are in phases following the research objectives and emerging themes. In the first phase, the theme question and associated finding are presented in a tabular form. In the second phase, the respondent's answers are presented word verbatim. In the final phase, a summary of the finding relating to the theme question presented and aligned with the literature study.

Prospects for small scale mining entrepreneurs in SA

In an attempt to establish the prospects small-scale mining entrepreneurs have, a question was formulated to capture such information. The interview findings are tabled below (Table 3).

The table presents prospects for small scale mining entrepreneurs. On the left, the table illustrates the prospects and on the right are the interview findings.

The question that respondents attempted to answer was: what are the prospects available for small-scale mining entrepreneurs in SA? The respondents felt there are numerous opportunities for emerging and small scale entrepreneurs. In particular they highlighted the following themes: growing demand, training, and financial support among others. The verbatim reports highlighting the various themes captured included the following:

What prospects are there for small-scale mining entrepreneurs?

- **Participant 1:** "the opportunities for small-scale mining entrepreneurs is that you get training from LIPSA before

Theme question: What are the prospects for small-scale mining entrepreneurs in SA?	
Domain	Interview findings
Opportunities	Forty five per cent (45%) of small-scale mining entrepreneurs suggested that there were plenty of opportunities for emerging small-scale mining entrepreneurs. Thirty six per cent (36%) of mining entrepreneurs revealed that there was a huge market for small-scale mining entrepreneurs, while 9% regarded the accessibility of mining permits as an opportunity. Furthermore, another 9% suggested free training from government as an opportunity for emerging entrepreneurs.
Exploitation of opportunities +	Fifty five per cent (55%) of small-scale mining entrepreneurs noted that, to exploit these opportunities one needed to have funds. Twenty seven per cent (27%) of small-scale mining entrepreneurs indicated that to exploit prospects in mining, small-scale mining entrepreneurs and would-be mining entrepreneurs had to be registered with the relevant authority. On the one hand, 9% of small-scale mining entrepreneurs revealed that in order for them to exploit these opportunities, companies needed to create joint ventures. On the other hand, 9% of mining entrepreneurs asserted that government should force big companies to purchase their products.
Accessibility of opportunities	Sixty four per cent (64%) of small-scale mining entrepreneurs agreed that it is easy to reap the benefit of the prospects in the mining industry while 36% of small-scale mining entrepreneurs claimed that it was very difficult to reap the benefits of prospects in the mining industry.

Table 3: Prospects for small scale mining entrepreneurs in SA.

starting a small-scale mine even when you have already started. The training is free of charge"

- **Participant 2:** "opportunities are there because err, I mean if the market is there it actually means there's a possibility of making good money there you can start small but after sometime then you grow bigger"

- **Participant 3:** "err the opportunities you get is sometimes the municipality, you find out that they are having projects where the construction needs to lay pavement of which they going to use river sand and sometimes they buy the paving bricks that we are manufacturing and last year we were busy with other they were building a plaza we were the ones who supplied the sand and stones"

- **Participant 4:** "I think opportunities are there, because in black areas we don't have competition and government is ordering sand from Polokwane instead of Lebowakgomo"

- **Participant 5:** "There are plenty of opportunities you just need to tap into the mining industry"

- **Participant 6:** "There are many opportunities ; community development and exposure"

- **Participant 7:** "There are many opportunities for emerging small-scale mining entrepreneurs. It is easy to get mining permits"

- **Participant 8:** "There are a lot of opportunities for local people and you need a lot of funds and support and you will create jobs"

- **Participant 9:** "It's a lot of opportunities, there are a lot of jobs in small-scale mining even local communities are engaging in illegal mining. Small-scale mining provides jobs for rural communities"

- **Participant 10:** "Opportunities are big, because as we speak everybody wants a structure made of sandstone. People come from as far as Johannesburg to purchase sandstone and we are told that people from Johannesburg export our minerals, so if things can be okay, we will export it ourselves"

- **Participant 11:** "Opportunities are huge, we can work together with small-scale mining entrepreneurs and create partnerships"

Summary of the findings and discussion of the verbatim responses: From a general perspective, the verbatim quotations indicate the opportunities recounted by the respondents come in different forms and are not limited to free training, preferential tenders, and an ever growing demand for mining products.

Aggregating the responses quantitatively, forty five per cent (45%) of mining entrepreneurs noted that there are plenty of opportunities in small-scale mining. Thirty six per cent (36%) of mining entrepreneurs revealed that there is a huge market for small-scale mining. On the one hand, 9% of small-scale mining entrepreneurs noted that obtaining mining permits for a small-scale mine was an opportunity on its own. On the other hand, 9% of small-scale mining entrepreneurs mentioned free training and grants as prospects.

Small-scale mining entrepreneurs noted that there are many opportunities for small-scale mining entrepreneurs and would-be entrepreneurs. More importantly, small-scale mining entrepreneurs were the leading employment provider in rural areas across the world [24,26]. This statement was supported by the fact that the majority of small-scale mining entrepreneurs in this study agreed that they were the major employer in the rural areas where this study was conducted. This finding is in line with those of Hentschel et al. [18]. Some small-scale mining entrepreneurs had diversified and had built toilets and tennis courts in the community, for instance. There was general agreement that small-scale mining offered many opportunities.

Challenges to small scale mining entrepreneurs

In this section the findings of the interviews are explored in relation to the themes that were identified:

The table (Table 4) presents challenges facing small scale mining entrepreneurs. On the left, the table illustrates the challenges and on the right are the interview findings.

The objective of the above questions was geared towards answering the main research question. The purpose of this question was to determine the challenges small-scale mining entrepreneurs face in SA. In accordance to theme, this is what the participants had to say;

Given that you currently operate a small-scale mine or you have done so in the past; what are the main financial challenges facing your business?

- ➤ **Participant 1:** "Our main financial challenge is the cost of repairing our equipment, so we end up making a loss "

- ➤ **Participant 2:** Initially, it was start-up capital. That was the most challenging. So we approached government and other private companies and then we formed a partnership.

- ➤ **Participant 3:** Our main financial challenge is that sometimes you find that illegal miners are selling their products at low prices and then people don't buy from us. Even our employees, are stealing our money.

Theme question: What are the challenges facing small-scale mining entrepreneurs in SA?	
Domain	Interview finding
Financial	Seventy three (73%) of small-scale mining entrepreneurs agreed that their main financial challenge was the lack of capital and not being able to purchase the desired equipment for their businesses. Nine per cent (9%) of small-scale mining entrepreneurs said their main financial challenge was not being able to make profit. Another 9% indicated that not being able to raise capital from financial institutions was a major problem. The remaining 9% suggested the start-up capital was their major issue as far as finance is concerned.
Geological	Ninety per cent (90%) of small-scale mining entrepreneurs asserted that they did not have any challenges as far as geology was concerned while only 10% indicated that they were either experiencing geological challenges at that point or had experienced them in the past.
Marketing	Fifty five per cent (55%) of small-scale mining entrepreneurs said they were not facing any marketing challenges, while 27% indicated that their main challenge was the lack of an advertising budget. The remaining 18% reported they experienced fierce competition from illegal miners.
Technical (equipment)	Only 9% reported that they had no challenges when it came to the technical aspect of their businesses. Seventy three per cent (73%) of small-scale mining entrepreneurs said they did not have access to appropriate equipment. A further 9% of the mining entrepreneurs indicated that their main challenge was using outdated equipment. The remaining 9% reported that they were using labour intensive equipment.
Environment	Twenty seven (27%) of small-scale mining entrepreneurs indicated that they had no environmental challenges. Eighteen per cent (18%) of small-scale mining entrepreneurs revealed their challenges revolved around climate issues. Another 18% of small-scale mining entrepreneurs acknowledged that they were polluting the environment. Yet another 9% of small-scale mining entrepreneurs indicated that their businesses had labour intensive productions, while the remaining 9% stated that their business faced rehabilitation challenges.

Table 4: Challenges to small-scale mining entrepreneurs in SA.

> **Participant 4:** We do get financial challenges, we started very small and even now we can't purchase the equipment that the mine needs. The money the mine makes is very small and you are unable to even fix your equipment.

> **Participant 5:** Lack of finance to purchase equipment for transporting the minerals for beneficiation.

> **Participant 6:** is that we don't get support from financial institutions; they just don't take us seriously, whether you have a grant or not, you can get top up from financial institutions.

> **Participant 7:** we sell our minerals at low prices because we don't have proper equipment, so make little money.

> **Participant 8:** IDC gave me R 1 million to start-up the business, thereafter I have been falling short of money to repay the money.

> **Participant 9:** Firstly when you starting a business, you need funds and a feasibility study. So I didn't have any funds for conducting a feasibility study so I resigned and took my package.

> **Participant 10:** We don't have finance to purchase equipment in order for us to cut stones.

> **Participant 11:** Our main financial challenges are setting up a processing plant and the handling cost of transporting our minerals.

Summary of the Challenges and discussions drawn from the verbatim quotations: Seventy three (73%) of small-scale mining entrepreneurs agreed that their main financial challenge was; the lack of finance and not being able to purchase the desired equipment for their businesses. Bradford [38]; Thwala and Phaladi [39]; Ledzani and Netswera [40]; and Mutemeri et al. [7] concur with the above findings. The premise statements are supported by the views held by Cant and Wiid [41]. According to Cant and Wiid [41] the lack of finance (apart from other challenges) facing small businesses in SA is a dominant challenge, therefore, contributing to the failure rate of small-small businesses. On a different note, Van Aardt Smit and Fatoki [42] are of the opinion that the challenges facing small businesses in SA not only limits the start and creation of business but also stagnates the growth of the business. As a result millions of Rands are therefore lost on business ventures due to avoidable mistakes and challenges [43].

Nine per cent (9%) of small-scale mining entrepreneurs said their main financial challenge was not being able to make profit. This could be attributable to various elements. However, this study believes that the lack of entrepreneurial flair and managerial competency; financial skills was the crux behind the finding. Small businesses owners in SA lack management skills; financial skills; marketing knowledge [34,38,41,44-46]. According to Fatoki [46] small businesses in SA do not engage in financial planning and control; investment appraisal and financial analysis. Fatoki [45] asserts that challenges facing small business in SA are financially integrated and managerial in nature.

Nine per cent (9%) indicated that being neglected by financial institutions was a major problem. In supporting this findings, one draws from the work of Ray [47]. According to Ray [47] financial institutions have a set of requirements which are often against applicants that have small-businesses in SA. For instance, In addition, the remaining nine per cent (9%) suggested the start-up capital was their major issue as far as finance is concerned. As a result of the various challenges of small-scale mining, it is estimated that the failure rate of small businesses in SA is between seventy per cent (70%) and eighty per cent (80%) [43].

Due to these hybrid financial challenges, small-scale mining entrepreneurs are not considered viable by financial institutions. Therefore, do not qualify for financial assistance, despite them having grants from government or even personal collateral, which is often rationally low. Therefore, the lack of finance as a predicament for small-scale mining entrepreneurs is perpetuating the struggle of; fulfilling obligations (loan repayments); access start-up capital and conducting feasibility studies.Most importantly, small-scale mining entrepreneurs could not save or perhaps raise money to purchase the desired equipment for their businesses despite being in operation for quite a number of years. As a direct consequence, small-scale mining entrepreneurs could not even raise money for transporting their minerals for beneficiation. In addition to that, small-scale mining entrepreneurs had to sell their minerals below market value due to market imperfections (illegal mining).

Overall, the most outstanding challenge facing small-scale mining entrepreneurs in SA is the lack of finance to purchase appropriate equipment for their respective businesses.

Conclusion

Although being a significant source of revenue for SA, the current state of the mining sector is one that does not directly benefit the previously disadvantaged. The aim of this study is to investigate the prospects for and challenges to small-scale mining entrepreneurs in

South Africa. Even though small scale mining entrepreneurs indicated that there are plenty of prospects for them, nonetheless a significant proportion revealed that the receptiveness of these prospects is constraint by the availability of funds. This paper thus demonstrated that the overarching challenge that small scale mining entrepreneurs face is the inadequate finance to purchase the requisite equipment needed for sustainability.

Limitations

Due to limited resources and time factor, this research was only limited to four provinces of SA, given the spatial distribution of minerals. Additionally, this study investigated prospects for and challenges to small scale mining entrepreneurs. Therefore, this research excluded non mining provinces and Black Economic Empowerment (BEE) mining entrepreneurs.

Recommendations

To harness challenges of small scale mining entrepreneurs, the supporting agencies of small scale mining entrepreneurs together with the South African government should provide entrepreneurial training prior granting any mining permits to ensure that small scale mining entrepreneurs are entrepreneurially intact prior to engaging in small scale mining. Furthermore, the South African government should ensure that the receptiveness of prospects are not only accessed by those with means to do so rather by every emerging small scale mining entrepreneurs to ensure business success.

- Future research should therefore investigate the complexity behind the receptiveness of the prospects available to small scale mining.
- Future research should also focus on prospects and challenges of BEE mining entrepreneurs.

References

1. Porter JL (2014) Presidential Address: Are efforts to mechanize SA mines too focused on machinery rather than technology? The Journal of the Southern African Institute of Mining and Metallurgy 114: 681-692.
2. Hilson G McQuicken J (2014) Four decades of support for artisanal and small-scale mining in sub-Saharan Africa: A critical review. The Extractive Industries and Society 1: 104-118.
3. Mkubukeli Z, Tengeh RK (2015) Small-scale mining in South Africa: an assessment of the success factors and support structures for entrepreneurs. Environmental Economics 6: 15-24.
4. Appiah H (1998) Organization of small scale mining activities in Ghana. The South African Institute of Mining and Metallurgy pp: 307-310.
5. Dondeyne S, Ndunguru E (2014) Artisanal gold mining and rural development policies in Mozambique: perspectives for the future. Futures p: 1.
6. Childs J (2014) A new means of government artisanal and small-scale mining? Fairtrade gold and development in Tanzania. Resources Policy 40: 128-136.
7. Mutemeri N, Sellick N, Mtegha H (2010) What is the status of small-scale mining in South Africa? Discussion document for the MQA SSM Colloquium.
8. Heemskerk M, van der Kooye R (2003) Challenges to sustainable small-scale mine development in Suriname. In Hilson G (ed.) The socioeconomic impacts of artisanal and small-scale mining in development countries. Leiden: Balkema pp: 661-678.
9. Avila EC (2003) Small-scale mining: a new entrepreneurial approach. Santiago: Natural Resources and Infrastructure division.
10. South Africa Department of Water Affairs and Forestry (2006) Small-scale mining (standard format): Best practice guidelines for water resources protection in the South African mining industry. Pretoria: Government Printer.
11. Phiri S (2011) Impact of artisanal small scale gold mining in the Umzingwane District (Zimbabwe), a potential for ecological disaster. Unpublished master's thesis, University of the Free State, Bloemfontein.
12. Van Straaten P (2000) Human exposure to mercury due to small scale gold mining in northern Tanzania. The Science of the Total Environment 259: 45-53.
13. Drasch-O'Reilly G, Bose-O'Reilly S, Beinhoff C, Roider G, Maydl S (2001) The Mt Diwata study on the Philippines 1999 - assessing mercury intoxication of the population by small scale gold mining. The Science of the Total Environment 267: 151-168.
14. Mothomogolo J (2012) Development of innovative funding mechanism for mining start-up: a South African case. The South African Institute of Mining and Metallurgy.
15. Mutemeri N, Petersen FW (2002) Small-scale mining in South Africa: past, present and future. Natural Resources Forum 26: 286-292.
16. Siegel S, Veiga MM (2009) Artisanal and small-scale mining as an extra-legal economy: De Soto and the redefinition of formalisation. Resources Policy 34: 51-56.
17. Barringer BR, Ireland RD (2010) Entrepreneurship: successfully launching new ventures. Upper Saddle River, New Jersey: Prentice Hall.
18. Hentschel T, Hruschka F, Priester M (2002) Global report on artisanal & small-scale mining. London: International Institute for Environment and Development and World Business Council for Sustainable Development.
19. Hilson G (2012) Family hardships and cultural values: child labour in Malian small scale gold mining communities. The University of Reading 40: 1663-1674.
20. Nieman G, Nieuwenhuizen C (2009) Entrepreneurship: a South African perspective. Van Schaik Publishers, Pretoria.
21. Evan D, Dean S (2002) Self-employment as a career choice: attitudes, entrepreneurial intentions and utility maximization. Entrepreneurial Theory and Practice 26: 81-90.
22. Shane S, Kolvereid L, Westhead P (1991) An exploratory examination of the reasons leading to new firm formation across and gender. Journal of Business Venturing 6: 431-446.
23. Kirkwood J (2009) Motivational factors in a push – pull theory of entrepreneurship. Gender in Management: An International Journal 24: 346-364.
24. Veiga MM, Maxson PA, Hylander LD (2006) Origin and consumption of mercury in small-scale gold mining. Journal of Cleaner Production 7: 436-447.
25. Werthman K (2009) Working in a boom-town: female perspective on gold-mining in Burkina Faso. Resources Policy 34: 18-23.
26. Hilson G (2009) Small-scale mining, poverty and economic development in sub-Saharan Africa: An overview. Resources Policy 34: 1-5.
27. Sousa R, Veiga M, Van Zyl D, Telmer K, Spiegel S (2011) Policies and regulations for Brazil's artisanal gold mining sector: analysis and recommendations. Journal of Cleaner Production 19: 742-750.
28. Chamber of Mines of South Africa (2013) South African Year Book 2012/2013. Johannesburg.
29. South Africa Department of Minerals Resources (2009) Mining charter impact assessment report. Pretoria: Department of Mineral Resources.
30. Glaser BG, Strauss AI (1967) The discovery of grounded theory: strategies for qualitative research. Aldine, Chicago IL.
31. Brynard PA, Hanekom SX (2006) Introduction to research in management-related fields. Van Schaik Publishers, Pretoria.
32. Dunn DS (2010) The practical researcher: a student guide to conducting psychological research. Chichester, West Sussex: Wiley-Blackwell.
33. Gravetter FJ, Forzano LB (2009) Research methods for the behavioural sciences. Wadsworth, California: Cengage Learning.
34. Blumberg B, Cooper DR, Schindler PS (2011) Business research methods. McGraw-Hill Education, Berkshire.
35. Anderson C (2010) Presenting and Evaluating Qualitative Research. American Journal of Pharmaceutical Education 74: 1-7.
36. Marshall B, Cardon P, Poddar A, Fontenot R (2013) Does sample size matter

in qualitative research? A review of qualitative interviews in research. Journal of Computer Information systems, 11-22.

37. Weerawarddena J, Mort GS (2006) Investigating social entrepreneurship: A multidimensional model. Journal of World Business 41: 21-35.

38. Bradford WD (2007) Distinguishing economically from legal formal firms: targeting business support to entrepreneurs in South Africa's townships. Journal of Small Business Management 45: 94-115.

39. Thwala WD, Phaladi MJ (2009) An exploratory study of problems facing small contractors in the North West Province of South Africa. African Journal of Business Management 3: 533-539.

40. Ladzani W, Netswera G (2009) Support for rural small businesses in Limpopo province, South Africa. Development Southern Africa 26: 225-239.

41. Cant MC, Wiid JA (2013) Establish the challenges affecting South Africa SMEs. International Business & Economics Research Journal 12: 707-716.

42. Fatoki OO, Van Aardt Smit A (2011) Constraints to credit access by new SMEs in South Africa: a supply-side analysis. African Journal of Business Management 5: 1413-1425.

43. Brink A, Cant M, Ligthelm A (2003) Problems experienced by small businesses in South Africa. Paper presented at the 16th Annual conference of Small Enterprise Association of Austrialia and New Zealand, University of Ballarat, Ballarat.

44. Lekhanya LM (2010) The use of marketing strategies by small, medium and micro enterprises in rural KwaZulu-Natal. Durban University of Technology, Durban.

45. Fatoki OO (2011) The impact of human, social and financial capital on the performance of small and medium-sized enterprises in South Africa. Journal of Social Science 29: 193-204

46. Fatoki OO (2012) An investigation into the financial management practices of new micro-enterprise in South Africa. Journal of Social Science 33: 179-188.

47. Ray DE (2009) Doing research in the real world. Thousand Acres, SAGE, CA.

Permissions

All chapters in this book were first published in JEOM, by OMICS International; hereby published with permission under the Creative Commons Attribution License or equivalent. Every chapter published in this book has been scrutinized by our experts. Their significance has been extensively debated. The topics covered herein carry significant findings which will fuel the growth of the discipline. They may even be implemented as practical applications or may be referred to as a beginning point for another development.

The contributors of this book come from diverse backgrounds, making this book a truly international effort. This book will bring forth new frontiers with its revolutionizing research information and detailed analysis of the nascent developments around the world.

We would like to thank all the contributing authors for lending their expertise to make the book truly unique. They have played a crucial role in the development of this book. Without their invaluable contributions this book wouldn't have been possible. They have made vital efforts to compile up to date information on the varied aspects of this subject to make this book a valuable addition to the collection of many professionals and students.

This book was conceptualized with the vision of imparting up-to-date information and advanced data in this field. To ensure the same, a matchless editorial board was set up. Every individual on the board went through rigorous rounds of assessment to prove their worth. After which they invested a large part of their time researching and compiling the most relevant data for our readers.

The editorial board has been involved in producing this book since its inception. They have spent rigorous hours researching and exploring the diverse topics which have resulted in the successful publishing of this book. They have passed on their knowledge of decades through this book. To expedite this challenging task, the publisher supported the team at every step. A small team of assistant editors was also appointed to further simplify the editing procedure and attain best results for the readers.

Apart from the editorial board, the designing team has also invested a significant amount of their time in understanding the subject and creating the most relevant covers. They scrutinized every image to scout for the most suitable representation of the subject and create an appropriate cover for the book.

The publishing team has been an ardent support to the editorial, designing and production team. Their endless efforts to recruit the best for this project, has resulted in the accomplishment of this book. They are a veteran in the field of academics and their pool of knowledge is as vast as their experience in printing. Their expertise and guidance has proved useful at every step. Their uncompromising quality standards have made this book an exceptional effort. Their encouragement from time to time has been an inspiration for everyone.

The publisher and the editorial board hope that this book will prove to be a valuable piece of knowledge for researchers, students, practitioners and scholars across the globe.

List of Contributors

Anifowose Oladotun Larry
Department of Entrepreneurship Management of Technology, Federal University of Technology, Akure, Ondo State, Nigeria

Golibjon Y
Tashkent State Institute of Oriental Studies, Uzbekistan

Fahad Bin Muhaya, Saad Haj Bakry and Suhail M AlAlmaee
King Saud University, Riyadh, Saudi Arabia

Yeter Demir U and Ufuk E
Giresun University Management, Ordu, Turkey

Bharti Motwani
Institute of Management and Research, Information Technology, Vijay Nagar Indore, Madhya Pradesh-452010, India

Walid Ghodbane
Department of Management Science, University of Tunis, Tunisia

Md. Joynal Abdin
Deputy Manager at SME Foundation in Dhaka, Bangladesh

Md. Mizanur Rahman
Assistant Manager at SME Foundation in Dhaka, Bangladesh

Rinne T
Department of Management Studies, Aalto University School of Business, P.O. BOX 21230, 00076 AALTO, Finland

Khet Raj Dahal
Centre for Post-Graduate Studies, Nepal Engineering College, Kathmandu, Nepal

Manoj KC
Civil Engineer, Kathmandu Valley Development Authority, Nepal

Siva Kumar A
Bharathidasan University, Environmental Engineering, Palkakalai Nagar, Pallavakam, Chennai, India

Sibylle Georgianna
Vanguard University of Southern California, Office of Graduate Studies, 55 Fair Drive, Costa Mesa, CA, USA

Jovi Dacanay C
School of Economics, University of Asia, The Pacific Pearl Drive Corner St. Josemaria Escriva Drive Ortigas Center (1605), Pasig City, Philippines

Muhammad Awais Siddiqui
Management department, Allama Iqbal Open University, Pakistan

Abdulwahab Bin Shmailan
Jubail Industrial College, Jubail Industrial, KSA

Matsuda N
Ministry of Economy, Trade and Industry, Japan

Matsuo Y
Faculty of Engineering, University of Tokyo, Japan

Mehmet Sahin G
Faculty of Business Administration, Gebze Technical University, Kocaeli, Turkey

Büşra K
Department of Administrative Science, Beykent University, Istanbul, Turkey

Rohr Ulrich P and Dieterle Thomas
Divisional Medical and Scientific Affairs, F. Hoffmann-La Roche Ltd, 4070 Basel, Switzerland

Schäfer H Hendrik
Filser Ludwig and Laubender Ruediger P
Roche Professional Diagnostics, Biostatistics and Data Management, 82377 Penzberg, Germany

Maitland Roger
Graduate School of Business, University of Cape Town, 8002 Cape Town, South Africa

Zaugg Christian E
Roche Professional Diagnostics, Global Medical and Scientific Affairs, 6343 Rotkreuz, Switzerland

Jui-Chih Ho
National Changhua University of Education, Graduate Institute of Human Resource Management, Taiwan

Soumyendra Kishore Datta and Tanushree De
Department of Economics Burdwan University West Bengal, India

List of Contributors

Lai Xiao-Dong
School of Tourism and Urban Management, Jiangxi University of Finance and Economics, Nanchang, China

Larry Anifowose
Department of Entrepreneurship Management Technology, The Federal University of Technology, Akure, Ondo State, Nigeria

Selvaraj N
Saraswathi Narayanan College, Madurai, Tamilnadu, India

Elvis Asiedu and Patrick Dede Nyarkoh
Servicio Nacional De Aprendizaje (SENA), Neiva, Huila, Colombia

Nichodemus Obioma Ejimabo
Wayland Baptist University Fairbanks, Alaska, USA

Yeboah AM and Alhaji A
Department Liberal Studies, Cape Coast Polytechnic, Cape Coast, Ghana

Berzin SC
Associate Professor, Boston College Graduate School of Social Work, 140 Commonwealth Avenue, Chestnut Hill, MA 02467, USA

Catsouphes MP
Associate Professor, GSSW and the Carroll School of Management, 140 Commonwealth Avenue, Chestnut Hill, MA 02467, USA

Selvaraj N
Department of Commerce, Saraswathi Narayanan College, Madurai, Tamilnadu, India

Francoise U, Donghong D and Janviere N
University of Science and Technology of China Hefei, Anhui, China

Selvaraj N
Assistant Professor of Commerce, Saraswathi Narayanan College, Madurai, Tamil Nadu, India

Balajikumar P
Assistant Professor of Management, Saraswathi Narayanan College, Madurai, Tamil Nadu, India

Zandisile Mkubukeli and Robertson Tengeh
Faculty of Business and Management Sciences, Cape Peninsula, University of Technology, South Africa

Index

A
Association of Southeast Asian Nations, 5

B
Banks, 63, 70-89, 99-100, 102, 105, 148-154, 162, 206-208, 210-211, 213-214
Basic Psychological Needs, 124-130
Business Initiative, 31, 179, 181-182, 184
Business Opportunity, 44, 47, 147

C
Career Development, 126, 200
Characteristics, 26, 43, 45, 48, 74, 76, 97-99, 102, 105-106, 111, 131, 140-141, 148, 161, 164-165, 171, 189, 200-204, 217
Cluster Development Model, 35
Cluster Development Process, 35, 37
Communication, 6, 9, 14, 18, 20-27, 29, 31-33, 37, 44-45, 47, 49, 53-54, 57, 59, 67-68, 76, 105-107, 112, 139, 142, 144, 166, 168-169, 171-177
Construction Enterprises, 138-146
Construction Industries, 49-51, 57, 139
Corporate Viability, 116
Cost-control, 116, 119-121
Cronbach's Alpha, 20, 22, 93, 132, 134-136, 181-182
Customer And Service, 150

D
Decision-making, 118, 122-124, 138, 141, 166, 168-169, 171-173, 177-179
Design Thinking, 186-187, 189-191
Diagnostic Industry, 116, 118-119, 121-122
Different Steps Of Cluster Development, 35

E
E-government: Importance, 9
Economic Development, 8, 35-36, 40, 49, 51, 60, 89, 138, 145, 156, 158, 164, 206, 223
Economic Mobility, 156, 160-161, 163-164
Economic Resources, 147, 164
Energy Resources, 15, 17
Entrepreneurial Intention, 200-203, 205
Entrepreneurial Outlook, 179-184
Entrepreneurial Skill Development, 1
Entrepreneurial Ventures, 156-159, 163-164
Ethics And Leadership Activities, 166
Experience Jel Classification L25, 104

F
Financial Independence, 156, 160-161, 163-164
Future Development, 9-10, 38, 138

G
Gifted Talent, 104, 106-107, 109
Green Energy, 15, 17

H
Health Care, 116-123, 188

I
Impression Management Motives, 124-125, 128, 130
Incubation Manager, 58
Industries, 7, 35-36, 49-51, 57, 65, 77, 94, 106, 108-109, 139, 145, 157, 163, 193, 199, 206-208, 210, 213-214, 223
Innovation, 2, 5-8, 29-31, 33-34, 39, 50, 60, 62, 65, 89, 97-98, 102, 116, 119, 122, 137-146, 149, 156, 165, 180, 184, 186-192, 197, 201, 204
Innovation And Small And Medium-sized Enterprises, 5
Innovation Development, 5
Innovation Management, 138-139, 141-145
Institutional Commitment, 111, 113-114
Intrapreneurship, 97, 186, 189, 191
Involvement And Personal Traits, 193

J
J24, 104
J.m. Model For Cluster Development, 35-36
Job Satisfaction, 65-66, 68-69, 111-115, 176, 201, 204

K
Knowledge Sharing, 9, 131, 133, 135-136

L
L26, 104
Leadership, 19, 28, 30-31, 33, 36, 38-40, 42, 47-57, 65-69, 101-102, 109, 111-115, 124, 130, 140, 156, 166-178, 186-187, 191-192, 200
Leadership Management, 49, 178

M
Management, 1-2, 4-5, 12, 15, 32, 36, 40, 49, 51, 53-54, 57, 60, 63, 69, 90, 97, 99, 101, 105, 122, 131, 134, 155, 160, 170, 179, 184, 186, 193, 199, 207, 215, 218, 224
Mba, 104-109, 162, 204
Medical Value, 116-119, 121, 123
Migration, 156-160, 163-165

N
Non-interest Banking, 147-149

O
Operational Self-sufficiency, 70-71, 73-74, 78-83, 85-88
Organizational Commitment, 67, 111-115
Organizational Growth, 166

P
Perceptions, 44, 98, 111, 150, 167, 169, 173-174, 177, 188-191, 197-198, 205, 219
Performers, 193-199
Personal Development, 200, 218
Policy, 5-7, 10, 12, 14, 34, 40, 49-52, 58, 70-72, 103, 110, 117, 123, 137, 142, 145, 164, 166-169, 172, 176, 184, 191, 195, 204, 216, 219, 223
Proactive Personality, 200
Psychological Need Satisfaction, 131, 200-201, 203-205

R
Regression, 33, 70-71, 76-78, 80-82, 84-90, 93-94, 107, 111, 114, 124, 128-129, 132, 135-136, 195-196, 198-199
Relational Capital, 132-137
Renewable Energy, 15, 17
Resource Orchestration, 42-43, 45-48
Restaurant Firms, 179-183

S
Self-leadership, 65-69
Selfdetermined Prosocial Motivation, 124
Service Business, 42, 99, 156, 162
Small And Medium-sized Enterprises Development, 5
Small Medium Businesses, 90
Small Scale Business, 1-2, 4
Small Scale Mining, 215-221, 223
Social Entrepreneurship, 97, 186, 224
Social Innovation, 186-187, 189, 191
Social Relationship, 156, 160
Societal Value, 116, 118, 122
Sources Of Finance And Trend Values, 206
Spillovers, 7, 70, 76-77, 79-82, 87-89
Steps And Phases Of Cluster Development, 35
Strategic Entrepreneurship, 42, 44, 48
Super-leadership, 65-69
Supervisor Support, 124-131

T
Teamwork, 166, 176
Technological Innovation, 29, 138-146
Technopreneurial, 29
Top 500, 138-140, 144
Transactions Cost, 70-71, 73-74, 76-82, 84-85, 87-89
Transnational Entrepreneurship, 156-165

V
Voice Behavior, 124-130, 177

W
Wind Power, 15-16

CPSIA information can be obtained
at www.ICGtesting.com
Printed in the USA
BVHW050807230519
548993BV00012B/40/P